THE (BUSN) SOLUTION

THIRD CANADIAN EDITION

KELLY WILLIAMS MacKENZIE SNOW

BUSN
INTRODUCTION TO BUSINESS

D0885099

Print

BUSN, Third Canadian Edition, delivers all the key terms and all the content for the **Introduction to Business** course through a visually engaging and easy-to-review print experience.

Digital

∴ MINDTAP

MindTap enables you to stay organized and study efficiently by providing a single location for all your course materials and study aids. Built-in apps leverage social media and the latest learning technology to help you succeed.

1 Open the Access Card included with this text.

2 Follow the steps on the card.

3 Study.

Student Resources

- Interactive Ebook
- Online Glossary
- Practice Quizzes
- Chapter Videos
- Flashcards
- Study Cards
- Concept Maps
- You Make the Decision Activities
- Chapter Case Studies
- Homework

Students: **nelson.com/student**

Instructor Resources

- Access to all Student Resources
- Engagement Tracker and Gradebook
- Instructor Companion Site
- Instructor's Manual
- Case Assignments
- Collaborative Learning Exercises
- PowerPoint Slides
- Video Guide
- Test Bank

Instructors: **nelson.com/instructor**

NELSON

BUSN, Third Canadian Edition

by Marce Kelly, Chuck Williams,
H.F. (Herb) MacKenzie, and Kim Snow

VP, Product and Partnership Solutions:
Anne Williams

Publisher, Digital and Print Content:
Anne-Marie Taylor

Marketing Manager:
Christina Koop

Content Development Manager:
Martina van de Velde

Photo and Permissions Researcher:
Karen Hunter

Senior Production Project Manager:
Imoinda Romain

Production Service:
MPS Limited

Copy Editor:
Matthew Kudelka

Proofreader:
MPS Limited

Indexer:
Becky Hornyak

Design Director:
Ken Phipps

Managing Designer:
Pamela Johnston

Interior Design Revisions:
Trinh Truong

Cover Design:
Ken Cadinouche

Cover Image:
Ben Miners/Getty Images

Compositor:
MPS Limited

Library and Archives Canada Cataloguing in Publication Data

Kelly, Marce, author
   BUSN / by Marce Kelly, Chuck Williams, H.F. (Herb) MacKenzie, and Kim Snow. — Third Canadian edition.

Includes bibliographical references and index.
ISBN 978-0-17-657034-7 (softcover).—ISBN 0-17-657034-9 (softcover)

   1. Business—Textbooks.
I. MacKenzie, H. F., author II. Williams, Chuck, 1959–, author III. Snow, Kim, author IV. Title. V. Title: Business.

HF1008.K44 2017   650
C2016-907594-X

ISBN-13: 978-0-17-657034-7
ISBN-10: 0-17-657034-9

BUSN

Brief Contents

BUSN

Herb MacKenzie

4 The World Marketplace: Business Without Borders 52

Photo Travel ViaD/Shutterstock.com

5 Business Formation: Choosing the Form That Fits 68

6 Small Business and Entrepreneurship: Economic Rocket Fuel 84

7 Accounting: Decision Making by the Numbers 98

8 Finance: Acquiring and Using Funds to Maximize Value 116

Norm Betts/Bloomberg via Getty Images

9 Financial Markets: Allocating Financial Resources 134

10 Marketing: Building Profitable Customer Connections 152

Tetra Images/Getty Images

11 Product and Promotion:
Creating and Communicating Value 170

12 Distribution and Pricing:
Right Product, Right Person, Right Place, Right Price 192

Audioundwerbung/Getty Images

ONLINE CHAPTER

Business Communication: Creating
and Delivering Messages That Matter

Letter to Students

We are confident that *BUSN* will meet your needs and that you will enjoy it. We have spent considerable time trying to make the materials student focused so that your first exposure to postsecondary business education in Canada will be exciting and rewarding for you. The short, lively text covers all of the key concepts—everything you will need for a first exposure to economics, global business, accounting, finance, marketing, management, operations, and more. At the same time, we have included many relevant and engaging examples—and a lot of visual content—that help make the book fun to read. But the text is only part of the package. You can access a rich variety of study tools via computer or iPhone—the choice is yours.

The third Canadian edition of this innovative, student-focused package was prepared by H.F. (Herb) MacKenzie and Kim Snow, the same team widely known for one of Canada's most popular marketing texts. The Canadian authors have many years of practical business experience, and both have been recognized for outstanding classroom teaching.

Dr. H.F. (Herb) MacKenzie is an associate professor of marketing at Brock University, St. Catharines, Ontario. Dr. MacKenzie received his BA from St. Francis Xavier University, his MBA from Saint Mary's University, and his PhD from the Ivey School of Business. He has taught in the undergraduate, graduate, and executive education programs at universities in Canada, Europe, and the Middle East and has provided consulting to both private and public sector businesses since 1985. He has over fifteen years of industrial sales and sales management experience and has published many cases, conference proceedings, and articles in the areas of sales management, buyer–seller relationships, and distribution channel management. He has also co-authored Canadian editions of textbooks on selling, sales management, and marketing and has edited five Canadian marketing casebooks. He has received numerous awards from his students, including Professor of the Year, Marketing Professor of the Year, and Faculty of Business Faculty Award of Excellence (twice).

Dr. Kim Snow is an associate professor of marketing at York University in Toronto. Dr. Snow received her Diploma in Business Administration from Wilfrid Laurier University and her MBA and PhD from the University of Bradford, UK. She has been a member of the faculty at York University since 1992. She has published numerous articles in the areas of service marketing, service quality, customer satisfaction, and marketing research. She has worked with the American Marketing Association Student Chapters and has participated in several advisory and editorial boards. Prior to joining York University, Dr. Snow spent seventeen years working in the financial services industry.

H. F. (Herb) MacKenzie

Kim Snow

We would appreciate any comments or suggestions you want to offer about this package. You can reach Herb MacKenzie at herb.mackenzie@brocku.ca and Kim Snow at kimsnow@yorku.ca. We wish you a fun, positive, productive term and look forward to your feedback.

1

Business Now:
Change Is the Only Constant

LEARNING OBJECTIVES
After studying this chapter, you will be able to...

1-1 Define business and discuss the role of business in the economy

1-2 Explain the evolution of modern business

1-3 Discuss the role of not-for-profit organizations in the economy

1-4 Outline the core factors of production and how they influence the economy

1-5 Describe today's business environment and discuss each key dimension

1-6 Explain how current business trends may influence your career choices

After you finish this chapter, go to page 15 for STUDY TOOLS

1-1 Business Now: Moving at Breakneck Speed

Day by day, the business world spins faster. Industries rise—and sometimes fall—in the course of a few short months. Technologies forge instant connections around the globe. Powerful new trends surface and submerge, sometimes within less than a year. In this fast-paced, fluid environment, change is the only constant. According to Charles Darwin, it is not the strongest of the species that survive, nor the most intelligent, but the ones most responsive to change. And so it is with business.

Successful firms lean forward and embrace the change. They seek the opportunities and avoid the pitfalls. They carefully evaluate risks. They completely understand their market, and they adhere to ethical practices. Their core goal: to generate long-term profits by delivering unsurpassed **value** to their customers.

Over the past few years, in today's dynamic business environment, the explosive growth in social media has been having a crucial impact on businesses and consumers alike. Digging deeper into current culture,

value The relationship between the price of a good or a service and the benefits it offers its customers.

Time magazine recently identified "10 Ideas That Are Changing Your Life." A few highlights:

- **Your Head Is in the Cloud.** Swamped every day by a startling surge of data (each day, the average person spends about 12 hours consuming information), we are increasingly offloading the task of remembering that information to search engines and smartphones. This process of "outsourcing our memory" is changing our cognitive habits; in fact, research shows that when we don't know the answer to a question, we now think about where we can find the nearest Web connection, rather than the subject of the question itself.[1]

- **Food That Lasts Forever.** No one wants to think about eating a sandwich that's five years old, but with our global population growing so rapidly, long-term food preservation may be essential to our very survival. In some developing countries today, food loss through rot and decay is as high as 70 percent. As of today, Twinkies (contrary to popular belief) are not even close to immortal—they have a shelf life of less than a month—but a well-sealed can of Spam can last more than a decade. Vacuum-packed tuna tastes fresh for about 30 months, while Thermos-stabilized pork chops apparently remain edible for about seven years. It will be hard to get past the yuck factor unless survival is at stake.[2]

Business is like riding a bicycle. Either you keep moving or you fall down.
Frank Lloyd Wright (1867–1959), architect, writer, and educator

■ **High Status Stress.** As people move up the ladder of affluence, you might expect the stress of having a lower income to fade away. In fact, research suggests that the opposite may be true: "life stress increases so dramatically that its toxic effects essentially cancel out many positive aspects of succeeding." One reason may be that the driven perfectionists who often make it to the top feel enormous pressure to be on call 24/7 via text, e-mail, and phone in order to simply survive professionally.[3]

■ **Privacy in Public.** In Canada—except in Quebec—there is no expectation of privacy in public. However, concern and uncertainty are common, and there are minor variations depending on city and province. Assuming no other laws are being broken, anyone may photograph anything that is visible to them, and publish where they wish. This includes photographs taken on public property, unless the photographer has been asked to cease. Any pictures taken prior to such notification, however, remain the property of the photographer, who may not be forced to delete or surrender it, and who owns copyright to it.[4]

■ **Nature Is Over.** Nearly 20 percent of vertebrate species are threatened, and that number seems sure to increase. And with the world population now topping 7 billion and still growing, a new approach to nature is crucial.[5]

■ **Niche Aging.** Back in the day, retirement dreams typically featured plenty of sunshine, sandy beaches, and lively bingo games. But while many Canadians do go south to retire, or at least for the winters, retirees today are likely to seek more specialized options, where they can grow old alongside others who share a specific interest such as country music or university-level learning. One expert in the field points out: "You're talking about the generation that created 12 different versions of Coca-Cola. They're not going to settle for one kind of retirement community."[6]

1-1a Business Basics: Some Key Definitions

While you can certainly recognize a business when you see one, more formal definitions may help as you read through this book. A **business** is any activity that provides goods and services in an effort to earn a profit. **Profit** is the financial reward that comes from starting and running a business.

> **business** Any activity that provides goods and services in an effort to earn a profit.
>
> **profit** The money a business earns in sales (or revenue) minus expenses, such as the cost of goods and the cost of salaries (Revenue – Expenses = Profit [or Loss]).

More specifically, a profit is the money that a business earns in sales (or revenue), minus expenses, such as the cost of goods and the cost of salaries. Clearly, not every business earns a profit all of the time. When a business brings in less money than it needs to cover expenses, it incurs a **loss**. If you launch a music label, for instance, you'll need to pay your artists, buy or lease a studio, and purchase equipment, among other expenses. If your label generates hits, you'll earn more than enough to cover all your expenses and make yourself rich. But a series of duds could leave you holding the bag.

Just the possibility of earning a profit provides a powerful incentive for people of all backgrounds to launch their own enterprises. For those considering doing so, now may be a challenging time, but things can change rapidly. At the start of 2016, the small business confidence index measured by the Canadian Federation of Independent Business dropped to 54.3 (an index above 50 indicates that most business owners expect stronger performance in the coming year). The highest expectations were in Nova Scotia (69.0), and the lowest were in Alberta (28.8—a record low that was 26 points below its score the previous year). The highest scores were in the hospitality and professional services sectors; the lowest, in the construction and natural resources sectors.[7] In Chapter 6 we will be discussing, in more detail, entrepreneurship and **entrepreneurs**—people who are willing to risk their time, money, and other resources to start and manage their own businesses.

Interestingly, as entrepreneurs create wealth for themselves, they produce a ripple effect that enriches everyone around them. For instance, if your new website becomes the next Facebook, who will benefit? Clearly, *you* will. And you'll probably spend at least some of that money enriching your local clubs, clothing stores, and car dealerships. But others will benefit, too, including your members, the advertisers on your site, the staff who support them, the contractors who build your facilities, and the government that collects your taxes. The impact of one successful entrepreneur can extend to the far reaches of the economy. Multiply the impact by thousands of entrepreneurs— each working in his or her own

> The entrepreneur always searches for change, responds to it, and exploits it as an opportunity.
>
> Peter Drucker, management consultant, educator, author

self-interest—and you can see how the profit motive benefits almost everyone.

Taking a broader perspective, business drives up the **standard of living** for people worldwide, contributing to a higher **quality of life**. Businesses provide not only the products and services people enjoy but also the jobs they need. Beyond the obvious, business contributes to society through innovation—think cars, TVs, and tablet computers. Business also helps raise the standard of living through taxes, which the government spends on projects ranging from streetlights to environmental cleanup. And socially responsible firms contribute even more by advocating for the well-being of the society that feeds their success.

1-2 The History of Business: Putting It All in Context

You may be surprised to learn that—unlike today—business hasn't always been focused on what the customer wants. In fact, business in Canada and the United States has changed rather dramatically over the past 200 to 300 years. Business historians typically divide our business history into five distinct eras, which overlap during the periods of transition.

- **The Industrial Revolution.** Technological advances fuelled a period of rapid industrialization from the mid-1700s to the mid-1800s. As mass production took hold, huge factories replaced skilled artisan workshops. The factories hired large numbers of semi-skilled workers, who specialized in a limited number of tasks. The result was unprecedented production efficiency, but also a loss of individual ownership and personal pride in the production process.

- **The Entrepreneurship Era.** Building on the foundation of the Industrial Revolution, large-scale entrepreneurs emerged in the second half of the 1800s, building business empires. These industrial titans created enormous wealth, raising the overall standard of living across the country. But many also dominated their markets, forcing out competitors, manipulating prices, exploiting workers, and decimating the environment. Towards the end of the 1800s, governments stepped into the business realm, passing laws to regulate business and protect consumers and workers, thus creating more balance in the economy.

loss When a business incurs expenses that are greater than its revenue.

entrepreneurs People who risk their time, money, and other resources to start and manage businesses.

standard of living The quality and quantity of goods and services available to a population.

quality of life The overall sense of well-being experienced by either an individual or a group.

- **The Production Era.** In the early 1900s, major businesses focused on further refining the production process and creating greater efficiencies. Jobs became even more specialized, increasing productivity and lowering costs and prices. In 1913, Henry Ford introduced the assembly line, which quickly became standard across major manufacturing industries. With managers focused on efficiency, the customer was an afterthought. But when customers tightened their belts during the Great Depression and the Second World War, businesses took notice. The "hard sell" emerged: aggressive persuasion designed to separate consumers from their cash.

- **The Marketing Era.** After the Second World War, the balance of power shifted away from producers and towards consumers, the producers flooded the market with enticing choices. To differentiate themselves from their competitors, businesses began to develop brands, or distinctive identities, to help consumers understand the differences among various products. The *marketing concept* emerged: a consumer focus that came to permeate successful companies in every department, at every level. This approach continues to influence business decisions today as global competition heats up to unprecedented levels.

- **The Relationship Era.** Building on the marketing concept, today's leading-edge firms are looking beyond each immediate transaction with their customers with the goal of building long-term relationships. Satisfied customers can become advocates for a business, spreading the word with more speed and credibility than even the best promotional campaign. Also, cultivating current customers is more profitable than constantly seeking new ones. A key tool is technology. With the Web and other digital resources, businesses can gather detailed information about their customers and use that information data to serve them better.

1-3 Not-for-Profit Organizations and the Economy: The Business of Doing Good

Not-for-profit organizations also play a critical role in the economy, often working hand in hand with business to improve the quality of life in our society. Focusing on areas such as health, human services, education, religion, and the arts, **not-for-profit organizations** are business-*like* entities, but their primary goals do not include profit. Chuck Bean, executive director of the Nonprofit Roundtable, explains: "By definition, non-profits are not in the business of financial gain. We're in the business of doing good. However, non-profits are still businesses in every other sense—they employ people, they take in revenue, they produce goods and services and contribute in significant ways to our region's economic stability and growth." Canada has around 170,000 not-for-profit and charity organizations. They contribute more to the Canadian gross domestic product (GDP) annually than the entire retail sector. Canada has the world's second largest not-for-profit sector, employing more than 2 million Canadians. Not-for-profit museums, schools, theatres, and orchestras have become economic magnets for many communities, drawing additional investment.[8] Not-for-profit organizations are discussed in greater detail in Chapter 5.

> **not-for-profit organizations** Business-*like* establishments that employ people and produce goods and services with the fundamental goal of contributing to the community rather than generating financial gain.

This McKay seven-seat touring car, manufactured in Nova Scotia in 1914, had a 40-horsepower engine.

Herb MacKenzie

Not-for-profits, such as Goodwill, employ about one in ten Canadian workers.

Herb MacKenzie

Dumb, Dumb, or Not So Dumb

In the wake of disastrous mistakes and outrageous mismanagement, it might be tough to remember that some mistakes are actually pretty amusing. Several examples might help to remind you.[9]

■ **If only they could have "Googled" the future...** In 1999, the founders of Google were seeking to sell their search engine. They approached George Bell, CEO of Excite, which was one of the hottest brands on the Internet in the 1990s, with an asking price of $1 million. But Bell turned them down, as did Yahoo!, both believing the acquisition would have been too pricey. Excite went bankrupt soon after, and Yahoo! now trails far behind Google. On February 2, 2016, the shares of Alphabet (a holding company formed in October 2015, and Google's parent) opened 3 percent higher, giving the company a market capitalization of $547.1 billion, making it the world's most valuable company.

■ **Accidental cybersnooping.** As Google sent its "Street View" cars all over the world collecting panoramic images for uploading to Google Maps, the firm "unintentionally" collected and retained, among other things, passwords and complete e-mail messages picked up from unsecured Wi-Fi networks.

■ **Clicking without thinking.** To test Google's ability to block harmful advertising, Belgian IT security consultant Didier Stevens posted an ad that read, "Is your PC virus-free? Get it infected here!" It was accepted by Google and displayed 259,723 times: 409 Web surfers actually clicked on the ad.

■ **Wasted time or well worthwhile?** To celebrate the 30th anniversary of Pac-Man in 2010, engineers at Google turned the site's home page into a fully functional version of the game, wasting an estimated 4.8 million hours of the world's time and more than US$120 million in lost productivity.

Sources: Ari Levy, "Google Parent Alphabet Passes Apple Market Cap at the Open," cnbc.com, February 2, 2016; "Excite declines buying Google", *Business Excellence* website, October 10, 2010; Marguerite Reardon, "Google: Oops, We Spied on Your Wi-Fi," cnet .com, May 14, 2010; Mitch Wagner, "Google's Pac-Man Cost $120M in Productivity," pcworld.com, n.d.; "101 Dumbest Moments in Business," fortune.com, January 16, 2008.

CHANGING *DON'T* TO *DO*

Herb MacKenzie

When in doubt, we usually don't! Most of us can probably think of a time when we should have taken some action, but instead we did nothing, because doing nothing was easier. Enter the choice architects: behavioural scientists who claim that businesses, governments, and other institutions can engineer our options to "nudge" us into making choices that are (ideally) more socially desirable or (from a business standpoint) more profitable than the choices we'd make on our own. Consider these examples:

■ **Better aim.** A sign sometimes seen in men's washrooms says: "We aim to please; you aim too, please." But, as most women who share toilets with men can attest, even the best-intentioned men don't seem to aim very well. In busy washrooms, this is more than just a gross annoyance; dirty bathrooms increase cleaning costs and undermine brand image. Aad Kiedboom, an economist who worked for Schiphol International Airport in Amsterdam, tackled this issue by etching the image of a black housefly onto the bowls of the airport's urinals, just to the left of the drain. As a result, "spillage" decreased by 80 percent.

■ **Green footprints.** Copenhagen has been ranked as one of the top six cleanest cities in Europe, but aspires to be first. An experiment conducted at Roskilde University demonstrated how to "nudge" people in the right direction. Students first handed out caramels to pedestrians and then took a benchmark reading of the number of wrappers discarded on the street. Then they placed a series of green footprints that led to a nearby garbage can and repeated the experiment. The result: 46 percent fewer wrappers were discarded on the street. Clearly, when people are thoughtlessly disrespectful, a little nudge can be a great reminder.[10]

1-4 Factors of Production: The Basic Building Blocks

Businesses and not-for-profit organizations both rely on **factors of production**—four fundamental resources—to achieve their objectives. Some combination of these factors is crucial for an economic system to work and create wealth. As you read through the factors, keep in mind that they don't come free of charge. Human resources, for instance, require wages, while entrepreneurs need a profit incentive.

- **Natural Resources.** This factor includes all inputs that offer value in their natural state, such as land, fresh water, wind, and mineral deposits. Most natural resources must be extracted, purified, or harnessed; people cannot actually create them. (Note that agricultural products, which people do create through planting and tending, are not a natural resource.) The value of all natural resources tends to rise with high demand, low supply, or both.

- **Capital.** This factor includes machines, tools, buildings, information, and technology—the synthetic resources that a business needs to produce goods or services. Computers and telecommunications capability have become pivotal elements of capital across a surprising range of industries, from financial services to professional sports. You may be surprised to learn that in this context, capital does not include money, but clearly, businesses use money to acquire, maintain, and upgrade their capital.

- **Human Resources.** This factor encompasses the physical, intellectual, and creative contributions of everyone who works within an economy. As technology replaces a growing number of manual labour jobs, education and motivation have become increasingly important to human resource development. Given the importance of knowledge to workforce effectiveness, some business experts, such as management guru Peter Drucker, have broken out knowledge as its own category, separate from human resources.

- **Entrepreneurship.** Entrepreneurs are people who take the risk of launching and operating their own businesses, largely in response to the profit incentive. They tend to see opportunities where others don't, and they use their own resources to capitalize on that potential. Entrepreneurial enterprises can kick-start an economy, creating a tidal wave of opportunity by harnessing the other factors of production. But entrepreneurs don't thrive in an environment that doesn't support them. The key ingredient is economic freedom: freedom of choice (whom to hire, for instance, or what to produce), freedom from excess regulation, and freedom from too much taxation. Protection from corruption and unfair competition is another entrepreneurial "must."

Clearly, all of these factors must be in place for an economy to thrive. But which factor is *most* important? One way to answer that question is to examine current economies around the world. Russia and China are both rich in natural resources and human resources. And both countries have a solid level of capital (growing in China and deteriorating in Russia). Yet neither country is wealthy; both rank relatively low in terms of gross national income per person. The missing ingredient seems to be entrepreneurship, which is limited in Russia largely through corruption and in China through government interference and taxes. Contrast those examples with, say, Hong Kong. The population there is small and the natural resources are severely limited, yet Hong Kong has consistently ranked among the richest regions in Asia. The reason? Operating for many years under the British legal and economic system, the government actively encouraged entrepreneurship, which fuelled the creation of wealth. Recognizing the potential of entrepreneurship, China has recently done more to relax regulations and support free enterprise. The result has been tremendous growth, which may yet bring China into the ranks of the wealthier nations.[11]

1-5 The Business Environment: The Context for Success

No business operates in a vacuum. External factors play a vital role in determining whether a given business succeeds or fails. Likewise, the broader **business environment** can make the critical difference in whether an overall economy thrives or disintegrates. The five key dimensions of the business environment are the economic environment, the competitive environment, the technological environment, the social environment, and the global environment, as shown in Exhibit 1.1.

factors of production Four fundamental elements—natural resources, capital, human resources, and entrepreneurship—that businesses need to achieve their objectives. Some combination of these factors is crucial for an economic system to create wealth.

business environment The setting in which business operates. The five key components are economic environment, competitive environment, technological environment, social environment, and global environment.

Exhibit 1.1

Each dimension of the business environment impacts both individual businesses and the economy overall.

Economic Environment

Social Environment

BUSINESS

Competitive Environment

Global Environment

Technological Environment

1-5a The Economic Environment[12]

Canada is a member of the G7—a group of industrialized nations that also includes France, Germany, Italy, Japan, the United Kingdom, and the United States. The finance ministers of these countries meet regularly to discuss economic issues. Since 2008, the global financial crisis—still a concern in 2016, and promising to continue well into the future—has been a major item on their agenda. The Canadian economy, while certainly affected by this crisis, has proven more resilient than the economies of many countries. However, Canada did experience a small economic recession in 2015. Growth in 2016 is expected to lag US growth, and if oil prices continue to decline, there is a chance of another recession.

The Canadian economy remains relatively strong in part because the government takes active steps to reduce the risks of starting and running a business. As a result, free enterprise and fair competition flourish. The federal government, largely through Industry Canada, promotes a number of agencies and initiatives to encourage economic development across the country. Meanwhile, provincial governments compete for business development by providing investment and tax incentives for new businesses or by making the tax environment more attractive for existing businesses, which can then keep more of their profits to reinvest for growth and job creation.

Another key element of the Canadian economic environment is legislation that supports enforceable contracts. For instance, if you contract a company to supply your silk screening business with 1,000 blank T-shirts at $4.00 each, that firm must comply or face legal consequences. The firm can't wait until a day before delivery and jack up the price to $8.00 each, because you would almost certainly respond with a successful lawsuit. Many Canadian residents take enforceable contracts for granted, but in a number of developing countries—which offer some of today's largest business opportunities—contracts are often not enforceable (at least not in day-to-day practice).

Corruption also plays a role in the economic environment. A low level of corruption and bribery dramatically reduces the risk of running a business. Fortunately, Canadian laws keep domestic corruption mostly—but not completely—at bay. Other ethical lapses can also increase the cost of doing business for everyone involved. In the wake of ethical meltdowns at major Canadian and US corporations such as Nortel, Enron, and WorldCom, the federal government has passed regulations to increase corporate accountability. If the legislation effectively curbs illegal and unethical practices, every business will have a fair chance at success.

Although the Canadian economy is strong overall, it is threatened by underlying issues. Personal incomes have risen, but personal debt has risen more rapidly. By 2016, the ratio of debt to personal disposable income had reached nearly 165 percent—in other words, the average household owed $1.65 in debt for each $1.00 of disposable income. If there is an unforeseen economic shock, some households may be forced to declare personal bankruptcy. The same may happen if interest rates rise too rapidly as the economy recovers. Regardless, as Canadians are forced to spend more to service debt, they will have less money to spend on new purchases, and this will slow economic recovery.

Meanwhile, government debt has been mushrooming as well. By 2016, combined federal and provincial debt will reach $1.3 trillion. Government debt has both short- and long-term effects. In the short term, governments will spend more to service debt and have less to spend on programs where it could be better spent. Research suggests that in the long term, growing government debt dampens economic growth. The federal government, for example, expects to spend $25.9 billion to service its debt in 2016, more than it spent the previous year on national defence. Provincially, Ontario spends more to service its debt than it spends on its entire welfare system. Going forward, it looks as if most if not all governments in Canada will go much more deeply into debt. Many economists do support governments taking on debt during poor economic times, to create jobs and spur growth. While it is very unlikely we will see a balanced federal budget by 2019–20, as the governing Liberals have promised, it is still possible that our debt-to-GDP ratio (another important economic indicator) can be lowered. The Bank of Canada has stated that the economic situation in Canada in early 2016 could put the government on track for an additional $90 billion in debt over the next four years.

Later chapters on economics and ethics will address these economic challenges and their significance in more depth. But, bottom line, we have reason for cautious (some would say *very* cautious) optimism. Our economy has not been battered as badly as the US economy, but it is unlikely to recover as quickly as that of our neighbour. The United States began increasing interest rates in 2015 in anticipation of economic growth. Since Canada is very much affected by economic conditions there, at least some sectors of our economy will strengthen in 2016 as a result.

1-5b The Competitive Environment

As global competition intensifies yet further, leading-edge companies have focused on customer satisfaction as never before. The goal: to develop long-term, mutually beneficial relationships with customers. Getting current customers to buy more of your product is a lot less expensive than convincing potential customers to try your product for the first time. And if you transform your current customers into loyal advocates—vocal promoters of your product or service—they'll get those new customers for you more effectively than any advertising or discount program. Companies such as Amazon, Coca-Cola, and Apple lead their industries in customer satisfaction, which translates into higher profits even when the competition is tough.[13]

Customer satisfaction comes in large part from delivering unsurpassed value. The best measure of value is the size of the gap between product benefits and price. A product has value when its benefits to the customer are equal to or greater than the price the customer pays. Keep in mind that the cheapest product doesn't necessarily represent the best value. If a $1 toy from Dollarama breaks in a day, customers may be willing to pay several dollars more for a similar toy from somewhere else. But if that $1 toy lasts all year, customers will be delighted by the value and will likely encourage their friends and family to shop at Dollarama. The key to value is quality, and virtually all successful firms offer top-quality products relative to their direct competitors.

A 2015 ranking of the best 100 global brands by the Interbrand consulting firm places 8 of the 10 top brands by brand value in the United States. Also included are Toyota (Japan) and Samsung (South Korea). The top Canadian brand, Thomson Reuters, ranked number 63.[14] Exhibit 1.2 shows the winners and their brand value as they race to capture the hearts, minds, and dollars of consumers around the world.

Leading Edge Versus Bleeding Edge **Speed-to-market**—the rate at which a firm transforms concepts

Exhibit 1.2

Global Brand Champions and Their Value

MOST VALUABLE BRANDS	BRAND VALUE IN $ BILLIONS (CHANGE IN BRAND VALUE IN %)
1. **Apple**	170.3 (+43)
2. **Google**	120.3 (+12)
3. **Coca-Cola**	78.4 (−4)
4. **Microsoft**	67.7 (+11)
5. **IBM**	65.1 (−10)
6. **Toyota**	49.0 (+16)
7. **Samsung**	45.3 (0)
8. **GE**	42.3 (−7)
9. **McDonald's**	39.8 (−6)
10. **Amazon**	37.9 (+29)

Source: Interbrand Releases 2015 Best Global Brands Report, Interbrand, October 4, 2015, http://interbrand.com/?newsroom=interbrand-releases-2015-best-global-brands-report, accessed February 9, 2016.

into actual products—can be another key source of competitive advantage. The pace of change just keeps getting faster. In this tumultuous setting, companies that stay ahead of the pack often enjoy a distinct advantage. But keep in mind that there's a difference between the leading edge and the bleeding edge. Bleeding-edge firms launch products that fail because they're too far ahead of the market. In the late 1990s, for instance, during the dot.com boom, Montreal-based Peachtree Network sold its services to many grocers across North America as it helped them sell to their customers online. But the firm went bankrupt in 2001, partly because customers weren't yet ready to dump traditional grocery stores in favour of cybershopping. Leading-edge firms, by contrast, offer products just as the market becomes ready to embrace them.[15]

Apple provides an excellent example of leading edge. You may be surprised to learn that Apple—which owns about 70 percent of the digital music player market—did not offer the first MP3 player. Instead, it surveyed the existing market to help develop a new product, the iPod, which was far superior in terms of design and ease of use. But Apple didn't stop with one successful MP3 player. Racing to stay ahead, it soon introduced the colourful, more affordable iPod Mini. And before sales reached their peak, it launched the iPod Nano, which essentially pulled the rug out from under the blockbuster iPod Mini just a few short months before

speed-to-market The rate at which a new product moves from conception to commercialization.

APPLE TARNISHED, APPLE POLISHED

Herb MacKenzie

Seems like it was long, long ago in a galaxy far, far away that Apple first introduced the iPad, but it was only in 2010 that everyone was making jokes that iPad sounded more like a feminine hygiene product than a tablet computer. In the first three years after its introduction, Apple built iPad into such a blockbuster that analysts for *Fortune* claim that if it were its own business, separate from Apple, it would rank 98 on the *Fortune* 500 list, higher than both McDonald's and Nike. But the iPhone 5 has not done nearly as well. In fact, *Consumer Reports* has given the iPhone 5 mediocre scores, calling it "the worst of the top smartphones." It scored at the bottom of the top three at two major phone carriers and wasn't even listed in the top three at another. Apple Maps software on the iPhone 5 was so bad that it misplaced entire towns, making it three times more likely to get you lost than Google Maps. Eventually, Apple replaced Apple Maps with Google Maps and issued a rare official apology. The iPhone 5 clearly tarnished Apple. In a technology market moving quickly towards greater dependence on mobile, another product failure and more negative reviews for the iPhone could have hurt Apple at its core, despite the overwhelming success of the iPad and the iPad mini.

Fortunately, a fix polished Apple: iPhone 6 and iPhone 6 Plus. In their first three days after launch, Apple sold 10 million units.[16]

the holiday selling season. Why? If Apple didn't do it, a competitor might well have done it instead. And Apple is almost maniacally focused on maintaining its competitive lead.[17]

1-5c The Workforce Advantage

Employees can contribute another key dimension to a firm's competitive edge. Recent research suggests that investing in worker satisfaction yields tangible bottom-line results. The researchers compared the stock prices of *Fortune* magazine's annual list of the "100 Best Companies to Work for in America" to the S&P 500, which reflects the overall market. The firms with the highest employee satisfaction provided a 10.3 percent annual return, compared to a 2.95 percent return for the firms in the S&P 500. In fact, from 1997 through 2012, the returns from the "100 Best" have quadrupled returns from the overall market. While the critical difference in performance most likely stemmed from employee satisfaction, other factors—such as excellent products and superb top management—likely *also* played a role in both employee satisfaction and strong stock performance.[18] As you will see in Chapter 14, employee happiness provides many benefits for the organization.

Finding and holding the best talent will likely become a crucial competitive issue over the next decade as the baby boom generation continues to retire. The 500 largest North American companies anticipate losing about half their senior managers over the next five to six years. Replacing them will be tough, for baby boomers will be succeeded by a much smaller cohort of workers. But the impact will be muted as long as the economy remains poor: A recent survey of more than 3,000 employees by the Canadian Payroll Association found that more than one in five respondents expected to work at least four years longer than they originally planned. Firms that cultivate human resources now will find themselves better able to compete as the market for top talent tightens.[19]

1-5d The Technological Environment

The broad definition of **business technology** includes any tools that businesses can use to become more efficient and effective. More specifically, in today's world, business technology usually refers to computers, telecommunications, and other digital tools. Over the past few decades, digital technology has had a transformative impact on business. New industries have emerged; others have disappeared. And some fields—such as travel, banking, and music—have changed dramatically. Even in categories with relatively unchanged products, companies have leveraged technology to streamline production and create new efficiencies. Examples include new processes such as computerized billing, digital animation, and robotic manufacturing. For fast-moving firms, the technological environment represents a rich source of competitive advantage; it

business technology Any tools—especially computers, telecommunications, and other digital products—that businesses can use to become more efficient and effective.

Google continues to be a powerhouse of innovation, in terms of both product development and employee benefits.

can also be a major threat for companies that are slow to adapt or to integrate new approaches.

The **World Wide Web** has transformed not only business but also people's lives. Anyone, anywhere, anytime, can use the Web to send and receive images and data (as long as access is available). One result is the rise of **e-commerce** (i.e., online sales), which allows businesses to tap into a worldwide community of potential customers. In the wake of the global economic crisis, e-commerce has slowed from the breakneck 20 percent–plus growth rates of recent years, but even so, analysts predict that solid single-digit growth will continue. Business-to-business selling comprises the vast majority of total e-commerce sales (and an even larger share of the profits). Also, a growing number of businesses have connected their digital networks with suppliers and distributors to create a more seamless flow of goods and services.[20]

Alternative selling strategies thrive on the Internet, giving rise to more individualized buying experiences. If you've browsed seller reviews on eBay or received shopping recommendations from Amazon, you have a sense of how personal Web marketing can feel. Online technology also allows leading-edge firms to offer customized products at prices comparable to those of standardized products. On the NikeID website, for instance, customers can "custom build" Nike shoes, clothing, and gear, all while sitting at home in their pyjamas.

As technology continues to evolve at breakneck speed, the scope of change—in both everyday life and business operations—will be almost unimaginable. In this environment, companies that welcome change and manage it well will clearly be the winners.

1-5e The Social Environment

The social environment encompasses the values, attitudes, customs, and beliefs shared by groups of people. It also covers **demographics**, or the measurable characteristics of a population. Demographic factors include population size and density as well as specific traits such as age, gender, race, education, and income. As one can expect, given all these influences, countries differ greatly from one another in terms of their social environments. Nations as diverse as Canada will have a number of different social environments. Instead of covering the full spectrum, this section focuses on the broad social trends that most strongly impact Canadian business. Understanding the various dimensions of the social environment is crucial for businesses, which must offer goods and services that respond to it if they are to succeed.

Diversity Canada today is one of the world's most ethnically diverse countries. More than 20 percent of Canadians were born in another country (about 11 percent of Americans were born outside the United States). Furthermore, while US multicultural policy has tended towards assimilation, Canada continues to encourage its citizens to retain and honour their cultural heritage. Another major difference between the United States and Canada is that the former has a few ethnic groups that make up the great majority of non-Caucasians, while Canada is now home to many (but smaller) ethnic groups. Exhibit 1.3 shows Canada's top four visible-minority groups and the numbers of each expected by 2017.

However, the national statistics are somewhat misleading because ethnic groups tend to cluster together. Canada's 15 largest cities

World Wide Web The service that allows computer users to easily access and share information on the Internet in the form of text, graphics, video, and animation.

e-commerce Business transactions conducted online, typically via the Internet.

demographics The measurable characteristics of a population. Demographic factors include population size and density and specific traits such as age, gender, and race.

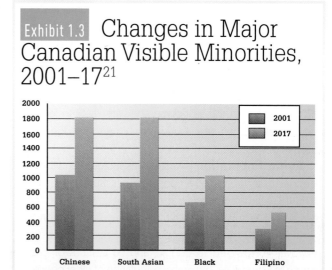

Exhibit 1.3 Changes in Major Canadian Visible Minorities, 2001–17[21]

Source: Statistics Canada, "Population Projections of Visible Minority Groups, Canada, Provinces, and Regions: 2001–2017", Catalogue no 91-541-XIE, based on the reference scenario.

are home to 90 percent of Canadians who were born abroad. Around half of the populations of Toronto and Vancouver are expected to comprise visible-minority groups by 2017, as will approximately one-quarter of the populations of Calgary, Ottawa, and Windsor.[22]

What does this mean for business? Growing ethnic populations offer robust profit potential for firms that pursue them. TD Canada Trust, for example, has 43 percent of the South Asian Canadian market and 29 percent of the Chinese Canadian market. It employs ethnic, bilingual, or multilingual staff to better serve Canada's ethnic markets, and it ensures that it has promotional material in all of its branches to meet their needs. More than 60 languages are spoken in TD branches, and more than 200 languages are available by phone. For other businesses in Canada, reaching ethnic markets is becoming increasingly easier. Rogers Communications has been actively targeting ethnic consumers and now has over 100 multicultural channels, which broadcast in more than 20 languages.[23]

Growing diversity also impacts the workforce. A diverse staff—one that reflects an increasingly diverse marketplace—can yield a powerful competitive advantage, for these employees are better able to serve a diverse customer base. There is considerable research that demonstrates a strong link between diversity and innovation. Decision-making and problem-solving skills are enhanced. From global behemoths such as Procter & Gamble to local corner stores, companies have taken proactive steps to hire and nurture people from a broad range of backgrounds. True diversity includes differences in gender, race, age, religion, and nationality, among others. Leading-edge firms that take a proactive approach to effective integration achieve greater employee performance and higher employee retention.[24]

Effectively managing diversity should become easier as time goes by. Multiple studies demonstrate that young Canadian adults are the most tolerant age group, and they are moving in a more tolerant direction than earlier generations regarding racial differences, immigration, and LGBTQ issues. As this generation gathers influence and experience in the workforce, they are likely to leverage diversity in their organizations to hone their edge in a fiercely competitive marketplace.[25]

Aging Population As lifespans increase and birth rates decrease, the Canadian population is rapidly aging. In 2015, the estimated median ages in Canada were 40.6 for men and 43.1 for women, and they're increasing monthly.[26] By mid-century the global population of people aged 60 and over is expected to double, and 60 percent of that growth will be in Asia. The global population of older people is expected to reach 2.3 billion by 2100, triple what it is now.[27]

Fast Food? Sometimes. Fast Computer? Awesome! Fast Fashion? Huh?

In most industries, faster is better, and those of you who have surfed the Web on a newer, faster device can certainly relate. And when you're hungry, it's great to get a pizza delivered in less than thirty minutes. But fashion has gotten faster, too, and in this case, faster may not be better. Mass market powerhouses, such as H&M, Forever 21, and Zara, can take a product quite literally from the drawing boards to store shelves around the world in about two weeks. And with rock-bottom prices, many consumers are able to buy more than ever before. In fact, Canadian consumers purchase billions of garments each year—about 64 items per person—and no matter how much they give away, this excess can lead to waste. According to Elizabeth Cline, author of *OverDressed*, "charities long ago passed the point of being able to sell all of our wearable used clothes." In part because of this surplus, every year billions of pounds of apparel end up in landfills. So it may be better for everyone involved—and for our planet—if it took a little longer for affordable versions of this year's fashions to make it from the pages of *Vogue* magazine to the hangers in your closet.[28]

Sources: Julian Sancton, "Book Review: 'Overdressed,' by Elizabeth L. Cline," bloomberg.com, June 21, 2012; Eliana Dockterman, "How U.S. Clothing Brands Are Getting Greener," August 20, 2012.

The rapidly aging population brings opportunities and threats for business. Companies in fields that cater to the elderly—such as health care, pharmaceuticals, travel, recreation, and financial management—will clearly boom. Creative companies in other fields will capitalize on this trend by reimagining their current products to serve older clients. Possibilities include books and movies—and perhaps even video games—with mature characters, low-impact fitness programs such as water aerobics, and smartphones and tablets with more readable screens. Again, the potential payoff of age diversity is clear: companies with older employees are more likely to find innovative ways to reach the aging consumer market.

But at the same time, surging retirement rates pose significant threats to overall business success. Because of the smaller labour pool, companies will need to compete even harder for top talent, and this will drive up recruitment and payroll costs. As governments at all levels stretch to serve the aging population, taxes may increase, placing an additional burden on business. And as mid-career workers spend more on eldercare, they may find themselves with less to spend on other goods and services, shrinking the size of the consumer market.

Sorting Through Shades of Green

Green is everywhere. Firm after firm—including Loblaws, Canadian Tire, and Toyota, among many others—have staked their future on green marketing, trumpeting claims that range from "locally grown" to "fully recyclable." If you can't figure out which to believe and which to blow off, you have plenty of company. Only about half of consumers believe green claims. Fortunately, there are a number of labels to help Canadians make better choices. One such label, EcoLogo—also known as Environmental Choice—identifies products that have been independently certified to be green throughout their entire life cycle, from production, to consumption, to disposal. Standards are sufficiently high that only the top 20 percent of products on the market can achieve this accreditation. More than 7,000 products, including draperies, lithium batteries, and toys, now carry this logo.

To provide additional help to confused consumers, TerraChoice, an environmental marketing agency, has laid out *The Six Sins of Greenwashing*. (Greenwashing is defined as false or misleading green claims.)

- *Sin of the Hidden Trade-Off.* Green claims based on a single environmental attribute, without attention to more important issues. Example: A paper company that promotes recycled products but doesn't mention how it impacts global warming.

- *Sin of No Proof.* Environmental claims without evidence or reliable certification. Example: Light bulb manufacturers that promote energy efficiency without documentation to support this claim.

- *Sin of Vagueness.* Green claims that are so broad or poorly defined that consumers are likely to misunderstand their real meaning. Example: Anything labelled "All Natural." Natural substances—such as arsenic—can be toxic, too.

- *Sin of Irrelevance.* Environmental claims that may be truthful but just don't matter. Example: Anything labelled "Chlorofuorocarbon (CFC) Free" is a bit silly because CFCs have been banned in Canada for several decades. No product should claim not to have them.

- *Sin of Lesser of Two Evils.* Green claims that may be true but distract consumers from the greater negative environmental impacts of the category as a whole. Example: Organic cigarettes. Enough said.

- *Sin of Fibbing.* Green claims that are out-and-out lies. Example: Some dishwashing detergents claim to be "Energy Star" registered, even though the official Energy Star website excludes them.

Finding products that meet the rigorous TerraChoice standards can be almost impossible, but you can still be a reasonably green consumer. First, recognize that green comes in many shades. A somewhat green product certainly beats a product that isn't green at all. And you can always encourage the companies you buy from to be honest and clear about how green they actually are.[29]

Rising Worker Expectations Workers of all ages continue to seek flexibility from their employers. Moreover, following massive corporate layoffs of the early 2000s, employees are much less likely to be loyal to their firms. According to Shannon Young, HR manager with Randstad Canada, more workers today, regardless of age, view themselves as "free agents" responsible for managing their own careers: "They work on maintaining cutting-edge skills and often don't feel any remorse about jumping ship if another job offers better pay or more growth opportunity."[30] Smart firms are responding to the change in worker expectations by forging a new partnership with their employees. The goal is greater mutual respect through open communication, information sharing, and training. The not-so-hidden agenda, of course, is stronger long-term performance.[31]

Ethics and Social Responsibility With high-profile ethical meltdowns dominating the headlines over the past few years, workers, consumers, and governments have begun to hold businesses—and the people who run them—to a higher standard. The laws that have been passed in the wake of recent accounting scandals demand transparent financial management and more accountability from senior executives. Recognizing their key role in business success, more and more consumers and workers have begun to insist that companies play a proactive role in making their communities—and often the world community—better places. Sustainability—doing business today without harming the ability of future generations to meet their needs—has become a core issue in the marketplace, driving business policies, investment decisions, and consumer purchases at unprecedented levels.[32]

1-5f The Global Environment

The Canadian economy operates in the context of the global environment, interacting continually with other economies. Over the past two decades, technology and free trade have blurred the lines between individual economies around the world. Technology has forged unprecedented links among countries, making it cost-effective—even efficient—to establish computer help centres in Mumbai to service customers in Toronto, or to hire

Herb MacKenzie

countries—took bold steps to lower tariffs (taxes on imports) and to reduce trade restrictions worldwide. As a result, goods are moving more freely across international boundaries. Individual groups of countries have gone even further, creating blocs of nations with virtually unrestricted trade. Mexico, Canada, and the United States have laid the groundwork for a free trade mega-market through the North American Free Trade Agreement (NAFTA). The European Union (EU) is a 28-nation politico-economic bloc, but it has been weakened in recent years, for its members are divided regarding how to manage its external borders in the wake of refugee immigration and terrorism. In a 2016 referendum in the United Kingdom (UK), nearly 52 percent of voters supporting an exit from the EU, resulting in considerable political upheaval, as Scotland, a major part of the United Kingdom, voted strongly to remain. What will happen now is uncertain, but should the UK invoke an agreement called Article 50, it will become the first country to withdraw from the EU and will have two years to negotiate its exit. Other free trade agreements continue to develop around the world. The free trade movement has lowered prices and increased quality across virtually every product category as competition becomes truly global. We'll discuss these issues and their implications in more depth in Chapter 4.

A Multipronged Threat In the past decade alone, war, terrorism, disease, and natural disasters have taken a horrific toll in human lives around the globe. The economic toll has been devastating as well. The 9/11 terrorist attacks in the United States in 2001 decimated the global travel industry. The deadly SARS epidemic of 2003 dealt a powerful blow to the economies of Hong Kong, Beijing, and Toronto. Less than two years later, the Indian Ocean tsunami wiped out the fishing industry along vast stretches of the Indian and Sri Lankan coasts and crippled the Thai tourism industry, which had been booming. The effects of the 2011 tsunami in Japan are still being felt around the world. At the start of 2016, the Zika virus seemed to be spreading to many countries of the world. While its effects are not usually severe, it does pose considerable risk for some segments of the population, especially pregnant women and children. The World Health Organization has declared it an international public health emergency, and as world travel declines, its economic impact will certainly be felt in many regions. With nationalism on the rise, and growing religious and ethnic tensions around the world, the global economy may continue to suffer collateral damage.[34]

programmers in Buenos Aires to make websites for companies in Stockholm. Not surprisingly, jobs have migrated to the lowest bidders with the highest quality, regardless of where those bidders are based.

Often, the lowest bidder is based in China or India; both economies supported by considerable foreign investment. China has been a magnet for manufacturing jobs because of its large population and low wages—ranging from CAD$2.31 to CAD$3.93 per hour, depending on region, versus $25.66 per hour in Canada. While China remains the world's largest manufacturing economy, it has slowed considerably in recent years. India has been especially adept at attracting high-tech jobs, in part because of its world-class, English-speaking university graduates, who are willing to work for less than their counterparts around the globe.[33]

The migration of jobs relates closely to the global movement towards **free trade**. In 1995, a renegotiation of the **General Agreement on Tariffs and Trade (GATT)**—signed by 125

> In Asia, the average person's living standards are currently set to rise by 10,000 percent in one lifetime!
>
> —Newsweek

free trade An international economic and political movement designed to help goods and services flow more freely across international boundaries.

General Agreement on Tariffs and Trade (GATT) An international trade agreement that has taken bold steps to lower tariffs and promote free trade worldwide.

1-6 Business and You: Making It Personal

Whatever your career choice—from video game developer, to real estate agent, to Web designer—business will impact your life. Both the broader economy and your own business skills will influence your personal financial success. In light of these factors, making the right career choice can be a bit scary. The good news is that experts advise graduating students to "do what you love." That is a hard-headed strategy, not soft-hearted puffery. Following your passion makes dollars and sense in today's environment, which values less routine abilities such as creativity, communication, and caring. Exercising these abilities tends to be more rewarding for most people than using routine, programmable skills that computers can easily emulate. Following your passion doesn't guarantee a fat paycheque, but it does boost your chances of both financial and personal success.[35]

THE BIG PICTURE

Business today is complex, global, and faster moving than ever before. Looking forward, the rate of change seems likely to accelerate even more. China and India seem poised to achieve economic clout, raising worldwide competition to a whole new level. Technology will continue to change the business landscape. And a new focus on ethics and social responsibility will likely transform the role of business in society. This book will focus on the impact of change in every facet of business, from management to marketing to money, with an emphasis on how the elements of business relate to one another and how business as a whole relates to you.

careers in business: Manager of New Media

Work with marketing team to determine what motivates and inspires consumers. Lead development and execution of digital marketing campaigns across a variety of platforms to build a deep, meaningful, and genuine relationship with consumers. Develop and manage interactive viral campaigns, integrate interactive media into the overall business strategy. According to SimplyHired.com, the average salary for new media managers in 2012 was $79,000, although there was significant variation based on company, location, industry, experience, and benefits. Most new media positions require experience in the field and a four-year degree in either business or communication. Many also prefer a master's degree in business (an MBA).

STUDY TOOLS 1

IN THE BOOK, YOU CAN:

☐ Rip out the Chapter Review card at the back of the book to have a summary of the chapter and key terms handy.

ONLINE AT NELSON.COM/STUDENT YOU CAN:

☐ Work through key concepts with a Guided Learning Question.

☐ Prepare for tests with quizzes.

☐ Review the key terms with Flash Cards (online or printer-ready).

☐ Explore practical examples of chapter concepts with Connect a Concept exercises.

2

Business Ethics and Social Responsibility:
Doing Well by Doing Good

LEARNING OBJECTIVES
After studying this chapter, you will be able to...

2-1 Define ethics and explain the concept of universal ethical standards

2-2 Describe business ethics and ethical dilemmas

2-3 Discuss how ethics relates to both the individual and the organization

2-4 Define social responsibility and examine the impact on stakeholder groups

2-5 Explain the role of social responsibility in the global arena

2-6 Describe how companies evaluate their efforts to be socially responsible

After you finish this chapter, go to page 33 for STUDY TOOLS

2-1 Ethics and Social Responsibility: A Close Relationship

Ethics and social responsibility—often discussed in the same breath—are closely related, but they are definitely not the same. Ethics are a set of beliefs about right and wrong, good and bad; business ethics involve the application of these issues in the workplace. Clearly, ethics relate to individuals and their day-to-day decision making. Just as clearly, the decisions of each individual can impact the entire organization.

Social responsibility is the obligation of a business to contribute to society. The most socially responsible firms feature proactive policies that focus on meeting the needs of all of their stakeholders—not only investors but also employees, customers, and the broader community. The company's stance regarding social responsibility sets the tone for the organization and clearly influences the decisions of individual employees.

While this chapter discusses ethics and social responsibility separately, keep in mind that the two areas have a dynamic, inter-active relationship that plays a vital role in building both profitable businesses and a vibrant community.

2-1a Defining Ethics: Murkier Than You'd Think...

In the most general sense, **ethics** are a set of beliefs about right and wrong, good and bad. Your individual ethics stem from who you are as a human being; that said, your family, your social group, and your culture also play a significant role in shaping your ethics. And therein lies the challenge: In Canada, people come from such diverse backgrounds that establishing broad agreement on specific ethical standards can be daunting. The global arena only amplifies the challenge.

A given country's legal system provides a solid starting point for examining ethical standards. The function of laws in Canada (and elsewhere) is to establish and enforce ethical norms that apply to everyone in our society. Laws provide basic standards of behaviour. But truly ethical behaviour goes beyond the basics. In other words, your actions can be completely legal yet still unethical. And because the legal system is far from perfect, in rare instances your actions can be illegal yet still ethical. Exhibit 2.1 shows some examples of how business conduct can fall within legal and ethical dimensions. Clearly, legal *and* ethical actions should be

ethics A set of beliefs about right and wrong, good and bad.

Exhibit 2.1 Legal–Ethical Matrix

LEGAL AND UNETHICAL	LEGAL AND ETHICAL
Promoting high-calorie/low-nutrient foods with inadequate information about the risks.	Producing high-quality products.
Producing products that you know will break before their time.	Rewarding integrity. Leading by example.
Paying non-living wages to workers in developing countries.	Treating employees fairly. Contributing to the community. Respecting the environment.

ILLEGAL AND UNETHICAL	ILLEGAL AND ETHICAL
Embezzling money.	Providing rock-bottom prices *only* to distributors in underserved areas.
Engaging in sexual harassment.	Collaborating with other medical clinics to guarantee low prices in low-income countries (collusion).
Practising collusion with competitors.	
Encouraging fraudulent accounting.	

your goal. Legality should be the floor—not the ceiling—for how to behave in business and elsewhere.

Do all actions have ethical implications? Clearly not. Some decisions fall within the realm of free choice, with no direct link to right and wrong, good and bad. Examples might include where you buy your morning coffee, what features your company includes on its new laptop computers, or what new machines your gym decides to purchase.

2-1b Universal Ethical Standards: A Reasonable Goal or Wishful Thinking?

Too many people view ethics as relative. In other words, their ethical standards shift depending on the situation and how it relates to them. Here are a few examples:

- "It's not okay to steal paper from the office supply store...*but* it's perfectly fine to 'borrow' supplies from the storage closet at work. Why? The company owes me a bigger salary."

- "It's wrong to lie...*but* it's okay to call in sick when I have personal business to take care of. Why? I don't want to burn through my limited vacation days."

- "Everyone should have a level playing field...*but* it's fine to give my brother the first shot at my company's contract. Why? I know he really needs the work."

This kind of two-faced thinking is dangerous because it can help people rationalize bigger and bigger ethical deviations. This problem can be fixed by identifying **universal ethical standards** that apply to everyone across a broad spectrum of situations. Some people argue that we could never find universal standards for a country as diverse as Canada. But the not-for-profit, nonpartisan Character Counts organization has worked with a diverse group of educators, community leaders, and ethicists to identify six core values, listed in Exhibit 2.2, that transcend political, religious, class, and ethnic divisions.

> **universal ethical standards** Ethical norms that apply to all people across a broad spectrum of situations.
>
> **business ethics** The application of right and wrong, good and bad in a business setting.
>
> **ethical dilemma** A decision that involves a conflict of values; every potential course of action has some significant negative consequences.

Herb MacKenzie

Exhibit 2.2 — Universal Ethical Standards[1]

TRUSTWORTHINESS	Be honest. Don't deceive, cheat, or steal. Do what you say you'll do.
RESPECT	Treat others how you'd like to be treated. Be considerate. Be tolerant of differences.
RESPONSIBILITY	Persevere. Be self-controlled and self-disciplined. Be accountable for your choices.
FAIRNESS	Provide equal opportunity. Be open-minded. Don't take advantage of others.
CARING	Be kind. Be compassionate. Express gratitude.
CITIZENSHIP	Contribute to the community. Protect the environment. Cooperate whenever feasible.

Source: Hanson, W. (ed.), *Making Ethical Decisions*, Josephson Institute, 2012. CHARACTER COUNTS! and The Six Pillars of Character are registered trademarks of the Josephson Institute of Ethics. ©2011 Josephson Institute. Reprinted from *Making Ethical Decisions* with permission. www.josephsoninstitute.org.

2-2 Business Ethics: Not an Oxymoron

Quite simply, **business ethics** is the application of right and wrong, good and bad, in a business setting. This isn't as straightforward as it may first seem. The most challenging business decisions seem to arise when values are in conflict—when whatever you do will have negative consequences, forcing you to choose among bad options. These are true **ethical dilemmas**. (Keep in mind that ethical *dilemmas* differ from ethical *lapses*, which involve clear misconduct.) Here are a couple of hypothetical examples of ethical dilemmas:

- You've just done a great job on a recent project at your company. Your boss has been highly vocal about acknowledging your work and the increased revenue that resulted from it. Privately, she says that you have clearly earned a bonus of at least 10 percent, but due to company politics, she is unable to secure the bonus for you. She also implies that if you were to submit inflated expense reports for the next few months, she would look the other way, and you could pocket the extra cash as well-deserved compensation for your contributions.

■ An engineer on your staff has an excellent job offer from another company and asks your advice on whether to accept the position. You need him to complete a project that is crucial to your company (and to your own career). You also have been told—in strictest confidence by senior management—that when this project is complete, the company will be laying off all internal engineers. If you advise him to stay, he will lose the opportunity (and end up without a job), but if you advise him to go, you will be violating the company's trust (and jeopardizing your own career).

BAD NEWS TODAY— WORSE NEWS TOMORROW!

Investigations into student attitudes and behaviours related to ethical conduct suggest that students are disturbingly willing to lie, cheat, and steal, despite a sky-high opinion of their own personal character. One study involved 30,000 US high school students; another involved 15,000 undergraduate students at 11 Canadian universities. Some highlights (or perhaps we should call them lowlights):

■ 55 percent of US students admitted to lying to a teacher about something significant in the previous year; 76 percent did so to parents.

■ 51 percent of US high school students admitted that they cheated on a test at school within the previous 12 months.

■ 73 percent of Canadian undergraduate students admitted that they had cheated on written work in high school; 53 percent admitted that they continued to do so at university.

■ 58 percent of Canadian undergraduate students admitted that they had cheated on exams in high school; the good news—or bad news—is that the rate dropped to only 18 percent among university students. (That means that if you are not a cheat, there is nearly a 50 percent chance that the person to your left or right is.)

■ 23 percent of US boys admitted to stealing from a store in the past year; 17 percent of girls did. 19 percent of boys admitted to stealing from a friend, compared to 10 percent of girls.

Sadly, the actual rates of bad behaviour are probably understated because 26 percent of respondents in one study admitted that they lied on one or two questions, and experts agree that dishonesty on surveys usually reflects an attempt to conceal misconduct.

Despite rampant lying, cheating, and stealing, 98 percent of respondents agreed that it's important to be a person of good character, and 77 percent rated their own character higher than that of their peers. Furthermore, 92 percent said they were satisfied with their personal character.

A number of analysts find it easy to dismiss the long-term implications of these findings, claiming that as teenagers mature, their judgment and morals will mature as well and their conduct will reflect stronger values. However, a more recent large-scale study by a major ethics institute found unequivocally that high school attitudes and behaviours are a clear predictor of adult behaviour across a range of situations. Cheaters in high school are far more likely as adults to lie to their spouses, customers, bosses, and employers and to cheat on expense reports, taxes, and insurance claims.

Clearly, now is the time for smart companies to clarify their standards and establish safeguards to head off costly ethical meltdowns in their future workforce. And maybe it's time for more postsecondary educational institutions to consider recording ethical lapses on student transcripts.[2]

Sources: "For the First Time in a Decade, Lying, Cheating, and Stealing Among American Students Drops," November 20, 2012, Josephson Institute website; Linette Ho, "Classroom Cheating On the Rise; School Isn't About Education Any More; It's About Getting Good Grades and That Increases the Pressure," *Vancouver Sun*, March 28, 2012.

Herb MacKenzie

2-3 Ethics: Multiple Touchpoints

Although each person must make his or her own ethical choices, the organization can have a significant influence on the quality of those decisions. The next two sections discuss the impact of both the individual and the organization on ethical decision making. As you read them, keep in mind that the interaction between the two is dynamic: sometimes it's hard to tell where one stops and the other starts.

2-3a Ethics and the Individual: The Power of One

Ethical choices begin with ethical individuals. Your personal needs, your family, your culture, and your religion all influence your value system. Your personality traits—self-esteem, self-confidence, independence, and sense of humour—play a significant role as well. These factors all come into play as you face ethical dilemmas. The challenge can be overwhelming, which has led a range of experts to develop frameworks for reaching ethical decisions. While the specifics vary, the key principles of most decision guides are very similar:

- Do you fully understand each dimension of the problem?

- Who would benefit? Who would suffer?

- Are the alternative solutions legal? Are they fair?

- Does your decision make you comfortable at a "gut feel" level?

- Could you defend your decision on the nightly TV news?

- Have you considered and reconsidered your responses to each question?

The approach seems simple, but in practice, it really isn't. Workers—and managers, too—often face enormous pressure to do what's right for the company or what's right for their career rather than simply what's right. And keep in mind that it's completely possible for two people to follow the framework and arrive at completely different decisions, each feeling confident that he or she has made the right choice.

2-3b Ethics and the Organization: It Takes a Village

Although each person is clearly responsible for his or her own actions, the organization can influence those actions to a startling degree. Not surprisingly, influence starts at the top, and actions matter far more than words. The president of the Ethics Resource Center states: "CEOs in particular must communicate their personal commitment to high ethical standards and consistently drive the message down to employees through their actions." Any other approach—even just the *appearance* of shaky ethics—can be deeply damaging to a company's ethical climate. Here are a couple of examples from the news:

- **High flyers:** When the CEOs of the Big Three automakers—hovering on the edge of bankruptcy—approached government to request a US$25 billion bailout package, they flew in three separate corporate jets at an estimated cost of $20,000 per round-trip flight. All three were operating in line with official corporate travel policies, but it just didn't look right. One lawmaker pointedly asked: "Couldn't you all have downgraded to first class or jet-pooled or something to get here? It would have at least sent a message that you do get it." Not surprisingly, the execs left empty-handed.[3]

- **Retirement perks:** When Jack Welch retired from his post as CEO of General Electric, the GE board awarded him a generous financial package and an eye-popping collection of perks. His perks ranged from use of a US$80,000 per month apartment, to food and wine for home entertainment, to corporate jet privileges. These perks did not represent an ethical breach—Welch negotiated them in good faith—but when the list surfaced in the press a year after his retirement, he voluntarily gave up his perks to mitigate a public relations problem that could have tarnished his reputation as a tough, ethical, and highly successful CEO.[4]

- **Gross excess:** In the mid-1990s, Disney CEO Michael Eisner hired his friend Michael Ovitz as Disney's president. Fourteen months later, Disney fired Ovitz for incompetence, and he walked away with a US$140 million settlement. Disgruntled shareholders sued the Disney board

for mismanagement, which led to the release of Ovitz's Disney expense account documents. In 14 months he had spent $4.8 million (that's about $80,000 per week!). Specifics included $54,330 for LA Lakers tickets, a $946 gun for Robert Zemeckis, and $319 for breakfast. Was he stealing? *No.* Was he unethical? You decide.[5]

Are these decisions wrong? Unethical? How do you feel about the business decisions in Exhibit 2.3?

2-3c Creating and Maintaining an Ethical Organization

Recent research from the Ethics Resource Center (ERC) suggests that organizational culture has more influence than any other variable on the ethical conduct of individual employees. According to the ERC, 66 percent of companies have a "strong" or "strong-leaning" ethics culture, and 81 percent of companies now offer ethics training to their employees.[7] Consider, for example, the following research results:

- Only 33 percent of employees reported observing misconduct in large companies that had an effective ethics program; 62 percent did so in similar companies without an effective ethics program.

- Only 4 percent of those who reported wrongdoing experienced retaliation in large companies that have an effective ethics program; 59 percent did so in similar companies without an effective ethics program.

- ERC research identifies two disturbing patterns. First, behavioural misconduct is often continuous and

---

Exhibit 2.3 Ethics at Work: The Good, the Bad, and the Ugly

How would you judge the actions of these people?[6]

Chris Spence The director of the Toronto District School Board resigned after it was alleged he "failed to maintain the standards of [his] profession." He admitted to plagiarism in speeches, blogs, and newspaper articles. The University of Toronto has opened a separate investigation alleging plagiarism in his doctoral dissertation, written nearly two decades ago. If guilty, he could lose his Ph.D.

Brian Mulroney The former prime minister of Canada admitted that he accepted $225,000 in cash from German businessman Karlheinz Schreiber. Mulroney stated that he placed the money in a home safe and a safety deposit box at a New York bank, where it sat for six years until he made a voluntary disclosure, which resulted in his paying tax on only half the money.

John Mackey The co-founder and CEO of Whole Foods—with stores in Canada, the United States, and the United Kingdom—was exposed as the contributor of thousands of anonymous comments on Yahoo! Finance hyping his company and occasionally attacking rival Wild Oats, which he hoped to purchase for an advantageous price.

Bill Gates As Microsoft CEO, Bill Gates made some ethically shaky moves, but he and his wife also established the Bill and Melinda Gates Foundation, which supports grantees in more than 100 countries around the globe. Working for the foundation, Gates applies his famous problem-solving skills to global health, global development, and education.

Martin Shkreli While CEO of Turing Pharmaceuticals, Shkreli raised the price of Daraprim from $13.50 to $750 per tablet (a 5,000 percent price increase) when his company acquired marketing rights for the drug. Many of the most vulnerable cancer patients—approximately 8,800 of them—who require the drug have no alternative. Shkreli says, "This isn't the greedy drug company trying to gouge patients; it is us trying to stay in business." Dubbed "the most hated man in America," Shkreli has since been charged with securities fraud, unrelated to the drug-price fiasco.

Sylvie Therrien Employed as an Employment Insurance (EI) fraud investigator, Sylvie blew the whistle in 2013 when she went public, claiming that the government forced her to meet aggressive savings quotas aimed at reducing payments to EI claimants. The government denied her assertions but quickly backtracked, stating that the $540,000 in annual savings were simply targets and not quotas. She lost her job when Service Canada accused her of breaching its employee code of conduct. So much for whistleblower protection. "I didn't do anything wrong," she says. "I was just following my conscience."

Sources: Vincent Donovan, "The Whistleblower," *Toronto Star*, January 30, 2016; Carly Weeks, "Experts Raise Alarm Over Drug Prices," *The Globe and Mail*, September 28, 2015; "'Most Hated Man in America' Resigns as Turing Pharmaceuticals CEO Day After Securities Fraud Arrest," *Telegraph-Journal* (Saint John, N.B.), December 19, 2015; Rosie DiManno, "2013 Was a Stuporific Year for Stupidity," Toronto Star, December 31, 2013; Megan O'Toole, "U of T to Review Spence's PhD Thesis for Plagiarism; May Lead to Hearing," *National Post*, January 12, 2013; Norma Greenaway, "Former PM Paid Taxes on Only Half of $225 000; Mulroney Grilled Over 'Good Deal' on Taxes," *Calgary Herald*, May 20, 2009; David Kesmodel and John Wilke, "Whole Foods Is Hot, Wild Oats a Dud—So Said 'Rahodeb,'" *The Wall Street Journal Online*, July 12, 2007.

Chapter 2 Business Ethics and Social Responsibility: Doing Well by Doing Good

ongoing. Only one-third of reported rule-breaking represented a one-time occurrence. Forty-one percent of respondents reported that observed misconduct was repeated a second time, and 26 percent reported that it was an ongoing pattern of behaviour. Second, managers were involved more frequently than non-managers, and the misconduct increased in tandem with the level of management involved. Senior managers were involved in 24 percent of observed misconduct, middle managers in 19 percent, and first-line managers in 17 percent.

A strong organizational culture works in tandem with a formal ethics program to create and maintain an ethical work environment. A written **code of ethics** is the cornerstone of any formal ethics program. The purpose of a written code is to give employees the information they need to make ethical decisions across a range of situations. Clearly, an ethics code becomes even more important for multinational companies because it lays out unifying values and priorities for divisions that are rooted in different cultures. However, a written code is worthless if it doesn't reflect living principles. An effective code of ethics flows directly from ethical corporate values and leads directly to ongoing communication, training, and action.

Specific codes of ethics vary greatly among organizations. Perhaps the best-known code is the Johnson & Johnson Credo, which has guided the company profitably—with a soaring reputation—through a number of crises that would have sunk lesser organizations. A striking element of the Credo is the strong focus on fairness. It carefully refrains from overpromising financial rewards, committing instead to a "fair return" for shareholders.

To bring a code of ethics to life, experts advocate a forceful, integrated approach to ethics that almost always includes the following steps:

1. Get executive buy-in and commitment to follow-through. Top managers need to communicate—even overcommunicate—about the importance of ethics. But talking works only when it's backed up by action: senior management must give priority to keeping promises and leading by example.

2. Establish expectations for ethical behaviour at all levels of the organization, from the CEO to the evening cleaning crew. Be sure that outside parties such as suppliers, distributors, and customers understand the standards.

3. Integrate ethics into mandatory staff training. From new employee orientation to ongoing training, ethics must play a role. Additional, more specialized training helps employees who face more temptation (e.g., purchasing agents, overseas sales reps).

4. Ensure that your ethics code is both global and local in scope. Employees in every country should understand both the general principles and the specific applications. Be sure to translate the code into as many languages as necessary.

5. Build and maintain a clear, trusted reporting structure for ethical concerns and violations. The structure should allow employees to seek anonymous guidance for ethical concerns and to anonymously report ethics violations.

6. Establish protection for **whistleblowers**—that is, for people who report illegal or unethical behaviour to the authorities or the media. Be sure that no retaliation occurs. Some have even suggested that whistleblowers receive a portion of the penalties levied against firms that violate the law.

7. Enforce the code of ethics. When people violate ethical norms, companies must respond immediately and (whenever appropriate) publicly in order to retain employee trust. Without enforcement, the code of ethics becomes meaningless.

> The evil that men do lives after them; The good is oft interred with their bones.
>
> William Shakespeare, *Julius Caesar*

code of ethics A formal, written document that defines the ethical standards of an organization and gives employees the information they need to make ethical decisions across a range of situations.

whistleblowers Employees who report their employer's illegal or unethical behaviour to either the authorities or the media.

social responsibility The obligation of a business to contribute to society.

2-4 Defining Social Responsibility: Making the World a Better Place

Social responsibility is the obligation of a business to contribute to society. As with ethics, the broad definition is clear but specific implementation can be complex. Obviously, the number one goal of any business is long-term profits; without profits, other contributions are impossible. But once a firm achieves a reasonable return, the balancing act begins: How can a company balance the need to

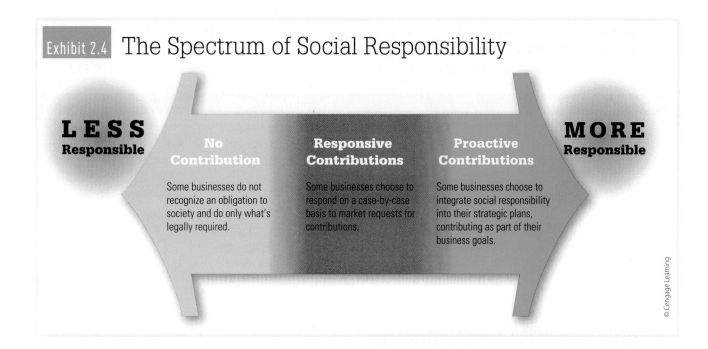

Exhibit 2.4 The Spectrum of Social Responsibility

LESS Responsible

MORE Responsible

No Contribution

Some businesses do not recognize an obligation to society and do only what's legally required.

Responsive Contributions

Some businesses choose to respond on a case-by-case basis to market requests for contributions.

Proactive Contributions

Some businesses choose to integrate social responsibility into their strategic plans, contributing as part of their business goals.

© Cengage Learning

contribute against the need to boost profits, especially when the two conflict? The answer depends on the business's values, mission, resources, and management philosophy, which lead in turn to its position on social responsibility. Business approaches fall along the spectrum from no contribution to proactive contributions, as shown in Exhibit 2.4.

2-4a The Stakeholder Approach: Responsibility to Whom?

Stakeholders are any groups (or individuals) that have a stake (or a personal interest) in the performance and actions of an organization. Different stakeholders have different needs, expectations, and levels of interest. The federal government, for instance, is a key stakeholder in pharmaceutical companies but a very minor stakeholder in local art studios. The community at large is a key stakeholder for a coffee shop chain but a minor stakeholder for a Web design firm. Enlightened organizations identify key stakeholders for their business and consider stakeholder priorities in their decision making. The goal is to balance their needs and priorities as effectively as possible, with an eye towards building their business over the long term. Core stakeholder groups for most businesses are employees, customers, investors, and the broader community.

Responsibility to Employees: Creating Jobs That Work Jobs alone aren't enough. The starting point for socially responsible employers is to meet legal stan-

Socially responsible employers provide safe workspaces for all of their employees.

Herb MacKenzie

dards, and in this case the requirements are significant. How would you judge the social responsibility of the firms listed in Exhibit 2.5? Employers must comply with laws relating to matters ranging from equal opportunity, to workplace safety, to minimum wage and overtime, to protection from sexual harassment, to family and medical unpaid leaves. We will be discussing these legal requirements (and others) in Chapter 14 on human resource management.

But socially responsible employers go far beyond the law. They create a workplace environment that respects the dignity and value

stakeholders Any groups that have a stake—or a personal interest—in the performance and actions of an organization.

Exhibit 2.5 Social Responsibility at Work

How would you judge the actions of these firms?[8]

THE CLOROX COMPANY

Clorox introduced a line of "99% natural" cleaning products called Green Works. This is the first such effort from a major consumer products company and the first time that the Sierra Club has endorsed a product line by allowing the use of its logo on the labels. In return, Clorox makes an annual contribution to the Sierra Club, the amount based on total Green Works sales.

TIM HORTONS

In 2016, Tim Hortons announced that it will exclusively use eggs produced by cage-free hens by 2025, throughout its North American operations. Currently, over 90 percent of hens used for eggs are crammed into battery cages: cages so small they cannot walk, spread their wings, or perform other natural behaviours. Many such hens become mangled and are often left in their cages after death. Battery cages were banned in the European Union and several US states. Many other popular fast food restaurants have recently made similar announcements.

VOLKSWAGEN AG

The world's second largest automobile manufacturer was caught using "cheat devices" on its cars to mask the extent of emissions during laboratory tests. As many as 11 million vehicles worldwide were affected. North American head Michael Horn blamed "a couple of software engineers" for the fraud. Stockholm entrepreneur and Audi A6 owner Linus Elmgren has a different view: "They've cheated the whole world and their sense of regret has been insufficient in my mind."

ORNGE

ORNGE, Ontario's air ambulance service, has been involved in suspicious activity almost since its inception. The agency established a complex web of private businesses and redirected monies to them over several years. In addition, following the purchase of 12 helicopters from an Italian supplier for $144 million—financed by Ontario taxpayers—one of the private businesses got a contract from the helicopter supplier for $6.7 million to research other potential global markets for air ambulance services. Key employees involved in the questionable research: the girlfriend of the ORNGE founder and the daughter of the ORNGE chairman.

KRAFT

As obesity among kids spirals out of control, Kraft has taken a brave stand: a pledge to stop advertising unhealthy—yet highly profitable—foods to young children. Kraft also plans to eliminate in-school marketing and drop some unhealthy snacks from school vending machines. As the king of the food business, Kraft has chosen what's right for kids over what's right for its own short-term profits.

SNC-LAVALIN

Canada's largest construction and engineering firm is missing $56 million. Reports are that the monies were secretly funnelled to Libya's Gaddafi family. CEO Pierre Duhaime breached the company's code of ethics and approved the payments after two other company executives refused to do so. Duhaime stepped down in 2012—or, according to SNC-Lavalin, retired—and has taken a $4.9 million package that was promised in his employment contract.

---

of each employee. They ensure that hard work, commitment, and talent pay off. They move beyond minimal safety requirements to establish proactive protections such as ergonomically correct chairs (i.e., chairs that won't hurt your back) and computer screens that reduce eye strain. And the best employers respond to the ongoing employee search for a balance between work and the rest of their lives. With an increasing number of workers facing challenges such as raising kids and caring for elderly parents, responsible companies are stepping in with programs such as on-site daycare, company-sponsored day camp, and referral services for eldercare.

SEVENLY IS HEAVENLY

Herb MacKenzie

Have you heard of Sevenly? To many not-for-profit organizations that benefit from its contributions, it is a heavenly company. In fact, the company name was chosen to play off the word heavenly. It was founded in 2011 by Dale Partridge, who has taken the title Chief World Changer, and his 19-year-old partner Aaron Chavez. Since then, the company has contributed nearly $4.5 million and has helped more than 1.5 million people. It was named "Mashable's Most Social Small Business of 2014," and Facebook named it "One of the Top Ten Stories of Facebook's First Ten Years."

Sevenly supports not-for-profits in seven chosen categories: hunger solutions, disaster assistance, poverty relief, medical causes, access to potable water, human trafficking and slavery prevention, and a general aid category that includes such things as suicide prevention and homelessness. Each week (seven days), the company features a "Cause of the Week" and donates $7 from the sale of a featured article that will only be sold for—you guessed it—seven days. The limited window for sales creates a sense of urgency to make a purchase. For sales of other products, Sevenly donates 7 percent of sales to one of its past charity partners. Approximately 28 percent of the company's revenue goes to social causes.

Sevenly uses premium fabrics and water-based inks for its many T-shirts and hoodies, and has them manufactured in Worldwide Responsible Accredited Production-certified child-labour-free facilities in China, Nicaragua, and Peru. Social media drive 85 percent of company sales. Through its own polls, the company has discovered that 94 percent of respondents report they are better educated about social causes because of Sevenly, and 73 percent say they are more likely to donate to or volunteer for charitable causes.

To reinforce its values and mission, the company keeps a complaining room. Employees whose attitude temporarily falls below positivity standards are sent there, where they can view pictures of children who are suffering from real problems. Dale Partridge says, "We are letting the world know, starting with our own staff, that there is more to life than us and you. Life is bigger than 'my cell phone died' and 'life sucks because I'm in traffic.'"[9]

Responsibility to Customers: Value, Honesty, and Communication A core responsibility of business is to deliver consumer value by providing quality products at fair prices. Honesty and communication are vital to this. Consumerism—a widely accepted social movement—suggests that consumer rights should be the starting point. In the early 1960s, US President John F. Kennedy defined these rights, which most American and Canadian businesses respect when it comes to both consumer expectations and legal requirements:

- **The right to be safe:** Businesses are legally responsible for injuries and damages caused by their products, even if they have no reason to suspect that their products might cause harm. This makes it easy for consumers to file suits. The drive to avert lawsuits has sometimes led to absurdities such as the warning on some coffee cups: "Caution! Hot coffee is hot!" (No kidding.)

- **The right to be informed:** The law requires firms in a range of industries—from mutual funds, to groceries, to pharmaceuticals—to provide the public with extensive information. Health Canada, for instance, requires most grocery foods to feature a very specific "Nutrition Facts" label. Beyond legal requirements, many firms use the Web to provide a wealth of extra information about their products. Pizza Hut, for example, offers an interactive Nutrition Calculator that works with all of its menu items (and it's fun to use, too).

- **The right to choose:** Freedom of choice is a fundamental element of the capitalist Canadian economy. Our economic system works largely because consumers freely choose to purchase the products that best meet their needs. As businesses compete, consumer value increases. Socially responsible firms support consumer choice by following the laws that prevent anticompetitive behaviour such as predatory pricing and collusion.

- **The right to be heard:** Socially responsible companies make

> **consumerism** A social movement that focuses on four key consumer rights: (1) the right to be safe, (2) the right to be informed, (3) the right to choose, and (4) the right to be heard.

it easy for consumers to express legitimate complaints. They also develop highly trained customer service people to respond to complaints. In fact, smart businesses view customer complaints as an opportunity to create better products and stronger relationships. Statistics suggest that 1 in 50 dissatisfied customers takes the time to complain. The other 49 quietly switch brands. By soliciting feedback, you're not only being responsible but also building your business.[10]

Delivering quality products is another key component of social responsibility to consumers. **Planned obsolescence**— deliberately designing products to fail in order to shorten the time between consumer repurchases— represents a clear violation of social responsibility. In the long term, the market itself weeds out offenders.

> **planned obsolescence**
> The strategy of deliberately designing products to fail in order to shorten the time between purchases.

> You show me a leader that can't look and say, "Boy, I made mistakes and I wish I could have done that differently." If you can't [admit that], you're a very dubious leader of anything, at any time, in any circumstance.
>
> Michael McCain, CEO, Maple Leaf Foods

After all, who would repurchase a product that meets a premature end? But in the short term, planned obsolescence thins consumer wallets and abuses consumer trust.

When businesses do make mistakes, apologizing to consumers doesn't guarantee renewed sales. But a sincere apology can definitely restore a company's reputation, which can ultimately lead to greater profits. Several examples make this point clear:

- When tainted meat at Maple Leaf Foods killed 22 Canadians, company president and CEO Michael McCain was quick to face the media. Against the advice of company lawyers, he apologized on television and took full responsibility for what happened. Maple Leaf Foods initiated a $30 million food recall, implemented more than 200 new operating procedures in its plants, and was quick to settle a class action lawsuit for more than $25 million. Many public relations professionals point to his actions as a case study in crisis management, and Michael McCain has since been recognized by several Canadian business schools for his corporate leadership. Have his actions helped McCain Foods? A lack of action might well have killed the company. But within only a few months, consumer confidence in the Maple Leaf brand rebounded from 64 to 91 percent.[11]

- When Johnson & Johnson discontinued the popular o.b. Ultra tampons, loyal users stripped the shelves of remaining stock (bidding the price of a box of Ultras up to more than $100 on eBay) and bombarded the manufacturer with complaints. Johnson & Johnson announced that Ultras would be back on store shelves within a year, and offered an apology video rife with every cliché imaginable, including a handsome, male singer. The music video was customizable; viewer names appeared throughout in the video, and the video closed with a coupon offer. The video was a masterful attempt to regain loyalty for a product that had yet to reappear on store shelves.[12]

- Chipotle Mexican Grill, with more than 2,000 locations in the United States and Canada, was hit with several outbreaks involving norovirus, salmonella, and E. coli. In the last half of 2015, almost 500 customers became ill. The company's stock price, which had exceeded $750 per share in August, dropped to less than $400 by

Herb MacKenzie

January 2016. Sales decline for the last quarter of 2015 was estimated to exceed $72 million. Founder and co-CEO Steve Ellis made a public apology in December, promising a comprehensive safety program involving not only its restaurants but also its supply chain and the farms where its products are sourced. This seems to have appeased shareholders—the company's stock price increased significantly in January. At least investors seem to be betting that customers will soon return.[13]

Responsibility to Investors: Fair Stewardship and Full Disclosure The primary responsibility of business to investors is clearly to make money—to create an ongoing stream of profits. But companies achieve and maintain long-term earnings in the context of responsibility to all stakeholders, which may mean trading short-term profits for long-term success. Responsibility to investors starts with meeting legal requirements, and in the wake of a number of large corporate scandals, the bar is higher than ever. The US **Sarbanes-Oxley Act** limits conflict-of-interest issues by restricting the consulting services that accounting firms can provide for the companies they audit. The same act requires that financial officers and CEOs personally certify the validity of their financial statements. Canadian regulators have been forced to adopt similar measures to preserve access to US financial markets. Nearly 200 Canadian businesses listed on the Toronto Stock Exchange are cross-listed on US stock exchanges and are, therefore, largely subject to the US requirements.

But beyond legal requirements, companies have a number of additional responsibilities to investors. Spending money wisely would be near the top of the list. For instance, are executive retreats to the South Pacific on the company tab legal? They probably are. Do they represent a responsible use of corporate dollars? Now that seems unlikely. Honesty is another key responsibility that relates directly to financial predictions. No one can anticipate exactly how a company will perform, and an overly optimistic or pessimistic assessment is perfectly legal. But is it socially responsible? It probably isn't, especially if it departs too far from the objective facts—which is, of course, a subjective call.

Responsibility to the Community: Business and the Greater Good Beyond increasing everyone's standard of living, businesses can contribute to society in two main ways: philanthropy and responsibility. **Corporate philanthropy** includes all business donations to not-for-profit groups, whether this involves money or products. A study of 93 of Canada's largest corporations—all with revenues over $25 million—found the median

Herb Mackenzie

value of reported contributions to be $340,000.[14] Corporate philanthropy also includes donations of employee time; in other words, some companies pay their employees to spend time volunteering at not-for-profit organizations. Timberland, an outdoor clothing company, is a leader in corporate philanthropy; it not only donates goods but also gives employees paid six-month sabbaticals to work for not-for-profit organizations.

Some companies contribute to not-for-profit organizations through **cause-related marketing**. This involves a partnership between a business and a not-for-profit organization, designed to spike sales for the company and to raise money for the not-for-profit organization. According to a 2015 Ipsos Marketing Canada poll, 95 percent of Canadians agree it is a good idea

Sarbanes-Oxley Act US federal legislation that sets higher ethical standards for public corporations and accounting firms. Key provisions limit conflict-of-interest issues and require financial officers and CEOs to certify the validity of their financial statements.

corporate philanthropy All business donations to not-for-profit groups, including money, products, and employee time.

cause-related marketing Marketing partnerships between businesses and not-for-profit organizations, designed to spike sales for the company and raise money for the not-for-profit organization.

for companies to support social causes, and 84 percent of them say they would switch to brands that do, if price and quality were similar. The most popular causes included poverty reduction (61 percent), environment (58 percent), child specific (56 percent), mental health (54 percent), and education (51 percent).[15] Unlike outright gifts, these dollars are not tax deductible for the company, but they can certainly build the company's brands.

Corporate responsibility relates closely to philanthropy but focuses on the actions of the business itself rather than donations of money and time. The Home Depot, for instance, employs more Olympic hopefuls than any other company through its Olympic Job Opportunities Program. The firm offers athletes full-time pay and benefits for a flexible 20-hour workweek to accommodate demanding training and competition schedules. Taking a different approach to corporate responsibility, Telus Corp. has created 11 Canadian and 4 international Community Boards that evaluate and provide funding to local grassroots causes in each region where the company operates. In the past decade, these boards have contributed over $53 million to more than 4,300 projects.[16] These programs ultimately benefit society as a whole.

Responsibility to the Environment Protecting the environment is perhaps the most crucial element of responsibility to the community. Business is a huge consumer of the world's limited resources, from oil, to timber, to fresh water, to minerals. In some cases, the production process decimates the environment and spews pollution into the air, land, and water, sometimes causing irreversible damage. And the products created by business can cause pollution as well, such as the smog generated by cars, and the sometimes toxic waste generated by junked electronic parts.

Governments at all levels—federal, provincial/territorial, and municipal—set minimum standards for environmental protection. And a growing number of companies are exceeding these standards, developing innovative strategies for building their businesses while protecting the environment. Many have embraced the idea of **sustainable development**: doing business to meet the needs of this generation without harming the ability of future generations to meet their needs. This means weaving environmentalism throughout the business decision-making process. Because sustainable development

corporate responsibility Business contributions to the community through the actions of the business itself rather than donations of money and time.

sustainable development Doing business to meet the needs of the current generation, without harming the ability of future generations to meet their needs.

Going Green—It's Not Just Governments

While governments and grassroots groups around the world have led the global push to "go green," make no mistake, multinational businesses have played a leadership role as well, making major contributions to the greening of the planet. Some examples from Canada[17]:

- HP Canada manages its "Eco Advocate Program," first established in Canada but now involving 2,500 employees worldwide. Nearly 300 advocates in Canada are among those who participate in such things as tree planting, organic gardening, and hosting bicycle tune-up clinics. HP continues its "HP Planet Partners" program, recycling its ink and laser cartridges, along with computer hardware and rechargeable batteries of all brands.

- Home Depot Canada, in 36 days, raised nearly $1.3 million through its "Orange Door Project," where customers were asked to contribute $2 to help eliminate youth homelessness. It also has a long-standing association with Habitat for Humanity and donates unsalable returned products to it: valued nearly $8 million in one recent year.

- IKEA Canada has installed 3,790 solar panels atop three of its Toronto-area stores (700,000 worldwide), collectively capable of generating enough electricity to power 100 homes. It has also purchased a 46-megawatt wind farm in Alberta, with expected annual production capacity equal to 60 percent of the company's North American needs.

- Labatt Breweries of Canada encourages employees to participate in an annual World Environment Day competition at each facility. Employees have participated in such things as the "Dash 4 Trash" clean-up in Creston, British Columbia, cleaning activities with the "Lake Ontario Waterkeepers" in Toronto, and the "Thames River Clean-up" in London, Ontario.

- TD Bank Group manages a "Green Nation" program that boasts over 17,500 members (about 20 percent of its workforce), who have pledged over 450,000 environmental actions at home, at work, and in their communities. Its "sustainable energy-efficient design" concept branch—the first of its kind in Canada—is expected to be about 45 percent more energy-efficient than a similar-size traditional branch.

- Hemlock Printers, in Burnaby, British Columbia, has for six consecutive years been named Most Environmentally Progressive Printer in Canada. The printer offers its Carbon Neutral Printing Program for customers who want to offset the amount of carbon emissions produced by their print job. Customers who participate can use the "Zero" brandmark on those materials to show commitment to a better environment.

Sources: "Canada's Greenest Employers," 2015 Winners: www.canadastop100.com/environmental/; Home Depot Canada website, www.homedepot.ca; IKEA Canada website, www.ikea.com; "Top 50 Socially Responsible Corporations: 2014," Maclean's.ca, June 5, 2014; Hemlock Printers website, www.hemlock.com.

can mean significant long-term cost savings, the economic crisis may even push forward environmentally friendly programs.

The results have been impressive across a range of industries. McDonald's, for instance, produces mountains of garbage each year, as do virtually all fast food chains. But the Golden Arches stands above the others in its efforts to reduce waste. The following are some encouraging examples:

- McDonald's, while recognizing that there are challenges to waste diversion owing to differences in local infrastructures in each market it serves, aspires to recycle 50 percent of its in-restaurant waste by 2020.

- In one four-year period, the company's delivery fleet travelled over 5 million kilometres on the biodiesel produced from converting used cooking oil at its UAE locations.

- McDonald's is currently piloting a composting program for coffee grounds—"Good Neighbor, Good Grounds"—to reduce the amount of organic waste from landfill sites.[18]

Herb MacKenzie

From Toilet to Tap

Practically everyone has watched a thirsty dog eagerly slurp water from an open toilet. Leaving the yuck factor aside, can all those dogs really be wrong? Both research and experience suggest that "toilet to tap" (or repurposing wastewater) may be the long-term solution to the looming worldwide fresh water shortage. In fact, recycled water has long been used for agriculture and industry. But the city-state of Singapore has been drinking what it calls NEWater for more than a decade and now gets 30 percent of its drinking water from recycled sewer water. It hopes to increase this to 55 percent by 2060 when its agreement for water supplies from neighbour Malaysia expires. Before the reclaimed water reaches the tap, it is mixed with other water sources to increase public acceptance. The business opportunities have already begun to emerge. Currently, companies such as GE Water and Siemens Water Technologies are doing advanced water research and helping design and build filtration facilities.

Several states in the United States, including California, are also repurposing waste water. However, the recycled water in California doesn't go directly to tap. It first gets pumped underground, where it mixes with the district's groundwater, and then goes to tap. If the thought upsets you, you might consider that currently, more than 200 wastewater treatment plants discharge sewage effluent into the river that is the primary source for drinking water in southern California. Where does your water come from?[19]

Sources: Elizabeth Weise, "In a Drought, Should We Drink Sewage? Singapore Does," usatoday.com; Meera Senthilingam, "Drinking Sewage: Solving Singapore's Water Problem," cnn.com.

Reducing the *amount* of garbage is better than recycling, but recycling garbage clearly beats dumping it in a landfill. McDonald's participates in this arena as well, through its extensive recycling programs, but more importantly as a big buyer of recycled products.

Taking an even broader perspective, some firms have started to measure their carbon footprint, with an eye towards reducing it. **Carbon footprint** refers to the amount of harmful greenhouse gases that a firm emits throughout its operations, both directly and indirectly. The ultimate goal is to become carbon neutral—either to emit zero harmful gases or to counteract the impact of emissions by removing a comparable amount from the atmosphere through projects such as planting trees. Tree Canada is a not-for-profit organization that helps businesses offset their carbon emissions. First, it facilitates an independent emission assessment

carbon footprint The amount of greenhouse gases that a firm emits throughout its operations, both directly and indirectly.

CHOOSING BETWEEN A LOAF OF BREAD AND A PACKET OF SHAMPOO

Three-quarters of the world's population—nearly 4 billion people—earn less than US$2.00 per day. C.K. Prahalad (1941–2010), a well-respected consultant and economist, claimed that if the "aspirational poor" had a chance to consume, they could add about US$13 trillion in annual sales to the global economy. Unilever, a global marketing company headquartered in Europe, has aggressively pursued this market with consumer products. Its customers might not have electricity, running water, or even enough for dinner, but many of them do have packets of Sunsilk Shampoo and Omo detergent. Electronics companies have experienced marketing success as well. In Dharavi, for instance—one of the largest urban slums in India—more than 85 percent of households own a television set.

Critics suggest that the corporate push to reach impoverished consumers will enrich multinationals at the expense of their customers, representing exploitation of the world's poorest people. Ashvin Dayal, East Asia director for the antipoverty group Oxfam UK, expressed concern to *Time* magazine that corporate marketing might unseat locally produced products or encourage overspending by those who truly can't afford it. Citing heavily marketed candy and soda, he pointed out that "companies have the power to create needs rather than respond to needs."

Prahalad countered that many people at the bottom of the economic pyramid accept that some of the basics—running water, for instance—are not likely to ever come their way. Instead, they opt to improve their quality of life through affordable "luxuries" such as single-use sachets of fragrant shampoo. He argued, "It's absolutely possible to do very well while doing good." Furthermore, he suggested that corporate marketing may kick-start the poorest economies, triggering entrepreneurial activity and economic growth. Since globalization shows no signs of slowing, let's hope that he was right.[20]

What do you think? Is targeting the poor with consumer goods exploitation or simply smart marketing?

Herb MacKenzie

---

that costs between $500 and $1,500, depending on complexity. Then it provides the participating company with a report that identifies the sources and amount of emissions, as well as the number of trees that would need to be planted to offset their harmful effects. If the company decides to proceed, Tree Canada arranges for the trees to be planted and monitored to ensure their successful growth. Then it certifies the company as carbon neutral. Tree Canada has planted nearly 80 million trees.[21]

More and more companies are using **green marketing** to promote their businesses. This means marketing environmental products and practices to gain a competitive edge. Patagonia, for example, markets outdoor clothing using 100 percent organic cotton and natural fibres such as hemp. But green marketing presents a tough challenge: while most people support the idea of green products, the vast majority won't sacrifice price, performance, or convenience to actually buy those products. Sometimes, however, green marketing can be quite consistent with profitability. The Toyota Prius hybrid car provides an interesting example. The Prius costs several thousand dollars more than a standard car, but as gas prices skyrocketed in the summer of 2008, consumers flooded dealerships, snapping up Prius hybrids faster than Toyota could ship them. Even so, when the economy dipped later that year, Toyota sales plummeted along with the rest of the industry, which suggests that the environment may be a fair-weather priority for consumers. By 2012, though, Prius sales were again soaring, especially with the introduction of the plug-in hybrid version.[22]

green marketing Developing and promoting environmentally sound products and practices to gain a competitive edge.

2-5 Ethics and Social Responsibility in the Global Arena: A House of Mirrors?

Globalization has made ethics and social responsibility even more complicated for workers at every level. Bribery and corruption are among the most challenging issues faced by individuals and companies that are involved in international business. Currently, more than 6 billion people live in countries where corruption is a serious problem. Transparency International, a leading anticorruption organization, publishes a yearly index of "perceived corruption" across 168 countries. No country scores a perfect 10 out of 10, but Canada ranked in 9th place in 2015 with a score of 83; and the United States, with a score of 75, ranked 16th. The four Scandinavian countries were ranked in the top five, although Norway was tied with Netherlands for fifth place. Not surprisingly, the world's poorest countries fall largely in the bottom half of the index, suggesting that rampant corruption is part of their business culture. North Korea and Somalia were tied for last place.[23]

Corruption wouldn't be possible if companies didn't offer bribes, so Transparency International also researched the likelihood of firms from 28 of the world's largest economies to pay bribes abroad. The results of its latest Bribe Payers Index indicated that firms from the Netherlands and Switzerland were the least likely to pay bribes, tied at 8.8. Canada, with a score of 8.5, was tied in sixth place with Australia. The United States ranked tenth. Businesses in Mexico (7.0), China (6.5), and Russia (6.1) were most likely to pay bribes.[24]

These statistics raise some thought-provoking questions:

- When does a gift become a bribe? The law is unclear, and perceptions differ from country to country.

- How can corporations monitor corruption and enforce corporate policies in their foreign branches?

- What are other ways to gain a competitive edge in countries where bribes are both accepted and expected?

Other challenging issues revolve around business responsibility to workers abroad. At minimum, businesses should pay a living wage for reasonable hours in a safe working environment. But exactly what this means is less clear-cut. Does a living wage mean enough to support an individual or a family? Does "support" mean enough to subsist day to day or enough to live in modest comfort? Should Canadian businesses mandate no child labour in countries where families depend on their children's wages to survive? Companies must address these questions individually, bringing together their own values with the laws of both Canada and their host countries.

The most socially responsible companies establish codes of conduct for their vendors, setting clear policies for human rights, wages, safety, and environmental impact. In 1991, Levi Strauss became the first global company to establish a comprehensive code of conduct for its contractors. Over the years, creative thinking has helped it maintain its high standards even in the face of cultural clashes. An example from Bangladesh, outlined in the *Harvard Business Review*, illustrates its preference for win–win solutions. In the early 1990s, Levi Strauss "discovered that two of its suppliers in Bangladesh were employing children under the age of 14—a practice that violated the company's principles but was tolerated in Bangladesh. Forcing the suppliers to fire the children would not have ensured that the children received an education, and it would have caused serious hardship for the families depending on the children's wages. In a creative arrangement, the suppliers agreed to pay the children's regular wages while they attended school and to offer each child a job at age 14. Levi Strauss, in turn, agreed to pay the children's tuition and provide books and uniforms." This creative solution allowed the suppliers to maintain their valuable contracts from Levi Strauss; at the same time, Levi Strauss upheld its values and improved the quality of life for its most vulnerable workers.[25]

Clearly, codes of conduct work best with monitoring, enforcement, and a commitment to finding solutions that work for all parties involved. Sears Canada has such a code and requires that it be posted in all vendors' factories where it does business. The code covers issues such as child labour, forced labour, health and safety, and discrimination. Sears is committed to sourcing all of its products in a fair and equitable manner. Violations to the code can be reported by phoning a special phone number at Sears.[26]

Sears Canada and Levi Strauss seem to be doing their part, but the world clearly needs universal standards and universal enforcement to ensure that the benefits of globalization don't come at the expense of the world's most vulnerable people.

> Successful people have a social responsibility to make the world a better place and not just take from it.
>
> Carrie Underwood, Singer

2-6 Monitoring Ethics and Social Responsibility: Who Is Minding the Store?

Actually, many firms are monitoring themselves. The process is called a **social audit**: a systematic evaluation of how well a firm is meeting its ethics and social responsibility objectives. Establishing goals is the starting point for a social audit; the next step is determining how to measure the achievement of those goals, and measurement can be a bit tricky. As You Sow, an organization dedicated to promoting corporate social responsibility, recommends that companies measure their success by evaluating a "double bottom line," one that accounts for traditional financial indicators such as earnings, and one that accounts for social responsibility indicators such as community involvement.

social audit A systematic evaluation of how well a firm is meeting its ethics and social responsibility goals.

Other groups are watching as well, which helps keep businesses on a positive track. Activist customers, investors, unions, environmentalists, and community groups all play a role. In addition, the threat of government legislation keeps some industries motivated to self-regulate. One example would be the entertainment industry, which uses a self-imposed rating system for both movies and TV, largely to fend off regulation. Many people argue that the emergence of salads at fast food restaurants represents an effort to avoid regulation as well.

Clearly, the primary goal of any business is to earn long-term profits for its investors. But profits alone are not enough. As active participants in society, firms must also promote ethical actions and social responsibility throughout their organizations and their corresponding customer and supplier networks. Although every area matters, a few warrant special mention:

- In tough economic times, effective business leaders focus more than ever on integrity, transparency, and a humane approach to managing the workforce—especially during cutbacks.
- Building or maintaining a presence in foreign markets requires particularly careful attention to human rights and local issues.
- Sustainable development and other environmentally sound practices are not only fiscally prudent and customer-friendly but also crucial for the health of our planet.

careers in business ethics and social responsibility: Ethics Officer

Work with senior management to provide leadership, advice, and guidance in all matters pertaining to ethics, including training, enforcement, financial disclosure, and gift rules. Ensure that the company's code of ethics remains in strict compliance with all relevant laws. Model the highest standards of honesty and personal ethics at all times to foster an ethical climate in the organization. Arrange and facilitate employee ethics training. Work with HR to examine ethics complaints and to ensure that all investigations of employee misconduct are handled fairly and promptly. Assist in the resolution of ethical dilemmas wherever needed throughout the organization.

STUDY TOOLS 2

IN THE BOOK, YOU CAN:

☐ Rip out the Chapter Review card at the back of the book to have a summary of the chapter and key terms handy.

ONLINE AT NELSON.COM/STUDENT YOU CAN:

☐ Work through key concepts with a Guided Learning Question.

☐ Prepare for tests with quizzes.

☐ Review the key terms with Flash Cards (online or printer-ready).

☐ Explore practical examples of chapter concepts with Connect a Concept exercises.

3

Economics:
The Framework for Business

LEARNING OBJECTIVES
After studying this chapter, you will be able to . . .

3-1 Define economics and discuss the global economic crisis

3-2 Analyze the impact of fiscal and monetary policy on the economy

3-3 Explain and evaluate the free market system and supply and demand

3-4 Explain and evaluate planned market systems

3-5 Describe the trend towards mixed market systems

3-6 Discuss key terms and tools to evaluate economic performance

After you finish this chapter, go to page 51 for STUDY TOOLS

3-1 Economics: Cloudy and Overcast across Canada[1]

You might wonder about the title of this section: it sounds like a weather report. What you might not realize is that the weather can have a significant impact on the economy. Consider the 2015 winter, during which much of Canada experienced unusually long, cold periods and, especially in eastern Canada, considerable snowfall. Consumer spending fell, and housing starts dropped. Economists estimate that at least one percentage point was chopped from US growth as the result of poor February weather. The effect was likely greater in Canada.

However, the two factors that will have a real impact on the Canadian economy going forward are the Canadian dollar, which was hovering around US $0.76 in late 2016, and the low price of oil on the world market. The price of oil dropped from over US$107 per barrel in the summer of 2014 to less than $30 in early 2016, and it is expected to rise only

> Nobody spends somebody else's money as carefully as he spends his own. Nobody uses somebody else's resources as carefully as he uses his own.
>
> Milton Friedman, economist

slowly going forward. In previous years, the Organization of the Petroleum Exporting Countries (OPEC) had cut oil production to help support higher prices, but it has recently decided to maintain production, forcing prices downward as world supply grows. Why the change in strategy? OPEC seems intent on keeping prices low to force high-cost producers (US shale, Canada's Oil Sands) to reconsider investing in new extraction technologies. An internal OPEC report sees oil prices remaining below US$76 as far out as 2025. That means that Oil Sands production in Canada will remain unprofitable for some time, as the breakeven price—the price at which producers do not lose money, but also do not make a profit—for new development in Canada is about US$80 per barrel.

There are both pros and cons to a lower Canadian dollar and to low oil prices, and we will explore these in more detail in the next section, where we also look more closely at what is happening around the world—the global economy—so that you will better appreciate how the world economies are becoming increasingly interdependent.

During an economic downturn, some businesses, such as fast food restaurants, may see increased sales.

Some basic definitions are required at this point. The **economy** is essentially a financial and social system. It represents the flow of resources through society, from production, to distribution, to consumption. **Economics** is the study of the choices that people, companies, and governments make in allocating those resources. The field of economics has two broad subfields: macroeconomics and microeconomics. **Macroeconomics** is the study of a country's overall economic issues, such as the employment rate, the GDP, and taxation policies. While macroeconomic issues may seem abstract, they directly affect your day-to-day life, influencing key variables such as what jobs will be available for you, how much cash you'll actually take home after taxes, and how much you can buy with that cash in any given month. **Microeconomics** focuses on smaller economic units such as individual consumers, families, and individual businesses. Both macroeconomics and microeconomics have played an integral role in the global economic crisis.

3-1a Global Economy: Slow Growth in the Near Future[2]

It's a commonly heard joke that economists have accurately predicted five of the last three recessions. Is there likely to be a global recession? Is Canada in for another recession (following a small recession in 2015)? Ask two economists; get three opinions. (Sorry, another economist joke.) The reality is that no one, not even an economist, can predict the future with certainty. Recession is, however, unlikely: predictions are that growth, although low by historic standards, will be positive in all global regions. Canada is not currently in danger of a recession, but some regions of the country no doubt will experience recession in 2016—especially Alberta, and possibly Newfoundland and Labrador.

Regarding the world economy, there has been considerable economic slowdown, and growth is predicted to be weak for some time. The Conference Board of Canada predicts that the global economy will grow by 2.8 percent in 2016. Growth is lower than the global average that prevailed prior to the world economic crisis of 2008–09. The European economy will continue to grow, but very slowly. Growth there is expected to remain well below

economy A financial and social system of how resources flow through society, from production, to distribution, to consumption.

economics The study of the choices that people, companies, and governments make in allocating society's resources.

macroeconomics The study of a country's overall economic issues, such as the employment rate, the gross domestic product, and taxation policies.

microeconomics The study of smaller economic units such as individual consumers, families, and individual businesses.

2 percent, led by Spain, the United Kingdom, and Germany. An issue in several countries is the low birth rate. Especially in Germany, Spain, and Italy, the rate is below 1.5, whereas the replacement rate needed to maintain a population is 2.1. Young migrant refugees could help ease this decline; they could also increase the tax base that is necessary to support soaring health care and pension expenditures. Latin America will see even lower economic growth—around 0.2 percent. Hardest hit will be those countries affected by dropping commodity prices: Venezuela, Brazil, and Argentina. A major issue in most Latin American countries is inflation; in that region, it rose from 13 percent in 2014 to 26 percent in 2015, and it is expected to decline only marginally in 2016. Recently, the worst inflation has been in Venezuela: 98.3 percent in 2015, and predicted to be the highest in the region again in 2016. Chile, too, will be hurt, for China's demand for its major export, copper, has dropped considerably; even so, its growth will likely be among the strongest in Latin America. Even Asia, the region with the fastest growth in recent years, has slowed considerably and is expected to see growth of only 5.7 percent. China, recently the fastest growing economy in the Asia–Pacific region, has been having difficulty moving from an economy dependent on export trade for growth, to one that is supported by domestic growth through consumer demand. Predictions are that its growth will be only 6.5 percent in 2016, below the 7–8 percent predicted for India. While the Chinese government has relaxed its one-child policy, the birth rate remains below the replacement rate of 2.1, and the average age of the population continues to rise.

How about the United States and Canada? The United States has largely led the world recovery following the global recession, but stunned analysts in early 2015 as its economy contracted by 0.7 percent. It did, however, post 2.5 percent growth in 2015, and it is expected to grow by 2.8 percent in 2016. Unemployment has dropped steadily, from over 9 percent in 2011 to just 5 percent in late 2015. It is on track to achieve full employment by mid-2016: an unemployment rate of 5 percent and an underemployment rate of 9 percent. The first figure has already been met; the second (underemployment rate) was 9.8 percent in early 2016, but dropping. Household debt has been falling from its peak in 2008, and housing starts are predicted to almost double to 1.9 million in 2016.

Canada's economy is also slowing rapidly. It grew by only 1.2 percent in 2015 and is expected to show a slight improvement to 1.7 percent in 2016. The falling Canadian dollar has been a mixed blessing. Canadians will be encouraged to vacation at home rather than visit the United States, while American tourists will be coming in increasing numbers to Canada, spending money on accommodations,

transportation, food, and entertainment. Canadian exports will become more attractive, so manufacturers will see increased sales to the United States. However, the cost of US-manufactured machinery will increase considerably. Canadian manufacturers are already producing at near capacity and will be hesitant to buy new machinery from the United States. So growth in manufacturing is unlikely to meet its full potential.

While there is some benefit to lower oil prices, the rapid decline has largely negative consequences for Canada's economy. Consumers benefit from lower gas prices at the pump, but that only helps the economy if they spend their savings in other ways. However, household debt levels are at an all-time high, unemployment has reached 7.2 percent and is expected to show only marginal improvement in the near future, wage gains are modest and expected to average only 2.3 percent in 2016, and there is a threat of continued job losses, especially in the oil-rich provinces. All of those things will help to keep consumer spending low. About one-third of business investment in Canada is in the oil and gas sector, and with profits in this sector down by more than $30 billion as a result of the recent oil price drop, future investment will be decidedly weak. Canada's other commodities have also seen considerable price declines over the past few years. Gold prices have dropped by more than 20 percent since 2011, copper and nickel are down by more than 35 percent, and iron ore has plunged by more than 60 percent. As a result, many mining projects are now losing money, and planned investments have been put on hold or simply cancelled.

Even the construction industry is having problems. Office vacancies are at their highest levels since 2010, and unemployment will restrain demand for new office space. Retail space is also in excess; several large chains have been closing stores, and it will be several years before new capacity is needed. Housing starts were low in the early part of 2015, partly due to the weather, but they did rebound later in the year. Even so, they remain below 2012 levels. One bright spot on the horizon: stronger housing starts in the United States will increase demand for Canadian lumber in 2016. The economy will likely be further helped by government spending. The federal government and some provincial governments have already announced they will be running fairly high deficits in the foreseeable future as they try to spur economic growth.

What does all of this mean? Well, today's economy is good *and* bad, but mostly it's cautiously good. And, certainly, it's complex. This section will expose you to what is happening in the economic world around you. It will help you appreciate the complex interdependence among world economies, between federal and provincial governments, between government and business, and between business and society. You will find plenty in this section to consider. As you read further in this chapter, you will develop a greater appreciation for economics, its complexities, and its importance to your life.

3-2 Managing the Economy through Fiscal and Monetary Policy

While market forces are what *drive* performance in a capitalist economy, proactive roles by the federal government and the Bank of Canada can help *shape* that performance. The goal is controlled, sustained growth, and both fiscal and monetary policy help achieve it.

3-2a Fiscal Policy

Fiscal policy refers to government efforts to influence the economy through taxation and spending decisions that are designed to encourage growth, boost employment, and curb inflation. Clearly, fiscal strategies are closely tied to political philosophy. But regardless of politics, most economists agree that lower taxes can boost the economy by leaving more money in people's pockets for them to spend or invest. Most also agree that government spending can boost the economy in the short term by providing jobs, such as mail carrier or national park ranger, and in the long term through investments in critical public assets, such as airports, highways, and renewable energy. Done well, both taxation and spending can offer economic benefits. The tricky part is finding the right balance between the two approaches. As economist Henry Hazlitt pointed out, it's important to keep in mind that "either immediately or ultimately, every dollar of government spending must be raised through a dollar of taxation; once we look at the matter in this way, the supposed miracles of government spending will appear in another light."

Every year, the government must draw up a budget—that is, a financial plan that outlines expected revenues from taxes and fees, as well as expected spending. If revenue is higher than spending, the government incurs a **budget surplus**. If spending is higher than revenue, the government incurs a **budget deficit** and must borrow money to cover the shortfall. The sum of all the money borrowed over the years and not yet repaid is the total **federal debt**. Exhibit 3.1 shows Canada's National Debt Clock, which changes in real time. Exhibit 3.2 shows key sources of revenue and key expenses for the federal government in 2014–15. Note that revenues exceeded expenses, meaning there was a budget surplus. Unlike the United States,

Courtesy of Canada's National Debt Clock http://www.nationaldebtclocks.org

Exhibit 3.1 National Debt Clock

where the national debt has grown annually for more than 50 years, Canada experienced a budget surplus in 1998—its first in 28 years—and in every year from then until 2008, which marked the start of a deep, serious recession. The government has run deficits for several years since, and as a result, the federal debt, which stood at $457.6 billion then, had grown to $612.3 billion at the end of 2014–15. (When provincial debt is included, total government debt in Canada exceeded $1.2 trillion; it is expected to exceed $1.3 trillion in 2016.) Actually, the federal government reported a very small surplus in 2014–15 (Exhibit 3.2), but it is projecting several years of large deficits going forward as it tries to spur economic growth in what has become a fairly stagnant economy.[3]

3-2b Monetary Policy

Monetary policy refers to actions that shape the economy by influencing interest rates and the supply of money. The federal government manages Canadian monetary policy through the Bank of Canada, the country's central bank. Besides setting monetary policy, the Bank of Canada provides banking services to member banks and to the federal government.

The Bank of Canada is headed by a 14-person board of directors. This board is composed of the governor, the senior deputy governor, and 12 directors from outside the bank, including the federal deputy finance minister, who sits as a non-voting member. Stephen S. Poloz,

fiscal policy Government efforts to influence the economy through taxation and spending.

budget surplus Overage that occurs when revenue is higher than expenses over a given period of time.

budget deficit Shortfall that occurs when expenses are higher than revenue over a given period of time.

federal debt The sum of all the money that the federal government has borrowed over the years and not yet repaid.

monetary policy Bank of Canada decisions that shape the economy by influencing interest rates and the supply of money.

A MILLION, A BILLION, A TRILLION: SAY WHAT?

Herb MacKenzie

When people talk about the global economy, they often use the words "million," "billion," and "trillion." Even if you don't have a million dollars, you can probably imagine what a million dollars will do. After all, people across Canada regularly win this amount—and much more—in various lotteries. But getting your mind around a trillion dollars may be a bit more difficult. No one in the world has a trillion dollars, even though some economies own several trillion dollars. To understand the true magnitude of a trillion dollars, consider this:

- If you had started spending a million dollars a day—every day, without fail—at the start of the Roman Empire, you still wouldn't have spent a trillion dollars by today; in fact, you'd have more than $250 billion left over, and that would make you a very rare person indeed.

- One trillion five-dollar bills—because we no longer have one-dollar bills in Canada—laid end to end, would stretch farther than the distance from the earth to the sun. You could also wrap your chain of bills more than 12,000 times around the earth's equator.

- If you flew a jet at the speed of sound, spooling out a roll of one trillion bills behind you, it would take you more than 14 years to release them. But your plane probably couldn't carry the roll because it would weigh more than a million tonnes.

Turning the global economy around may take much more than a trillion dollars, but make no mistake when you hear those numbers thrown around on the news—a trillion dollars is an awful lot of money!

Exhibit 3.2 Federal Government 2014–15 Revenue and Expenses ($billions)[4]

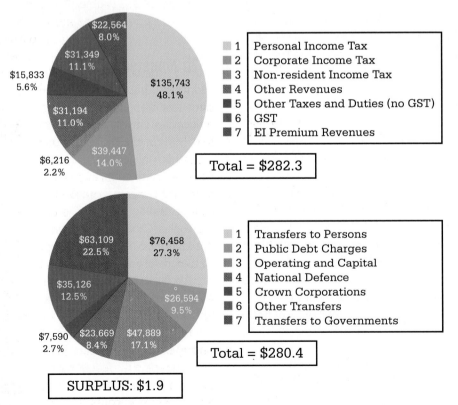

1 Personal Income Tax
2 Corporate Income Tax
3 Non-resident Income Tax
4 Other Revenues
5 Other Taxes and Duties (no GST)
6 GST
7 EI Premium Revenues

$135,743 48.1%
$39,447 14.0%
$6,216 2.2%
$31,194 11.0%
$15,833 5.6%
$31,349 11.1%
$22,564 8.0%

Total = $282.3

1 Transfers to Persons
2 Public Debt Charges
3 Operating and Capital
4 National Defence
5 Crown Corporations
6 Other Transfers
7 Transfers to Governments

$76,458 27.3%
$26,594 9.5%
$47,889 17.1%
$23,669 8.4%
$7,590 2.7%
$35,126 12.5%
$63,109 22.5%

Total = $280.4

SURPLUS: $1.9

appointed in 2013, is the present governor. All members of the board are appointed by the federal finance minister. The governor and senior deputy governor serve seven-year terms; all other directors serve three-year terms. Board members are eligible for reappointment.

The Bank of Canada can have a tremendous impact on the Canadian economy. Ever since the responsibilities of the Bank of Canada were defined in the *Bank of Canada Act*, which received Royal Assent in 1934, the purpose of the institution has remained the same. There have been many amendments to the act, but the Bank of Canada still exists "to regulate credit and currency in the best interests of the economic life of the nation." The actions taken by the Bank of Canada directly influence inflation, employment, and production and therefore affect the standard of living of all Canadians. Arguably, the governor of the Bank of Canada could be considered the second most powerful person in the country.

The Bank of Canada helps guide the economy by influencing the size of the **money supply**—that is, the total amount of money in the overall economy. The two most commonly used definitions of the money supply are M1 and M2:

- **M1**: All currency—paper bills and metal coins—plus chequing accounts and traveller's cheques.

- **M2**: All M1 plus most savings accounts, money market accounts, and certificates of deposit (low-risk savings vehicles with a fixed term, typically less than one year).

In 2015, the M1 money supply totalled more than $771 billion, and the M2 version of the money supply exceeded $1.3 trillion.[5] In practice, the term *money supply* most often refers to M2. Note that credit cards are not part of the money supply, although they do have an unmistakable impact on the flow of money through the economy.

The Bank of Canada attempts to reduce the money supply when prices begin to rise. Ideally, if less money is available, interest rates will rise. This will reduce spending, which should bring inflation under control. But when the economy is too sluggish, the Bank of Canada typically increases the money supply. If more money is available, interest rates usually drop, encouraging businesses to expand and consumers to spend. Specifically, the Bank of Canada uses two key tools that expand and contract the money supply:

- Open market operations
- Discount rate changes

Open Market Operations This is the Bank of Canada's most frequently used tool. **Open market operations** involve buying and selling government securities, which include treasury bonds, notes, and bills. These securities are the IOUs the government issues to finance its deficit spending.

How do open market operations work? When the economy is weak, the Bank of Canada *buys* government securities on the open market. When the Bank of Canada pays the sellers of these securities, money previously held by the Bank of Canada is put into circulation. This directly stimulates spending. In addition, any of the additional funds supplied by the Bank of Canada that are deposited in banks will allow banks to make more loans, making credit more readily available. This encourages even more spending and further stimulates the economy.

When inflation is a concern, the Bank of Canada *sells* securities. Buyers of the securities write cheques to the Bank of Canada to pay for the securities they have bought, and the Bank of Canada withdraws these funds from banks. Because they have fewer funds, banks must cut back on the loans they make, credit becomes tighter, and the money supply shrinks. This reduces spending and cools off the inflationary pressures in the economy.

Discount Rate Changes Just as you can borrow money from your bank, your bank can borrow funds from the Bank of Canada. And just as you must pay interest on your loan, your bank must pay interest on loans from the Bank of Canada. The **bank rate**—the interest rate the Bank of Canada charges on its loans to commercial banks—is established on eight fixed dates each year. In January 2016, the bank rate stood at 0.50 percent, a low rate by historical standards. When the Bank of Canada has a low discount rate, banks can obtain funds at a lower cost and use these funds to make more loans to their own customers. When the cost of acquiring funds from the Bank of Canada is lower, interest rates on bank loans also tend to fall. The result: businesses and individuals are more likely to borrow money and spend it, which stimulates the economy. Clearly, the Bank of Canada is most likely to reduce the discount rate during recessions. But in response to inflation—usually a sign of a rapidly expanding economy—the Bank of Canada usually increases the discount rate. Banks react by raising the interest rates they charge their customers. Fewer businesses and individuals are willing to take loans, which ultimately slows down the economy and reduces inflation.[6]

Reserve Requirement Changes Many central banks also manage the money supply by managing cash reserves. They require member banks to hold

money supply The total amount of money within the overall economy.

M1 money supply Includes all currency plus chequing accounts and traveller's cheques.

M2 money supply Includes all of M1 money supply plus most savings accounts, money market accounts, and certificates of deposit.

open market operations The Bank of Canada function of buying and selling government securities, which include treasury bonds, notes, and bills.

bank rate The rate of interest the Bank of Canada charges when it loans funds to banks.

FROM DISRUPTIVE DEMOGRAPHIC TRENDS TO ECONOMIC AFTERSHOCKS

Herb MacKenzie

Data from the 2011 Census suggest that a profoundly different Canada will emerge over the next 50 years. Canada's population will become older and more diverse and will shift westward geographically. Here are some highlights:

- By 2063, the population could reach 63.5 million people, compared to 35.2 million in 2013.

- Alberta's population will grow significantly and will likely surpass British Columbia's by 2038. Several scenarios suggest there will be population declines in New Brunswick, Nova Scotia, and Newfoundland and Labrador.

- Nunavut will have the youngest population in Canada by 2038, and Newfoundland and Labrador will have the oldest. By 2038 about 25 percent of Canadians will be seniors, but that will likely surpass 30 percent in Newfoundland and Labrador.

- The number of people over 100 years old—centenarians—will increase from roughly 7,000 today to 62,000 by 2063. People over 80 will increase from 4.1 percent of the population to 9.6 percent by 2045.

- There will be 6,775,800 Canadians who were born outside Canada: 20.6 percent, more than one in five. This is the highest percentage among all G7 countries.

These trends will bring both opportunities and challenges for businesses. For instance, marketers will need to customize their pitches for more different target customers. Educated, high-income, older Canadians will drive demand for new consumer electronics and other high-tech products related to "elder care." Meanwhile, a more diverse, multicultural population will require companies to develop new strategies both for attracting customers and for managing their workforces.[7]

---

funds, called *reserves*, equal to a stated percentage of the deposits held by their customers. This percentage is called the **reserve requirement** (or the required reserve ratio). Reserves help protect depositors who may want to withdraw their money without notice. As reserve requirements increase, banks hold more funds, meaning that they will have fewer funds available for making loans. This makes credit tighter and causes interest rates to rise. As reserve requirements decrease, some of the funds that banks were holding become available for loans. This increases the availability of credit and causes interest rates to drop. Currently, banks in the United States are required to maintain about a 10 percent reserve ratio. The Bank of Canada, however, eliminated reserve requirements so that Canada's large banks could compete effectively with other financial institutions that are not required to carry reserves. Canadian banks generally maintain a reserve ratio of about 2 percent. However, to help ensure that banks manage their reserves

reserve requirement A rule that specifies the minimum amount of reserves (or funds) a bank must hold, expressed as a percentage of the bank's deposits.

effectively, the Bank of Canada charges member banks a penalty when they must borrow to cover withdrawals.

Other Bank of Canada Functions Besides setting monetary policy, the Bank of Canada has several other core functions. These include providing banking services for both the government and banks. In its role as a banker for banks, the Bank of Canada coordinates the cheque-clearing process for cheques on behalf of any banks that are willing to pay its fees. And as the government's bank, the Bank of Canada maintains the federal government's chequing account and keeps the Canadian currency supply in good condition.

3-3 Capitalism: The Free Market System

It's a simple fact, more clear now than ever before: no one can get everything they want all of the time. We live in a world of finite resources, which means that societies

"LOOKING TO MULTIPLY YOUR MONEY? LOOK NO FURTHER THAN YOUR FINANCIAL INSTITUTION!"

Everyone knows that banks and credit unions help people save money, but most people don't realize that they actually *create* money. The process is complex, but a simplified example illustrates the point: Say you deposit $5,000 in your local credit union branch. How much money do you have? You obviously have $5,000. Now imagine that your friend, Shuang Li, goes there for a loan. If your credit union keeps a reserve ratio of 2 percent, then it has $4,900 to loan Shuang. She uses the money to buy a used car from your neighbour Mohamed, who deposits the $4,900 in his local bank. How much money does Mohamed have? Clearly, he has $4,900. How much money do you have? You still have $5,000. Thanks to the system, our "money supply" has increased from $5,000 to $9,900. Multiply this phenomenon times millions of such financial transactions, and you can see why cold hard cash accounts for only a small percentage of total Canadian M2 money supply.

But what happens if everyone wanted to withdraw their money at the same time? The financial system would clearly collapse. And in fact, during the Great Depression there were many bank failures in the United States. Canadian banks were larger and more diversified and did not experience as many failures. A few small banking institutions did fail, in the 1980s and 1990s, but not one penny in insurable bank deposits was lost because the **Canada Deposit Insurance Corporation (CDIC)**, a federal Crown corporation created by Parliament in 1967, insures eligible deposits held in Canadian dollars from $1 to $100,000 at CDIC member institutions. Credit union customers are similarly protected by provincial agencies, which vary depending on the jurisdiction involved.

Herb MacKenzie

must determine how to distribute resources among their members. An **economic system** is a structure for allocating limited resources. Over time and around the globe, nations have instituted different economic systems. A careful analysis suggests that no system is perfect, which may explain why there isn't one standard approach. The next sections of this chapter examine each basic type of economic system and explore the trend towards mixed economies.

A hallmark of the free market system is the consumer's right to choose.

Herb MacKenzie

The economic system of Canada is called **capitalism**, also known as a *private enterprise system* or a *free market system*. Brought to prominence by Adam Smith in the 1700s, capitalism is based on private ownership, economic freedom, and fair competition. A core capitalist principle is the paramount importance of individuals, innovation, and hard work. In a capitalist economy—such as Canada—individuals, businesses, or not-for-profit organizations privately own the vast majority of enterprises (only a small fraction are owned by the government). These private sector businesses are free to make their own choices regarding everything from what they will produce, to how much they will charge, to whom they will hire and fire. Correspondingly, individuals are free to choose what they will buy, how much they are willing to pay, and where they will work.

To thrive in a free enterprise system, companies must offer value to their customers—otherwise, their customers will choose to go elsewhere. Businesses must also offer value to their employees

economic system
A structure for allocating limited resources.

Canada Deposit Insurance Corporation (CDIC)
A federal Crown corporation that insures deposits in banks and thrift institutions for up to $100,000 per customer, per bank.

capitalism An economic system—also known as the private enterprise or free market system—based on private ownership, economic freedom, and fair competition.

and suppliers in order to attract top-quality talent and supplies. As companies compete to attract the best resources and offer the best values, quality goes up, prices remain reasonable, and choices proliferate, raising the standard of living in the economy as a whole.

3-3a The Fundamental Rights of Capitalism

For capitalism to succeed, the system must ensure some fundamental rights—or freedoms—to all of the people who live within the economy:

- **The right to own a business and keep after-tax profits:** Remember that capitalism doesn't guarantee that anyone will actually *earn* profits. Nor does it promise there won't be taxes. But if you do earn profits, you get to keep your after-tax income and spend it however you see fit (within the limits of the law, of course). This right acts as a powerful motivator for business owners in a capitalist economy; the lower the tax rate, the higher the motivation. The Canadian government strives to maintain low tax rates to preserve the after-tax profit incentive that plays such a pivotal role in the free enterprise system.

- **The right to private property:** This means that individuals and private businesses can buy, sell, and use property—which includes land, machines, and buildings—in any way that makes sense to them. This right also includes the right to will property to family members. The only exceptions to private property rights are minimal government restrictions designed to protect the greater good. You can't, for instance, use your home or business to produce cocaine, abuse children, or spew toxic smoke into the air.

- **The right to free choice:** Capitalism relies on economic freedom. People and businesses must be free to buy (or not buy) according to their wishes. They must be free to choose where to work (or not work) and where to live (or not live). Freedom of choice directly feeds competition, creating a compelling incentive for business owners to offer the best goods and services at the lowest prices. Canadian government trade policies boost freedom of

pure competition A market structure with many competitors selling virtually identical products. Barriers to entry are quite low.

choice by encouraging a wide array of both domestic and foreign producers to compete freely for our dollars.

- **The right to fair competition:** A capitalist system depends on fair competition among businesses to drive higher quality and lower prices and provide more choices. Capitalism can't achieve its potential if unfair practices—such as deceptive advertising, predatory pricing, and broken contracts—mar the free competitive environment. The government's role is to create a level playing field by establishing regulations and monitoring the competition to ensure compliance.

Adam Smith (1723–90) has often been called the "father of economics."

Georgios Kollidas/Shutterstock.com

3-3b Four Degrees of Competition

While competition is essential for the free market system to function, not all competition works the same. Different industries experience different degrees of competition, ranging from pure competition to monopolies.

- **Pure competition** is a market structure with many competitors selling virtually identical products. Because customers can't (or won't) distinguish one product from another, no single producer has any control over the price. Also, new producers can easily enter and leave purely competitive markets. In today's Canadian economy, examples of pure competition have virtually disappeared. Agriculture probably comes closest—corn is basically corn, for example—but with the dramatic growth of huge corporate farms and the success of major cooperatives such

Herb MacKenzie

as Sunkist, the number of competitors in agriculture has dwindled and new farmers are having trouble entering the market. Not only that, but segments of the agriculture market—such as organic farms and hormone-free dairies—have emerged with hit products that command much higher prices than the competition.

- **Monopolistic competition** is a market structure with many competitors selling differentiated products. (Caution! Monopolistic competition is quite different from a *monopoly*, which we will cover shortly.) Producers have some control over the price of their wares depending on the value they offer their customers. Also, new producers can fairly easily enter categories marked by monopolistic competition. In fact, if a monopolistic category takes off, it typically attracts a number of new suppliers quite quickly. Examples of monopolistic competition include the clothing industry and the restaurant business. Think about the clothing business, for a moment, in local terms. How many firms do you know that sell T-shirts? You could probably think of at least 50 without too much trouble. And the quality and price are all over the board: Designer T-shirts can sell for well over $100, but plenty of options go for less than $10. How hard would it be to start your own T-shirt business? Probably not hard at all. In fact, chances are strong that you know at least one person who sells T-shirts on the side. In terms of product and price variation, number of firms, and ease of entry, the T-shirt business clearly demonstrates the characteristics of monopolistic competition.

- **Oligopoly** is a market structure with only a handful of competitors selling products that are either similar or different. The retail gasoline business and the car manufacturing industry, for instance, are both oligopolies, even though gas stations offer very similar products, and car companies offer quite different models and features. Other examples of oligopoly include the soft drink industry, the computer business, and network television. Breaking into a market characterized by oligopoly can be tough because it typically requires a huge upfront investment. You could start making T-shirts in your kitchen, for instance, but you'd need a pretty expensive facility to start manufacturing cars. Oligopolies typically avoid intense price competition because they have nothing to gain—every competitor simply makes less money. When price wars do flare up, the results can be devastating for entire industries.

- **Monopoly** is a market structure with just a single producer completely dominating the industry,

leaving no room for any significant competitors. Monopolies usually aren't good for anyone but the company that has control; without competition there isn't any incentive to hold down prices or increase quality and choices. Because monopolies can harm the economy, most capitalist countries have enacted pro-competition legislation. In the past, Canadians faced a monopoly service provider for package delivery (Canada Post), for telephone service (Bell Canada), and for air travel (Air Canada). All of these service providers now have competition, and Canadian consumers are better off. But Canada's largest monopoly service provider still exists: health care—a public system in which the government will not allow private competition. A 2013 report by the Organisation for Economic Co-operation and Development (OECD) found that despite having a per capita cost 36 percent higher than the OECD average, Canada had the longest wait times for elective surgery. A second report—the 2014 Commonwealth Fund Report—ranked Canada's health care performance well behind that of Australia and many European countries. Pressure is building: a rapidly aging population and increased costs for new technologies and drugs will force governments to reconsider how health care is delivered across Canada, and consumers will likely have greater choice in the not-too-distant future.[8]

But in a few situations, the government not only allows monopolies but actually encourages them. This usually occurs when it would be too inefficient for each competitor to build its own infrastructure to serve the public. A **natural monopoly** then arises. Cable television offers a clear example. Would it really make sense for even a handful of competitors to wire neighbourhoods separately for cable? Clearly, that's not practical—just imagine the chaos! Instead, the government has granted cable franchises—or monopolies—to individual companies and then regulated them (with mixed results) to ensure that they don't abuse the privilege. Besides natural monopolies, the government grants patents and copyrights, which create artificial monopoly situations (at least temporarily), in order to encourage innovation.

monopolistic competition A market structure with many competitors selling differentiated products. Barriers to entry are low.

oligopoly A market structure with only a handful of competitors selling products that are either similar or different. Barriers to entry are typically high.

monopoly A market structure with one producer completely dominating the industry, leaving no room for any significant competitors. Barriers to entry tend to be virtually insurmountable.

natural monopoly A market structure with one company as the supplier of a product because the nature of that product makes a single supplier more efficient than multiple, competing ones. Most natural monopolies are government sanctioned and regulated.

Herb MacKenzie

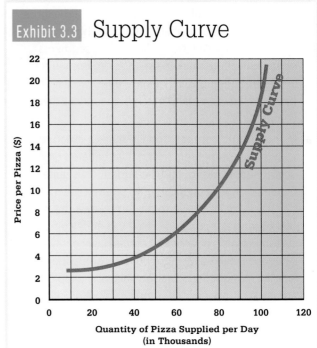

Exhibit 3.3 Supply Curve

© Cengage Learning

3-3c Supply and Demand: Fundamental Principles of a Free Market System

In a free market system, the continual interplay between buyers and sellers determines the selection of products and prices available in the economy. If a business makes something that few people actually want, sales will be low and the firm will typically yank the product from the market. Similarly, if the price of a product is too high, low sales will dictate a price cut. But if a new good or service becomes a hit, you can bet that similar offerings from other firms will pop up almost immediately (unless barriers—such as government-granted patents—prevent new entrants). The concepts of demand and supply explain how the dynamic interaction between buyers and sellers directly impacts the range of products and prices in the free market.

Supply **Supply** refers to the quantity of products that producers are willing to offer for sale at different market prices. Because businesses seek to make as much profit as possible, they are likely to produce more of a product that commands a higher market price and less of a product that commands a lower price. Think about it in terms of pizza. Assume that it costs a local restaurant about $5 to make a pizza. If the market price for pizza hits, say, $20, you can bet that a restaurant will start cranking out pizza. But if the price drops to $6, the restaurant has much less incentive to focus on pizza and will probably invest its limited resources in cooking other dishes.

The relationship between price and quantity from a supplier standpoint can be shown on a graph called the **supply curve**. The supply curve maps quantity on the *x*-axis (or horizontal axis) and price on the *y*-axis (or vertical axis). In most categories, as the price rises, the quantity produced rises correspondingly, yielding a graph that curves up as it moves to the right. Exhibit 3.3 shows a possible supply curve for pizza.

Demand **Demand** refers to the quantity of products that consumers are willing to buy at different market prices. Because consumers generally seek the products they need (or want) at the lowest possible prices, they tend to buy more of products with lower prices and less of products with higher prices. Pizza and tacos, for instance, are both popular meals. But if pizza costs a lot less than tacos, most people will get pizza more often than tacos. Likewise, if the price of pizza were out of hand, people would probably order tacos (or some other option) more often, reserving their pizza eating for special occasions.

The relationship between price and quantity from a demand standpoint can be shown on a graph called the **demand curve**. Like the supply curve, the demand curve maps quantity on the *x*-axis and price on the *y*-axis. But different from the supply curve, the demand curve for most goods and services slopes down as it moves to the right, for quantity demanded tends to drop as prices rise. Exhibit 3.4 shows how a demand curve for pizza could look.

Equilibrium Price It's important to remember that supply and demand don't operate in a vacuum. The constant interaction between the two forces helps determine the market price in any given category. In theory, the actual

supply The quantity of products that producers are willing to offer for sale at different market prices.

supply curve The graphed relationship between price and quantity from a supplier standpoint.

demand The quantity of products that consumers are willing to buy at different market prices.

demand curve The graphed relationship between price and quantity from a customer demand standpoint.

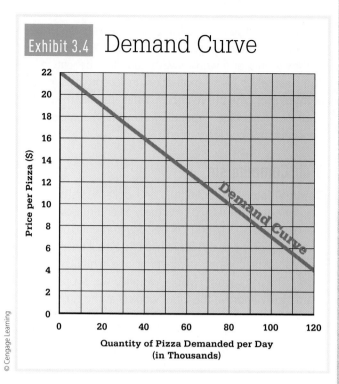

Exhibit 3.4 Demand Curve

Price per Pizza ($) / Quantity of Pizza Demanded per Day (in Thousands)

© Cengage Learning

market price occurs at the point where the supply curve and the demand curve intersect (see Exhibit 3.5). The price associated with this point of intersection—the point where the quantity demanded equals the quantity supplied—is called the **equilibrium price**, and the quantity associated with this point is called the *equilibrium quantity*.

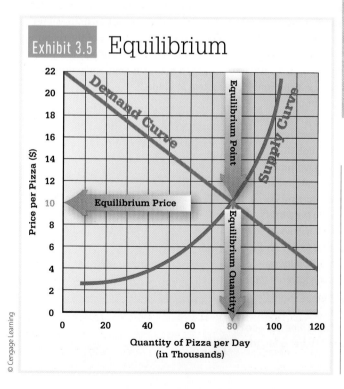

Exhibit 3.5 Equilibrium

Price per Pizza ($) / Quantity of Pizza per Day (in Thousands)

© Cengage Learning

Pay as You Throw

Admit it! Every so often, you've thrown away a can or a bottle that you really should have recycled, right? Would you have made the same choice if you had to pay your municipality for every piece of trash you threw away? A growing number of communities across Canada are implementing "pay as you throw" (PAYT) programs that charge residents for waste collection based on the amount of waste they throw away—in the same way that residents are charged for electricity, gas, and other utilities. In some municipalities, residents are charged for each bag of waste. In others, a limited number of bags—usually one or two—is collected free and charges are incurred for additional bags. Finally, in some regions, residents pay a fee for a garbage container, depending on its size. The more waste you "throw," the larger the container you need, and the higher the price you pay. As a result of PAYT programs, residents are motivated not only to recycle more but also to think about ways to generate less waste in the first place. In fact, communities with PAYT programs report average reductions in waste amounts ranging from 25 to 35 percent. Recycling tends to increase significantly as well, further cutting down on the amount of waste requiring disposal. This can mean lower disposal costs, savings in waste transportation expenses, potentially greater revenues from the sale of recovered materials, and other cost savings. In addition, while every 9,000 tonnes of solid waste going to landfills creates one job, that same amount of waste kept out of landfills can create 10 recycling jobs or 75 materials reuse jobs. In fact, a recent study showed that a stronger recycling economy would create more than 1.5 million new jobs across Canada and the United States, in manufacturing, collection, and other careers with family-supporting wages. Obviously, PAYT programs work for the environment, but more recycling also works for the economy. So next time you're tempted to chuck an empty bottle or a finished newspaper, take an extra moment and find a recycling bin.[9]

Sources: "Creating Green Jobs Through Recycling", *EPA Region 9 Newsletter*, February, 2011, EPA website; *Pay as You Throw Fact Sheet for State Officials*, updated July 26, 2011, EPA website; "More Recycling Will Create 1.5 Million New U.S. Jobs", November 14, 2011, *Recycling Works Campaign* website.

3-4 Planned Economies: Socialism and Communism

In capitalist economies, private ownership is paramount. Individuals own businesses, and their personal fortunes depend on their success in the free market. But in planned economies, the government plays a more heavy-handed role in controlling the economy. The two key categories of planned economies are socialism and communism.

equilibrium price The price associated with the point at which the quantity demanded of a product equals the quantity supplied.

3-4a Socialism

Socialism is an economic system based on the principle that the government should own and operate key enterprises that directly affect public welfare, such as utilities, telecommunications, and health care. Although the government's goal is to run these enterprises in the best interest of the overall public, inefficiencies and corruption often interfere with effectiveness. Socialist economies also tend to have higher taxes, which are designed to distribute wealth more evenly through society. Tax revenues typically fund services that citizens in free enterprise systems would have to pay for themselves in countries with lower tax rates. Examples range from free child care, to free university education, to free public health care systems.

Most Western European countries—from Sweden, to Germany, to the United Kingdom—developed powerful socialist economies in the second half of the 20th century. But more recently, growth in these countries has languished. Although many factors have contributed to the slowdown, the impact of high taxes on the profit incentive and of lavish social programs on the work incentive has clearly played a role. Potential entrepreneurs may migrate to countries that let them keep more of their profits, and workers with abundant benefits may find themselves losing motivation. In recent years, many of these economies have imposed stiff austerity measures to control government spending, eliminating some public benefits many took for granted.

> **socialism** An economic system based on the principle that the government should own and operate key enterprises that directly affect public welfare.

> **communism** An economic and political system that calls for public ownership of virtually all enterprises, under the direction of a strong central government.

3-4b Communism

Communism is an economic and political system that calls for public ownership of virtually all enterprises, under the direction of a strong central government. The communist concept was the brainchild of political philosopher Karl Marx, who outlined its core principles in his *Das Kapital* (1867). The communism Marx envisioned was supposed to dramatically improve the lot of workers at the expense of the super-rich.

But the countries that adopted communism in the 1900s—most notably the former Soviet Union, China, Cuba, North Korea, and Vietnam—did not thrive. Most of them imposed authoritarian governments that suspended individual rights and choices. People were unable to make even basic choices such as where to work or what to buy. Without the free market to establish what to produce, crippling shortages and surpluses developed. Corruption infected every level

LUNCH? ✓
PENCIL? ✓
DESK? CHAIR?

Herb Mackenzie

As students started school in one impoverished township in central China recently, many of them could be spotted lugging a ragtag assortment of beat-up old desks and chairs to their school, which cannot afford places for 60 percent of its students. When Chinese microbloggers tweeted photos of grandmothers hauling school desks through the countryside, rage at the government ensued. Leading intellectuals began making pointed public comments such as: *China has become the world's second largest economy; it throws its money to African countries to pay for the construction of their school buildings and school buses. In Macheng, more than three thousand pupils have to bring their own desks to school for class. It brings shame on the image of the Chinese.* Soon after, the top official in Macheng found the money for the desks, but this sort of social media commotion undermines the power and legitimacy of the ruling socialist government and may pave the way for a new economic and political system in China.[10]

of government. Under enormous pressure from their own populations and the rest of the world, Europe's communist regimes—and even the Soviet Union—began to collapse at the end of the 1980s, and were replaced with democracy and free markets. Over the past two decades, China has also introduced significant free market reforms across much of the country, fuelling its torrid growth rate. And in the 1990s, Vietnam launched free market reforms, stimulating rapid, sustained growth. The remaining communist economic systems—North Korea and Cuba—continue to falter, with their people facing drastic shortages and even starvation.

3-5 Mixed Economies: The Story of the Future

In today's world, pure economies—either market or planned—are practically nonexistent, as each would fall far short of meeting the needs of its citizens. A pure market economy would make insufficient provision for the old, the young, the sick, and the environment. A pure planned economy would not create enough value to support its people over the long term. Instead, most of today's nations have **mixed economies**, falling somewhere along a spectrum that ranges from pure planned at one extreme to pure market at the other.

Even Canada—one of the most market-oriented economies in the world—does not have a *pure* market economy. The various branches of the government own or regulate a number of major enterprises, including the postal service, schools, parks, libraries, entire systems of universities, health care facilities, and the military. In fact, the federal government is the nation's largest employer, providing jobs for more than 400,000 Canadians, three-quarters of them in census metropolitan areas.[11] The government also intervenes extensively in the free market by creating regulations that stimulate competition and protect both consumers and workers.

Over the past 30 years, most economies of the world have begun moving towards the market end of the spectrum. Government-owned businesses have converted to private ownership through a process called **privatization**. Socialist governments have reduced red tape, cracked down on corruption, and created new laws to protect economic rights. Extravagant human services—from free health care to education subsidies—have shrunk. And far-reaching tax reforms have created new incentives for both domestic and foreign investment in once-stagnant planned economies.

Unfortunately, the price of economic restructuring has been a fair amount of social turmoil in many nations undergoing market reforms. Countries from France to China have experienced sometimes violent demonstrations in response to social and employment program cutbacks. Change is challenging, especially when it redefines economic winners and losers. But countries that have taken strides towards the market end of the spectrum—from small players such as the Czech Republic to large players such as China—have seen the payoff in rejuvenated growth rates that have raised the standard of living for millions of people.

3-6 Evaluating Economic Performance: What's Working?

Clearly, economic systems are complex—very complex. So you probably won't be surprised to learn that no single measure captures all the dimensions of economic performance. To get the full picture, you need to understand a range of terms and measures, including gross domestic product, employment level, the business cycle, inflation rate, and productivity.

3-6a Gross Domestic Product

Real **gross domestic product**, or **GDP**, measures the total value of all final goods and services produced within a nation's physical boundaries over a given period of time, adjusted for inflation. (Nominal GDP does not include an inflation adjustment.) All domestic production is included in the GDP, even when the producer is foreign-owned. The Canadian GDP, for instance, includes the value of Honda vehicles built in Canada, even though Honda is a Japanese firm. Likewise, the Malaysian GDP includes the value of Teknion office furniture built in Malaysia, even though Teknion is a Canadian firm.

GDP is a vital measure of economic health. Businesspeople, economists, and political leaders use GDP to measure the economic performance of individual nations and to compare the growth among nations. Interestingly, GDP levels tend to be somewhat understated because they don't include any illegal activities—such as paying undocumented nannies and gardeners or selling illegal drugs—which can represent a significant portion of some countries' production.

mixed economies Economies that embody elements of both planned and market-based economic systems.

privatization The process of converting government-owned businesses to private ownership.

gross domestic product (GDP) The total value of all final goods and services produced within a nation's physical boundaries over a given period of time.

Manufacturing in Canada has been in decline for decades. Abandoned manufacturing sites can be found across the country.

job loss is called *frictional unemployment*, and it tends to be ultimately positive. *Structural unemployment*, on the other hand, is usually longer term. This category includes people who don't have jobs because the economy no longer needs their skills. In Canada over the past decade, more and more workers have found themselves victims of structural unemployment as manufacturing jobs have moved overseas. Often their only option is expensive retraining. Two other categories of unemployment are *cyclical*, which involves layoffs during recessions, and *seasonal*, which involves job loss related to the time of year. In some parts of the country, construction and agricultural workers are seasonally unemployed. But perhaps the best example may be the department store Santa, who has a job only during the holiday season!

The GDP also ignores legal goods that are not reported to avoid taxation, as well as output produced within households. In 2014, Canada's GDP was USD$1.79 trillion, just off its 2013 record high of $1.84 trillion.[12]

3-6b Employment Level

The overall level of employment is another key element of economic health. When people have jobs they have money, which allows them to spend and invest, fuelling economic growth. Most nations track employment levels largely through the **unemployment rate**, which includes everyone of employment age who doesn't have a job and is actively seeking one. Between 1966 and 2015, Canada's unemployment rate averaged 7.7 percent, from a high of 13.1 percent in December 1982 to a low of 2.9 percent in June 1966. In January 2016, the unemployment rate in Canada was 7.2 percent.[13]

Interestingly, some unemployment is actually good—it reflects your freedom to change jobs. If you have an awful boss, for instance, you can just quit. Are you unemployed? Of course, you are. Are you glad? You probably are, and the chances are good that you'll find another position that's a better fit for you. This type of

unemployment rate
The percentage of people in the labour force of employment age who do not have jobs and are actively seeking employment.

business cycle The periodic contraction and expansion that occurs over time in virtually every economy.

contraction A period of economic downturn, marked by rising unemployment and falling business production.

recession An economic downturn marked by a decrease in the GDP for two consecutive quarters.

depression An especially deep and long-lasting recession.

recovery A period of rising economic growth and employment.

3-6c The Business Cycle

The **business cycle** is the periodic contraction and expansion that occurs over time in virtually every economy. But the word "cycle" may be a little misleading because it implies that the economy contracts and expands in a predictable pattern. In reality, the phases of the cycle are different each time they happen, and—despite the efforts of countless experts—no one can accurately predict when changes will occur or how long they will last. Those who make the best guesses stand to make fortunes, whereas bad bets can be financially devastating. The two key phases of the business cycle are contraction and expansion, as shown in Exhibit 3.6.

- **Contraction** is a period of economic downturn marked by rising unemployment. Businesses cut back on production, and consumers shift their buying patterns to more basic products and fewer luxuries. The economic "feel-good factor" simply disappears. Economists declare an official **recession** when GDP decreases for two consecutive quarters. A **depression** is an especially deep and long-lasting recession. Fortunately, economies seldom spiral into full-blown depressions, thanks in large part to proactive intervention from the government. The last depression in Canada was the Great Depression of the 1930s. Whether a downturn is mild or severe, the very bottom of the contraction is called the *trough*, as shown in Exhibit 3.6.

- **Recovery** is a period of rising economic growth and increasing employment following a contraction. Businesses begin to expand. Consumers start to regain confidence, and spending begins to rise. The recovery is essentially the transition period between contraction and expansion.

Exhibit 3.6 Business Cycle

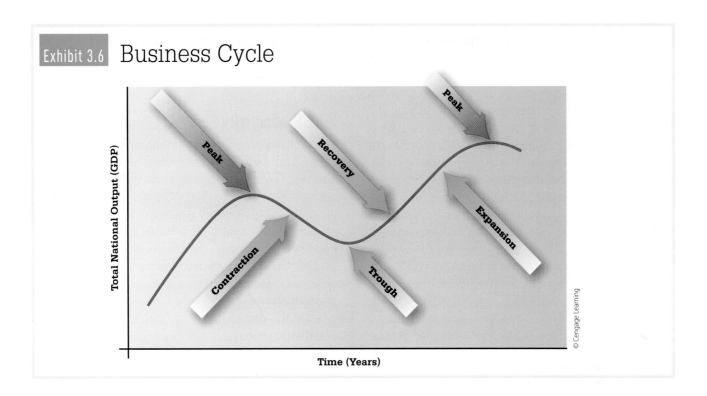

Time (Years)

© Cengage Learning

- **Expansion** is a period of robust economic growth and high employment. Businesses expand to capitalize on emerging opportunities. Consumers are optimistic and confident, which fuels purchasing, which fuels production, which fuels further hiring. As Exhibit 3.6 demonstrates, the height of economic growth is called the *peak* of the expansion. The Canadian economy has been growing between 2 and 3 percent in recent years. The Canadian economy as a whole grew 2.5 percent in 2014. Looking forward several years, national growth projections are lower. Oil-consuming provinces will benefit from lower oil prices, but the economies of oil-producing provinces, particularly Alberta and Newfoundland and Labrador, will contract. British Columbia is expected to lead Canada's growth in the near term.[14]

3-6d Price Levels

The rate of price changes across the economy is another basic measure of economic well-being. **Inflation** means that prices on average are rising. Much as with unemployment, a low level of inflation is not so bad. It reflects a healthy economy—people have money and are willing to spend it. But when the Bank of Canada—the nation's central bank—manages the economy poorly, inflation can spiral out of control, which can lead to **hyperinflation**, when average prices increase more than 50 percent per month. In Hungary, for example,

inflation in its unstable, post–Second World War economy climbed so quickly that prices doubled every 15 hours in 1945–46. More recently, prices in the war-torn former Yugoslavia doubled every 16 hours between October 1993 and January 1994.

When the rate of price increases slows down, the economy is experiencing **disinflation**, which was the situation in Canada in the mid-1990s. But when prices actually decrease, the economy is experiencing **deflation**, typically a sign of economic trouble that goes hand in hand with very high unemployment. People don't have money and simply won't spend unless prices drop. During the Great Depression of the 1930s, the Canadian economy experienced deflation. In fact, average prices in Canada were 37 percent lower in 1933 than in 1920. In recent years, inflation in the Canadian economy has been quite stable, ranging from 1 to 3 percent. The Canadian inflation rate (measured by the Consumer Price Index) was 1.6 percent in 2015.[15]

The government uses two major price indexes to evaluate inflation: the **consumer price index (CPI)**

expansion A period of robust economic growth and high employment.

inflation A period of rising average prices across the economy.

hyperinflation An average monthly inflation rate of more than 50 percent.

disinflation A period of slowing average price increases across the economy.

deflation A period of falling average prices across the economy.

consumer price index (CPI) A measure of inflation that evaluates the change in the weighted-average price of goods and services that the average consumer buys each month.

and the **producer price index (PPI)**. The CPI measures the change in weighted-average price over time in a consumer "market basket" of goods and services that the average person buys each month. Statistics Canada creates the basket—which includes more than 600 goods and services such as housing, transportation, haircuts, wine, and pet care. It updates what is included in the basket periodically to reflect changes in consumer spending habits. While the market basket is meant to represent the average consumer, keep in mind that the "average" includes a lot of variation, so the CPI may not reflect your personal experience. If you don't have a pet, for example, changes in veterinary costs won't affect you, although they would (slightly) impact the CPI.

The PPI measures the change over time in weighted-average wholesale prices, or the prices that businesses pay one another for goods and services. Changes in the PPI can sometimes predict changes in the CPI because producers tend to pass on price increases (and sometimes also price decreases) to consumers within a month or two of the changes.

producer price index (PPI) A measure of inflation that evaluates the change over time in the weighted-average wholesale prices.

productivity The basic relationship between the production of goods and services (output) and the resources needed to produce them (input), calculated via the following equation: Output / Input = Productivity.

3-6e Productivity

Productivity refers to the relationship between the goods and services an economy produces and the resources needed to produce them. The amount of output—goods and services—divided by the amount of input (e.g., hours worked) equals productivity. The goal, of course, is to produce more goods and services, using fewer hours and fewer other inputs. A high level of productivity typically correlates with healthy GDP growth, while low productivity tends to correlate with a more stagnant economy.

Over the past couple of decades, Canada has experienced strong, sustained productivity growth, due largely to infusions of technology that help workers produce more output, more quickly. But keep in mind that that productivity doesn't measure quality. That's why it's so important to examine multiple measures of economic health rather than relying on simply one or two dimensions.

From your standpoint as a business person, a key goal of economics is to guide your decision making by offering a deeper understanding of the broad forces that affect both your business and your personal life. Knowing even basic economic principles can help you make better business decisions in virtually every area—from production, to marketing, to accounting, to name just a few—regardless of your specific function or level within an organization. But you won't find an economics department within many (if any) businesses—rather, you'll find people across the organization applying economic theories and trends to their work, even in the face of continual economic flux. As you read through the other chapters in this book, take a moment to consider the macroeconomic and microeconomic forces that affect each area you study. You're likely to find a surprising number of examples.

careers in economics: Business Economist

Collect, analyze, and distribute data to explain economic phenomena and forecast economic trends, particularly with regard to supply and demand. Create and present clear, concise reports on economic trends to senior management on a monthly basis. Manage and motivate a small team of financial analysts and statisticians.

STUDY TOOLS 3

IN THE BOOK, YOU CAN:

☐ Rip out the Chapter Review card at the back of the book to have a summary of the chapter and key terms handy.

ONLINE AT NELSON.COM/STUDENT YOU CAN:

☐ Work through key concepts with a Guided Learning Question.

☐ Prepare for tests with quizzes.

☐ Review the key terms with Flash Cards (online or printer-ready).

☐ Explore practical examples of chapter concepts with Connect a Concept exercises.

4

The World Marketplace:
Business Without Borders

LEARNING OBJECTIVES
After studying this chapter, you will be able to . . .

4-1 Discuss business opportunities in the world economy

4-2 Explain the key reasons for and against international trade

4-3 Describe the tools for measuring international trade

4-4 Analyze strategies for reaching global markets

4-5 Discuss barriers to international trade and strategies to surmount them

4-6 Describe the free trade movement and discuss key benefits and criticisms

After you finish this chapter, go to page 67 for STUDY TOOLS

4-1 An Unprecedented Opportunity . . .

As access to technology skyrockets and barriers to trade continue to fall, individual economies around the world have become more interdependent than ever before. The result is a tightly woven global economy marked by intense competition and huge, shifting opportunities. The potential for Canadian business is enormous. The global economic crisis of 2008 caused the world GDP to contract in 2009 for the first time since the Second World War, compared to average increases of about 3.5 percent per year since 1946. However, world GDP growth turned positive again in 2010 and 2011, led by growth in emerging markets nearly twice that of growth in advanced economies.[1] See Exhibit 4.1 for a sampling of some specific higher and lower growth countries.

A quick look at population trends underscores the opportunities enjoyed today by the global business community, especially in developing nations. With more than 35 million people, Canada accounts for only a small percentage of the world's population.[2] However, billions of people live beyond our borders, all of them potential customers for Canadian firms. But even though the growth

rates in many high-population countries are strong, most of these nations remain behind North America in terms of development and prosperity, and this poses considerable challenges for foreign firms. (Put simply, most of their populations may not have the resources to buy even basic goods and services.) Exhibit 4.1 compares the world's five largest economies to Canada in terms of population, per capita GDP, and GDP growth rate. Note that even though North American consumers clearly have money, China and India represent a much bigger opportunity in terms of size and economic growth.

The world is more malleable than you think and it's waiting for you to hammer it into shape.

Bono, musician and humanitarian

Monkey Business Images/Shutterstock.com

Exhibit 4.1 | Selected Population and GDP Figures[3]

NATION	POPULATION	PER CAPITA GDP ($US)	GDP GROWTH RATE
CANADA	34,837,841	43,100	1.6
CHINA	1,355,692,576	9,800	7.7
INDIA	1,236,344,631	4,000	3.2
EUROPEAN UNION	511,434,812	34,500	.1
UNITED STATES	318,892,103	52,800	1.6
INDONESIA	253,609,643	5,200	5.3

Cellphones offer an interesting indicator of economic growth. Several recent studies have found that in a country that increases cellphone penetration by 10 percentage points, GDP is likely to increase by anywhere from 0.5 percent to 1.2 percent. That may seem small, but it equates to somewhere between $49 and $118 billion for an economy the size of China.

Not surprisingly, cellphone penetration in India and China is skyrocketing. China currently boasts the world's largest base of cellphone users—about one billion—and that growth will likely continue. India's current subscriber base is more than 900 million; it has grown explosively over the past five years, and that growth seems likely to continue over the next decade. Indeed, this growth may well continue until China and India both hit the 100 percent cellphone penetration rates that characterize a number of developed nations such as Taiwan, Hong Kong, Germany, and Argentina, which have more than one phone per person.

In the North America, Europe, and Japan, cellphones followed landlines. Many developing nations aren't bothering to build conventional phone service; instead, they're moving directly to cellphone networks. This trend is especially

FACING FACTS: FACEBOOK AROUND THE WORLD

Facebook has almost 1.4 billion active users each month, so it shouldn't be any surprise that Facebook accounts for one of every seven minutes spent on the Web. Nor should it be surprising that there are only five countries in the world where Facebook isn't the most popular social network. One of those countries is China, which is a closed society that officially bans Facebook. The ban has not stopped Facebook from trying, because as Sheryl Sandburg, Facebook's COO, says, "If your mission is to connect the entire world…you can't connect the whole world and not China." The other countries where Facebook does not (yet) rule are Japan, Russia, South Korea, and Vietnam. These all represent fast-growing Facebook markets, which suggests that Facebook is poised for global dominance, especially versus local competitors. In some countries such as the United States and Canada—where Facebook may appear to have maxed out—continued growth potential comes from the mobile market. Building a better mobile experience is one of Facebook's top priorities, which certainly makes sense since half of Facebook's users access the site at least once a month through mobile devices, and more than 10 percent of the site's members only use Facebook's mobile site. Already, the Facebook mobile app ranks among the top five apps for both iOS and Android. Facebook, despite its somewhat disappointing stock performance, is the only truly global social network in a world where social media have become the new norm of communication.[4]

© Cienpies Design/Shutterstock.com

marked across Africa, where cellphone penetration rates are more than double the penetration rates for landlines. By the end of 2012, cellphone penetration in Africa's 54 countries had surpassed 76 percent and was poised to eclipse 80 percent in early 2013. David Knapp, general director of Motorola Vietnam, points out that many developing nations "can leapfrog technology." And Vietnamese micro-entrepreneur Nguyen Huu Truc says: "It's no longer something that only the rich can afford. Now, it's a basic means of communication." As more people get connected, better communication will likely feed economic growth. According to Muhammad Yunis, founder of Grameen Bank in Bangladesh, "a mobile phone is almost like having a card to get you out of poverty in a couple of years." As a consequence, millions of people worldwide will have a higher standard of living.[5]

4-2 Key Reasons For and Against International Trade

Companies engage in global trade for a variety of reasons besides the obvious one: the opportunity to tap into huge and growing new markets. The benefits include better access to factors of production, reduced risk, and an inflow of new ideas.

- **Access to factors of production:** International trade offers a valuable opportunity for individual firms to capitalize on factors of production that simply aren't present in the right amounts at the right prices in their home countries. India, China, and the Philippines, for example, attract multibillion-dollar investments because of their large cohorts of technically skilled university graduates, who work for about one-fifth the pay of comparable Canadian workers. Russia and the OPEC nations offer abundant supplies of oil, and Canada, like other forested nations, boasts plenty of timber. Canada also offers plentiful capital, which is less available in other parts of the world. International trade helps even out some of the resource imbalances among nations.

- **Reduced risk:** Global trade reduces dependence on one economy, and this in turn reduces the economic risk for multinational firms. When the Japanese economy entered a deep, sustained slump in the 1990s, for instance, Sony and Toyota thrived by focusing on other, healthier markets around the world.

GLOBAL BRANDING

Every year, Interbrand, the branding consulting company, ranks the best brands in the world. Interbrand's methodology ensures that only truly global companies are eligible. To appear on the list, a brand must derive at least 30 percent of its earnings from outside its home country, be recognizable beyond its base of customers, and have publicly available marketing and financial data. The top 10 global brands in 2014 were:

1. Apple
2. Google
3. Coca-Cola
4. IBM
5. Microsoft
6. General Electric
7. Samsung
8. Toyota
9. McDonald's
10. Mercedes-Benz

In the wake of the worldwide global economic recovery, top global brands are laser-focused on building and, in some cases, *re*building the trust of their consumers. According to one brand consultant, "Trust is what drives profit margin and share price." Because today's consumers have access to so much information, transparency and openness are critical components of trust. Another marketing executive commented: "Consumers are telling companies in a thousand ways that if you aren't open with me, then I won't trust you." Brands that succeed at building trust may well top the Interbrand list for years to come.[6]

Nywlt-art/Shutterstock.com

But a word of caution: as national economies continue to integrate, an economic meltdown in one part of the world can have far-reaching impacts elsewhere. For example, after the banking crisis in the United States in 2008, nations around the world felt the economic repercussions along with the United States.

- **Inflow of innovation:** International trade offers companies an invaluable source of new ideas. Japan, for instance, is far ahead of the curve regarding cellphone service. Japanese cellphone "extras," including games, ringtones, videos, and stylish new accessories, are setting the standard for cellphone service around the world. In Europe, consumers are showing a growing interest in traditional and regional foods. Companies with a presence in foreign markets experience budding trends like these first-hand, giving them a jump in other markets around the world.

Most people agree that free trade has benefited most countries, but it does have some negative aspects. These include the loss of certain jobs, the loss of industries, and the increase in foreign ownership.

- **Loss of jobs:** When trade opens up across borders, many manufacturing jobs move to the country with the lowest paid workers. This often means that higher paying manufacturing jobs from one country move to

another. This can result in high unemployment among workers in those industries.

- **Loss of industries:** In some cases, entire industries will move to countries with lower paid workers. This can have a significant impact on the supply of products in those countries that have "lost" the jobs.

- **Increase in foreign ownership:** For countries that have a wealth of natural resources, free trade can result in a large number of domestic resource companies being purchased by foreign individuals or corporations. Some argue that foreign ownership can weaken a country's national security.[7]

4-2a Competitive Advantage

Industries tend to succeed on a worldwide basis in countries that enjoy a competitive advantage. To understand competitive advantage, you first need to understand how **opportunity cost** relates to international trade. When a country produces more of one good, it must produce less of another good (assuming that resources are finite). The value of the second-best choice—the value of the production that a country gives up in order to produce the first product—represents the opportunity cost of producing the first product.

> **opportunity cost** The opportunity of giving up the second-best choice when making a decision.

A country has an **absolute advantage** when it can produce more of a good than other nations, using the same amount of resources. China, for example, has an absolute advantage in terms of clothing production relative to Canada. But having an absolute advantage isn't always enough. Unless they face major trade barriers, the industries in any country tend to produce products for which they have a **comparative advantage**—meaning that they tend to turn out those goods that have the lowest opportunity cost compared to other countries. Canada, for instance, boasts a comparative advantage in natural resources, Germany has a comparative advantage in the production of high-performance cars, and South Korea enjoys a comparative advantage in electronics.

Michael Porter, a Harvard professor, developed a model for evaluating industries in order to determine which ones would provide a comparative advantage. His model is shown in Exhibit 4.2. In his view, the following factors influenced the competitiveness of an industry*:

1. *The power of suppliers:* Are there enough suppliers for the industry?

2. *The power of buyers:* Do the buyers have bargaining power? Is there enough information available for buyers to make informed decisions?

3. *The threat of new entrants:* Is there a long learning curve? Are there high investment requirements or economies of scale related to the industry that would make it difficult for new companies to start up?

4. *The threat of substitute products:* Are substitute products available? Are there high switching costs associated with the product?

5. *The degree of rivalry:* The above four factors influence the degree of rivalry within an industry. The level of rivalry within an industry can affect the growth of the industry.[8]

But keep in mind that comparative advantage seldom remains static. As technology changes and the workforce evolves (through factors such as education and experience), nations may gain or lose comparative advantage in various industries. China and India, for example, are both seeking to build a comparative advantage versus other nations in technology production by investing in their infrastructure and their institutions of higher education.

absolute advantage The benefit a country has in a given industry when it can produce more of a product than other nations using the same amount of resources.

comparative advantage The benefit a country has in a given industry if it can make products at a lower opportunity cost than other countries.

Exhibit 4.2 **Porter's Five Forces Model of Competition**

Buyers
- Number of buyers
- Switching costs to use another product or supplier
- Brand identity
- Threat of backward integration

Substitute Products
- Price difference
- Quality difference
- Performance difference
- Cost of switching
- Buyers' willingness to substitute

Competitive Rivalry
- Number of competitors
- Significance of competition (e.g., size)
- Product differentiation
- Cost for buyer to go to the competition
- Exit barriers

The Industry

Supplier Power
- Number of suppliers
- Size suppliers
- Product differentiation
- Buyers' switching costs
- Ability to substitute

Threat of New Competition Barriers to Entry
- Capital requirements
- Economies of scale
- Legal/regulatory issues
- Access to distribution channels
- Buyers' switching costs

Source: From unknown, http://college.cengage.com/business/resources/casestudies/students/porter.htm. © Cengage Learning.

4-3 Global Trade: Taking Measure

Global trade was significantly affected by the 2008 financial crisis. By the end of 2010, world trade was showing a slow recovery, but it has yet to return to pre-crisis levels. Global trade is expected to continue to slowly improve as the economies of the United States and the EU continue to recover. Measuring the impact of international trade on individual nations requires a clear understanding of balance of trade, balance of payments, and exchange rates.[9]

* Michael Porter, *The Competitive Advantage of Nations*, The MacMillan Press Ltd, pp. 73–74.

4-3a Balance of Trade

The **balance of trade** is a basic measure of the difference between a nation's exports and imports. If the total value of exports is higher than the total value of imports, the country has a **trade surplus**. If the total value of imports is higher than the total value of exports, the country has a **trade deficit**. Balance of trade includes the value of both goods and services, and it incorporates trade with all foreign nations. A trade deficit signals that an economy is wealthy enough to buy huge amounts of foreign products; however, a large deficit can be destabilizing. After all, as goods and services flow into a nation, money flows out, and this can pose a challenge with regard to long-term economic health. At the end of 2008, Canada experienced a trade deficit for the first time since early 1999. That trend continued through 2014, except in 2011, when the Canadian economy showed a small surplus.[10]

4-3b Balance of Payments

Balance of payments is a measure of the total flow of money into or out of a country. Clearly, the balance of trade plays a central role in determining the balance of payments. But the balance of payments also includes other financial flows such as foreign borrowing and lending, foreign aid payments and receipts, and foreign investments. A **balance of payments surplus** means that more money flows in than out, while a **balance of payments deficit** means that more money flows out than in. Keep in mind that the balance of payments typically corresponds to the balance of trade because trade is, in general, the largest component.

4-3c Exchange Rates

Exchange rates measure the value of one nation's currency relative to the currencies of other nations. Exchange rates do not directly measure global commerce, but they powerfully affect trading nations. The exchange rate of a given currency is expressed relative to other currencies. For example, when the US dollar began to show strength against a variety of world currencies (e.g., the euro, the Japanese yen, the Chinese yuan, and the Mexican peso), a number of American corporations took a significant earnings hit. Companies with a strong international presence, including P&G, PepsiCo, Kimberly Clark, Colgate Palmolive, Coca-Cola, McDonald's, and Ford, were all affected by the strengthening US dollar. Many firms choose to present their earnings reports stripped of the effects of currency translations, but in today's global economy, that clearly offers a misleading picture of performance.[11]

Here are some examples of how the exchange rate can affect the economy, using the Canadian dollar and the euro.

STRONG DOLLAR VERSUS EURO: WHO BENEFITS? (EXAMPLE: $1.00 = 1.20 EUROS)	WEAK DOLLAR VERSUS EURO: WHO BENEFITS? (EXAMPLE: $1.00 = .60 EUROS)
Canadian travellers to Europe: Their dollars can buy more European goods and services.	*European travellers to Canada:* Their dollars buy more Canadian goods and services.
Canadian firms with European operations: Operating costs—from buying products to paying workers—are lower.	*European firms with Canadian operations:* Operating costs—from buying products to paying workers—are lower.
European exporters: Their products are less expensive in Canada, so Europe exports more and we import more.	*Canadian exporters:* Their products are less expensive in Europe, so we export more and Europe imports more.

4-3d Countertrade

A thorough evaluation of global trade must also consider exchanges that don't actually involve money. A surprisingly large chunk of international commerce—as much as 25 percent—involves the barter of products for products. Companies typically engage in **countertrade** to meet the needs of customers—usually in developing countries—who don't have access to hard currency or credit. Individual countertrade agreements range from simple barter to a complex web of exchanges that end up meeting the needs of multiple parties. Done poorly, countertrading can be a confusing nightmare for everyone involved. But done well, countertrading is a powerful tool for gaining customers and products that would not otherwise be available.[12] Not surprisingly, barter opportunities tend to increase during economic downturns. For example, during the latest economic downturn, ads began to appear both in Russian newspapers and online, such as one that offered "2,500,000 rubles' worth of premium underwear for

balance of trade A basic measure of the difference in value between a nation's exports and imports, including both goods and services.

trade surplus Overage that occurs when the total value of a nation's exports is higher than the total value of its imports.

trade deficit Shortfall that occurs when the total value of a nation's imports is higher than the total value of its exports.

balance of payments A measure of the total flow of money into or out of a country.

balance of payments surplus Overage that occurs when more money flows into a nation than out of that nation.

balance of payments deficit Shortfall that occurs when more money flows out of a nation than into that nation.

exchange rates A measurement of the value of one nation's currency relative to the currency of other nations.

countertrade International trade that involves the barter of products for products rather than for currency.

any automobile." Another offered "lumber in Krasnoyarsk for food or medicine."[13]

4-4 Seizing the Opportunity: Strategies for Reaching Global Markets

There is no one right way to seize the opportunity in global markets. In fact, the opportunity may not even make sense for every firm. International trade can offer new profit streams and lower costs, but it also introduces higher levels of risk and complexity. For a firm to succeed in reaching global markets, it must be prepared.

Firms with overseas ambitions have a number of options for moving forward. One way is to seek foreign suppliers through outsourcing and importing. Another possibility is to seek foreign customers through exporting, licensing, franchising, and direct investment. These market development options fall along a spectrum from low cost–low control to high cost–high control, as shown in Exhibit 4.3. In other words, companies that choose to export products to a foreign country spend less to enter that market than companies that choose to build their own factories. But companies that build their own factories have a lot more control than exporters over how their business unfolds. Keep in mind that profit opportunity and risk—which vary along with cost and control—also play a critical role in how firms approach international markets.

Smaller firms tend to begin with exporting and move along

foreign outsourcing
Contracting with foreign suppliers to produce products, usually at a fraction of the cost of domestic production (also called contract manufacturing).

Exhibit 4.3 Market Development Options

LOWER Risk — HIGHER Risk

Exporting Licensing Franchising Direct Investment

LESS Control — MORE Control

© Cengage Learning

the spectrum as the business develops. Larger firms may jump straight to the strategies that give them more control over their operations. Large firms are also likely to use a number of different approaches in different countries, depending on the goals of the firm and the structure of the foreign market. Regardless of the specific strategy, most large companies—such as General Electric, Nike, and Disney—both outsource with foreign suppliers and sell their products to foreign markets.

4-4a Foreign Outsourcing and Importing

Foreign outsourcing means contracting with foreign suppliers to produce products, usually at a fraction of the cost of domestic production. Gap, for instance, relies on a network of manufacturers in 50 different countries, mostly in less developed parts of the world, from Asia, to Africa, to Central America. Apple depends on firms in China and Taiwan to produce the iPhone. Countless small companies contract with foreign manufacturers as well. The key benefit, of course, is dramatically lower wages, which drives down the cost of production.

But while foreign outsourcing lowers costs, it also involves significant risk. Quality control typically requires very detailed specifications to ensure that a company gets what it actually needs. Another key risk of foreign outsourcing involves social responsibility. A firm that contracts with foreign producers has an obligation to ensure that those factories adhere to ethical standards. Deciding what those standards should be is often quite tricky, given different cultures, expectations, and laws in different countries. And policing the factories on an ongoing basis can be even harder than determining the standards. Companies that don't get it right face the threat of significant consumer backlash in North America and Europe. This has been a particular issue with products produced in China. Over the past few years, for instance, product defects have forced North American firms to recall a host of Chinese-produced toys, including Thomas

© David Roark/UPPA/Photoshot

the Tank Engine trains, which were coated with toxic lead paint, ghoulish fake eyeballs, which were filled with kerosene, and small dolls that posed a swallowing hazard.[14]

Many North Americans have become personally familiar with the quality/cost tradeoff as more and more companies have outsourced customer service to foreign call centres. Research suggests that the cost of offering a live, North American-based, customer service agent averages about $7.50 per call, while outsourcing those calls to live agents in another country drops the average cost down to about $3.25 per call. But customers end up paying the difference in terms of satisfaction; they report high levels of misunderstanding, frustration, and inefficiency. A number of firms have enjoyed the best of both worlds by outsourcing customer service calls to North American agents who work from their own homes.[15]

Importing means buying products domestically that have been produced or grown in foreign nations rather than contracting with overseas manufacturers to produce special orders. Imported products, of course, don't carry the brand name of the importer, but they also don't carry as much risk. Pier 1 Imports, a large retail chain, has built a powerful brand around the importing concept, creating stores that give the customer the sense of a global shopping trip without the cost or hassle of actually leaving the country.

4-4b Exporting

Exporting is the most basic level of international market development. It simply means producing products domestically and selling them abroad. Exporting represents an especially strong opportunity for small and mid-sized companies. One North American hair care company developed a line of products specifically for customers of African heritage. Recognizing opportunity abroad, the company now exports its products to Africa and the Caribbean.[16]

4-4c Foreign Licensing and Foreign Franchising

Foreign licensing and foreign franchising, the next level of commitment to international markets, are quite similar. **Foreign licensing** involves a domestic firm granting a foreign firm the right to produce and market its product or to use its trademark/patent rights in a defined geographic area. The company that offers the rights, or the *licensor*, receives a fee from the company that buys the rights, or the *licensee*. This approach allows firms to expand into foreign markets with little or no investment; it also helps circumvent government restrictions on importing in closed markets. But maintaining control of licensees can be a significant challenge. Licensors also run the risk that unethical licensees may become their competitors, using information they have

gained from the licensing agreement. Foreign licensing is especially common in the food and beverage industry. The most high-profile examples include Coke and Pepsi, which grant licences to foreign bottlers all over the world.

Foreign franchising is a specialized type of licensing. A firm that expands through foreign franchising, called a *franchisor*, offers other businesses, or *franchisees*, the right to produce and market its products if the franchisee agrees to specific operating requirements—a complete package of how to do business. Franchisors also often offer their franchisees management guidance, marketing support, and even financing. In return, franchisees pay both a start-up fee and an ongoing percentage of sales to the franchisor. A key difference between franchising and licensing is that franchisees take over the identity of the franchisor. A McDonald's franchise in Paris, for instance, is clearly a McDonald's, not, say, a Pierre's Baguette outlet that also carries McDonald's products.

4-4d Foreign Direct Investment

Direct investment in foreign production and marketing facilities represents the deepest level of global involvement. The cost is high, but companies with direct investments have more control over how their businesses operate in a given country. The high dollar commitment also represents significant risk if the business doesn't go well. Most direct investment takes the form of either acquiring foreign firms or developing new facilities from the ground up. Another increasingly popular approach is strategic alliances or partnerships, which allow multiple firms to share risks and resources for mutual benefit.

Foreign acquisitions enable companies to gain a foothold quickly in new markets. For example, Italian carmaker Fiat took over struggling auto giant Chrysler, with plans to more fully exploit the North American market. A number of other global giants, such as Microsoft, General Electric, and Nestlé, tend to follow a foreign acquisition strategy.[17]

Developing new facilities from scratch—or *offshoring*—is the most costly form of direct investment. It also involves significant risk. The benefits include complete control over how the facility develops and the potential for high profits, which

importing Buying products domestically that have been produced or grown in foreign nations.

exporting Selling products in foreign nations that have been produced or grown domestically.

foreign licensing Authority granted by a domestic firm to a foreign firm for the rights to produce and market its product or to use its trademark/patent rights in a defined geographic area.

foreign franchising A specialized type of foreign licensing in which a firm expands by offering businesses in other countries the right to produce and market its products according to specific operating requirements.

direct investment When firms either acquire foreign firms or develop new facilities from the ground up in foreign countries (also called foreign direct investment).

VEGGIE SURPRISE, ANYONE?

Vincent Thian/AP Photo

Travel around the world and you're likely to see North American fast food franchisees in virtually every city. Although you'll surely recognize the names of these fast food companies, you may not be as familiar with the food they serve because many of the dishes have been completely changed in response to local culture.

Some favourites from the Domino's international menus:

- **Japan: squid pizza**
- **England: tuna and sweet corn pizza**
- **Guatemala: black beans**
- **Netherlands: grilled lamb pizza**

Pizza Hut:

- **Japan: crust stuffed with shrimp nuggets and injected with mayonnaise**
- **South Korea: crust filled with sweet potato mousse**
- **China: lemon-flavoured salmon pastry roll and scallop croquettes with crushed seaweed**

- **Middle East: "Crown Crust": a pizza/cheeseburger hybrid studded with "cheeseburger gems," which are cheeseburger sliders attached to the outside of a meaty pizza that's topped with lettuce and tomato and drizzled with "special sauce"**

KFC:

- **China: spicy tofu chicken rice, rice porridge breakfast (congee)**
- **India: Chana Snacker (a chickpea burger topped with Thousand Island sauce)**

McDonald's:

- **India: paneer salsa wrap (cottage cheese with Mexican-Cajun coating)**
- **Australia: bacon and egg roll ("rashers of quality bacon and fried egg")**
- **Kuwait: veggie surprise burger (no detailed description . . . yikes!)**
- **Brazil: cheese quiche**[18]

---

makes the approach attractive for corporations that can afford it. Intel, for instance, plans to build a $2.5 billion specialized computer chip manufacturing plant in northeastern China. And foreign car companies, from Daimler-Benz (Germany), to Hyundai (Korea), to Toyota (Japan), have built factories in Canada and the United States.[19]

Joint ventures involve two or more companies joining forces—sharing resources, risks, and profits but without merging companies—to pursue specific opportunities. A formal, long-term agreement is usually called a **partnership**; a less formal, less encompassing agreement is usually called a **strategic alliance**. Joint ventures are a popular, although controversial, means of entering foreign markets. Often a foreign company connects with a local firm to ease its way into the market. In fact, some countries, such as Malaysia, require that foreign investors have local partners. Recent research has found that joint ventures between multinational firms and domestic partners can be more costly and less rewarding than they initially appear. This suggests that joint ventures make sense only in countries that require local political and cultural knowledge as a core element of doing business.[20]

4-5 Barriers to International Trade

Every business faces challenges, but international firms face more hurdles than domestic firms. Understanding and surmounting those hurdles is the key to success in global markets. Most barriers to trade fall into the following categories: sociocultural differences, economic differences, and legal/political differences. As you think about these barriers, keep in mind that each country has a different mix of barriers. Often countries with the highest barriers have the least competition, which can be a real opportunity for the first international firms to break through.

4-5a Sociocultural Differences

Sociocultural differences include differences among countries in language, attitudes, and values. Specific and

joint ventures When two or more companies join forces—sharing resources, risks, and profits but not actually merging companies—to pursue specific opportunities.

partnership A voluntary agreement under which two or more people act as co-owners of a business for profit.

strategic alliance An agreement between two or more firms to jointly pursue a specific opportunity without actually merging their businesses. Strategic alliances typically involve less formal, less encompassing agreements than partnerships.

sociocultural differences Differences among cultures in language, attitudes, and values.

Oops! What were they thinking?

Saudi Women's Superpower?

Many people may not be surprised to learn that Saudi Arabian women do not have much political or economic power. But a look at one recent IKEA catalogue suggests that they may have an unusual superpower—the ability to become invisible. The IKEA catalogue is sent all over the world with minor changes in the images, typically made to suit local market fashion-related tastes. But in one issue of the catalogue the photos in the Saudi version were virtually identical to the standard version except that in several of the images, the photos of the women had completely disappeared—which was odd (and completely unnecessary), given that women are not prohibited from appearing in marketing materials. Saudi Arabia has been criticized for its treatment of women. Swedish trade Minister Ewa Bjorling, for example, commented, "You cannot remove or retouch women out of reality." IKEA was dismayed, especially since the company has a long history of avoiding the political spotlight whenever possible. An IKEA spokesperson commented: "We regret the current situation...and we should have reacted and realized that excluding women from the Saudi Arabian version of the catalogue is in conflict with the IKEA Group values."[21]

---

perhaps surprising elements that impact business include nonverbal communication, forms of address, attitudes towards punctuality, religious celebrations and customs, business practices, and expectations regarding meals and gifts. For firms that operate in multiple countries, it is vital to understand and respond to sociocultural factors. But because the differences often operate at a subtle level, they can undermine relationships before anyone is aware that this is happening. The best way to jump over sociocultural barriers is to conduct thorough consumer research, cultivate first-hand knowledge, and practise extreme sensitivity. The payoff can be a sharp competitive edge. Hyundai, for instance, enjoys a whopping 18 percent share of the passenger car market in India. It beat the competition with custom features that reflect Indian culture, such as elevated rooflines to provide more headroom for turban-wearing motorists.[22]

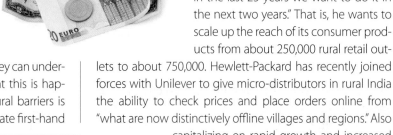

4-5b Economic Differences

Before entering a foreign market, it's vital to understand and evaluate the local economic conditions. Key factors to consider include population, per capita income, economic growth rate, currency exchange rate, and stage of economic development. But keep in mind that low scores for any of these measures doesn't necessarily equal a lack of opportunity. In fact, some of today's biggest opportunities are in countries with low per capita income. For example, the Indian division of global giant Unilever gets 50 percent of its sales from rural India by selling products to individual consumers in tiny quantities, such as two-cent sachets of shampoo. The rural Indian market has been growing so dramatically that the chairman of Hindustan Unilever declared: "What we have done in the last 25 years we want to do it in the next two years." That is, he wants to scale up the reach of its consumer products from about 250,000 rural retail outlets to about 750,000. Hewlett-Packard has recently joined forces with Unilever to give micro-distributors in rural India the ability to check prices and place orders online from "what are now distinctively offline villages and regions." Also capitalizing on rapid growth and increased demand, Samsung has introduced Guru, a mobile phone that can be charged with solar power, to rural India.[23]

Serving less developed markets effectively requires innovation and efficiency. Consumers in emerging markets often need different product features, and they almost always need lower costs. C.K. Prahalad, an influential business scholar, believes that forward-thinking companies can make a profit in developing countries if they make advanced technology affordable. Many markets are so large that high-volume sales can make up for low profit margins.

Overall, the profit potential is clear and growing. As consumers in developing countries continue to gain income, companies that establish their brands early will have a critical edge over firms that enter the market after them.

Infrastructure should be another key economic consideration when entering a foreign

> In 2014, Canada exported $526.5 billion worth of merchandise to the world.
>
> Statistics Canada

infrastructure A country's physical facilities that support economic activity.

market. Infrastructure refers to a country's physical facilities that support economic activity. It includes basic systems in each of the following areas:

- Transportation (e.g., roads, airports, railways, and ports)
- Communication (e.g., TV, radio, Internet, and cellphone coverage)
- Energy (e.g., utilities and power plants)
- Finance (e.g., banking and credit)

The level of infrastructure can vary dramatically among countries. For example, only 26 percent of Africans are Internet users, compared to the 87 percent in North America. In Vietnam and Thailand, many consumers buy products directly from vendors in small boats, rather than from "land" stores, as in Europe. Although credit card purchases are still relatively low in much of the world, especially in Asia, recent growth has been explosive and will probably continue for the next few years.[24]

4-5c Political and Legal Differences

Political regimes obviously differ around the world, and their policies have a dramatic impact on business. The laws and regulations that governments create around business are often less than clear, yet they can still represent a significant barrier to international trade. To compete effectively—and to reduce risk—managers must carefully evaluate these factors and make plans to respond to them both now and as they change.

Laws and Regulations International businesses must comply with international legal standards, the laws of their own countries, and the laws of their host countries. This can be a challenge, because many developing countries change business regulations with little notice and less publicity. The justice system can pose another key challenge, especially with regard to legal enforcement of ownership and contract rights. Since 2003, the World Bank has published a "Doing Business" report that ranks the ease of doing business for small and medium-sized companies in 189 different countries. The 2015 "Doing Business" report showed that Singapore leads in ease of doing business, followed by New Zealand, Hong Kong, and Denmark. Canada was 16th on the list, and the United States was 7th. Overall, Eastern Europe and Sub-Saharan Africa had improved the most. The "Doing Business" project examines the ease of doing business from ten different angles, including contract enforcement, the tax regime, and construction permits. An effective legal system reduces risk for both domestic and foreign businesses.[25]

Bribery (i.e., the payment of money for favourable treatment) and corruption (i.e., the solicitation of money for favourable treatment) are also major issues around the

Troubled Waters

Planet Earth does not produce more fresh water—it simply recycles what it has—which isn't nearly enough in light of the planet's exploding human population. In fact, according to the World Health Organization, more than 2.4 million people die every year from lack of access to clean water—the overwhelming majority in the developing world—and the problem will only worsen. By 2050, one in five developing countries will face water shortages, many of them severe. By 2030, China, the world's most populous country, may no longer be self-sufficient in terms of wheat and corn production. Clearly, the growing water shortage is a human crisis, but it also will be a business crisis. Obviously, food and beverage companies depend on water. But when it comes right down to it, every industry from pharmaceuticals to semiconductors, to mining, to clothing manufacturing, depends on water at some point in its supply or usage chain. *Fortune* magazine suggests that agricultural firms can begin preparing now by investing in the development of GMO crops, precision agriculture, and high-tech irrigation. According to brand consultancy *Interbrand*, other businesses would also be wise to prepare by designing and executing an enterprise-wide strategy for water stewardship—not just for their own operations, but for their entire value chains.[26]

world. While both are technically illegal in almost every major country, they are often accepted as a standard way of doing business. Regardless, Canadian corporations and Canadian citizens are subject to prosecution by Canadian authorities if they offer bribes in any nation. See Chapter 2 for more details.

Political Climate The political climate deeply influences whether a country is attractive to foreign business. Stability is crucial. When a country faces strife from civil war, riots, or other violence, this creates huge additional risk for foreign business. Yet figuring out how to operate in an unstable environment such as Russia, Bolivia, or the Middle East can give early movers a real advantage. Coca-Cola's regional manager for Russia commented: "The politics do concern us." But having snagged 50 percent of the $1.9 billion carbonated soft drink market, he concluded that "the opportunity far outweighs the risk." Poor enforcement of intellectual property rights across international borders is another tough issue for business. The Business Software Alliance piracy tracking study found that worldwide piracy rates are remaining level at 42 percent, with piracy in emerging markets towering over what is found in mature markets—68 percent versus 24 percent. The countries with the highest piracy rates are Georgia, Zimbabwe, Bangladesh, Moldova, and Libya, all over 90 percent.[27]

Exhibit 4.4 Arguments For and Against Trade Restrictions

REASONS TO *CREATE* TRADE RESTRICTIONS	REASONS TO *ELIMINATE* TRADE RESTRICTIONS
Protect domestic industry (e.g., the steel industry)	Reduce prices and increase choices for consumers by encouraging competition from around the world
Protect domestic jobs in key industries (but perhaps at the cost of domestic jobs in other industries)	Increase domestic jobs in industries with a comparative advantage versus other countries
Protect national security interests	Increase jobs—both at home and abroad—from foreign companies
Retaliate against countries that have engaged in unfair trade practices	Build exporting opportunities through better relationships with other countries
Pressure other countries to change their policies and practices	Use resources more efficiently on a worldwide basis

International Trade Restrictions National governments have the power to erect barriers to international business through a variety of trade restrictions. The arguments for and against trade restrictions—also called **protectionism**—are summarized in Exhibit 4.4. As you read, note that most economists find the reasons for eliminating trade restrictions are much more compelling than the reasons for creating them.

Trade restrictions have a range of motivations. They also take a variety of forms. The most common trade restrictions are tariffs, quotas, voluntary export restraints, and embargoes.

- **Tariffs** are taxes levied against imports. Governments tend to use protective tariffs either to shelter fledgling industries that couldn't compete without help or to shelter industries that are crucial to the domestic economy. In Canada, tariffs are administered by the Foreign Affairs, Trade and Development Canada through the Export and Import Controls Bureau. An Import Control List identifies those products subject to import restrictions.

- **Quotas** are limitations on the amount of specific products that may be imported from certain countries during a given time period. Russia, for example, has specific quotas for meat imports from the United States.

- **Voluntary export restraints (VERs)** are limitations on the amounts of specific products that one nation will export to another nation. Although the government of the exporting country typically imposes VERs, they usually do so out of fear that the importing country would impose even more onerous restrictions. As a result, VERs often aren't as "voluntary" as the name suggests. The United States, for instance, insisted on VERs with Japanese auto exports in the early 1980s (which many economists believe ultimately precipitated the decline of the US auto industry).

- An **embargo** is a total ban on international trade in a certain item or a total halt in trade with a particular nation. The intention of most embargoes is to pressure the targeted country to change political policies or to protect national security. The US embargo on trade with Cuba offers a high-profile example. Recently the United States has taken steps to open up trade with Cuba.

Embargoes, VERs, and quotas are relatively rare compared to tariffs, and tariffs are falling to new lows. But as tariffs decrease, some nations are seeking to control imports through nontariff barriers such as the following:

- Requiring red tape–intensive import licences for certain categories.

- Establishing nonstandard packaging requirements for certain products.

- Offering less favourable exchange rates to certain importers.

- Establishing standards regarding how certain products are produced or grown.

- Promoting a "buy national" consumer attitude among local people.

Nontariff barriers tend to be fairly effective because complaints about them can be hard to prove and easy to counter.[28]

protectionism National policies designed to restrict international trade, usually with the goal of protecting domestic businesses.

tariffs Taxes levied against imports.

quotas Limitations on the amount of specific products that may be imported from certain countries during a given time period.

voluntary export restraints (VERs) Limitations on the amount of specific products that one nation will export to another nation.

embargo A complete ban on international trade of a certain item or a total halt in trade with a particular nation.

4-6 Free Trade: The Movement Gains Momentum

Perhaps the most dramatic change in the world economy has been the global move towards **free trade**—the unrestricted movement of goods and services across international borders. Even though *complete* free trade is not a reality, the emergence of regional trading blocs, common markets, and international trade agreements has moved the world economy much closer to that goal.

4-6a GATT and the World Trade Organization (WTO)

The **General Agreement on Tariffs and Trade (GATT)**, is an international trade accord designed to encourage worldwide trade among its members. Established in 1948 by 23 nations, GATT has undergone a number of revisions. The most significant changes stemmed from the 1986–94 Uruguay Round of negotiations, which took bold steps to slash average tariffs by about 30 percent and to reduce other trade barriers among the 125 nations that signed.

The Uruguay Round also created the **World Trade Organization (WTO)**, a permanent global institution to promote international trade and to settle international trade disputes. The WTO monitors provisions of the GATT agreements, promotes further reduction of trade barriers, and mediates disputes among members. The WTO's decisions are binding, which means that all parties involved in disputes must comply in order to maintain good standing in the organization.

Ministers of the WTO meet every two years to address current world trade issues. As the world economy has shifted towards services rather than goods, the emphasis of WTO meetings has followed suit. Controlling rampant piracy of intellectual property is a key concern for developed countries. For less developed countries, agricultural subsidies (such as those in Europe) are a central issue because these may unfairly distort agricultural prices worldwide.

Both the broader agenda and the individual decisions of the WTO have become increasingly controversial over the past decade. Advocates for less developed nations are deeply concerned that free trade is clearing the path for major multinational corporations to push local businesses into economic failure. A local food stand, for instance, probably won't have the resources to compete with a global giant like McDonald's. If the food stand closes, the community has gained inexpensive hamburgers, but the entrepreneur has lost a livelihood and the community has lost the local flavour that contributes to its unique culture. Other opponents of the WTO worry that the acceleration of global trade is encouraging developing countries to fight laws that protect the environment and workers' rights. They fear that such laws will cost them their low-cost advantage on the world market. These concerns have sparked significant protests during the past few meetings of the WTO ministers, and the outcry may well grow louder as developing nations gain economic clout.

4-6b The World Bank

Established in the aftermath of the Second World War, the **World Bank** is an international cooperative of 188 member countries working together to reduce poverty in the developing world. The World Bank influences the global economy by providing financial and technical advice to the governments of developing countries for projects in a range of areas including infrastructure, communications, health, and education. The financial assistance usually comes in the form of low-interest loans. But to secure a loan, the borrowing nation must often agree to conditions that can involve rather arduous economic reforms.

4-6c The International Monetary Fund (IMF)

Like the World Bank, the **International Monetary Fund (IMF)** is an international organization accountable to the governments of its 188 member nations. The IMF's basic mission is to promote international economic cooperation and stable growth. Funding comes from the member nations. To achieve these goals, the IMF does the following:

free trade The unrestricted movement of goods and services across international borders.

General Agreement on Tariffs and Trade (GATT) An international trade treaty designed to encourage worldwide trade among its members.

World Trade Organization (WTO) A permanent global institution to promote international trade and to settle international trade disputes.

World Bank An international cooperative of 188 member countries working together to reduce poverty in the developing world.

International Monetary Fund (IMF) An international organization of 188 member nations that promotes international economic cooperation and stable growth.

The World Bank and the IMF both require a remarkable degree of international communication.

Stephen Jaffe/Handout/MF/Getty Images

- Supports stable exchange rates.
- Facilitates a smooth system of international payments.
- Encourages member nations to adopt sound economic policies.
- Promotes international trade.
- Lends money to member nations to address economic problems.

Although all of its functions are important, the IMF is best known as a lender of last resort to nations in financial trouble. This policy has come under fire in the past few years. Critics accuse the IMF of encouraging poor countries to borrow more money than they can ever hope to repay, which actually cripples their economies over the long term, creating even deeper poverty.

The IMF has responded to its critics by implementing a historic debt relief program for poor countries. Under this program, which has since been expanded to include other agencies, the IMF and its partners have extended 100 percent debt forgiveness to 36 poor countries, erasing about $75 billion in debt. The managing director of the IMF has pointed out that the cancelled debt will allow these countries to increase spending in priority areas to reduce poverty and promote growth (although some experts worry that debt cancellation has set a troubling precedent for future lending). The result should be a higher standard of living for some of the poorest people in the world.[29]

4-6d Trading Blocs and Common Markets

Another major development over the past decade has been the emergence of regional **trading blocs**, or groups of countries that have reduced or even eliminated all tariffs, allowing for the free flow of goods among the member nations. A **common market** goes even further than a trading bloc by attempting to harmonize all trading rules. Canada, the United States, and Mexico have formed the largest trading bloc in the world, and the 28 countries of the European Union have formed the largest common market. The European Union may be reduced to 27 countries now that the British have voted to leave.

NAFTA The **North American Free Trade Agreement**, or **NAFTA**, is the treaty that created the free trade zone among Canada, the United States, and Mexico. The agreement took effect in 1994, gradually eliminating trade barriers and investment restrictions over a 15-year period. Despite dire predictions of Canadian jobs flowing to Mexico, the Canadian economy has grown significantly since the implementation of NAFTA. The American and Mexican economies have thrived as well.

NAFTA critics point out that the US trade deficit with both Mexico and Canada has skyrocketed. Exports to both nations have increased, but imports from them have grown far more quickly, increasing the US trade deficit and threatening the long-term health of the American economy. Other criticisms of NAFTA include increased pollution and worker abuse. Companies that move their factories to Mexico to benefit from lower costs are also taking advantage of looser environmental and worker protection laws, and this generates serious ethical concerns. The full impact of NAFTA—for better or for worse—is difficult to evaluate as so many other variables affect all three economies.[30]

European Union Composed of 28 nations and over half a billion people, and boasting a combined GDP of more than $15 trillion, the **European Union (EU)** is the world's largest common market. Exhibit 4.5 shows a map of the EU countries as of 2015 plus the six countries that have applied to join.[31]

The EU's overarching goal is to bolster Europe's trade position and to increase its international political and economic power. To help make this happen, the EU has removed all trade restrictions among member nations and unified internal trade rules, allowing goods and people to move freely among EU countries. The EU has also created standardized import and export policies among EU countries and the rest of the world, giving the member nations more clout as a bloc than each would have had on its own. Perhaps the EU's most economically significant move was to introduce a single currency, the euro, in 2002. Of the 15 EU members at the time, 12 adopted the euro (exceptions were the United Kingdom, Sweden, and Denmark). The EU has impacted the global economy with its leading-edge approaches to environmental protection, quality production, and human rights.

The EU has faced some challenges caused by the global recession. In 2011, some EU nations faced debt crises that threatened the stability not only of the EU but of other financial markets as well. Greece, Ireland, Portugal, and Italy all faced financial problems requiring action by other European countries. During this time, some critics predicted the demise of the EU; others suggested that these challenges could result in a stronger union after controls were implemented to correct problems.[32]

trading bloc A group of countries that has reduced or even eliminated tariffs, allowing for the free flow of goods among the member nations.

common market A group of countries that has eliminated tariffs and harmonized trading rules to facilitate the free flow of goods among the member nations.

North American Free Trade Agreement (NAFTA) The treaty among Canada, the United States, and Mexico that eliminated trade barriers and investment restrictions over a 15-year period starting in 1994.

European Union (EU) The world's largest common market, composed of 28 European nations.

CREATIVE COUNTDOWN

viche81/Shutterstock.com

In a world economy that's driven by new ideas, it stands to reason that the most creative countries will have an edge, so it's not surprising that a study by the Martin Prosperity Institute, ranking 82 countries on their creativity, uncovered great correlations between creativity and economic progress, entrepreneurship, human development, and happiness, among other factors. Greater levels of creativity also correspond on balance to greater levels of economic equality, suggesting that "sustained economic progress can no longer tolerate the waste of human talent, but must increasingly turn on the full development of each and every human being." Here are the top ten most creative countries:

10. Netherlands
9. Singapore
8. Norway
7. Canada
6. New Zealand
5. Australia
4. Denmark
3. Finland
2. United States
1. Sweden[33]

Exhibit 4.5 European Union 2015

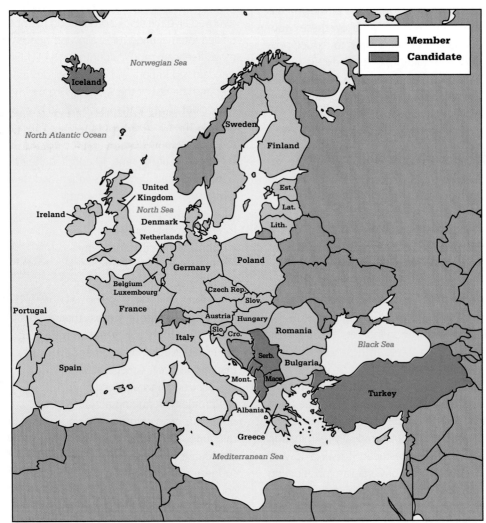

Source: Europa http://europa.eu/about-eu/countries/index_en.htm.

The last decade has been marked by extraordinary changes in the world economy. The boundaries between individual countries have fallen lower than ever before, creating a new level of economic connectedness. The growing integration has created huge opportunities for visionary companies of every size. But integration also means risk. The dangers became clear in 2008, when the economic crisis in the United States rapidly reverberated around the globe, fuelling a deep, worldwide recession.

To succeed abroad—especially in tough economic times—individual firms must make the right choices about how to structure their operations, surmount barriers to trade, meet diverse customer needs, manage a global workforce, and handle complex logistics. Human rights and environmental protection continue to be especially critical for international businesses. Both are vital components of social responsibility and will only gain importance as advocates raise awareness around the world. In the face of economic, political, and social flux, effective global business leaders must master both strategy and implementation at a deeper level than ever before.

THE BIG PICTURE

careers in international business: International Sports Marketing Manager

Implement marketing plans outside of Canada with a focus on the United States, Europe, Australia, and New Zealand. Work with global brand marketing team to develop and execute events that incorporate athletes. Participate in the scouting process to identify and pursue up-and-coming athletes in relevant sports. Provide support for the endorsement contract negotiation process.

STUDY TOOLS 4

IN THE BOOK, YOU CAN:
- ☐ Rip out the Chapter Review card at the back of the book to have a summary of the chapter and key terms handy.

ONLINE AT NELSON.COM/STUDENT YOU CAN:
- ☐ Work through key concepts with a Guided Learning Question.
- ☐ Prepare for tests with quizzes.
- ☐ Review the key terms with Flash Cards (online or printer-ready).
- ☐ Explore practical examples of chapter concepts with Connect a Concept exercises.

5

Business Formation:
Choosing the Form That Fits

LEARNING OBJECTIVES

After studying this chapter, you will be able to...

5-1 Describe the characteristics of the three basic forms of business ownership

5-2 Discuss the advantages and disadvantages of a sole proprietorship

5-3 Evaluate the pros and cons of the partnership as a form of ownership

5-4 Explain why corporations have become the dominant form of business ownership

5-5 Describe three additional corporate forms: cooperatives, not-for-profit corporations, and Crown corporations

5-6 Evaluate the advantages and disadvantages of franchising

After you finish this chapter, go to page 82 for STUDY TOOLS

5-1 Business Ownership Options: The Big Three

One of the most important decisions that entrepreneurs make when they start a new business is which form of ownership they'll use. The form they choose will affect virtually every aspect of establishing and operating the firm, including the initial cost of setting up the business, the way the profits are distributed, the types of taxes (if any) the business must pay, and the types of regulations it must obey. Choice of ownership also determines the degree to which each owner is personally liable for the firm's debts and the sources of funds available to the firm to finance future expansion.

Businesses in Canada are owned and organized under one of three forms:

1. A **sole proprietorship** is a business that is owned,

sole proprietorship A form of business ownership with a single owner who usually actively manages the company.

partnership A voluntary agreement under which two or more people act as co-owners of a business for profit.

general partnership A partnership in which all partners can take an active role in managing the business and have unlimited liability for any claims against the firm.

corporation A form of business ownership in which the business is considered a legal entity that is separate and distinct from its owners.

and usually managed, by a single individual. As far as the law is concerned, a sole proprietorship is simply an extension of the owner. Company earnings are treated as income of the owner; likewise, any debts the company incurs are considered to be the owner's personal debts.

2. A **partnership** is a voluntary agreement under which two or more people act as co-owners of a business for profit. As we'll see later in the chapter, there are several types of partnerships. In its most basic form, known as a **general partnership**, each partner has the right to participate in the company's management and share in profits—but also has unlimited liability for any debts the company incurs.

3. A **corporation** is recognized as a legal entity separate from its owners, either by the *Canada Business Corporations Act* if it has been incorporated federally or by one or more provincial statutes if it has been incorporated provincially. It is a business entity created by filing a form (known as the **articles of incorporation**) in the appropriate jurisdiction where the corporation wishes to do business, paying the appropriate incorporation fees, and meeting certain other requirements (the specifics vary among jurisdictions). Unlike a sole proprietorship or a partnership, a corporation is considered

to be a legal entity that is separate and distinct from its owners. In many ways, a corporation is like an artificial person. It can legally engage in virtually any business activity a natural person can pursue. For example, a corporation can enter into binding contracts, borrow money, own property, pay taxes, and initiate legal actions (such as lawsuits) in its own name. It can even be a partner in a partnership or an owner of another corporation. Because of a corporation's status as a separate legal entity, the owners of a corporation have **limited liability**—meaning that they aren't personally responsible for the debts and obligations of their company.

5-2 Advantages and Disadvantages of Sole Proprietorships

More than 32 percent of all Canadian businesses are sole proprietorships. In fact, there are 1,107,982 of them.[1] They are numerous, but they are small. Why? A look at the advantages and disadvantages of sole proprietorships can help answer why.

5-2a Advantages

Sole proprietorships offer some very attractive advantages to people starting a business:

- **Ease of formation:** Compared to the other forms of ownership we'll discuss, the paperwork and costs involved in forming a sole proprietorship are minimal. No special forms must be filed, and no special fees must be paid. Entrepreneurs who are eager to get a business up and running quickly can find this a compelling advantage.

- **Retention of control:** As the only owner of a sole proprietorship, you're in control. You have the ability to manage your business the way *you* want. If you want to "be your own boss," a sole proprietorship may look very attractive.

- **Pride of ownership:** One of the main reasons many people prefer a sole proprietorship is the feeling of pride and the personal satisfaction they gain from owning and running their own business.

articles of incorporation The document filed with the appropriate government to establish the existence of a new corporation.

limited liability When owners are not personally liable for claims against their firm. Limited liability owners may lose their investment in the company, but their personal assets are protected.

- **Retention of profits:** If your business is successful, *all* the profits go to you—minus your personal taxes, of course.

- **Possible tax advantage:** No taxes are levied directly on the earnings of sole proprietorships as a business. Instead, the earnings are taxed only as income of the proprietor. As we'll see when we discuss corporations, this avoids the undesirable possibility of double-taxation of earnings.

5-2b Disadvantages

Entrepreneurs thinking about forming a sole proprietorship should also be aware of some serious drawbacks:

- **Limited financial resources:** Raising money to finance growth can be tough for sole proprietors. Because only one owner is responsible for a sole proprietor's debts, banks and other financial institutions are often reluctant to lend them money. Likewise, suppliers may be unwilling to provide supplies on credit. This leaves sole proprietors dependent on their own wealth plus the money their firms generate.

- **Unlimited liability:** Because the law views a sole proprietorship as an extension of its owner, the firm's debts become the personal debts of the owner. If someone sues your business and wins, the court could seize your personal possessions—even those that have nothing to do with your business—and sell them to pay the damages. This unlimited personal liability means that operating as a sole proprietorship is a risky endeavour.

- **Limited ability to attract and maintain talented employees:** Most sole proprietors are unable to pay the high salaries and offer the perks that highly qualified, experienced employees get when they work for big, well-established companies.

- **Heavy workload and responsibilities:** Being your own boss can be very rewarding, but it can also mean very long hours and a lot of stress. Sole proprietors—as the ultimate authority in their business—often must perform tasks or make decisions in areas where they lack expertise.

- **Lack of permanence:** Because a sole proprietorship is just an extension of the owner, it lacks permanence. If the owner dies, retires, or must withdraw from the business for some other reason, the company legally ceases to exist. Even when the company continues to operate under new ownership, in the eyes of the law it is a different firm.

Partnerships: Two Heads (and Bankrolls) Can Be Better Than One

Partnerships are much less common in Canada than sole proprietorships. Partnerships tend to be both larger and more profitable than sole proprietorships. There are 209,748 partnerships in Canada—one-fifth as many as sole proprietorships—but they generate, on average, considerably more total revenue.[2] There are several types of partnerships, each with its own specific characteristics. We'll focus our discussion mainly on the most basic type, known as a general partnership, but we'll also take a quick look at limited partnerships and limited liability partnerships.

5-3a Formation of General Partnerships

There is no limit on the number of partners that can participate in a general partnership, but most partnerships consist of only a few partners—often just two. The partnership is formed when the partners enter into a voluntary partnership agreement. It is legally possible to start a partnership on the basis of a verbal agreement, but doing so is often a recipe for disaster. It's much safer to get everything in writing and to seek expert legal assistance when drawing up the agreement. A typical partnership agreement spells out such details as the initial financial contributions each partner will make, the specific duties and responsibilities each will assume, how they will share profits (and losses), how they will settle disagreements, and how they will deal with the death or withdrawal of one of the partners. A well-written agreement can prevent a lot of misunderstandings.

Herb MacKenzie

5-3b Advantages of General Partnerships

Partnerships offer some key advantages relative to both sole proprietorships and corporations:

- **Ability to pool financial resources:** With more people investing in the company, a partnership is likely to have a stronger financial base than a sole proprietorship.

- **Ability to share responsibilities and capitalize on complementary skills:** Partners can share the burden of running the business, which can ease the workload. They can also benefit from complementary skills and interests; the partners can split up the tasks so that they use their skills to best advantage.

- **Ease of formation:** In theory, forming a partnership is easy. As we've already noted, it's possible (but not advisable) to establish a partnership based on a simple verbal agreement. But we shouldn't overemphasize this advantage. Working out all of the details of a partnership agreement can be a complex and time-consuming process.

- **Possible tax advantages:** Much as with a sole proprietorship, the earnings of a partnership "pass through" the business—untouched by the Canada Revenue Agency—and are taxed only as the partners' personal income. Again, this avoids the potential for double-taxation faced by corporations.

> Forty for you, sixty for me. And equal partners we will be.
>
> Joan Rivers, comedian

5-3c Disadvantages of General Partnerships

General partnerships also have some serious disadvantages. As you read about them, keep in mind that a well-written partnership agreement can mitigate some of the drawbacks:

- **Unlimited liability:** As a general partner you're liable not only for your own mistakes but also for those of your partners. In fact, all general partners have unlimited liability for the debts and obligations of their business. So if the assets they've invested in the business aren't sufficient to meet these claims, the personal assets of the partners are at risk. When someone sues a partnership, the lawsuit can target *any* individual partner or group of partners. In fact, lawsuits often go after the partners with the deepest pockets, even if they did not personally participate in the act that caused the legal action. In other words, if you have more personal wealth than the other partners, you could lose more than they do, even if they were at fault!

- **Potential for disagreements:** If general partners can't agree on how to run the business, the conflict can complicate and delay decision making. A well-drafted partnership agreement usually specifies how disputes will be resolved, but disagreements among partners can create friction and hard feelings that harm morale and undermine the cooperation needed to keep the business on track.

- **Difficulty in withdrawing from a partnership:** A partner who withdraws from a partnership remains personally liable for any debts or obligations the firm had *at the time of withdrawal*—even if those obligations were created by the actions of other partners.

- **Lack of continuity:** If a current partner withdraws from the partnership, the relations among the participants will clearly change, potentially ending the partnership. This creates uncertainty about how long a partnership will remain in business.

5-3d Limited Partnerships

The risks associated with unlimited liability make general partnerships unattractive to many individuals who would otherwise be interested in joining a business partnership. Fortunately, two other types of partnerships allow some partners to limit their personal liability to some extent, although each comes with particular requirements.

The first of these, known as a limited partnership, is a partnership arrangement that includes at least one general partner *and* at least one limited partner. Both types of partners contribute financially to the company and share in its profits. But in other respects they play different roles:

- General partners have the right to participate fully in managing the partnership, but they also assume unlimited personal liability for any of its debts—just like the partners in a general partnership.

- Limited partners *cannot* actively participate in management, but they have the protection of limited liability. This means that, as long as they do not actively participate in managing the company, their personal wealth is not at risk.

5-3e Limited Liability Partnerships

The **limited liability partnership (LLP)** is another form of partnership. It is similar to a limited partnership in some ways, but it has the advantage of allowing *all* partners to take an active role in management while also offering *all* partners some

limited partnership A partnership that includes at least one general partner who actively manages the company and accepts unlimited liability and one limited partner who gives up the right to actively manage the company in exchange for limited liability.

limited liability partnership (LLP) A form of partnership in which all partners have the right to participate in management and have limited liability for company debts.

DIVORCING YOUR BUSINESS PARTNER

Herb MacKenzie

Business partnerships end, just like marriages, sometimes with bitterness that hurts not only the partners but also their children (in this case, the business they started). So, what can be done to make the dissolution less acrimonious for the partners and less disruptive to the business?

First, plan for a separation from the start with a shareholder agreement. Michael Tolkin, of the Merchant Exchange, says: "Though nobody likes to think about, much less plan for, a dissolution, agreeing on an exit plan should be part of the earliest partnership discussions. That way, no matter how heated things get, both you and your partner are protected and forced to abide by terms upon which you agreed when cooler heads prevailed." Shareholder agreements, which are similar to prenuptial agreements, often include items such as non-compete restrictions.

Use a neutral third-party arbitrator, such as a lawyer or accountant. Business owner Derek Johnson says: "If you have the resources, both parties should hire an attorney the minute it's decided that it's needed to dissolve a partnership. This allows both parties to negotiate at arm's length, without being slowed down by partner emotions."

Resentment sometimes motivates spurned business partners to be uncooperative or, worse, to seek revenge by running up debts, locking up financial resources, or restricting access to assets that provide competitive advantage. So, get access to key financial accounts, passwords, and intellectual property before discussing the breakup with your business partner.

Debie Rothenburger found out the hard way. She asked a long-time friend to form a partnership in a picture framing business in Winnipeg, Manitoba. When her partner wanted out, the two couldn't agree on a fair price for the partner's share of the business. Ultimately, Rothenburger had to start all over with a new business, under a new company name, and with a new phone number. She said: "The last week of our partnership was like a divorce. It does get personal."[3]

---

form of limited liability. In other words, there's no need to distinguish between limited and general partners in an LLP.

Limited liability partnerships are generally available only to professional groups, such as accountants, architects, doctors, and lawyers. The degree of liability protection and who can form a limited liability partnership vary across Canada as these partnerships are covered by provincial and territorial legislation. In Ontario, for example, only lawyers and certified professional accountants may form limited liability partnerships.

5-4 Corporations: The Advantages and Disadvantages of Being an Artificial Person

Canada has 2,113,183 corporations.[4] They account for nearly 62 percent of all Canadian businesses, and they generate more revenue than all other business forms combined. The fact that corporations are the dominant form of ownership when it comes to income and employment should not be surprising when you consider the size of Canada's largest corporations. By 2016, Loblaw Companies Limited, for example, employed more than 192,000 full- and part-time employees across more than 2,300 corporate, franchised, and associate-owned locations. Sales revenue in 2014 was $42.6 billion.[5] It would take many sole proprietorships or partnerships to achieve comparable revenues or employment. But don't assume that all corporations are large. A corporation can be formed by an individual, who may operate the firm with or without any paid employees.

There are two types of corporations in Canada. **Public corporations** are firms whose shares of stock, or stocks, are widely held by the public. **Private corporations** are owned by only a few shareholders, and their shares of stock are not publicly traded. Corporate ownership will be discussed in greater depth shortly.

5-4a Forming a Corporation

As we mentioned earlier, the formation of a corporation requires filing articles of incorporation and paying filing fees. It also requires the adoption of **corporate bylaws**, which are detailed rules that govern the way the corporation is managed and operates. Because of these requirements, forming a corporation is more complex than forming a sole proprietorship or partnership. The exact requirements for incorporating a company vary from province to province. Some provinces have simple forms, inexpensive fees, low corporate tax rates, and "corporation-friendly" laws and court systems. In these provinces, forming a corporation is not much harder or more expensive than setting up a sole proprietorship. Some provinces have special reporting requirements and make operating a corporation considerably more demanding.

Corporations that operate only in one or two provinces may decide to incorporate only in those provinces where they intend to do business. Those that choose to operate in multiple jurisdictions will benefit from federal incorporation, which then gives them the right to conduct business across Canada. However, there are advantages to federal incorporation even for small corporations, as Mark Blumes discovered. He opened his first Work Wearhouse store in Calgary, Alberta. However, when his company expanded to Ontario, another company was operating there under a similar name, so he was forced to change his company name—something he did not want to do—and the company became Mark's Work Wearhouse.[6] The company was later purchased by Canadian Tire and is now simply called Mark's. When companies become incorporated, they must add "Incorporated" (Inc.), "Limited" (Ltd.), or "Corporation" (Corp.) after their name to indicate clearly to suppliers and customers that the liability of the owners does not extend beyond the assets of the firm.

5-4b Ownership of a Corporation

Ownership of corporations is represented by shares of stock, so owners are called **shareholders** (or stockholders). Common stock represents the basic ownership interest in a corporation, but some firms also issue preferred stock. One key difference between the two types of stock involves voting rights: common shareholders normally have the right to vote in shareholders' meetings; preferred shareholders do not.

Some large public corporations issue millions—or even billions—of shares of stock. They may be owned by thousands of people, who may buy or sell their shares on the open stock market. Had you bought 1,000 shares of Sherritt International (S.TO) on the Toronto Stock Exchange (TSX) at its highest price during the one-year period ending January 18, 2016, you would have paid $3,240. You would also be a part-owner of the company, albeit a very small part. (There are nearly 300 million shares outstanding, and nearly 900,000 shares are traded daily.) Unfortunately for you, had you decided to sell your shares at their lowest price during that same period, you would have received only $530. Of course, once you sold your shares, you would no longer be a part-owner of Sherritt International Corp. And you would have learned an important lesson about trading shares on the stock market: you don't always win.[7] Shares of many Canadian public corporations are traded daily on securities exchanges such as the TSX. Many smaller corporations are owned by just a handful of shareholders who don't actively trade their stock. It's even possible for individuals to incorporate their business and be the sole shareholder in their corporation.

Shareholders don't have to be individuals. Organizations such as mutual funds, insurance companies, pension funds, and endowment funds pool money from a large number of individual contributors and use these funds to buy stocks and other securities. These organizations, called **institutional investors**, own the majority of stock in many large corporations.

Ownership of private corporations is different. Restrictions are often placed on who may own shares of stock and how those shares may be bought or sold. Often, ownership is restricted to the founders of the business, their families, or close friends and associates. Kroeker Farms employs between 60 and 160 people depending on the time of year and has been operating for more than 60 years in Winkler, Manitoba. Shares of stock are held entirely by senior employees or by the children, grandchildren, and great-grandchildren of the founder and their spouses.[8]

> "Corporation: an ingenious device for obtaining profit without individual responsibility."
>
> Ambrose Bierce, 19th-century compiler of *The Devil's Dictionary*

> A corporation's primary goal is to make money. Government's primary role is to take a big chunk of that money and give it to others.
>
> Larry Ellison, CEO, Oracle Corporation

public corporation A corporation whose shares of stock are widely held by the public.

private corporation A corporation owned by only a few shareholders and whose shares of stock are not publicly traded.

corporate bylaws The basic rules governing how a corporation is organized and how it conducts its business.

shareholder An owner of a corporation.

institutional investor An organization that pools contributions from investors, clients, or depositors and uses these funds to buy stocks and other securities.

CHAIR OF THE BOARD: EVEN THE CEO NEEDS A BOSS

Herb MacKenzie

n most companies, the CEO is hired and fired by the board of directors, a group of independent advisers elected or appointed to oversee company performance. The board is led by its chair, who is typically elected by the board. But what if, as in nearly 80 percent of large companies, the CEO is also the chair of the board?

Gary Wilson, who has served on the Disney and Yahoo! boards and has also chaired the board of Northwest Airlines (now merged with Delta), argues that "America's most serious corporate governance problem is the Imperial CEO—a leader who is both chairman of the company's board of directors as well as its chief executive officer. Such a CEO can dominate his board and is accountable to no one." Wilson explains that "this arrangement creates a conflict of interest, because the chairman is responsible for leading an independent board of directors. The board's primary responsibility,

on behalf of the owners, is to hire, oversee and, if necessary, fire the CEO. If the CEO is also the chairman, then he leads a board that is responsible for evaluating, compensating, and potentially firing himself."

In short, a CEO also serving as board chair doesn't have a boss.

The solution? Simple: keep the board independent and the CEO accountable by appointing a separate, outside board chair. General Motors has waffled frequently on this issue. When it split the roles in the 1990s, while the company was close to financial collapse, the move was hailed by corporate governance experts. However, since Mary Barra became the company CEO in 2013, she has been hailed for producing strong financial results, for quelling a shareholder revolt, and for deftly managing a product recall scandal. In 2016, she was named CEO and board chair. As long as things are rosy, she won't have to consider firing herself.[9]

5-4c The Role of the Board of Directors

It's not practical for all of the shareholders of a large corporation to participate actively in the management of their company. Besides, most shareholders don't have the time, management skills, or desire to effectively manage such a complex business enterprise. Thus, in accordance with corporate bylaws, the shareholders elect a **board of directors** and rely on this board to oversee the operations of their company and protect their interests.

The board of directors establishes the corporation's mission and sets its broad objectives but seldom takes an active role in the day-to-day management of the company. Instead, in accordance with corporate bylaws, the board appoints a chief executive officer (CEO) and other corporate officers and delegates the responsibility for detailed management of the corporation to them. The board also sets the level of compensation for these officers and monitors their performance to ensure that they act in a manner consistent with shareholder interests. It also provides advice to these officers on broad policy issues, approves their major proposals, and ensures that the company adheres to major regulatory requirements.

board of directors The individuals who are elected by shareholders of a corporation to represent their interests.

5-4d Advantages of Corporations

There are several reasons why corporations have become the dominant form of business ownership:

- **Limited liability:** Because a corporation is legally separate from its owners, shareholders are not personally liable for the debts of their company. If a corporation goes bankrupt, the shareholders may find that their stock is worthless, but their other personal assets are protected.

- **Permanence:** Unless the articles of incorporation specify a limited duration, corporations can continue operating as long as they remain financially viable and the majority of shareholders want the business to continue. Unlike a sole proprietorship or a partnership, a general corporation is unaffected by the death or withdrawal of an owner.

- **Ease of transfer of ownership:** It's easy for shareholders of publicly traded general corporations to withdraw from ownership—they simply sell their shares of stock.

- **Ability to raise large amounts of financial capital:** Corporations can raise large amounts of financial capital by issuing shares of stock or by selling long-term IOUs called *corporate bonds*. The ability to raise money by issuing these securities gives corporations a major financial advantage over most other forms of ownership.

- **Ability to make use of specialized management:** Large corporations often find it easier than proprietorships and partnerships to hire highly qualified professional managers. Major corporations can typically offer attractive salaries and benefits, and their permanence and potential for growth offer managers opportunities for career advancement.

> All I mean is that a board of directors is one or two ambitious men—and a lot of ballast.
>
> Ayn Rand, *The Fountainhead*

5-4e Disadvantages of Corporations

In addition to their significant benefits, corporations also have a number of drawbacks:

- **Expense and complexity of formation and operation:** As we've already seen, establishing a corporation is more complex and expensive than forming a sole proprietorship or a partnership. Corporations are also subject to more formal operating requirements. For example, they are required to hold regular board meetings and keep accurate minutes.

- **Complications when operating in more than one province:** When a business that's incorporated in one province does business in other provinces, it's called a "*domestic* corporation" in the province where it's incorporated and a "*foreign* corporation" in the other provinces. A corporation must register or qualify to do business as a foreign corporation in order to operate in any province other than the one in which it incorporated. This typically requires additional paperwork, fees, and taxes. But registration as a foreign corporation is only necessary if the company is involved in substantial business activities within the province. Businesses that only engage in minor business activities typically are exempt from the registration requirement. For example, a firm operating a production facility or maintaining a district office in a province other than its corporate home would need to register as a foreign corporation, but a firm that simply held a bank account or solicited sales to customers in that province through the mail would not be required to do so.

- **Double-taxation of earnings and additional taxes:** The Canada Revenue Agency considers a general corporation to be a separate legal entity and taxes its earnings accordingly. Then, any dividends (earnings the corporation distributes to shareholders) are taxed *again* as the personal income of the shareholders. This double-taxation can take a big bite out of the company's earnings that are distributed to shareholders. (But note that corporations often reinvest some or all of their profits back into the business. Shareholders don't pay income taxes on these retained earnings.)

- **More paperwork and more regulation:** Corporations are more closely regulated than other forms of business. Large, publicly traded corporations are required to submit an **annual report**—a yearly statement of the firm's financial condition and its future expectations—to shareholders and to various government and regulatory agencies. Quarterly reports, submitted at three-month intervals, provide more current information concerning a corporation's financial condition. Anyone can look at these reports, which makes it difficult to keep key information secret from competitors.

- **Possible conflicts of interest:** The corporate officers appointed by the board are supposed to further the interests of shareholders. But some top executives pursue policies that further their *own* interests (such as prestige and power, job security, and attractive financial perks) at the expense of the shareholders. The board of directors has an obligation to protect the interests of shareholders, but in recent years the boards of several major corporations have come under criticism for failure to exercise proper oversight.

5-4f Corporate Restructuring

Large corporations constantly look for ways to grow and achieve competitive advantages. Some corporations work to achieve these goals at least in part through mergers, acquisitions, and divestitures. We'll close our discussion of corporations by taking a quick look at these forms of corporate restructuring.

Mergers and Acquisitions In the news and in casual conversation, the terms *merger* and *acquisition* are often used interchangeably. However, there's a difference. An **acquisition** occurs when one firm buys another firm. The firm making the purchase is called the *acquiring firm*, and the firm being purchased is called the *target firm*. After the acquisition, the target firm ceases to exist while the acquiring firm continues in operation and its stock is still traded. Not all acquisitions

annual report A yearly statement of the firm's financial condition and its future expectations.

acquisition A corporate restructuring in which one firm buys another. After the acquisition, the target firm (the one being purchased) ceases to exist as an independent entity, while the acquiring firm continues to operate.

LOWERING APPLE'S TAX BITE

Herb MacKenzie

Although double-taxation is a major drawback to corporate ownership, tax laws provide corporations with ways to reduce their tax liabilities, such as incorporating or doing business in low-tax locations.

Apple's most creative tax strategy is the "Double Irish with a Dutch Sandwich." No, that's not a double Irish whiskey with an Uitsmitjer, a Dutch sandwich with meat, cheese, and fried eggs. Facebook, Google, and Microsoft also do this, but here's how it works at Apple specifically. Apple Sales International (ASI), located in Ireland, is registered to Baldwin Holdings, an Apple subsidiary in the British Virgin Islands that has no corporate taxes. Apple Sales International owns the rights to the international sale of Apple's technology patents, which are worth billions per year. Yet, rather than selling them, it licenses them to Ireland-based Apple Operations International (AOI), which then sells Apple's technology globally. AOI's profits are then transferred to Apple's Dutch subsidiary (i.e., the Dutch sandwich). This avoids an Irish withholding tax because the European Union views this as an internal company transfer. Finally, the Dutch subsidiary transfers the profits back to Bermuda and Baldwin Holdings.

Confused? Just know that like you, companies go to great lengths to legally reduce their taxes. You do so to increase your tax refund, but companies do so to increase dividends that can be paid to shareholders and to retain earnings that can be reinvested in the company.[10]

---

merger A corporate restructuring that occurs when two formerly independent business entities combine to form a new organization.

are on friendly terms. When the acquiring firm buys the target firm despite the opposition of the target's board and top management, the result is called a *hostile takeover*.

In a **merger**, instead of one firm buying the other, the two companies agree to a combination of equals, joining together to form a new company out of the two previously independent firms. Exhibit 5.1 describes the three most common types of mergers and acquisitions.

Exhibit 5.1 Types of Mergers and Acquisitions

TYPE OF MERGER/ ACQUISITION	DEFINITION	COMMON OBJECTIVE	EXAMPLE
HORIZONTAL MERGER/ ACQUISITION	Combination of firms in the same industry.	Increase size and market power within industry. Improve efficiency by eliminating duplication of facilities and personnel.	$12.4 billion purchase of Shoppers Drug Mart by Loblaw Companies in 2013.
VERTICAL MERGER/ ACQUISITION	Combination of firms at different stages in the production of a given good or service so that the firms have a *buyer–seller* relationship.	Provide tighter integration of production and increased control over supply of crucial inputs.	1996 merger of Time Warner (a major provider of cable television) with Turner Broadcasting (owner of several US-based cable networks such as CNN and TNT).
CONGLOMERATE MERGER/ACQUISITION	Combination of firms in unrelated industries	Reduce risk by making the firm less vulnerable to adverse conditions in any single market.	The 2006 acquisition by Berkshire Hathaway (a highly diversified company that holds stock in many firms) of Iscar, a privately held company that makes cutting tools.

© Cengage Learning

SHAREHOLDER'S "SAY ON PAY"

A corporation's board of directors is ethically bound to put the financial interests of shareholders who own the company above all else. Critics charge, however, that boards have too often increased executive pay regardless of company performance. CEO compensation in Canada has increased 47 percent between 2008 and 2014. But there is a movement towards shareholder input on executive compensation. Say-on-pay votes are required in the United States, Great Britain, and Australia but so far, they are voluntary in Canada. Paul Gryglewicz, senior partner at Global Governance Advisors, expects this will change before 2020.

How well are say-on-pay votes catching on in Canada? In 2011, only 35 of the 100 largest companies on the TSX held a say-on-pay vote. In 2015, 64 did so, and for the first time, three Canadian companies failed to get 50 percent support for their proposed CEO compensation package: Canadian Imperial Bank of Commerce, Barrick Gold, and Yamana Gold. Most companies and outside groups, such as independent advisory firm Institutional Shareholder Services, treat anything less than 70 percent approval as problematic. When only 58 percent of Allstate's shareholders approved executive compensation plans, CEO Tom Wilson communicated with 30 percent of shareholders to

Herb MacKenzie

learn why people were concerned: "My job is to make our shareholders happy."

So, what typically leads to rejection or low levels of approval? In short, paying managers much more than comparable managers at similar companies, not linking executive pay to company performance, excessive severance pay (more than three times annual salary plus bonus), exorbitant benefits, or giving executives additional compensation to pay personal taxes (i.e., tax gross-ups).

Solutions are straightforward. Like Allstate's Wilson, communicating with shareholders is key. Then make sure pay is comparable, transparent, and easily understood by shareholders, and that it increases or decreases along with goals related to long-term company financial performance. And sometimes, it's not just financial performance that's considered. The board of directors at Canadian National Railway Company reduced the annual bonus of CEO Claude Morgeau for 2014 because train derailments were up 73 percent over the previous year, and employee injuries had also risen.

Are say-on-pay votes making a difference? Early results suggest so. A recent survey found that 12 new CEOs of major Canadian companies were paid, on average, 31 percent less than their predecessors.[11]

Divestitures: When Less Is More Sometimes corporations restructure by subtraction rather than by addition. A **divestiture** occurs when a firm transfers total or partial ownership of some of its assets to investors or to another company. Firms often use divestitures to rid themselves of a part of their company that no longer fits well with their strategic plans. This allows them to streamline their operations and focus on their core businesses. In many (but not all) cases, divestitures involve the sale of assets to outsiders; this raises financial capital for the firm.

One common type of divestiture, called a *spin-off*, occurs when a company issues stock in one of its own divisions or operating units and sets it up as a separate company, complete with its own board of directors and corporate officers. It then distributes the stock in the new

company to its existing shareholders. After the spin-off, the shareholders end up owning two separate companies rather than one. They can then buy, sell, or hold either or both stocks as they see fit. While a spin-off allows a corporation to eliminate a division that no longer fits in its plans, it doesn't actually generate any additional funds for the firm.

A *carve-out* is like a spin-off in that the firm converts a particular unit or division into a separate company and issues stock in the newly created corporation. However, instead of distributing the new stock to its current stockholders, it sells the stock to outside investors, thus raising additional financial capital. In many cases, the firm sells only a minority of the total shares so that it maintains majority ownership.

> **divestiture** The transfer of total or partial ownership of some of a firm's assets to investors or to another company.

5-5 Other Types of Corporations: Same but Different

Now that we have described general corporations, let's take a quick look at three other types of corporations that are popular in Canada: cooperatives, not-for-profit (or non-profit) corporations, and Crown corporations.

5-5a Cooperatives[12]

Many Canadians are familiar with the cooperative (or co-op) form of corporation. In fact, there are approximately 9,000 co-ops in Canada. Together, they provide products and services to 18 million members and support more than 600,000 jobs. The UN General Assembly, with the support of the Canadian government, declared 2012 as the UN International Year of Cooperatives, hoping to raise public awareness of the social and economic contributions of the cooperative business model. More than 250 million people worldwide earn their living as employees or members of cooperatives. The top 300 co-ops generate more than US$2.3 billion annually.

What is unique about a co-op? **Cooperatives** are owned by their members and are formed to meet the common needs of those members, who may be producers such as farmers or consumers such as you. Members may also be small businesses that have formed a co-op to increase their purchasing power so that they can compete with larger private corporations. Co-ops have a different control structure from other businesses. Each co-op member has equal ownership of the co-op and has an equal voice in how the co-op is run. Cooperatives can be for-profit or not-for-profit. With for-profit co-ops, profits are distributed to members based on how much they use the co-op, not on how many shares they hold. Furthermore, these profits are provided to members as patronage dividends, which reduces the taxable income for the co-op. Taxes are then paid only by the individual member. Here is a small sample of Canadian co-ops:

cooperative A corporation formed to meet the common needs of its members, where it is owned equally by each of them.

not-for-profit corporation A corporation that does not seek to earn a profit and that differs in several fundamental respects from general corporations.

Crown corporation A government-owned organization that provides services to Canadians where it would not be possible for other firms to do so.

- *Mountain Equipment Co-op* is Canada's largest retail cooperative. In 2014, it had 4.3 million members, making it the fourth largest polity (i.e., entity with voters) in Canada, behind Canada itself, Ontario, and Quebec. Sales were $336 million.

- *Home Hardware* is a wholesale co-op, owned by nearly 1,100 independent hardware store owners, who share in the savings from volume purchases and national advertising, which would not otherwise be available to individual members. Members operate under one of four banners: Home Hardware, Home Hardware Building Centre, Home Building Centre, and Home Furniture.

- *Federated Co-operatives* is a co-op of co-ops. That is, it is owned by 220 retail co-ops that operate in more than 500 communities across western Canada. Sales in 2014 were $10.8 billion, which ranked it 45th among Canada's top 500 corporations. Patronage refunds to members were $451 million.

- *Ocean Spray* is a producer co-op founded more than 80 years ago. It is North America's leading producer of fruit juices and is owned by more than 700 cranberry and 45 grapefruit growers in Canada and the United States. Around 60 percent of all cranberries in Canada are grown for Ocean Spray.

5-5b Not-for-Profit (or Non-profit) Corporations[13]

Not-for-profit corporations do not have profit goals or objectives. This does not mean they do not have a concern with finances; they need money to meet their social goals, which after all are their raison d'être. These organizations operate in the public *and* private sectors. The Canada Border Services Agency, for example, is a public not-for-profit organization that provides border security services and helps facilitate the flow of people and products across the border. The Canadian Cancer Society operates in the private sector. It supports cancer research and provides services for Canadians living with cancer and for their caregivers, family, and friends.

Canada has an estimated 170,000 not-for-profit and charity organizations; they employ 2 million Canadians and benefit from more than 13 million volunteers. They contribute 8.1 percent of total Canadian GDP, which is more than the retail industry. Canada's not-for-profit sector is the second largest in the world, behind that of the Netherlands. The United States ranks fifth. Not-for-profit business is "big" business in Canada, and these organizations must compete not only for the financial resources they need to provide their services but also for skilled business managers and others if they are to succeed.

5-5c Crown Corporations

Crown corporations are government-owned enterprises, although most operate at arm's length from the government. These corporations provide services to Canadians in sectors where private industry cannot, either because the service is unlikely to be profitable or because it is extremely difficult to provide such a service. Examples of federal Crown corporations include Atomic Energy of Canada, the Business Development Bank of Canada, Marine Atlantic, and the Canadian Broadcasting Corporation. Each province also owns Crown corporations. Examples include Tourism British Columbia, Manitoba Hydro, the New Brunswick Liquor Corporation, SaskTel, and Loto-Québec. As noted in Chapter 4, governments have been reducing their role in the economy through privatization. Many former Crown corporations have been sold, including Air Canada, the Canadian National Railway, Canada Post, Nova Scotia Power, and BC Rail.

5-6 Franchising: Proven Methods for a Price

A **franchise** is a licensing arrangement under which one party (the **franchisor**) allows another party (the **franchisee**) to use its name, trademark, patents, copyrights, business methods, and other property in exchange for monetary payments and other considerations. Franchising has become a very popular way to operate a business. Franchising is *not* a form of ownership like the sole proprietorships, partnerships, and corporations we've already described. Instead, it's a very popular way to *operate* a business. Canada has around 1,300 franchise brands that oversee more than 78,000 franchise units. Franchising employs more than one million people—that is, one of every 14 working Canadians. The industry generates about $68 billion annually.[14]

The two most popular types of franchise arrangements are **distributorships** and **business format franchises**. In a distributorship, the franchisor makes a product and grants distributors a licence to sell it. The most common example of this type of franchise is the arrangement between automakers and the dealerships that sell their cars. In a business format franchise, the franchisor grants the franchisee the right to both make *and* sell its good or service. Under this arrangement the franchisor usually provides a wide range of services to the franchisee, such as site selection, training, and help in obtaining financing, but it also requires the franchisee to follow very specific guidelines while operating the business. You're no doubt very familiar with business format franchises; examples include Tim Hortons, Rona, Canadian Tire, M&M Meat Shops, and Molly Maid.

5-6a Franchising in Today's Economy

Franchising is now a well-established method of operating a business, but that doesn't mean it's static. Let's look at some ways the world of franchising is changing.

One of the biggest trends in franchising for the past several years has been an expansion into overseas markets. Franchisors in a variety of industries have found that opportunities for franchise growth are greater overseas because competition is less intense and markets are less saturated. US franchisors, because of their size in their own domestic market, have been especially aggressive—and successful—opening franchise locations outside their home country. Many choose Canada as the country for their first international expansion. McDonald's now has more than 33,000 locations in 119 countries and serves nearly 64 million people each day.[15] Restaurant Brands International—owner of Tim Hortons and Burger King—operates more than 19,000 restaurants and generates more than $23 billion in annual sales across nearly 100 countries. Nearly 2 billion cups of Tim Hortons coffee are sold each year, including 8 out of every 10 cups of out-of-home coffee sold in Canada.[16] Even much smaller Canadian franchisors have been seeking franchising opportunities outside Canada. Wee Piggies & Paws, for example, started as a small, home-based business in St. Catharines, Ontario. Shortly afterwards, owner Debbie Cornelius decided there was an opportunity to franchise her business to other "mom-preneurs." The company now has around 70 franchise locations in Canada and the United States.[17] Of course, operating in foreign countries can pose special challenges. There are often differences in culture, language, laws, demographics, and economic development. As a result, franchisors, like other types of business owners, must adjust their business methods—and the specific products they offer—to meet the needs of foreign consumers.

Another notable trend has been the growth in the number of women franchisees. Hard data are difficult to find, but the International Franchising Association (IFA) estimates that women now own about 30 percent of all franchises, and anecdotal evidence suggests that the trend towards more women-owned franchises is continuing. A number of women, such as JoAnne Shaw (founder of the Coffee Beanery) and Maxine Clark (founder of Build-A-Bear), also have become very successful

franchise A licensing arrangement whereby a franchisor allows franchisees to use its name, trademark, products, business methods, and other property in exchange for monetary payments and other considerations.

franchisor The business entity in a franchise relationship that allows others to operate their business using resources it supplies in exchange for money and other considerations.

franchisee The party in a franchise relationship that pays for the right to use resources supplied by the franchisor.

distributorship A type of franchising arrangement in which the franchisor makes a product and licenses the franchisee to sell it.

business format franchise A broad franchise agreement in which the franchisee pays for the right to use the name, trademark, and business and production methods of the franchisor.

franchisors. But despite these highly visible success stories, the number of women franchisors hasn't grown nearly as quickly as the number of women-owned franchises.[18]

5-6b Advantages of Franchising

Both the franchisee and the franchisor must believe they'll benefit from the franchise arrangement; otherwise, they wouldn't participate. For the franchisor, the advantages of franchising are fairly obvious. It allows the franchisor to expand the business and bring in additional revenue (in the form of franchising fees and royalties) without investing its own capital. Also, franchisees—business owners who are motivated to earn a profit—may be more willing than salaried managers to do whatever it takes to maximize the success of their outlets.

From the franchisee's perspective, franchising offers several advantages:

- **Less risk:** Franchises offer access to a proven business system and product. The systems and methods offered by franchisors have an established track record. People who are interested in buying a franchise can do research to see how stores in the franchise have performed and can talk to existing franchisees before investing.

- **Training and support:** The franchisor normally provides the franchisee with extensive training and support. For example, Subway offers two weeks of training at its headquarters and additional training at meetings. It also sends out newsletters, provides Internet support, maintains a toll-free number for phone support, and provides on-site evaluations.[19]

- **Brand recognition:** Operating a franchise gives the franchisee instant brand name recognition, which can be a big help in attracting customers.

- **Easier access to funding:** Bankers and other lenders may be more willing to loan you money if your business is part of an established franchise than a new, unproven business.

5-6c Disadvantages of Franchising

Franchising also has some drawbacks. From the franchisor's perspective, operating a business with perhaps thousands of semi-independent owner-operators can be complex and challenging. With such a large number of owners it can be difficult to keep all of the franchisees satisfied, and disappointed franchisees sometimes go public with their complaints, damaging the reputation of the franchisor. In fact, it isn't unusual for disgruntled franchisees to sue their franchisors.

Franchisees are also likely to find some disadvantages:

- **Costs:** The typical franchise agreement requires franchisees to pay an initial franchise fee when they enter into the franchise agreement and an ongoing royalty (usually a percentage of monthly sales revenues) to the franchisor. In addition, the franchisor may assess other fees to support national advertising campaigns or for other purposes. These costs vary considerably, but for high-profile franchises they can be substantial. Tim Hortons requires its potential franchisors to have $1.5 million in net worth, including $500,000 in liquid assets. The franchise fee is currently $50,000, and the weekly royalty is 6 percent of gross sales. There is also a 4 percent fee to cover advertising costs.[20] Lower-profile franchise operations are less costly. Molly Maid—started in Canada but now operating in the United States, the United Kingdom, Portugal, and Japan—charges $19,000 to purchase a franchise opportunity in a new territory plus a royalty fee equal to 6 percent of revenue. However, a franchisee who wishes to buy an existing location may pay up to $100,000 plus royalties.[21]

- **Lack of control:** The franchise agreement usually requires the franchisee to follow the franchisor's procedures and methods to the letter. People who want the freedom and flexibility to be their own boss can find these restrictions frustrating.

- **Negative halo effect:** The irresponsible or incompetent behaviour of a few franchisees can create a negative perception that adversely affects not only the franchise as a whole but also the success of other franchisees.

- **Growth challenges:** While growth and expansion are possible in franchising (many franchisees own multiple outlets), strings are attached. Franchise agreements usually limit the franchisee's territory and require franchisor approval before any expansion into other areas.

- **Restrictions on sale:** Franchisees are prohibited from selling their franchises to other investors without prior approval from the franchisor.

Herb MacKenzie

WHAT HAPPENS WHEN FRANCHISEES SUE THEIR FRANCHISORS?

To maintain quality across stores, franchise agreements require franchisees to strictly follow the franchisor's procedures for making or delivering a product or service. That consistency is why McDonald's fries and Subway sandwiches taste the same whether you buy them in Vancouver, British Columbia, or Saint John, New Brunswick. But what happens when franchisees don't want to follow the franchisor's recommendations?

For example, the Burger King (BK) National Franchisee Association sued BK for requiring franchised stores to sell double cheeseburgers for $1 as part of the chain's value menu. BK franchisees argued they lost money on every $1 double cheeseburger, which usually sold for between $1.89 and $2.39, and that the BK franchise agreement didn't give the company the right to determine prices, which, historically, local franchisees controlled. BK countered that franchisees that didn't comply with its pricing "may be declared in default of their franchise agreement."

Twice before, BK had asked BK franchisees to approve a $1 double cheeseburger, and both times the franchisees' answer was "No." But this time, BK didn't ask, and BK franchisees responded with a lawsuit.

BK solved the conflict by following a strategy that McDonald's used to avoid an identical problem with its franchises. BK renamed the double cheeseburger the Dollar Double and reduced franchisee costs by requiring only one rather than two cheese slices. In theory, franchise agreements dictate nearly every way in which franchisors and franchisees work together. But, they can't anticipate everything. When conflicts occur, successful franchisors and franchisees strive for mutually beneficial solutions.[22]

Sources: R. Gibson, "Franchising—Have It Whose Way? At Burger King, Management and Franchisees are Locked in Battle Over the Company's Direction," *The Wall Street Journal*, May 17, 2010; R. Gibson, "Burger King Franchisees Can't Have It Their Way," *The Wall Street Journal*, January 21, 2012; S. Needleman, "Tough Times for Franchising—As Business Disputes Spark Tensions, Some Franchisees Take Franchisers to Court," *The Wall Street Journal*, February 9, 2012; P. Ziobro & K. Benn, "Burger King to Raise Price of Its $1 Double Cheeseburger," *The Wall Street Journal*, February 17, 2010.

Herb MacKenzie

- **Poor execution:** Not all franchisors live up to their promises. Sometimes the training and support are of poor quality, and sometimes the company does a poor job of screening franchisees, leading to the negative halo effect we mentioned earlier.

These considerations suggest that before buying a franchise, potential owners should carefully research the franchise opportunity.

5-6d Entering Into a Franchise Agreement

To obtain a franchise, the franchisee must sign a **franchise agreement**. This agreement is a legally binding contract that specifies the relationship between the franchisor and the franchisee in great detail. There's no standard form for the contract, but it normally covers the following items:

- **Terms and conditions:** The franchisee's rights to use the franchisor's trademarks, patents, and signage and any limitations or restrictions on those rights. It also covers how long the agreement will last and under what terms and conditions it can be renewed.

- **Fees and other payments:** The fees the franchisee must pay for the right to use the franchisor's products and methods and when these payments are due.

- **Training and support:** The types of training and support the franchisor will provide to the franchisee.

- **Specific operational requirements:** The methods and standards established by the franchisor that the franchisee is required to follow.

- **Conflict resolution:** How the franchisor and franchisee will handle disputes.

- **Assigned territory:** The geographic area in which the franchisee will operate and whether the franchisee has exclusive rights in that area.

It's vital that franchisees read through the franchise agreement carefully before signing on the dotted line. In fact, it's a good idea to have a lawyer who is knowledgeable about franchise law review it. You'll have to pay for any legal advice, but entering into a bad franchise agreement can be a lot more expensive (and stressful) than a lawyer's fees.

> It's not hard to meet expenses. They're everywhere.
>
> Anonymous franchisee

> **franchise agreement** The contractual arrangement between a franchisor and franchisee that spells out the duties and responsibilities of both parties in detail.

THE BIG PICTURE

This chapter has discussed the three major forms of business ownership. Each form of ownership has both advantages and limitations, so no single form of ownership is the best in all situations.

Sole proprietorships are appealing to entrepreneurs who want to start a business quickly, with few formalities or fees, and who want to be their own boss. But sole proprietorships aren't well suited for raising financing from external sources, so growth opportunities are limited. And sole proprietors have unlimited liability for their company's debts and obligations.

General partnerships allow two or more owners to pool financial resources and take advantage of complementary skills. But each owner must assume the risk of unlimited liability, and disagreements among partners can complicate and delay important decisions.

Corporations are more complex and expensive to create than other forms of business. Another potentially serious drawback is the double-taxation of earnings. But corporations have the greatest potential for raising financial capital; they also provide owners with the protection of limited liability.

Three additional types of corporations are cooperatives, not-for-profit corporations, and Crown corporations. Finally, franchising is an increasingly popular business format in Canada.

careers in franchising: Franchise Store Manager

Responsible for running day-to-day retail store operations. Required to open and close the store; manage schedules and productivity; provide world-class customer service; monitor cost control, payroll, and expenses; provide weekly and monthly reports to the franchise owner; recruit, train, and coach employees; and develop and implement the store marketing program.

Ultimately accountable for profit/loss, continuous improvement, service delivery levels, personnel management, and business development. The ideal candidate has a college degree, a dynamic personality, two years' retail store operations experience, strong management skills, and excellent computer knowledge, and is a good listener who can motivate a team and run good meetings.

STUDY TOOLS 5

IN THE BOOK, YOU CAN:

☐ Rip out the Chapter Review card at the back of the book to have a summary of the chapter and key terms handy.

ONLINE AT NELSON.COM/STUDENT YOU CAN:

☐ Work through key concepts with a Guided Learning Question.

☐ Prepare for tests with quizzes.

☐ Review the key terms with Flash Cards (online or printer-ready).

☐ Explore practical examples of chapter concepts with Connect a Concept exercises.

Learning like never before.

nelson.com/student

6

Small Business and Entrepreneurship:
Economic Rocket Fuel

LEARNING OBJECTIVES
After studying this chapter, you will be able to...

6-1 Explain the key reasons to launch a small business

6-2 Describe the typical entrepreneur's mindset and characteristics

6-3 Discuss funding options for small businesses

6-4 Analyze the opportunities and threats that small businesses face

6-5 Discuss ways to become a new business owner and tools to facilitate success

6-6 Explain the size, scope, and economic contributions of small business

After you finish this chapter, go to page 97 for STUDY TOOLS

6-1 Launching a New Venture: What's in It for Me?

Entrepreneurial activity has played a powerful, positive role in the Canadian economy. Despite the past recession, new business creation has been increasing steadily. Who's responsible for the increased entrepreneurial activity in Canada? You might be surprised. Provincially, British Columbia leads the country: 3.7 percent of its workers own a startup business (i.e., one that is less than two years old). Alberta and Saskatchewan are in second and third place, respectively. With respect to age, Canadians over 50 are the fastest growing segment: they own nearly 30 percent of startups. And you can't ignore Generation Y. Over the past five years, they have increased their ownership of startups by 10 percent. Consider here that they watched Mark Zuckerberg, the founder of Facebook, quickly become one of the richest people on the planet. However, most startups begin as small businesses, and many remain so throughout their existence. There are 1.1 million small businesses across Canada: 36.3 percent in the four western provinces, 35.0 percent in Ontario, 21.4 percent in

entrepreneurs People who risk their time, money, and other resources to start and manage a business.

Quebec, 7.0 percent in the four Atlantic Provinces, and 0.3 percent in Yukon, the Northwest Territories, and Nunavut combined.

Self-employment is also growing in Canada: 2.7 million Canadians are self-employed, and a million more work for one of the 610,000 businesses that employ four or fewer people. Make no mistake: starting a new business is tough—very tough. Yet for the right person, the advantages of business ownership far outweigh the risks and the hard work that is involved. People start their own ventures for a variety of reasons, but most are seeking some combination of independence and freedom (57.3 percent), or greater financial success (45.3 percent), or they want to exploit a business opportunity (44.4 percent). Others are simply seeking survival (7.7 percent).[1]

6-1a Greater Financial Success

Although you can make a pretty good living working for someone else, your chances of getting really rich may be higher if you start your own business. The *Forbes* annual list of the 400 richest businesspeople is dominated by **entrepreneurs** such as Bill Gates and Paul Allen (founders of Microsoft), Phil Knight (founder of Nike), Michael Dell (founder of Dell Inc.), and Sergey Brin and

Larry Page (founders of Google). Many people feel that their chances of even moderate financial success are higher if they're working for themselves rather than for someone else. The opportunity to make more money is a primary motivator for many entrepreneurs, although other factors clearly play a role as well.[2]

6-1b Independence

Being your own boss is a huge benefit of starting your own business. You answer to no one except yourself and any investors you have invited to participate in your business. Bottom line: you are the only one who is ultimately responsible for your success or failure. This setup will be especially compelling if you, because of your personality, have trouble being a subordinate (and we all know people who fit that description!). But while independence is nice, it's important to keep in mind that every business succeeds by meeting the needs of its customers, who can be even more demanding than the toughest boss.

> Obviously everyone wants to be successful, but I want to be looked back on as being very innovative, very trusted and ethical and ultimately making a big difference in the world.
>
> Sergey Brin, co-founder, Google

6-1c Flexibility

The ability to set your own hours and control your own schedule is hugely appealing for many business owners, especially parents who are seeking more time with their kids, or retirees looking for extra income. Given current technological tools—from e-mail to eBay—it's easy for small business owners to manage their firms on the go or after hours. Of course, there's often a correlation between hours worked and dollars earned. (It's rare to work less and earn more.) But when more money isn't the primary goal, the need for flexibility can be enough to motivate many entrepreneurs to launch their own enterprises.

6-1d Challenge

Running your own business provides a level of challenge unmatched by many other endeavours. Most business owners—especially new business owners—never find themselves bored! Also, starting a business offers endless opportunities for learning that can provide greater satisfaction for many people than grinding out the hours as an employee.

6-1e Survival

Although most entrepreneurs launch their business in response to an opportunity and in hopes of improving their lives, some entrepreneurs launch an enterprise because they believe that starting their own business is their only economic option. This segment of "necessity entrepreneurs" includes a range of people, from middle-aged workers laid off from corporate jobs, to new immigrants with limited English, to those who experience discrimination in the standard workplace. For each of these people, small business ownership can be the right choice in the face of few other alternatives.

> Whatever you're thinking, think bigger.
>
> Tony Hsieh, founder, Zappos.com

6-2 The Entrepreneur: A Distinctive Profile

Successful entrepreneurs tend to stand out from the crowd in terms of both their mindset and their personal characteristics. As you read this section, consider whether you fit the entrepreneurial profile.

6-2a The Entrepreneurial Mindset: A Matter of Attitude

Almost every entrepreneur starts as a small business person—either launching a firm or buying a firm—but not every small business person starts as an entrepreneur. The difference is a matter of attitude. From day one, a true entrepreneur—such as Sam Walton of Walmart, Steve Jobs of Apple, or Jeff Bezos of Amazon—aims to change the world through blockbuster goods or services. That isn't the case for all small business owners. Most people who launch new firms expect to better themselves, but they don't expect huge, transformative growth. In fact, less than 60 percent of Canadian small business owners desire to grow their business.[3]

However, classic entrepreneurs who deliver on the promise of their best ideas can dramatically change the world's economic and social landscape. Examples of business owners who thought and delivered big include Henry Ford, founder of the Ford Motor Company; Bill Gates, founder of Microsoft; Richard Branson, founder of Virgin Enterprises; and Stephenie Meyer, creator of the *Twilight* franchise. Canadian examples include Mike Lazaridis, founder of BlackBerry; James Pattison, founder of the Jim Pattison Group; Frank Stronach, founder of Magna International; and Lise Watier, founder of Lise Watier Cosmétiques Inc.

6-2b Entrepreneurial Characteristics

While experts sometimes disagree about the specific characteristics of successful entrepreneurs, almost all mention vision, self-reliance, energy, confidence, tolerance of uncertainty, and tolerance of failure (see Exhibit 6.1). Most successful entrepreneurs have all of these qualities and more, but they come in a huge variety of combinations that highlight the complexity of personality: there is no single successful entrepreneurial profile.

Vision Most entrepreneurs are wildly excited about their own new ideas, which many seem to draw from a bottomless well. Entrepreneurs find new solutions to old problems, and they develop brand-new products that we didn't even know we needed until we had them. And entrepreneurs stay excited about their ideas, even when friends and relatives think they're crazy. For instance,

Exhibit 6.1 Entrepreneurial Characteristics

Vision · Self-Reliance · Energy · Confidence · Tolerance of Uncertainty · Tolerance of Failure

Herb MacKenzie

APP-SURD? OR NOT SO MUCH?

Herb MacKenzie

Facebook's purchase of Instagram for a cool billion dollars added fuel to the already overheated market for mobile apps. In fact, in the race to create the next killer app, *The Wall Street Journal* reports that "it is getting tough to tell the difference between a joke and the next big thing." For instance, iPoo, a social-networking app that connects people sitting on toilets, sounds like a joke, but it really exists. In the first three years after it was created by Amit Khanna of Markham, Ontario, and two friends, nearly 100,000 people per year have each paid $1 to download iPoo through Apple's iTunes. Apple takes 30 percent of the profits, but, even so, the developers made enough to help put one of them through Harvard Business School. And they claim that tens of thousands actually use it every day. Let's not forget the Passion app, which charges $0.99 and uses the iPhone's microphone and accelerometer to somehow evaluate your sexual performance (no thank you!), which you can then compare against the other people using the app. Another spoof app that made it big is Jotly, a rate-anything app that lets users rate anything they can photograph, from "personal hiding places," to good meals, to whatever … While Jotly started as a digital designer's joke, within a couple of months, it had thousands of users and two legitimate venture-backed competitors. The idea certainly sounds app-surd, but perhaps Instagram didn't sound so great either before it took the iPhone world by storm.[4]

Fred Smith, founder of the FedEx empire, traces the concept for his business to a term paper he wrote at Yale, which supposedly received a C from a skeptical professor. But that didn't stop him from creating a business logistics system that transformed the industry, and along with UPS, enabled e-commerce to flourish.

Self-Reliance As an entrepreneur, the buck stops with you. New business owners typically need to do everything themselves, from getting permits, to motivating employees, to keeping the books—all in addition to producing the product or service that made them start the business in the first place. Self-reliance seems to come with an **internal locus of control**, or a deep-seated sense that the individual is personally responsible for what happens in his or her life. When things go well, people with an internal locus of control feel that their efforts have been validated, and when things go poorly, those same people feel that they need to do better next time. This sense of responsibility encourages positive action. In contrast, people with an **external locus of control** rely less on their own efforts and feel buffeted by forces such as random luck and the actions of others, which they believe will ultimately control their fate.

Energy Entrepreneurs simply can't succeed without an enormous amount of energy. Six or seven 12-hour workdays are not atypical in the startup phase of running a business. In fact, 61 percent of small business owners report working six or more days per week, compared to only 22 percent of workers in the general population. And for small business owners, even a day off isn't *really* off—Discover Financial Services learned that only 27 percent of small business owners describe a day off as not working at all, while 57 percent of small business owners say they always or most of the time work on holidays. But small business owners seem to find it worthwhile: 47 percent said that if they won $10 million in the lottery, they would still work in their current job. Only 9 percent would stop

Herb MacKenzie

> **internal locus of control** A deep-seated sense that the individual is personally responsible for what happens in his or her life.
>
> **external locus of control** A deep-seated sense that forces other than the individual are responsible for what happens in his or her life.

WHAT NOT TO DO

Guy Kawasaki, former Chief Evangelist of Apple, venture capitalist, and bestselling author, recently offered advice to aspiring entrepreneurs by sharing *The Top Ten Mistakes of Entrepreneurs* in a business school presentation. Highlights of the presentation:

- **Scaling too soon:** Don't spend money ramping up the size of the operation until the sales have actually appeared. That could be a shortcut to an early bankruptcy.

- **Pitching instead of prototyping:** In the past, entrepreneurs raised money by developing great pitches, but now funders expect *working* prototypes, especially since, in today's world, many of the other things a new business needs are available for free, thanks to open source software, the Cloud, and a great comfort level with virtual teams/offices. Developing a working prototype of a product reduces the risk that an entrepreneur cannot deliver.

Herb MacKenzie

- **Too many slides and too small a font:** Kawasaki recommends following the 10/20/30 rule when raising money. Never use more than ten slides, never speak for more than 20 minutes, and always use a 30-point font or larger. Another way of looking at font size: use a font size no smaller than half the age of the oldest person in the room. You want to hold the attention of potential funders throughout your presentation.

- **Hiring in your own image:** Many entrepreneurs are tempted to hire people just like themselves, but this can create glaring weaknesses in an organization. Virtually every firm must cover three fundamental functions—making it, selling it, and collecting the money—and these require three different skill sets, and often three personality types.[5]

If you are intrigued by Kawasaki's approach, consider reading one of his books. They are filled with practical advice on how to succeed as an entrepreneur.

---

working, and 8 percent would combine work, volunteering, and other areas of interest.[6]

Confidence Successful entrepreneurs typically have confidence in their own ability to achieve, and their confidence encourages them to act boldly. But too much confidence has a downside. Entrepreneurs must take care not to confuse likelihood with reality. In fact, many could benefit from the old adage "Hope for the best and plan for the worst." A study confirmed that entrepreneurs are typically overconfident regarding their own abilities. As a result, they're willing to plunge into a new business, but they don't always have the skills to succeed.[7]

Tolerance of Uncertainty More often than others, entrepreneurs see the world in shades of grey rather than simply black and white. They tend to embrace uncertainty in the business environment, turning it to their advantage rather than shying away. Uncertainty also relates to risk, and successful entrepreneurs tend to more willingly accept risk—financial risk, for instance, such as mortgaging their home for the business, and professional risk, such as staking their reputation on the success of an unproven product.

Tolerance of Failure Even when they fail, entrepreneurs seldom label themselves losers. They tend to view failure as a chance to learn rather than as a sign that

they just can't do it (whatever "it" may be for them at any given moment). Their resilience allows them to bounce back, using the knowledge gained from their failure to help ensure their future success. For these entrepreneurs, failure can actually be an effective springboard for achievement.[8]

A surprising number of entrepreneurial stars experienced significant failure in their careers yet bounced back to create wildly successful ventures. Early in his career, for instance, Walt Disney was fired from an ad agency (in hindsight, a rather foolish ad agency) for a "singular lack of drawing ability." Ray Kroc, the man who made McDonald's into a fast-food empire, couldn't make a go of real estate, so he sold milkshake machines for much of his life. He was 52 years old, and in failing health, when he discovered the McDonald brothers' hamburger stand and transformed it into a fast-food empire. Steve Jobs, founder of Apple computer, found himself unceremoniously dumped by his board of directors less than 10 years after introducing the world's first personal computer. After another decade, he returned in triumph, restoring Apple's polish with blockbuster new products such as the iPod and the iPhone. And J.K. Rowling, creator of the $15 billion Harry Potter empire, had her initial book rejected by 12 short-sighted publishers. So next time you fail, keep your eyes open for opportunity—your failure may be the first step towards the next big thing.[9]

WHAT TIME OF DAY ARE YOU MOST CREATIVE?

Herb MacKenzie

Probably not when you think you are ... Research suggests that most people are best able to solve insight problems—the kind of problems where the answer comes in a single "aha" moment or flash of insight, or creativity—during the time of day when they are typically least alert. In other words, morning people tend to be most creative in the evening, and vice versa.

Check out these insight problems. If you don't get the answers right away, try again during your least alert time of day, before you look at the answers at the bottom of the box.

Insight problem 1. Water lilies double in this area every 24 hours. At the beginning of summer there is one water lily on the lake. It takes 60 days for the lake to become completely covered with water lilies. On which day is the lake half covered?

Insight problem 2. Three members of MENSA (restricted to people with high IQs) were having breakfast at a 1960s-style diner when one of them noticed that the salt shaker was filled with pepper, and vice versa. They immediately decided they must correct the situation, but that they must do so without contaminating the contents. Eventually they had a solution that involved a cup, a paper napkin, and two plastic straws. Assuming you were one of these three people, how would you solve the problem?

Clearly, entrepreneurship requires creativity. Knowing your most creative time of day may help you buff up your own creative prowess before you take the leap into small business ownership.[10]

Source: "Creativity Happens When You Least Expect It", by Sian Beilock, February 8, 2012, *Psychology Today* website, http://www.psychologytoday.com/ blog/choke/201202/creativity-happens-when-youleast- expect-it, accessed March 30, 2015.

(Answers: Insight problem 1: Day 59. Insight problem 2: Do what the waitress did: reverse the tops of the two shakers.)

6-3 Finding the Money: Funding Options for Small Business

For many entrepreneurs, finding the money to fund their business is the top challenge of their startup year. The vast majority of new firms are funded by the personal resources of their founder. In fact, 95 percent of entrepreneurs raise startup funds from personal accounts, family, and friends. Other key funding sources include bank loans, angel investors, and venture capital firms.[11]

6-3a Personal Resources

While the idea of using just your own money to open a business sounds great, the financial requirements of most new firms typically force entrepreneurs to also tap personal resources such as family, friends, and credit cards. According to *Consumer Reports*, 68 percent of total startup financing comes from personal resources.[12] Almost every small business expert recommends that if you do borrow from family or friends, you keep the relationship as professional as possible. If the business fails, a professional agreement can preserve personal ties. And if the business succeeds, you'll need top-quality documentation of financing from family and friends to get larger-scale backing from outside sources.

Personal credit cards can be an especially handy—although highly risky—financing resource. A recent survey found that nearly half of all startups are funded with plastic. (It's no wonder, given that those solicitations just keep on coming.) Credit cards do provide fast, flexible money, but watch out—if you don't pay back your card company fast, you'll find yourself socked with financing fees that can take years to pay off.[13]

6-3b Loans

Getting commercial loans for a new venture can be tough. Banks and other lenders are understandably hesitant to fund a business that doesn't have a track record. And when they do, they require a lot of paperwork and, often, a fairly long waiting period. Given these hurdles, only 20 percent of new business owners launch with commercial loans. And virtually no conventional lending source—private or government—will lend 100 percent of the startup dollars for a new business. Most require the entrepreneur to provide a minimum of 25–30 percent of total startup costs from personal resources.[14]

Other sources of financing include the Business Development Bank of Canada, Export Development Canada, and the Canada Small Business Financing Program (CSBF), which helps small businesses gain loans they might not otherwise get. Businesses with revenues less than $5 million may apply through the program for loans of up to $500,000, but they must do so through regular financial institutions—banks, credit unions, or *caisses populaires*. Around 10,000 loans are arranged annually through this program, worth more than $1 billion. Various regional sources of funding can also be found on the Canada Business Network website (www.canadabusiness.ca).[15]

Peer-to-peer lending offers yet another potential funding source for new business startups. LendingClub.com is one of several, and by far the largest, US sites that brings together borrowers and investors so that both can benefit financially. Canada's first such marketplace lender is Vancouver-based Grouplend, established in 2014; there, Canadians can borrow as much as $30,000. Many entrepreneurs have found this to be an easier way to get money, at more favourable terms, than through more established sources.[16]

6-3c Angel Investors

Angel investors aren't as saintly—or as flighty—as they sound. Angels are wealthy individuals who invest in promising startup companies for one basic reason: to make money for themselves. Angel investors usually have a short-to-medium time horizon. That is, they wish to recoup their investment and make a profit within two to eight years. On average, angels do quite well, but not without risk. More than half of investments end with a loss of invested principal. In 2014, Michelle Scarborough founded what she believes is Canada's first angel group specifically for women angels. Women are a small part of the angel investor community but are becoming increasingly influential. What does it take to become an angel? Under Canadian securities law, an accredited investor must have access to a minimum of $1 million in investable assets. There are as many as 500,000 accredited investors in Canada, but only a small percentage are angels.

Anecdotal evidence suggests that angel investors who work in groups outperform individuals. Teamwork saves time finding suitable investments; it also reduces risk; furthermore, groups benefit from members' cross-industrial expertise. The number of angel groups has been steadily growing across Canada. There are now more than 30, and most belong to the National Angel Capital Organization (NACO) (www.angelinvestor.ca), which represents more than 2,100 members. NACO reports steady growth in the number and size of investments made by its members: 71 investments totalling $35.7 million in 2011, 139 investments totalling $40.5 million in 2012, and 199 investments totalling $89.0 million in 2013.[17]

6-3d Venture Capital

Venture capital firms fund high-potential new companies in exchange for a share of ownership, which can sometimes be as high as 60 percent. Venture capital firms sometimes become heavily involved in the operations of the business, and when they control majority ownership, this can have a significant impact on the business, as Mark Blumes found out. After starting Mark's Work Wearhouse, he eventually had a significant disagreement with the management put in place as part of the venture capital agreement, and he was ousted. In the end, the company was bought by Canadian Tire and renamed Mark's.

Venture capital investment in Canada in 2014 was $1.9 billion and involved 379 deals, somewhat down from the 452 deals valued at a total of $2 billion in 2013. However, the average size of deals rose to $5 million from $4.4 million. According to the Canadian Venture Capital and Private Equity Association (www.cvca.ca), popular investment targets included virtually all technology sectors: information and communications technology ($1.1 billion), life sciences ($423 million), and clean technology ($133 million).[18]

6-4 Opportunities and Threats for Small Business: A Two-Sided Coin

Most small businesses enjoy a number of advantages as they compete for customers. But they also must defuse a range of threats in order to succeed long term.

6-4a Small Business Opportunities

Small businesses enjoy a real competitive edge across a range of different areas. Because of their size, many small firms can exploit narrow but profitable **market niches**, offer personal customer service, and maintain lower overhead costs. And due to advances in technology, small firms can compete more effectively than ever in both global and domestic markets.

Market Niches Many small firms are uniquely positioned to exploit small but profitable market niches.

angel investors Individuals who invest in start-up companies with high growth potential in exchange for a share of ownership.

venture capital firms Companies that invest in start-up businesses with high growth potential in exchange for a share of ownership.

market niches Small segment of a market with fewer competitors than the market as a whole. Market niches tend to be quite attractive to small firms.

NUTTY MARKET NICHES

Herb MacKenzie

Small businesses can do especially well in market niches, even niches that initially seem somewhat wacky. Here are a handful of wacky businesses that have really worked:

- **Neuticles:** Did you worry about your dog's self-esteem after he got neutered? Entrepreneur Greg Miller did, which was why he invented Neuticles, artificial testicular implants for dogs. Despite the giggle factor, Neuticles have become a huge commercial success although, he points out, many people initially thought the idea was nuts.

- **The Smashing Place:** Ever been so mad you just wanted to smash something? If you live in Tokyo, you're in luck! You can just visit The Smashing Place, buy a plate or a cup of your choice, and smash it against a concrete wall—the staff will even cheer you on, and recycle the scraps afterwards.

- **Rent-a-Chicken:** Your first question may be why? As interest in local food and urban farming has grown, more families have shown interest in keeping chickens, which can be a bit of a commitment—especially baby chicks. That's where Rent-a-Chicken can help, by providing two full-grown hens and everything needed to keep them for the summer. Founder Leslie Suitor claims, "Chickens are about as easy as goldfish. Really. Families can expect to gather about a dozen eggs a week." That's eggcellent![19]

So the next time inspiration strikes, you may want to write down your idea and get to work, no matter how wacky it may initially seem.

These sparsely occupied spaces in the market tend to have fewer competitors because they simply aren't big enough—or high enough in profile—for large firms. An attractive niche sometimes appears when a larger firm decides to exit a market. For example, when John Wiley & Sons decided to stop publishing books in Canada, Figure 1 Business saw a void. The Vancouver-based company specializes in business books written by Canadian authors. It launched in March 2015 with 10 books. Chris Labonte, one of the partners, sees business memoirs and corporate histories as a solid niche in business book publishing.[20]

Personal Customer Service With a smaller customer base, small firms can develop much more personal relationships with individual customers. In many small businesses, the owner—who often is also the president—often becomes the external face for the company. Harry McWatters, co-founder of Sumac Ridge Estate Winery in British Columbia, sums up the selling lessons he learned over his career: ENTREPRENEUR = SALESPERSON.[21] The personal touch can be especially beneficial in some foreign markets, where clients prize the chance to deal directly with top management.

> Anything that's really awesome takes a lot of work.
>
> Mark Zuckerberg, founder, Facebook

Lower Overhead Costs Because entrepreneurs wear so many hats, from CEO to customer service rep, many small firms have lower overhead costs. They can hire fewer managers and fewer specialized employees. Perhaps more importantly, smaller firms—due to a lack of resources—tend to work around costs with tactics such as establishing headquarters in the owner's garage or offering employees flexible schedules instead of costly extended health care benefits.

Technology The Internet has played a powerful role in opening new opportunities for small business. Using a wealth of online tools, from eBay to eMachineShop, companies of one can create, sell, publish, and even manufacture goods and services more easily than ever before. Also, the Web has created international opportunities, transforming small businesses into global marketers. The London-based Anything Left-Handed retail store, for instance, evolved into an award-winning global wholesaler of left-handed items within a year of launching its website. Founder Keith Milsom comments: "Our website has allowed us to communicate with potential customers and market our business worldwide at very little cost, making international development possible."[22]

6-4b Small Business Threats

While small businesses do enjoy some advantages, they also face intimidating obstacles, from a high risk of failure to too much regulation.

High Risk of Failure Starting a new business involves risk—a lot of risk—but the odds improve significantly if you make it past the five-year mark. Exhibit 6.2 shows the survival rates of Canadian employer businesses with fewer than 250 employees.

These numbers may look daunting, but it's important to remember that owners shut down their businesses for many reasons other than the failure of the firm itself. The possibilities include poor health, divorce, better opportunities elsewhere, and, interestingly, an unwillingness to commit the enormous time it takes to run a business. Small business expert David Birch jokingly calls this last reason—which is remarkably common—the "I had no idea!" syndrome. It highlights the importance of anticipating what you're in for before you open your doors.[23]

Lack of Knowledge and Experience People typically launch businesses because they either have expertise in a particular area—such as designing websites or cooking Vietnamese food—or because they have a breakthrough idea—such as a new way to develop computer chips or run an airline. But in-depth knowledge in a specific area doesn't necessarily mean expertise in running a business. Successful business owners must know everything from finance to human resources to marketing.

Too Little Money The media are filled with stories of business owners who made it on a shoestring; that said, lack of startup money is a major issue for most new firms. Ongoing profits don't usually begin for a while, which means that entrepreneurs must plan on some lean months—or even years—as the business develops momentum. That means a real need to manage money wisely and to resist the temptation to invest in fixed assets, such as fancy offices and advanced electronics, before sufficient regular income warrants it. It also requires the nerve to stay the course despite initial losses.[25]

Bigger Regulatory Burden Complying with federal regulations can be challenging for any business, but it can be downright overwhelming for small firms. On average, Canadian small businesses spend 18 hours each year complying with government regulations. A Canadian study that investigated the cost to small businesses of meeting federal information-reporting requirements found that firms with fewer than 5 employees spent approximately 8 percent of revenue; firms with 5 to 19 employees spent 3.8 percent; firms with 20 to 49 employees spent 2.4 percent; and firms with 50 to 99 employees spent 1.8 percent.[26]

Costs of Employee Extended Benefits Programs Administrative and real costs for employee extended benefits plans are higher than for large businesses, making it even tougher for small firms to offer coverage to their employees. While a Manulife Financial survey of Canadian small business owners found that 86 percent of them feel an obligation to provide benefits for their employees, fewer than 60 percent offer health benefits, 20 percent offer group RRSPs, and only 15 percent offer an employee pension plan. Given that many employees value these benefits, small business owners are at a real disadvantage in terms of building a competitive workforce.[27]

6-5 Launch Options: Reviewing the Pros and Cons

When you imagine starting a new business, the first thought that comes to mind would probably be the process of developing your own big idea from an abstract concept to a thriving enterprise. But that's not the only option. In fact, it may make more sense to purchase an established business or even buy a franchise such as a Tim Hortons or Subway outlet. Each choice, of course, has its pros and cons. The trick is finding the best fit for you: the combination that offers you the least harmful downsides and the most meaningful upsides. Broadly speaking, it's less risky to buy an

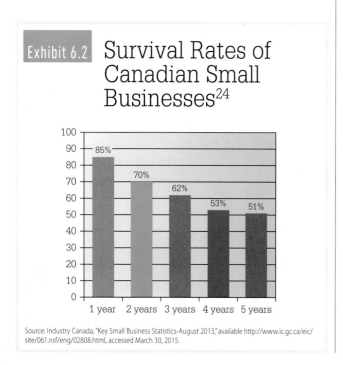

Exhibit 6.2 Survival Rates of Canadian Small Businesses[24]

Source: Industry Canada, "Key Small Business Statistics-August 2013," available http://www.ic.gc.ca/eic/site/061.nsf/eng/02808.html, accessed March 30, 2015.

Exhibit 6.3 Pros and Cons of Starting a Business from Scratch versus Buying an Established Business[28]

STARTING YOUR BUSINESS FROM SCRATCH

KEY PROS	KEY CONS
It's all *you*. Your concept, your decisions, your structure, and so on.	It's all *you*. That's a lot of pressure.
You don't have to deal with the prior owner's bad decisions.	It takes time, money, and sheer sweat equity to build a customer base.
	Without a track record, it's harder to get credit from both lenders and suppliers.
	From securing permits to hiring employees, the logistics of starting a business can be challenging.

BUYING AN ESTABLISHED BUSINESS

KEY PROS	KEY CONS
The concept, organizational structure, and operating practices are already in place.	Working with someone else's idea can be a lot less fun for some entrepreneurs.
Relationships with customers, suppliers, and other stakeholders are established.	You may inherit old mistakes, which can range from poor employee relations to pending lawsuits.
Getting financing and credit is less challenging.	

BUYING A FRANCHISE

KEY PROS	KEY CONS
In most cases, you're buying your own piece of a well-known brand and proven way of doing business.	You have less opportunity for creativity because most agreements tie you to franchise requirements.
Typically, management expertise and consulting come with the franchise package.	If something goes wrong with the national brand (e.g., *E. coli* at a burger joint), your business will suffer too.
Franchisors occasionally offer not just advice but also the financing that can make the purchase possible.	The initial purchase price can be steep, and that doesn't include the ongoing percentage-of-sales royalty fee.
These advantages add up to a very low 5 percent first-year failure rate.	

established business or franchise, but it can be more satisfying to start from scratch. Exhibit 6.3 offers a more detailed overview of the pros and cons.

6-5a Making It Happen: Tools for Business Success

Whichever way you choose to become a small business owner, several strategies can help you succeed in the long term: gain experience in your field, learn from others, educate yourself, access **Canada Business Network** resources, and develop a business plan.

Gain Experience Getting roughly three years of experience working for someone else in the field that interests you is a good rule of thumb. That way, you can learn what does and doesn't fly in your industry with relatively low personal risk (and you'd be making any mistakes on someone else's dime). You can also start developing a vibrant, relevant network before you need to ask for favours. But if you stay much longer than three years, you may get too comfortable to take the plunge and launch your own venture.

Learn from Others You should actively seek opportunities to learn from people who've succeeded in your field. If you don't know anyone personally, use your network to get introductions. And don't forget industry associations, local events, and other opportunities to build relationships. Also, remember that people who failed in your field may be able to give you valuable

Canada Business Network
A federal government service designed to maintain and strengthen the nation's economy by aiding, counselling, assisting, and protecting the interests of small businesses.

insights. (Why make the same mistakes they did?) As a bonus, they may be more willing to share their ideas and their gaffes if they're no longer struggling to develop a business of their own.

Educate Yourself The opportunities for entrepreneurial learning have exploded in the past decade. Many colleges and universities now offer full-blown entrepreneurship programs that help students both develop their plans and secure their initial funding. But education shouldn't stop there. Seek out relevant press articles, workshops, websites, and blogs so that your ongoing education will continue to boost your career.

Access Resources The Government of Canada, through the Canada Business Network, offers many resources for entrepreneurs and small business owners. The Canada Business Network website (www.canadabusiness.ca) provides a wealth of information on starting a business, financing, taxes and GST/HST, licences and permits, managing a business, research and statistics, selling to government, and much more. Some of its information is targeted at specific groups who can benefit from the available government resources: women, youth, Aboriginal peoples, persons with disabilities, and entrepreneurs in rural and northern communities. The Canada Business Network also works hand in hand with provincial and territorial governments and provides links on its website to government information specific to each region of Canada.

Develop a Business Plan Can a business succeed without a plan? Of course. Many do just fine by simply seizing opportunity as it arises and changing direction as needed. Some achieve significant growth without a plan. But a **business plan** does provide an invaluable way to keep you and your team focused on success. And it's absolutely crucial for obtaining outside funding, which is why many entrepreneurs write a business plan after they've used personal funding sources (such as savings, credit cards, and money from family and friends) to get themselves up and running. Even then, the plan may be continually in flux if the industry is rapidly changing.

Writing an effective business plan, which is usually 25–50 pages long, takes about six months. While the specifics may change by industry, the basic elements of any business plan answer these core questions:

> More than 30 percent of the richest people in the world do not have a college degree, but 57 percent of those who start a business in high-income countries do have a college degree.
>
> Global Entrepreneurship Monitor and *Forbes*

- What service or product does your business provide, and what needs does it fill?
- Who are the potential customers for your product or service, and why will they purchase it from you?
- How will you reach your potential customers?
- Where will you get the financial resources to start your business?
- When can you expect to achieve profitability?

The final document should include all of the following information:

- Executive summary (2–3 pages)
- Description of business (include both risks and opportunities)
- Marketing
- Competition (don't underestimate the challenge)
- Operating procedures
- Personnel
- Complete financial data and plan, including sources of startup money (be realistic!)
- Appendix (be sure to include all your research on your industry)[29]

Check out the information and advice available through the Canada Business Network and on many regional websites. On the Canada Business Network website, click on "Planning" to see sample business plans and a number of templates to help you create your own business plan.

business plan A formal document that describes a business concept, outlines core business objectives, and details strategies and timelines for achieving those objectives.

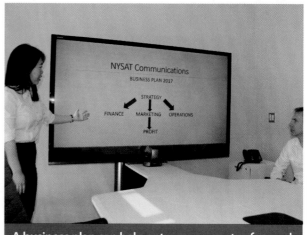

A business plan can help entrepreneurs stay focused.

Herb MacKenzie

ACCIDENTAL INVENTIONS

Every new business begins with a great idea, but not all great ideas begin with careful planning—a number of successful businesses have been built on inventions that happened by accident. But that doesn't mean you shouldn't be prepared; first-century philosopher Seneca said, "Luck is what happens when preparation meets opportunity." A sampling of "accidental inventions":

- **Microwave Ovens.** When Second World War scientist Percy Spencer was inspecting a magnetron tube at a Raytheon lab, he noticed that a candy bar in his pocket had melted, which sparked the idea of using microwaves for cooking. Originally called a "radarange," more than 90 percent of households today have a microwave oven.

Herb MacKenzie

- **Popsicles.** In 1905, 11-year-old Frank Epperson "invented" the Popsicle when he left a powdered drink and water concoction outside overnight, and it froze with the stir stick still in it. By the time he filed the patent 18 years later, his own children had started calling the "Eppsicle" the Popsicle.

- **Post-it Notes.** 3M scientist Spencer Silver developed the repositionable adhesive for Post-it Notes. But they didn't become a product until his co-worker, Art Fry, was looking for a sticky, reusable bookmark to replace the paper bookmarks that kept slipping out of his church hymnal. Fry proposed the product, which quickly became a worldwide hit for 3M.[30]

6-6 Small Business and the Economy: An Outsized Impact

The most successful entrepreneurs create goods and services that change the way people live. Many have built blockbuster corporations that today power the stock market and dominate pop culture through ubiquitous promotion. But small businesses—despite their lower profile—also play a vital role in the Canadian economy. Here are a few statistics from Industry Canada, Small Business and Tourism Branch:

- Canada has more than 1.1 million small businesses; 98 percent of all businesses in Canada have fewer than 100 employees.

- Business bankruptcies have fallen considerably in recent years in Canada, and numbered only 3,200 in 2012.

- Around 78 percent of these businesses operate in the service sector; the rest produce goods.

- Just over 10 percent of small- and medium-sized businesses exported in 2011, but they exported more than $150 billion, over 40 percent of Canada's total exports by value.

- Regarding business entries and exits, the latest statistics indicate that the number of small businesses has increased by more than 20,000 per year.

- Depending on estimates, small businesses contribute between 25 and 41 percent to Canada's annual GDP.[31]

The statistics, of course, depend on the definition of small business. Industry Canada defines small business as companies with fewer than 100 employees if they operate in the goods-producing sector, but fewer than 50 employees if they are service-producing firms. But Industry Canada also points out that other institutions define small business differently depending on their unique needs. For example, Export Development Canada defines small business as companies that export less than $1 million. The Canadian Bankers Association defines small business as companies that qualify for loans of less than $250,000. Regardless of the definition used, this fact is clear: Small business is a big player in the Canadian economy. Beyond the sheer value of the goods and services they generate, small businesses make a powerful contribution to the Canadian economy in terms of creating new jobs, fuelling innovation, and providing opportunities for women.

- **Creating new jobs:** Small businesses employ over 7.7 million Canadians, which is nearly 70 percent of the total private sector labour force. Between 2002 and 2012, 78 percent (more than 100,000) of all new jobs in the private sector were created by small businesses. As pointed out previously (see Exhibit 6.2), nearly 70 percent of micro-enterprises and about 85 percent of other small businesses survive after two years. At the same time, the number of bankruptcies in Canada has been steadily declining—down by more than 50 percent—over a recent 10-year period, which suggests that many of the new jobs they create remain stable. But while small businesses are quick to add new jobs, they're often the first to contract when times are tough: instability comes with the territory. Unfortunately, employees of small businesses earn about 10 percent less than the Canadian average.[32]

- **Fuelling innovation:** Small businesses spend around $5 billion annually on research and development, more than 30 percent of total expenditures in Canada. Small patenting firms are more likely to produce "scientifically important" innovations and have produced 13 to 14 times more patents per employee. Small firms tend to be effective innovators for a number of reasons. Perhaps most important, their very reason for existence often ties to a brand new idea. In the early years, they need innovation simply in order to survive. And they often display a refreshing lack of bureaucracy that allows new thinking to take hold.[33]

- **Creating opportunities for women and older Canadians:** Almost 14 percent of Canadian small businesses are wholly owned by women; an additional 18 percent are owned in equal partnership between women and men. Nearly 80 percent of small business owners have more than 10 years' business experience, and nearly 50 percent are between the ages of 50 and 64. Canadian women and older Canadians are a big force in small business.[34]

6-6a Entrepreneurship Around the World

Research suggests that entrepreneurship is having an economic impact in countries around the world. For more than a decade, the Global Entrepreneurship Monitor (GEM) has measured the annual rate of new business startups across a range of countries, adding new countries each year. The 16th annual GEM study included 73 countries, covering 72.4 percent of the world's population and 90 percent of the world's GDP. The results indicate that entrepreneurship is a global phenomenon. The entrepreneurial activity rate varies dramatically from country to country, ranging from a high of 37.4 percent in Cameroon to a low of 2.1 percent in Suriname. Exhibit 6.4 shows the 10 economies with the highest and lowest entrepreneurship rates, measured as total early-stage entrepreneurial activity: a combination of businesses that are currently in the business formation stage and those businesses that have been operating for less than three-and-a-half years.[35]

The differences among countries seem to depend on a number of interrelated factors: What is the national per capita income? What will the entrepreneur need to give up (i.e., the opportunity costs)? How strongly do the national culture and political environment support business startups?

- **Per capita income:** In low-income countries such as Cameroon and Ecuador, a high percentage of entrepreneurs start their own businesses because they simply have no other options. This contributes heavily to the startlingly high overall level of entrepreneurship. The rate of such "necessity entrepreneurship" declines in higher income countries like Canada and the United States, where entrepreneurs are more likely to strike out on their own in response to an opportunity they have spotted in the marketplace.

- **Opportunity costs:** Entrepreneurship rates are significantly lower in countries that provide a high level of employment protection (it's hard to get fired) and strong unemployment insurance (financial support if you do

Exhibit 6.4	Early Phase Entrepreneurship Rates, 2014[36]		
TOP TEN ENTREPRENEURSHIP RATES (%)		**BOTTOM TEN ENTREPRENEURSHIP RATES (%)**	
COUNTRY	**RATE**	**COUNTRY**	**RATE**
Cameroon	37.4	Suriname	2.1
Uganda	35.5	Japan	3.8
Botswana	32.8	Kosovo	4.0
Ecuador	32.6	Italy	4.4
Peru	28.8	Russia	4.7
Bolivia	27.4	France	5.3
Chile	26.8	Germany	5.3
Thailand	23.3	Belgium	5.4
Burkina Faso	21.7	Denmark	5.5
Angola	21.5	Spain	5.5

Note: The rate for Canada was 13.0 percent; for the United States: 13.8 percent.

© Cengage Learning

Herb MacKenzie

get fired). When these benefits are in place, the sense of urgency regarding entrepreneurship tends to fall. The European Union provides a number of clear examples.

- **Cultural/political environment:** Extensive, complex regulations can hinder entrepreneurship by raising daunting barriers. And a lack of cultural support only compounds the problem. These factors certainly contribute to the relatively low entrepreneurship rates in much of the European Union and Japan. Entrepreneurs in more supportive nations such as Canada, the United States, and New Zealand get a boost from limited regulation and strong governmental support. A thriving "cowboy culture" helps, too—standout individuals who break free of old ways attract attention and admiration in many of the countries with higher entrepreneurship rates.

THE BIG PICTURE

Successful entrepreneurs need more than simply a great idea. Bringing that idea to market—and earning a profit in the process—requires deep knowledge of every area of business. Finding money, attracting customers, and absorbing risk are only some of the challenges. But for the right person, the payoff can be huge in terms of everything from financial success to scheduling flexibility. The key is finding something you love to do that offers value to others. While that doesn't guarantee success, building on a passion suggests that you'll at least enjoy the journey. Looking forward as the global economy continues to recover, entrepreneurship seems likely to become a way of life, either part-time or full-time, for a growing swath of the population. The ideal result would be a higher standard of living—and a higher quality of life—for business owners and their customers worldwide.

careers in entrepreneurship: Clothing Company Founder

Design unique items that appeal to young people via innovative styles, attention-grabbing slogans, and distinctive fabrics. Build relationships with business funders. Oversee suppliers to ensure timely order delivery and ethical manufacturing practices. Build solid base of retail accounts. Develop a creative social media marketing campaign to boost sales. Meet profitability goals every quarter.

STUDY TOOLS 6

IN THE BOOK, YOU CAN:

- ☐ Rip out the Chapter Review card at the back of the book to have a summary of the chapter and key terms handy.

ONLINE AT NELSON.COM/STUDENT YOU CAN:

- ☐ Work through key concepts with a Guided Learning Question.
- ☐ Prepare for tests with quizzes.
- ☐ Review the key terms with Flash Cards (online or printer-ready).
- ☐ Explore practical examples of chapter concepts with Connect a Concept exercises.

7

Accounting:
Decision Making by the Numbers

LEARNING OBJECTIVES

After studying this chapter, you will be able to…

7-1 Define accounting and explain how accounting information is used by a variety of stakeholders

7-2 Identify the purposes and goals of accounting standards

7-3 Describe the key elements of the major financial statements

7-4 Describe several methods stakeholders can use to obtain useful insights from a company's financial statements

7-5 Explain the role of managerial accounting and describe the various cost concepts identified by managerial accountants

7-6 Describe how financial managers use key ratios to evaluate their firm

After you finish this chapter, go to page 115 for STUDY TOOLS

7-1 Accounting: Who Needs It— and Who Does It?

Accounting is a system for recognizing, organizing, summarizing, analyzing, and reporting information about the financial transactions that affect an organization. The goal of this system is to provide its users with relevant, timely information that allows them to make better economic decisions.

Who uses the information that accounting provides? It's a long list because everyone wants to make good decisions. In fact, a variety of business stakeholders rely so heavily on accounting information that it's sometimes called the language of business. Key users of accounting information include:

■ *Managers:* Marketing managers, for instance, need information about sales in various regions and for various product lines. Financial managers need up-to-date facts about debt, cash, inventory, and capital.

■ *Shareholders:* As owners of the company, most shareholders

accounting A system for recognizing, organizing, analyzing, and reporting information about the financial transactions that affect an organization.

have a keen interest in its financial performance, especially as indicated by the firm's financial statements. Has management generated a strong enough return on their investment?

■ *Employees:* Strong financial performance would help employees make their case for nice pay raises and hefty bonuses. But if earnings drop—especially multiple times—layoffs may be in the offing, and many employees may decide to polish their résumés.

■ *Creditors:* Bankers and other lenders want to assess a firm's creditworthiness by examining its accounting statements before granting a loan.

■ *Suppliers:* Like bankers, companies that provide supplies want to know that the company can pay for the orders it places.

■ *Government agencies:* Accurate accounting information is critical for meeting the reporting requirements of the Canada Revenue Agency, the securities exchanges, and other federal and provincial agencies.

A number of other groups—including the news media, competitors, and unions—may also have a real

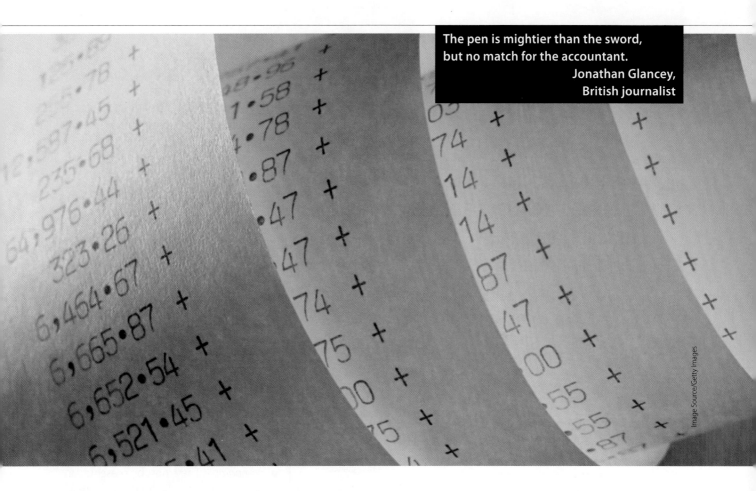

Image Source/Getty Images

interest in a firm's accounting information—whether the firm wants them to have it or not. If you have any interest in managing, investing in, or working for a business, the ability to understand accounting information is extremely valuable.

7-1a Accounting: Who Does It?

Accountants work in a variety of positions to provide all of this information. Let's take a quick look at some of the roles accountants play.

Many accountants work within an organization, preparing reports and analyzing financial information specific to that organization. These accountants perform a wide variety of tasks, including cost management, asset management, and budget development. They often prepare reports for managers and financial statements for owners and other stakeholders.

Other accountants provide a broad range of accounting and consulting services to clients on a fee basis. These clients may be individuals, corporations, not-for-profit organizations, or government agencies. Typical services include income tax preparation, external auditing, and consultation on a variety of accounting issues and problems. These accountants often help new companies

design their accounting systems and procedures, and help mature companies update and improve their accounting systems.

Another group of accountants work for a wide variety of government agencies at the local, provincial, and federal levels. In general, they perform tasks similar to those of public and private accountants. Many of these accountants work to ensure that government agencies properly manage

Wavebreakmedia/Shutterstock.com

A variety of business stakeholders, managers, shareholders, employees, creditors, suppliers, and government agencies use accounting information.

and account for the public funds they use. Others are employed by government regulatory agencies to audit the finances of private firms or individuals to ensure that government regulations are met and that all appropriate taxes are paid.

7-2 Financial Accounting: Intended for Those on the Outside Looking In

Financial accounting is the branch of accounting that addresses the needs of external stakeholders, including shareholders, creditors, and government regulators. These stakeholders are seldom interested in detailed accounting information about a company's individual departments or divisions. Instead, they're interested in the financial performance of the firm as a whole. They often want to know how a firm's financial performance has changed over a period of several years or to compare its results with those of other firms in the same industry. The major output of financial accounting is a set of financial statements designed to provide this broad type of information. We'll describe these statements in the next section.

> If my father had hugged me even once, I'd be an accountant now.
>
> Ray Romano, comedian

7-2a Role of the Accounting Principles

Imagine how confused and frustrated investors, creditors, and regulators would become if every firm could just make up its own financial accounting rules as it went along and change them whenever it wanted. To reduce confusion and provide external stakeholders with consistent and accurate financial statements, the accounting profession has adopted a set of **International Financial Reporting Standards (IFRS)** that guide the practice of financial accounting. Before January 1, 2011, Canadian companies used a different set of standards called **generally accepted accounting principles (GAAP)**, and some

countries, such as the United States, continue to use GAAP. Public companies (i.e., those that trade stocks on one of the stock exchanges) are required to follow the IFRS; other companies have the option to do so. Companies that fit into the optional categories are those that are privately owned, as well as not-for-profit organizations, which have another set of standards. The International Accounting Standards Board (IASB) is responsible for developing the IFRS.[1]

Through the IFRS, accountants aim to ensure that financial statements are:

- *relevant:* They must contain information that helps the user understand the firm's financial performance and condition.

- *reliable:* They must provide information that is objective, accurate, and verifiable.

- *consistent:* They must provide financial statements based on the same core assumptions and procedures over time. If a firm introduces any significant changes in how it prepares its financial statements, the company is required to clearly identify and describe these changes.

- *comparable:* They must be presented in a reasonably standardized way, so that users can track the firm's financial performance over a period of years and compare its results to those for other firms.

The IASB is constantly modifying, clarifying, and expanding IFRS as business practices evolve and new issues arise. Perhaps the IASB's most important focus in recent years has been on finding ways to make accounting practices more consistent with those in other nations.

7-2b Ethics in Accounting

Even clear and well-established accounting principles won't result in accurate and reliable information if managers and accountants flaunt them. A series of accounting scandals have shocked the business world over the past couple of decades. Several large corporations were implicated in major scandals. In many cases, these firms overstated earnings by billions of dollars or hid billions of dollars in debts. Once their accounting improprieties became known, most of these firms suffered severe financial difficulties. Some of the companies went bankrupt, leaving shareholders with worthless stock and employees without jobs or pension plans.[2]

These scandals served as a wake-up call to the accounting profession that their ethical training and standards

financial accounting The branch of accounting that prepares financial statements for use by owners, creditors, suppliers, and other external stakeholders.

International Financial Reporting Standards (IFRS) An international set of accounting standards that are used in the preparation of financial reports.

generally accepted accounting principles (GAAP) A set of accounting standards that is used in the preparation of financial statements. Replaced in Canada on January 1, 2011, with International Financial Reporting Standards (IFRS).

ACCOUNTING FRAUD, THE NOT-SO-USUAL SUSPECTS: FRIENDS, NEIGHBOURS, CO-WORKERS, BOSSES, AND RELATIVES

Image Source/Getty Images

Stealing cash, faking bills or expense reports, or falsifying revenues or expenses to misstate profits, is accounting fraud. According to one accounting expert, it "can happen to people who are otherwise good-intentioned; maybe they are trying to make a mortgage payment or put food on the table. These aren't hardened or overly sophisticated criminals." A legal expert explains: "People don't just set out and say, 'I'm going to commit a fraud.' Most of the time they're good people who have complied with the rules. Then pressure sets in, and they go closer and closer to the line." Many cases have involved family members, people who have known each other since childhood, or even the best man at your wedding. According to one study, 85 percent of those committing fraud are doing so for the first time, and you wouldn't normally suspect them. The typical fraud lasts 18 months before being detected, costs a company 5 percent of annual revenues, and averages $140,000 per incident. Also, there's only a 50 percent chance of recovering what's been stolen.

So if 85 percent of the people who commit fraud have never done so before, how can you detect who is committing fraud? The experts say: "There are three factors usually associated with fraud—opportunity, the ability to rationalize it, and financial need." Opportunity means "no one is watching." So hire an accountant to conduct a fraud audit to identify weaknesses and recommend strong accounting controls and procedures, such as dual signoffs for all transactions. Rationalization and financial need are evident in 81 percent of fraud cases: people were living above their means, experiencing financial difficulties, or had unusually close associations with vendors or customers, which gave them opportunity. Finally, since most fraud is initially detected by tips from employees, customers, or vendors, establish and publicize an independent hotline that people can call to report suspicions.[3]

needed major improvement. In the wake of the scandals, many accounting boards passed new ethics-related requirements.

7-3 Financial Statements: Read All about Us

A key responsibility of financial accounting is the preparation of three basic financial statements: balance sheet, income statement, and statement of cash flows. Taken together, these financial statements provide external stakeholders with a broad picture of an organization's financial condition and its recent financial performance. Large corporations with publicly traded stock must send an annual report containing financial statements to all shareholders. The *Canada Business Corporations Act* and various provincial corporation and securities laws cover specific requirements for annual reports. Let's take a look at the information each of these statements provides.

7-3a The Balance Sheet: What We Own and How We Got It

The **balance sheet** summarizes a firm's financial position at a specific point in time. Although the balance sheets of different firms vary in specifics, all of them are organized to reflect the most famous equation in all of accounting—so famous that it is usually referred to simply as the **accounting equation**:

$$\text{Assets} = \text{Liabilities} + \text{Owners' equity}$$

balance sheet A financial statement that reports the financial position of a firm at a particular point in time by identifying and reporting the value of the firm's assets, liabilities, and owners' equity.

accounting equation Assets = Liabilities + Owners' equity. This states that the value of a firm's assets is, by definition, exactly equal to the financing provided by creditors and owners for the purchase of those assets.

DOUBLE-ENTRY BOOKKEEPING: "ONE OF THE FINEST INVENTIONS OF MANKIND"

ra2studio/Shutterstock

The invention of double-entry bookkeeping, often attributed to Franciscan friar Luca Pacioli in 1494, was key to the expanding trade of Italian merchants, for otherwise "it would be impossible for them to conduct their business, for they would have no rest and their minds would always be troubled."

Double-entry bookkeeping requires that every accounting transaction be in balance and have two entries, a debit on the left and a credit on the right. For example, a $1 million bank loan is recorded as a $1 million debit in cash and a $1 million credit for notes payable.

	Debit	Credit
Cash	$1,000,000	
Notes Payable		$1,000,000

As shown in the "T account" above, the transaction balances because the company has $1 million in cash, but owes $1 million to pay off the loan.

Likewise, if you sell $75,000 in goods and receive a cash payment, the balanced journal entry looks like this:

	Debit	Credit
Cash	$75,000	
Sales Revenue		$75,000

reflecting the increase in cash as a function of making the sale.

Most students find debits and credits confusing at first. Even so, double-entry bookkeeping was a breakthrough because it facilitated error checking with every single accounting entry, and in so doing, according to Pacioli, it allowed Italian merchants "to make a lawful and reasonable profit so as to keep up his business."

Double-entry bookkeeping has been called one of "finest inventions of mankind." Italian economist Antonio Martino agreed: "Without double-entry bookkeeping, the rational conduct of business, and the pursuit of profit, modern civilization would not exist."[4]

Exhibit 7.1 shows a simplified balance sheet for Bigbux, a hypothetical company we'll use to illustrate the information provided by financial statements. As you look over this exhibit, keep in mind that real-world balance sheets may include additional accounts and that different firms sometimes use different names for the same type of account. Setting aside these differences, Exhibit 7.1 should help you understand the basic structure common to all balance sheets. Notice that the three main sections of this statement reflect the key terms in the accounting equation. Once we've defined each of these terms, we'll explain the logic behind the accounting equation and how the balance sheet illustrates this logic.

- **Assets** are things of value that the firm owns. Balance sheets usually classify assets into at least two major

assets Resources owned by a firm.

In Canada, all professional accounting associations (Chartered Accountants, Certified Management Accountants, and Certified General Accountants) have joined together and will be called Chartered Professional Accountants.

Chartered Professional Accountants

categories. The first category, *current assets*, consists of cash and other assets that the firm expects to use up or convert into cash within a year. For example, in Bigbux's balance sheet the value for *accounts receivable* refers to money owed to Bigbux by customers who purchased its goods on credit. These receivables are converted into cash when customers pay their bills. *Inventory* is the other current asset listed on Bigbux's balance sheet. For a wholesale or retail company, inventory consists of the stock of goods it has available for sale. For a manufacturing firm, inventory includes not only finished goods but also materials and parts used in the production process, as well as any unfinished goods.

Plant, property, and equipment is the other major category of assets shown on most balance sheets. This category lists the buildings, land, machinery, equipment, and other long-term assets that Bigbux owns. With the exception of

Exhibit 7.1 Balance Sheet for Bigbux

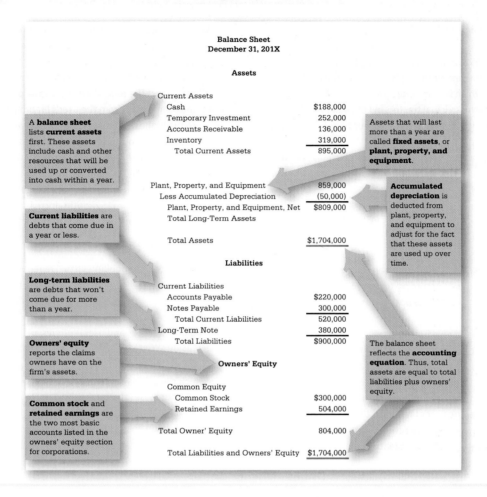

Balance Sheet
December 31, 201X

Assets

A **balance sheet** lists **current assets** first. These assets include cash and other resources that will be used up or converted into cash within a year.

Current Assets	
Cash	$188,000
Temporary Investment	252,000
Accounts Receivable	136,000
Inventory	319,000
Total Current Assets	895,000

Assets that will last more than a year are called **fixed assets**, or **plant, property, and equipment**.

Plant, Property, and Equipment	859,000
Less Accumulated Depreciation	(50,000)
Plant, Property, and Equipment, Net	$809,000
Total Long-Term Assets	
Total Assets	$1,704,000

Accumulated depreciation is deducted from plant, property, and equipment to adjust for the fact that these assets are used up over time.

Current liabilities are debts that come due in a year or less.

Long-term liabilities are debts that won't come due for more than a year.

Liabilities

Current Liabilities	
Accounts Payable	$220,000
Notes Payable	300,000
Total Current Liabilities	520,000
Long-Term Note	380,000
Total Liabilities	$900,000

The balance sheet reflects the **accounting equation**. Thus, total assets are equal to total liabilities plus owners' equity.

Owners' equity reports the claims owners have on the firm's assets.

Owners' Equity

Common stock and **retained earnings** are the two most basic accounts listed in the owners' equity section for corporations.

Common Equity	
Common Stock	$300,000
Retained Earnings	504,000
Total Owner' Equity	804,000
Total Liabilities and Owners' Equity	$1,704,000

land, all of these assets have a limited useful life, so accountants subtract *accumulated depreciation* from the original value of these assets to reflect the fact that these assets are being used up over time.

Although Bigbux doesn't do so, some companies list a third category of assets, called *intangible assets*. These are assets that have no physical existence—you can't see or touch them—but that still have value. Examples include patents, copyrights, trademarks, and even the goodwill a company develops with its stakeholders.

- **Liabilities** indicate what the firm owes—in other words, the claims against the firm's assets. Balance sheets usually organize liabilities into two broad categories: current liabilities and long-term liabilities. *Current liabilities* are debts that come due within a year of the date on the balance sheet. Accounts payable—what the firm owes suppliers when it buys supplies on credit—is a common example of a current liability. Wages payable, which indicates what the firm owes to workers for work they have already performed, is another example.

Long-term liabilities are debts that don't come due until more than a year after the date on the balance sheet. The only long-term liability that Bigbux lists is a long-term loan, which is a formal written IOU with a due date more than a year after the date on the balance sheet.

- **Owners' (or shareholders') equity** refers to the claims the owners have against their firm's assets. The specific accounts listed in the owners' equity section of a balance sheet depend on the form of business ownership. As Exhibit 7.1 shows, *common stock* is a key owners' equity account for corporations. So for corporations such as Bigbux, the owners' equity section is usually titled *shareholders' equity*. *Retained earnings*, which are the accumulated earnings reinvested in the company (rather than paid to owners), are another major component of the owners' equity section.

liabilities Claims against the firm's assets.

owners' equity The claims a firm's owners have against their company's assets (often called shareholders' equity on balance sheets of corporations).

Just because they can, doesn't mean they should.

Zynga, the billion-dollar company responsible for popular online social games such as Farmville, makes money two ways. First, by selling advertising, including banner ads, video ads, and product placement within its games. The second way, which is much more profitable, is by selling in-game items, such as virtual tractors in Farmville, which are paid for with Facebook credits, PayPal accounts, or FarmCash, all linked to credit card payments.

From an accounting perspective, Zynga's business seems straightforward. Buy $20 of FarmCash to spend in Farmville, and Zynga earns $20 in revenue. Well, not quite.

Zynga has your $20, but the $20 of FarmCash is like a gift card for a retail store. The retailer has $20, but now owes you $20 in merchandise. So until FarmCash is spent in the game, it has to be treated as deferred revenue.

So, given these accounting rules, how should Zynga's earnings be determined? According to Ernst & Young, a global accounting firm, there are three options for booking virtual goods revenue.

With game-based revenue, revenues are spread over the game life. If the game is estimated to last five years, then $20 of virtual revenue in year 1 would be booked as $4 in each of the five years.

User-based revenue is a quicker approach: revenues are spread over the average user's lifetime. If the average user plays for two years, then $20 of virtual revenue is booked at $10 per year, leading to higher revenue estimates.

With item-based revenue, the type of virtual item determines when revenue is booked. For consumables used only once, book the revenue when the item is used in the game. For durable items used over time, such as a virtual tractor in Farmville, subtract the date of first purchase, perhaps two months into game play, from the user's lifetime, two years, leading to the highest estimates of annual revenue over the shortest period, 22 months.

The risk with all three methods is that revenue estimates can be manipulated by changing estimated game life or user life. Zynga reported a 19-month user life in 2011, and 15 months in 2012. The shorter time, 15 months, increased reported revenues by $27 million, turning a loss into a gain.

What do YOU think?

- Which approach to booking virtual revenue seems the fairest and most accurate—game-based, user-based, or item-based?

- Based on your experience with online gaming, do you think that game lifetimes and user lifetimes are increasing or decreasing? Why?

- How sustainable is Zynga's "freemium" business model, in which the game is free but revenues are derived from in-game purchases that make the game quicker or more powerful or more fun. Are you more or less likely to play an online game based on an annual fee, or based on the freemium model? Why?[5]

The logic behind the accounting equation is based on the fact that firms must finance the purchase of their assets, and owners and non-owners are the only two sources of funding. The accounting equation tells us that the value of a firm's assets must equal the amount of financing provided by owners (as measured by owners' equity) plus the amount provided by creditors (as indicated by the firm's liabilities) to purchase those assets. Because a balance sheet is based on this logic, it must *always* be in balance. In other words, the dollar value of the assets *must* equal the dollar value of the liabilities plus owners' equity. This is true for *all* firms, from the smallest sole proprietorship to the largest multinational corporation. Notice in Exhibit 7.1 that the $1,704,000

income statement The financial statement that reports the revenues, expenses, and net income that resulted from a firm's operations over an accounting period.

> After the accounting associations in Canada united there were over 190 000 Canadians with the CPA designation.
>
> Chartered Professional Accountants of Canada

in total assets listed on Bigbux's balance sheet matches the $1,704,000 in liabilities plus owners' equity.

7-3b The Income Statement: How Did We Do?

The **income statement** summarizes the financial results of a firm's operations over a given period of time. (Exhibit 7.2 shows the income statement for our fictional Bigbux firm.) The figure that attracts the most attention on the income statement is net income, which measures the company's profit or loss. In fact, another name for the income statement is the *profit and loss statement* (or, informally, the P&L). Just as with the balance sheet, we can use a simple equation to illustrate the logic behind the organization of the income statement:

Revenue − Expenses = Net income

In this equation:

- **Revenues** represent the increase in the amount of cash and other assets (such as accounts receivable) the firm earns in a given time period as a result of its business activities. A firm normally earns revenue by selling goods or by charging fees for providing services (or both). Accountants use **accrual basis accounting** when recognizing revenues. Under the accrual approach, revenues are recorded when they are earned and payment is reasonably assured. It's important to realize that this is not always when the firm receives cash from its sales. For example, if a firm sells goods on credit, it reports revenue before it receives cash. (The revenue would show up initially as an increase in accounts receivable rather than as an increase in cash.)

- **Expenses** indicate the cash a firm spends, or other assets it uses up, to carry out the business activities necessary to generate its revenue. Under accrual basis accounting, expenses aren't necessarily recorded when cash is paid. Instead, expenses are matched to the revenue they help generate. The specific titles given to the costs and expenses listed on an income statement vary among firms, as do the details provided. But the general approach remains the same: costs are deducted from revenue in several stages to show how net income is determined. The first step in this process is to deduct *costs of goods sold*, which are costs directly related to buying, manufacturing, or providing the goods and services the company sells. (Manufacturing companies often use the term *cost of goods manufactured* for these costs.) The difference between the firm's revenue and its cost of goods sold is its *gross profit*. The next step is to deduct *operating expenses* from gross profit. Operating expenses are costs the firm incurs in the regular operation of its business. Most income statements divide operating expenses into *selling expenses* (such as salaries and commissions paid to salespeople and advertising expenses) and *general* (or *administrative*) *expenses* (such as rent, insurance, utilities, and office supplies). The difference between gross profit and operating expenses is *net operating income*. Finally, interest expense and taxes are deducted from net operating income to determine the firm's net income.

- **Net income** is the profit or loss the firm earns in the time period covered by the income statement. If net income is positive, the firm has earned a profit. If it's negative, the firm has suffered a loss. Net income is called the "bottom line" of the income statement because it is such an important measure of the firm's operating success. But income statements usually include additional information below the net income, so it isn't literally the bottom line. For example, the income statement for Bigbux indicates how much of the net income was retained and how much was distributed to shareholders in the form of dividends.

Take a look at Exhibit 7.2 to see how the income statement for Bigbux is organized. See if you can identify the accounts that represent the revenue, expense, and income concepts we've just described.

> Happiness is a positive cash flow.
>
> Fred Adler

7-3c Statement of Cash Flows: Show Me the Money

The last major financial statement is the **statement of cash flows**. Cash is the lifeblood of any business organization. A firm must have enough cash to pay what it owes to workers, creditors, suppliers, and taxing authorities—hopefully with enough left to pay its owners a return on their investment. So it's not surprising that a firm's stakeholders want to know not only *how much* the firm's cash balance changed over the accounting period but also *why* it changed. The statement of cash flows provides this information by identifying the amount of cash that flowed into and out of the firm from three types of activities:

1. Cash flows from *operating activities* show the amount of cash that flowed into the company from the sale of goods or services, as well as cash from dividends and interest received from ownership of the financial securities of other firms. It also shows the amount of cash Bigbux used to cover expenses resulting from operations and any cash payments to purchase securities held for short-term trading purposes. Remember that under the accrual method not all revenues and expenses on the income statement represent cash flows, so operating cash flows may differ substantially from the revenues and expenses shown on the income statement.

2. Cash flows from investing activities show the amount of cash received from the sale of fixed assets (such as land and buildings) and financial assets purchased as longterm investments. It also shows any cash used to buy fixed assets and long-term financial investments.

revenues Increases in a firm's assets that result from the sale of goods, provision of services, or other activities intended to earn income.

accrual-basis accounting The method of accounting that recognizes revenue when it is earned and matches expenses to the revenues they helped produce.

expenses Resources that are used up as the result of business operations.

net income The difference between the revenue a firm earns and the expenses it incurs in a given time period.

statement of cash flows The financial statement that identifies a firm's source and uses of cash in a given accounting period.

Exhibit 7.2 # Bigbux's Income Statement

Revenue is the increase in resources, such as cash and accounts receivable, a firm earns from the sale of goods over the specified time period.

Cost of goods sold is the cost of merchandise or the costs directly involved in producing the goods the firm sells.

Operating expenses are incurred in the process of earning sales revenue but are not directly tied to producing or acquiring goods. Examples include salaries and commissions, clerical costs, advertising costs, insurance, and depreciation.

Bigbux, Inc.
Income Statement
For Year Ending December 31, 201X

Sales Revenue		$890,000.00
Cost of Goods Sold		550,000.00
Gross profit		340,000.00
Selling Expenses	75,000.00	
Administrative Expenses	80,000.00	
Depreciation	10,000.00	
Total Operating Expenses		165,000.00
Net Operating Income		175,000.00
Interest		12,000.00
Taxable Income		163,000.00
Taxes		62,000.00
Net Income		101,000.00
Dividends		55,000.00
Transfer to Retained Earnings		46,000.00

Gross profit is found by subtracting the cost of goods sold from revenue.

Net operating income is found by subtracting total operating expenses from gross profit.

Net income is the bottom line— the after-tax profit the firm earns.

The last two items show what the firm did with the earnings. **Dividends** are earnings distributed to the shareholders, while the **transfer to retained earnings** shows the amount reinvested in the company. (This is the amount by which the retained earnings listed on the balance sheet increases.)

3. Cash flows from *financing activities* show the cash the firm received from issuing additional shares of its own stock or from taking out long-term loans. It also shows cash outflows from payment of dividends to shareholders and to repay principal on loans.

Exhibit 7.3 shows the statement of cash flows for Bigbux. You can see that Bigbux experienced a substantial increase in its total cash balance. You can also see that this increase in cash was primarily due to two factors. First, a look at operating cash flows shows that the cash Bigbux collected from customer payments exceeded its cash payments for inventory and operating expenses by a significant margin. Second, the section on financing activities shows that Bigbux took out a large long-term loan. The net increases in cash from these sources more than offset the net cash outflow from investing due to the purchase of new equipment. Note that the cash balance at the end of the period matches the amount of cash reported in the current balance sheet (see Exhibit 7.1 again)—as it always should.

7-3d Other Statements

In addition to the three major statements we've just described, firms usually prepare either a statement of retained earnings or a shareholders' equity statement. Let's take a quick look at each of these statements.

The *statement of retained earnings* is a simple statement that shows how retained earnings have changed from one accounting period to the next. The change in retained earnings is found by subtracting dividends paid to shareholders from net income.

Firms that have more complex changes in the owners' equity section sometimes report these changes in notes to the financial statements in the annual report. But they often disclose these changes by providing a *shareholders' equity statement*. Like the statement of retained earnings, this statement shows how net income and dividends affect retained earnings. But it also shows other changes in shareholders' equity, such as those that arise from the issuance of additional shares of stock.

7-4 Interpreting Financial Statements: Digging Beneath the Surface

The financial statements we've just described contain a lot of important information. But they don't necessarily tell the whole story. In fact, the numbers they report can be misleading if they aren't put into proper context. So in

Exhibit 7.3 Statement of Cash Flows for Bigbux

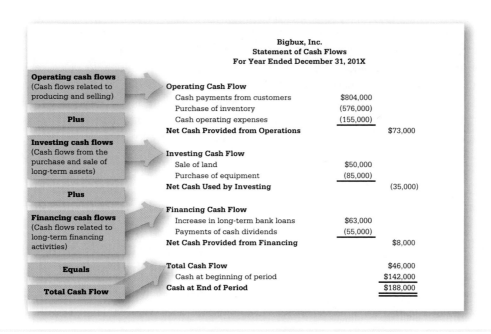

Bigbux, Inc.
Statement of Cash Flows
For Year Ended December 31, 201X

Operating cash flows (Cash flows related to producing and selling)	**Operating Cash Flow**		
Plus	Cash payments from customers	$804,000	
	Purchase of inventory	(576,000)	
	Cash operating expenses	(155,000)	
	Net Cash Provided from Operations		$73,000
Investing cash flows (Cash flows from the purchase and sale of long-term assets)	**Investing Cash Flow**		
Plus	Sale of land	$50,000	
	Purchase of equipment	(85,000)	
	Net Cash Used by Investing		(35,000)
Financing cash flows (Cash flows related to long-term financing activities)	**Financing Cash Flow**		
	Increase in long-term bank loans	$63,000	
	Payments of cash dividends	(55,000)	
	Net Cash Provided from Financing		$8,000
Equals	**Total Cash Flow**		$46,000
Total Cash Flow	Cash at beginning of period		$142,000
	Cash at End of Period		$188,000

addition to looking at the statements, it's also important to check out the independent auditor's report and the notes that accompany these statements. It's also a good idea to compare the figures reported in current statements to those from earlier statements to see how key account values have changed.

7-4a The Independent Auditor's Report: A Necessary Stamp of Approval

Every publicly traded corporation in Canada is required to have a qualified accountant perform an annual external audit of its financial statements. And many companies that aren't publicly traded also obtain external audits, even though they aren't required to do so.

The purpose of the audit is to verify that the company's financial statements were properly prepared in accordance with accounting standards and that they fairly present the financial condition of the firm. So external auditors don't just check the figures, they also examine the accounting *methods* the company used to *obtain* those figures. For example, auditors interview the company's accounting and bookkeeping

staff to verify that they understand and properly implement procedures that are consistent with accounting standards. They also examine a sample of specific source documents (such as sales receipts or invoices) and verify that the transactions they represent were properly posted to the correct accounts. Auditors also look for signs of fraud or falsified records. They often conduct an actual physical count of goods or supplies in inventory to determine the accuracy of the figures reported in the company's inventory records

In the most recent annual survey conducted by the Chartered Professional Accountants of Canada, 32% of Canadians have been a victim of financial fraud.

Chartered Professional Accountants of Canada

© John Knill/Photodisc/Getty Images

and contact the company's bank to verify its account balances. The audit process is rigorous, but it's important to realize that in large, public companies, it would be impossible for auditors to check the accuracy of every transaction.

The results of the audit are presented in an independent auditor's report, which is included in the annual report the firm sends to its shareholders. If the auditor doesn't find any problems with the way a firm's financial statements were prepared and presented, the report will offer an *unqualified opinion* (also referred to as a *clean opinion*). An unqualified opinion is by far the most common outcome. If the auditor identifies some minor concerns but believes that on balance the firm's statements remain a fair and accurate representation of the company's financial position, the report will express a *qualified opinion*. But when auditors discover more serious and widespread problems with a firm's statements, they offer an *adverse opinion*. An adverse opinion indicates that the auditor believes the financial statements are seriously flawed and that they may be misleading and unreliable. (An adverse opinion must include an explanation of the specific reasons for the opinion.) Adverse opinions are very rare, so when an auditor renders one it should set off alarm bells, warning others to view the information in the firm's financial statements with real skepticism.

In order for accounting firms to perform audits with integrity, they must be independent of the firms they audit. During the 1990s, many of the major accounting firms entered into highly lucrative consulting contracts with some of the businesses they were auditing. It became increasingly difficult for these accounting firms to risk losing these high-paying contracts by raising issues about accounting practices when they audited the books of their clients. In other words, the auditors ceased to be truly independent and objective. The lack of rigorous oversight by external auditors contributed to the accounting scandals we mentioned earlier in this chapter.

7-4b Notes to Financial Statements: Reading the Fine Print

Some types of information can't be adequately conveyed by numbers alone. Annual reports include notes (often

BEYOND THE NUMBERS: WHY YOU SHOULD READ THE ANNUAL REPORT

Feng Yu/Shutterstock.com

Understanding a company's financial performance is easier when you understand how its business works. To do that, read the annual report. Below are some excerpts from McDonald's annual report.

- Item 1: *Business.* This section describes the company, its customers, and its operations. Here we learn that "the Company owns the land and building or secures long-term leases for both Company-operated and conventional franchised restaurant sites." This explains why the biggest item on McDonald's balance sheet is $38.49 billion for property, plant, and equipment. With 31,000 restaurants around the world, McDonald's is one of the largest corporate owners of real estate in the world.

- Item 1A: *Risk Factors.* This section describes possible threats to the company's performance. McDonald's explains that "persistently high unemployment rates" and "declining economic growth rates" have made consumers price-sensitive, leading to "flat or contracting" revenues for fast food suppliers. Add in rising labour

and commodity prices, and there are understandable pressures on profits. Accordingly, while McDonald's revenues were $27.6 billion in 2012, up from $27 billion in 2011, net income of $5.4 billion in 2012 was down from $5.5 billion in 2011, despite a $600 million increase in revenues. The annual report explains why.

- Item 7: *Management's Discussion and Analysis.* This section describes trends and events affecting the company. For example, with only 32 percent of revenue coming from the United States, McDonald's is a truly global company. Europe, for instance, is a significantly larger and more profitable market. Why? One reason is that 90 percent of its European restaurant exteriors, and 50 percent of its interiors, have been modernized or "reimaged." Also, 1,600 McCafé coffee bars in those restaurants are driving European sales.

So if you want to understand balance sheets and income and cash flow statements, learn the story behind the numbers by reading the annual report.[6]

CSI ACCOUNTING

dragon_fang/Shutterstock.com

A forensic accountant is an expert at finding white-collar criminals and retrieving incriminating evidence. Businesses, lawyers, and government agencies, including the Royal Canadian Mounted Police, hire these financial investigators to follow the money trail when there is a suspected problem with the accounting records.

What do forensic accountants do? Forensics involves applying scientific knowledge to legal problems, so forensic accountants investigate business fraud. While lawyers look for motive and opportunity, forensic accountants look for incentive, opportunity, rationalization, and capability. While chartered professional accountants look for signs of good accounting practice, forensic accountants actively look for signs of fraud, such as laundering profits.

Multinational corporations hire forensic accountants to investigate internal fraud. For example, Siemens, which has operations in 191 countries, paid forensic accountants and lawyers $100 million to investigate bribes its employees paid to government officials around the world.

Also, companies hire forensic accountants to scrub the notoriously unreliable books of Chinese companies before acquiring or doing business with them. Similarly, firms in countries where corrupt business practices are common, such as eastern Europe and Africa, hire forensic accountants to prove their financial reports are accurate so that banks and potential partners will do business with them.

Finally, forensic accountants are often hired in divorce proceedings to verify disputed financial assets. Heather Mills, ex-wife of former Beatle Paul McCartney, whom she believed was worth $1.6 billion, hired forensic accountants after he claimed to be worth only $800 million (which the court ruled was correct).

Will the need for forensic accountants dry up with increasing government oversight and the emergence of highly skilled numbers investigators? According to one expert, it is unlikely, because "fraud is a growth industry. There's never been a shortage of bad people doing bad things."[7]

---

many pages of notes) that disclose additional information about the firm's operations and accounting practices, as well as any special circumstances that clarify and

Jose Luis Pelaez/Iconica/Getty Images

External auditors carefully examine a company's financial records before rendering their opinion.

supplement the numbers reported on the financial statements. These notes can be *very* revealing. For example, accounting standards often allow firms to choose among several options when it comes to certain accounting procedures—and the choices the firm makes can affect the value of assets, liabilities, and owners' equity on the balance sheet and the revenues, costs, and net income on the income statement. The notes to financial statements explain the specific accounting methods used to recognize revenue, value inventory, and depreciate fixed assets. They may also provide details about the way the firm funds its pension plan or health insurance for its employees. They must also disclose *changes* in accounting methods that could affect the comparability of the current financial statements to those of previous years. Even more interesting, the notes may disclose important facts about the status of a lawsuit against the firm or other risks the firm faces. Stakeholders who ignore these notes are likely to miss out on important information.

Another important source of information is the section of the annual report usually titled "Management's Discussion and Analysis." As its name implies, this is where the top management team provides its take on the financial condition of the company. Accounting guidelines require top management to disclose any trends, events, or risks likely to have a significant impact on the firm's financial condition in this section of the report.

7-4c Comparative Statements: Trendy Analysis

The IFRS require publicly traded corporations to provide information about previous accounting periods in their financial statements. Most companies do this by providing statements that list two or three years of figures side by side, making it possible to see how account values have changed over a period of time. Many firms that aren't publicly traded also present comparative statements, even though they are not required to do so by the IFRS.

Comparative balance sheets allow users to trace what has happened to key assets and liabilities over the past two or three years and whether its owners' equity had increased. Comparative income statements allow users to determine whether the firm's net income had increased or decreased and what has happened to revenues and expenses in recent years. Using comparative statements to identify changes in key account values over time is called **horizontal analysis**.

horizontal analysis
Analysis of financial statements that compares account values reported on these statements over two or more years to identify changes and trends.

managerial (or management) accounting
The branch of accounting that provides reports and analysis to managers to help them make informed business decisions.

7-5 Inside Intelligence: The Role of Managerial Accounting

Now that we've looked at financial accounting, let's turn our attention to the other major branch of accounting, **managerial** (or **management**) **accounting**. As its name implies, this branch of accounting is designed to meet the needs of a company's managers, although in recent years many firms have empowered other employees and given them access to this information as well. Exhibit 7.4 identifies several ways that managerial accounting differs from financial accounting.

Managers throughout an organization rely on information created by managerial accountants to make important decisions. The accuracy and reliability of this information can make a huge difference in the performance of a firm. In fact,

Exhibit 7.4 Comparison of Financial and Managerial Accounting		
	FINANCIAL ACCOUNTING	**MANAGERIAL ACCOUNTING**
PURPOSE	Primarily intended to provide information to external stakeholders such as shareholders, creditors, and government regulators. Information provided by financial accounting is available to the general public.	Primarily intended to provide information to internal stakeholders such as the managers of specific divisions or departments. This information is proprietary, meaning that it isn't available to the general public.
TYPE OF INFORMATION PRESENTED	Focuses almost exclusively on financial information.	Provides both financial and non-financial information.
NATURE OF REPORTS	Prepares a standard set of financial statements.	Prepares customized reports to deal with specific problems or issues.
TIMING OF REPORTS	Presents financial statements on a predetermined schedule (usually quarterly and annually).	Creates reports upon request by management rather than according to a predetermined schedule.
ADHERENCE TO ACCOUNTING STANDARDS	Governed by a set of accounting principles or standards (IFRS).	Uses procedures developed internally that are not required to follow accounting standards.
TIME PERIOD FOCUS	Summarizes past performance and its impact on the firm's present condition.	Provides reports dealing with past performance, but also involves making projections when dealing with planning issues.

many firms view their management accounting systems as a source of competitive advantage and regard the specifics of these systems as highly valuable company secrets.[8]

It's impossible to describe all the functions performed by managerial accountants in a single chapter. So we'll be selective and focus on only two of them—but the two we'll discuss often play a crucial role in managerial decision making. They are measuring and assigning costs, and developing budgets.

7-5a Cost Concepts: A Cost for All Reasons

Without good information on costs, managers would be operating in the dark as they try to set prices, determine the most desirable mix of products, and locate areas where efficiency is lagging. A firm's management accounting system helps managers throughout an organization measure costs and assign them to products, activities, and even whole divisions.

Accountants define **cost** as the value of what is given up in exchange for something else. Depending on the type of problem they are analyzing, managerial accountants actually measure and evaluate several different types of costs. We'll begin our discussion by describing some of the cost concepts commonly used by managerial accountants.

At the most basic level, accountants distinguish between out-of-pocket costs and opportunity costs. **Out-of-pocket costs** (also called *explicit costs*) are usually easy to measure because they involve actual expenditures of money or other resources. The wages a company pays its workers, the payments it makes to suppliers for raw materials, and the rent it pays for office space are examples.

But accountants realize that not all costs involve a monetary payment; sometimes what is given up is the *opportunity* to use an asset in some alternative way. Such costs are often referred to as **implicit costs**. For example, suppose a couple of lawyers form a partnership and set up their office in a building one of the partners already owns. They feel good about their decision because they don't have to make any out-of-pocket payments for rent. But a good managerial accountant would point out to the partners that they still incur an implicit cost, because by using the building themselves they forgo the opportunity to earn income by renting the office space to someone else.

Managerial accountants also distinguish between fixed costs and variable costs. As the name implies, **fixed costs** don't change when the firm changes its level of production. Fixed costs include interest on a bank loan, property insurance premiums, rent on office space, and other payments that are set by a contract or by legal requirements. Many fixed costs are really only fixed for some "relevant range" of output. For example, if a company sees a dramatic rise in sales, it may have to move into bigger facilities, thus incurring a higher rent.

Variable costs are costs that rise (vary) when the firm produces more of its goods and services. As a company ramps up its production, it is likely to need more labour and materials and to use more electrical power. Thus payments for many types of labour, supplies, and utilities are variable costs.

7-5b Assigning Costs to Products: As (Not So) Simple as ABC?

Finally, accountants often want to assign costs to specific *cost objects*, such as one of the goods or services their firm produces. When they assign costs to specific cost objects, they distinguish between *direct costs* and *indirect costs*. **Direct costs** are those that can be directly traced to the production of the product. For example, the wage payments made to workers directly involved in producing a good or service would be a direct cost for that product. On the other hand, the costs a firm incurs for plant maintenance, quality control, or depreciation on office equipment are usually classified as **indirect costs** since they tend to be the result of the firm's general operations rather than the production of any specific product.

Direct costs for labour and materials are usually easy to measure and assign, since they have an easily identifiable link to the object. Unfortunately, indirect costs aren't tied in such a simple and direct way to the production of a specific product. In the past, managerial accountants usually relied on simple rules to assign indirect costs to different products—and in some cases they still do. One such approach is to allocate indirect costs in proportion to the number of direct labour hours involved in the production of each product. Under this method, products that require the most labour to produce are assigned the most indirect costs. But, while this approach is

Tetra Images/Jupiterimages

cost The value of what is given up in exchange for something.

out-of-pocket cost A cost that involves the payment of money or other resources.

implicit cost The opportunity cost that arises when a firm uses owner-supplied resources.

fixed costs Costs that remain the same when the level of production changes within some relevant range.

variable costs Costs that vary directly with the level of production.

direct costs Costs that are incurred directly as the result of some specific cost object.

indirect costs Costs that are the result of a firm's general operations and are not directly tied to any specific cost object.

Budgeting encourages communication and coordination among managers and employees.

simple, it can provide very misleading information. There is simply no logical reason for many types of indirect costs to be related to the amount of direct labour used to produce a product.

In recent years, managerial accountants have developed more sophisticated ways to allocate costs. One relatively new method is called **activity-based costing (ABC)**.

This approach is more complex and difficult to implement than the direct labour method. Basically, it involves a two-stage process. The first stage is to identify specific activities that create indirect costs and then determine the factors that "drive" the costs of these activities. The second stage is to tie these cost drivers to the production of specific goods (or other cost objects). Once the relationships between cost drivers and specific products are identified, they can be used to determine how much of each indirect cost is assigned to each product.

Clearly, ABC is much more complex to implement than a system that assigns costs based on a simple "one-size-fits-all" rule, such as the direct labour method. However, it's likely to provide more meaningful results because it is

based on a systematic examination of how indirect costs are related to individual goods.

7-6 Evaluating Performance: Where Do We Stand?

7-6a Using Ratio Analysis to Identify Current Strengths and Weaknesses

One way in which financial managers evaluate a firm's current strengths and weaknesses is by computing ratios that compare values of key accounts listed on their firm's financial statements—mainly its balance sheet and income statement. This technique is called **financial ratio analysis**. Over the years, financial managers have developed an impressive array of specific ratios. The most important fall into four basic categories: liquidity, asset management, leverage, and profitability. Because financial needs differ across industries—for example, the automobile industry is capital intensive (it takes billions of dollars to design new cars and build or refurbish factories), whereas the software industry is not (the marginal cost of producing another copy of a software program or app is close to zero)—it's standard practice to compare a firm's financial ratios to industry averages. We will work through the financial ratios below by continuing our financial analysis of the income statements, balance sheets, and cash flows.

1. *Liquidity ratios:* In finance, a **liquid asset** is one that can be quickly converted into cash with little risk of loss. **Liquidity ratios** measure the ability of an organization to convert assets into the cash it needs to pay off liabilities that come due in the next year.

One of the simplest and most commonly used liquidity ratios is the *current ratio*, which is computed by dividing a firm's current assets by its current liabilities. Current assets include cash and other assets expected to be converted into cash in the next year, while current liabilities are the debts that must be repaid in the next year. The larger the current ratio, the easier it should be for a firm to obtain the cash needed to pay its short-term debts. A current ratio below 1.0 signifies that a company does not have enough current assets to pay short-term liabilities. For the Bigbux company, the current ratio is 1.72. The company has current assets of $895,000 and current liabilities of $520,000 (895,000 / 520,000 = 1.72). This current ratio means that the Bigbux company has 72 percent more current assets than current liabilities. Bigbux would also

activity-based costing (ABC) A technique to assign product costs based on links between activities that drive costs and the production of specific products.

financial ratio analysis Computing ratios that compare values of key accounts listed on a firm's financial statements.

liquid asset An asset that can quickly be converted into cash with little risk of loss.

liquidity ratios Financial ratios that measure the ability of a firm to obtain the cash it needs to pay its short-term debt obligations as they come due.

compare this ratio to the industry average. As we'll explain when we discuss how firms manage cash and other liquid assets in the next chapter, it is also possible to have too much liquidity.

2. *Asset management ratios:* **Asset management ratios** (also sometimes called *activity ratios*) provide measures of how effectively an organization is using its assets to generate net income. For example, the *inventory turnover ratio*—computed by dividing the firm's cost of goods sold by average inventory—measures how many times a firm's inventory is sold and replaced each year. For example, if a company keeps an average of 100 finished widgets in inventory each month, and it sold 1,000 widgets this year, then it turned its inventory 10 times. A high turnover ratio is good because it indicates that a firm can continue its daily operations with a small amount of inventory on hand. It's expensive to have unsold inventory sitting on shelves—that is, low inventory turns. Companies with high inventory turns, and that replenish inventory levels more frequently, have less cash tied up in inventory, which means those funds can be used elsewhere. However, inventory turnover ratios can be *too* high. When that happens, the company isn't keeping enough goods in stock, causing stockouts, which frustrates customers and results in lost sales if they take their business elsewhere.

For firms that sell a lot of goods on credit, the *average collection period* is another important asset management ratio. This ratio is computed by dividing accounts receivable by average daily credit sales. A value of 45 for this ratio means that customers take 45 days (on average) to pay for their credit purchases. In general, the smaller the ratio the better it is for the firm. A lower value for the average collection period indicates that the firm's customers are paying for their purchases more quickly. But we'll see in our discussion of working capital management that low collection periods can also have drawbacks.

3. *Leverage ratios:* **Financial leverage** is the use of debt to meet a firm's financing needs; a *highly leveraged* firm is one that relies heavily on debt. While the use of leverage can benefit a firm when times are good, a high degree of leverage is very risky. The extensive use of financial leverage played a major role in the financial meltdown that began during the latter part of the last decade.

Leverage ratios measure the extent to which a firm is employing financial leverage. One common measure of leverage ratios is the *debt-to-asset ratio* (sometimes just called the *debt ratio*), which is computed by dividing a firm's total liabilities by its total assets. If a firm financed half its assets with debt and half with owners' equity, its debt ratio would be .5 (or 50 percent). The higher the debt-to-asset ratio, the more heavily leveraged the firm is. The Bigbux's debt-to-asset ratio is 52.8 percent ($900,000 in liabilities divided by $1,704,000 in assets). The Bigbux Company would compare this figure to its results from previous years and to the ratios of other companies in the same industry.

4. *Profitability ratios:* Firms are in business to earn a profit, and **profitability ratios** provide measures of how successful they are at achieving this goal. There are many different profitability ratios, but we'll look at just a couple of examples. *Return-on-equity (ROE)*, calculated by dividing net income (profit) by owners' equity, measures the income earned per dollar invested by the shareholders. The return-on-equity ratio for the Bigbux company is 12.5 percent (net income of $101,000 divided by $804,000). If a firm issues both common and preferred stock, the computation of this ratio typically measures only the return to the common shareholders because they are considered to be the true owners of the company. Thus, dividends paid to preferred shareholders are subtracted from net income in the numerator when computing ROE because these dividends aren't available to common shareholders. Similarly, the denominator of this ratio includes only equity provided by common shareholders and retained earnings.

Another profitability ratio, called *earnings per share (EPS)*, indicates how much net income a firm earned per share of common stock outstanding. It is calculated by dividing net income minus preferred dividends by the average number of shares of common stock outstanding.

Exhibit 7.5 summarizes the ratios mentioned and describes a few other ratios as well. Interpreting ratios correctly isn't always easy. For one thing, there's no single "best" value for a specific ratio; whether a particular ratio value is good or bad depends, in part, on the industry. For example, grocery stores normally have high inventory turnover ratios, meaning that goods move through them quickly—a good thing, as few people want to buy bananas, bread, milk, or tomatoes that have been sitting in the store for several months! But it's not unusual for a furniture store or art gallery to have some expensive and distinctive pieces in stock for months before they are sold.

A comparison of a firm's ratios with the average ratios for other

asset management ratios Financial ratios that measure how effectively a firm is using its assets to generate revenues or cash.

financial leverage The use of debt in a firm's capital structure.

leverage ratios Ratios that measure the extent to which a firm relies on debt financing in its capital structure.

profitability ratios Ratios that measure the rate of return a firm is earning on various measures of investment.

Chapter 7 Accounting: Decision Making by the Numbers

Exhibit 7.5 Key Financial Ratios

RATIO	TYPE	WHAT IT MEASURES	HOW IT IS COMPUTED
CURRENT	Liquidity: measures ability to pay short-term liabilities as they come due.	Compares current assets (assets that will provide cash in the next year) to current liabilities (debts that will come due in the next year).	$\dfrac{Current\ Assets}{Current\ Liabilities}$
INVENTORY TURNOVER	Asset management: measures how effectively a firm is using its assets to generate revenue.	How quickly a firm sells its inventory to generate revenue.	$\dfrac{Cost\ of\ Goods\ Sold}{Average\ Inventory}$
AVERAGE COLLECTION PERIOD	Asset management: measures how effectively a firm is using its assets to generate revenue.	How long it takes for a firm to collect from customers who buy on credit.	$\dfrac{Accounts\ Receivable}{\left(\dfrac{Annual\ Credit\ Sales}{365}\right)}$
DEBT-TO-EQUITY	Leverage: measures the extent to which a firm relies on debt to meet its financing needs.	Compares the total amount of debt financing to the amount of equity (owner-provided) financing. A high ratio indicates that the firm is "highly leveraged."	$\dfrac{Total\ Debt}{Total\ Owner's\ Equity}$
DEBT-TO-ASSETS	Leverage: measures the extent to which a firm relies on debt to meet its financing needs.	Similar to debt-to-equity but compares debt to assets rather than equity. This is another way of measuring the degree of financial leverage, or debt, the firm is using.	$\dfrac{Total\ Debt}{Total\ Assets}$
RETURN ON EQUITY	Profitability: compares the amount of profit to some measure of resources invested.	Indicates earnings per dollar invested by the owners of the company. Because common shareholders are the true owners, preferred shareholders' dividends are deducted from net income before this ratio is computed.	$\dfrac{Net\ Income\ -\ Preferred\ Dividends}{Average\ Common\ Stock\ Equity}$
RETURN ON ASSETS	Profitability: compares the amount of profit to some measure of resources invested.	Indicates the amount of profit earned on each dollar the firm has invested in assets.	$\dfrac{Net\ Income}{Average\ Total\ Assets}$
EARNINGS PER SHARE	Profitability: compares the amount of profit to some measure of resources invested.	Measures the net income per share of common stock outstanding.	$\dfrac{Net\ Income\ -\ Preferred\ Dividend}{Average\ Number\ of\ Common\ Shares\ Outstanding}$

firms in the same industry (or with the ratios for a firm recognized as an industry leader) can help determine whether they're in the right ballpark. But even these comparisons can be misleading if they aren't carefully interpreted. The accounting profession allows firms some flexibility in such matters as how they measure inventory and cost of goods sold and how they depreciate their assets. Because of this flexibility, two firms in the *same* industry with very similar real-world performance could report very different values for profitability or asset management ratios simply because they used different—but equally acceptable—accounting methods to develop their statements.

Comstock/Jupiterimages

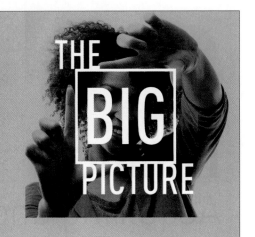

Accounting provides vital information to both the internal and external stakeholders of a firm. The balance sheet, income statement, and statement of cash flow—the main outputs of financial accounting—help external stakeholders, such as owners and creditors, evaluate the financial performance of a firm. Managerial accounting helps managers throughout an organization make better decisions by providing them with relevant and timely information about the costs and benefits of the choices they have to make. Clearly, a basic knowledge of accounting concepts will help you succeed in just about any career path you choose.

careers in accounting: Company Accountant

Responsible for daily cash reconciliation, preparation of monthly financial reports, including balance sheets and income statements, preparing spreadsheets and financial forecasts and analyses for the accounting manager and/or controller, and ensuring compliance with International Financial Reporting Standards. The ideal candidate has a bachelor's or master's degree in accounting, technical accounting knowledge, strong oral and written communication skills, a problem-solving attitude, and the ability to prioritize tasks and work under deadlines, pays close attention to detail, and is eligible to qualify for the Chartered Professional Accountants (CPA) designation or is CPA certified.

STUDY TOOLS 7

IN THE BOOK, YOU CAN:

☐ Rip out the Chapter Review card at the back of the book to have a summary of the chapter and key terms handy.

ONLINE AT NELSON.COM/STUDENT YOU CAN:

☐ Work through key concepts with a Guided Learning Question.

☐ Prepare for tests with quizzes.

☐ Review the key terms with Flash Cards (online or printer-ready).

☐ Explore practical examples of chapter concepts with Connect a Concept exercises.

8

Finance:
Acquiring and Using Funds to Maximize Value

LEARNING OBJECTIVES
After studying this chapter, you will be able to...

8-1 Identify the goal of financial management and explain the issues financial managers confront as they seek to achieve this goal

8-2 Explain how the budget process can help managers plan, motivate, and evaluate their organization's performance

8-3 Evaluate the major sources of funds available to meet a firm's short-term and long-term financial needs

8-4 Identify the key issues involved in determining a firm's capital structure

8-5 Describe how financial managers acquire and manage current assets

8-6 Explain how financial managers evaluate capital budgeting proposals to identify the best long-term investment options for their company

After you finish this chapter, go to page 133 for STUDY TOOLS

8-1 What Motivates Financial Decisions?

Financial capital refers to the funds a firm uses to acquire its assets and finance its operations. Firms use some of their capital to meet short-term obligations, such as paying bills from suppliers, meeting payroll, repaying loans from banks, and paying taxes owed to the government. Other funds are used to finance major long-term investments, such as the purchase of a plant and equipment or the launch of a new product line. And, of course, firms need some funds to pay a return to the owners for their investment in the company.

Companies also have a variety of ways to acquire the financial capital they need: direct contributions by owners, reinvestment of earnings, loans from banks, credit provided by suppliers, and (for corporations) newly issued stocks or bonds. This isn't a complete list by any means—in fact, we'll discuss additional sources later in the chapter—but you get the idea: firms often have several ways to raise money.

In a nutshell, **finance** is the functional area of business that is responsible for finding, among all these alternatives, the best sources of funds and the best ways to use them. But which sources and uses are "best" depends on the goals of the financial managers. Historically, the most widely accepted goal of financial management has been to *maximize the value of the firm to its owners*. For corporations with publicly traded stock, this translates into finding the sources and uses of financial capital that will maximize the market price of the company's common stock.

Financial managers emphasize the goal of maximizing the market price of stock because they have a legal and ethical obligation (called a *fiduciary duty*) to make decisions consistent with the financial interests of their firm's owners. After all, the shareholders are the ones with their money at risk. The managers who work for the company have a fiduciary responsibility to act in the best interests of the shareholders, and that means increasing the value of their investment in the company.

Another reason for emphasizing shareholder wealth is more pragmatic. Firms that fail to create shareholder wealth are unlikely to be viewed as attractive investments. So, to continue attracting the financial capital needed to achieve its other goals, a firm must provide value to its shareholders.

But finding the mix of sources and uses of funds that maximize shareholder value isn't a simple process. Let's

> **financial capital** The funds a firm uses to acquire its assets and finance its operations.
>
> **finance** The functional area of business that is concerned with finding the best sources and uses of financial capital.

> **Money is like a sixth sense—and you can't make use of the other five without it.**
> **William Somerset Maugham,**
> **English playwright, novelist,**
> **and short story writer**

look at two major issues that confront financial managers as they seek to achieve their primary goal.

8-1a Shareholder Value and Social Responsibility: Does Good Behaviour Pay Off?

The emphasis that financial managers place on maximizing shareholder value may seem to conflict with the modern view that a socially responsible firm has an obligation to respect the needs of *all* stakeholders—not just its owners, but also its employees, customers, creditors, suppliers, and even society as a whole. The good news is that being socially responsible *can* be (and often is) a good strategy for also achieving the goal of shareholder wealth maximization—especially if managers take a *long-term* perspective.

When a company respects the needs of customers by providing high-quality goods and services at competitive prices, and when it listens and responds fairly to their concerns, those customers are more likely to keep coming back—and to recommend the company to friends and relatives. Similarly, when a firm provides its employees with a good work environment, those employees are likely to have better morale and greater loyalty, resulting in higher

productivity and lower employee turnover. And when a company supports its local community through corporate philanthropy or cause-related marketing, the resulting goodwill may boost sales and create a more favourable business climate. All of these outcomes suggest that a commitment to meeting social responsibilities can contribute to a more profitable company and an increase in shareholder value.[1]

But things aren't always that simple. Being socially responsible requires a long-term commitment to the needs of many different stakeholders. Unfortunately, the incentives provided to top executives (in the form of raises, bonuses, and other perks) are often tied to their firm's *short-term* performance. In such cases, some managers focus on policies that make their firm's stock price rise in the short run but that are unsustainable over the long haul. And when managers fix their attention on raising the market price of the company's stock in the next year (or next quarter), concerns about social responsibility sometimes get lost in the shuffle.

It is also worth noting that responding to the needs of all stakeholders isn't always a simple and straightforward task. Diverse stakeholder groups can have very different goals, and finding the right balance among the competing interests of these groups can be difficult. For example, a

Chapter 8 Finance: Acquiring and Using Funds to Maximize Value firm's managers might believe they can increase profits (and the value of its stock) by shutting down a plant in Canada and outsourcing the work to China. While this might benefit shareholders, it would clearly be detrimental to its Canadian workforce and the community in which that current plant is located. When conflicts arise between the long-term interests of owners and those of other stakeholders, financial managers generally adopt the policies they believe are most consistent with the interests of ownership.

8-1b Risk and Return: A Fundamental Tradeoff in Financial Management

One of the most important lessons in financial management is that there is a tradeoff between risk and return. In financial management, **risk** refers to the degree of uncertainty about the actual outcome of a decision. The **risk-return tradeoff** suggests that sources and uses of funds that offer the potential for high rates of return tend to be more risky than sources and uses of funds that offer lower returns.

Financial managers want to earn an attractive rate of return for shareholders. But they also must realize that the higher the expected return they seek, the more they expose their company to risk.

8-2 Budgeting: Planning for Accountability

Managerial accounting provides much of the information used to develop budgets. **Budgeting** is a management tool that explicitly shows how firms will acquire and use the resources it needs to achieve its goals over a specific time period. The budgetary process facilitates planning by requiring managers to translate goals into measurable quantities and to identify the specific resources needed to achieve these goals. But budgeting offers other advantages as well. If done well, budgeting does the following:

- It helps managers clearly specify how they intend to achieve the goals they set during the planning process. This should lead to a better understanding of how the organization's limited resources will be allocated.

risk The degree of uncertainty regarding the outcome of a decision.

risk-return tradeoff The observation that financial opportunities that offer high rates of return are generally riskier than opportunities that offer lower rates of return.

budgeting A management tool that explicitly shows how firms will acquire and use the resources needed to achieve its goals over a specific time period.

- It encourages communication and coordination among managers and employees in various departments within the organization. For example, the budget process can give middle and first-line managers and employees an opportunity to provide top managers with important feedback about the challenges of their specialized areas and the resources they need to meet those challenges. But, as we will explain in the next section, the extent to which this advantage is realized depends on the specific approach used in the budgeting process.

- It serves as a motivational tool. Good budgets clearly identify goals *and* demonstrate a plan of action for acquiring the resources needed to achieve them. Employees tend to be more highly motivated when they understand the goals their managers expect them to accomplish and when they view these goals as ambitious but achievable.

- It helps managers to evaluate progress and performance. Managers can compare actual performance to budgetary figures to determine whether various departments and functional areas are making adequate progress towards achieving their organization's goals. If actual performance falls short of budgetary goals, managers know to look for reasons and take corrective action.

8-2a Preparing the Budget: Top Down or Bottom Up?

There are two broad approaches to budget preparation. In some organizations, top management prepares the budget with little or no input from middle and supervisory managers—a process known as *top-down budgeting*. Supporters of this approach point out that top management knows the long-term strategic needs of the company and is in a better position to see the big picture when making budget decisions.

The other approach to budget development is called *bottom-up* or *participatory budgeting*. Organizations that use a participatory process allow middle and supervisory managers to actively participate in the creation of the budget. Proponents of this approach maintain that it has two major advantages. First, lower level managers are likely to know more about the issues and challenges facing their departments—and the resources it will take to address them—than top management. Second, middle and first-line managers are likely to be more highly motivated to achieve budgetary goals when they have a say in how those goals are developed. On the negative side, the bottom-up approach is more time-consuming and resource-intensive to carry out than the top-down approach. Also, some middle managers may be tempted to overstate their needs or set low budget goals in order to make their jobs easier—an outcome known as *budgetary slack*.[2] Despite these drawbacks, the participatory approach currently is more common than the top-down process.

8-2b Developing the Key Budget Components: One Step at a Time

The budgeting process actually involves the preparation of several different types of budget documents. But all of these individual budgets can be classified into two broad categories: operating budgets and financial budgets.

Operating budgets are budgets that identify projected sales and production goals and the various costs the firm will incur in order to meet these goals. These budgets are developed in a specific order, with the information from earlier budgets used in the preparation of later budgets.

The preparation of operating budgets begins with the development of a *sales budget* that provides quarterly estimates of the number of units of each product the firm expects to sell, the selling price, and the total dollar value of expected sales. The sales budget must be created first because the production and cost figures that go into other operating budgets depend directly or indirectly on the level of sales. Once the sales budget is complete, the budgeted sales level can be used to develop the production, administrative expenses, and selling expenses budgets. Once the production budget is completed, the information it contains is used to prepare budgets for direct labour costs, direct materials costs, and manufacturing overhead. The final stage in the preparation of operating budgets is the creation of a *budgeted income statement*.

Financial budgets focus on the firm's financial goals and identify the resources needed to achieve these goals. The two main financial budget documents are the *cash budget* and the *capital expenditure budget*. The cash budget identifies short-term fluctuations in cash flows, which helps managers identify times when the firm might face cash flow problems—or when it might have extra cash that it could invest. The capital expenditure budget identifies the firm's planned investments in major fixed assets and long-term projects. The information from these two financial budgets and the budgeted income statement are combined to construct the *budgeted balance sheet*.

The firm's **master budget** organizes the operating and financial budgets into a unified whole, representing the firm's overall plan of action for a specified time period. In other words, the master budget shows how all of the pieces fit together to form a complete picture. Exhibit 8.1 shows all of the budget documents that are included in a

operating budgets Budgets that communicate an organization's sales and production goals and the resources needed to achieve these goals.

financial budgets Budgets that focus on the firm's financial goals and identify the resources needed to achieve these goals.

master budget Presentation of an organization's operational and financial budgets that represents the firm's overall plan of action for a specified time period.

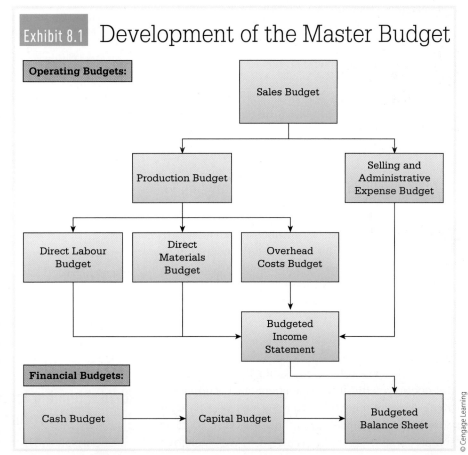

Exhibit 8.1 Development of the Master Budget

Operating Budgets:
- Sales Budget
- Production Budget
- Selling and Administrative Expense Budget
- Direct Labour Budget
- Direct Materials Budget
- Overhead Costs Budget
- Budgeted Income Statement

Financial Budgets:
- Cash Budget
- Capital Budget
- Budgeted Balance Sheet

© Cengage Learning

The housing boom that occurred in the United States between 2003 and 2007 seemed like a win–win situation for everyone. The surge in housing construction created jobs and stimulated economic growth. Millions of Americans who had never owned a home found themselves moving into their dream house. Even Americans who already owned homes saw the value of their houses soar. And lenders in the mortgage market made huge profits.

But in reality, the gains in the United States housing market were the result of an unsustainable bubble, arising in part because of the shortsighted—and sometimes unethical—behaviour of mortgage brokers who arranged housing loans and the lenders who provided the funds. These brokers and lenders increasingly tapped what the US financial community called the subprime mortgage market, consisting of borrowers who lacked the financial capacity to qualify for conventional loans. To make these loans *appear* affordable, brokers pushed variable-rate mortgages with very low initial rates. They knew that subprime borrowers would be unable to make the higher payments if interest rates rose, but they often neglected to explain this fact to the borrowers. They also pushed many unsophisticated borrowers into mortgage agreements that generated high fees, which they folded into the mortgage. The result: more income for the brokers and lenders and higher payments for the borrower.

Such policies increased the profits of brokers and lenders at first, but were unsustainable in the long run. When interest rates on variable-rate mortgages increased, a huge number of subprime borrowers defaulted on their loans. In many areas, the surge in foreclosures contributed to a steep decline in housing prices. Mortgage lending collapsed, and many of the most aggressive firms in the subprime market were wiped out.

Many observers believe that more ethical mortgage lending practices could have resulted in a better outcome. As Nobel Prize–winning economist Joseph Stiglitz put it: "Had the designers of these mortgages focused on the ends—what we actually wanted from our mortgage market—rather than how to maximize *their* revenues, then they might have devised products that *permanently* increased homeownership. They could have 'done well by doing good.'"[3]

What do YOU think?

- What ethical responsibilities do mortgage brokers and lenders have to their borrowers?
- What responsibility did subprime borrowers have to "read the fine print" in their loan agreements?
- How do the lessons of the mortgage crisis illustrate the need to focus on the long-term consequences of financial decisions?
- What can Canadian mortgage lenders do to prevent a similar problem happening here?

---

typical master budget. The arrows indicate the order in which the budgets are developed, starting with the sales budget and ending with the budgeted balance sheet.

8-2c Being Flexible: Clearing Up Problems with Static

The budget process, as we've described it so far, results in a *static* budget, meaning that it is based on a single assumed level of sales. Static budgets are excellent tools for planning, but they have weaknesses when they are used to measure progress, evaluate performance, and identify problem areas that need correcting.

The problem with a static budget is that real-world sales can (and often do) vary considerably from their forecasted value—often for reasons that aren't under the control of the firm's management. For example, the collapse of the world economy into a deep recession, beginning in late 2007, caused sales to drop sharply and unexpectedly even at many well-managed companies.

As we mentioned earlier, many cost figures in budgets are based on the level of sales specified in the sales budget. When actual sales differ significantly from the sales volume assumed in a static budget, all of these related budget figures will be erroneous. Using these inaccurate figures to evaluate real-world performance is likely to result in very poor assessments.

One common way managerial accountants avoid this problem is by developing a *flexible budget* for control purposes. A flexible budget is one that isn't based on a single assumed level of sales. Instead, it is developed over a *range* of possible sales levels, for the purpose of showing the appropriate budgeted level of costs for each different level of sales. This flexibility enables managers to make more meaningful comparisons between actual costs and budgeted costs.

8-2d Planning Tools: Creating a Road Map for the Future

Financial planning is an important part of the firm's overall planning process. Assuming that the overall planning

process has established appropriate goals and objectives for the firm, financial planning must answer the following questions:

- What specific assets must the firm obtain in order to achieve its goals?

- How much additional financing will the firm need to acquire these assets?

- How much financing will the firm be able to generate internally (through additional earnings), and how much must it obtain from external sources?

- When will it need to acquire external financing?

- What is the best way to raise these funds?

The planning process involves input from a variety of areas. Besides seeking input from managers in various functional areas of their business, financial managers usually work closely with the firm's accountants during the planning process.

8-2e Basic Planning Tools: Budgeted Financial Statements and the Cash Budget

The budgeting process provides financial managers with much of the information they need for financial planning. The **budgeted income statement** and **budgeted balance sheet** are two key financial planning tools. Also called *pro forma financial statements*, they provide a framework for analyzing the impact of the firm's plans on the financing needs of the company.

- The budgeted income statement uses information from the sales budget and various cost budgets (as well as other assumptions) to develop a forecast of net income for the planning period. This can help the firm

evaluate how much internal financing (funds generated by earnings) will be available.

- The budgeted balance sheet forecasts the types and amounts of assets a firm will need to implement its plans. It also helps financial managers determine the amount of additional financing (liabilities and owners' equity) the firm must arrange in order to acquire those assets.

The **cash budget** is another important financial planning tool. Cash budgets normally cover a one-year period and show projected cash inflows and outflows for each month. Financial managers use cash budgets to get a better understanding of the *timing* of cash flows within the planning period. This is important because most firms experience uneven inflows and outflows of cash over the course of a year, which can lead to cash shortages and cash surpluses. Projecting cash flows helps financial managers determine when the firm is likely to need additional funds to meet short-term cash shortages, and when surpluses of cash will be available to pay off loans or to invest in other assets.

Even firms with growing sales can experience cash flow problems, especially if many of their customers buy on credit. In order to achieve higher sales levels, growing firms must hire more labour and buy more supplies. The firm may have to pay for these additional inputs *before* its credit customers pay their bills, leading to a temporary cash crunch.

Exhibit 8.2 illustrates this type of situation by presenting a partial cash budget for a hypothetical firm called Oze-Moore. The cash budget shows that, despite its increasing sales, Oze-Moore will have cash shortages in March and April. Knowing this in advance gives financial managers time to find the best sources of short-term financing to cover these shortages. The cash budget also shows that Oze-Moore will experience a big cash surplus in May as the customers start paying for the purchases they made in March and April. Knowing this ahead of time helps managers forecast when they will be able to repay the loans they took out to cover their previous cash shortages. It also gives them time to evaluate short-term interest-earning investments they could make to temporarily "park" their surplus cash.

budgeted income statement A projection showing how a firm's budgeted sales and costs will affect expected net income (also called a pro forma income statement).

budgeted balance sheet A projected financial statement that forecasts the types and amounts of assets a firm will need to implement its future plans and how the firm will finance those assets (also called a pro forma balance sheet).

cash budget A detailed forecast of future cash flows that helps financial managers identify when their firm is likely to experience temporary shortages or surpluses of cash.

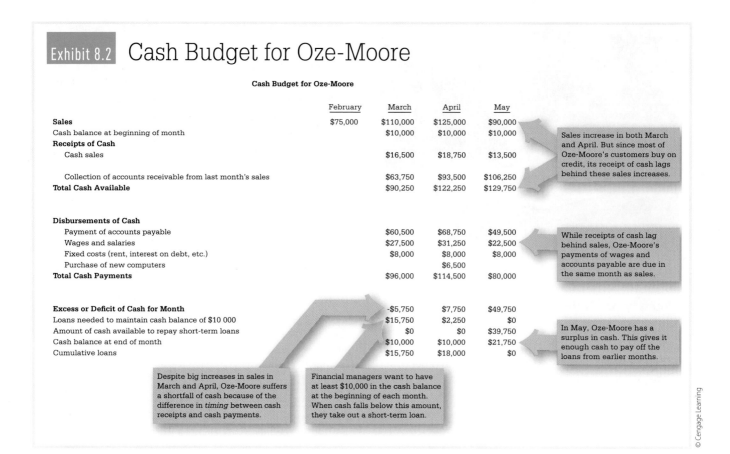

Exhibit 8.2 Cash Budget for Oze-Moore

Cash Budget for Oze-Moore

	February	March	April	May
Sales	$75,000	$110,000	$125,000	$90,000
Cash balance at beginning of month		$10,000	$10,000	$10,000
Receipts of Cash				
Cash sales		$16,500	$18,750	$13,500
Collection of accounts receivable from last month's sales		$63,750	$93,500	$106,250
Total Cash Available		$90,250	$122,250	$129,750
Disbursements of Cash				
Payment of accounts payable		$60,500	$68,750	$49,500
Wages and salaries		$27,500	$31,250	$22,500
Fixed costs (rent, interest on debt, etc.)		$8,000	$8,000	$8,000
Purchase of new computers			$6,500	
Total Cash Payments		$96,000	$114,500	$80,000
Excess or Deficit of Cash for Month		-$5,750	$7,750	$49,750
Loans needed to maintain cash balance of $10 000		$15,750	$2,250	$0
Amount of cash available to repay short-term loans		$0	$0	$39,750
Cash balance at end of month		$10,000	$10,000	$21,750
Cumulative loans		$15,750	$18,000	$0

Sales increase in both March and April. But since most of Oze-Moore's customers buy on credit, its receipt of cash lags behind these sales increases.

While receipts of cash lag behind sales, Oze-Moore's payments of wages and accounts payable are due in the same month as sales.

In May, Oze-Moore has a surplus in cash. This gives it enough cash to pay off the loans from earlier months.

Despite big increases in sales in March and April, Oze-Moore suffers a shortfall of cash because of the difference in *timing* between cash receipts and cash payments.

Financial managers want to have at least $10,000 in the cash balance at the beginning of each month. When cash falls below this amount, they take out a short-term loan.

8-3 Finding Funds: What Are the Options?

Once financial managers have identified the amount of financial capital needed to carry out their firm's plans, the next step is to determine which sources of funds to tap. The most appropriate sources of funds for a business depend on several factors. One of the most important considerations is the firm's stage of development. Start-up firms face different challenges and have different needs than more established firms. Another factor is the reason the funds are needed. Funds used to meet short-term needs, such as meeting payroll, paying suppliers, or paying taxes, typically come from different sources than funds used to finance major investments in plant, property, and equipment.

The financing options available to new firms are generally much more limited than those available to more mature firms with an established track record. In fact, for startup firms the main source of funds is likely to be the personal wealth of the owner (or owners), supplemented by loans from relatives and friends. Given how risky new business ventures are, banks and other established lenders often hesitate to make loans to new, unproven companies. As a firm grows and becomes more established, it typically is able to obtain financing from other sources.

Some startups with the potential for generating rapid growth may be able to attract funds from wealthy individuals, or from venture capital firms. Venture capitalists typically invest in risky opportunities that offer the possibility of high rates of return and typically provide funds in exchange for a share of ownership.

8-3a Sources of Short-Term Financing: Meeting Needs for Cash

Firms that have survived the startup phase of the business life cycle often have several sources of short-term financing. Let's take a look at some of the most common options.

Trade Credit One of the most important sources of short-term financing for many firms is **trade credit**, which arises when suppliers ship materials, parts, or goods to a firm without requiring payment at the time of delivery. By allowing the firms to "buy now, pay later," they help the firm conserve its existing cash and thereby avoiding having to acquire funds from other sources.

trade credit Spontaneous financing granted by sellers when they deliver goods and services to customers without requiring immediate payment.

Is Donating to Charity Socially Responsible or Good for Business?

According to Nobel Prize–winning economist Milton Friedman, the only social responsibility organizations have is satisfying company shareholders by maximizing profits, the company's stock price, and the value of the firm.

If that's the case, then why do companies like Tim Hortons, McDonald's, and Unilever all donate time and money to worthy causes each year? Shouldn't these companies reinvest those funds back into the business (i.e., retained earnings) or distribute profits as dividends to shareholders? Yet each of these companies has chosen to support at least one charity.

Tim Hortons has the Tim Hortons Children's Foundation and Timbit Hockey program. The Tim Hortons Children's Foundation sponsors camp programs for children who would otherwise not be able to attend summer or winter camp, and the Timbit Hockey program provides support to children's sport teams. McDonald's also supports the Ronald McDonald House Charities. The Ronald McDonald House Charities provide accommodation to families with sick children while they are in hospital.

Unilever, producers of the Dove line of products, wants to change the way young women view themselves in their Campaign for Real Beauty. That campaign uses several techniques to broaden the definition of beauty and promote self-esteem.

Milton Friedman would say that while companies like Tim Hortons, McDonald's and Unilever make contributions that look like social responsibility, they're really just a means to maximize profits by enhancing the company's reputation. So are these companies "doing good" or are they trying to increase profits? Which comes first, profits or social responsibility? What do you think?[4]

Sources: J. Mackey, M. Friedman, and T. Rodger, "Rethinking the Social Responsibility of Business," *Reason*, October 1, 2005; The Dove Campaign for Real Beauty website; Tim Hortons company website; McDonald's company website,.

In most cases, the terms of trade credit are presented on the invoice the supplier includes with the shipment. For example, the invoice might list the terms as 2/10 net 30. The "net 30" indicates that the supplier allows the buyer 30 days before payment is due. The "2/10" tells the buyer that the supplier is offering a 2 percent discount off the invoice price if the buyer pays within 10 days.

At first glance, the 2 percent discount in our example may not seem like a big deal. But failing to take the discount can be very costly. Consider the terms we mentioned above: 2/10, net 30. If the firm fails to pay within 10 days, it loses the discount and must pay the full amount

20 days later. Paying 2 percent more for the use of funds for only 20 days is equivalent to an *annual* finance charge of over 37 percent![5]

Suppliers will grant trade credit only after they've evaluated the creditworthiness of the firm. But once they've granted this credit to a company, they generally continue offering it as long as the firm satisfies the terms of the credit arrangements. Trade credit is sometimes called **spontaneous financing** because it is granted when the company places its orders without requiring any additional paperwork or special arrangements. The level of trade credit automatically adjusts as business conditions change and the company places larger or smaller orders with its suppliers.

Although firms of all sizes use this type of financing, trade credit is a particularly important source of financing for small businesses. One study found that about 60 percent of small firms rely on trade credit as a major source of short-term financial capital.[6]

Factoring The money that customers owe a firm when they buy on credit shows up in accounts receivable on the company's balance sheet. A **factor** buys the accounts receivables of other firms. The factor makes a profit by purchasing the receivables at a discount and collecting the full amount from the firm's customers.

Although firms that use factors don't receive the full amount their customers owe, factoring offers some definite advantages. Instead of having to wait for customers to pay, the firm gets its money almost immediately. Also, since the factor is responsible for collection efforts, the firm using the factor may be able to save money by eliminating its own collection department. Finally, the factor typically assumes the risk for bad debts on any receivables it buys. (However, factors typically perform a careful evaluation of the quality of accounts receivable before they buy them and may refuse to buy receivables that are high risk.)

Short-Term Bank Loans Banks are another common source of short-term business financing. Short-term bank loans are usually due in 30 to 90 days, although they can be up to a year in length. When a firm negotiates a loan with a bank, it signs a *promissory note*, which specifies the length of the loan, the rate of interest the firm must pay, and other terms and conditions of the loan. Banks sometimes require firms to pledge collateral, such as inventories or accounts receivable, to back the loan. That way, if the borrower fails

spontaneous financing Financing that arises during the natural course of business without the need for special arrangements.

factor A company that provides short-term financing to firms by purchasing their accounts receivables at a discount.

to make the required payments, the bank has a claim on specific assets that can be used to pay off the amount due.

Rather than going through the hassle of negotiating a separate loan each time they need more funds, many firms work out arrangements with their bankers to obtain preapproval so that they can draw on funds as needed. One way they do this is by establishing a **line of credit**. Under this arrangement, a bank agrees to provide the firm with funds up to some specified limit, as long as the borrower's credit situation doesn't deteriorate.

A **revolving credit agreement** is similar to a line of credit, except that the bank makes a formal, legally binding commitment to provide the agreed-upon funds. A revolving credit agreement is like a *guaranteed* line of credit. In exchange for the binding commitment to provide the funds, the bank requires the borrowing firm to pay a commitment fee based on the *unused* amount of funds. Thus, under the terms of a revolving credit agreement, the firm will pay interest on any funds it borrows and a commitment fee on any funds it does not borrow. The commitment fee is lower than the interest on the borrowed funds, but it can amount to a fairly hefty charge if the firm has a large unused balance.

Commercial Paper Well-established corporations have some additional sources of short-term financial capital. For instance, many large corporations with strong credit ratings issue **commercial paper**, which consists of short-term promissory notes (IOUs). Historically, commercial paper issued by corporations has been unsecured—meaning it isn't backed by a pledge of collateral. Because it is normally unsecured, commercial paper is only offered by firms with excellent credit ratings; firms with less-than-stellar financial reputations that try to issue unsecured commercial paper are unlikely to find buyers. In recent years, a new class of commercial paper has emerged, called *asset-backed commercial paper*, which, as its name implies, is backed by some form of collateral.

line of credit A financial arrangement between a firm and a bank in which the bank preapproves credit up to a specified limit, provided that the firm maintains an acceptable credit rating.

revolving credit agreement A guaranteed line of credit in which a bank makes a binding commitment to provide a business with funds up to a specified credit limit at any time during the term of the agreement.

commercial paper Short-term (and usually unsecured) promissory notes issued by large corporations.

Commercial paper can be issued for up to 270 days, but most firms typically issue it for much shorter periods—typically 30 days, but sometimes for as little as two days. One key reason commercial paper is popular with companies is that it typically carries a lower interest rate than banks charge on short-term loans. By far the biggest issuers of commercial paper are financial institutions, but other large corporations also use this form of financing.

Why use commercial paper? According to one source, "The commercial paper market works like a credit card for big companies. Some days they have money, and some days they do not. So if they need money Tuesday, but will have money Friday, they'll go to the commercial paper market and borrow some money. Then on Friday they will pay back the money, plus interest."[7]

8-3b Sources of Long-Term Funds: Providing a Strong Financial Base

The sources of financial capital we've looked at so far have been appropriate for dealing with cash needs that arise from short-term fluctuations in cash flows. But financial managers typically seek more permanent funding to finance major investments and provide a secure financial base for their company. Let's take a look at some of the more common sources of long-term funds.

Direct Investments from Owners One key source of long-term funds for a firm is the money the owners themselves invest in their company. For corporations, this occurs when it sells *newly issued* stock—and it's important to realize that the *only* time the corporation receives financial capital from the sale of its stock is when it is initially issued. If Google issued new shares of stock that you bought, the funds would go to Google. But once

you own Google's stock, if you decide to sell your shares to another investor, Google gets nothing.

Another way firms can meet long-term financial needs is by reinvesting their earnings. The profits that a firm reinvests are called **retained earnings**. This source isn't a pool of cash; it simply reflects the share of the firm's earnings used to finance the purchase of assets, pay off liabilities, and reinvest in the business. If you want to know how much cash a firm has, check the figure in the cash account at the top of its balance sheet. You'll typically find that the value in the firm's cash account is quite different from the amount listed as the retained earnings! For example, in 2014, Google had $75.7 billion in retained earnings compared to $18.3 billion in cash and cash equivalents.[8]

Retained earnings are a major source of long-term capital for many corporations, but the extent to which they are used depends on the state of the economy. When the economy is booming and profits are high, retained earnings tend to soar. But when the economy slides into a recession, most corporations find they have few earnings to reinvest.

The decision to retain earnings involves a tradeoff because firms have another way to use their earnings: they can pay out some or all of their profits to their owners by declaring a dividend. You might think that shareholders would be unhappy with a firm that retained most of its earnings, since that would mean receiving a smaller dividend. But many shareholders actually prefer their companies to reinvest earnings—at least if management invests them wisely—because doing so can help finance their firm's growth. And a growing, more profitable firm usually translates into an increase in the market price of the firm's stock.

Billionaire Warren Buffet's company, Berkshire Hathaway, has never paid dividends, choosing to reinvest all of its substantial profits. This strategy paid off handsomely for shareholders. During the ten-year period between March 24, 2003, and March 24, 2013, Berkshire's stock soared from $68,000 to $153,741 per share.[9] By May 2015 the price had reached $217,000.[10] Even though it paid them no dividend, you can bet that most of Berkshire's shareholders were pleased with the capital gains that resulted from this strategy.

Long-Term Debt Credit In addition to contributions from owners, firms can raise long-term funds by borrowing from banks and other lenders or by issuing bonds.

Term Loans There are many different types of long-term loans, but the most typical arrangement—sometimes simply called a *term loan*—calls for a regular schedule of fixed payments sufficient to ensure that the

principal (the amount initially borrowed) and interest are repaid by the end of the loan's term.

Lenders often impose requirements on long-term loans to ensure repayment. Most lenders require that the loans be backed by a pledge of some type of collateral. Banks and other lenders also often include *covenants* in their loan agreements. A **covenant** is a requirement a lender imposes on the borrower as a condition of the loan. One common covenant requires the borrower to carry a specified amount of liability insurance. Another requires the borrower to agree not to borrow any *additional* funds until the current loan is paid off. Covenants sometimes even restrict the size of bonuses or pay raises the firm can grant to employees. The purpose of covenants is to protect creditors by preventing the borrower from pursuing policies that might undermine its ability to repay the loan. While covenants are great for lenders, borrowers often view them as highly restrictive.[11]

Corporate Bonds Rather than borrow from banks or other lenders, corporations sometimes issue their own formal IOUs, called *corporate bonds*, which they sell to investors. Bonds often have due dates (maturities) of ten or more years after issuance. Like corporate stock, bonds are marketable, meaning that bondholders can sell them to other investors before they mature. But it is important to realize that unlike shares of stock, which represent ownership in a corporation, bonds are certificates of debt.

> When you combine ignorance and leverage, you get some pretty interesting results.
>
> —Warren Buffet

8-4 Leverage and Capital Structure: How Much Debt Is Too Much Debt?

Most firms use a combination of **equity** and **debt financing** to acquire needed assets and to finance their operations. Owners provide equity financing, while creditors (lenders) provide debt financing. Thus, when a company issues and sells new stock or uses retained earnings to meet its financial needs, it is using equity financing. But when it takes out a bank loan, or issues and sells corporate bonds, it is relying on debt financing.

retained earnings The part of a firm's net income it reinvests.

covenant A restriction that lenders impose on borrowers as a condition of providing long-term debt financing.

equity financing Funds provided by the owners of a company.

debt financing Funds provided by lenders (creditors).

Both equity and debt financing have advantages and drawbacks. A firm's **capital structure** refers to the extent to which it relies on various forms of debt and equity to satisfy its financing needs. To simplify our discussion, we'll focus mainly on the capital structure of corporations, but many of the basic principles apply to other forms of ownership.

8-4a Pros and Cons of Debt Financing

When a firm borrows funds, it enters into a contractual agreement with the lender. This arrangement creates a *legally binding* requirement to repay the money borrowed (called the principal) *plus interest*. These payments take precedence over any payments to owners. Lenders often require the firm to pledge collateral, such as real estate, financial securities, or equipment, to back the loan. Should the firm be unable to make the required payments, the lenders can use this collateral to recover what they are owed.

Debt financing offers some advantages to firms. For instance, the interest payments a firm makes on debt are a tax-deductible expense. So the Government of Canada (in the form of Revenue Canada) subsidizes the interest payments. For example, if the corporation's tax rate is 30 percent, then each dollar of interest expense reduces the firm's taxes by $.30—meaning the true cost to the firm of each dollar of interest is only $.70.

Another advantage of debt is that it enables the firm to acquire additional funds without requiring existing shareholders to invest more of their own money or the sale of shares to new investors (which would dilute the ownership of existing owners). Moreover, if the firm invests the borrowed funds profitably, the use of debt can substantially improve the return on equity to the shareholders. We'll illustrate this result in our discussion of financial leverage.

One obvious disadvantage of debt is the requirement to make fixed payments. This can create real problems when the firm finds itself in an unexpectedly tight financial situation. In bad times, required interest payments can eat up most (or all) of the earnings, leaving little or no return to the firm's owners. And if the firm is unable to meet these payments, its creditors can force it into bankruptcy.

As we mentioned earlier, another disadvantage of debt financing is that creditors often impose covenants on the borrower. These covenants can hamper the firm's flexibility and may result in unintended problems. For example, a covenant that restricts bonuses and pay raises to employees may undermine the morale of key workers and tempt them to seek employment elsewhere. Similarly, restrictions on dividends or on the ability of the firm to borrow additional funds may make it difficult for the firm to raise more money.

capital structure The mix of equity and debt financing a firm uses to meet its permanent financing needs.

8-4b Pros and Cons of Equity Financing

For corporations, equity financing comes from two major sources: retained earnings and money directly invested by shareholders who purchase newly issued stock. Equity financing is more flexible and less risky than debt financing. Unlike debt, equity imposes no required payments. A firm can skip dividend payments to shareholders without having to worry that it will be pushed into bankruptcy. And a firm doesn't have to agree to burdensome covenants in order to acquire equity funds.

On the other hand, equity financing doesn't yield the same tax benefits as debt financing. In addition, existing owners may not want a firm to issue more shares, since doing so may dilute their share of ownership. Finally, a company that relies mainly on equity financing forgoes the opportunity to use financial leverage. But as we've already noted, leverage can be a two-edged sword. We'll illustrate the risks and rewards of leverage in our next section.

8-4c Financial Leverage: Using Debt to Magnify Gains (and Losses)

Firms that rely on a lot of debt in their capital structure are said to be *highly leveraged*. The main advantage of financial leverage is that it magnifies the return on the shareholders'

Most firms use equity financing, from the business owners, and debt financing, from lenders, to acquire the capital needed to finance operations and purchase key assets.

Konstantin Chagin/Shutterstock.com

investment when times are good. Its main disadvantage is that it also reduces the financial return to shareholders when times are bad.

Let's illustrate both the advantages and disadvantages of financial leverage with a simple example. Exhibit 8.3 shows the revenues, expenses, and earnings that two firms—Eck-Witty Corporation and Oze-Moore International—would experience for two different levels of sales, one representing a strong year and the other a weak year. To make the impact of leverage easy to see, we'll assume that Eck-Witty and Oze-Moore are *identical* in all respects *except* their capital structure. In particular, our example assumes that the two companies have the same amount of assets and experienced exactly the same *earnings before interest and taxes* (abbreviated as EBIT). Thus, any differences in the net income of these firms will result from differences in their use of debt and equity financing. We'll use return on equity (ROE) to measure the financial return each firm offers its shareholders. (See Chapter 7 if you need a reminder about how to interpret or compute this ratio.)

Note that *both* firms have a total of $1 million in assets, but they've financed the purchase of their assets in very different ways. Eck-Witty used only common stock and retained earnings in its capital structure, so it has $1 million in equity financing and no debt. Oze-Moore's capital structure consists of $200,000 in owners' equity and $800,000 in debt, so it is highly leveraged. The interest rate on its debt is 10 percent, so Oze-Moore has to make required interest payments of $80,000 per year to its lenders. Both companies must pay taxes equal to 25 per-

cent of their earnings, but Oze-Moore's total tax bill will be lower than Eck-Witty's because its interest payments are tax-deductible.

As Exhibit 8.3 shows, when sales are strong, Oze-Moore's use of leverage really pays off. Eck-Witty's ROE of 12 percent under the strong sales scenario isn't bad, but it pales in comparison to the 30 percent return Oze-Moore generates for its owners under the same scenario. Oze-Moore's higher ROE occurs because its interest payments are *fixed*. It pays its creditors $80,000—no more, no less—whether EBIT is high or low. When Oze-Moore can borrow funds at an interest rate of 10 percent and invest them in assets that earn *more* than 10 percent (as it does in the strong sales scenario), the extra return goes to the *owners* even though creditors provided the funds. This clearly gives a significant boost to the returns enjoyed by the shareholders.

But in the weak sales scenario, the results are quite different. In this case, the $80,000 of *required* interest payments eats up all of Oze-Moore's earnings, leaving it with no net income for its owners, so its ROE is zero. If EBIT had been anything less than $80,000, Oze-Moore wouldn't have had enough earnings to cover the interest—and if it failed to come up with the money to pay its creditors, they could force it into bankruptcy. This illustrates the risk associated with financial leverage. In comparison, notice that Eck-Witty still earns a positive ROE for its owners in the weak sales scenario; granted, an ROE of 6 percent isn't spectacular, but it sure beats the 0 percent return that Oze-Moore experienced!

Exhibit 8.3 How Financial Leverage Affects the Return on Equity

Eck-Witty (Capital structure is all only equity)

Equity (Funds supplied by owners)		$1,000,000
Debt (Funds obtained by borrowing)		$0

	Strong Sales	Weak Sales
EBIT	$160,000	$80,000
Interest	0	0
Taxable Income	160,000	80,000
Taxes	40,000	20,000
After Tax Earnings	120,000	60,000
ROE	12.0%	6%

Eck-Witty's use of only equity financing results in a lower ROE than Oze-Moore's when sales are strong. But it enjoys better ROE than Oze-Moore when sales are weak.

Oze-Moore (Capital structure is 20% equity and 80% debt)

Equity (Funds supplied by owners)		$200,000
Debt (Funds obtained by borrowing)		$800,000

	Strong Sales	Weak Sales
EBIT	$160,000	$80,000
Interest	80,000	80,000
Taxable Income	80,000	0
Taxes	20,000	0
After Tax Earnings	60,000	0
ROE	30.0%	0.0%

Oze-Moore's use of leverage magnifies ROE when sales are strong. But the required interest payments of $80,000 completely wipes out taxable income and after tax earnings.

TWITTER SELLS MILLIONS OF SHARES ON THE FIRST DAY

TWITTER, TWEET, RETWEET and the Twitter logo are trademarks of Twitter, Inc. or its affiliates. Courtesy of Twitter.

An IPO or initial public offering occurs when companies who have only used debt financing issue shares for the first time on the stock market. This is what Twitter did in 2013 when the firm wanted to expand.

Like Google, Twitter makes money through advertising. It uses promoted tweets, which are sent out to twitter users, and promoted accounts, which Twitter promotes to encourage new Twitter followers. When the first shares of Twitter were sold, the company was not even making a profit. That did not seem to matter to investors. Twitter priced the shares at $26 and by the end of the first day of sales the company had sold 70 million shares, adding $1.8 billion to the company. This level of activity would have suggested that investors thought the company was going to be profitable in the future.

By May 2015, the company shares were worth $36 and earnings per share had fallen over 8 percent from the previous year. At the same time, the company had a debt-to-equity ratio of .43. This ratio was higher than the industry average, indicating that Twitter may need to better manage the level of debt the company had. The company did have good liquidity, as shown by a current ratio of 10.8.

Twitter has a growth strategy of developing new technology internally and purchasing other companies that fit with its future plans.[12]

8-5 Acquiring and Managing Current Assets

Let's turn our attention to how a firm determines the amount and type of current assets to hold. As we'll see, holding current assets involves a tradeoff; either too much or too little of these assets can spell trouble.

8-5a Managing Cash: Is It Possible to Have Too Much Money?

A company must have cash to pay its workers, suppliers, creditors, and taxes. Many firms also need cash to pay dividends. And most firms also want to hold enough cash to meet unexpected contingencies. But cash has one serious shortcoming compared to other assets: it earns little or no return. If a firm holds much more cash than needed to meet its required payments, shareholders are likely to ask why the excess cash isn't being invested in more profitable assets. And if the firm can't find a profitable way to invest the money, the shareholders are likely to ask management why it doesn't use the excess cash to pay them a higher dividend—most shareholders can think of plenty of ways *they*'d like to use the cash!

In the narrowest sense, a firm's cash refers to its holdings of currency (paper money and coins issued by the government) plus demand deposits (the balance in its chequing account). However, most firms, when reporting their cash holdings on their balance sheet, take a broader view, including **cash equivalents** along with their actual cash. Cash equivalents are very safe and highly liquid assets that can be converted into cash quickly and easily. Commercial paper, Treasury Bills (T-bills), and money market mutual funds are among the most popular cash equivalents. The advantage of these cash equivalents is that they offer a better financial return (in the form of interest) than currency or demand deposits.

As we explained in our discussion of short-term sources of funds, major corporations with strong credit ratings often *sell* commercial paper to raise needed short-term funds. On the other side of such transactions are firms that *buy* commercial paper as part of their portfolio of cash equivalents because—at least under normal economic conditions—it is a safe and liquid way to earn some interest. But during economic downturns, the appeal of commercial paper as a cash equivalent plummets, due to increased risk.

Treasury bills, or **T-bills**, are short-term IOUs issued by the government. Most T-bills mature (come due) in 4, 13, or 26 weeks. There is a very active secondary market for T-bills, meaning that their owners can sell them to other investors before they mature. Thus, T-bills are highly liquid. And, unlike commercial paper, T-bills are backed by the government, so they are essentially risk-free. The safety and liquidity of T-bills make them very attractive cash equivalents even in times of economic distress.

Money market mutual funds raise money by selling shares to large numbers of investors. They then pool these

cash equivalents Safe and highly liquid assets that many firms list with their cash holdings on their balance sheet.

Treasury bills (T-bills) Short-term marketable IOUs issued by the government.

money market mutual funds A mutual fund that pools funds from many investors and uses these funds to purchase very safe, highly liquid securities.

PAN AM/ PARAPAN AM GAME PLANNING

n July and August 2015, the athletes of 41 nations arrived in Toronto and surrounding communities to compete in the Pan Am and Parapan Am Games. According to Barb Anderson, the CFO for the games, planning, organizing, and carrying out the games was a six-year project. The project began even before November 6, 2009, the date Toronto was awarded the games. The organizing committee for the games, headed by David Peterson, developed what is called a Bid Book providing a basic concept for the games.

The real work started after November 2009, when the organizing committee took the $1.4 billion budget and turned the concept into a reality. The $1.4 billion was contributed by three levels of government: federal, provincial, and municipal. This money was divided evenly between capital development projects, building new sports facilities, and operations.

The end result was impressive. The Pan Am Games involved 36 sports and another 15 for the Parapan Am Games. These events were spread over 30 venues, 10 of which were new. Another 15 existing facilities required renovations. Also, an athlete's village was built for the games. The venues were spread over 16 municipalities. The number of people involved in the games was equally impressive—more than 10,000 athletes, 23,000 volunteers, and roughly 25,000 spectators.

Planning, organizing and delivering projects like the Pan Am/Parapan Am Games requires the same budgeting skills as running a business, the only difference being that at the end of the games, the project ends.[13]

---

funds to purchase a portfolio of short-term, liquid securities. (In fact, money market mutual funds often include large holdings of commercial paper and T-bills.) Money market mutual funds are an affordable way for small investors to get into the market for securities, which would otherwise be beyond their means. This affordability also makes these funds a particularly attractive cash equivalent for smaller firms.

> Debt is one person's liability, but another person's asset.
>
> Nobel Prize-winning economist Paul Krugman

8-5b Managing Accounts Receivable: Pay Me Now or Pay Me Later

Accounts receivable represents what customers who buy on credit owe the firm. Allowing customers to buy on credit can significantly increase sales. However, as our discussion of the cash budget showed, credit sales can create cash flow problems because they delay the receipt of cash the firm needs to meet its financial obligations. Customers who pay late or don't pay at all only exacerbate the problem. So it's important for firms to have a well-thought-out policy that balances the advantages of offering credit with the costs. The key elements of this policy should include:

- *Setting credit terms:* For how long should the firm extend credit? What type of cash discount should the firm offer to encourage early payments?

- *Establishing credit standards:* How should the firm decide which customers qualify for credit? What type of credit information should it require? How strict should its standards be?

- *Deciding on an appropriate collection policy:* How aggressive should the firm be at collecting past-due accounts? At what point does it make sense to take (or at least threaten to take) legal action against late-paying customers, or to turn over the accounts to collection agencies? When does it make sense to work out compromises?

In each area, financial managers face tradeoffs. For example, a firm that extends credit for only 30 days will receive its payments sooner than a firm that allows customers 90 days. But setting short credit periods may also result in lost sales. Similarly, setting high credit standards reduces the likelihood a firm will have problems with customers who pay late (or not at all). However, strict standards may prevent many good customers from getting credit, resulting in lower sales. Finally, an aggressive collection policy may help the firm collect payments that it would otherwise lose. But an aggressive policy is costly, and it can alienate customers who make honest mistakes, causing them to take future business to competitors.

Some small businesses have found that being flexible and creative about the form of payment can help them get at least some of what they are owed. Barter arrangements sometimes work better than demanding cash—especially in troubled times. For example, a health spa took payments from one of its customers in the form of hundreds of granola bars. Similarly, the owner of a bookkeeping firm agreed to accept payment from a veterinarian in the form of emergency surgery on her pet cat![14]

8-5c Managing Inventories: Taking Stock of the Situation

Inventories are stocks of finished goods, work-in-process, parts, and materials that firms hold as a part of doing business. Clearly, businesses must hold inventories to operate. For example, you'd probably be disappointed if you visited a Best Buy store and were confronted with empty shelves rather than with a wide array of electronic gadgets to compare and try out. Similarly, a manufacturing firm wouldn't be able to assemble its products without an inventory of parts and materials.

But for many firms, the costs of storing, handling, and insuring inventory items are significant expenses. In recent years, many manufacturing firms have become highly aggressive about keeping inventories as low as possible in an attempt to reduce costs and improve efficiency. Such "lean" inventory policies can be very effective, but they leave the firm vulnerable to supply disruptions. Honda had to shut down some of its assembly lines for eight days after 15 feet of floodwater swamped the Taiwanese factories of key suppliers, delaying shipments of four-wheel drive systems for its cars. If Honda held larger inventories, it might have been able to continue operating its assembly lines until its Taiwanese suppliers could resume shipments.[15]

8-6 Capital Budgeting: In It for the Long Haul

We'll conclude the chapter with a look at how firms evaluate proposals to invest in long-term assets or undertake major new projects. **Capital budgeting** refers to the procedure a firm uses to plan for its investment in assets or projects that it expects will yield benefits for more than a year. The capital budgeting process evaluates proposals such as these:

capital budgeting The process a firm uses to evaluate long-term investment proposals.

time value of money The principle that a dollar received today is worth more than a dollar received in the future.

- Replacing existing machinery and equipment with more advanced models to reduce costs and improve the efficiency of current operations.

- Buying additional machinery and equipment to expand production capacity.

- Investing in new factories, property, and equipment needed to expand into new markets.

- Introducing new or modifying existing factories or equipment to achieve goals not directly related to expanding production, such as reducing pollution or improving worker safety.

The number of capital budgeting proposals a firm considers each year can be quite large. But it's unlikely that all proposals will be worth pursuing. How do financial managers decide whether to accept a proposal?

8-6a Evaluating Capital Budgeting Proposals

Financial managers measure the benefits and costs of a long-term investment proposal in terms of the cash flows it will generate. These cash flows are likely to be negative at the start of a project because money must be spent to get a long-term investment project up and running before it begins generating positive cash flows. But a project must eventually generate enough positive cash flows to more than offset these negative initial cash outflows if it is to benefit the company.

8-6b Accounting for the Time Value of Money

One of the most challenging aspects when it comes to evaluating a long-term project's cash flows is that they are spread out over a number of years. When comparing cash flows that occur at different times, financial managers must take the **time value of money** into

Capital budgeting helps managers evaluate the desirability of investments in long-term assets.

FOR A SOCIALLY RESPONSIBLE FIRM IN NEED OF FUNDS, THERE'S NO NEED TO FEAR

Venture capital (VC) firms have long been an important source of financing for hot new companies offering the potential for rapid growth. VCs are limited partnerships or limited liability companies that pool funds from wealthy individuals and institutional investors (such as pension funds) and invest those funds in firms with high profit potential. Many of today's best-known corporations, including Staples, Google, Apple, and Starbucks, got their first major funding from venture capitalists.

Traditional venture capital firms focus almost exclusively on the bottom line. They are willing to invest in "green" companies (and often do), but only if the firms offer potentially high (and quick) returns. But over the past decade a new breed of "green" VC firms has emerged. These new firms still seek a solid financial return, but that isn't their *only* goal. They exist to fund firms that pursue worthy social and environmental goals—and they do so even if the expected financial return is a bit lower and they have to wait longer to receive it.

One such venture capital firm in Canada is Investeco. Investeco describes itself as Canada's first environmental investment company. Established in 2003 by Andrew Heintzman and Michael de Pencier, the company invests in alternative power, water technologies, and organic and natural foods. In 2011 the company started a new $40 million fund in order to invest in companies producing healthy food. Investeco felt that this industry was a good investment because of the trend towards eating healthy foods. Many companies in the natural food industry have difficulty getting financial help from banks, which leaves them struggling to grow. Investeco not only provides the funding to allow companies to grow but also provides advice from industry experts.[16]

© D-BASE/Photodisc/Jupiterimages

account. The time value of money reflects the fact that, from a financial manager's perspective, a dollar received today is worth *more* than a dollar received in the future because the sooner you receive a sum of money, the sooner you can put that money to work to earn even *more* money.

Suppose you were given the choice between receiving $1,000 today or the same amount one year from today. If you think like a financial manager, this choice is a no-brainer. Let's be conservative and say that if you receive the money today you can deposit it in an insured one-year investment at your local bank that pays 4 percent interest. Your 4 percent investment means that a year from today you would have $1,040 (the $1,000 you deposited plus $40 in interest). If you wait until next year to receive the $1,000, you'll lose the opportunity to earn that $40 in interest. Clearly, receiving the cash today is the better option.

Because money has a time value, a cash flow's value depends not only on the *amount* of cash received but also on *when* it is received. Financial managers compare cash flows occurring at different times by converting

them to their present values. The **present value** of a cash flow received in a future time period is the amount of money that, if invested *today* at an assumed rate of interest (called the *discount rate*), would grow to become that future amount of money. Exhibit 8.4 shows that $10,000 invested today at 3 percent grows to a future value of $11,254.09 in four years. Thus, $10,000 is the present value of $11,254.09 received in four years.

8-6c The Risk–Return Tradeoff Revisited

Unfortunately, financial managers don't have crystal balls, so they don't know the *actual* cash flows a proposed project will generate. Instead, they base their analysis on the cash flows the proposal is *expected* to generate. Once a company actually invests in a project, it may find that the *actual* cash flows are quite different from these estimated flows. This uncertainty means that capital budgeting decisions must consider risk.

> **present value** The amount of money that, if invested today at a given rate of interest, would grow to become some future amount in a specified number of time periods.

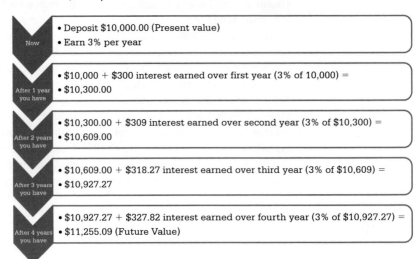

Exhibit 8.4 How a Present Value of $10,000 Grows to a Future Value of $11,254.09 in Four Years

Now
- Deposit $10,000.00 (Present value)
- Earn 3% per year

After 1 year you have
- $10,000 + $300 interest earned over first year (3% of 10,000) =
- $10,300.00

After 2 years you have
- $10,300.00 + $309 interest earned over second year (3% of $10,300) =
- $10,609.00

After 3 years you have
- $10,609.00 + $318.27 interest earned over third year (3% of $10,609) =
- $10,927.27

After 4 years you have
- $10,927.27 + $327.82 interest earned over fourth year (3% of $10,927.27) =
- $11,255.09 (Future Value)

In general, projects with the potential for high returns are also the projects with a high degree of uncertainty and risk. This is another example of the risk–return tradeoff we introduced at the beginning of this chapter. Clearly, financial managers must take this tradeoff into account when they compare different capital budgeting proposals; they must determine whether riskier proposals generate a high enough expected return to justify their greater risk.

One common way financial managers try to do this is to use a higher discount rate when computing the present values of cash flows for risky projects than when computing present values for less risky projects. This reflects the idea that a higher return is required to compensate for the greater risk.

of its estimated future cash flows and subtracting the initial cost of the investment from the sum. A positive NPV means that the present value of the expected cash flows from the project is greater than the cost of the project. In other words, the benefits from the project exceed its costs even after accounting for the time value of money. Financial managers approve projects with positive NPVs. A negative NPV means that the present value of the expected future cash flows from the project is less than the cost of the investment. This would indicate that the cost of the project outweighs its cash flow benefits. Financial managers would reject proposals with negative NPVs (see Exhibit 8.5).

8-6d Net Present Value: A Decision Rule for Capital Budgeting

net present value (NPV)
The sum of the present values of expected future cash flows from an investment minus the net cost of that investment.

The most common method financial managers use to evaluate capital budgeting proposals is to compute their **net present value (NPV)**. The NPV of an investment proposal is found by adding the present values of all

Exhibit 8.5 Decision Rule for Capital Budgeting

RESULT OF NPV CALCULATION	DECISION
NPV ≥ 0	Accept proposal ✓
NPV < 0	Reject proposal ✗

I n this chapter we discussed the tasks that financial managers perform as they attempt to find the best sources and uses of financial resources—meaning those that will maximize the value of the firm to its owners. We saw that in their attempts to achieve this goal, financial managers face two challenges. The first is to balance the needs of owners against those of the other stakeholders; the second is to balance the potential rewards of their decisions against the risks.

Recent history illustrates how important sound financial management is to the success of a firm—and how devastating poor financial decisions can be. Indeed, the recent decline and fall of some of the biggest and best-known corporations can be traced in large measure to poor financial decisions—especially decisions that failed to adequately take risk into account, resulting in the use of too much leverage.

These lessons from the recent past will probably result in a different approach to financial management over the next several years. While memories of the recession are still relatively fresh, firms may be more conservative in their view of what constitutes the best sources and uses of funds. Firms are likely to shy away from excessive debt and put more emphasis on equity financing. They also are less likely to use their funds to invest in highly risky or speculative assets.

careers in finance: Financial Analyst

Responsible for financial planning, preparing complex financial analyses and recommendations, establishing and maintaining internal financial controls, creating and analyzing monthly, quarterly, and annual reports, ensuring financial information has been recorded accurately, and working closely with business unit leaders to align company and financial goals. The ideal candidate has a bachelor's or master's degree in finance, expert spreadsheet and analytical skills, strong oral and written communication skills, strong understanding of financial analysis and reporting, and effective time and project management skills, including the ability to simultaneously manage multiple projects and priorities as well as to work under pressure to meet deadlines.

STUDY TOOLS 8

IN THE BOOK, YOU CAN:

☐ Rip out the Chapter Review card at the back of the book to have a summary of the chapter and key terms handy.

ONLINE AT NELSON.COM/STUDENT YOU CAN:

☐ Work through key concepts with a Guided Learning Question.

☐ Prepare for tests with quizzes.

☐ Review the key terms with Flash Cards (online or printer-ready).

☐ Explore practical examples of chapter concepts with Connect a Concept exercises.

9

Financial Markets:
Allocating Financial Resources

LEARNING OBJECTIVES
After studying this chapter, you will be able to...

9-1 Explain the role of financial markets in the economy and identify the key players in these markets

9-2 Identify the key regulations that govern the way financial markets operate

9-3 Describe and compare the major types of securities that are traded in securities markets

9-4 Explain how securities are issued in the primary market and traded on secondary markets

9-5 Compare several strategies that investors use to invest in securities

9-6 Interpret the information provided in the stock quotes available on financial websites

After you finish this chapter, go to page 151 for STUDY TOOLS

9-1 The Role of Financial Markets and Their Key Players

Financial markets perform a vital function: they transfer funds from savers (individuals and organizations willing to defer using some of their income to earn a financial return and build their wealth) to borrowers (individuals and organizations that need additional funds to achieve their financial goals). Without these markets, companies would find it difficult to obtain the financial resources needed to meet payrolls, invest in new facilities, develop new products, and compete effectively in global markets.

But it's not just businesses that benefit from these markets. You do, too, through your involvement in both sides of financial markets. You participate as a borrower when using your credit card to finance daily purchases or when taking out a loan for college or university tuition. You also participate as a saver when depositing money into a savings account to accumulate the down payment for your first house,

financial markets Markets that transfer funds from savers to borrowers.

depository institution A financial intermediary that obtains funds by accepting chequing and savings deposits and then lending those funds to borrowers.

or when investing in stocks and bonds to build a nest egg for your retirement years.

In Canada and other well-developed market economies, the vast majority of financing occurs indirectly, with *financial intermediaries* coming between the ultimate savers and borrowers. We'll see that they perform a variety of functions, but what they all have in common is that they help channel funds from savers to borrowers.

9-1a Depository Institutions

Depository institutions are financial intermediaries that obtain funds by accepting chequing and savings deposits from individuals, businesses, and other institutions, and then lending those funds to borrowers.

- Banks are the most common depository institutions. When you make a deposit into a chequing or savings account at your bank, you are providing funds that the bank can use for making loans to businesses, governments, or other individuals.

  In Canada there are six large banks and 75 smaller banks. The World Economic Forum has rated the Canadian banking system as the most sound in the world. Canadian banks make a significant contribution

The Toronto Stock Exchange was established in 1852.
Toronto Stock Exchange website

Andrew Francis Wallace/Toronto Star via Getty Images

to the Canadian economy, accounting for just over 3 percent of GDP and employing more than 275,000 Canadians. The six largest Canadian banks paid almost $8 billion in taxes and over $20 billion in salaries to employees in one year.[1]

- In many ways, **trust companies** are similar to banks. They take deposits from customers and lend money out for mortgages and loans. The mortgages and loans given out by trust companies are mostly to individuals rather than to businesses. Trust companies can also act as trustees for estates, personal trusts, and pension plans. With the financial industry changing over the past several decades, most of the large trust companies have been purchased by the banks or other corporations.[2]

Credit unions and **caisse populaires** are cooperatives, which means that they are owned by their depositors. People who deposit money into a credit union or *caisse populaire* are shareholders and can vote on how the financial institution is run.

Credit unions and *caisses populaires* are much smaller players in financial markets than banks, but roughly one-third of all Canadians have an account at one of these. Credit unions can found across the country; *caisses populaires* are found mostly in Quebec.[3]

9-1b Nondepository Financial Institutions

Besides banks and other depository institutions, a number of other financial intermediaries play important roles in financial markets.

- **Institutional investors** don't accept deposits; however, they amass huge pools of financial capital from other sources and use these funds to acquire portfolios of many different assets. Mutual funds obtain money by selling shares to investors; insurance companies obtain money by collecting premiums from policyholders; and pension funds obtain money by collecting the funds that employers and their employees contribute for the employees' retirement. These institutions invest heavily in corporate stock; indeed, institutional investors hold the majority of shares in most major corporations. They are also major holders of corporate bonds and government securities.

trust company A financial intermediary similar to a bank that obtains funds by accepting chequing and savings deposits and then lending those funds to borrowers.

credit union A depository institution that is organized as a cooperative, meaning that it is owned by its depositors.

caisse populaires A depository institution that is organized as a cooperative, meaning that it is owned by its depositors.

WOOF! DIVIDENDS AND DOGS OF THE DOW

Erik Lam/Shutterstock.com

Stock returns come in two forms. If a stock grows in value after being purchased, the price appreciation is called a capital gain. Historically, most investors prefer such growth stocks. If a corporation distributes part of its earnings to shareholders, a stock dividend is paid for each share of stock. Unfortunately, most investors don't include dividend-paying stocks in their portfolios. That's a mistake. Since 1927, non–dividend-paying stocks have earned an average annual return of 8.4 percent, while stocks with small dividend payouts have averaged 10.2 percent, stocks with moderate dividends have averaged 10.2 percent, and stocks with large dividends have averaged 11.1 percent.

While there aren't any guarantees, companies that start paying dividends often go to great lengths to continue doing so. Procter & Gamble has paid dividends each year since 1890, and General Mills since 1899. Procter & Gamble has been increasing its dividends annually since 1957.

How can you take advantage of dividend-paying stocks in your investment portfolio? One simple strategy is the "Dogs of the Dow," in which you buy the ten highest yielding dividend stocks listed on the Dow Jones Industrial Average. Such stocks have high dividends relative to their stock prices, which are lower than they should be. This approach gives you a strong dividend and a likelihood that the stock price will appreciate off its lows. Invest equally in each "dog." Hold them for a year. Then replace those that are no longer dogs with that year's new dogs. Sometimes this strategy underperforms the market, but over 20 years, it has matched the returns of the Dow Jones Industrial Average and slightly exceeded Standard & Poor's.

Most stock advisers, though, recommend a mix of growth stocks and dividend-paying stocks. They also caution that dividend-paying stocks are not a substitute for bonds, which typically pay higher yields against much lower risk.[4]

■ **Securities brokers** act as agents for investors who want to buy or sell financial securities, such as corporate stocks or bonds. Besides handling the trades, many brokers provide their clients with additional services, such as financial planning and market research. Brokers are compensated by charging fees and commissions for the services they provide.

> **securities broker** A financial intermediary that acts as an agent for investors who want to buy and sell financial securities. Brokers earn commissions and fees for the services they provide.

> **securities dealer** A financial intermediary that participates directly in securities markets, buying and selling stocks and other securities for its own account.

> **investment bank** A financial intermediary that specializes in helping firms raise financial capital by issuing securities in primary markets.

■ **Securities dealers** participate directly in securities markets, buying and selling stocks and bonds for their own account. They earn a profit by selling securities for higher prices than they paid to purchase them. (The difference between the prices at which they buy and sell securities is called the *spread*.)

■ **Investment banks** are financial intermediaries that help firms issue new securities to raise financial capital. Sometimes investment banks actually buy the newly issued securities themselves; in other cases, they simply help arrange for their sale. Today's investment banks aren't actually independent companies. Rather, they are typically divisions of huge bank holding companies that also own commercial banks.

9-2 Regulating Financial Markets to Protect Investors and Improve Stability

Financial markets work well only when savers and borrowers have confidence in the soundness of key financial institutions and in the fairness of the market outcomes. When depositors lose confidence in their banks, or when investors discover that financial markets are rigged by practices such as insider trading or unethical and deceptive accounting, the financial system breaks down. To ensure that this confidence is justified, a mix of federal, provincial, and private efforts regulate financial institutions and the markets.

9-2a Regulations for Depository Institutions

Every country regulates the national banking system using a variety of regulations and controls. The international financial crisis of 2008 is only the latest example of how financial markets can malfunction. Canada's financial markets weathered the recent financial market meltdown better than those of most countries. The stability of Canada's financial markets was due in part to the risk management programs put in place by the federal government.

In 1987 the federal government created an agency, the Office of the Superintendent of Financial Institutions (OSFI), to supervise private pension plans and financial institutions. This agency monitors and assesses financial institutions to ensure that the companies have adequate risk management and corporate governance programs in place. The OSFI reports to the federal government through the finance minister.[5]

The Financial Consumer Agency of Canada is another federal government agency that supervises federally regulated financial institutions. This agency focuses on protecting consumer rights and educating consumers about financial matters in Canada.[6]

There are also several pieces of legislation that relate to financial institutions. The *Bank Act* governs banks and federal credit unions in Canada. The *Trust and Loan Act* applies to federally regulated trust and loan companies across Canada. The *Insurance Companies Act* relates to federally registered insurance companies. Not all financial institutions are federally registered. If a financial institution is not federally registered, it will be governed by legislation in the province in which it is registered.[7]

9-2b Regulation for Securities Markets

While many countries have a national body that regulates security markets, Canada has provincial and territorial security commissions. Each province and territory has its own security act, which sets out the rules to protect investors. Most of these acts are similar in nature. Generally, provincial acts require people selling securities to be honest and knowledgeable in security trading. Companies are required to provide investors with published financial statements that conform to the accounting rules and that are audited by independent accountants. All provincial and territorial commissions have the authority to enforce the rules of their commission.

Canada is moving towards one regulatory body across the country. This move has been slow mainly because it requires the agreement of all provincial and territorial bodies. The first step in this direction was the *passport system*. The passport system allows a company wanting to enter the securities market to deal with only one provincial securities commission. This system improves market efficiency, reduces duplication, and reduces the costs. In effect, the passport system accomplishes what a single regulatory body would do without the provinces having to give up their authority. To introduce this system, the provincial and territorial bodies

have agreed to work towards uniform regulations. Uniform regulations across Canada are important, but because so many Canadian companies are closely linked to companies in the United States, it is important that Canadian requirements be similar to the regulations south of the border.[8]

As they have moved towards a single regulatory body, British Columbia, Ontario, Saskatchewan, New Brunswick, Prince Edward Island, and Yukon have set up the Cooperative Capital Markets Regulatory System. This group is encouraging the regulatory agencies across the country to join. The aim of this group is to enact the *Capital Markets Act*, which will modernize capital market regulations.[9]

9-2c The Role of Self-Regulatory Organizations

Although the individual security commissions retain ultimate control over the securities markets, they rely on **self-regulatory organizations (SROs)** to oversee the operations of these markets. SROs are non-governmental organizations that develop and enforce the rules governing the behaviour of their members.

In Canada, the Canadian Securities Administrators (CSA) plays an important role in improving, coordinating, and harmonizing regulations for capital markets. The CSA is a voluntary organization with representatives from each province and territory. It has several committees that develop policy and deliver regulatory programs. These committees cover topics such as enforcement of regulation, investor education, and registrant regulation.[10]

The Investment Industry Regulatory Organization of Canada (IIROC) is another self-regulatory organization. It was established in 2008 when the Investment Dealers Association of Canada and Market Regulatory Services Inc. merged. This organization sets regulations and standards that ensure the efficient operation of markets and that protect investors.[11]

9-3 Investing in Financial Securities: What Are the Options?

Financial securities markets are vital to corporations, which rely on them to obtain much of their long-term financial capital. They also provide one of the most important venues that individuals can use to build their long-term wealth and earn significant financial returns.

self-regulatory organizations (SROs) Non-governmental organizations operating in the securities industry that develop and enforce rules and standards governing the behaviour of their members.

9-3a Common Stock

Common stock is the basic form of ownership in a corporation. Exhibit 9.1 shows a stock certificate representing ownership in Yahoo! Inc. Owners of common stock have certain key rights.

- **Voting rights:** Owners of common stock have the right to vote on important issues at the annual shareholders' meeting. One key issue that shareholders vote on is the selection of members to the corporation's board of directors. They also may vote on other major issues, such as to approve a merger with another firm or a change in the corporation's bylaws. Under the most common arrangement, shareholders can cast one vote for each share of stock they own.

- **Right to dividends:** A dividend is a distribution of profits to the corporation's shareholders. Common shareholders have the right to receive a dividend if the company's board of directors declares one. Of course, if a firm has a bad year, there may not be any profits to distribute. And even if the company is profitable, the board may choose to reinvest the earnings in the company rather than distribute them as dividends. Thus, *there is no guarantee that shareholders will receive a dividend.*

common stock The basic form of ownership in a corporation.

capital gain The return on an asset that results when its market price rises above the price the investor paid for it.

preferred stock A type of stock that gives its holder preference over common shareholders in terms of dividends and claims on assets.

- **Capital gains:** Shareholders also may receive another type of return on their investment, called a **capital gain**, if the price of the stock rises above the amount they paid for it. Capital gains can create very attractive returns for shareholders. Of course, there is no guarantee the stock's price will rise. If it falls, shareholders will experience a capital loss rather than a capital gain.

- **Pre-emptive right:** If a corporation issues new stock, existing shareholders may have a pre-emptive right to purchase new shares in proportion to their existing holdings before the stock is offered to the general public. For example, if you own 5 percent of the existing shares of stock, then the pre-emptive right gives you the right to purchase 5 percent of the new shares. This could be important for large shareholders that want to maintain control over a significant share of votes.

- **Right to a residual claim on assets:** The final shareholder right is a residual claim on assets. If the corporation goes out of business and liquidates its assets, shareholders have a right to share in the proceeds in proportion to their ownership. But note that this is a *residual* claim—it comes *after all other claims* have been satisfied. In other words, the firm must pay any back taxes, legal expenses, wages owed to workers, and debts owed to creditors before the owners get anything. By the time all of these other claims have been paid, little or nothing may be left for the owners.

9-3b Preferred Stock

Common stock is the basic form of corporate ownership, but some companies also issue **preferred stock**, so named because—compared to common stock—it offers its holders preferential treatment in two respects:

- **Claim on assets:** Holders of preferred stock have a claim on assets that comes before common shareholders if the company goes out of business. This gives preferred shareholders a better chance than common shareholders of recovering their investment if the company goes bankrupt.

- **Payment of dividends:** Unlike dividends on common stock, dividends on preferred stock are usually a stated amount. And a company that issues preferred stock can't pay *any* dividend to its common shareholders unless it pays the full stated dividend on preferred stock. Still, it is important to note that a corporation has no *legal* obligation to pay a dividend

Exhibit 9.1 Common Stock Certificate: A Share of Corporate Ownership

Caro/Sueddeutsche Zeitung Photo/The Image Works

INVEST IN BONDS, BUT BEWARE OF CREDIT AND INTEREST RATE RISKS

REWARD ▶

BUSINESS

◀ RISK

DelMosz/Shutterstock.com

Because stock investing is inherently risky, financial advisers recommend diversifying investment portfolios by including bonds to generate a steady flow of income. But that doesn't mean bonds are risk free. In fact, bonds are subject to substantial credit and interest rate risks.

Credit risk affects bond investors when companies in financial difficulties are at risk of default—that is, of not paying the bond interest and principal. An example is Kodak, the struggling photography company. Investors worried that Kodak, which had just $1.3 billion in cash on hand and was burning through $300 million in cash per quarter, would not be able to pay the $350 million in bond interest when it became due. As a result, the value of Kodak bonds plunged to just 16 cents on the dollar. One financial analyst commented: "There's not enough to cover the debt under a worst case scenario, which I think is where we're headed."

Bonds are also affected by interest rate risk. For example, when the economy is not growing rapidly and the rate of inflation is about 2 percent per year, bond interest rates tend to be very low, with 10-year notes paying 1.75 percent and 30-year notes paying just over 3 percent. However, if the economy heats up and prices rise (i.e., inflation), bonds will have to pay higher interest rates to attract investors. If that happens, the prices of low-interest-paying bonds will drop—after all, why buy bonds paying 3 percent when you can get bonds paying 5 percent?

Should you invest in bonds? Absolutely. But take credit risk and interest rate risk into account when you do.[12]

---

to *any* shareholders, not even those who hold preferred stock.

Preferred stock often includes a *cumulative feature*. This means that when the firm skips a preferred dividend in one period, the amount it must pay the next period is equal to the dividend for that period *plus* the amount of the dividend it skipped in the previous period. Any additional skipped dividends continue to accumulate, and the firm can't pay *any* dividends to common shareholders until *all* of the accumulated dividends are paid to preferred shareholders. A cumulative provision gives the board a strong incentive to make regular dividend payments to preferred shareholders.

Preferred stock isn't necessarily "preferred" to common stock in all respects. For example, preferred shareholders normally don't have voting rights, so they can't vote on issues that come up during shareholders' meetings. And even though preferred shareholders are more likely to receive a dividend, there is no guarantee that the fixed dividend paid to preferred shareholders will always be greater than the dividend the board declares for common shareholders. Finally, when a company experiences strong

earnings, the market price of its common stock can—and often does—appreciate more in value than the price of its preferred stock. Once capital gains are taken into account, the overall return that common shareholders earn can be much greater than the total return earned by preferred shareholders.

9-3c Bonds: Earning Your Interest

A **bond** is a formal IOU issued by a corporation or governmental entity. Bonds come in many different varieties. Our discussion will focus on the basic characteristics of long-term bonds issued by corporations.

The date the bond comes due is called the **maturity date**, and the amount the issuer owes the bondholder at maturity is called the bond's **par value** (or face value). Long-term bonds issued by corporations usually mature 10 to 30 years after issuance, but longer maturities are possible. Recently, several major corporations, including Disney and

> **bond** A formal debt instrument issued by a corporation or government entity.
>
> **maturity date** The date when a bond will come due.
>
> **par value (of a bond)** The value of a bond at its maturity; what the issuer promises to pay the bondholder when the bond matures.

IBM, issued *century bonds* that mature 100 years after their issue. The par value of bonds is usually $1,000 or some multiple of that amount.[13]

Bondholders can sell their bonds to other investors before they mature, but the price they receive may not correspond to the bond's par value because bond prices fluctuate with conditions in the bond market. When a bond's market price is above its par value, it is selling at a *premium*; when its price is below par value, it is selling at a *discount*.

Most bonds require their issuers to pay a stated amount of interest to bondholders each year until the bond matures. The **coupon rate** on the bond expresses the annual interest payment as a percentage of the bond's par value. For example, investors who own a bond with a par value of $1,000 and a coupon rate of 7.5 percent receive $75 in interest (7.5 percent of $1,000) each year until the bond reaches maturity—or until they sell their bonds to someone else. But because bonds can sell at a premium or a discount, the coupon rate doesn't necessarily represent the rate of return that investors earn on the amount they actually *paid* for the bond. The **current yield** expresses a bond's interest payment as a percentage of the bond's current market price rather than its par value. If the market price of the bond in our example was $833.33, then the current yield would be 9 percent (found by dividing the $75 interest payment by $833.33).

Unlike with dividends on stock, a firm has a *legal obligation* to pay interest on bonds—and to pay the bondholder the par value of the bond when it matures. Thus, bondholders are more likely to receive a financial return than shareholders. But that doesn't mean that bonds are without risk. Corporations that get into serious financial difficulties sometimes *default* on their bonds, meaning that they are unable to make required payments. When that happens, bankruptcy proceedings usually allow bondholders to recover some (but not all) of what they are owed. Historically, the average amount recovered has been about 72 cents on the dollar. While that is better than

what shareholders can expect when a company goes through bankruptcy, it is far short of being risk free![14]

9-3d Convertible Securities: The Big Switch

Corporations sometimes issue **convertible securities**. These are bonds or preferred stock that investors are allowed to exchange for a stated number of shares of the corporation's common stock. The *conversion ratio* states the number of shares of common stock exchanged for each convertible security. For example, if the conversion ratio is 20, then each convertible security can be exchanged for 20 shares of common stock. The ratio is set at the time the convertible securities are issued so that it is only financially desirable to convert the securities if the price of the common stock increases.

Owning a convertible security allows investors to take advantage of a rise in stock prices, while limiting their risk if stock prices fall. If the price of the common stock increases, the holders of convertible securities can convert them into the now more valuable stock. But if the price of the company's common stock falls, investors can continue to hold their convertible securities and collect their interest or preferred dividends.

The firm also can benefit from issuing convertible bonds, because the popularity of this feature with investors allows it to offer a lower coupon rate on convertible bonds (or a lower dividend on preferred stock), thus reducing its fixed payments. Also, if the investor exchanges the securities for stock, the firm no longer has to make these fixed payments at all. But there is one important group that may be unhappy with this arrangement; the corporation's existing shareholders may be displeased by the fact that the new stock issued to convertible securities dilutes their share of ownership—and their share of any profits.

Mutual Funds and Exchange Traded Funds (ETFs): Diversification Made Easy Financial **diversification**—the practice of holding many different securities in many different sectors—is generally considered a desirable strategy because it helps reduce (but not completely eliminate) risk. If you hold many different securities in different sectors of the economy, then losses on some securities may be offset by gains on others.

Many investors who want to hold diversified portfolios find that investing in large numbers of individual stocks and bonds is prohibitively expensive. And even if they could afford to do so, investors often lack the time and expertise to select a large number of individual securities. Faced with these limitations, many investors find that **mutual funds** and exchange-traded funds are attractive options.

---

coupon rate The interest paid on a bond expressed as a percentage of the bond's par value.

current yield The amount of interest earned on a bond expressed as a percentage of the bond's current market price.

convertible security A bond or share of preferred stock that gives its holder the right to exchange it for a stated number of shares of common stock.

financial diversification A strategy of investing in a wide variety of securities in order to reduce risk.

mutual fund An institutional investor that raises funds by selling shares to investors and uses the accumulated funds to buy a portfolio of many different securities.

net asset value per share The value of a mutual fund's securities and cash holdings minus any liabilities, divided by the number of shares of the fund outstanding.

Mutual Funds: Portfolios Made Easy There are two ways mutual funds can be structured. A *closed-end fund* issues a fixed number of shares and invests the money received from selling these shares in a portfolio of assets. Shares of closed-end funds can be traded among investors much like stocks. An *open-end mutual fund* doesn't have a fixed number of shares, nor are its shares traded like stocks. Instead, the fund issues additional shares when demand increases and redeems (buys back) old shares when investors want to cash in.

The price at which shares of an open-end mutual fund are issued and redeemed is based on the fund's **net asset value per share** (NAVPS), which is computed by dividing the total value of the fund's cash, securities, and other assets (less any liabilities) by the number of fund shares outstanding. Although the NAVPS is the basis for the price of a fund's shares, investors often also pay commissions and purchase fees.

Several features make mutual funds a popular choice for investors:

- **Diversification at relatively low cost:** By pooling the funds of thousands of investors, mutual funds have the financial resources to invest in a broader portfolio of securities than individual investors could afford. This high level of diversification can help reduce risk.

- **Professional management:** Most mutual funds are managed by a professional fund manager who selects the assets in the fund's portfolio. This can be appealing to investors who lack the time and expertise to make complex investment decisions.

- **Variety:** Whatever your investment goals and philosophy, you can probably find a fund that's a good match. There are many different types of funds; some invest only in certain types of securities (such as municipal bonds or stocks of large corporations), others invest in specific sectors of the economy (such as energy, technology, or health care), and still others seek more balanced and broad-based portfolios. Some funds simply invest in a portfolio of stocks that matches those in a specific stock index, such as the S&P/TSX Composite Index and the Standard & Poor 500. These *index funds* have become very popular in recent years.

- **Liquidity:** It's easy to withdraw funds from a mutual fund. For a closed-end fund, you simply sell your shares. For an open-end fund, you redeem your shares from the fund itself. However, regardless of when you initiate your withdrawal, redemptions of an open-end fund are not carried out until its NAVPS is determined after the *next* trading session is completed.

How Does "Being Green" Affect Company and Investment Performance and Investor Behaviour?

Is it a good investment strategy to go "green"? Let's examine what the research tells us about company performance, investment performance, and how investors actually behave.

First, there is no tradeoff between social responsibility and company financial performance. The higher costs of being socially responsible can be offset by a better product or corporate reputation, leading to stronger sales or higher profit margins. Still, social responsibility doesn't guarantee profitability. All companies experience challenges and threats, and ups and downs. So while being socially responsible may be the right thing to do, it won't necessarily help or hurt business success.

Second, most examinations of the financial performance of green investment funds are limited to just a small number of mutual funds. However, a study comparing 131 green investment funds found that they significantly underperformed average market returns over five-year (2.22 vs. 3.45 percent), and 10-year (3.92 vs. 5.10 percent) periods. The differences were smaller but similar over three-year (2.65 vs. 3.42 percent) and 15-year (6.53 vs. 6.93 percent) periods. Green mutual funds were also more expensive to run. The authors concluded: "Green mutual funds have to date achieved relatively poor risk-adjusted returns."

Third, a study of individual investor behaviour compared environmentalists, strong supporters of environmental issues, to typical investors. Environmentalists indicated that it was important to invest in companies that don't sell weapons, experiment on animals, or pollute. But when asked to hypothetically invest up to $5,000 into 22 mutual funds, environmentalists, like typical investors, consistently ranked financial performance criteria as most important. This suggests that even environmentally minded investors are concerned foremost with earning good returns.

What's the takeaway? Socially responsible or environmentally minded companies are just as likely to be profitable—or unprofitable—as other companies. Green investment funds, so far, are more expensive and produce slightly lower returns. Even environmentalists want their portfolios to earn substantial returns.[15]

Sources: C. Chang, W. Nelson, and D. White, "Do Green Mutual Funds Perform Well?" *Management Research Review*, 35 (2012); M. Orlitzky, "Payoffs to Social and Environmental Performance," *Journal of Investing* 14 (2005); M. Orlitzky, F. Schmidt, and S. Rynes, "Corporate Social and Financial Performance: A Meta-Analysis," *Organization Studies* 24 (2003); V. Vyvyan, C. Ng, and M. Brimble, "Socially Responsible Investing: The Green Attitudes and Grey Choices of Australian Investors," *Corporate Governance* 15 (2007).

Mutual funds do have some drawbacks. Perhaps the most serious is that the professional management touted by many funds doesn't come cheap. Investors in mutual funds pay a variety of fees that typically range from 1 percent to 3 percent of the amount invested. The fees charged by mutual funds can make a serious dent in the overall return received by the fund's investors. And funds assess these fees even when they perform poorly. One reason for the popularity of index funds is that they don't require professional management, so their fees are lower.

Another drawback of actively managed funds is that when their professional managers engage in a lot of trading, significant tax consequences are associated with those financial gains. It is also important to realize that some of the specialized mutual funds that invest in only one sector of the economy or only one type of security may not provide enough diversification to reduce risk significantly.

Exchange Traded Funds: Real Basket Cases (and We Mean That in a Good Way) An **exchange-traded fund (ETF)** is similar to a mutual fund in some respects but differs in how it is created and how its shares are initially distributed. ETFs allow investors to buy ownership in what is called a *market basket* of many different securities. In fact, the market basket for most ETFs reflects the composition of a broad-based stock index, much like an index mutual fund. But in recent years more specialized ETFs that focus on narrower market baskets of assets have appeared on the market. Like closed-end mutual funds—but unlike the more common open-end funds—ETFs are traded just like stocks. Thus, you can buy and sell ETFs any time of the day.

Compared to most actively managed mutual funds, ETFs usually have lower costs and fees. However, since ETFs are bought and sold like stocks, you do have to pay brokerage commissions every time you buy or sell shares.

exchange traded fund (ETF) Shares traded on securities markets that represent the legal right of ownership over part of a basket of individual stock certificates or other securities.

primary securities market The market where newly issued securities are traded. The primary market is where the firms that issue securities raise additional financial capital.

secondary securities market The market where previously issued securities are traded.

public offering A primary market issue in which new securities are offered to any investors who are willing and able to purchase them.

private placement A primary market issue that is negotiated between the issuing corporation and a small group of accredited investors.

initial public offering (IPO) The first time a company issues stock that may be bought by the general public.

9-4 Issuing and Trading Securities: The Primary and Secondary Markets

There are two distinct types of securities markets: the primary securities market and the secondary securities market. The **primary securities market** is where corporations raise additional financial capital by selling *newly issued* securities. The **secondary securities market** is where *previously issued securities* are traded.

9-4a The Primary Securities Market: Where Securities Are Issued

There are two methods of issuing securities in the primary market:

- In a **public offering**, securities may be sold to anyone in the investing public who is willing (and financially able) to buy them.

- In a **private placement**, securities are sold directly to one or more private investors (who may be individuals or institutions) under terms negotiated between the issuing firm and the private investors.

Public Offerings Many corporations are initially owned by a small number of people who don't actively trade the stock to outsiders. But growing corporations often need to obtain more financial capital than such a small group can provide. Such firms may decide to *go public* by issuing additional stock and offering it to the general public. The first time a corporation sells its stock in a public offering, the sale is called an **initial public offering (IPO)**.

Going public is a complicated and high-stakes process; obtaining sufficient funds in an IPO is often critical to the firm's success. Most firms that go public seek the help of financial advisers such as investment dealers, securities law firms, accountants, and investor relations professionals. These advisers assist the firm at every step of the IPO, from planning and market assessment until the day of the actual offering.

A key decision for the company is how to arrange for the actual sale of the securities. The company typically uses either a *best efforts* or a *firm commitment* approach. Under the best efforts approach, the company advisers provide assistance with pricing and marketing, as well as with finding potential buyers. But there is no guarantee that the firm will sell all of its securities at a high enough price to meet its financial goals. The company assisting with the sale of the stock earns a commission on all of the shares sold under a best efforts approach. Under a *firm commitment* arrangement, the firm assisting with the sale of the stock is also responsible for **underwriting** the issue. This means that the investment company helping with the sale purchases *all* of the shares, which guarantees that the firm issuing the stock will receive a known amount of new funds directly from the investment company, which will then seek to make a profit by reselling the stock to investors at a higher price.

Before going public, a firm must get approval from the provincial securities commission and register each security with the commission. The registration statement provides a detailed description of the firm, as well as the financial information and background of the company and the officers of the company. The registration statement is called the *prospectus*. Firms must give a copy of the final prospectus to all investors who are interested in purchasing the shares.

Private Placements Private placements are usually quicker, simpler, and less expensive than public offerings. In a private placement, the issuing firm negotiates the terms of the offer directly with a small number of investors. An investment dealer often helps the firm identify and contact potential investors and helps the firm negotiate the terms of the offer.

One reason private placements are simpler and less expensive than public offerings is that privately placed securities are exempt from the requirement to prepare a prospectus. The ability to obtain financing without having to prepare complex registration documents can be a real attraction. A significant drawback is that private placements normally don't raise as much money as public offerings.

Private placements can be offered only to *accredited investors*. In Canada, the private placement market is relatively small compared to the United States or the United Kingdom and involves knowledgeable investors. Most private placements in Canada involve pension plans, which are required to hold the shares for a specific period before reselling them.

9-4b Secondary Securities Markets: Let's Make a Deal

Firms that issue stocks and bonds don't receive any additional funds when their securities are traded in the secondary markets. But secondary markets still matter to the corporations that issue these securities. The price of a firm's stock in the secondary market directly reflects investor opinion about how well the firm is being managed. Also, few investors would want to buy securities issued in the primary markets without the possibility of earning capital gains by selling these securities in the secondary markets.

Aaron Harris/Bloomberg via Getty Images

Stock (Securities) Exchanges The stocks of most largely traded corporations are listed and traded on a **stock (or securities) exchange**. A securities exchange (or stock exchange) is an organization that provides a venue for stockbrokers or securities dealers to trade listed stocks and other securities for clients. Each stock exchange establishes requirements for the stocks it lists. Specific listing requirements vary among the exchanges, but they're typically based on the earnings of the company, the number of shares of stock outstanding, and the number of shareholders. In addition to meeting listing requirements, exchanges also require firms to pay an initial fee at the time their securities are first listed and an annual listing fee to remain listed on the exchange.

In Canada, the TMX Group owns and operates the **Toronto Stock Exchange** and the **TSX Venture Exchange**. The Toronto Stock Exchange is for more established companies; the TSX Venture Exchange is for early-stage companies. As companies grow they will move from the TSX Venture Exchange to the Toronto Stock Exchange. Not surprisingly, these exchanges have a large number of mining and energy companies listed.

The Toronto Stock Exchange started in 1852 when a group of businessmen formed an Association of Brokers. By 1901, there were 100 stocks listed on the exchange. In 1997, the Toronto Stock Exchange became an electronic trading environment and closed its trading floor. However, 1999 is the year when major changes occurred for stock markets across Canada. In that year, the Toronto Stock Exchange became Canada's only exchange for senior stock; the Montreal exchange took over trading in

underwriting An arrangement under which an investment dealer agrees to purchase all the shares of a public offering at an agreed-upon price.

stock (or securities) exchange An organized venue for trading stocks and other securities that meet its listing requirements.

Toronto Stock Exchange Canada's stock exchange for larger companies.

TSX Venture Exchange Canada's stock exchange for smaller companies.

derivatives; and Vancouver, Alberta, and Winnipeg joined together to form an exchange for junior stock. Shortly after these changes, the Toronto Stock Exchange became a for-profit company and the market for junior stock became the TSX Venture Exchange.

The New York Stock Exchange is part of the Euronext group of stock exchanges. Euronext group is a global network that includes eleven stock exchanges in the United States and Europe. There are more than 12,000 stocks listed on the Euronext exchanges, and each day, more than 15 million individual trades take place. NASDAQ is part of NASDAQ OMX, which runs exchanges in the United States and 26 other countries. NASDAQ began 40 years ago as the National Association of Securities Dealers, or NASD.[16]

Trading on early stock exchanges occurred at physical locations, where brokers met on trading floors to buy and sell securities for their clients. Some exchanges still maintain actual trading floors, but most trading on today's exchanges is done electronically. The participants in these markets carry out their trades mainly via computer networks.

The trend towards electronic trading began in 1971 with the establishment of NASDAQ, which initially was just a system used to report stock prices electronically. But over the years, it evolved into a complete market with formal listing requirements and fees. The stocks of many of today's high-profile technology companies, such as Apple, Google, and Microsoft, are traded on the NASDAQ market.

The key players in the NASDAQ market are known as **market makers**. These are securities dealers that make a commitment to continuously offer to buy and sell (make a market in) specific NASDAQ-listed stocks. Each NASDAQ stock has several market makers who compete against one another by posting two prices for each stock: the *bid price* indicates how much the market maker will pay per share to buy a stated quantity of the stock, while the *ask price* indicates the price per share at which it will sell the same stock. The ask price is higher than the bid price; the difference is called the *bid/ask spread* (or just the *spread*) and is the source of the market maker's profit.

The Over-the-Counter Market Many corporations with publicly traded stock don't meet the requirements to have their shares listed on an organized exchange;

Chris Cheadle/Getty Images

some are too small, and others haven't experienced satisfactory business performance. Other corporations meet requirements to list on a stock exchange but choose not to do so because they don't want to pay the listing fees the exchanges charge. The **over-the-counter market (OTC)** is where the stocks of such companies are traded. OTC stocks are traded through a system of market makers much like stocks are traded on the NASDAQ exchange. However, the market for most OTC stocks is much less active than for stocks listed on the major exchanges. Because of this, most stocks listed on the OTC have only a few market makers. The lack of competition often leads to much higher spreads between bid and ask prices for stocks traded in the OTC than normally exist for stocks traded on the NASDAQ exchange.

Electronic Communications Networks The newest development in stock market technology involves the rise of **electronic communications networks** (ECNs). ECNs are classified as alternative trading systems because they represent an alternative to established stock exchanges as a venue for buying and selling securities. ECNs are entirely automated and computerized trading systems

market makers Securities dealers that make a commitment to continuously offer to buy and sell the stock of a specific corporation listed on the NASDAQ exchange or traded in the OTC market.

over-the-counter market (OTC) The market where securities that are not listed on exchanges are traded.

electronic communications network (ECN) An automated, computerized securities trading system that automatically matches buyers and sellers, executing trades quickly and allowing trading when securities exchanges are closed.

that allow traders to bypass the market makers used in the NASDAQ and OTC markets. However, individuals can only take advantage of this venue by opening an account with a broker-dealer that subscribes to an ECN.

If you place an order to buy a security on an ECN, the computer system checks to see if there is a matching order from another trader to sell the same security. If so, it immediately and automatically executes the transaction in a process that typically takes less than a second to complete. ECNs obviously speed up transactions. They also make it possible for investors to trade securities "after hours" when the exchanges are closed.

9-5 Personal Investing

Would investing in stocks, bonds, and other securities make sense for you? If so, how could you get started? What are the potential risks and rewards of various investment strategies?

Investing in securities requires you to think carefully about your specific situation and your personal goals and attitudes:

- What are your short-term and long-term goals?

- Given your budget, how much are you able to invest?

- How long can you leave your money invested?

- How concerned are you about the tax implications of your investments?

- How much tolerance do you have for risk?

The best types of securities for you, and the best investment strategies for you to use, will depend in large part on your answers to questions such as these.

Notice that the last question deals with your attitude towards risk. Most people are not comfortable with high levels of risk. But no investment strategy completely avoids risk. And in general, the riskier the approach, the greater the *potential* rewards. To achieve your goals, you'll need to find the balance between risk and return that works for you.

9-5a Choosing a Broker

Members of the general public cannot directly trade stocks and other securities on the exchanges, the over-the-counter market, or the ECNs we described earlier in

the chapter. Thus, most investors enlist the services of a brokerage firm to carry out these trades. Choosing the right broker is the first step in implementing your investment plans.

A full-service broker provides a wide range of services—such as market research, investment advice, and tax planning—in addition to carrying out your trades. Discount brokers provide the basic services needed to buy and sell securities but offer fewer additional services. They may also restrict your ability to trade certain types of securities. For example, some discount brokers don't offer the ability to buy and sell foreign securities. Discount brokers tend to charge significantly lower commissions than full-service brokers. In fact, many discount brokers charge flat fees of only a few dollars per trade for basic transactions. But discount brokerage firms also charge a variety of fees, and once these fees are considered, brokerage firms that offer low commissions may not be as inexpensive as they first appear!

In recent years, competition among brokerage firms has blurred the distinction between full-service and discount brokers. To stop clients from defecting to discount brokers, many full-service firms have lowered their commissions. At the same time, many discount brokers have begun offering a broader range of services to attract more clients. Now many brokerage firms offer investors the choice of discount or full-service accounts.

Once you've decided on a broker, you need to open an account. This is a fairly simple process; it requires filling out some forms (usually available online) and making an initial investment. The minimum initial investment varies, but $1,000 to $3,000 is fairly typical.

> Investors must keep in mind that there's a difference between a good company and a good stock. After all, you can buy a good car but pay too much for it.
>
> Richard Thaler

9-5b Buying Securities: Let's Make a Deal

Once you've set up your account, you can trade securities be contacting your broker and indicating the security you want to trade and the quantity you want to buy or sell. You can also specify the type of order you want to place. The most common types of orders are market orders and limit orders:

- **Market orders** instruct the broker to buy or sell a security at the current market price. Placing a market order virtually guarantees that

market order An order telling a broker to buy or sell a specific security at the best currently available price.

INDEX FUNDS CERTAINLY AREN'T AVERAGE!

PeskyMonkey/iStockphoto.com

ndex funds match or mirror the stock market, or a particular segment of it. For instance, the CIBC Canadian Index Fund holds stocks from companies that mirror the Canadian equity market, including some of the largest companies listed on the Toronto Stock Exchange. Roughly 30 percent of the fund comprises stocks from financial companies such as the Royal Bank of Canada; another 20 percent represents energy firms, including Enbridge. So when market weightings change, index funds buy and sell stocks proportionate to those changes.

Index funds provide three great benefits for investors.

Because they don't employ expensive fund managers to decide which stocks to buy or sell, costs are often lower. While professional money managers charge an annual fee between 2 percent and 2.5 percent per year, the CIBC Canadian Index Fund charges a fee of 1.14 percent per year. For an investor with $100,000 invested, that's the difference between an annual fee of $2,000 or $2,500 and $1,140!

Next, compared to managed funds, which often buy and sell stocks (called turnover), index funds make infrequent changes to the stocks they hold. Since buying and selling stocks incurs additional costs, this means that index funds are cheaper to administer.

Finally, because they mirror the market, index funds almost always match average market performance.

Simple. Cheap. Index funds are gaining popularity among investors.[17]

---

your order will be executed. The downside is that you may end up buying at a higher price than you expected to pay (or selling your stock for less than you expected to receive).

- **Limit orders** place limits on the prices at which orders are executed. A buy limit order tells a broker to buy a stock *only* if its price is at or below a specified value. You'd use this approach if you wanted to make sure you didn't pay more for the stock than you thought it was worth. A sell limit order tells your broker to sell the shares *only* if the price is at or above a specified value. This prevents your broker from selling your stock at a price you believe is too low.

9-5c Strategies for Investing in Securities

There are several strategies you can use to guide your investment decisions. We'll provide an overview of the more common approaches, but none of these approaches is foolproof—alas, there is no known strategy that is guaranteed to earn you millions.

Investing for Income
Some investors focus on buying

limit order An order to a broker to buy a specific stock only if its price is below a certain level, or to sell a specific stock only if its price is above a certain level.

Tetra Images/Getty Images

Stockbrokers place orders to buy and sell stocks and other securities for their clients.

Just because they can, doesn't mean they should.

For decades, investors started their day reading the *Wall Street Journal's* Heard on the Street column, making it one of the most influential financial columns in the world. The stocks mentioned in it often rose or fell depending on the news.

In the 1980s, R. Foster Winans, who then wrote the column, began leaking news about company stocks to a stockbroker *before* the column appeared in print. Armed with insider information ahead of the public, the broker purchased stocks more cheaply *before* prices rose on good news, and sold stocks *before* prices dropped on bad news. The broker netted $690,000 from these insider trades, $31,000 of which he funnelled back to Winans.

Insider information undermines securities markets because it gives unfair advantage to investors who have knowledge that hasn't yet become public. Insider trading is illegal in Canada, as it is in the United States, and can result in a prison sentence of up to 10 years. Information is considered to insider information if it could reasonably be expected to influence the price of a stock and is not available to the general public. Insider information could be information available to a shareholder, obtained because of a business relationship, obtained through the process of a takeover or similar transaction, or obtained through employment. It is also illegal in Canada for someone in a position to have insider information to pass it along to someone else who could have an advantage in buying or selling a stock.

Not all insider trading is illegal. For example, CEOs and other company leaders may buy and sell their companies' stocks as long as they are not acting on nonpublic information and register their transactions with the Canadian Securities Administrators. The Canadian Securities Administrators provide an online System for Electronic Disclosure by Insiders (SEDI), the purpose of which is to provide information regarding the trading activities of the company insiders.

What do YOU think?

- Should CEOs and other company insiders be allowed to buy and sell their companies' stocks?
- What steps can be taken to further discourage insider trading?
- What kind of penalties should those guilty of insider trading be subject to?[18]

---

bonds and preferred stocks in order to generate a steady, predictable flow of income. Recall that bonds pay a stated amount of interest each year and that preferred stock usually pays a fixed dividend on a regular basis. These investors may also buy common stock in large, well-established firms with a reputation for paying regular dividends. This approach is popular with retirees who want to supplement their retirement income. The drawback is that the return on such low-risk securities is relatively low, and their market value seldom increases much over time. Thus, it probably isn't the best strategy for younger investors who are trying to accumulate wealth.

Market Timing Investors who rely on market timing use a variety of analytical techniques to try to predict when prices of specific stocks are likely to rise and fall. Market timers try to make quick gains by buying low and selling high over a relatively short time horizon.

The problem with market timing is that so many factors can influence stock prices—some of them random in nature—that it's tough to consistently identify the timing and direction of changes in stock prices. Market timing also requires investors to make frequent trades. Given the commissions and fees the investor pays on every trade, this approach may do a better job of enriching the broker than enriching the investor!

Value Investing Investors who favour value investing try to find stocks that are undervalued in the market. They believe other investors will eventually recognize the true value of these stocks. When this happens, the demand for the stocks will increase and the market value will rise, generating an attractive return. This approach requires a lot of research to identify discrepancies between a company's true (or intrinsic) value and its current market price.

The drawback with value investing is that you are in competition with thousands of other investors trying to do the same thing, so the competition to locate good buys is intense. Unless you're among the first to discover an undervalued stock, the investors who beat you to it will rush to buy up the stock, increasing demand and driving up the stock's price so that it is no longer undervalued.

Investing for Growth Investors who focus on growth look for companies that have the potential to grow much faster than average for a sustained period of time, which they believe will lead to stock price growth. Investors using this strategy often invest in stocks of relatively small new companies with innovative products in a hot sector of the economy.

Investing for growth entails significant risk. By their very nature, small new companies don't have an established track record. Rapidly expanding industries also tend to attract a lot of start-up companies, so competition can be intense. It's hard to predict which firms will be winners; even experts often make the wrong choice.

Buying and Holding If you're a patient person with steady nerves, a buy-and-hold approach may appeal to you. This strategy involves purchasing a diversified set of securities and holding them for a long period of time. Investors who use the buy-and-hold approach don't usually worry about detailed analysis of individual stocks. Instead, they invest in a broad range of securities and put their faith in the ability of the *overall market* to continue the long-run upward trend it has exhibited throughout its history. One way that many buy-and-hold investors do this is by investing in index mutual funds and ETFs. The buy-and-hold strategy seldom enables someone to "get rich quick," but it does usually result in an attractive financial return over the long haul.

> I will tell you how to become rich. Close the doors. Be fearful when others are greedy. Be greedy when others are fearful.
>
> Warren Buffet

Obviously, the buy-and-hold strategy will work only if you can afford to leave your money invested for a long time. When the stock market takes a dive, it can sometimes take years for stocks to recover and start to show solid returns. Some people who think they're comfortable with a buy-and-hold strategy end up getting "happy feet" after a few days of declining stock prices. They panic and sell off their stock—often just days before the market starts to rise again! For the buy-and-hold strategy to work, you've got to have the patience and mental toughness to ride out short-term downturns in the market.

stock index A statistic that tracks how the prices of a specific set of stocks have changed.

Dow Jones Industrial Average An index that tracks stock prices of 30 large, well-known corporations.

Standard & Poor's 500 (S&P 500) A stock index based on prices of 500 major US corporations in a variety of industries and market sectors.

S&P/TSX Composite Index A benchmark used to measure the price performance of Canadian stock trading on the Toronto Stock Exchange.

9-6 Keeping Tabs on the Market

Once you've begun to invest in securities, you'll want to keep track of how your investments are doing. Using the Internet, you can easily access information about both general market trends and the performance of specific securities.

9-6a Stock Indices: Tracking the Trends

One of the most common ways to track general market conditions and trends is to follow what's happening to various stock indices. A **stock index** provides a means of tracking the prices of a large group of stocks that meet certain defined criteria. Many investors like to see how the stocks in their own portfolio compare to the performance of these broad indices. Let's look at some of the best-known and most widely followed indices:

- The **Dow Jones Industrial Average**: Often called the "DJIA" or just "the Dow," this is the most widely followed stock index. The Dow is based on the adjusted average price of 30 stocks picked by the editors of the *Wall Street Journal*. All of the Dow firms are huge, well-established corporations, such as American Express, General Electric, Coca-Cola, Hewlett-Packard, and Disney.

- The **Standard & Poor's 500 (S&P 500)**: With 500 stocks instead of just 30, the S&P 500 is a much broader index than the DJIA. Still, like the Dow, all of the companies included in the S&P 500 are large, well-established American corporations.

- The **S&P/TSX Composite Index**: This index is composed of four other indices—equity indices, income trust indices, GIC indices, and market cap indices. The S&P/TSX Composite Index includes Canadian senior stocks listed on the Toronto Stock Exchange and is used to measure the performance of that market.

Exhibit 9.2 identifies several other well-known indices, including some that track prices of stocks in foreign securities markets.

9-6b Tracking the Performance of Specific Securities

Many financial websites offer detailed stock quotes that provide the current price of a company's stock and a wealth of related information. To check out a specific stock, you simply type the stock symbol—a short combination of

Exhibit 9.2 | Major Stock Price Indices

INDEX	WHAT IT TRACKS
NASDAQ COMPOSITE	All of the domestic and foreign common stocks traded on the NASDAQ exchange.
WILSHIRE 5000	Stock prices of all U.S. corporations with actively traded stock. Despite the 5000 in its name, this index actually includes well over 6,000 stocks. (The exact number changes frequently.)
RUSSELL 2000	Stock prices of 2000 relatively small but actively traded US corporations.
FTSE 100	Stock prices of 100 of the largest and most actively traded companies listed on the London Stock Exchange.
NIKKEI 225	Stock prices of 225 of the largest and most actively traded companies listed on the Tokyo Stock Exchange.
SSE COMPOSITE	Stock prices of all stocks listed on the Shanghai Stock Exchange.

©Cengage Learning

letters that uniquely identifies a corporate security—into a "Get Quote" box. (Don't worry if you don't know the symbol; most sites have a look-up feature that finds the symbol if you type in the company's name.)

Exhibit 9.3 illustrates the way one financial website, the Toronto Stock Exchange (http://tmx.quotemedia.com), displays information about a specific stock. (Many other financial websites provide very similar information.) Some of the key figures reported on these sites include:

- **Last trade:** The price of the common stock for the last trade of the day.
- **Change:** The closing price of the stock for the day.
- **Bid and ask:** The highest price a buyer is offering for the stock, and the lowest price a seller is willing to accept for the stock.
- **Day's range:** The highest and lowest price for the stock during the day.

Exhibit 9.3 | Stock Quote on the TMX Group Inc.

Reproduced with permission from TMX Group, Inc.

- **52-week range:** The highest and lowest price for the stock over the previous 52 weeks.

- **Volume:** The number of shares of the stock that were traded during the day.

- **Market cap:** The total market value of all shares of the common stock outstanding. This is found by multiplying the price per share times the number of shares of common stock outstanding.

- **P/E:** The price/earnings ratio is found by dividing the price per share by the stock's earnings per share. However, the P/E ratio for companies with negative earnings per share is usually reported as N/A. In general, a higher P/E ratio means that investors expect a greater growth in earnings over time.

- **EPS (earnings per share):** The earnings per share of common stock outstanding. EPS is computed by dividing the net income available to common shareholders by the number of shares of common stock outstanding.

- **Div and Yield:** The sum of dividends per share paid by the company over the past 12 months. Yield is found by dividing the dividend per share by the previous day's price per share. It tells us the percent of return to the investor based on the price the stock was on that day and the dividend paid by the company. (But keep in mind that the dividend isn't the only return investors might earn. In fact, when stocks are rising in value, the capital gain may offer a much greater return than the dividend.)

Financial websites also have information about other types of securities such as mutual funds, ETFs, and bonds.

Many different organizations participate in financial markets, including banks, finance companies, securities brokers and dealers, investment banks, and institutional investors such as mutual funds, insurance companies, and pension funds. Although they differ in their functions, each of these participants helps financial markets achieve their primary purpose of channelling funds from savers to borrowers.

In this chapter, we focused on one particular type of financial market, namely the market for financial securities. The financial capital that corporations raise when they issue stocks and bonds in these markets is critical to every functional area of their operations. Without these funds, the marketing department would lack the resources needed to develop new products, information technology professionals would be unable to update hardware and software, and operations managers would be unable to acquire the machinery and equipment needed to produce the goods and services the company sells to earn its profits.

On the other side of these markets, investors who buy corporate securities do so to acquire assets that they believe will help them achieve their own financial goals. But investing in securities involves risk. Over any short-run period, there is simply no guarantee that stocks and bonds will provide investors with the returns they expect. The good news—at least if you plan to invest—is that history shows that, over the long run, the return on these securities is positive. Given enough time and patience, investing in stocks and other securities is likely to result in a substantial increase in wealth.

careers in finance: Financial Advisor/Securities Broker

Responsible for meeting and getting to know clients and their financial needs, offering financial advice on investment recommendations (for a diversified mix of stocks, fixed-income investments including bonds and certificates of deposit, mutual funds and annuities, as well as a wide range of insurance options, including life insurance, long-term disability, and long-term care), and placing trades. The ideal candidate has a bachelor's or master's degree, Canadian Securities Certification, a strong sales and/or management background, strong interpersonal skills that provide the ability to develop meaningful relationships, and the drive to set and achieve goals in a performance-driven atmosphere.

STUDY TOOLS 9

IN THE BOOK, YOU CAN:

☐ Rip out the Chapter Review card at the back of the book to have a summary of the chapter and key terms handy.

ONLINE AT NELSON.COM/STUDENT YOU CAN:

☐ Work through key concepts with a Guided Learning Question.

☐ Prepare for tests with quizzes.

☐ Review the key terms with Flash Cards (online or printer-ready).

☐ Explore practical examples of chapter concepts with Connect a Concept exercises.

10 Marketing:

Building Profitable Customer Connections

LEARNING OBJECTIVES

After studying this chapter, you will be able to...

10-1 Discuss the objectives, the process, and the scope of marketing

10-2 Identify the role of the customer in marketing

10-3 Explain each element of marketing strategy

10-4 Describe the consumer and business decision-making process

10-5 Discuss the key elements of marketing research

10-6 Explain the roles of social responsibility and technology in marketing

After you finish this chapter, go to page 168 for STUDY TOOLS

10-1 Marketing: Getting Value by Giving Value

What comes to mind when you hear the term **marketing**? Most people think of the radio ad they heard this morning or the billboard they saw while driving to school. But advertising is only a small part of marketing; the whole story is much bigger. The American Marketing Association, to which most professors from Canada, the United States, and many other countries belong, defines marketing as *the activity, set of institutions, and processes for creating, communicating, delivering, and exchanging offerings that have value for customers, clients, partners, and society at large.*

The ultimate benefit that most businesses seek from marketing is long-term profitability. But attaining this benefit is impossible without first delivering value to customers and other stakeholders. A successful marketer delivers value by filling customers' needs in ways that exceed their expectations. As a result, you get sales today and sales tomorrow and sales the next day, which—across the days and months and years—can translate into long-term profitability. Alice Foote MacDougall, a successful entrepreneur in the 1920s, understood this thinking early on: "In business you get what you want by giving other people what they want." **Utility** is the ability of goods and services to satisfy these wants. And because there is a wide range of wants, products can provide utility in a number of different ways:

- **Form utility** satisfies wants by converting inputs into a finished form. Clearly, the vast majority of products provide some kind of form utility. For example, Jamba Juice blends fruit, sherbet, juices, and frozen yogurt into delicious smoothies, and Swiss Chalet mixes red onions, tomatoes, olives, cucumber, and other ingredients to make its tasty Greek salads.

- **Time utility** satisfies wants by providing goods and services at a convenient time for customers. For example, FedEx delivers some parcels on weekends, many dry cleaners offer one-hour service, 7-Eleven opens early and closes late, and e-commerce, of course, provides the ultimate 24/7 convenience.

marketing The activity, set of institutions, and processes for creating, communicating, delivering, and exchanging offerings that have value for customers, clients, partners, and society at large.

utility The ability of goods and services to satisfy consumer "wants."

form utility The power of a good or a service to satisfy customer "wants" by converting inputs into a finished form.

time utility The power of a good or a service to satisfy customer "wants" by providing goods and services at a convenient time for customers.

- **Place utility** satisfies wants by providing goods and services at a convenient place for customers. For example, ATMs offer banking services in many large supermarkets, Comfort Inn lodges tired travellers and businesspeople at many convenient locations, and vending machines refuel tired students at virtually every university and college campus.
- **Ownership utility** satisfies wants by smoothly transferring ownership of goods and services from seller to buyer. Virtually every product provides some degree of ownership utility, but some offer more than others. Honda Canada, and many other car dealerships, offers financing options.

Satisfying customer wants—in a way that exceeds expectations—is a job that never ends. Jay Levinson, a recognized expert in breakthrough marketing, comments: "Marketing is … a process. You improve it, perfect it, change it, even pause it. But you never stop it completely."

10-1a The Scope of Marketing: It's Everywhere!

For many years, businesspeople have actively applied the principles of marketing to goods and services ranging from cars, to fast food, to liquor, to computers, to movies. But within the past decade or two, other organizations have successfully adopted marketing strategies and tactics to further their goals.

Not-for-profit organizations—in the private *and* public sectors—play a significant role in our economy. These organizations use marketing, sometimes quite assertively, to achieve their objectives. The Government of Canada—the largest advertiser in Canada—spent $75.2 million on advertising in 2013–14, 46.5 percent of it on television advertising and 27.1 percent of it on Internet advertising. This was considerably less than the $136.3 million spent in 2009–10. Your own college or university probably markets itself to both prospective students and potential alumni donors. Private sector not-for-profit organizations also use marketing strategies for everything from marshalling hockey coaches for kids, to boosting attendance at the local zoo, to planning cultural events.[1]

Not-for-profit organizations have played a pivotal role in the expansion of marketing across our economy to include people, places, events, and ideas. But for-profit enterprises have also begun to apply marketing strategies and tactics beyond simply goods and services.

place utility The power of a good or a service to satisfy customer "wants" by providing goods and services at a convenient place for customers.

ownership utility The power of a good or a service to satisfy customer "wants" by smoothly transferring ownership of goods and services from seller to buyer.

- **People marketing:** Politics, sports, and the arts dominate in this category. Countless politicians, athletes, and entertainers have used people marketing to their advantage. Consider, for example, Paris Hilton, who appeared to build her early career on promotion alone, eventually parlaying the media attention into a successful line of perfumes and fashion items. Hilton clearly has no doubt about her abilities, declaring: "I am a marketing genius." In fact, as you pursue your personal goals—whether you seek a new job or a Friday night date—people marketing principles can help you achieve your objective. Start by figuring out what your "customer" needs and then ensure that your "product" (you!) delivers above and beyond expectations.

- **Place marketing:** This category involves drawing people to a particular place. Provinces and cities use place marketing to attract businesses. Manitoba, for example, is "Friendly Manitoba." Nova Scotia is "Canada's Ocean Playground." Consider "Beautiful British Columbia." Montreal has its International Jazz Festival, Toronto has its International Film Festival, and Calgary has its Stampede.

    Provinces and territories, cities and municipalities—and even Canada—use place marketing to attract tourists. There are expected to be 100 million annual outbound travellers from China by 2020. Canada has launched a major campaign in China with the tagline "Say Hello to Canada," hoping to attract many Chinese tourists to Niagara Falls, Ottawa, Whistler, and Banff.[2]

- **Event marketing:** This category includes the marketing—or sponsoring—of athletic, cultural, or charitable events. One of the most heavily promoted events ever was the 2015 "Fight of the Century" between Floyd Mayweather Jr. and Manny Pacquiao, which broke the all-time pay-per-view record and resulted in a payout of $250 to $275 million for Mayweather. Pacquiao, the loser, earned only $170 to $190 million, or, about $5 million per minute.[3] Partnerships between the public and private sectors are increasingly common in event marketing. Examples include the Olympics, the Grey Cup, and the many benefit concerts and telethons held across Canada each year to raise charity funds.

- **Idea marketing:** A whole range of public and private organizations market ideas that are meant to change how people think or act. Buckle your seatbelt, support our political party, recycle, donate blood, don't pollute, don't smoke—all are examples of popular causes. Often, idea marketing and event marketing are combined, as we see in the annual Avon Walk for Breast Cancer. The planners actively market the idea of annual mammograms as they solicit contributions for breast cancer research and participation in the event itself.

10-1b The Evolution of Marketing: From the Product to the Customer

The current approach to marketing evolved through a number of overlapping stages, as you'll see in Exhibit 10.1. But as you read about these eras, keep in mind that some businesses have remained lodged—with varying degrees of success—in the thinking of a past era.

Production Era Marketing didn't always begin with the customer. In fact, in the early 1900s, the customer was practically a joke. Henry Ford summed up the prevailing mindset when he reportedly said: "You can have your Model T in any colour you want as long as it's black." This attitude made sense from a historical perspective since consumers didn't have the overwhelming number of choices that are currently available; most products were purchased as soon as they were produced and distributed to consumers. In this context, the top business priority was to produce large quantities of goods as efficiently as possible.

Selling Era By the 1920s, production capacity had increased dramatically. For the first time, supply in many categories exceeded demand, which caused the emergence of the hard sell. The selling focus gained momentum in the 1930s and 1940s, when the Depression and the Second World War made consumers even more reluctant to part with their limited funds.

Marketing Era The landscape changed dramatically in the 1950s. Many factories that had churned out military goods converted to consumer production, flooding the market with choices in almost every product category. An era of relative peace and prosperity emerged, and as soldiers returned from the war, marriage and birth rates soared. To compete for the consumer's dollar, marketers

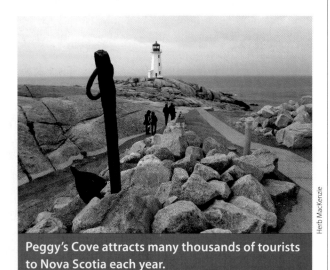

Herb MacKenzie

Peggy's Cove attracts many thousands of tourists to Nova Scotia each year.

The Evolution of Marketing

ERA	Production	Sales	Marketing	Relationship	Social
PREVAILING ATTITUDE	"A good product will sell itself."	"Creative advertising and selling will overcome consumers' resistance and persuade them to buy."	"The consumer rules! Find a need and fill it."	"Long-term relationships with customers and other partners lead to success."	"Connecting to consumers via Internet and social media sites is an effective tool."
APPROXIMATE TIME PERIOD	Prior to 1920s	Prior to 1950s	Since 1950s	Since 1990s	Since 2000s

attempted to provide goods and services that met customer needs better than anything else on the market. As a result, the marketing concept materialized in the 1950s. The **marketing concept** is a philosophy that makes customer satisfaction—now and in the future—the central focus of the entire organization. Companies that embrace this philosophy strive to delight customers, integrating this goal into all business activities. The marketing concept holds that delivering unmatched value to customers is the only effective way to achieve long-term profitability.

Relationship Era The marketing concept has gathered momentum across the economy, leading to the current era, unfolding over the last decade, which zeros in on long-term customer relationships. Acquiring a new customer can cost five times more than keeping an existing customer. Retaining your current customers—and getting them to spend additional dollars—is clearly cost-effective. Moreover, satisfied customers can develop into advocates for your business, becoming powerful generators of positive "word of mouth."

Social Era The social era began shortly after the rise of the Internet, and in the middle of the second decade of the 21st century, its impact on marketing has become ubiquitous. In its early years, the Internet was viewed simply as another communication tool and as an enabler of e-commerce, but the development of social media has demonstrated that it can facilitate not only promotion and online business, but also marketing research and relationship building. Businesses and consumers are able to develop and exchange information, ideas, and audiovisual content through virtual communities and networks using Facebook, Twitter, YouTube, LinkedIn, Instagram, Pinterest, Snapchat, and other mobile and Web-based social media. Businesses now routinely connect with consumers through social media as a way to market goods and services, and to more deeply understand consumer attitudes and behaviours.

10-2 The Customer: Front and Centre

10-2a Customer Relationship Management (CRM)

Customer relationship management (CRM) is the centrepiece of successful 21st-century marketing. Broadly defined, CRM is the ongoing process of acquiring, maintaining, and growing profitable customer relationships by delivering unmatched value. CRM works best when marketers combine marketing communication with one-on-one personalization. Amazon is a champion player at CRM, greeting customers by name, recommending specific products, and providing streamlined checkout. Clearly, information is an integral part of this process—you simply can't do CRM without collecting, managing, and applying the right data at the right time for the right person (and every repeat customer is the "right person").

> **marketing concept**
> A business philosophy that makes customer satisfaction—now and in the future—the central focus of the entire organization.
>
> **customer relationship management (CRM)**
> The ongoing process of acquiring, maintaining, and growing profitable customer relationships by delivering unmatched value.

Limited Relationships The scope of your relationships will depend not just on the data you gather but also on your industry. Colgate-Palmolive, for example, can't forge a close personal bond with every person who buys a bar of Irish Spring soap. But it does invite customers to call its toll-free line with questions or comments, and it maintains a vibrant website with music, an e-newsletter, special offers, and an invitation to contact the company. You can bet that the company actively gathers data and pursues a connection with customers who do initiate contact.

Full Partnerships If you have a high-ticket product and a smaller customer base, you're much more likely to pursue a full partnership with each of your key clients. Colgate-Palmolive, for instance, has dedicated customer service teams working with key accounts such as Walmart and Costco. With a full partnership, the marketer gathers and leverages extensive information about each customer and often includes the customer in key aspects of the product development process.

Value You know you've delivered **value** when your customers believe that your product has a better relationship between cost and benefits than any competitor. By this definition, low cost does not always mean high value. In fact, a recent survey suggests that loyal customers are often willing to pay *more* for their products rather than switch to lower cost competitors. Apple provides a clear example. We probably all personally know at least a handful of Apple fanatics who gladly pay far more for their Apple Watch (or iPhone or iPad) than they would pay for a competing product.

10-2b Perceived Value versus Actual Value

The operative idea here is *perceived*. Simply creating value isn't enough; you also must help customers believe that your product is uniquely qualified to meet their needs. This becomes a particular challenge when you're a new business competing against a market leader with disproportionately strong perceived value.

10-2c Customer Satisfaction

You know you've satisfied your customers when you deliver perceived value above and beyond their expectations. But achieving

value A customer perception that a product has a better relationship than its competitors between the cost and the benefits.

customer satisfaction When customers perceive that a good or service delivers value above and beyond their expectations.

customer loyalty When customers buy a product from the same supplier again and again—sometimes even paying more for it than they would for a competitive product.

marketing plan A formal document that defines marketing objectives and the specific strategies for achieving those objectives.

market segmentation Dividing potential customers into groups of similar people, or segments.

customer satisfaction can be tricky. Less savvy marketers often fall into one of two traps:

- The first trap is *overpromising*. Even if you deliver more value than anyone else, your customers will be disappointed if your product falls short of overly high expectations. The messages you send regarding your product influence expectations—keep them real!

- The second trap is *underpromising*. If you don't set expectations high enough, too few customers will be willing to try your product. The result will be a tiny base of highly satisfied customers, which usually isn't enough to sustain a business.

Finding the right balance is tricky but clearly not impossible. Judging by their high scores on the American Customer Satisfaction Index, the following companies have come close to mastering the art of customer satisfaction: Costco, Amazon, Lowe's, and L Brands (Victoria's Secret, Bath & Body Works).[4]

10-2d Customer Loyalty

Customer loyalty is the payoff from delivering value and generating satisfaction. Loyal customers purchase from you again and again—and they sometimes even pay more for your product. They forgive your mistakes. They provide valuable feedback. They may require less service. They refer their friends (and sometimes even strangers). Moreover, studying your loyal customers can give you a competitive edge for acquiring new ones because people with a similar profile would likely be a great fit for your products.[5]

10-3 Marketing Strategy: Where Are You Going and How Will You Get There?

In marketing terms, the question becomes: Who is your target audience and how will you reach them? Many successful firms answer this question by developing a formal **marketing plan**, updated on a yearly basis; other firms handle their planning on a more informal basis. But regardless of the specific approach, the first step in planning your marketing strategy should be to determine where to target your efforts. Who are those people who are most likely to buy your products? The first step is **market segmentation**—dividing your market into groups of people who are similar to one another and different from everyone else (i.e., segments). One or more of these segments will be your target market. Once you've identified your target market, your next step is to determine how you can best use marketing tools to reach them. And finally, you need to anticipate and respond to changes in the external environment. This section will define a target market, explain market segmentation, introduce the marketing mix, and review the key factors in the marketing environment. Taken together, these elements will shape an effective marketing strategy, as shown in Exhibit 10.2.

10-3a Target Market

Your **target market** is the group of people who are most likely to buy your product. This is where you should concentrate your marketing efforts. But why not target your efforts towards everyone? After all, even if most middle-aged moms wouldn't buy purple polka-dotted miniskirts, an adventurous few just might do it. Well, you can always hope for the adventurous few, but virtually every business has limited resources, and marketing towards the people who are most likely to buy your flamboyant minis—say, teenage girls—will maximize the impact of each dollar you spend. A well-chosen target market embodies the following characteristics:

- **Size:** There must be enough people in your target group to support a business.

- **Profitability:** The people must be willing and able to spend more than the cost of producing and marketing your product.

- **Accessibility:** Your target must be reachable through channels that your business can afford.

- **Limited competition:** Look for markets with limited competition; a crowded market is much tougher to crack.

10-3b Consumer Markets Versus Business Markets

Consumer marketers (B2C) direct their efforts to people who are buying products for personal consumption (e.g., candy bars, shampoo, and clothing), whereas **business marketers (B2B)** direct their efforts to customers who are buying products to use either directly or indirectly to produce other products (e.g., tractors, steel, and cash registers). But keep in mind that the distinction between the market categories is not in the products themselves; rather, it lies in how the buyer will use the product. For instance, shampoo that you buy for yourself is clearly a consumer product, but shampoo that a hair stylist buys for a salon is a business product. Similarly, a computer you buy for yourself is a consumer product, but a computer your school buys for the computer lab is a business product. Both B2C and B2B marketers need to choose the best target, but they tend to follow slightly different approaches.

10-3c Consumer Market Segmentation

Choosing the best target market (or markets) for your product begins with dividing your market into segments, or groups of people who have similar characteristics. But people can be similar in a number of different ways, so, not surprisingly, marketers have several options for segmenting potential consumers.

Demographic Segmentation Demographic **segmentation** refers to dividing the market based on measurable characteristics about people, such as age, income, ethnicity, and gender. Demographics are a vital starting point for most marketers. Chapstick, for instance, targets young women with the Shimmer version of its lip balm, and Chevy Camaro targets young men who have money. Sometimes the demographic makeup of a given market is tough to discern; black artists, for

target market The group of people who are most likely to buy a particular product.

consumer marketers (aka business-to-consumer or B2C) Marketers who direct their efforts towards people who are buying products for personal consumption.

business marketers (aka business-to-business or B2B) Marketers who direct their efforts towards people who are buying products to use either directly or indirectly to produce other products.

demographic segmentation Dividing the market into smaller groups based on measurable characteristics about people, such as age, income, ethnicity, and gender.

Exhibit 10.2 Marketing Strategy

The marketer creates the marketing mix but responds to the marketing environment with a single-minded focus on the target market.

Competitive
Social/Cultural
Product Strategy
Pricing Strategy
Economic
TARGET MARKET
Promotion Strategy
Distribution Strategy
Technological
Political/Legal

© Cengage Learning

COLOUR ME... HUNGRY?!

Have you ever noticed that fast food restaurants typically feature vivid shades of red, yellow, and orange in both their logos and their decor? Think McDonald's, KFC, Burger King, and Pizza Hut. The colour choice is no coincidence.

Marketing researchers have learned that consumers associate red with energy, passion, and speed. Yellow suggests happiness and warmth, while orange suggests playfulness, affordability, and fun. A simulated cocktail party study found that partygoers in red rooms

Herb MacKenzie

reported feeling hungrier and thirstier than others, and guests in yellow rooms ate twice as much as others. The implication: Surrounding customers with red, yellow, and orange encourages them to eat a lot quickly and leave, which aligns nicely with the goals of most fast food chains.

Colour psychology is a powerful—although often overlooked—marketing tool. Colours evoke emotions and trigger specific behaviours, which can dramatically influence how people buy your product. Here is a list of common colours and some of their associations in Canadian mainstream culture.

Keep in mind that while some colour associations are universal, others can differ significantly among cultures, and Canada is a land with many diverse cultures. White, for instance, signifies death

and mourning in Chinese culture, while purple represents death in Brazil.

RED ---------- Love, passion, warmth, food, excitement, action, danger, need to stop

BLUE ---------- Power, trustworthiness, calm, success, seriousness, boredom

GREEN ---------- Money, nature, health, healing, decay, illness

ORANGE ---------- Playfulness, affordability, youth, fun, low quality, cheap

PURPLE ---------- Royalty, luxury, dignity, spirituality, nightmares, craziness

WHITE ---------- Purity, innocence, simplicity, mildness

BLACK ---------- Sophistication, elegance, seriousness, sexuality, mystery, evil

As a marketer, your goal should be to align your colour choice with the perceptions of your target market and the features of your product. The result should be more green for your bottom line![6]

© Cengage Learning

---

instance, create the bulk of rap music, yet Caucasian suburban males form the bulk of the rap music market.

Geographic Segmentation Geographic segmentation refers to dividing the market based on where consumers live. This process can incorporate countries, cities, or population density as key factors. For instance, Ford Expedition does not concentrate on European markets, where tiny, winding streets and nonexistent parking are common in many cities. Cosmetic surgeons tend to market their services more heavily in urban rather than rural areas. And finding a great snowboard is easy in Whistler, BC, but more challenging in Regina, Saskatchewan.

geographic segmentation Dividing the market into smaller groups based on where consumers live. This process can incorporate countries, cities, or population density as key factors.

psychographic segmentation Dividing the market into smaller groups based on consumer attitudes, interests, values, and lifestyles.

Psychographic Segmentation Psychographic segmentation refers to dividing the market based on consumer attitudes, interests, values, and lifestyles. Toyota Prius, for instance, targets consumers who care about protecting the environment. A number of companies have found a highly profitable niche providing upscale wilderness experiences for people who seek all the pleasure with none of the pain (you enjoy the great outdoors, while someone else lugs your gear, pours your wine, slices your goat cheese, and inflates your extra-comfy air mattress). Both magazine racks and the Internet are filled with products geared towards psychographic segments, from Sports Illustrated, to InfoWorld, to Canadacomputers.com, to CanadianBusiness.com. Note: Marketers typically use psychographics to complement other segmentation approaches rather than to provide the core definition.

Consumers with shared attitudes, interests, values, and lifestyles often buy similar products.

Herb MacKenzie

Behavioural Segmentation Behavioural **segmentation** refers to dividing the market based on how people behave towards various products. This category includes both the benefits that consumers seek from products and how consumers use the product. The Neutrogena Corporation, for example, built a multimillion-dollar hair care business by targeting consumers who wanted an occasional break from their favourite shampoo. Countless products such as Miller Lite actively target the low-carbohydrate consumer. But perhaps the most common type of behavioural segmentation is based on usage patterns. Fast food restaurants, for instance, actively target heavy users (who, ironically, tend to be slender): young men in their 20s and 30s. This group consumes about 17 percent of their total calories from fast food, compared to 12 percent for adults in general. Understanding the usage patterns of your customer base gives you the option of either focusing on your core users or trying to pull light users into your core market.

10-3d **Business Market Segmentation**

B2B marketers typically follow a similar process in segmenting their markets, but they use slightly different categories:

B2B Geographic Segmentation This refers to dividing the B2B market based on the concentration of customers. Many industries tend to be highly clustered in certain areas, such as technology in Waterloo, Ontario, and oil exploration in Alberta and in Newfoundland and Labrador. Geographic segmentation, of course, is especially common on an international basis, given that variables such as language, culture, income, and regulatory differences can play a crucial role.

B2B Customer-Based Segmentation This refers to dividing the B2B market based on the characteristics of customers. This approach includes a range of possibilities. Some B2B marketers segment based on customer size. Others segment based on customer type. Johnson & Johnson, for example, has a group of salespeople dedicated exclusively to retail accounts such as Shoppers Drug Mart and Walmart, while other salespeople focus solely on motivating doctors to recommend their products. Other potential B2B markets include institutions—schools and hospitals, for instance, are key segments for Heinz Ketchup—and the government.

B2B Product Use-Based Segmentation This refers to dividing the B2B market based on how customers will use the product. Small and mid-sized companies find this strategy especially helpful in narrowing their target markets. Possibilities include developing the ability to support certain software packages or production systems, or to serve certain customer groups such as long-distance truckers or restaurants that deliver food.

10-3e **The Marketing Mix**

Once you've clearly defined your target market, your next challenge is to develop compelling strategies for product, price, distribution, and promotion. The blending of these elements becomes your **marketing mix**, as shown in Exhibit 10.3.

■ **Product strategy:** Your product involves far more than simply a tangible good or a specific

behavioural segmentation Dividing the market based on how people behave towards various products. This category includes both the benefits that consumers seek from products and how consumers use the product.

marketing mix The blend of marketing strategies for product, price, distribution, and promotion.

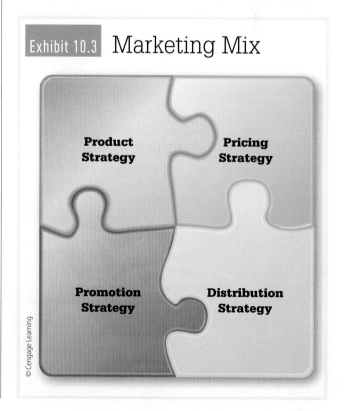

Exhibit 10.3 Marketing Mix

Product Strategy

Pricing Strategy

Promotion Strategy

Distribution Strategy

© Cengage Learning

service. Product strategy decisions range from brand name, to product image, to package design, to customer service, to guarantees, to new product development, and more. Designing the best product clearly begins with understanding the needs of your target market.

- **Pricing strategy:** Pricing is a challenging area of the marketing mix. To deliver customer value, your prices must be fair relative to the benefits of your product. Other factors include competition, regulation, and public opinion. Your product category plays a critical role as well. A low-cost desk, for instance, might be appealing, but who would want discount-priced knee surgery?

- **Promotion strategy:** Promotion includes all of the ways that marketers communicate about their products. The list of possibilities is long and growing, especially as the Internet continues to evolve at breakneck speed. Key elements today include advertising, personal selling, sales promotion, public relations, word of mouth, and product placement. Successful promotional strategies typically evolve in response to both customer needs and competition. A number of innovative companies are even inviting their customers to participate in creating their advertising through venues such as YouTube. Check out Exhibit 10.4 to see how easily you can analyze promotional strategies.

- **Distribution strategy:** The goal is to deliver your product to the right people, in the right quantities, at the

> Don't find customers for your products; find products for your customers.
>
> Seth Godin,
> entrepreneur and author

right time, in the right place. The key decisions include shipping, warehousing, and selling outlets (e.g., the Web versus network marketing versus bricks-and-mortar stores). The implications of these decisions for product image and customer satisfaction can be significant.

10-3f The Global Marketing Mix

As you decide to enter foreign markets, you'll need to re-evaluate your marketing mix for each new country. Should it change? If so, how should it change? Many business goods simply don't require much change in the marketing mix because their success isn't dependent on culture. Examples include heavy machinery, cement, and farming equipment. Consumer products, however, often require completely new marketing mixes to reach consumers effectively.

Nike's approach to marketing in China offers an interesting example of how one firm managed the complex process of building a successful business in a foreign market. When Nike first entered China in the 1990s, the company seemed to face an insurmountable challenge: not only did a pair of Nike sneakers cost twice the Chinese average monthly salary, but most Chinese just didn't play sports, according to Terry Rhoads, then director of Nike sports marketing. So he boldly set out to change that. Rhoads created a Nike high school basketball league, which has since spread to 17 cities. To loosen up fans, he blasted canned cheering during games and arranged for

---

Exhibit 10.4 Analyzing Promotional Strategies

How does Honda position its Civic and Accord vehicles? How does the target market differ for each of the two models?

SOME SECRETS MIGHT BE BETTER KEPT SECRET

Ever wonder if your fast food favourites just don't have quite enough fat and calories? Well, you could always get more, if only you knew what to ask for. A surprising number of fast food chains offer "secret menus" that include interesting (and sometimes horrifying) new combinations of food and beverages. They aren't available at all locations, but if any of them appeal to you, it can't hurt to ask, next time you have the munchies. A sampling:

- **Burger King Suicide Burger:** four beef patties, four slices of cheese, plenty of bacon, and BK's special sauce. Or try the Noah's Ark Burger: two fish burgers with two Whopper patties, two chicken patties, two veggie burger patties, and four slices of bacon added. (Build it at your table.)
- **Starbucks Raspberry Cheesecake Frappuccino:** This decadent delight can be had for the asking, along with the Captain Crunch Frappuccino, the Cinnamon Roll Frappuccino, and several other surprising concoctions.
- **Tim Hortons:** The next time you order a Double Double, ask for half of it to be filled with hot chocolate. You now have a cheap mocha, and you can ask for whipped cream on top.
- **Wendy's Barnyard Burger:** a spicy chicken filet, a burger patty,

Herb MacKenzie

ham, and bacon, with a slice of cheese between each.

- **McDonald's Land, Sea, and Air Burger:** a beef patty, a Filet O' Fish patty, and a chicken patty, drenched in tartar sauce and huddled between two buns. Or, try the Mc10:35 burger, so named because you can only get it during the transition period between breakfast and lunch: egg and ham from a McMuffin between two patties in a McDouble burger.

So why all the secrecy? Having a secret menu makes loyal customers feel "in the know." A secret menu is not publicly posted and therefore not subject to government regulation. Many options on the secret menus do not align with the more healthy images that the firms are attempting to convey. Maybe they are ashamed. In any event, according to restaurant industry analyst Bonnie Riggs, "fast food is trying any way they can to compete with fast casual."[8]

Sources: Arti Patel, "20 Tim Hortons Secret Menu Items Approved by Readers," *The Huffington Post Canada*, July 15, 2015 Debbie Siegelbaum, "Secret Menus: Fast Food 'Hacks' for In-the-Know Customers," *BBC News*, September 3, 2014; Dan Myers, "Wild Fast-Food Secret Menu Items," foxnews.com, October 30, 2013; Alaina McConnell, "14 Secret Menu Items You Can Order at Fast Food Restaurants," *Financial Post*, December 22, 2012.

national TV coverage of the finals. He even leveraged connections with the NBA to bring Michael Jordan for visits.

The gamble quickly paid off as the Chinese middle class emerged, along with more individualistic values, which are a strong fit with the Nike ethos. By 2001, Nike had dubbed its marketing approach "hip hoop," describing it as an effort to "connect Nike with a creative lifestyle." Sales in 2014 exceeded US$2.5 billion, driven largely by footwear. Nike currently is striving to build Chinese sales on its existing basketball fans by further developing an individual and team sports culture. Nike executive Don Blair comments: "China has one of the biggest populations who are tuned in to sports, but they aren't yet participants."[7]

10-3g The Marketing Environment

While marketers actively influence the elements of the marketing mix, they must anticipate and respond to the elements of the external environment, which they typically cannot control. **Environmental scanning** is a key tool; the goal is simply to continually collect information from sources ranging from informal networks, to industry newsletters, to the general press, to customers, to suppliers, to the competition, among others. The key components of the external environment include the following:

Competitive The dynamic competitive environment probably affects marketers on a day-to-day basis more than any other element. Understanding the competitive environment often begins with analysis of **market share**, or the percentage of the marketplace that each firm controls. To avoid ambushes, and to uncover new opportunities, you must continually monitor how both dominant and emerging competitors handle each element of

> **environmental scanning** The process of continually collecting information from the external marketing environment.
>
> **market share** The percentage of a market controlled by a given marketer.

their marketing mix. And don't forget indirect competitors, who meet the same consumer needs as you but with a completely different product (e.g., Altoids versus Scope).

Economic The only certainty in the economic environment is change, but the timing of expansions and contractions is virtually impossible to predict. Your goal as a marketer is to identify and respond to changes as soon as possible, keeping in mind that a sharp eye sees opportunity even in economic downturns. For instance, affordable luxuries and do-it-yourself enterprises can thrive during recessions.

Social/Cultural The social/cultural element covers a vast array of factors including lifestyle, customs, language, attitudes, interests, and population shifts. Trends can change rapidly, with a dramatic impact on marketing decisions. Anticipating and responding to trends can be especially important in industries such as entertainment, fashion, and technology. When Facebook removed some key privacy controls from its News Feed, the social media giant did not anticipate the black eye it would quickly receive from outraged consumers who believed that Facebook had violated their privacy. Facebook was also surprised that the privacy controls it later implemented—which required consumers to opt out of sharing—would not be enough to appease privacy advocates.[9]

Technological Changes in technology can be highly visible to consumers (e.g., the introduction of the Apple Watch). However, technology often impacts marketers in ways that are less visible. For example, today's technology allows for the mass customization of Levi's blue jeans at a reasonable price; it also facilitates just-in-time inventory management for countless companies, which see the results in their bottom line.

Political/Legal The political/legal area includes laws, regulations, and the political climate. Most Canadian laws and regulations are clear (e.g., impaired driving is illegal in all provinces and territories), but others are complex and evolving (e.g., qualifications for certain tax breaks). The political climate includes changing levels of governmental support for various business categories. Clearly, political/legal issues affect heavily regulated sectors (e.g., telecommunications and pharmaceuticals) more than others.

10-3h The Global Marketing Environment

As the Internet has grown, the world market has become accessible to almost every business. This has boosted the importance of understanding each element of the marketing environment—competitive, economic, social/cultural, technological, and political/legal—in each of your key markets. The biggest global challenges include finding ways to research opportunities in other countries and to deliver your products to customers in those countries.

10-4 Customer Behaviour: Decisions, Decisions, Decisions!

If successful marketing begins with the customer, then understanding the customer is critical. Why do people buy one product but not another? How do they use the products they buy? When do they get rid of them? Knowing the answers to these questions will clearly help you better meet customer needs.

10-4a Consumer Behaviour

Consumer behaviour refers specifically to how people act when they are buying products for their own personal consumption. The decisions they make often seem spontaneous (after all, how much thought do you give to buying a pack of gum?), but they often result from a complex set of influences, as shown in Exhibit 10.5.

Marketers, of course, add their own influence through the marketing mix. For instance, after smelling pretzels in the mall and tasting pretzel morsels from the sample tray, many of us will at least be tempted to cough up the cash for a hot, buttery pretzel of our own—regardless of any other factors. Similarly, changes in the external environment—for example, a series of floods in Manitoba—dramatically affect consumer decisions about items such as rubber boots, sump pumps, and batteries.

All of these forces shape consumer behaviour in each step of the process of making a purchase decision. Exhibit 10.6 shows how the consumer decision process works.

Clearly, marketing can influence the purchase decision every step of the way, from helping consumers identify needs (or problems) to resolving that awful feeling of **cognitive dissonance** (or second-guessing oneself) after a major purchase. Some marketers address cognitive dissonance by developing specific programs to help customers validate their purchase choices. One example is post-purchase mailings that highlight the accolades received by an expensive product.

consumer behaviour
Description of how people act when they are buying, using, and discarding goods and services for their own personal consumption. Consumer behaviour also explores the reasons behind people's actions.

cognitive dissonance
Consumer discomfort with a purchase decision, typically for a major purchase.

Exhibit 10.5 — Elements That Influence the Consumer Decision-Making Process

INFLUENCE	DESCRIPTION
CULTURAL	*Culture:* The values, attitudes, and customs shared by members of a society *Microculture:* A smaller division of the broader culture *Social class:* Societal position driven largely by income and occupation
SOCIAL	*Family:* A powerful force in consumption choices *Friends:* Another powerful force, especially for high-profile purchases *Reference groups:* Groups that give consumers a point of comparison
PERSONAL	*Demographics:* Measurable characteristics such as age, gender, or income *Personality:* The mix of traits that determine who you are
PSYCHOLOGICAL	*Motivation:* Pressing needs that tend to generate action *Attitudes:* Lasting evaluations of (or feelings about) objects or ideas *Perceptions:* How people select, organize, and interpret information *Learning:* Changes in behaviour based on experience

© Cengage Learning

But does every consumer go through every step of the process all the time? Clearly not. People make low-involvement decisions (such as buying that pack of gum) according to habit, or even just on a whim. But when the stakes are high—be they financial or social—most people move through the five steps of the classic decision-making process. For example, most of us wouldn't think of buying a car, a computer, or the "right" pair of blue jeans without walking ourselves through the decision-making process.

10-4b Business Buyer Behaviour

Business buyer behaviour refers to how people act when they're buying products to use either directly or indirectly (i.e., to produce other products, such as chemicals, copy paper, and computer servers). Business buyers typically have purchasing training and apply rational criteria to their decisions. They usually buy according to purchase specifications and objective standards, with a minimum of personal judgment or whim. Often, business buyers are integrating input from a number of internal sources, based on a relatively formal process. And finally, business buyers tend to seek (and often secure) highly customized goods, services, and prices.

Exhibit 10.6 — Consumer Decision Process

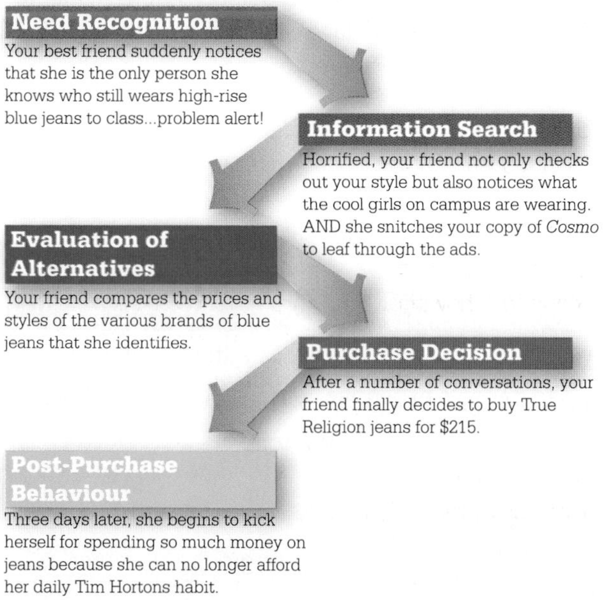

Need Recognition
Your best friend suddenly notices that she is the only person she knows who still wears high-rise blue jeans to class...problem alert!

Information Search
Horrified, your friend not only checks out your style but also notices what the cool girls on campus are wearing. AND she snitches your copy of *Cosmo* to leaf through the ads.

Evaluation of Alternatives
Your friend compares the prices and styles of the various brands of blue jeans that she identifies.

Purchase Decision
After a number of conversations, your friend finally decides to buy True Religion jeans for $215.

Post-Purchase Behaviour
Three days later, she begins to kick herself for spending so much money on jeans because she can no longer afford her daily Tim Hortons habit.

© Cengage Learning

10-5 Marketing Research: So What Do They *Really* Think?

If marketing begins with the customer, marketing research is the foundation of success. **Marketing research** involves gathering, interpreting, and applying

business buyer behaviour How people act when they are buying products to use either directly or indirectly to produce other products.

marketing research The process of gathering, interpreting, and applying information to uncover marketing opportunities and challenges and to make better marketing decisions.

information to uncover opportunities and challenges. The goal, of course, is better marketing decisions: more value for consumers and more profits for businesses that deliver. Companies use marketing research for the following reasons:

- To identify external opportunities and threats (from competition to social trends).
- To monitor and predict customer behaviour.
- To evaluate and improve each area of the marketing mix.

Most successful marketers rely on research to develop breakthrough products and effective marketing programs. But research will never replace the creative potential of the gifted individual. Steve Jobs, founder of Apple, famously declared: "A lot of times, people don't know what they want until you show it to them."

10-5a Types of Data

There are two main categories of marketing research data—**secondary data** and **primary data**—each with its own set of benefits and drawbacks, as shown in Exhibit 10.7.

secondary data Existing data that marketers gather or purchase for a research project.

primary data New data that marketers compile for a specific research project.

observation research Marketing research that does not require the researcher to interact with the research subject.

Clearly, it makes sense to gather secondary data before you invest in primary research. Look at your company's internal information. What does previous research say? What does the press say? What can you find on the Web? Once you've looked at the secondary research, you may find that primary research is unnecessary. But if not, your secondary research will guide your primary research and make it more focused and relevant, which ends up saving time and money.

10-5b Primary Research Tools

There are two basic categories of primary research: observation and survey. **Observation research** happens when the researcher *does not* directly interact with the research subject. The key advantage of watching versus asking is that what people actually *do* often differs from what they *say*—sometimes quite innocently. For instance, when an amusement park employee stands outside an attraction and records which way people turn when they exit, he may be conducting observation research to determine where to place a new lemonade stand. In this case, watching is better than asking because many people could not honestly say which way they're likely to turn. Examples of observation research include the following:

- Scanner data from retail sales
- Traffic counters to determine where to place billboards
- Garbage analysis to measure recycling compliance

Observation research can be both cheap and amazingly effective. A car dealership, for instance, might survey the preset radio stations on every car that comes in for service. That information will then help them choose which stations to use for advertising. The main downside of observation research is that it doesn't yield any information on consumer motivation—the reasons behind consumer decisions. The preset radio stations won't matter, for example, if the bulk of drivers listen only to their iPods in the car.

Exhibit 10.7 Research Data Comparison	
SECONDARY DATA	**PRIMARY DATA**
Existing data that marketers gather or purchase	New data that marketers compile for the first time
Tends to be lower cost	Tends to be more expensive
May not meet your *specific* needs	Customized to meet your needs
Frequently outdated	Fresh, new data
Available to your competitors	Proprietary—no one else has it
Examples: Statistics Canada, *Globe and Mail*, *Canadian Business*, your product sales history	Examples: Your own surveys, focus groups, customer comments, mall interviews

© Cengage Learning

Oops! What were they thinking?

"If you can't be a good example, then you'll just have to serve as a horrible warning."

Even the heavy hitters make marketing gaffes. Their biggest mistakes are often entertaining, but they also serve as a powerful warning to consult with the customer *before* taking action. A few amusing examples:

- In 2010, Gap, a company known for basic, everyday clothing, tried to update its image to appeal to the trendy, more contemporary crowd. Unfortunately, it lost sight of its strength among its existing target market. The consumer backlash was swift, and after only two days, Gap reverted to its older logo—one that had served it well for more than two decades. There are many instances throughout marketing history where companies decided to update their brand or brand image but upset their target existing customers; Campbell's, Quaker Oats, and Coca-Cola provide other examples.

- In 2012, Direct Energy sent letters to some 500 000 Ontario customers. Bolded sections of the letter promised customers a number of benefits, including a service guarantee and inflation price protection. Unfortunately, an unbolded section that followed informed customers that the terms and conditions of the new contract that was attached would come into effect shortly if the customer did not call and specifically request to remain on their old contract. The problem: With the new contract, customers risked being billed from a few hundred dollars to more than $3000 if they decided to drop Direct Energy. The company's phone lines became so jammed by angry callers that the hate factor increased when many could not get through to the company. It's a good guess that the company's attempt to protect its market share has cost it considerably.

- In 2014, Coors Light ran a promotion where it left suitcases bearing the brewer's logo around several Canadian cities. Finders could tweet a picture of themselves with a special code, and subsequently receive prizes. In Toronto, an off-duty police officer spied one suitcase attached to a metal railing and decided it was suspicious. The resulting traffic mayhem that resulted as police investigated the package caused considerable confusion. One irate commuter tweeted, "Awesome. You're the reason it took me an extra 20 minutes to get home from work. I'll continue avoiding your beer."

These fiascos only highlight the importance of *marketing research*. But sometimes, of course, even research isn't enough to identify marketing issues before they hit. At that point, the priority should shift to dealing with the mistake openly, honestly, and quickly, which can help a company win the game, despite the gaffe.[10]

Sources: Jacquelyn Stevens and Marc McAree, "'Greenwashing' Environmental Claims Give Rise to Legal Liability," Fabricare Canada, September/October 2014; Rebecca Harris, "Greenwashing: Cleaning Up by 'Saving the World,'" *Marketing*; Adam Kingsmith, "Pretty Little Industrial liars, Pt. 1," DeSmog Canada; *CBC Marketplace*.

With **survey research**, the researcher *does* interact with research subjects. The key advantage is that you can secure information about what people are thinking and feeling, beyond what you can observe. For example, a carmaker might observe that most of its purchasers are men. It could then use this information to tailor its advertising to men, or it could do survey research and possibly learn that although men do the actual purchasing, women often make the purchase decision—a very different scenario! The main downside of survey research is that many people aren't honest or accurate about their experiences, opinions, and motivations, which can make survey research quite misleading. Examples of survey research include the following:

- Telephone and online questionnaires
- Door-to-door interviews
- Mall-intercept interviews
- Focus groups
- Mail-in questionnaires

10-5c An International Perspective

Conducting marketing research across multiple countries can be an overwhelming challenge. In parts of Latin America, for instance, many homes don't have telephone connections, so the results from telephone surveys can be very misleading. Door-to-door tends to be a better approach, but in parts of the Middle East, researchers could be arrested for knocking on a stranger's door, especially if they aren't dressed according to local standards. Because of these kinds of issues, many companies hire research firms with a strong local presence (often based in-country) to handle their international marketing research projects.

> **survey research** Marketing research that requires the researcher to interact with the research subject.

10-6 Social Responsibility and Technology: A Major Marketing Shift

Two key factors have had a dramatic impact on marketing over the last couple of decades: a surge in the social responsibility movement, and the dramatic rise of the Internet and digital technology. This section covers how each factor has influenced marketing.

10-6a Marketing and Society: It's Not Just about You!

Over the past couple of decades, the social responsibility movement has accelerated in Canada, demanding that marketers actively contribute to the needs of the broader community. Leading-edge marketers have responded by setting higher standards in key areas such as environmentalism, the abolishment of sweatshops, and involvement in the local community. Loblaw Companies Limited, for instance, publishes on its website a formal corporate social responsibility report that explains what it is doing to benefit its communities. Walmart Canada does the same. Canadian Tire highlights its corporate citizenship initiatives on its website; so do many other influential businesses that operate in Canada.

Green Marketing Companies are employing **green marketing** when they actively promote the ecological benefits of their products. Toyota has been especially successful promoting the green benefits of its Prius (although like all carmakers, Toyota has struggled during the global financial crisis and, more recently, as a consequence of the Japanese earthquake and tsunami). Its strategy highlights fuel economy *and* performance, implying that consumers can "go green" without making any real sacrifices. Environmentally friendly fashion offers another emerging example of green marketing. Over the past few years, a number of designers have rolled out their versions of upscale eco-fashion. In addition to clothing from organic cotton, recent entries include vegan stilettos with four-inch heels, bamboo dresses, biodegradable umbrellas, and solar-powered jackets (these jackets feature solar cells, integrated into the collar, that collect solar energy and route it to charge devices). Green marketing items are aimed at a growing number of consumers who make purchase decisions based (at least in part) on their convictions. But reaching these consumers may

green marketing The development and promotion of products with ecological benefits.

Whitewashing with a Green Paint Brush

If you are truly concerned about the environment—and many Canadians are—you need to start asking questions when you see "green" claims. Many consumers have been buying "natural," "environmentally friendly," and "sustainable" products unaware that they are actually hurting the environment. Marketers are only too willing to put a word on a package or in an advertisement if they believe it will result in increased sales, but in many instances their claims are unsubstantiated. The Greendex, an annual study conducted across 17 countries, found Canadians to be among the most environmentally concerned but also among the least likely to make green choices. Cost and inconvenience are reasons often given, but the most common reason was a belief that many manufacturers are simply greenwashing—whitewashing with a green paintbrush. This was further supported by BrandSpark, which found that 60 percent of Canadians believed green claims were often misleading or exaggerated. Proof that Canadian consumers are wise to be skeptical: environmental advocacy firm TerraChoice investigated 2219 products making green claims in North America. All but 25 were guilty of at least one of the "seven sins of greenwashing": vagueness, lack of proof, fibbing, fake and false label certifications, irrelevance, "hidden tradeoffs," or "the lesser of two evils." A couple of greenwashing examples:

Dawn antibacterial soap. The company promised, "Dawn helps save wildlife," and showed ducklings and seals on some packaging and in some promotions. A CBC *Marketplace* investigation found one ingredient to be triclosan, an antibacterial agent declared toxic to marine life.

Organic Melt ice remover. The company advertised an environmentally safe "agricultural-based product" with sugar beets. The company disclosed to CBC's *Marketplace* that only 3 percent of its product by weight was sugar beets and that 97 percent was simply regular rock salt.

P.V.I. International. The company claimed that its device reduced emissions, was US-government certified, and improved fuel efficiency by 22 percent. Canada's Competition Tribunal fined the company $75,000 (and two of the company officers $25,000 each) for engaging in deceptive marketing practices. The company could not produce research to substantiate its claims.

The biggest threat of greenwashing is that legitimate companies—those that have products and practices that benefit the environment—will be tarnished with the same brush. If you are concerned for the environment—and hopefully you are—keep searching for and using green alternatives, but be wary of corporate greenwashers.[11]

Sources: "Environment a fair-weather priority for consumers", June 3, 2008, Penn, Schoen & Bergland Press Release, Penn, Schoen & Bergland website; "Green Fashion: Is It More Than Marketing Hype?" by Gloria Sin, May 28, 2008, *Fast Company* website; "Green Fashion," *Formerly Hippie, Now Hip!* February 21, 2008, *CBS News* website.

be an increasing challenge in tough economic times, when low prices trump all other considerations for a growing number of people.[12]

10-6b Technology and Marketing: Power to the People!

The digital age has revolutionized every element of marketing. Perhaps the most dramatic change has been a shift in power from producers to customers. The Internet gives customers 24/7 access to information and product choices from all over the world. In response, competition has intensified as marketers strive to meet an increasingly high standard of value.

But technology has also created *opportunities* for marketers. The Internet has opened the door for **mass customization**: creating products tailored for individual consumers on a mass basis. Using sophisticated data collection and management systems, marketers can now collect detailed information about each customer, which allows them to develop one-on-one relationships and to identify high-potential new customers. Through the Web, marketers can tap into (or even create) communities of users in order to gather valuable information about their goods and services. Technology also helps marketers lower costs so that they can deliver greater value to their customers.

The digital boom has also created an abundance of promotional opportunities as marketers reach out to consumers via new tools such as interactive advertising, virtual reality displays, text messaging, and video kiosks. We'll discuss these tools in more detail in Chapter 11.

> Just over 20% of people say they think most creatively in their cars, while 5% say they think most creatively in the shower, and—surprisingly—only 1% say they think most creatively while listening to music.
>
> M.I.T. Invention Index

mass customization The creation of products tailored for individual consumers on a mass basis.

INNOVATION UNLEASHED!

Herb MacKenzie

In today's hypercompetitive marketplace, businesses must differentiate their products from an astonishing array of alternatives. Life-changing innovation is rare; many successful products simply provide a new twist on an existing product. Examples include Wish-Bone's salad dressing spritzers, Nike's neon-coloured Flyknit athletic shoes, and Nabisco's 100-Calorie cookie packs.

To help you make those kinds of jumps, the game in this box uses rebus puzzles to stretch your creativity. Rebus puzzles present common words and phrases in novel orientation to one another. The goal is to determine the meaning. The puzzles are below, and the answers are at the bottom of the box.

ARREST YOU'RE	HISTORY HISTORY HISTORY	SK8 iiiiiiiiiiiii iiiiiiiiiiiii	print	BAN ANA	Shut Sit
funny funny words words words words	ST4ANCE	herring	MEREPEAT	Jack	Symphon

Answers: You're under arrest, too funny for words, history repeats itself, for instance, skate on thin ice, red herring, small print, repeat after me, banana split, Jack-in-the-Box, sit down and shut up, unfinished symphony

---

Because the ultimate goal of most marketing is long-term profitability, a core marketing principle must infuse every facet of a successful organization: the need to deliver products that exceed customer expectations. The customer must come first for *every* department—including finance, accounting, engineering, manufacturing, and human resources—although the specifics of how that plays out will clearly differ for each organizational function. Competition in the future will only intensify. Customer choices will continue to multiply as globalization and technology march forward. While these forces will weed out the weaker players, firms with a deeply engrained marketing orientation and a strong customer focus will continue to flourish—delivering value to their stakeholders and dollars to their bottom line.

careers in finance: Brand Manager

Drive the overall performance and profitability of a brand or group of brands. Establish the brand image and position in relation to competitors. Formulate and implement creative and effective marketing strategies. Manage and motivate creative teams that support the brand's development. Understand and integrate overall corporate goals into brand strategies. Communicate brand performance to senior management. Communicate key brand information to both internal and external stakeholders.

STUDY TOOLS 10

IN THE BOOK, YOU CAN:

☐ Rip out the Chapter Review card at the back of the book to have a summary of the chapter and key terms handy.

ONLINE AT NELSON.COM/STUDENT YOU CAN:

☐ Work through key concepts with a Guided Learning Question.

☐ Prepare for tests with quizzes.

☐ Review the key terms with Flash Cards (online or printer-ready).

☐ Explore practical examples of chapter concepts with Connect a Concept exercises.

Education has changed.
Your textbook should too.

4LTR
PRESS

nelson.com/student

11 Product and Promotion: Creating and Communicating Value

LEARNING OBJECTIVES

After studying this chapter, you will be able to …

11-1 Explain "product" and identify product classifications

11-2 Describe product differentiation and the key elements of product planning

11-3 Discuss innovation and the product life cycle

11-4 Analyze and explain promotion and integrated marketing communications

11-5 Discuss development of the promotional message

11-6 Discuss the promotional mix and the various promotional tools

After you finish this chapter, go to page 191 for STUDY TOOLS

11-1 Product: It's Probably More Than You Thought

When most people hear the term *product*, they immediately think of the material things that we buy and use and consume every day—for example, a Samsung Galaxy smartphone. But from a marketing standpoint, product means much more. A **product** can be anything that a company offers to satisfy consumer needs and wants; the possibilities include not only physical goods, but also services and ideas. A charity event, cosmetic surgery, and a cooking lesson all qualify as products.

When you buy a product, you also "buy" all of the attributes associated with it. These encompass a broad range of qualities such as the brand name, the image, the packaging, the reputation, and the guarantee. From a consumer standpoint, these attributes (or the *lack* of these attributes) are part of the product purchase, even if they don't add to its value. As a marketer, it's worth your while to carefully consider each element of your product to ensure that you're maximizing value without sacrificing profitability. For example, with the introduction of

product Anything that an organization offers to satisfy consumer needs and wants, including both goods and services.

the translucent, multicoloured iMac computers in 1998, Apple established its reputation for creating value through product design—an attribute that other PC manufacturers completely overlooked as they churned out their inventories of boring, beige boxes. Over the years, Apple has continued to polish its reputation by introducing sleek, elegantly designed products such as its iPad tablet and its iPhone.

11-1a Services: A Product by Any Other Name . . .

If a "product" includes anything that satisfies consumer needs, services clearly fit the bill. But services obviously differ from tangible goods. You often cannot see, hear, smell, taste, or touch a service, and you can almost never "own" it. After a haircut, for example, you might possess great-looking hair, but you don't own the haircutting experience (at least not literally). Most services embody these qualities:

■ **Intangibility:** You typically cannot see, hear, smell, taste, or touch a service before you buy it. Clearly, this creates a lot of uncertainty with consumers. Will the purchase really be worthwhile? Smart marketers mitigate the uncertainty by offering clues that suggest value. For example, if you walk into your local hairstylist,

you are likely to see pictures of models with perfect hairstyles, providing "evidence" of their styling abilities.

■ **Inseparability:** Try as you might, you simply can't separate the buyer of a service from the person who renders it. Delivery requires interaction between the buyer and the provider, and the customer directly contributes to the quality of the service. Consider a trip to the doctor. If you accurately describe your symptoms, you're likely to get a correct diagnosis. But if you simply say, "I just don't feel *normal*," the outcome is likely to be different.

■ **Variability:** This one is closely tied to inseparability. A talented masseuse will probably help you relax, whereas a mediocre one may actually make you more tense. And even a talented masseuse may give better service at the end of the day than at the beginning, or worse service on the day she breaks up with her boyfriend. Variability also applies to the differences among providers. A massage at a top-notch spa, for example, is likely to be better than a massage at your local gym.

■ **Perishability:** Marketers cannot store services for delivery at peak periods. A restaurant, for instance, has only so many seats; it can't (reasonably) tell its 8 p.m. dinner customers to come back the next day at 5 p.m. Similarly, major tourist destinations, such as Las Vegas, can't store an inventory of room

service deliveries or performances of Cirque du Soleil. This creates obvious cost issues; is it worthwhile to prepare for a peak crowd if it means losing money when it's slow? The answer depends on the economics of your business.

11-1b Goods versus Services: A Mixed Bag

Identifying whether a product is a good or a service can pose a considerable challenge because many products contain elements of both. A meal at your local Italian restaurant, for instance, obviously includes tangible goods: You definitely own that calzone. But someone took your order, brought it to the table, and (perhaps most importantly) did the dishes! Service was clearly a crucial part of the package.

A goods and services spectrum can provide a valuable tool for analyzing the relationship between the two (see Exhibit 11.1). At one extreme, **pure goods** don't include any services. Examples include a bottle of shampoo or a package of pasta. At the other extreme, **pure services** don't include any goods. Examples include financial consulting or math tutoring. Other products— such as a meal at Pizza Hut—fall somewhere between the poles.

> **pure goods** Products that do not include any services.
>
> **pure services** Products that do not include any goods.

Exhibit 11.1 Goods and Services Spectrum

Pure Goods

Bottle of Shampoo
Can of Cola

Financial Consulting
Math Tutoring

Pure Service

© Cengage Learning

11-1c Product Layers: Peeling the Onion

When customers buy products, they actually purchase more than just the good or service itself. They buy a complete product package that includes a core benefit, the actual product, and product augmentations. Understanding these layers is valuable because the most successful products delight consumers at each layer.

Core Benefit At the most fundamental level, consumers buy a core benefit that satisfies their needs. When you go to a concert, the core benefit is entertainment. When you buy a smartphone, the core benefit is communication. And when you go to the gym, the core benefit is fitness. Most products also provide secondary benefits that help distinguish them from other goods and services that meet the same customer needs. A secondary benefit of a smartphone might include entertainment, because it probably plays your music, too.

Actual Product The *actual product* layer, of course, is the product itself: the physical good or the delivered service that provides the core benefit. A live concert is the actual "service" that provides a music experience. Identifying the actual product is sometimes tough when the product is a service. For example, the core benefit of personal training might be weight loss, but the actual product may be some very fit person haranguing you to do 10 more sit-ups. Keep in mind that the actual product includes all of the attributes that make it unique, such as the brand name, the features, and the packaging.

> Quality means doing it right when no one is looking.
>
> Henry Ford

consumer products
Products purchased for personal use or consumption.

business products
Products purchased to use either directly or indirectly in the production of other products.

Augmented Product Most marketers wrap their actual products in additional goods and services, called the *augmented product*, that sharpen their competitive edge. Augmentations come in a range of different forms. Most smartphones come with a warranty or insurance and offer at least some customer service.

11-1d Product Classification: It's a Bird, It's a Plane...

Products fall into two broad categories—consumer products and business products—depending on the reason for the purchase. **Consumer products** are purchased for personal use or consumption, while **business products** are purchased to use either directly or indirectly in the production of another product. The bag of chips you buy to eat, for instance, is a consumer product, while the bag of chips a Subway owner buys to sell is a business product.

Consumer Product Categories Marketers further divide consumer products into several subcategories, as shown below. Understanding the characteristics of the subcategories can help marketers develop better strategies.

■ *Convenience products* are the inexpensive goods and services that consumers buy often with limited consideration and analysis. Distribution tends to be widespread, with promotion by the producers. Examples include staples such as milk and toothpaste, impulse items such as chocolate bars and magazines, and emergency products such as headache tablets and plumbing services.

- *Shopping products* are the more expensive products that consumers buy less often. Typically, as consumers shop, they search for the best value and learn more about features and benefits through the shopping process. Distribution is widespread, but more selective than for convenience products. Both producers and retailers tend to promote shopping products. Examples include computers, smartphone services, and athletic shoes.

- *Specialty products* are those much more expensive products that consumers seldom purchase. Most people perceive specialty products as being so important that they are unwilling to accept substitutes. Because of this, distribution tends to be highly selective (consumers are willing to go far out of their way for the "right" brand). Both producers and retailers are likely to promote specialty products, but to a highly targeted audience. Some examples of specialty products are Lamborghini sports cars, Tiffany jewellery, and Rolex watches.

- *Unsought products* are the goods and services that hold little interest (or even negative interest) for consumers. Price and distribution vary wildly, but promotion tends to be aggressive to drum up consumer interest. Home warranties and blood donations are some examples.

Business Product Categories Marketers also divide business products into subcategories. Here, too, understanding the subcategories can lead to better marketing strategies.

- *Installations* are large capital purchases designed for a long productive life. The marketing of installations emphasizes personal selling and customization. Examples include industrial robots, new buildings, and railway cars.

- *Accessory equipment* includes smaller, movable capital purchases, designed for a shorter productive life than installations. Marketing focuses on personal selling but includes less customization than installations. Examples include personal computers, power tools, and furniture.

- The *maintenance, repair, and operating products* category consists of small ticket items that businesses consume on an ongoing basis but that don't become part of the final product. Marketing tactics emphasize efficiency. Examples include cleaning supplies, nails, pens, and lubricants.

- *Raw materials* include the farm and natural products used in producing other products. Marketing emphasizes price and service rather than product differentiation. Examples include milk, cotton, turkeys, oil, and iron.

- *Component parts* and *processed materials* include finished (or partly finished) products used in producing

other products. Marketing emphasizes product quality as well as price and service. Examples include batteries for cars and aluminum ingots for pop cans.

- *Business services* are those services that businesses purchase to facilitate operations. Marketing focuses on quality and relationships; the role of price can vary. Examples include payroll services, marketing research, and legal services.

11-2 Product Differentiation and Planning: A Meaningful Difference

While some products have succeeded with little or no forethought, you'll dramatically boost your chances of a hit with careful planning. **Product differentiation** should be a key consideration. Winning products must embody a real or perceived difference from the glut of goods and services that compete in virtually every corner of the market. But different alone isn't enough; *different from* and *better than* the competition are both critical if you want to create the shortest path to success. A quick look at some high-profile product failures illustrates the point.

- **Clear beer:** In the 1990s, several companies introduced clear beers, reflecting an ill-fated obsession with clear products, including shampoo, soap, and the short-lived Crystal Pepsi.

- **Funky french fries:** In 2002, Ore-Ida, a division of Heinz, introduced Funky Fries. The flavours included cinnamon-sugar, chocolate, and "radical blue." Not surprisingly, they were off the market in less than a year.

11-2a Product Quality

Product quality relates directly to product value, which comes from understanding your customer. Peter Drucker, a noted business thinker, writer, and educator, declared:

> *Quality in a product or service is not what the supplier puts in. It's what the customer gets out and is willing to pay for. A product is not quality because it is hard to make and costs a lot of money . . . this is incompetence. Customers pay only for what is of use to them and gives them value. Nothing else constitutes quality.*

In other words, a high-quality product does a great job of meeting customer needs. Siemens, a huge electronics conglomerate, embodies this thinking in its approach to

product differentiation
The attributes that make a good or service different from other products that compete to meet the same or similar customer needs.

quality: "Quality is when our customers come back and our products don't."

But the specific definition of quality—and the attributes that indicate quality—change across product categories. A few examples are shown in Exhibit 11.2.

Regardless of product category, the two key aspects of quality are level and consistency. **Quality level** refers to how well a product performs its core functions. You might think that smart companies deliver the highest possible level of performance, but this is seldom profitable or even desirable. For instance, only a tiny group of consumers would pay for a speedboat that goes 200 km/h, when 80 km/h offers a comparable thrill (at least for most of us!). The right level of product performance is the level that meets the needs of your consumers, and those needs include price. Decisions about quality level must also consider the competition. The goal is to outperform the other players in your category while maintaining profitability.

The second dimension of quality is **product consistency**. How consistently does your product actually deliver the promised level of quality? With a positive relationship between price and performance, consistent delivery can offer a competitive edge at almost any quality level.

Honda offers an excellent example. When people consider the Accord, the Civic, and the CRV—all Honda-owned models—quality quickly comes to mind. And all three dominate their markets. But clearly, the quality level (and price) is different for each. The Accord serves the upper, more conservative end of the market; the Civic tends to appeal

quality level How well a product performs its core functions.

product consistency How reliably a product delivers its promised level of quality.

product features The specific characteristics of a product.

customer benefit The advantage a customer gains from specific product features.

Exhibit 11.2 Product Quality Indicators

PRODUCT CATEGORY	SOME QUALITY INDICATORS
INTERNET SEARCH ENGINES	Fast, relevant, far-reaching results
CHILDREN'S TOYS	Safety, expert endorsements, educational, and entertainment
COFFEE	Taste, brand, price, country of origin, additives (or lack of)
ROLLER COASTERS	Thrill factor, design, and setting
CHAINSAWS	Effectiveness, safety, and reliability

© Cengage Learning

to younger, hipper, more budget-minded consumers; and the CRV tends to appeal to middle-of-the-road shoppers seeking a small, reliable SUV. In short, Honda succeeds at delivering product consistency at several markedly different quality levels.

11-2b Features and Benefits

Product features are the characteristics of the product you offer. When a product is well designed, each feature corresponds to a meaningful **customer benefit**. The marketer's challenge is to design a package of features that offers the highest level of value for an acceptable price. And the equation must also account for profitability goals.

One winning formula may be to offer at least some low-cost features that correspond to high-value benefits. Creating an "open kitchen" restaurant, for instance, has limited impact on costs but gives patrons an exciting, up-close view of the drama and

Agricultural products such as milk and beef are classified as raw materials.

© Getty Images/liquidlibrary/Jupiterimages

hustle of professional food preparation. Exhibit 11.3 lists some other product features and their corresponding customer benefits.

11-2c Product Lines and the Product Mix

Some companies focus all of their efforts on one product, but most offer a number of different products to enhance their revenue and profits. A **product line** is a group of products that are closely related to one another, in terms of either how they work or the customers they serve. Indigo's first product line, for instance, was books. To meet the needs of as many book lovers as possible, Indigo carries well over a million different books in its product line. A **product mix** is the total number of product lines and individual items sold by a single firm. Indigo's product mix includes a wide range of product lines, from books, to electronics, to toys (to name just a few!).

Decisions regarding how many items to include in each product line and in the overall product mix can have a huge impact on a firm's profits. When there are too few items in each line, the company may be leaving money on the table. When there are too many items, the company may be spending unnecessarily to support its weakest links.

One reason why firms add new product lines is to reach completely new customers. Gap, for instance, added Old Navy to reach younger, lower income customers and Banana Republic to reach older, higher income customers. Each line includes a range of different products designed to meet the needs of specific customers. But the risk of adding new lines—especially lower priced lines—is **cannibalization**, which happens when a new entry "eats" the sales of an existing line. This is especially dangerous when the new products are lower priced than the current ones. You can see the problem, for instance, if a $20 jean purchase from Old Navy replaces a $50 jean purchase from

> In the factory, we make cosmetics; in the store, we sell hope.
>
> Charles Revson, founder, Revlon Cosmetics

Gap; the company has lost more than half its revenue on the sale. Like other companies with multiple lines, Gap carefully monitors the cannibalization issue and works to differentiate its lines as fully as possible.

11-2d Branding

At the most basic level, a **brand** is a product's identity. That is, a brand is what sets a product apart from others in the same category. Typically, brands represent a combination of elements such as product name, symbol, design, reputation, and image. But today's most powerful emerging brands go far beyond the sum of their attributes. They project a compelling group identity that creates brand fanatics: loyal customers who advocate for the brand better than any advertising a marketer could buy. The overall value of a brand to an organization—the extra money that consumers will spend to buy that brand—is called **brand equity**.

Since 2001, *BusinessWeek* and *Interbrand*, a leading brand consultancy, have teamed up to publish a ranking of the 100 Best Global Brands by dollar value. The top ten brands are listed in Exhibit 11.4. You can find the complete list on Interbrand's website.

Brand Name A catchy, memorable name is among the most powerful elements of your brand. While the right name will never save a bad business, it can launch a good business to new heights. But finding the right name can be tough. According

---

product line A group of products that are closely related to one another, in terms of either how they work or the customers they serve.

product mix The total number of product lines and individual items sold by a single firm.

cannibalization When a producer offers a new product that takes sales away from its existing products.

brand A product's identity—including product name, symbol, design, reputation, and image—that sets it apart from other players in the same category.

brand equity The overall value of a brand to an organization.

Exhibit 11.3 Product Features and Customer Benefits

PRODUCT	PRODUCT FEATURE	CUSTOMER BENEFIT
SUBWAY SANDWICHES	Lower fat	Looser pants
CONTACT LENSES	Different colours	A new-looking you
HIGH-DEFINITION TV	46-inch screen	The party's at your house
HYBRID CAR	Better gas mileage	More cash for other needs
TRIPLE LATTE	Caffeine, caffeine, caffeine	More time to, uh, study

© Cengage Learning

Indigo's product line and product mix

Exhibit 11.4 Interbrand Top Ten Global Brands 2014

BRAND	WORTH (MILLIONS)
Apple	118.8
Google	107.4
Coca-Cola	81.5
IBM	72.2
Microsoft	61.1
GE	45.4
Samsung	45.4
Toyota	42.3
McDonald's	42.2
Mercedes-Benz	34.3

2. Unique within the industry: Think Apple, Yahoo!, and Victoria's Secret.

3. Good alliteration, especially for long names: The words should roll off your tongue. Some examples are Coca-Cola, Weight Watchers, and Minute Maid.[1]

4. Brand names typically fall into four categories, as described in Exhibit 11.5.

Line Extensions Versus Brand Extensions

As companies grow, marketers look for opportunities to grow their businesses. **Line extensions** are similar products offered under the same brand name. Possibilities include new flavours, sizes, colours, ingredients, and forms. One example is Coca-Cola, which offers versions with lemon, with lime, with vanilla, with caffeine, without caffeine, with sugar, and without sugar. The marketing challenge is to ensure that line extensions steal market share from competitors rather than from the core brand.

to one consulting group, the following characteristics can help:

line extensions Similar products offered under the same brand name.

1. Short, sweet, and easy to pronounce and spell: Examples include Dell, Gap, Dove, Tide, and Kool-Aid.

Exhibit 11.5 Brand Name Categories

CATEGORY	DESCRIPTION	EXAMPLES
LOCATION-BASED	Refers to either the area served or the place of origin	Air Canada, Bank of Montreal, Best Western Hotels
FOUNDER'S NAME	Can include first name, last name, or both	McDonald's, Tim Hortons, Ford, Disney, Hewlett-Packard
DESCRIPTIVE OR FUNCTIONAL	Describes what the product is or how it works	eBay, GoodLife Fitness, Weight Watchers
EVOCATIVE	Communicates an engaging image that resonates with consumers	Yahoo!, Craftsman, Virgin, Intel, Lunchables, Cosmopolitan, Starbucks

Brand extensions, on the other hand, involve launching a product in a new category under an existing brand name. The Bic brand, for instance, is quite elastic, stretching nicely to include diverse products such as pens, glue, lighters, and disposable razors. The Virgin brand demonstrates similar elasticity, covering more than 350 companies that range from airlines, to phones, to soft drinks, to cars. But the concept of brand extension becomes clearest (and most entertaining) when we examine brand extension failures. Examples include Bic perfume, Budweiser Dry, and Harley Davidson cologne.[2]

Licensing Some companies opt to license their brands to other businesses. **Licensing** means purchasing—often for a substantial fee—the right to use another company's brand name or symbol. The benefits, of course, are instant name recognition, an established reputation, and a proven track record. On a worldwide basis, the best-known licensing arrangements are probably character names, which range from Mickey Mouse to Bart Simpson and appear on everything from cereal, to toys, to underwear. Many movie producers do high-profile licensing, turning out truckloads of merchandise that features movie properties such as *Harry Potter* and *Twilight*.

Another fast-growing area is the licensing of corporate names. Coca-Cola, for instance, claims to have more than 300 licensees who sell more than a billion dollars' worth of licensed merchandise each year. The potential benefits for Coca-Cola are clear: more promotion, increased exposure, and enhanced image. But the risk is significant. If licensed products are poor quality or overpriced, the consumer backlash hits the core brand rather than the producer of the licensed product.

Cobranding **Cobranding** is when established brands from different companies join forces to market the same product. This cooperative approach has a long history but is currently enjoying a new popularity. Examples include the following:

- Canadian Tire markets Debbie Travis products.
- Michaels craft stores market Martha Stewart products.

Cobranding can offer huge advantages to both partners by leveraging their strengths to enter new markets and gain more exposure. But cobranding can be risky. If one partner makes a major mistake, the fallout can damage the reputation of the other partner as well.

Many national brand names are recognizable around the world.

mikeledray/Shutterstock.com

National Brands Versus Store Brands **National brands**, also called manufacturers' brands, are brands the producer owns and markets. Many are well-known and widely available, such as Tide detergent and Pepsi-Cola. Although most retailers carry lots of national brands, more and more have opted to also carry their own versions of the same products, called **store brands**, or private labels. Deep discounters such as Walmart and Costco have had particular success with their private-label brands (e.g., Sam's Choice). Private labels play a growing role in grocery stores as well. A recent study revealed an increase in the rate of product development for store brands and an increase in sales for store brands.[3]

At the upper end of the market—especially in the clothing business—key retailers specialize in private brands to create and protect a consistent, upscale image.

11-2e Packaging

Great packaging does more than just hold the product. It can protect the product, provide information, facilitate storage, suggest product uses, promote the product brand, and attract buyer attention. Great packaging is especially important in the crowded world of grocery stores and mass merchandisers. In the average supermarket, the typical shopper passes about 300 items per minute and makes anywhere from 20 to 70 percent of purchases on sheer impulse. In this environment, your package must call out to your target customers and differentiate your product from all the others lined up beside it. But in attracting consumer attention, a good package cannot sacrifice the basics, such as protecting the product.[4]

Bottom line: Great packaging stems from consumer needs, but it usually includes at least a smidge of creative brilliance. Examples include yogurt in a pouch that doesn't need a spoon, soup to go that can be microwaved in the can,

brand extension A new product, in a new category, introduced under an existing brand name.

licensing Purchasing the right to use another company's brand name or symbol.

cobranding When established brands from different companies join forces to market the same product.

national brands Brands that the producer owns and markets.

store brands Brands the retailer both produces and distributes (also called private labels).

and single-serving cheese and cracker packets that parents can toss into kids' lunches.

11-3 Innovation and the Product Life Cycle: Nuts, Bolts, and a Spark of Brilliance

For a business to thrive long term, effective new product development is vital. And the process works only if it happens quickly. As technological advances hit the market at breakneck speed, current products are becoming obsolete faster than ever before. The need for speed compounds as hungry competitors crowd every niche of the market. But the rush is risky because new product development costs can be in the millions, and the success rate is less than one-third. Marketers who succeed in this challenging arena devote painstaking effort to understanding their customers, but they also nurture the creativity they need to generate new ideas. An example of how this can work: The 3M Corporation—makers of Post-it notes and Scotch Tape—introduces about 500 new products per year by pushing its employees to "relentlessly ask 'What if?'" 3M also encourages workers to spend 15 percent of their work time (*paid* work time!) on projects of personal interest.[5]

11-3a Types of Innovation

Clearly, the first personal computer represented a higher degree of newness than the first personal computer with a colour screen. And the computer with a colour screen represented a higher degree of newness than the first low-cost knockoff. Levels of innovation fall along a spectrum, as shown in Exhibit 11.6.

Discontinuous Innovation *Discontinuous innovations* are brand-new ideas that radically change how people live. Examples include the first car, the first television, and the first computer. These dramatic innovations require extensive customer learning, which should guide the marketing process.

Dynamically Continuous Innovation *Dynamically continuous innovations* are characterized by marked changes to existing products. Examples include cellphones, MP3 players, and digital cameras. These types of innovations require a moderate level of consumer learning in exchange for significant benefits.

Continuous Innovation A slight modification of an existing product is called a *continuous innovation*. Examples include new sizes, flavours, shapes, packaging, and design. The goal of continuous innovation is to distinguish

Exhibit 11.6 Levels of Innovation

Discontinuous Innovation

Dynamically Continuous Innovation

Continuous Innovation

© Cengage Learning

a product from the competition. The goal of a knockoff is simply to copy a competitor and offer a lower price.

11-3b The New Product Development Process

An efficient, focused development process will boost your chances of new product success. The standard model includes six stages as shown in Exhibit 11.7.

Each stage requires management to "green light" ideas before moving forward to ensure that the company doesn't waste resources on marginal concepts.

- **Idea generation:** Some experts estimate that it takes 50 ideas for each new product that makes it to market, so you should definitely cast a wide net. Ideas can come from almost anywhere, including customer research, customer complaints, salespeople, engineers, suppliers, and competitors.

- **Idea screening:** The purpose of this stage is to weed out ideas that don't fit with the company's objectives

WACKY LABELS

© Login/Shutterstock.com

As product recalls and lawsuits take on a life of their own, manufacturers are responding with warning labels that seem increasingly wacky. To call attention to this trend, an anti-lawsuit group sponsors the annual Wacky Warning Label Contest. Top finishers over the past few years included the following gems:

- A toilet brush tag that says "Do not use for personal hygiene."

- An electric shaver for men warns: "Never use while sleeping."

- An electric frying pan warns: Caution: "Griddle surface may be hot during and after cooking."

- A label on a personal water craft that cautions: "Never use a lit match or open flame to check fuel level."

- A label on a baby stroller with a small storage pouch that warns "Do not put child in bag."[6]

Source: Wacky Warning Labels 2009 Winners Announced, August 16, 2009, Foundation for Fair Civil Justice website; *Wacky Warning Labels Show* "Toll of Frivolous Lawsuits", by Bob Dorigo Jones, June 8, 2012, Bob Dorigo Jones website; Deadline for Entering 15th Annual Wacky Warning Labels™ Contest Is May 15, by Bob Dorigo Jones, May 7, 2012, Bob Dorigo Jones website.

Exhibit 11.7 Product Development Flow

© Cengage Learning

and ideas that would clearly be too expensive to develop. The Walt Disney Company, for instance, would certainly eliminate the idea of an X-rated cable channel because it just doesn't fit its mission.

- **Analysis:** The purpose of the analysis stage is to estimate costs and forecast sales for each idea to get a sense of the potential profit and of how the product might fit within the company's resources. Each idea must meet rigorous standards to remain a contender.

- **Development:** The development process leads to detailed descriptions of each concept, with specific product features. New product teams sometimes also make prototypes, or samples, that consumers can actually test. The results help fully refine the concept.

- **Testing:** This stage involves the formal process of soliciting feedback from consumers by testing the product. Do they like the features? Are the benefits meaningful? What price makes sense? Some companies also test-market their products or sell them in a limited area to evaluate the consumer response.

- **Commercialization:** This stage entails introducing the product to the general market. Two key success factors are gaining distribution and launching promotion. But a product that tested well doesn't always mean instant success. Coke, for example, tested its New Coke and found customers liked it better than the original, but it failed when the company brought it to the market.

11-3c New Product Adoption and Diffusion

In order to succeed commercially, new products must spread throughout a market after they are introduced. That process is called *diffusion*. But, clearly, diffusion happens at different speeds, depending on the individual consumer and on the product itself.

Product Adoption Categories Some consumers like to try new things; others seem terrified of change. These attitudes clearly impact the rate at which individuals are willing to adopt (or begin buying and using) new products. Consumer innovators, about 2.5 percent of the total, are adventurous risk takers. Laggards, about 16 percent of the total, sometimes adopt products so late that earlier adopters have already moved to the next new thing. The rest of the population falls somewhere in between. Keep in mind that individuals tend to adopt new products at different rates. For instance, we probably all know someone who is an innovator in technology but a laggard in fashion, or vice versa.

Product Diffusion Rates Some new products diffuse into the population much more quickly than others. For example, Apple iPods and Segway human transporters appeared on the market around the same time, but iPods have become a pop culture icon, while Segways remain on the fringe. What accounts for the difference? Researchers have identified five product characteristics that affect the rate of adoption and diffusion. The more characteristics a product has, the faster it will diffuse into the population.

> You can't wait for inspiration, you have to go after it with a club.
>
> Jack London, author

- **Observability:** How visible is the product to other potential consumers? Some product categories are easier to observe than others. If you adopt a new kind of car, for instance, the whole neighbourhood will know, as well as anyone else who sees you on the streets and highways.

- **Trialability:** How easily can potential consumers sample the new product? Trial can be a powerful way to create new consumers, which is why many grocery stores fill their aisles with sample tables during popular shopping hours. Other trial-boosting strategies include test-driving cars, sampling music, and testing new fragrances.

- **Complexity:** Can potential consumers easily understand what your product is and how it works? If your product confuses people—or if they find it hard to explain to others—adoption

product life cycle A pattern of sales and profits that typically changes over time.

rates will slow. For example, many people who test-ride Segway human transporters love the experience, but they have trouble explaining to others how it works or why it beats other transportation options.

- **Compatibility:** How consistent is your product with the existing way of doing things? Cordless phones, for example, caught on almost instantly because they were completely consistent with people's prior experiences—only better!

- **Relative advantage:** How much better are the benefits of your new product compared to existing products? When gas prices climb, for example, the benefits of a hybrid car take on a much higher value relative to standard cars. As a result, demand skyrockets.

11-3d The Product Life Cycle: Maximizing Results over Time

When marketers introduce a new product, they hope it will last forever, generating sales and profits for years to come. But they also realize that all products go through a **product life cycle**—that is, a pattern of sales and profits that typically changes over time. The life cycle can be dramatically different across individual products and product categories, and predicting the exact shape and length of the life cycle is virtually impossible. But most product categories do move through the four distinct stages shown in Exhibit 11.8.

- **Introduction:** This is a time of low sales and nonexistent profits as companies invest in raising awareness about the product and the product category. Some categories, such as the microwave, languish in this phase for years, while other categories, such as computer memory sticks, zoom through this phase. And some categories, of course, never get beyond introduction.

- **Growth:** During the growth period, sales continue to rise, although profits usually peak. Typically, competitors begin to notice emerging categories during the growth phase. They enter the market, often with variations on existing products that further fuel the growth. Hybrid cars are currently in the growth phase, and a number of competitors have recently entered the market.

- **Maturity:** During maturity, sales usually peak. Profits decline as competition intensifies. Once a market is mature, the only way to gain more users is to steal them from competitors rather than bring new users

Anna Bryukhanova/iStockphoto.com

Exhibit 11.8 Product Life Cycle for a Typical Product Category

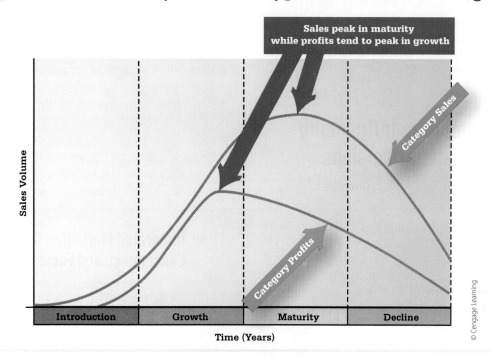

Sales peak in maturity while profits tend to peak in growth

Category Sales

Category Profits

Sales Volume

Introduction | Growth | Maturity | Decline

Time (Years)

© Cengage Learning

into the category. Weaker players begin to drop out of the category. Gasoline-powered cars and network TV are in maturity in North America.

■ **Decline:** During this period, sales and profits begin to decline, sometimes quite rapidly. The reasons usually relate to either technological change or change in consumer needs. For instance, the introduction of word processing pushed typewriters into

> In 2009, Canadian companies spent over $1.7 billion advertising on the Internet.
>
> Canadian Media Directors' Council Media Digest

decline, and a change in consumer tastes and habits pushed hot cereal into decline. Competitors continue to drop out of the category.

Familiarity with the product life cycle helps marketers plan effective strategies for existing products and identify profitable categories for new products. Exhibit 11.9 summarizes typical marketing strategies and offers examples for each phase.

Exhibit 11.9 The Product Life Cycle and Marketing Strategies

PHASE	EXAMPLES	SALES/PROFITS	KEY MARKETING STRATEGIES
INTRODUCTION	Virtual reality games, fuel cell technology, "smart" glasses	Low sales, low profits	Build awareness, trial, and distribution
GROWTH	Hybrid cars, flat screen TVs, tablet computers	Rapidly increasing sales and profits	Reinforce brand positioning, often through heavy advertising
MATURITY	Airlines, DVD players, personal computers, online stock trading, energy drinks	Flat sales and declining profits	Target competitors, while defending franchise with new product features, competitive advertising, promotion, and price cuts
DECLINE	Pagers, videocassettes	Declining sales and profits	Reduce spending and consider terminating the product

© Cengage Learning

Individual products also have life cycles, which usually follow the category growth pattern but sometimes vary dramatically. Clearly, it's in the marketer's best interest to extend the profitable run of an individual product as long as possible. There are several ways to make this happen: finding new uses for the product, changing the product, and changing the marketing mix.

11-4 Promotion: Influencing Consumer Decisions

Promotion is intended to influence consumers—to remind them, to inform them, to persuade them. The best promotion goes one step further, building powerful consumer bonds that draw your customers back to your product again and again. But don't forget that great promotion works only with a great product. One ad industry expert has captured this concept: "A great ad campaign will make a bad product fail faster. It will get more people to know it's bad."

Marketers can directly control most promotional tools. From TV advertising to telephone sales, the marketer creates the message and communicates it directly to the target audience. But ironically, marketers *cannot* directly control the most powerful promotional tools: publicity, such as a comment on a talk show or a review in *Consumer Reports*; and word of mouth, such as a recommendation from a close friend or even a casual acquaintance. Marketers can only influence these areas through creative promotional strategies.

11-4a Promotion in Chaos: Danger or Opportunity?

Not coincidentally, the Chinese symbol for crisis resembles the symbols for danger and opportunity—a perfect description of promotion in today's market. The pace of change is staggering. Technology has empowered consumers to choose how and when they interact with media, and they are grabbing control with dizzying speed. Cable-based, on-demand video continues to soar, and digital movie downloads are poised for explosive growth. Canadians are heavy Internet users. Roughly 80 percent of Canadians use the Internet, and each of them spends more than 17 hours a week online. Meanwhile, more passive forms of entertainment, such as network television, are slowly losing their audience. And those people who do still watch TV are gleefully changing the schedules and zapping the ads with DVRs or similar devices. As media splinter across an array of entertainment options, usage patterns have changed as well: tech-savvy viewers are more likely to consume media in on-the-fly snacks rather than sit-down meals. Also, services such as Netflix streaming have led to an increase in binge viewing of entire seasons of TV shows. Rising consumer power and the breakneck pace of technology have created a growing need—and a stunning opportunity—for marketers to zero in on the right customers, at the right time, with the right message.[7]

11-4b Integrated Marketing Communication: Consistency and Focus

Bloomberg/Getty Images

Dell promotes its brand heavily and effectively through its website.

How many marketing messages have you received in the past 24 hours? Did you flip on the TV or radio? Surf the Web? Notice a billboard? Glance at the logo on a T-shirt or cap? Chat with a friend about some product he likes? Marketing exposure quickly snowballs: the typical consumer receives about 3,000 advertising messages each day. Some of those messages are hard to avoid as marketers find new, increasingly creative ways to promote their products to a captive audience. The venues include elevators, taxis, golf carts, and other surprising settings.[8]

Given the confounding level of clutter, smart companies are using **integrated marketing communication** to coordinate their messages through every promotional vehicle—advertising, websites, salespeople, and so on—in order to create a coherent impression in the minds of their customers. Why bother coordinating all of these elements? The answer is clear. Consumers don't think about the specific source of the communication; instead, they combine—or integrate—the messages from *all* the sources to form a unified impression about your product. If the messages are out of sync or confusing, busy consumers won't bother to crack the code. They'll simply move on to the next best option.

Can you really control every message that every consumer sees or hears about your product? It's not likely. But if you accurately identify the key points of contact between your product and your target market, you can focus on those areas with remarkable effectiveness. For instance, the most

promotion Marketing communication designed to influence consumer purchase decisions through information, persuasion, and reminders.

integrated marketing communication The coordination of marketing messages through every promotional vehicle to communicate a unified impression about a product.

common points of contact for McDonald's are probably advertising and the in-store experience. From upbeat commercials, to smiling employees, to brightly striped uniforms, the company spends millions of dollars to support its core message of fast, tasty food in a clean, friendly environment. And that message is heavily concentrated in the areas that are key to its brand.

Other companies are likely to encounter the bulk of their customers through different channels. You would probably learn about Dell computers, for example, through either its website or word of mouth. Dell has invested heavily in both areas. The company maintains an innovative, user-friendly website that allows even novice users to create customized systems. And Dell delivers award-winning customer service and technical support, which encourages its customers to recommend the company's products to family and friends.

11-4c Coordinating the Communication

Even after you've identified the key points of contact, coordinating the messages remains a challenge. In many companies, completely different teams develop the different promotional areas. Salespeople and brand managers often have separate agendas, even when the same executive manages both departments. Frequently, disconnected outside agencies handle advertising, Web development, and sales promotion programs. Coordinating the messages will happen only with solid teamwork, which must begin at the top of the organization.

Information also plays a crucial role. To coordinate marketing messages, everyone who creates and manages them must have free access to knowledge about the customer, the product, the competition, the market, and the organization's strategy. Some of this information, such as strategic goals, will come from the top down, but a fair amount, such as information about the customer, should come from the bottom up. Information must also flow laterally, across departments and agencies. The marketing research department, for instance, may have critical information about product performance, which could help the Web management agency create a feature page that responds to competitive threats identified by the sales force. When all parties have access to the same data, they are much more likely to remain on the same page.

11-5 A Meaningful Message: Finding the Big Idea

Your promotional message begins with understanding how your product is different from and better than the competition. But your **positioning statement**—a brief statement that articulates how you want your target market to envision your product relative to the competition—seldom translates directly into the promotional message. Instead, it marks the beginning of the creative development process, often spearheaded by ad agency creative professionals. When it works, the creative development process yields a *big idea*—a meaningful, believable, and distinctive concept that cuts through the clutter. Big ideas are typically based on either a rational or an emotional premise. Here are a few examples:

Rational	*Science:* Clinique: "Allergy tested. 100% fragrance free." *Price:* Walmart: "Save money. Live better." *Engineering:* BMW: "The ultimate driving experience."
Emotional	*Imagination:* GE: "Imagination at work." *Security:* Allstate: "You're in good hands." *Fun:* Nintendo: "Born to play."

Not surprisingly, funny ads are a consumer favourite, although humour can be risky. For a record 10 years in a row, from 1998 through 2008, Budweiser—known for using humour effectively—nabbed the top spot in the annual consumer ranking of Super Bowl ads. But in 2009, a hilarious "Free Doritos" ad—created by talented amateurs in an online contest sponsored by Frito-Lay—knocked Budweiser off its pedestal. Budweiser regained the top spot in 2011, sharing the honour with Doritos, which, once again, took the top prize with a customer-created ad. Doritos used the same strategy to score a third win in 2012. In 2013, Budweiser held on to the top spot with a heart-warming spot about the bond between a trainer and his horse, while Doritos—again using the same strategy—fell to eighth place.[9]

The best big ideas have entrenched themselves in popular

> **positioning statement** A brief statement that articulates how the marketer would like the target market to envision a product relative to the competition.

culture, spawning both imitators and parodies. A small sampling includes the following:

- Nike: "Just do it."
- The Energizer Bunny.
- "Got Milk?"
- Budweiser: "Whasssssuuup?!"
- Motel 6: "We'll leave the light on for you."

11-5a An International Perspective

Some big ideas translate well across cultures. McDonald's, for instance, promotes family-friendly restaurants around the world. Other big ideas don't travel as smoothly. DeBeers, for example, tried running ads in Japan using its proven strategy in the West: fabulously dressed women smiling and kissing their husbands who have just given them glittering diamonds. The ads failed in Japan because a Japanese woman would be more likely to shed a few tears and feign anger that her husband would spend so much money. The revised DeBeers campaign featured a hard-working husband and wife in their tiny apartment. Receiving a diamond, the wife chides her extravagant husband: "Oh, you stupid!" The campaign was a wild success. Taking a big idea to a foreign market can mean big money and a powerful brand, but careful research should still be your first step.[10]

11-6 The Promotional Mix: Communicating the Big Idea

Once you've nailed your message, you need to communicate the big idea to your target market. The traditional communication tools—or **promotional channels**—include advertising, sales promotion, direct marketing, and personal selling. More recently, a number of new tools have emerged, ranging from advergaming to Internet minimovies. The *combination* of communication tools you choose to promote your product is called your *promotional mix*.

promotional channels Specific marketing communication vehicles, including traditional tools, such as advertising, sales promotion, direct marketing, and personal selling, and newer tools, such as product placement, advergaming, and online minimovies.

product placement The paid integration of branded products into movies, television, and other media.

11-6a Emerging Promotional Tools: The Leading Edge

Over the last decade, the promotional landscape has changed dramatically. Consumer empowerment and expectations have skyrocketed. Consumer tolerance for impersonal corporate communication has fallen. And digital technology has surged forward at breakneck speed. As a result, new promotional tools have emerged and previously minor tools have burst into the mainstream. This section covers several leading-edge promotional tactics, but keep in mind that other tools—such as mobile phone promotion, social media (e.g., Facebook), and widget-based marketing—are growing explosively too.

Internet Advertising Internet advertising has been highly visible for more than a decade. But the industry has moved far beyond simple banner ads and annoying pop-up ads. The highest growth areas include paid search advertising, search engine optimization, and online video advertising.

Paid search advertising includes sponsored links on search engines such as Google that relate to the topic you've searched, as well as targeted text ads on a number of different websites. Paid search seems to be an especially attractive tactic because it offers high accountability—marketers can tell exactly how well their limited advertising dollars are working.[11] Search engine optimization (SEO) is also showing strong growth. SEO involves taking specific steps to ensure that your website appears high on the list when customers look for your product or service via an Internet search engine such as Google or Yahoo!. Typically, the higher a firm appears, the more traffic that site will receive from potential customers.[12] Online video advertising includes the increasingly popular "pre-roll" ads, the 15- to 30-second spots that viewers often sit through before watching online video on sites such as YouTube. Canadian companies have increased their spending on online video advertising, and industry experts expect this growth to continue.[13]

Social Media Clearly, social media—including Facebook, Twitter, Blogger, Tumblr, Foursquare, and many others—are not a fad; in fact, they amount to a paradigm shift in how successful businesses market themselves. "You can't buy attention anymore," says one advertising expert. "Having a huge budget doesn't mean anything in social media…The old media paradigm was PAY to play. Now you get back what you authentically put in." And the evidence is building that social media offer a truly impressive return on investment, especially compared to traditional media. Smart marketers of both large and small businesses are investing their limited resources in social marketing and reaping unprecedented returns. In doing so, they are forging the future of marketing promotion.[14]

Product Placement Product placement— paying to integrate branded products into movies and TV—came to big-screen prominence in 1982, when Reese's Pieces played a highly visible role in Steven Spielberg's blockbuster *E.T.* Reese's Pieces sales shot up 65 percent

MULTICULTURAL PROMOTIONS

Canada is a multicultural nation, and the number of new Canadians from many different cultural backgrounds is increasing each year. Currently one in every five Canadians was born in a country other than Canada. Statistics Canada predicts that by 2031, the number of foreign-born Canadians will reach one in every three Canadians, and Canada's largest cities will have more than 50 percent of their populations coming from cultural groups other than French and English. Currently, the two largest cultural groups in Canada are South Asian and Chinese.

Marketers are paying attention to this change in the Canadian demographic environment. They know that different cultural groups relate differently to marketing communications and to the medium used to deliver marketing messages. For example, Canadians with a Chinese background are heavy Internet users, and Chinese and South Asians have a higher smartphone penetration rate than the rest of the Canadian population. However, these two cultural groups don't listen to the radio or read magazines as much as other Canadian cultures do.

Marketers who understand how different cultural groups get information can design better promotional strategies to get their messages out.[15]

David Cooper/Toronto Star via Getty Images

Sources: Eric Caron Malenfant, André Lebel, Laurent Martel, "Projections of the Diversity of the Canadian Population, 2006 to 2031," Statistics Canada; Howard Lichtman, "Ethnic Media and Cultural Diversity," *The Canadian Director's Council Media Digest 2014–2015*; Sarah Cunningham-Scharf, "5 Multicultural Marketing Pitfalls to Avoid," *Marketing Magazine*.

(a major embarrassment for the marketers of M&Ms, who passed on the opportunity). Over the years, product placement in movies has moved rapidly into the limelight.[16]

Product placement works best for marketers if the product seamlessly integrates into the show as a player rather than simply a prop. Whether in TV or movies, product placement offers marketers huge sales potential in a credible environment. But product placement is risky—if your show is a dud, your placement is worthless. And the cost is high and growing, which only increases the financial risk. Also, the benefits of product placement are tough to measure, especially for existing brands. In the end, the only measure that really counts is consumer acceptance, which may disappear if product placement intrudes too much on the entertainment value of movies and TV.

Advergaming Interactive games have exploded into pop culture; at least 41 percent of Canadians own a gaming system. Not surprisingly, marketers have followed closely behind, developing a new promotional channel: **advergaming**. The advergame industry generated $10 million in 2013.[17]

According to Massive, an advertising network that specializes in video games, advergaming works. Gamers exposed to embedded ads show a 64 percent increase in brand familiarity, a 37 percent increase in brand rating, and a 41 percent increase in purchase consideration; furthermore, rather than despising the ads, 55 percent of gamers said they "look cool." Despite the strong research results, analysts anticipate that advergaming will move in a new direction over the next few years, with deals that link brands to tangible rewards for players.[18]

Buzz Marketing A recent study defined "buzz" as the transfer of information from someone who is in the know to someone who isn't. Buzz marketing is essentially word-of-mouth marketing, which now influences two-thirds of all consumer product purchases. And it makes sense: in a world that's increasingly complex, people turn to others they know and trust to help sort the garbage from the good stuff. Other popular terms for **buzz marketing** are guerrilla marketing and viral marketing. Innovative buzz campaigns often cost significantly less than more traditional approaches.

Sponsorships **Sponsorships** are among the fastest-growing categories of promotional spending. The reason is clear: sponsorships, which usually involve cultural or sporting events, provide a deep association between a marketer and a partner. Usually, sponsors can't provide more than their logo or slogan; even so, consumers tend to view them in a positive light because they are clearly connected to events that matter to the target audience. The best sponsorship investments, of course, occur when the target audience for the marketer completely overlaps the target audience for the event. The high level of integration between sponsor and event provides valuable media coverage, justifying the hefty price.

advergaming Video games created as a marketing tool, usually with brand awareness as the core goal.

buzz marketing The active stimulation of word of mouth via unconventional and often relatively low-cost tactics. Other terms for buzz marketing are guerrilla marketing and viral marketing.

sponsorship A deep association between a marketer and a partner (usually a cultural or sporting event), which involves promotion of the sponsor in exchange for either payment or the provision of goods.

DID YOU GET PUNK'D?

Computer nerds aren't widely known for their sense of humour, but when they are being funny, watch out . . . cuz they may be laughing at YOU!! Every year on April Fool's Day, the geeks at Google design a prank—often a number of different pranks—designed to amuse, entertain, and punk their users (and probably to gain reams of free media coverage). After purchasing YouTube, they introduced the tradition on the video sharing giant, too. A small sampling of favourite hoaxes from around the Web:

- **Google:** First prank, April Fool's Day, 2000, introduced the MentalPlex, which invited users to visualize what they wanted to find while staring at a mesmerizing animation of swirling neon colours. The results page included the following "error" messages:
  - Weak or no signal detected. Upgrade transmitter and retry.
  - Multiple transmitters detected. Silence voices in your head and try again.

- Brainwaves received in analog. Please rethink in digital.
- Searching on this topic is prohibited under international law.
- Query is unclear. Try again after removing hat, glasses and shoes.
- Insufficient conviction. Please clap hands 3 times, while chanting "I believe" and try again.

- **YouTube:** One year, YouTube offered viewers *The YouTube Collection on DVD*, billed as a way to gain "the complete YouTube experience, completely offline." Simple. Economical. Convenient. Delivery options included a fleet of YouTube trucks directly to your home, plus a new truckload every week.

A good lesson for gullible users may be that if something seems a bit wonky on your favourite website, you may want to check the date before you start sniffing the screen, submitting an order, or doing anything other than enjoying a good laugh![19]

11-6b Traditional Promotional Tools: A Marketing Mainstay

Although new tools are gaining prominence, traditional promotional tools—advertising, sales promotion, public relations, and personal selling—remain powerful. Many marketers use the new tools in conjunction with the traditional ones to create a balanced, far-reaching promotional mix.

Advertising The formal definition of **advertising** is paid, nonpersonal communication, designed to influence a target audience with regard to a product, service, organization, or idea. Most major brands use advertising not only to drive sales but also to build their reputation, especially with a broad target market. Television remains the number-one advertising medium, with newspapers and online following close behind. As mass media prices increase and audiences fragment, fringe media are roaring towards the mainstream. Measurement is tough, however, because alternative media tactics are buried in other categories, including magazines, outdoor, and Internet. Overall media spending patterns for 2013 are shown in Exhibit 11.10.

> **advertising** Paid, nonpersonal communication, designed to influence a target audience with regard to a product, service, organization, or idea.

Each separate medium offers advantages and drawbacks, as summarized in Exhibit 11.11. Your goal as a marketer should be to determine which media options reach your target market efficiently and effectively, within the limits of your budget.

Exhibit 11.10 Media Spending Patterns[20]

MEDIA	2013 NET ADVERTISING REVENUE ($ MILLIONS)	PERCENTAGE OF TOTAL
TV	3,387	26
NEWSPAPERS	3,226	25
RADIO	1,600	13
MAGAZINES	558	4
OUTDOOR	514	4
ONLINE	3,082	24
MOBILE	443	4

Geowulf/iStockphoto.com

Exhibit 11.11 Major Media Categories

MAJOR MEDIA	ADVANTAGES	DISADVANTAGES
BROADCAST TV	*Mass audience:* Top-rated shows and special events garner millions of viewers. *High impact:* TV lends itself to vivid, complex messages that use sight, sound, and motion.	*Disappearing viewers:* With so many digital options available for viewers, regular programming has fewer viewers. *Jaded viewers:* Consumers who aren't zapping ads with DVRs are prone to simply tuning them out. *High cost:* A 30-second ad running during the Super Bowl could cost millions, and a typical prime-time ad could cost hundreds of thousands.
CABLE TV	*Targeted programming:* Cable helps advertisers target highly specialized markets. (Zhong Tian Channel, anyone?) *Efficient:* The cost per contact is relatively low, especially for local buys. *High impact:* Cable offers the same sight, sound, and motion benefits as broadcast.	*DVRs:* As with broadcast TV, many viewers simply aren't watching ads. *Uneven quality:* Many cable ads are worse than mediocre, providing a seedy setting for quality products.
NEWSPAPERS	*Localized:* Advertisers can tailor their messages to meet local needs. *Flexible:* Turnaround time for placing and pulling ads is very short. *Consumer acceptance:* Readers expect and even seek newspaper ads.	*Short lifespan:* Readers quickly discard their papers. *Clutter:* It takes 2 or 3 hours to read the average paper from cover to cover. Almost no one does it. *Quality:* Even top-notch colour newsprint leaves a lot to be desired.
DIRECT MAIL	*Highly targeted:* Direct mail can reach very specific markets. *International opportunity:* Less jaded foreign customers respond well to direct mail. *E-mail option:* Opt-in e-mail can lower direct mail costs.	*Wastes resources:* Direct mail uses a staggering amount of paper. And most recipients don't even read it before they toss it. *High cost:* Cost per contact can be high, although advertisers can limit the size of the campaign. *Spam:* Unsolicited e-mail ads have undermined consumer tolerance for all e-mail ads.
RADIO	*Highly targeted:* In one geographic area the dial ranges from special talk show to dance music, each station with dramatically different listeners. *Low cost:* Advertisers can control the cost by limiting the size of the buy. *Very flexible:* Changing the message is quick and easy.	*Low impact:* Radio relies only on listening. *Jaded listeners:* Many of us flip stations when the ads begin.
MAGAZINES	*Highly targeted:* From *Cosmopolitan* to *Computerworld*, magazines reach very specialized markets. *Quality:* Glossy print sends a high-quality message. *Long life:* Magazines tend to stick around homes and offices.	*High cost:* A full-page, four-colour ad in a popular magazine can cost as much as $300, 000. *Inflexible:* Advertisers must submit artwork months before publication.
OUTDOOR	*High visibility:* Billboards and building sides are hard to miss. *Repeat exposure:* Popular locations garner daily viewers. *Breakthrough ideas:* Innovative approaches include cars and buses "wrapped" in ads, video billboards, and blimps.	*Simplistic messages:* More than an image and a few words will get lost. *Visual pollution:* Many consumers object to outdoor ads. *Limited targeting:* It's hard to ensure that the right people see your ad.
DIGITAL	*24/7 global coverage:* Offers a remarkable level of exposure. *Highly targeted:* Search engines are especially strong at delivering the right ad to the right person at the right time. *Self-directed:* Consumers can choose which ads they want to view. *Interactive:* Can empower consumers.	*Intrusive:* There is an annoyance factor. Pop-up ads and unwanted smartphone messages alienate and infuriate many consumers. *Limited readership:* Web surfers simply ignore the vast majority of ads.

© Cengage Learning

RIGHT IDEA. WRONG PLACES.

Your AD here

Roman Sigaev/Shutterstock.com

Finding the right Big Idea to promote a product can be an enormous challenge. But the work doesn't stop even after a great Big Idea becomes a brilliant ad. Even the best ad won't work if it doesn't find the right place in the clutter of the overcrowded promotional environment. Less vigilant marketers have found themselves stuck with some amusingly bad placement:

- If your Starbucks ad is designed for the side of a van, made sure that when the door slides open, the "S" doesn't join with the "UCKS."

- Don't put an ad for fancy underwear on the side of a bus unless you're sure that the mud flaps on the bus tires will *always* prevent *all* mud from splashing on the pristine image of the underwear.

- Make sure that your billboard that touts two greasy breakfast sandwiches for $3 isn't right next to a billboard that announces that one in 3 people will die from heart disease.

You can't always know what will be around your ad, but it's always possible — and certainly worthwhile—to at least ask the question.[21]

Sales Promotion Sales promotion stimulates immediate sales activity through specific short-term programs aimed at either consumers or distributors. Sales promotion has long been subordinate to other promotional tools, but spending has accelerated in the past decade. Sales promotion falls into two categories: consumer promotion and trade promotion.

Consumer promotion is designed to generate immediate sales. Consumer promotion tools include premiums, promotional products, samples, coupons, rebates, and displays.

- *Premiums* are items that consumers receive free of charge—or for a lower-than-normal cost—in return for making a purchase.

- *Promotional products* are essentially gifts to consumers of merchandise that advertises a brand name. Promotional products work best when the merchandise relates to the brand, and when it's so useful or fun that consumers will opt to keep it around.

- *Samples* reduce the risk of purchasing something new by allowing consumers to try a product before committing their cash.

- *Coupons* offer immediate price reductions to consumers.

But the downside is huge. Marketers who depend on coupons encourage consumers to focus on price rather than value, which make it harder for consumers to differentiate brands and build loyalty.

- *Rebates,* common in the car industry and the electronics business, entice consumers with cash-back offers. Rebates provide an incentive for marketers as well: breakage. Most people who buy a product because of the rebate don't actually follow through and do the paperwork to get the money.

- *Displays* generate purchases in store. Most experts agree that consumers make most of their purchase decisions as they shop, which means that displays can play a crucial role in sales success.

Trade promotion is designed to stimulate wholesalers and retailers to push specific products more aggressively. Special deals and allowances are the most common form of trade promotion, especially for consumer products. The idea is that if you give your distributors a temporary price cut, they will pass the savings on to consumers via a short-term "special."

Trade shows are another popular form of trade promotion. Usually organized by industry trade associations, trade shows give exhibitors a chance to display and promote their products to their distributors. Other forms of trade promotion include contests, sweepstakes, and special events for distributors.

Public Relations In the broadest sense, **public relations** (or **PR**) involves the ongoing effort to create positive relationships with all of a firm's different "publics," including customers, employees, suppliers, the community, the general public, and the government. But in a more focused sense, PR aims to generate positive

sales promotion Marketing activities designed to stimulate immediate sales activity through specific short-term programs aimed at either consumers or distributors.

consumer promotion Marketing activities designed to generate immediate consumer sales, using tools such as premiums, promotional products, samples, coupons, rebates, and displays.

trade promotion Marketing activities designed to stimulate wholesalers and retailers to push specific products more aggressively over the short term.

public relations (PR) The ongoing effort to create positive relationships with all of a firm's different "publics," including customers, employees, suppliers, the community, the general public, and the government.

publicity, that is, unpaid stories in the media that create a favourable impression about a company or its products. The goal, of course, is to boost demand.

The biggest advantage of publicity is that it is usually credible. Think about it: Are you more likely to buy a product featured on the news or a product featured in a 30-second ad? Are you more likely to read a book reviewed by a major newspaper or one that is featured on a billboard? Publicity is credible because most people believe that information presented by the media is based on legitimate opinions and facts rather than on the drive to make money. It also helps that publicity is close to free (excluding any fees for a PR firm).

But publicity has a major downside: the marketer has no control over how the media present the company or its products. Despite the drawbacks to publicity, it has never been more popular with companies. The reason for the increased use of publicity is the popularity of smartphones. In the past, marketers had to count on the news media to be available to carry the story; today, anyone with a smartphone can video an event and broadcast it over the Internet within minutes.[22]

Personal Selling **Personal selling**—the world's oldest form of promotion—is person-to-person presentation of products to potential buyers. But successful selling typically begins long before the actual presentation and ends long afterwards. In today's competitive environment, selling means building long-term relationships. Creating and maintaining a quality sales force is expensive. Experts estimate that each business-to-business sales call can cost several hundred dollars. So why are so many Canadians employed in sales? Because nothing works better than personal selling for high-ticket items, complex products, and high-volume customers. In some companies, the sales team works directly with customers; in other firms, the sales force works with distributors who buy large volumes of products for resale.

Salespeople fall along a spectrum that ranges from order takers, who simply process sales, to order seekers, who use creative selling to persuade customers. Most department stores, for instance, hire order takers who stand behind the counter and ring up sales. But some hire creative order seekers who actively garner sales by offering extra services such as tasteful accessory recommendations for a clothing shopper.

A separate category of salespeople focuses on *missionary selling*, which means promoting goodwill for a company by providing information and assistance to customers. The pharmaceutical industry, for instance, hires a small army of missionary salespeople who call on doctors to explain and promote their products, even though the actual sales move through pharmacies.

The sales process typically follows six key stages. As we explore each one, keep in mind that well before the process begins, effective salespeople seek a complete understanding of their products, their industry, and their competition. A high level of knowledge permeates the entire selling process.

1. **Prospect and qualify:** Prospecting means identifying potential customers. Qualifying means choosing those who are most likely to buy your product.

2. **Prepare:** Before making a sales call, research is critical, especially in a business-to-business environment.

3. **Present:** You've probably heard that you don't get a second chance to make a good first impression, and that's especially true in sales. Your presentation itself should match the features of your product to the benefits your customer seeks (a chance to use all that preparation).

4. **Handle objections:** The key to success here is to view objections as opportunities rather than as criticism. Objections give you a chance to learn more about the needs of your prospects and to elaborate on the benefits of your product.

5. **Close sale:** Closing the sale—or asking the prospect to buy—is at the heart of the selling process. The close should flow naturally from the prior steps, but often it doesn't—sealing the deal can be surprisingly tough.

6. **Follow-up:** The sales process doesn't end when the customer pays. The quality of service and support plays a crucial role in future sales from the same customer, and getting those sales is much easier than finding brand-new prospects. Also, great relationships with current customers lead to testimonials and referrals that build momentum for long-term sales success.

> **publicity** Unpaid stories in the media that influence perceptions about a company or its products.
>
> **personal selling** The person-to-person presentation of products to potential buyers.

Tetra Images/Jupiter Images

HOOTSUITE: CANADA'S SOCIAL MEDIA MANAGEMENT PLATFORM

As more companies increase their use of social media marketing, it becomes important to have a way to monitor and manage the promotional material. Many companies and organizations, including nearly 80 percent of the largest firms in the United States and the Canadian prime minister's office, use the tools developed by HootSuite.

HootSuite is a Vancouver-based company that was started in 2008 by Ryan Holmes. HootSuite provides social media solutions for managing all social media communications through a single dashboard. A firm can receive an in-depth analysis of its social media programs, allowing it to identify areas of its promotional strategy that are not working as well as expected. HootSuite also provides companies with the opportunity to find out what is being said about them and their brands by monitoring various social media.

HootSuite has expanded rapidly into international markets. The company has more than 10 million users and has opened additional offices. Holmes vows to keep the company in Canada, but admits that finding sufficient people with social media skills sets can be challenging, particularly since the company hires five to ten new employees a week.[23]

Two personal selling trends are gathering momentum in a number of organizations: consultative selling and team selling. *Consultative selling* involves shifting the focus from the products to the customers. On a day-to-day basis, the practice involves a deep understanding of customer needs. Through lots and lots of active listening, consultative salespeople offer practical solutions to customer problems—solutions that use their products. Consultative selling generates powerful customer loyalty; however, it also involves a significant—and expensive—time investment from the sales force.

Team selling tends to be especially effective for large, complex accounts. This approach includes a group of specialists from key functional areas of the company—not just sales but also engineering, finance, customer service, and others. The goal is to uncover opportunities and respond to needs that would be beyond the capacity of a single salesperson. In these situations, a key part of the salesperson's role is to connect and coordinate the right network of contacts.

push strategy A marketing approach that involves motivating distributors to heavily promote—or "push"—a product to the final consumers, usually through heavy trade promotion and personal selling.

pull strategy A marketing approach that involves creating demand from the ultimate consumers so that they "pull" your products through the distribution channels by actively seeking them.

11-6c Choosing the Right Promotional Mix: Not Just a Science

There are no fail-safe rules for choosing the right combination of promotional tools. The mix varies dramatically, not only among various industries but also within specific industry segments. The best approach may be to consider the following questions in developing the mix that works best for your products.

- **Product characteristics:** How can you best communicate the features of your product? Is it simple or complex? Is it high priced or inexpensive? A specialized, high-priced item, for example, might require an investment in personal selling, whereas a simple, low-cost product might lend itself to billboard advertising.

- **Product life cycle:** Where does your product stand in its life cycle? Are you developing awareness? Are you generating desire? What about driving purchases? And building loyalty? The answers will clearly impact your promotional focus. For instance, if you're developing awareness, you might focus more on advertising, but if you're aiming to drive immediate sales, you'll probably emphasize sales promotion.

- **Target audience:** How big is your target audience? Where do they live and work? A small target audience—especially if it's geographically dispersed—lends itself to personal selling or direct mail. A sizable target audience suggests advertising as an effective way to reach large numbers. Audience expectations should also play a role in your promotional mix decisions.

- **Push versus pull:** Does your industry emphasize push or pull strategies? A **push strategy** involves motivating distributors to "push" your product to the final consumers, usually through heavy trade promotion and personal selling. A **pull strategy** involves creating demand from your final consumers so that they "pull" your products through the distribution channels. Many successful brands use a combination of push and pull strategies to achieve their goals.

- **Competitive environment:** How are your key competitors handling their promotional strategies? Would it make more sense for you to follow their lead or to forge your own promotional path? If all your competitors offer coupons, for instance, your customers may expect you to offer them as well. Or if the environment is cluttered, you may want to focus on emerging promotional approaches such as advergaming.

- **Budget:** What are your promotional goals? How much money will it take to achieve them?

(Answering this question is tough, but it's clearly important.) How much are your competitors spending in each area of the mix? And how much money do you have for promotion? Even though the available budget shouldn't drive the promotional mix, it plays a crucial role, especially for smaller businesses.

The possibilities in both product development and promotional strategy have rapidly multiplied in the past few years. But companies can't deliver on the potential without well-oiled teamwork throughout the organization. For instance, the operations group must focus on quality, the accounting group must focus on cost, and the finance group must focus on funding. From a big-picture standpoint, all groups must work towards the same overarching goal: maximizing customer value. Promotion also requires coordination within the organization and among the outside suppliers who provide promotional services. Finally, the best ideas for both product and promotion can come from any department. Marketers who stay ahead of the curve will sharpen their competitive edge in the decade to come.

careers in product and promotion:
Pharmaceutical Sales Representative

Build effective long-term business relationships with health care providers. Develop and deliver sales presentations to health care professionals. Distribute product information and samples in order to encourage more prescriptions and recommendations. Answer questions from health care professionals in a timely manner. Keep current about clinical data, competitive offerings, and health care organizations, issues, and events, particularly in area of specialty. Organize group events for health care professionals. Create and maintain detailed records of all contacts and meetings.

STUDY TOOLS 11

IN THE BOOK, YOU CAN:

☐ Rip out the Chapter Review card at the back of the book to have a summary of the chapter and key terms handy.

ONLINE AT NELSON.COM/STUDENT YOU CAN:

☐ Work through key concepts with a Guided Learning Question.

☐ Prepare for tests with quizzes.

☐ Review the key terms with Flash Cards (online or printer-ready).

☐ Explore practical examples of chapter concepts with Connect a Concept exercises.

12

Distribution and Pricing:
Right Product, Right Person, Right Place, Right Price

LEARNING OBJECTIVES
After studying this chapter, you will be able to...

12-1 Define distribution and differentiate between channels of distribution and physical distribution

12-2 Describe the various types of wholesale distributors

12-3 Discuss strategies and trends in store and nonstore retailing

12-4 Explain the key factors in physical distribution

12-5 Outline core pricing objectives and strategies

12-6 Discuss pricing in practice, including the role of consumer perceptions

After you finish this chapter, go to page 206 for STUDY TOOLS

12-1 Distribution: Getting Your Product to Your Customer

Next time you go to the grocery store, look around—the average Canadian supermarket carries about 45,000 different products.[1] Is your favourite brand of soda part of the mix? Why? How did it get from the factory to your neighbourhood store? Where else could you find that soda? How far would you be willing to go to get it? These are marketing distribution questions that contribute directly to the **distribution strategy**—that is, a plan for getting the right product to the right person at the right place at the right time.

The distribution strategy has two elements: channels of distribution and physical distribution. A **channel of distribution** is the path a product takes from the producer to the consumer, while **physical distribution** is the actual movement of products along that path. Some producers choose to sell their products directly to their customers through a **direct channel**. No one stands between the producer and the customer. Examples range from Dell computers (which today are also sold through retailers), to local farmers' markets, to factory outlet stores. But most producers use **channel intermediaries** to help their products move more efficiently and effectively from their factories to their consumers. GreenWorks, for example, sells lawn mowers, chainsaws, hedge trimmers, and other yard tools to Canadian Tire—a channel intermediary—which may in turn sell them to you.

12-1a The Role of Distributors: Adding Value

You may be asking yourself why we need distributors. Wouldn't it be a lot less expensive to buy directly from the producers? The answer, surprisingly, is no. Distributors add value—additional benefits—to products. They charge for adding that value, but typically they charge less than it would cost for consumers or producers to add that value on their own. When distributors add to the cost of a product without providing comparable benefits, the intermediaries don't stay in business. Fifteen years ago, for instance, most people bought plane tickets from travel agents. Then

distribution strategy A plan for delivering the right product to the right person at the right place at the right time.

channel of distribution The network of organizations and processes that links producers to consumers.

physical distribution The actual, physical movement of products along the distribution pathway.

direct channel A distribution process that links the producer and the customer with no intermediaries.

channel intermediaries Distribution organizations—informally called middlemen—that facilitate the movement of products from the producer to the consumer.

the Internet reduced the cost and inconvenience of buying tickets directly from airlines, and thousands of travel agencies lost their customers.

One core role of distributors is to reduce the number of transactions—and the associated costs—for goods to flow from producers to consumers. As Exhibit 12.1 shows, even one marketing intermediary in the distribution channel can funnel goods from producers to consumers with far fewer costly transactions.

Distributors add value, or **utility**, in a number of different ways: form, time, place, ownership, information, and service. Sometimes the distributors deliver the value (rather than adding it themselves), but often they add new utility that wouldn't otherwise be present. As you read through the various types of utility, keep in mind that they are often interrelated, building on one another to maximize value.

Form Utility Form utility provides customer satisfaction by converting inputs into finished products. Clearly, form utility is primarily a part of manufacturing. Nabisco provides form utility by transforming flour and sugar into cookies. But retailers can add form utility as well. Your favourite pizzeria, for example, converts dough, tomato paste, cheese, and other ingredients into a pizza.

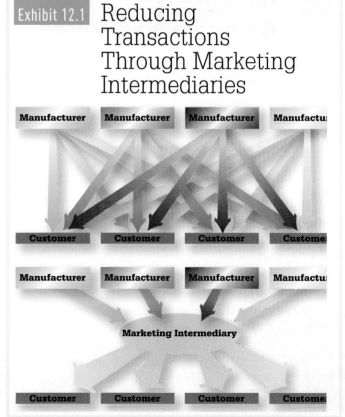

Exhibit 12.1 Reducing Transactions Through Marketing Intermediaries

© Cengage Learning

ATMs provide time and place utility, offering customers 24/7 access to cash in a variety of convenient locations.

Who's the real hog in the food distribution system?

Today, if you crave a fresh peach in the middle of winter, you can probably buy it at the supermarket, thanks to modern agribusiness, technology, and transportation. Some might say this makes you an energy hog because that peach was likely shipped from the Southern Hemisphere, and you could just as easily have chosen locally grown produce from your neighbourhood farmer's market. They may support their argument by pointing out that the food at the supermarket has travelled, on average, about 2,400 kilometres to get there.

But locally grown does not mean environmentally friendly—harmful pesticides can be used in any location. The biggest part of fossil fuel use in industrial farming is not transportation or machinery, it's chemicals. As much as 40 percent of the energy used in the food system goes to produce fertilizers and pesticides.

But you're still not off the hook—no matter where you buy your produce, you're probably still an energy hog, simply by virtue of our food storage and preparation systems. A single 10 kilometre round trip by car to the farmers market will easily burn in excess of 22,000 calories of fossil fuel energy. Refrigerator and freezer storage plus cooking also add energy hits. In total, household usage accounts for approximately 22 percent of all the energy expenditures.

So what's the best approach? While many people argue we should grow produce close to the point of consumption, others disagree. One expert advocates that all produce should be grown where it grows best—or most efficiently—as we do with almost everything else we produce. We pay a relatively small energy cost to get produce to market. That may mean growing produce in Canada, but it could also mean growing produce in Mexico or elsewhere in the world.[2]

Time Utility Time utility adds value by making products available at a convenient time for consumers. In our 24/7 society, consumers feel entitled to instant gratification, a benefit that distributors can provide more easily than most producers. Consider one-hour dry cleaning or even vending machines. These distributors provide options for filling your needs at a time that works for you.

Place Utility Place utility satisfies customer needs by providing the right products in the right place. Gas stations and fast food, for instance, often cluster conveniently at the bottom of highway ramps. ATMs—essentially electronic distributors—are readily available in locations that range from grocery stores to college and university cafeterias.

Ownership Utility Ownership utility adds value by making it easier for customers to actually possess the goods and services they purchase. Providing credit, cashing cheques, and delivering products are all examples of how distributors make it easier for customers to own their products.

utility The value, or usefulness, that a good or a service offers a customer.

Information Utility Information utility boosts customer satisfaction by providing helpful information. EB Games, for instance, hires gaming experts to guide its customers to the latest games and systems. Similarly, most skateboard stores hire skater salespeople, who gladly help customers find the best board for them.

Service Utility Service utility adds value by providing fast, friendly personalized service. Examples include placing a special order for that part you need to customize your car or giving you a makeover in your favourite retail store. Distributors that provide service utility typically create a loyal base of customers.

12-1b The Members of the Channel: Retailers versus Wholesalers

Many producers sell their goods through multiple channels of distribution. Some channels have many members, while others have only a few. The main differences among channel members relate to whether they are retailers or wholesalers. **Retailers** are the distributors that most of us know and use on a daily basis. They sell products directly to final consumers. Examples include 7-Eleven markets, Tim Hortons, and Canadian Tire. **Wholesalers**, on the other hand, buy products from producers and sell them to retailers, other wholesalers, or business users—which could include manufacturers, governments, not-for-profit organizations, and institutional accounts. To complicate this fairly simple concept, some distributors act as both wholesalers and retailers. Costco, for example, sells directly to businesses *and* to consumers.

12-2 Wholesalers: Sorting Out the Options

Some wholesalers are owned by producers, and others are owned by retailers, but the vast majority—accounting for about two-thirds of all the wholesale trade—are **independent wholesaling businesses**. These companies represent a number of different producers and distribute their goods to a range of customers. Independent wholesalers fall into two categories: (1) **merchant wholesalers**, which take legal possession, or title, of the goods they distribute, and (2) **agents/brokers**, which don't take title of the goods.

12-2a Merchant Wholesalers

Merchant wholesalers comprise about 80 percent of all wholesalers. By taking legal title to the goods they distribute, merchant wholesalers reduce the risk for producers that their products might be damaged or stolen—or even that they just won't sell. Taking title also allows merchant wholesalers to develop their own marketing strategies, including price.

- Full-service merchant wholesalers provide a complete array of services to the retailers or business users that typically purchase their goods. This includes warehousing, shipping, promotional assistance, product repairs, and credit.

- Limited-service merchant wholesalers provide fewer services to their customers. For example, some of them warehouse products but don't deliver them. Others warehouse and deliver but do not provide credit or marketing assistance. Limited-service merchant wholesalers include the following:

  - *Drop shippers:* Drop shippers take legal title of the merchandise but never physically possess it. They simply organize and facilitate product shipments directly from the producers to their customers. Drop shippers are common in industries with bulky products, such as coal or timber. Amazon, however, successfully pioneered the use of drop shipping in e-commerce, where it has become a standard shipping method for a number of major websites.

  - *Cash and carry wholesalers:* These distributors service customers that are too small to merit in-person sales calls from wholesaler reps. Customers must make the trip to the wholesaler themselves and cart their own products back to their stores. They are becoming less popular in Canada but are still common in Europe. (When Costco sells to businesses, it is cash and carry.)

  - *Truck jobbers:* Typically working with perishable goods such as bread, truck jobbers drive their products to their customers, which are usually smaller grocery stores. Their responsibilities often include checking the stock, suggesting reorder quantities, and removing out-of-date goods.

12-2b Agents and Brokers

Agents and brokers connect buyers and sellers and facilitate transactions in exchange for commissions. But they do *not* take legal ownership of the goods they distribute. Many insurance companies, for instance, distribute via agents, while brokers often handle real estate as well as seasonal products such as fruits and vegetables.

12-3 Retailers: The Consumer Connection

Retailers represent the last stop on the distribution path: they sell goods and services directly to final consumers. Given their tight consumer connection, retailers must keep in especially close touch with rapidly changing consumer needs and wants.

Smart retailers gain a competitive edge by providing more utility, or added value, than their counterparts. Low prices are only part of the equation. Other elements

retailers Distributors that sell products directly to the ultimate users, typically in small quantities that are stored and merchandised on the premises.

wholesalers Distributors that buy products from producers and sell them to other businesses such as retailers, not-for-profit organizations, institutional accounts, and the government.

independent wholesaling businesses Independent distributors that buy products from a range of different businesses and sell those products to a range of different customers.

merchant wholesalers Independent distributors that take legal possession, or title, of the goods they distribute.

agents/brokers Independent distributors that do not take title of the goods they distribute (even though they may take physical possession on a temporary basis).

Herb MacKenzie

clearly include customer service, product selection, advertising, and location. The look and feel of the retailer—whether online or on-ground—is another critical element.

Retailing falls into two main categories: store and non-store. But as we discuss each type, keep in mind that the lines between them are not always clear. In fact, **multichannel retailing**—or encouraging consumers to buy through different venues—is an emerging phenomenon. Some marketers have sold their products through multiple channels for many years. For example, on any given day, you could purchase a Coke from a grocery store, a restaurant, or a vending machine. The emergence of the Internet has provided a host of new opportunities for firms that hadn't previously considered a multichannel approach. An active relationship between on-ground and online outlets has become pivotal for many retailers.

12-3a Store Retailers

While other retail channels are growing, traditional stores remain the 800-pound gorilla of the retail industry, accounting for well over 90 percent of total retail. Stores range in size from tiny mom-and-pop groceries to multi-acre superstores dwarfed only by their parking lots. Exhibit 12.2 provides examples of different store types.

Exhibit 12.2 Retail Store Categories

STORE TYPE	STORE DESCRIPTION	EXAMPLES
CATEGORY KILLER	Dominates its category by offering a huge variety of one type of product.	Home Depot, Best Buy, PetSmart
CONVENIENCE STORE	Sells a small range of everyday and impulse products, at easy-to-access locations with long hours and quick checkout.	7-Eleven and a wide range of local stores
DEPARTMENT STORE	Offers a wide variety of merchandise (e.g., clothes, furniture, cosmetics), plus (usually) a high level of service.	The Bay, Sears
DISCOUNT STORE	Offers a wide array of merchandise at significantly lower prices and with less service than most department stores.	Walmart, Target
OUTLET STORE	Producer-owned store sells directly to the public at a huge discount. May include discontinued, flawed, or overrun items.	Nike, Gap, Versace, Calvin Klein, GUESS
SPECIALTY STORE	Sells a wide selection of merchandise within a narrow category, such as auto parts.	La Senza, Running Room, Lenscrafters, Mark's
SUPERMARKET	Offers a wide range of food products, plus limited non-food items (e.g., toilet paper).	Loblaws, Sobeys, No Frills
SUPERCENTRE	Sells a complete selection of food and general merchandise at a steep discount in a single enormous location.	Walmart Supercentres
WAREHOUSE CLUB	Sells discounted food and general merchandise in a large warehouse format to club members.	Costco, Sam's Club

© Cengage Learning

Both retailers and the producers that distribute through them must carefully consider their distribution strategy. The three key strategic options are *intensive*, *selective*, and *exclusive*.

Intensive Distribution Intensive distribution involves placing your products in as many stores as possible (or placing your stores themselves in as many locations as possible). This strategy makes the most sense for low-cost convenience goods that consumers won't travel too far to find. Marketers have chosen this strategy for Tim Hortons, Crest toothpaste, and *Maclean's* magazine, among thousands of other examples.

Selective Distribution Selective distribution means placing your products only with preferred retailers (or establishing your stores only in limited locations). This approach tends to work best for medium- and higher priced products and for stores that consumers don't expect to find on every street corner. Marketers have chosen this strategy for Nikon, LG, and most brands of paintball equipment.

Exclusive Distribution Exclusive distribution means establishing only one retail outlet in a given area. Typically that one retailer has exclusive distribution rights and provides exceptional service and selection. This strategy tends to work for luxury goods providers, whose customer bases actively seek their products. Examples include top-end cars such as Lamborghini and fashion trendsetters such as Versace.

Another key strategic consideration involves the **wheel of retailing**. The wheel is a classic theory that suggests that retail firms—sometimes even entire retail categories—become more upscale as they pass through their life cycles. For instance, it's easiest to enter a business on a shoestring, gaining customers by offering low prices. But eventually businesses trade up their selection, service, and facilities in order to maintain and build their customer base. Higher prices then follow, creating vulnerability to new, lower-priced competitors. And thus the wheel keeps rolling.

The wheel of retailing theory does describe many basic retail patterns, but it doesn't account for stores that launch at the high end of the market (e.g., Whole Foods) and those that retain their niche as deep discounters (e.g., Dollarama or Giant Tiger). However, the wheel theory does underscore the core principle that retailers must meet changing consumer needs in a relentlessly competitive environment.

12-3b Nonstore Retailers

While most retail dollars flow through bricks-and-mortar stores, a growing number of sales are going through other channels, or nonstore retailers. The key players in this development are online retailing, direct response retailing, direct selling, and vending.

Online Retailing Also known as e-tailing, online retailing grew at the astonishing rate of nearly 25 percent per year for most of the 2000s. But the torrid pace began to slow in 2008 with the onset of the recession. Growth began to increase again in 2009, and analysts now predict that it will continue in the high single digits for some time as e-commerce continues to mature. Much of this growth will likely come at the expense of on-ground retail as consumers continue to shift to online channels. The bigger name brands—including online-only brands, such as Amazon, and on-ground brands with a strong Web presence, such as Canadian Tire and Walmart—seem poised to benefit the most because cautious consumers are most familiar with them. Amazon.ca has out-distanced all other Canadian online retailers, with an estimated $1.5 billion in annual sales.[3] Estimates are that online sales in Canada will reach $34 billion by 2018.[4]

Online retailers, like their on-ground counterparts, have learned that great customer service can be a powerful differentiator. Simply "getting eyeballs" isn't enough because fewer than 5 percent of the people visiting a typical website convert into paying customers. Overstock.com has been a pioneer in online customer service, hiring and training 60 specialists who engage customers in live chats, available 24/7. When a customer has a live chat with one of their specialists, the average purchase amount doubles. In fact, shoppers are increasingly identifying Internet-only retailers as among those who offer the best customer service. In a recent survey, three online retailers—Amazon.com, Zappos.com, and Overstock.com—were ranked among the top five for the best customer service in any retail format.[5]

Online retailers face two major hurdles. The first is that products must be delivered, and even the fastest delivery services typically take at least a couple of days. But the truly daunting hurdle is the lack of security on the Web. As online retailers and software developers create increasingly secure systems, hackers are developing more sophisticated tools to crack their new codes.

Direct Response Retailing This category includes catalogues, telemarketing, and advertising (such as infomercials) meant to elicit direct consumer sales. While many traditional catalogue retailers have also established successful websites, the catalogue

multichannel retailing Providing multiple distribution channels for consumers to buy a product.

wheel of retailing A classic distribution theory that suggests that retail firms and retail categories become more upscale as they go through their life cycles.

side of the business continues to thrive. Victoria's Secret, for instance, sends out a mind-boggling 400 million catalogues each year—that's four catalogues for every woman between the ages of 15 and 64 in Canada and the United States. Telemarketing, both inbound and outbound, also remains a potent distribution channel, despite Canada's popular National Do Not Call list established in 2008.

Direct Selling This channel includes all methods of selling directly to customers in their homes or workplaces. Door-to-door selling has enjoyed a resurgence in the wake of Canada's National Do Not Call list, but the real strength of direct selling lies in multilevel marketing, or MLM. Multilevel marketing involves hiring independent contractors to sell products to their personal network of friends and colleagues and to recruit new salespeople in return for a percentage of their commissions. Mary Kay Cosmetics, Stella & Dot, and The Pampered Chef have all enjoyed enormous success in this arena, along with pioneering companies such as Tupperware.

> Marine transportation accounts for over 95 percent of the 180 million tonnes of goods Canada exports each year. Canadian ports are expected to double their trade volume over the next 15 to 20 years.

Association of Canadian Port Authorities

Vending Until about a decade ago, vending machines in Canada mostly sold soft drinks and snacks. But more recently, the selection has expanded (and the machines have gone more upscale) as marketers recognize the value of providing their products as conveniently as possible to their target consumers. iPods and other electronic devices are now being sold from vending machines at busy airports in Canada and the United States. Other countries are far ahead of Canada in the vending arena. In Japan, for instance, people buy everything from blue jeans to beef from vending machines. As technology continues to roll forward, Canadian consumers are likely to see a growing number of vending machines for products as diverse as "fresh-baked" pizza, digital cameras, and specialty coffee drinks.

supply chain All organizations, processes, and activities involved in the flow of goods from their raw materials to the final consumer.

supply chain management (SCM) Planning and coordinating the movement of products along the supply chain, from the raw materials to the final consumers.

logistics A subset of supply chain management that focuses largely on the tactics involved in moving products along the supply chain.

12-4 Physical Distribution: Planes, Trains, and Much, Much More

Determining the best distribution channels for your product is only the first half of your distribution strategy. The second half is physical distribution strategy: determining *how* your product will flow through the channel from the producer to the consumer.

The **supply chain** for a product includes not only its distribution channels but also the string of suppliers that deliver products to the producers (see Exhibit 12.3). Planning and coordinating the movement of products along the supply chain—from the raw materials to the final consumers—is called **supply chain management** or **SCM. Logistics** is a subset of SCM that focuses more on tactics (the actual movement of products) than on strategy.

At one time, relationships among the members of the supply chain were contentious. But these days, companies that foster collaboration rather than competition have typically experienced more success. Vendor-managed inventory is an emerging strategy—pioneered by Walmart—that allows suppliers to determine buyer needs and automatically ship product. This strategy saves time and money but also requires an extraordinary level of trust and information sharing among members of the supply chain.

Herb MacKenzie

More than 800,000 Canadians sell products for multilevel marketing companies—such as Nature's Sunshine—and generate over $2 billion in sales each year.

Exhibit 12.3 Elements of the Supply Chain

The supply chain highlights the links among the various organizations in the production and distribution process.

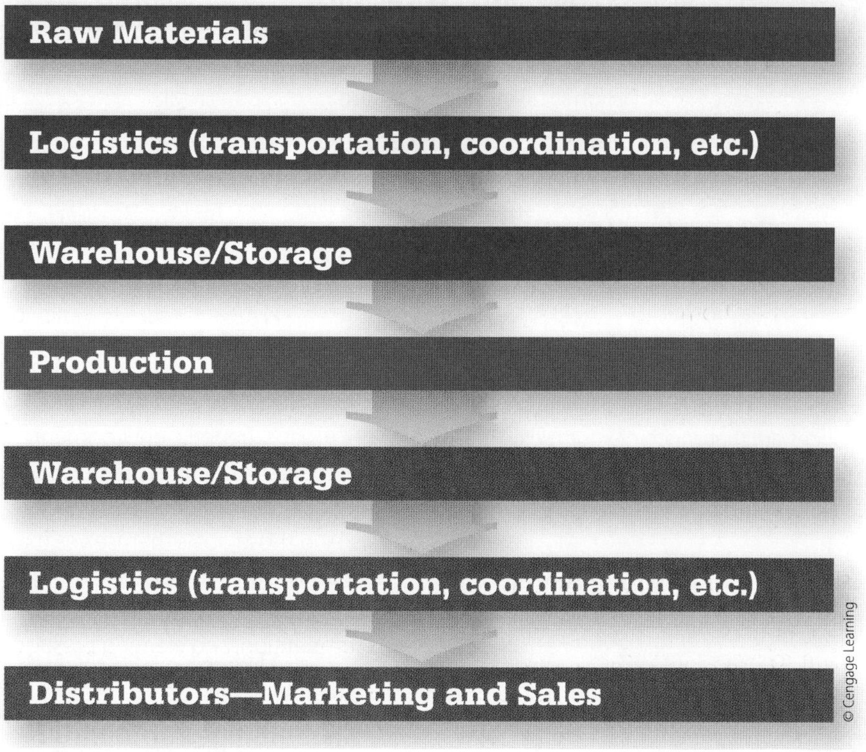

Raw Materials

Logistics (transportation, coordination, etc.)

Warehouse/Storage

Production

Warehouse/Storage

Logistics (transportation, coordination, etc.)

Distributors—Marketing and Sales

© Cengage Learning

In our turbo-charged 24/7 society, supply chain management has become increasingly complex. Gap, for instance, contracts with more than 3,000 factories in more than 50 different countries and distributes its products to 3,300 corporate and 400 franchise stores in five different countries. The coordination requirements are mind-boggling. Key management decisions include the following:

■ **Warehousing:** How many warehouses do we need? Where should we locate our warehouses?

■ **Materials handling:** How should we move products within our facilities? How can we best balance efficiency with effectiveness?

■ **Inventory control:** How much inventory should we keep on hand? How should we store and distribute it? What about costs such as taxes and insurance?

■ **Order processing:** How should we manage incoming and outgoing orders? What would be most efficient for our customers and suppliers?

■ **Customer service:** How can we serve our customers most effectively? How can we reduce waiting times and facilitate interactions?

■ **Transportation:** How can we move products most efficiently through the supply chain? What are the key tradeoffs?

■ **Security:** How can we keep products safe from vandals, theft, and accidents every step of the way?

Fragile or perishable products, of course, require even more consideration.

12-4a Transportation Decisions

Moving products through the supply chain is so important that it deserves its own section. The various options—trucks, planes, and railways, for instance—are called **modes of transportation**. To make smart decisions, marketers must consider what each mode offers in terms of cost, speed, dependability, flexibility, availability, and frequency of shipments. The right choice, of course, depends on the needs of the business and on the product itself. See Exhibit 12.4 for a description of the transportation options.

Depending on factors such as warehousing, docking facilities, and

> **modes of transportation**
> The various transportation options—such as planes, trucks, and railways—for moving products through the supply chain.

Exhibit 12.4 Modes of Transportation

MODE	COST	SPEED	ON-TIME DEPENDABILITY	FLEXIBILITY IN HANDLING	FREQUENCY OF SHIPMENTS	AVAILABILITY
RAIL	Medium	Slow	Medium	Medium	Low	Extensive
TRUCK	High	Fast	High	Medium	High	Most extensive
SHIP	Lowest	Slowest	Lowest	Highest	Lowest	Limited
PLANE	Highest	Fastest	Medium	Low	Medium	Medium
PIPELINE	Low	Slow	Highest	Lowest	Highest	Most limited

© Cengage Learning

accessibility, some distributors use several different modes of transportation. If you own a clothing boutique in Saskatchewan, for example, chances are that much of your merchandise travels by boat from China to Vancouver and then by truck from Vancouver to Saskatchewan.

12-4b Proactive Supply Chain Management

More and more marketers are turning to supply chain management to build a competitive edge through greater efficiency. But given the complexity of the field, many firms have chosen to outsource this challenge to experts rather than handle it internally. Companies that specialize in helping other companies manage the supply chain—such as UPS—have done particularly well in today's market.

12-5 Pricing Objectives and Strategies: A High-Stakes Game

Pricing strategy clearly has a significant impact on the success of any organization. Price plays a key role in determining demand for your products, which directly influences a company's profitability. Most people, after all, have a limited amount of money and a practically infinite number of ways they could spend it. Price impacts their spending choices at a more fundamental level than most other variables.

penetration pricing A new-product pricing strategy that aims to capture as much of the market as possible through rock-bottom prices.

But ironically, price is perhaps the toughest variable for marketers to control. Both legal constraints and marketing intermediaries (distributors) play a role in determining the final prices of most products. Marketers must also consider costs, competitors, investors, taxes, and product strategies.

In today's frenetic environment, stable pricing is no longer the norm. Smart marketers continually evaluate and refine their pricing strategies to ensure that they meet their goals. And those goals themselves may shift in response to the changing market. Common objectives and strategies include building profitability, boosting volume, matching the competition, and creating prestige.

12-5a Building Profitability

Because long-term profitability is a fundamental goal of most businesses, profitability targets are often the starting point for pricing strategies. Many firms express these goals in terms of either return on investment (ROI) or return on sales (ROS). Keep in mind that profitability is the positive difference between revenue (or total sales) and costs. Firms can boost profits by increasing prices or decreasing costs because either strategy will lead to a greater spread between the two. Doing both, of course, is tricky, but companies that succeed—such as Apple—typically dominate their markets.

12-5b Boosting Volume

Companies usually express volume goals in terms of market share—the percentage of a market controlled by a company or a product. Amazon.com, for example, launched with volume objectives. Its goal was to capture as many "eyeballs" as possible, in hopes of later achieving profitability through programs that depend on volume, such as advertising on its site. A volume objective usually leads to one of the following strategies.

Penetration Pricing Penetration pricing, a strategy for pricing new products, aims to capture as much of the market as possible through rock-bottom prices. Each individual sale typically yields a tiny profit; the real money

PRICING FOR PUBLICITY

Most marketers will tell you not to make low price your point of difference, because competitors can easily match it, and price wars are bad for everyone involved (except consumers!). But some low pricing can be interesting enough to attract publicity on its own. Some examples:

- **Demand-based pricing:** This was carried to an extreme in one bar in Barcelona, Spain. Bar Dow Jones treated all of its drinks like stocks, which increase in price when the demand goes up. If you bought a Heineken, for example, the next person who bought one would have to pay more—unless, of course, there was a crash!—in which case, the next buyer would get that beer at a bargain price.

- **External-factor based pricing:** Possibilities here include weather, stock exchange closing price, game results, and anything else the marketer can think of. One example is Coca-Cola–owned Limon Y Nada vending machines in Spain, which charge a different price based on the current temperature—the hotter the weather, the more expensive the soda! Another example is Bull & Bear Steakhouse, which attached cocktail prices to Facebook stock price changes in an effort to draw a younger crowd into the bar.

- **Customer-specific pricing:** Australia-based Kogan Electronics became the most talked about company on Twitter the day after it announced that it would charge shoppers who used Internet Explorer 7 instead of an updated version a 6.8 percent "tax," which it claimed would help cover the cost of the "antique" browser incurred by developers. The charge was accompanied by a snide message that said, in part, "It appears that you or your system administrator has been in a coma for over five years …"[6]

Sources: Allison Rice, "Unique Pricing Strategies that Get Publicity and New Customers," April 10, 2012, *Amsterdam Printing Blog; Yahoo! Celebrity Philippines* website, "Twitter Index: Tax on IE7, Drake vs Chris Brown," June 14, 2012.

Sebastian Kaulitzki/Fotolia

comes from the sheer volume of sales. A key benefit of this strategy is that it tends to discourage competitors, who may be scared off by the slim margins. But penetration pricing makes sense only in categories that don't have a significant group of consumers who would be willing to pay a premium price (otherwise, the marketer would be leaving money on the table). For obvious reasons, companies that use penetration pricing are usually focused on controlling costs. WestJet is a key example. Its prices are often unbeatable, but it strictly controls costs by using a single kind of jet, optimizing turnaround times at the gate, and using many non-major airports.

Everyday Low Pricing Also known as *sustained discount pricing*, **everyday low pricing (EDLP)** aims to achieve long-term profitability through volume. Walmart is clearly the king of EDLP with its slogan, "Save money. Live better." But Costco uses the same strategy to attract a much more upscale audience. The difference between the two customer groups quickly becomes apparent when you glance at the cars in the two stores' respective parking lots. Costco customers are typically seeking everyday discounts because they want to, not because they need to. The product mix—eclectic and upscale—reflects the customer base. (Costco sells diamond jewellery, high-end electronics, books, and low-priced rotisserie chickens.) Costco posted years of healthy, sustained growth before running into trouble at the end of 2008. As the recession tightened its grip, sales began to soften, especially in non-food categories, suggesting that EDLP may be most effective for less upscale products.[7] Within a few years, sales had recovered, and Costco continued on its previous growth trajectory.

High/Low Pricing The **high/low pricing** strategy tries to increase traffic in retail stores by special sales on a limited number of products and higher everyday prices on others. Often used—and overused—in grocery stores, drug stores, and department stores, this strategy can alienate customers who feel cheated when a product they bought for full price goes on sale soon after. High/low pricing can also train consumers to buy only when products are on sale.

Loss Leader Pricing Closely related to high/low pricing, **loss leader pricing** involves pricing a handful of items—or loss

> **everyday low pricing (EDLP)** Long-term discount pricing, designed to achieve profitability through high sales volume.
>
> **high/low pricing** A pricing strategy designed to drive traffic to retail stores by special sales on a limited number of products and higher everyday prices on others.

"Slippery Finger" Pricing Goofs

If a price seems too good to be true, it probably is. But seeking an incredible bargain can still make sense—dollars and cents. Due to "slippery finger" typos, frequent price changes, and programming glitches, online retailers are especially vulnerable to pricing mistakes. Without human cashier confirmation, it's tough to catch the goofs. And to magnify the problem, quick communication on the Web almost ensures a flood of customers placing orders as soon as the wrong price goes live. The biggest ever pricing mistake: In 2009, Best Buy advertised a Samsung television that retailed at $16,666 for $9.99.

A sampling of recent online "deals":

- Free flights from Los Angeles to Fiji
- Round-trip tickets from San Jose, California, to Paris for $27.98
- $2,999 fridges for $298 at Lowe's
- $1,329 Lenovo Y410P laptops for $279
- $379 Axim X3i PDAs wrongly priced at $79 on Dell's site
- Five watches, worth $11,332, briefly sale priced at $0.0 (with free shipping) on Ashford.com

Since the first few high-profile pricing disasters, online retailers have taken steps to protect themselves through specific disclaimers in their terms of use. And the courts have generally ruled that a company need not honour an offer if a reasonable person would recognize that it was a mistake.

But disclaimers and legal protections won't protect a retailer from customers who feel cheated. So companies that post pricing mistakes must choose between losing money by honouring offers or losing customer goodwill by cancelling them—there simply isn't a winning option. But Travelocity—home of those unintended free tickets from Los Angeles to Fiji—has at least found a way to handle snafus with grace. Its Travelocity Guarantee program notes, "If, say, we inadvertently advertise a fare that's just 'too good to be true,' like a free trip to Fiji, we'll work with you and our travel partners to make it up to you and find a solution that puts a smile on your face." So, happy shopping![8]

Sources: Chris Morran, "Don't Be Shocked When Lowe's Won't Sell You a $2,999 Fridge Mistakenly Priced at $298," consumerist.com, April 17, 2015; Pete Evans, "Lenovo Offers $100 for Laptop Pricing Glitch," *CBC News*, May 27, 2014; Bob Tedeschi, "Pricing Errors on the Web Can Be Costly," *The New York Times* website; All You Ever Wanted To Know About the Travelocity "Guarantee," *FlyerTalk Forum*; *Money Super Market* website, "8 Biggest Pricing Errors in History," undated.

---

leaders—temporarily below cost in order to drive traffic. The retailer loses money on the loss leaders but aims to make up the difference (and then some) on other purchases. To encourage other purchases, retailers typically place loss leaders at the back of the store, forcing customers to navigate past a tempting array of more profitable items. The loss leader strategy has been used effectively by producers as well. Gillette, for instance, gives away some shavers practically for free but reaps handsome profits as consumers buy replacement blades. Similarly, Microsoft has sold its Xbox systems at a loss in order to increase potential profits from high-margin video games.[9]

loss leader pricing Closely related to high/low pricing, loss leader pricing means pricing a handful of items—or loss leaders—temporarily below cost to drive traffic.

skimming pricing A new-product pricing strategy that aims to maximize profitability by offering new products at a premium price.

12-5c Matching the Competition

The key goal when matching the competition is to set prices based on what everyone else is doing. Usually, the idea is to wipe out price as a point of comparison, so that customers choose their product based on other factors. Examples include Coke and Pepsi, Honda and Toyota, Petro-Canada and Esso, Loblaws and Sobeys. Sometimes, one or two competitors emerge to drive pricing for entire industries.

12-5d Creating Prestige

This approach uses pricing to send consumers a message about the high quality and exclusivity of a product—the higher the price, the better the product. Of course, this strategy works only if the product actually delivers top quality; otherwise, nobody would buy more than once (and those who do so will clearly spread the word). Rolex watches, Mont Blanc pens, and Bentley cars all use prestige pricing to reinforce their image.

Skimming Pricing This new-product pricing strategy is a subset of prestige pricing. **Skimming pricing** involves offering new products at a premium price. The idea is to entice price-insensitive consumers—music fanatics, for example—to buy high when a product first enters the market. Once these customers have made their purchases, marketers will often introduce lower priced versions of the same product to capture the bottom of the market. Apple used this strategy with its iPod,

WHEN THE BOTTOM FALLS OUT

There's an old saying that a mine is simply a hole in the ground into which you pour money. Two Asian companies—one from China and one from Japan—learned this first-hand. They jointly acquired Calgary, Alberta-based Grand Cache Coal Corp. for $1 billion in a deal that closed in March 2012. At the time, metallurgical coal was selling for $300 per tonne, but it has since dropped to $120. Up Energy Development Group of China agreed to buy the Canadian mine in 2014 for $2: $1 to each of its owners (plus it agreed to assume the company's debts).

On the consumer side, the most expensive dogs in the world were Tibetan mastiffs, which sold for several hundred thousand dollars in 2014. One golden-haired puppy reportedly sold at a premium pet fair for US$2 million to a Chinese property developer; he also purchased its red-haired brother for an additional $1 million. Liu Na, the fair organizer, said prices usually depend on the breeder's expectations, the buyer's appreciation of the dog, and the bargaining process.

Come forward to 2015: one year later. Beijing animal activists rescued 170 dogs—including more than 20 Tibetan mastiffs—stuffed into metal chicken crates. The dogs were on their way to northeastern China, where, for approximately $5 each, they would be rendered into hot pot ingredients—that is, food. When rescued, the dogs had been several days without food or water and many had broken limbs, and over one-third of them were dead. A slowing economy is partly at blame for their demise, but so too is a government austerity program. Consumers who make such extravagant purchases have become the target for anti-corruption investigators. By 2015, the price of Tibetan mastiffs has dropped to about $2,000, but many can be purchased for much less. This is about the same price that Portuguese Water Dogs sell for in Canada.[10]

Herb MacKenzie

introducing a premium version for a hefty price tag. Once it had secured the big spenders, Apple introduced the lower priced iPod Nanos and Shuffles, with a powerful market response. But keep in mind that skimming works only when a product is tough to copy in terms of design, brand image, technology, or some other attribute. Otherwise, the fat margins will attract a host of competitors.

12-6 Pricing in Practice: A Real-World Approach

At this point, you may be wondering about economic theory. How do concepts such as supply and demand and price elasticity affect pricing decisions?

Most marketers are familiar with economics, but they often don't have the information they need to apply it to their specific pricing strategies. Collecting data for supply-and-demand curves is expensive and time consuming; also, it may be unrealistic for rapidly changing markets. From a real world standpoint, most marketers consider market-based factors—especially customer expectations and competitive prices—but they rely on cost-based

pricing. The key question is this: What price levels will allow me to cover my costs and achieve my objectives?

12-6a Breakeven Analysis

Breakeven analysis is a relatively simple process that determines the number of units a firm must sell to cover all costs. Sales above the breakeven point will generate a profit; sales below the breakeven point will lead to a loss. The actual equation looks like this:

$$\text{Breakeven Point (BP)} = \frac{\text{Total fixed costs (FC)}}{\text{Price/Unit (P)} - \text{Variable cost/unit (VC)}}$$

If you are selling sandwiches, for example, your fixed costs are perhaps $400,000 per year. Fixed costs stay the same no matter how many sandwiches you sell. Specific fixed costs include the mortgage, staff, equipment payments, advertising, insurance, and taxes. Suppose your variable cost per sandwich—the cost of the ingredients—is $3.00 per sandwich. If your customers are willing to pay $8 per sandwich, you can use the breakeven equation to determine how many sandwiches you'll need to sell in a year so that your

> **breakeven analysis** The process of determining the number of units a firm must sell to cover all costs.

total sales are equal to your total expenses. Remember that a company that is breaking even is not making a profit.

Here's how a breakeven analysis will work for our sandwich business:

$$BP = \frac{FC}{P - VC} = \frac{\$400,000}{\$8 - \$3} = \frac{\$400,000}{\$5} = 80,000 \text{ sandwiches}$$

Over a one-year horizon, 80,000 sandwiches will translate to about 220 sandwiches per day. Is that reasonable? Could you do better? If so, go for it! If not, you have several choices, each with its own set of considerations:

- **Raise prices:** How much do similar sandwiches in your neighbourhood cost? Are your sandwiches better in some way? Would potential customers be willing to pay more?

- **Decrease variable costs:** Could you use less expensive ingredients? Is it possible to hire less expensive help? How would these changes impact quality and sales?

- **Decrease fixed costs:** Should you choose a different location? Can you lease cheaper equipment? Would it make sense to advertise less often? How would these changes impact your business?

Clearly, there isn't one best strategy, but a breakeven analysis helps marketers get a sense of where they stand and the hurdles they need to clear before actually introducing a product.

12-6b Fixed Margin Pricing

Many firms determine upfront how much money they need to make for each item they sell. The **profit margin**—which is the gap between the cost and the price on a per product basis—can be expressed as a dollar amount, but more often it is expressed as a percentage. There are two key ways to determine margins:

- **Cost-based pricing:** The most popular method of establishing a fixed margin starts with determining the actual cost of each product. The process is more complex than it may initially seem because fixed costs must be allocated on a per product basis and some variable costs fluctuate dramatically on a daily or weekly basis. But once the per-product cost is set, the next step is to layer the margin on the

profit margin The gap between the cost and the price of an item on a per product basis.

odd pricing The practice of ending prices in numbers below even dollars and cents in order to create a perception of greater value.

> There are two kinds of fools in any market. One doesn't charge enough. The other charges too much.
>
> Russian proverb

cost to determine the price. Costco, for instance, has a strict policy that no branded item can be marked up by more than 14 percent and no private-label item by more than 15 percent. Supermarkets, on the other hand, often mark up merchandise by 25 percent and department stores by 50 percent or more. Margins in other industries can be much thinner.[11]

- **Demand-based pricing:** This approach begins by determining what price consumers would be willing to pay. With that as a starting point, marketers subtract their desired margin, which yields their target costs. This method is more market focused than cost-based pricing, but it's also more risky because profits depend on achieving those target costs. A number of Japanese companies such as Sony have been very successful with this approach, achieving extraordinarily efficient production.

12-6c Consumer Pricing Perceptions: The Strategic Wild Card

You just don't know if you've found the right price until you figure out how consumers perceive it. And those perceptions can sometimes defy the straightforward logic of dollars and cents. Two key considerations are price–quality relationships and odd pricing.

The link between price and perceived quality can be powerful. Picture yourself walking into a local sporting goods store, looking for a new snowboard. The store has several models of your favourite brand, most priced at around $450. But then you notice another option—same brand, same style—marked down to $79. Would you buy it? If you are like most consumers, you'll probably assume that something is wrong with a board that cheap. Would you be right? It's hard to know. Sometimes the relationship between price and quality is clear and direct, but that is not always the case. Regardless, consumers will use price as an indicator of quality unless they have additional information to guide their decision. Savvy marketers factor this tendency into their pricing strategies.

Marketers also must weigh the pros and cons of **odd pricing**, or ending prices in numbers below even dollars and cents. A Hoover steam mop at Canadian Tire, for instance, is $199.99. Gasoline, of course, often uses odd pricing, frequently ending in ".9." But wouldn't a round number be easier? Does that extra penny or fraction of a penny

WHEN SUPPLY IS LOW AND DEMAND IS HIGH

Herb MacKenzie

What happens when supply is low and demand is high? Of course, price goes up. And, sometimes, way up!

Going forward, prices are likely to climb for luxury assets: classic cars, art, wine, coins, and stamps are the most popular examples. The Knight Frank Luxury Investment Index (KFLII) tracks the performance of these and several other "investments of passion" over time. Between 2004 and 2014, classic cars appreciated 469 percent, followed by art and wine, both at 226 percent. Coins and stamps were not far behind. During the same period, the FTSE 100—the 100 companies with the largest market capitalization on the London Stock Exchange—increased by 51 percent.

What could you expect to pay for the highest-priced item in each asset class? Well, for antique cars, 53 of the 100 highest priced cars ever sold at auction (and 9 of the top 10) were Ferraris, one of which sold in 2014 for US$34.7 million ($38.1 million, including buyer's premium). However, another Ferrari sold in a private sale in 2013 for US$52 million.

Not expensive enough for you? In 2015, Pablo Picasso's 1955 painting "Women of Algiers" sold at auction for US$179.4 million. If you can't afford either of these, stamps or coins might be worth considering. In 2014, the British Guiana 1856 1c black on magenta stamp sold for only US$9.5 million, while a rare Edward VIII Gold Sovereign coin went for just under $800,000.

For those who are considering a new wealth creation strategy, investing money in luxury assets might be the answer. Just be careful not to pay too much![12]

Sources: Andrew Shirley, "Knight Frank Luxury Investment Index update 2014," knightfrankblog.com; Katya Kazakina and Mary Romano, "These 10 Pieces of Art Just Sold for Almost $800 Million," www.blomberg.com; *Gizmag* website, "The Top 100 Most Expensive Cars of All Time," November 13, 2014.

---

really make a difference? While the research is inconclusive, many marketers believe that jumping up to the "next" round number sends a message that prices have hit a whole new level. In other words, they believe that the *perceived* gap between $199.99 and $200.00 is much greater than the *actual* gap of one cent. And it certainly makes sense from an intuitive standpoint.

Odd prices have also come to signal a bargain. This is often—but not always—a benefit for the marketer. For instance, a big-screen TV for $999.99 might seem like a great deal, while knee surgery for $4,999.99 sounds kind of scary—you'd probably rather pay $5,000. Likewise, a fast food joint might charge $3.99 for its value meal, while fine restaurants almost always end their prices in zeros. The most exclusive restaurants sometimes simply show dollars: Caesar salad—$11. Marketers can determine whether odd pricing would work for them by evaluating the strategy in light of the messages it sends to the target market.

Distribution and pricing are two fundamental elements of the marketing mix. In today's frenzied global economy, marketers are seeking a competitive edge through distribution management. Creating a profitable presence in multiple retail venues requires constant focus throughout the organization. And managing the supply chain—how products move along the path from raw materials to the final consumer—plays a crucial role in controlling costs and providing great customer service. Integrating effective technology during the entire process can separate the winners from the losers.

Pricing objectives and strategies are also pivotal because they directly impact both profitability and product image. As the market changes, successful companies continually re-evaluate and modify their approach, working hand in hand with their accountants.

Looking ahead, a growing number of companies will probably move towards collaboration rather than competition as they manage their supply chains. And pricing will likely become even more dynamic in response to the changing market.

THE BIG PICTURE

careers in distribution and pricing: Warehouse Manager

Oversee the safe receipt, storage, retrieval, and timely transmission of goods. Oversee computerized inventory management system. Comply with federal, provincial, and municipal laws regarding warehousing, material handling, and shipping. Plan the arrangement of goods within the warehouse and handle requirements for specialized stock (e.g., chilled goods or fragile products). Keep current with all relevant legislation and industry trends. Ensure security in all aspects of warehouse operation. Maintain physical condition of warehouse. Create and track warehousing budget to meet financial objectives. Hire, manage, and motivate warehouse staff.

STUDY TOOLS 12

IN THE BOOK, YOU CAN:

☐ Rip out the Chapter Review card at the back of the book to have a summary of the chapter and key terms handy.

ONLINE AT NELSON.COM/STUDENT YOU CAN:

☐ Work through key concepts with a Guided Learning Question.

☐ Prepare for tests with quizzes.

☐ Review the key terms with Flash Cards (online or printer-ready).

☐ Explore practical examples of chapter concepts with Connect a Concept exercises.

13

Management, Motivation, and Leadership:
Bringing Business to Life

LEARNING OBJECTIVES
After studying this chapter, you will be able to…

13-1 Discuss the role of management and its importance to organizational success

13-2 Explain key theories and current practices of motivation

13-3 Outline the categories of business planning and explain strategic planning

13-4 Discuss the organizing function of management

13-5 Explain the role of managerial leadership and the key leadership styles

13-6 Describe the management control process

After you finish this chapter, go to page 223 for STUDY TOOLS

13-1 Bringing Resources to Life

To grow and thrive, every business needs resources—money, technology, materials—and an economic system that helps enterprise flourish. But those resources, or factors of production, are nothing without **management** to bring them to life. Managers provide vision and direction for their organizations, decide how to use resources to achieve goals, and inspire others—both inside and outside their companies—to follow their lead. By formal definition, managers achieve the goals of an organization through planning, organizing, leading, and controlling organizational resources, including people, money, and time.

In simple terms, **planning** means figuring out where to go and how to get there. **Organizing** means determining a structure for both individual jobs and the overall organization. **Leading** means directing and motivating people to achieve organizational goals. And **controlling** means checking performance and making adjustments as needed. In today's chaotic, hypercompetitive business environment, managers face daunting challenges. But for the right people, management positions can provide an exhilarating—although sometimes exhausting—career.

As the business pace accelerates and the environment continues to morph—especially in the wake of economic turmoil—the role of management has radically transformed. The successful manager has changed from boss to coach, from disciplinarian to motivator, from dictator to team builder. But the bottom-line goal has remained the same: to create value for the organization.

13-1a Management Hierarchy: Levels of Responsibility

Most medium-sized and large companies have three basic levels of management: **top management**, **middle management**, and **first-line (or supervisory) management**. The levels typically fall into a pyramid of sorts, with a small number of top managers and a

management Achieving the goals of an organization through planning, organizing, leading, and controlling organizational resources, including people, money, and time.

planning Determining organizational goals and action plans for how to achieve those goals.

organizing Determining a structure for both individual jobs and the overall organization.

leading Directing and motivating people to achieve organizational goals.

controlling Checking performance and making adjustments as needed.

> The man who rolls up his sleeves seldom loses his shirt.
>
> Thomas Cowan, Scottish footballer

Alex Pettes, president of TFI Food Equipment Solutions, motivates himself by reciting his personal mission statement three times each day.

larger number of supervisory managers. Responsibilities shift as managers move up the hierarchy, and the skills they use must shift accordingly. Here are the three key levels:

- **Top management** sets the overall direction of the firm. Top managers must articulate a vision, establish priorities, and allocate time, money, and other resources. Typical titles include chief executive officer (CEO), president, and vice-president.

- **Middle management** manages the managers. (Say that three times!) Middle managers communicate up and down the pyramid, and their primary contribution often involves coordinating teams and special projects with their peers from other departments. Typical titles include director, division head, and branch manager.

- **First-line management** manages the people who do the work. First-line managers must train, motivate, and evaluate nonmanagement employees, so they are heavily involved in day-to-day production issues. Typical titles include supervisor, foreperson, and section leader.

Smaller companies usually don't have a hierarchy of management. Often the owner must act as the top, middle, and first-line manager, all rolled into one. This clearly requires enormous flexibility and well-developed management skills.

13-1b Management Skills: Having What It Takes to Get the Job Done

Given the turbulence of today's business world, managers must draw on a staggering range of skills to do their jobs efficiently and effectively. Most of these abilities cluster into three broad categories: technical skills, human skills, and conceptual skills.

- **Technical skills** refer to expertise in a specific functional area or department. Keep in mind that technical skills don't necessarily relate to technology. People can have technical skills—or specific expertise— in virtually any field, from sales, to copy writing, to accounting, to airplane repair, to computer programming.

- **Human skills** refer to the ability to work with and through other people in a range of different relationships. Human skills include

top management Managers who set the overall direction of the firm, articulating a vision, establishing priorities, and allocating time, money, and other resources.

middle management Managers who supervise lower level managers and report to higher level managers.

first-line management Managers who directly supervise non management employees.

technical skills Expertise in a specific functional area or department.

human skills The ability to work effectively with and through other people in a range of different relationships.

communication, leadership, coaching, empathy, and team building. A manager with strong human skills can typically mobilize support for initiatives and find win–win solutions for conflicts.

- **Conceptual skills** refer to the ability to grasp a big-picture view of the overall organization and the relationships among its various parts. Conceptual skills also help managers understand how their company fits into the broader competitive environment. Managers with strong conceptual skills typically excel at strategic planning.

All three categories of skill are essential for management success. But their importance varies according to the level of the manager. Front-line managers must have a high degree of technical skills, which help them hire, train, and evaluate employees, avoid mistakes, and ensure high-quality production. Middle-level managers need an especially high level of human skills. They typically act as the bridge between departments, coordinating people and projects that sometimes have mismatched priorities. Top-level managers must demonstrate excellent conceptual skills in order to formulate a vision, interpret marketplace trends, and plan for the future. To move up in an organization, managers must constantly learn and grow, nurturing skills that reflect their new tasks.

Across all three skill sets, critical thinking and decision-making abilities have become increasingly important. Critical thinking helps managers find value in even an overload of information. Part of how information overload plays out is in e-mail management; according to *Fortune* magazine, the average knowledge worker now spends an astounding 28 percent of his or her work time managing e-mail. Simply deleting unwanted e-mails could take more than 16 hours per year! Strong decision-making skills help managers respond wisely and rapidly to all of this information, with an unwavering focus on customer satisfaction.

Managers who expect to grow in the company hierarchy must expect to foster new skills. Too often, workers get promotions because of great technical skills— for example, the top salesperson lands the sales manager slot— but they struggle to move further because they don't fully develop their human and conceptual skills.

> Any business that pays its eagles with chicken feed will soon find its eagles fly away and only its chickens remain.

conceptual skills The ability to grasp a big-picture view of the overall organization, the relationship between its various parts, and its fit in the broader competitive environment.

Maslow's hierarchy of needs theory Motivation theory that suggests human needs fall in a hierarchy and that as each need is met, people become motivated to meet the next highest need in the pyramid.

13-2 Motivation: Lighting the Fire

Standout managers motivate others to reach for their best selves—to accomplish more than they ever thought possible. Motivated workers tend to feel great about their jobs, and workers who feel great tend to produce more. But the thinking about *how* to motivate workers has changed dramatically over time. In the early 1900s, key management thinkers focused on efficiency and productivity, dictating precisely how workers should perform each element of their jobs. But more recent research suggests that people's thoughts and feelings play a vital role in motivation. This has led to a range of new theories.

13-2a Theories of Motivation

Maslow's Hierarchy of Needs Theory Noted psychologist Abraham Maslow theorized that people are motivated to satisfy only unmet needs. He proposed a hierarchy of human needs—from basic to abstract— and suggested that as each need is met, people become motivated to meet the next highest need in the pyramid. **Maslow's hierarchy of needs theory** proposes five specific needs, which are shown in Exhibit 13.1. While he didn't develop his theory based on the workplace, Maslow's ideas can illuminate the needs behind motivation at work.

From a workplace perspective, the idea that people are motivated only by unmet needs clearly holds true for the first two levels of the hierarchy. Finding a job that pays the bills, for instance, is the primary motivator for most people who don't have any job at all. People who have a job but no dental care would find dental insurance much more motivating than, say, a company picnic geared towards meeting social needs.

But once physiological and safety needs are met, the other needs are motivating to different degrees in different people. An employee with strong social connections outside work, for instance, might be more motivated by a promotion that meets esteem needs than by a company outing that meets social needs. A number of firms actually use self-actualization needs as a starting point for motivating employees, by creating a mission statement that communicates the importance of the work. Katimavik, for instance, has a mission "to prepare youth to become responsible citizens who make positive change

THE POWER OF ONE

Herb MacKenzie

Some people seem compelled to succeed no matter what ... and those are the folks who tend to drive the economy. A quick survey of some well-known super-achievers suggests that a high level of motivation was part of their personality from the very beginning:

- *Mark Zuckerberg, Facebook founder:* Before he went to college, Mark was recruited to work for Microsoft and AOL. As a toddler, he found a screwdriver and dismantled his crib when he thought he was too old for a "baby bed."

- *Howie Mandel, Canadian-born game and talk-show host and television producer:* Mandel began his career as a door-to-door carpet salesman and built the business into a two-store successful retail operation. On a business trip, he participated in a comedy amateur night and was hired to appear on his first comedy game show.

- *Justin Trudeau, prime minister of Canada:* Trudeau's first career was teaching high school in Vancouver, BC. Eventually returning to Montreal, he chaired the board of Katimavik, a youth service organization founded in 1977 by former prime minister Pierre Elliott Trudeau, his father. He travelled across the country promoting volunteerism to Canadian youth.

- *Chris Rock, comedian:* Chris's first job was at Red Lobster. "The thing about Red Lobster is that if you work there, you can't afford to eat there," he once told Jay Leno. "You're making minimum wage. A shrimp costs minimum wage."

But keep in mind that some high achievers don't gear up until well after childhood. True motivation requires clear goals, which people can develop at any point in their lives. When meaningful goals merge with energy and determination, anything becomes possible.[1]

---

in their lives and communities." More than 35,000 young Canadians have volunteered their services to improve communities across the country and have benefited themselves through the development of transferable employment skills.[2]

13-2b Theory X and Theory Y

Psychologist Douglas McGregor, one of Maslow's students, studied workplace motivation from a different angle. He posited that management attitudes towards workers

---

Exhibit 13.1 Maslow's Hierarchy of Needs Relates to the Workplace

MASLOW'S NEED	DESCRIPTION	WORKPLACE EXAMPLES
PHYSIOLOGICAL	Need for basic survival—food, water, clothing, and shelter	A job with enough pay to buy the basics
SAFETY	Need to feel secure—free of harm and free of fear	Safety equipment, health care plans, life insurance, retirement plans, job security, gym membership
SOCIAL (BELONGING)	Need to feel connected to others—accepted by family and friends	Teamwork, positive corporate culture, company lunchroom, uniforms, department outings
ESTEEM	Need for self-respect and respect from others—recognition and status	Acknowledgment, feedback, promotions, perks, raises
SELF-ACTUALIZATION	Need for fulfillment, the need to realize one's fullest potential	Challenging, creative jobs; meaningful work that ties to a greater good; volunteer opportunities

© Cengage Learning

Bad Decisions, Big Impacts

Every day, managers around the globe make high-stakes decisions, from expanding overseas, to introducing new products, to closing factories. The great decisions have become the stuff of legends, shaping the business world as we know it today. Bad choices also abound, although we tend to hear a lot less about them. Consider these five business decisions that made history for their silliness:

- Faced with the opportunity to buy rights to the telephone in 1876, Western Union, the telegraph behemoth, rejected the newfangled device: "This 'telephone' has too many short-comings to be seriously considered as a means of communication. The device is inherently of no value to us."

- In 1899, two young lawyers approached Asa Chandler—owner of the briskly selling new fountain drink Coca-Cola—with an innovative proposal to bottle the beverage. Chandler sold them exclusive rights to bottle Coke for the grand sum of $1. Oops.

- In 1975, Eastman Kodak invented the digital camera, but opted not to invest in it for fear of undermining its film business. By the time Kodak finally did invest in the digital market in the mid-1990s, Sony and Fuji already had too much of a lead on the product that Kodak had actually invented. Then the digital camera market began to wane as smartphones and tablets took over. Eastman Kodak filed for bankruptcy in 2011.

- In 1999, the fledgling search engine Excite rejected an offer to buy Google because it considered the $1 million asking price to be too high. Google is now worth nearly $300 billion, and Excite is defunct.

- Mike Smith, one of the executives in charge of evaluating new talent for the London office of Decca Records, rejected the Beatles in 1962 with the now infamous line: "Groups are out; four-piece groups with guitars particularly are finished." Not so much . . .

With the help of hindsight, momentous decisions may seem almost inevitable. But these bloopers clearly show that in the fog of the moment, the right choice can be anything but clear.[3]

Theory X and Theory Y Motivation theory that suggests that management attitudes towards workers fall into two opposing categories based on management assumptions about worker capabilities and values.

job enrichment The creation of jobs with more meaningful content, under the assumption that challenging, creative work will motivate employees.

directly affected worker motivation. His research suggested that management attitudes fall into two opposing categories, which he called **Theory X and Theory Y**, described in Exhibit 13.2.

McGregor proposed that managers should employ Theory Y assumptions in order to capitalize on the imagination and intelligence of every worker. In Canadian business today, some organizations use a Theory X approach, but a growing number have begun to at least experiment with Theory Y, tapping into a rich pool of employee input.

Job Enrichment A number of researchers have focused on creating jobs with more meaningful content, under the assumption that challenging, creative work will motivate employees to give their best effort. **Job enrichment** typically includes the following factors:

1. **Skill variety:** Workers can use a range of different skills.

2. **Task identity:** Workers do complete tasks with clear beginnings and endings.

Exhibit 13.2 Theory X and Theory Y

THEORY X ASSUMPTIONS ABOUT WORKERS	THEORY Y ASSUMPTIONS ABOUT WORKERS
■ Workers dislike work and will do everything they can to avoid it.	■ Work is as natural as play or rest—workers do not inherently dislike it.
■ Fear is motivating—coercion and threats are vital to get people to work towards company goals.	■ Different rewards can be motivating—people can exercise self-direction and self-control to meet company goals.
■ People prefer to be directed, avoiding responsibility and seeking security.	■ People can accept and even seek responsibility.
	■ The capacity for imagination, creativity, and ingenuity is widely distributed in the population.
	■ The intellectual capacity of the average worker is underutilized in the workplace.

© Cengage Learning

3. **Task significance:** Workers understand the impact of the task on others.
4. **Autonomy:** Workers have freedom and authority regarding their jobs.
5. **Feedback:** Workers receive clear, frequent information about their performance.

Richard Branson, maverick founder of the Virgin Group, relies on job enrichment—especially autonomy and feedback—to keep people motivated at his 350-company empire (which includes a startling range of firms, such as Virgin Atlantic Airlines, Virgin Music, Virgin mobile phones, and Virgin Galactic space travel). Branson gives his managers a stake in their companies and then tells them "to run it as if it's their own." He says: "I intervene as little as possible. Give them that, and they will give everything back." According to Virgin's website, "we pretty much practise a collaborative and supportive style of custodianship." Due in large part to Branson's motivational approach, the Virgin workforce is fully engaged with the company, contributing to its remarkable long-term success.[4]

Expectancy Theory Usually attributed to researcher Victor Vroom, **expectancy theory** deals with the relationships among effort, performance, and reward. The key concept is that a worker will be motivated if he or she believes that effort will lead to performance and performance to a meaningful reward. Imagine that you studied very hard for your exam (effort) but that you achieved a grade much lower than you expected (reward). What went wrong? As noted, expectancy theory does not propose that effort leads to reward; rather, effort leads to performance, and it is performance that leads to reward. Your effort may not have led to performance. Now you need to ask whether you were providing the right effort—that is, studying effectively.

Effort → Performance → Reward

The theory suggests that if any link in the chain is broken, the employee will not be motivated. And, of course, the employee must value the reward. Otherwise he or she will not be motivated to achieve it. Imagine if your company offers an all-expense paid trip for two to Paris for the top sales performer. If you are afraid to fly, you may not be motivated to win.

Equity Theory Pioneered by J. Stacy Adams, **equity theory** proposes that perceptions of fairness directly affect worker motivation. The key idea is that people won't be motivated if they believe that the relationship between what they contribute and what they earn is different from the relationship between what others contribute and what others earn. For example, if you work 10-hour days and earn

less than the guy in the next cubicle who works seven-hour days, you probably think it is pretty unfair. To restore a sense of balance, you might:

- demand a raise;
- start coming in late, leaving early, and taking longer lunch hours;
- convince yourself that the other guy is about to be fired; or
- look for another job.

The response to perceived inequity almost always involves trying to change the system, changing your own work habits, distorting your perceptions, or leaving the company.

But keep in mind that equity theory is based on perceptions, which are not always on the mark. People are all too prone to overestimate their own contributions, which throws perceived equity out of balance. The best way to combat equity issues is through clear, open communication from management.[5]

13-2c **Motivation Today**

Companies today use a range of approaches to motivation, although several key themes have emerged. Most firms no longer seek to make their employees happy; instead, they want their workers to be productive and engaged. Yet for employees, work is about more than just productivity. Business professor David Ulrich points out that even in today's hypercompetitive environment, "people still want to find meaning in their work and in the institutions that employ them."[6]

A growing emphasis on corporate culture has captured the best of both worlds for companies that do it right. A distinctive, positive culture tends to create productive employees who are deeply attached to their work and their companies. WestJet Airlines has been recognized a number of times on lists of Canada's best employers. Employees and their families get discounts on tickets and packaged holidays. They can purchase WestJet shares, and the company matches their investment up to 20 percent of the employee's salary. An internal "care team" organizes more than 200 events for employees: ice cream days, wine tastings, ski days, softball tournaments, and so on.[7]

McDonald's Restaurants of Canada has been on the *Canadian Business* list of Canada's top 50 large employers (more than 400 employees) for 13 years. Employees receive an annual $800 allowance

expectancy theory Motivation theory that deals with the relationships among individual effort, individual performance, and individual reward.

equity theory Motivation theory that proposes perceptions of fairness directly affect worker motivation.

for fitness equipment or health-club memberships. Every 10 years, employees get a paid eight-week sabbatical, plus their regular vacation and, on their fifth, 15th, 25th, and 35th anniversary, they get an additional week of paid vacation. The company also has a promote-from-within culture so that 90 percent of managers and half of franchisees (and three Canadian presidents) began their career serving customers. At Chubb Insurance Co. of Canada, in addition to an annual fitness allowance, employees get in-house yoga and massages and subsidized social events. Employees can take up to five paid volunteer days each year, and the company matches employee donations. Workers also get to customize their individual benefits and pension plans. Chubb double-matches employee contributions to a company retirement savings program.[8]

Finally, a growing number of businesses have expanded their range of employee incentives beyond just cash. While money certainly matters, *Fortune* points out that "telling employees they're doing a great job costs nothing but counts big." Employee training is a noncash motivational tactic gaining momentum across the economy in response to the growing array of complex skills needed by the workforce. The emphasis on training and education is especially motivating given that more and more employees identify themselves based on their field of expertise rather than their organization.[9]

> Leadership is a hot topic. Searching the term in Google gets about 640 million results. A search on Amazon.com gets more than 179,672 books (February 7, 2016).
>
> Google and Amazon

change, and economic uncertainty. The best plans keep the organization on track, without sacrificing flexibility and responsiveness; they incorporate ways to respond to change both inside and outside the organization.[10]

Although all managers engage in planning, the scope of the process changes according to the manager's position within the organization. Top-level managers focus on **strategic planning**. They establish a vision for the company, define long-term objectives and priorities, determine broad action steps, and allocate resources. Middle managers focus on **tactical planning**, or applying the strategic plan to their specific areas of responsibility. And first-line managers focus on **operational planning**, or applying the tactical plans to daily, weekly, and monthly operations. Successful firms often encourage a flow of feedback up and down the organization to ensure that all key plans are sound and that all key players "buy in." Some typical planning decisions and timeframes are shown in Exhibit 13.3.

A fourth category of planning has been gaining prominence: **contingency planning**, or planning for unexpected events. Senior management usually spearheads contingency planning, but with input from the other levels of management. Contingency plans consider what might go wrong—both inside the business and with the outside environment—and develop responses. Potential issues include the following:

- How should we respond if our competitors knock off our bestselling product?
- What should we do if the government regulates our industry?

strategic planning High-level, long-term planning that establishes a vision for the company, defines long-term objectives and priorities, determines broad action steps, and allocates resources.

tactical planning More specific, shorter-term planning that applies strategic plans to specific functional areas.

operational planning Very specific, short-term planning that applies tactical plans to daily, weekly, and monthly operations.

contingency planning Planning for unexpected events, usually involving a range of scenarios and assumptions that differ from the assumptions behind the core plans.

13-3 Planning: Figuring Out Where to Go and How to Get There

The planning function—figuring out where to go and how to get there—is the core of effective management. The *Wall Street Journal* found that 80 percent of executives identify planning as their most valuable management tool. But even though planning is critical, it's also highly risky in light of cutthroat competition, rapid

Herb MacKenzie

Exhibit 13.3 | Managerial Planning

TYPE OF PLANNING	MANAGEMENT LEVEL	SCOPE OF PLANNING	EXAMPLES OF PLANNING QUESTIONS AND CONCERNS
STRATEGIC PLANNING	Senior management	Typically five-year time frame	Should we acquire a new company? Should we begin manufacturing in China? Should we take our company public?
TACTICAL PLANNING	Middle management	Typically one-year time frame	Should we invest in new production equipment? Should we spend more time servicing each customer? Should we spend fewer ad dollars on TV and more on the Web?
OPERATIONAL PLANNING	First-line management	Daily, weekly, and monthly time frame	How should we schedule employees this week? When should we schedule delivery for each batch of product? How should customer service people answer the phones?

© Cengage Learning

- How can we respond if our data management/computer system fails or is otherwise compromised?
- How can we rebuild our business if a natural disaster destroys our plant or supply channels?

Clearly, anticipating every potential problem is impossible (and impractical!). Instead, effective contingency plans tend to focus only on the issues that are most probable, or most potentially harmful, or both (see Exhibit 13.4). For example, a wilderness resort in British Columbia might focus its contingency plans on forest fires, while Air Canada might focus its plans on responding to a pilots' strike.

Exhibit 13.4 | Contingency Planning Paradigm

Businesses tend to focus their contingency plans on issues that are most probable _and_ most potentially harmful.

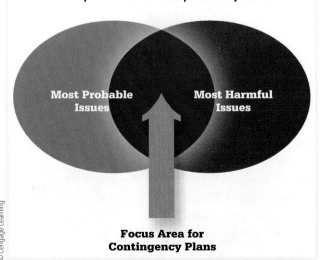

Most Probable Issues

Most Harmful Issues

Focus Area for Contingency Plans

© Cengage Learning

13-3a Strategic Planning: Setting the Agenda

Strategic planning is the most fundamental part of the planning process because all other plans—and most major management decisions—stem from the strategic plan. The strategic planning process typically includes these steps:

1. Define the mission of the organization.
2. Evaluate the organization's competitive position.
3. Set goals for the organization.
4. Create strategies for competitive differentiation.
5. Implement strategies.
6. Evaluate results and incorporate lessons learned.

Defining Your Mission The mission of an organization articulates its essential reason for being. The **mission** defines the organization's purpose, values, and core goals, providing the framework for all other plans (see Exhibit 13.5). Most large companies present their mission as a simple, vivid, compelling statement that everyone involved with the company—from the janitor to the CEO, from customers to investors—can easily understand. Mission statements tend to vary in their length, their language, and even their name, but they share a common goal: to provide a clear, long-term focus for the organization.

Evaluating Your Competitive Position Strategy means nothing in a vacuum—every firm must plan in the context of the marketplace. Many companies use a **SWOT analysis** (strengths, weaknesses, opportunities, and threats) to evaluate where they stand relative to the competition. Strengths and weaknesses

> **mission** The definition of an organization's purpose, values, and core goals, which provides the framework for all other plans.
>
> **SWOT analysis** A strategic planning tool that helps management evaluate an organization in terms of internal strengths and weaknesses and external opportunities and threats.

SLACKERS? NOT SO MUCH...

Generation Y—those born between 1978 and 1998—is changing the face of the workforce. These self-confident, outspoken young people have posed a new set of challenges for managers across the economy. A quick profile of Generation Y—also known as Gen Yers, "millennials," "echo-boomers," and "Gen F" (for Facebook)—highlights their key characteristics. Keep in mind that no general overview can clearly describe each member of Generation Y. Yet chances are strong that Gen Yers will recognize at least parts of themselves in the following profile. Companies that understand Gen Yers—and figure out how to harness their talents—will find themselves with a sharp competitive edge in the years to come.

- **Goal-driven:** Gen Yers expect to have to perform for their rewards. But they tend to find smaller, short-term goals much more motivating than long-term goals. The reason: A week in their fast-paced world is more like a year was for their parents.

- **Facebook-focused:** On average, Gen Yers have 696 Facebook friends, and 16 of them are work friends.

- **Change-oriented:** Gen Yers actively embrace change and excitement. Many anticipate changing jobs frequently and even hope to do so. They don't share the expectation of long-term employment that disillusioned so many of their parents.

- **Tech Savvy:** Gen Yers are masters of the Internet and the iPod. They often expect top technology in the workplace, and they use virtually all of it (often at the same time!) to boost their performance.

- **Diverse:** Gen Y is among the most diverse demographic groups—one in three is a minority—and most don't believe that their ethnicity defines their character. Many were born in other countries and speak multiple languages fluently.

- **Entrepreneurial:** Only 7 percent of Gen Yers work for a Fortune 500 company because start-ups are dominating the workforce. Even though most of their companies won't succeed, they are demonstrating an unprecedented entrepreneurial spirit. Companies can allow Gen Yers to operate entrepreneurially within the corporation by giving them control over their time, activities, and budgets as much as possible.

- **Fulfillment-focused:** Gen Yers tend to deeply value their families and their personal lives. They fully expect to achieve their lofty career goals without sacrificing time for themselves and the people they care about.[11]

Herb MacKenzie

are internal to the organization, and include factors that would either build up or drag down the firm's performance. Opportunities and threats are external, and include factors that would affect the company's performance but are typically out of the company's control. Exhibit 13.6 offers some examples.

Initial information about internal strengths and weaknesses usually comes from careful analysis of internal

Exhibit 13.5 Examples of Mission Statements

CANADIAN CANCER SOCIETY	The Canadian Cancer Society is a national community-based organization of volunteers whose mission is the eradication of cancer and the enhancement of the quality of life of people living with cancer.
RETAIL COUNCIL OF CANADA	To advance, promote, and protect the interests of our members through effective advocacy, communications, and education.
HOME HARDWARE CANADA	Home Hardware's mission as a Dealer-Owned company is to supply Home Dealers with quality products and services, to assist them with programs to operate effective and efficient stores at a profitable level, thereby allowing them to serve the customer with competitive prices and superior service.

Courtesy of Canadian Cancer Society; Retail Council of Canada; Home Hardware Canada. All used with permission.

Exhibit 13.6 SWOT Analysis Examples

POTENTIAL INTERNAL STRENGTHS	POTENTIAL EXTERNAL OPPORTUNITIES
■ Premium brand name	■ Higher consumer demand
■ Proven management team	■ Complacent competitors
■ Lower costs/higher margins	■ Growth in foreign markets
■ Diverse workforce	■ New social trends

POTENTIAL INTERNAL WEAKNESSES	POTENTIAL EXTERNAL THREATS
■ Low employee satisfaction	■ A powerful new competitor
■ Inadequate financial resources	■ A deep recession
■ Poor location	■ New government regulations
■ Poor safety record	■ Costly new taxes

© Cengage Learning

Exhibit 13.7 Goal Setting: Getting It Right

WEAK GOAL	POWERFUL GOAL
Become more innovative	Introduce one new product each quarter for the next three years
Reduce delinquent accounts	Reduce delinquent accounts to no more than 1% of the total accounts receivable by the end of the second quarter
Increase market share	Become the #1 or #2 brand in each market where we compete by the end of 2020

© Cengage Learning

reports on topics such as budget and profitability. But to better understand strengths and weaknesses, executives should actively seek firsthand information—on a personal basis—from key people throughout the company, from front-line workers to the board of directors.

Gathering information about external opportunities and threats can be more complex because these areas include both current and potential issues (which can be tough to predict). Information about external factors can come from many different sources, including the news, government reports, customers, and competitors.

Setting Your Goals Strategic goals represent concrete benchmarks that managers can use to measure performance in each key area of the organization. They must fit the firm's mission and tie directly to its competitive position. The most effective goals are as follows:

1. **Specific and measurable:** Whenever possible, managers should define goals in clear numerical terms that everyone understands.

2. **Tied to a timeframe:** To create meaning and urgency, goals should be linked to a specific deadline.

3. **Realistic but challenging:** Goals that make people stretch can motivate exceptional performance.

Exhibit 13.7 offers examples of how weak goals can be transformed into powerful goals.

Creating Your Strategies Strategies are action plans that help the organization achieve its goals by forging the best fit between the firm and the environment. The underlying aim, of course, is to create a significant advantage versus the competition. Sources of competitive advantage vary, ranging from better product quality, to better technology, to more motivated employees. The most successful companies build their advantage across several fronts. WestJet, for example, has a more motivated workforce and a lower cost structure. H&M has lower prices and more fashionable clothing. And Procter & Gamble has more innovative new products and strong core brands.

The specifics of strategy differ by industry and by company, but all strategies represent a road map. The SWOT analysis determines the starting point, and the objectives signify the immediate destination. Because speed matters, you must begin mapping the next leg of the journey even before you arrive. For added complexity, you never know—given the turbulent environment—when you might hit roadblocks. This means that strategies must be dynamic and flexible. Top managers have responded to this challenge by encouraging front-line managers to participate in the process more than ever before.

Implementing Your Strategies Implementation should happen largely through tactical planning. Middle managers in each key area of the company must develop plans to carry out core strategies in their area. If the strategic plan, for example, calls for more new products, marketing will need to generate ideas, finance will need to find funding, and sales will need to prepare key accounts. And all of these steps will require tactical planning.

strategic goals Concrete benchmarks that managers can use to measure performance in each key area of the organization.

strategies Action plans that help the organization achieve its goals by forging the best fit between the firm and the environment.

Evaluating Your Results and Incorporating Lessons Learned Evaluation of results should be a continual process, handled by managers at every level as part of their controlling function, covered further in this chapter. But for evaluation to be meaningful, the lessons learned must be analyzed objectively and factored back into the next planning cycle.

13-4 Organizing: Fitting Together the Puzzle Pieces

The organizing function of management means creating a logical structure for people, their jobs, and their patterns of interaction. And clearly, the pieces can fit together in a number of different ways. In choosing the right structure for a specific company, management typically considers many factors, including the goals and strategies of the firm, its products, its use of technology, its size, and the structure of its competitors. Given the potential for rapid change in each of these factors, smart companies continually re-examine their structure and make changes whenever necessary. Microsoft, for instance, restructures its organization every couple of years as new challenges emerge.

But to be effective, reorganizations—and their purpose—must be clear to employees throughout the company. Former Xerox CEO Anne Mulcahy learned the hard way. Her comments: "During the 1990s, we had lots of consultants on organizational effectiveness. We sliced and diced the business into industries, product lines, and geographies … you name it. It looked good on paper, but fell apart in implementation. I found myself in a job where I couldn't look anybody in the eye and feel clear accountability for anything … I'll trade off organizational design for clarity and accountability any day of the week!"[12]

To help employees understand how they and their jobs fit within the broader organization, most firms issue an **organization chart**, or a visual representation of the company's formal structure, as shown in Exhibit 13.8.

Looking at the company represented by Exhibit 13.8, you would probably assume that the vice-president of production has more power than a regular employee in the marketing department. And in terms of formal power, you'd be absolutely right. But if the marketing employee babysits on the weekend for the president's granddaughter, the balance of power may actually be a bit different than it seems. Make no mistake—the formal structure matters. But knowing how power flows on an informal basis can dramatically increase your effectiveness as well by helping you target your ideas to the right managers and marshal the support of the most influential employees.

13-4a Key Organizing Considerations

In developing the organizational structure, management must make decisions about the degree of centralization, the span of management control, and the type of departmentalization that makes the most sense at any given time.

Centralization The **degree of centralization** relates directly to the source of power and control. In centralized companies, a small number of people at the top of the organization have the power to make decisions. This approach is simple and efficient, and the result tends to be a strong corporate image and a uniform customer approach across the front lines. The downside is that centralized companies typically respond more slowly to customer needs and have lower employee morale. The tradeoff may be worthwhile in steady, stable markets, but those are rare.

Faced with today's turbulent environment, most firms are moving towards greater decentralization, pushing power to the lower levels of the organization. Employees

organization chart A visual representation of the company's formal structure.

degree of centralization The extent to which decision-making power is held by a small number of people at the top of the organization.

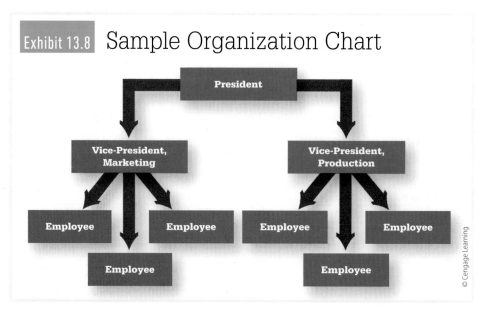

Exhibit 13.8 **Sample Organization Chart**

President

Vice-President, Marketing

Vice-President, Production

Employee

Employee

Employee

Employee

Employee

Employee

© Cengage Learning

WANNA BE MORE PRODUCTIVE? RELAX!!

Herb MacKenzie

ronically, a growing body of research suggests rather strongly that the best way to get more done may be to spend more time doing less. This can include daytime workouts, short afternoon naps, longer sleep hours at night, and longer, more frequent vacations. Despite misguided efforts to make it otherwise, time is definitely finite; energy, on the other hand, can be renewed, which is why a study by Harvard University estimated that sleep deprivation (less than six hours per night) costs American businesses US$63.2 billion annually in lost productivity.

Many studies of vacation show that taking more vacation days has a dramatic positive impact on worker performance. Despite this, people in many parts of the world fail to take all of the vacation time to which they are entitled. The good news is that Canadians take more of their vacation time than Americans, although many still do not take the average 15 days per year available to them. The most vacation-deprived workers in the world are in South Korea; they take 6 of the 15 days they are offered annually. Across 26 countries, 15 percent of respondents say they would change jobs if offered more vacation time; however, 69 percent would choose a raise over more days off. Only in India did more people prefer vacation time to money.

Another approach to more vacation is to allow more days per week off. Entrepreneur Katie Fang, a graduate of the University of British Columbia's Sauder School of Business, initially worked six or seven days a week to get her Web-based business, SchooLinks, started. Now, she limits her staff to a four-day workweek. She has noticed a boost in productivity, but, perhaps more important, she has found that many of them were reading about programming or working on related projects during their days off and that this was helping them build skills that indirectly benefited the company.[13]

---

with the power to make decisions can respond to customer needs more quickly and effectively. They can also capitalize on opportunities that would likely vaporize in the time it would take to get permission to act. But for decentralization to work, every employee must fully understand the firm's mission, goals, and strategy; otherwise, the company could develop a fragmented image, which would undermine its strength in the long term. Also, active communication across departments is essential so that all employees can benefit from innovations in other parts of the organization.

Span of Control The **span of control**, or span of management, refers to the number of people a manager supervises. There is no ideal number for every manager. The "right" span of control varies based on the abilities of both the manager and the subordinates, the nature of the work being done, the location of the employees, and the need for planning and coordination. The general trend among industries has been towards wider spans of control; a growing number of companies are pruning layers of middle management to the bare minimum.

Departmentalization **Departmentalization** means breaking workers into logical groups. A number of different options make sense, depending on the organization.

- **Functional:** Dividing employees into groups based on area of expertise, such as marketing, finance, and engineering, tends to be efficient and easy to coordinate. For those reasons, it works especially well for small to medium-sized firms.

- **Product:** Dividing employees into groups based on the products a company offers helps workers develop expertise about products, which often results in especially strong customer relations.

- **Customer:** Dividing employees into groups based on the customers a company serves helps companies focus on the needs of specific customer groups. Many companies have separate departments for meeting the needs of business and consumer users. This approach is related to product departmentalization.

- **Geographic:** Dividing employees into groups based on where customers are located can help different departments better serve specific regions within one country. Similarly, many international firms create a separate department for each country they serve.

- **Process:** Dividing into groups based on what type of work employees do is common in manufacturing, where

span of control Span of management; refers to the number of people a manager supervises.

departmentalization The division of workers into logical groups.

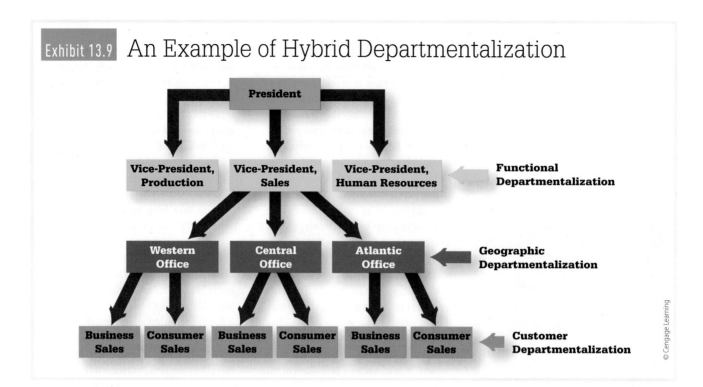

Exhibit 13.9 An Example of Hybrid Departmentalization

President

Vice-President, Production | Vice-President, Sales | Vice-President, Human Resources ← Functional Departmentalization

Western Office | Central Office | Atlantic Office ← Geographic Departmentalization

Business Sales | Consumer Sales | Business Sales | Consumer Sales | Business Sales | Consumer Sales ← Customer Departmentalization

© Cengage Learning

management may divide departments by processes such as cutting, dyeing, and sewing.

As companies get larger, they usually adopt several different types of departmentalization at different levels of the organization. This approach, shown in Exhibit 13.9, is called *hybrid departmentalization*.

13-4b Organization Models

Company structures tend to follow one of three different patterns: line organizations, line-and-staff organizations, and matrix organizations. But these organizational models are not mutually exclusive. In fact, many management teams build their structure using elements of each model at different levels of the organization.

Line Organizations A **line organization** typically has a clear, simple chain of command from top to bottom. Each person is directly accountable to the person immediately above, which means quick decision making and no fuzziness about who is responsible for what. The downside is a lack of specialists to provide advice or support for line managers. This approach tends

to work well for small businesses, but for medium-sized and large companies, the result can be inflexibility, too much paperwork, and even incompetence because experts aren't available to give their input into key decisions.

Line-and-Staff Organizations A **line-and-staff organization** incorporates the benefits of a line organization without all the drawbacks. **Line managers** supervise the functions that contribute directly to profitability: production and marketing. **Staff managers**, on the other hand, supervise the functions that provide advice and assistance to the line departments. Examples include legal, accounting, and human resources. In a line-and-staff organization, the line managers form the primary chain of authority in the company. Staff departments work alongside line departments, but there is no direct reporting relationship (except at the top of the company). Because staff people don't report to line people, their authority comes from their know-how. This approach, which overlays fast decision making with additional expertise, tends to work well for medium-sized and large companies. But in some firms, the staff departments gain so much power that they become dictatorial, imposing unreasonable limitations on the rest of the company.

Matrix Organizations **Matrix organizations** build on the line-and-staff approach by adding a lot more flexibility. A matrix structure brings together specialists from different areas of the company to work on individual projects on a temporary basis. A new product development team, for instance, might include representatives from sales, engineering, finance, purchasing, and

line organizations
Organizations with a clear, simple chain of command from top to bottom.

line-and-staff organizations Organizations with line managers forming the primary chain of authority in the company and staff departments working alongside line departments.

line managers Managers who supervise the functions that contribute directly to profitability: production and marketing.

staff managers Managers who supervise the functions that provide advice and assistance to the line departments.

matrix organizations Organizations with a flexible structure that brings together specialists from different areas of the company to work on individual projects on a temporary basis.

advertising. For the course of the project, each specialist reports to the project manager and to the head of his or her own department (e.g., the vice-president of marketing). The matrix approach has been particularly popular in the high-tech and aerospace industries.

The matrix structure offers several key advantages. It encourages teamwork and communication across the organization. It offers flexibility in deploying key people. It lends itself to innovative solutions. And not surprisingly, the matrix structure when managed well creates a higher level of motivation and satisfaction for employees. But these advantages have a clear flip side. The need for constant communication can bog down a company in too many meetings. The steady state of flux can be overwhelming for both managers and employees. And having two bosses can cause conflict and stress for everyone.

> The factory of the future will have only two employees, a man and a dog. The man will be there to feed the dog. The dog will be there to keep the man from touching the equipment.
>
> Warren Bennis, organizational consultant and author

alities, characteristics, and backgrounds. Most researchers agree that true leaders are trustworthy, visionary, and inspiring. After all, we don't follow people who don't know where they're going, and we definitely don't follow people we don't trust. Other key leadership traits include empathy, courage, creativity, intelligence, and fairness.

13-5a Leadership Style

How a leader uses power defines his or her leadership style. While the range of specific styles is huge, most seem to cluster into three broad categories: autocratic, democratic, and free rein. The categories fall along a continuum of power, with the manager at one end and the employees at the other, as shown in Exhibit 13.10.

Autocratic leaders hoard decision-making power for themselves, and they typically issue orders without consulting their followers. **Democratic leaders** share power with their followers. Even though they still make final decisions, they typically solicit and incorporate input from their followers. **Free-rein leaders** set objectives for their followers but give them freedom to choose how they accomplish those goals.

Interestingly, the most effective leaders don't use just one approach. They tend to shift their leadership style, depending on the followers and the situation. When a quick decision is paramount, autocratic leadership may make the most sense. An army officer, for example, probably shouldn't take a vote on whether to storm a hill in the middle of a firefight. But when creativity is the top priority—during new-product brainstorming, for instance—free-rein management probably works best. Likewise, a brand-new worker might benefit from autocratic (but friendly) management, while a talented, experienced employee would probably work best under free-rein leadership.

Another vital consideration is the customer. When the customer seeks consistency in the delivery of the product—in fast food, for instance—the autocratic leadership style may be appropriate. But when the customer needs flexibility and problem-solving

13-5 Leadership: Directing and Inspiring

While most people easily recognize a great leader, defining the qualities of leaders can be more complex because successful leaders have a staggering range of person-

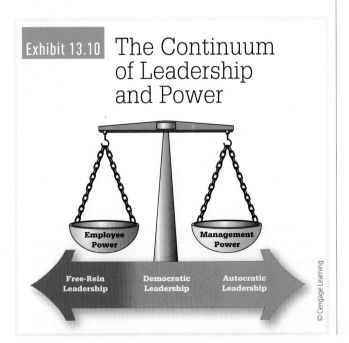

Exhibit 13.10 The Continuum of Leadership and Power

Employee Power

Management Power

Free-Rein Leadership

Democratic Leadership

Autocratic Leadership

© Cengage Learning

autocratic leaders Leaders who hoard decision-making power for themselves and typically issue orders without consulting their followers.

democratic leaders Leaders who share power with their followers. While they still make final decisions, they typically solicit and incorporate input from their followers.

free-rein leaders Leaders who set objectives for their followers but give them freedom to choose how they accomplish those goals.

HUMAN MACHINES

Herb MacKenzie

Over the past couple of decades, technology has replaced many onerous mechanical jobs. But technology has also changed how managers do their work, by making it much easier to track employees—everything from how much time they spend talking to coworkers to how much time they spend in the washroom. Efficiency skyrockets, but so does stress, and job satisfaction plummets correspondingly. In one warehouse operation, workers must wear headphones, and through the headset, the boss tells them what to do and how much time they have to do it each step of the way. From a worker standpoint, the system feels grossly impersonal. "They don't care whether you feel good, or if you're having a bad day." At another firm, workers are tracked via GPS and have been disciplined for driving too slowly or for taking an extra ten minutes for lunch on a tough day. Said one, "You're always so worried that you're not doing your job correctly. It makes you stressed out, and there's so much pressure to rush." Awareness Technologies, which produces software that can monitor employee activity online and remotely

disable inappropriate devices or block inappropriate websites, has grown rapidly since its founding. Satisfied clients report big jumps in employee productivity.

Many companies seem to support this approach, but many others do not. Anxiety, depression, and stress-related ailments cost the Canadian economy $52 billion each year. Many startups are beginning to focus on workplace atmosphere and how it can be improved; among them are Know Your Company, Niko Niko, Officevibe, Plasticity Labs, TinyPulse, and Waggl. Happy employees are more creative, experience less burnout, require fewer doctor visits, have greater job satisfaction, are more committed to their employer, and produce more and better results. Workplace consultant Jessica Pryce-Jones discovered that the happiest employees spend 80 percent of their time doing what they are supposed to be doing; the least content spend only half as much time.[14]

As a potential future manager, do you believe that the tradeoffs between productivity and employee job satisfaction are worthwhile? Why or why not?

---

assistance—a consulting client, for example—the free-rein leadership style may be most effective. The democratic leadership style typically provides customers with a balance of consistency and flexibility, which works across a wide range of industries.

13-6 Controlling: Making Sure It All Works

Controlling may be the least glamorous of the management functions, but don't be fooled: It's critically important. Controlling means monitoring performance of the firm—or individuals within the firm—and making improvements when necessary. As the environment changes, plans change. And as plans change, the control process must change as well, to ensure that the company achieves its goals. The control process includes three key steps:

1. Establish clear performance standards.

2. Measure actual performance against standards.

3. Take corrective action if necessary.

Establishing clear standards—or performance goals—begins with planning. At every level of planning, objectives should emerge that are consistent with the company's mission and strategic plan. The objectives must be (1) specific and measurable, (2) realistic but challenging, and (3) tied to a time frame. Individual managers may need to break these goals into smaller parts for specific employees, but the subgoals should retain the same three qualities as the original objective.

Measuring performance against standards should happen well before the end of the time frame attached to the goal. A strong information tracking system is probably management's best tool in this phase of the control process.

If the company or individual is not on track to meet the goals, management's first response should be communication. Employees with full information are far more likely to improve their performance than employees who never learn that they're falling behind. But sometimes workers need more than information—they may need additional resources or coaching in order to meet their goals. Apple's Steve Jobs was often accused of being a tyrannical boss—especially in the employee evaluation process—but he defended himself by saying: "My job is not to be easy on people. My job is to make them better." If they still don't succeed, perhaps the goals themselves need re-examination as part of a dynamic planning process. Given the expense in both human and financial terms, disciplining employees for poor performance should come only after exploring the reasons why they did not meet goals, then making changes as necessary.

Over the past decade, management has become more complex and demanding than ever before. Managers in every area of the business must carry out their roles—planning, organizing, leading, and controlling—in a relentlessly fast-paced world that seethes with constant change. While management isn't for everyone, it's often a fit for people with vision, courage, integrity, energy, and a passionate commitment to their companies.

The role of management will continue to evolve in response to the environment. Regardless of how the changes unfold, several key factors will be absolutely vital for successful managers in the 21st century: a constant focus on the customer, a commitment to globalization, excellent judgment, and the right mix of talented, motivated employees.

careers in management: Manager

Define strategic and tactical objectives for the organization or business unit. Develop plans to meet those objectives. Coach, counsel, motivate, and develop employees. Maintain and allocate resources as necessary to attain goals. Monitor achievement of objectives and make changes as necessary. Create and oversee a business unit budget. Ensure product and service quality by setting and enforcing standards. Foster a business culture that aligns with the broader organizational culture. Communicate and collaborate as appropriate throughout the organization. Maintain current professional and technical knowledge.

STUDY TOOLS 13

IN THE BOOK, YOU CAN:

☐ Rip out the Chapter Review card at the back of the book to have a summary of the chapter and key terms handy.

ONLINE AT NELSON.COM/STUDENT YOU CAN:

☐ Work through key concepts with a Guided Learning Question.

☐ Prepare for tests with quizzes.

☐ Review the key terms with Flash Cards (online or printer-ready).

☐ Explore practical examples of chapter concepts with Connect a Concept exercises.

14

Human Resource Management:
Building a Top-Quality Workforce

LEARNING OBJECTIVES
After studying this chapter, you will be able to …

14-1 Explain the importance of human resources to business success

14-2 Discuss key human resource issues in today's economy

14-3 Outline challenges and opportunities that the human resources function faces

14-4 Discuss human resource planning and core human resources responsibilities

14-5 Explain the key federal legislation that affects human resources

After you finish this chapter, go to page 240 for STUDY TOOLS

14-1 Human Resource Management: Bringing Business to Life

As competition accelerates around the globe, companies are changing their human resource policies because they recognize the value of being employee-centred when it comes to recruiting and retaining the best workers at all levels of the organization. Samsung Canada provides covered bicycle racks and preferred parking spaces for employees who carpool or who drive hybrid cars. Once inside, they have gym equipment, shower facilities, a dedicated room for meditation and prayer, subsidized healthy food options, and an employee lounge. On-site yoga and Zumba classes are also available. The company encourages community involvement by giving each employee two paid days to volunteer for a number of local charities. Not surprisingly, it was recently recognized as one of the ten best companies to work for in Canada.[1]

human resource (HR) management The management function focused on maximizing the effectiveness of the workforce by recruiting world-class talent, promoting career development, and determining workforce strategies to boost organizational effectiveness.

Companies that get the most from their people often consider their human resources their biggest investment. They view the core goal of **human resource (HR) management** in a similar light: to nurture their human investment so that it yields the highest possible returns. HR can achieve that goal by recruiting world-class talent, promoting career development, and boosting organizational effectiveness. But clearly, this can happen only in partnership with key managers throughout the company, especially senior executives. (In smaller companies, of course, the owners usually do HR management in addition to their other responsibilities.)

14-2 Human Resource Management Challenges: Major Hurdles

Building a top-quality workforce can be tougher than it may first seem. HR managers, and their counterparts throughout the company, face huge challenges. The best strategies still aren't clear, but forward-thinking firms tend to experiment with new approaches.

Award and recognition lunches help build top-quality workforces.

Herb MacKenzie

14-2a Older Workers

As the oversized baby boom generation enters its 60s, its employers—which include almost every major Canadian company—face a potential crisis: the loss of key talent and experience through retirements. Enlightened companies have responded with programs to retain their best employees through flexible schedules, training opportunities, and creative pay schedules. The threat posed by massive retirements has been somewhat mitigated in Canada by the elimination of a mandatory retirement age. The Canadian government also allows Canadians older than 65 to defer the receipt of their old age security payments for up to 60 months, with an increase in benefits for each month of deferral. Beginning in 2023—and becoming fully implemented in 2029—the eligibility age for old age security will be increased from 65 to 67.[2]

14-2b Younger Workers

As 20-somethings enter the workforce, they often bring optimism, open minds, technological know-how, a team

> If something goes wrong, it's my problem; if something goes right, it's their success.
>
> Pamela Fields, CEO, Stetson

orientation, a proven ability to multi-task, and a multicultural perspective. But a number of them also bring an unprecedented sense of entitlement. This can translate into startlingly high expectations for their pay, their responsibilities, and their job flexibility but little willingness to "pay dues." Many have no expectation that their employers will be loyal to them, and they don't feel that they owe their companies strong loyalty. Managing this group can sometimes be a challenge, but companies that do it well stand to deliver results for years to come.[3]

14-2c Women Workers

Over the past few decades, women have made enormous strides in terms of workplace equality. But several large-scale studies confirm that women continue to face daunting discrimination in terms of both pay and promotions. A Conference Board of Canada report suggests that women are still disadvantaged when it comes to gaining management positions; the proportion of women in both middle- and senior-management positions remains

HUMBLE BEGINNINGS

Everyone starts somewhere. Not even the rich and famous always had glamour jobs. In today's challenging economy, getting any job at all can be tough for young people, but whatever work you do get, consider that it might be the first step on the road to the next big thing. Some early job examples of the rich and famous:

- **Shania Twain (songwriter, singer):** At 18, she moved to Toronto, but found she had to supplement her singing career with a number of odd jobs, including time at McDonald's. When her parents died in a car crash, she returned to Timmins, Ontario, to support her three younger siblings, and took a job singing at a local resort.

- **Jim Carrey (actor, comedian):** At 15, Jim did stand-up comedy in a Toronto comedy club, but soon took a janitor job to help support his family.

- **Oprah Winfrey (media mogul):** Oprah began working at the corner grocery store next to her father's barber shop . . . and she hated every minute of it.

- **Michael Dell (founder, Dell Computer Corporation):** Dishwasher at a Chinese restaurant. Memorable proverb learned at work: "Do work you love and you'll never work a day in your life."

- **Sean Connery (actor):** Before earning his international licence to kill as James Bond, Connery worked as a truck driver, a bricklayer, a milkman, and a coffin polisher.

- Tommy Hilfiger sold jeans from the trunk of his car; Madonna sold coffee at Dunkin' Donuts; Jerry Seinfeld sold light bulbs by telephone; Garth Brooks sold boots in a retail store.[4]

Herb MacKenzie

virtually unchanged over the past 20 years. Men have been two to three times more likely to be promoted to senior management and 1.5 times more likely to be promoted to middle management.[5] Many women have responded to the unfriendly business environment by leaving the workforce to raise children, start their own companies, or pursue other interests. As a result, we are experiencing a harmful, ongoing brain drain. HR managers can help mitigate this issue by implementing specific retention plans for valued women workers and by taking proactive steps to reintegrate returning women back into the workforce.[6]

14-2d Work–Life Balance

Over the past decade, workers across all ages and both genders have actively pursued more flexibility and work–life balance in their jobs. With the 2008 economic downturn, many companies reduced their workforces, causing remaining employees to feel overworked and overwhelmed. Nearly 50 percent reported that they experienced high stress at work. At the same time, 3 of 10 people in the 45–64 age range comprise the "sandwich generation." They have children under the age of 25 at home, while they also must serve as caregivers to one or more elderly family members. Unfortunately, many managers view flexible working arrangements as simply an employee benefit. Research

has increasingly demonstrated the value of flex-time for reducing employee stress and for promoting motivation and productivity. As a result, insightful HR managers are trying harder to offer enough flexibility to keep their best workers without jeopardizing their company's business goals. At DLGL, a Quebec-based HR software developer, workers are expected to work, on average, 38 hours per week. If an employee works significantly more than that, it gets flagged for investigation. The company's concern for work–life balance has likely contributed to the 17-year average tenure of its employees.[7]

14-2e Wage Gap

Comparing CEO pay to worker pay brings to light a startling wage gap. In 2014, Canada's 100 top-paid CEOs earned, on average, $9 million—184 times the wage of the average Canadian worker. John Chen, Blackberry's CEO, was at the top: $89.7 million. He eclipsed Magna International's Donald Walker, who was number two on the list with $23.4 million. Only two women made the list: Linda Hasenfratz of Linamar ($10.1 million) and Dawn Farrell of TransAlta Corp. ($4.5 million).[8] Most observers don't object to the pay gap when top CEO pay ties to top performance. But when the link is missing, the gap can demoralize workers, infuriate shareholders, and even undermine corporate performance. It clearly represents a strategic challenge for HR management.

14-2f Layoffs and Outsourcing

As high-tech, high-end jobs follow low-tech, low-end jobs out of the country—or even just to local contractors—human resources find themselves in turmoil. Many jobs have disappeared altogether as companies continue to downsize in response to unfavourable economic conditions. How can companies boost the morale of the employees who are left behind? Does less job security translate to less worker loyalty? How can HR continue to add value as the ground shifts beneath workers, who wonder how long their own jobs will last?

14-2g Lawsuits

Canada is becoming a more litigious society, with employees, customers, and shareholders launching more and more lawsuits against firms of all sizes. But we are still well behind the United States, where, even though many lawsuits are legitimate—and some are profoundly important—a good number are just plain silly. But even if a lawsuit is frivolous, even if it's thrown out of court, it can still cost a company millions of dollars. Even more importantly, a frivolous lawsuit can cost a business its reputation. Avoiding employee lawsuits by knowing the law and encouraging legal practices is a growing HR challenge.

> HR matters enormously in good times. It defines you in bad times.
>
> Jack and Suzy Welch

14-3 Human Resources Managers: Corporate Black Sheep?

14-3a The Problem

The HR management *function* is clearly important, and HR *departments*—and the people who work in them—face major challenges. Leading-edge firms expect every department to offer strategic, "big picture" contributions that boost company value. Yet a report in *Fast Company* suggests that most HR professionals lack sufficient strategic skills. The report quotes a respected executive at a top North American company as arguing that business acumen is the single biggest factor that HR professionals lack today.

But even highly qualified, strategically focused HR managers face daunting perception problems. A management professor at a leading school comments:

"The best and the brightest just don't go into HR." Once in the workforce, many employees see the HR department as irrelevant or, even worse, as the enemy. This perception clearly undermines their effectiveness.

14-3b The Solution

To gain respect from both senior management and their own peers, HR executives must earn a seat at the table. The first step is to know the company. What are the strategic goals? Who is the core customer? Who is the competition? Respected HR departments typically figure out ways to quantify their impact on the company in dollars and cents. They determine how to raise the value of the firm's human capital, which in turn increases the value of the firm itself. Effective HR people also remain open to exceptions even as they enforce broad company policies.

But clearly, these solutions will work only if senior management recognizes the potential value of effective HR management. One simple test of senior management commitment is the reporting relationship. If the HR department reports to the CFO, it may be on the fast track to outsourcing. But if the HR department reports to the CEO, the strategic possibilities are unlimited.

14-4 Human Resource Planning: Drawing the Map

Great HR management begins with great planning: Where should you go? And how should you get there? Your objectives, of course, should flow from the company's master plan, and your strategies must reflect company priorities.

One of the first steps in the HR planning process should be to figure out where the company stands in terms of human resources. What skills does the workforce already have? What skills do they need? A company-wide **job analysis** often goes hand in hand with evaluating the current workforce. Job analysis examines what exactly needs to be done in each position to maximize the effectiveness of the organization, independent of who might be holding each job at any specific time. Smaller companies often handle job analysis on an informal basis, but larger

> **job analysis** The examination of specific tasks that are assigned to each position, independent of who might be holding the job at any specific time.

Exhibit 14.1 Job Description and Job Specifications: Band Manager

JOB DESCRIPTION	JOB SPECIFICATIONS
Work with the music group to help make major decisions regarding the creative and business direction of the band	A bachelor's degree in music management
Negotiate recording contracts and engagement fees	A minimum of three years of experience managing a high-profile band
Help band members understand their rights and responsibilities	Excellent communication and networking skills

© Cengage Learning

Exhibit 14.2 Human Resource Management

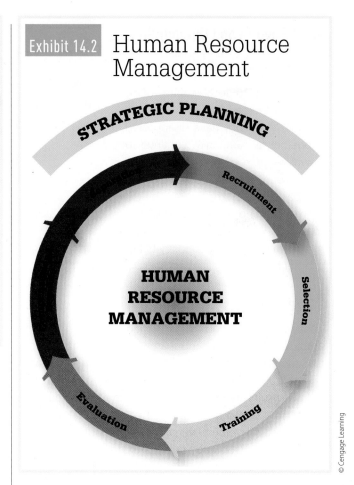

© Cengage Learning

companies typically specify a formal **job description** and **job specifications** (or "specs").

A job description defines the job holder's *responsibilities*, and the job specs define the *qualifications* for doing the job. Consider the job of band manager. The job description might include finding engagements for the band and settling disputes among band members. The job specs might include the type of education and teaching experience required. Taken together, the two might look something like Exhibit 14.1.

The next step is to forecast future HR requirements. The forecasting function requires a deep understanding of the company's goals and strategies. HR managers must also assess the future supply of workers. Assessing supply can be a real challenge since the size of the workforce shifts continually, as does its quality. But key considerations should include retirement rates, graduation rates in relevant fields, and the pros and cons of the international labour market.

A complete HR plan—which falls under the company's strategic planning umbrella—must cover each core area of HR management (see Exhibit 14.2):

- Recruitment
- Selection
- Training
- Evaluation
- Compensation
- Benefits
- Separation

job description An explanation of the responsibilities for a specific position.

job specifications The specific qualifications necessary to hold a particular position.

internal recruitment The process of seeking employees who are currently within the firm to fill open positions.

14-4a Recruitment: Finding the Right People

Finding people to hire is easy, but finding *qualified* employees can be tough. Many of Canada's fastest growing fields of employment will require higher education levels. Fortunately, the number of Canadians who hold postsecondary degrees has been increasing rapidly. In 1995, only 635,000 Canadians had a university degree. By 2005, the number had grown to 1.3 million, and by 2015, there were 2.1 million university-educated Canadians.[9] Colleges across Canada have also been increasing the skill levels of many young Canadians who seek to enter the labour force. And as highly trained, highly educated baby boomers hit retirement, HR recruiters will face a real hiring crunch. Even in the face of a shortage, recruiters also must find new employees who fit with the company culture in terms of personality and style.

New employees come from two basic sources: internal and external. **Internal recruitment** involves transferring or promoting employees from other positions within the company. This approach offers several advantages:

- It boosts employee morale by reinforcing the value of experience within the firm.

- It reduces risk for the firm because current employees have a proven track record.
- It lowers costs of both recruitment and training.

But companies often find that they don't have the right person within their organization. The firm may be too small, or perhaps no one has the right set of skills to fill the immediate needs. Or perhaps the firm needs the fresh thinking and energy that can come only from outside. When this is the case, companies turn to **external recruitment**.

External recruitment, or looking for employees outside the firm, usually means tapping into a range of different resources. The possibilities include employment websites, newspaper ads, trade associations, college and university employment centres, and employment agencies. But the most promising source of new hires may be referrals from current employees. More and more organizations are offering their current employees a cash bonus—typically $1,000 to $2,000—for each person they refer to the company who makes it past a probationary period. As an added benefit, employees who come through referrals have an excellent chance at success because the person who recommended them has a stake in their progress. Employee referral programs also represent a real bargain for employers, compared to the average cost per new hire of more than $4,000. Not surprisingly, a higher level of employee referrals correlates with a higher level of shareholder returns, although lack of diversity may become a long-term problem when employee referrals are relied on.[10]

14-4b Selection: Making the Right Choice

Once you have a pool of qualified candidates, your next step is to choose the best person for the job. This, too, is

> # A company is known by the people it keeps.
>
> Meehan & Meehan

easier said than done, yet making the *right* selection is crucial. The costs of a bad hire—both the direct costs such as placing ads and the intangibles such as lost productivity and morale—can drain company resources. A typical selection process includes accepting applications, interviewing, testing, checking references and background, and making the job offer. Keep in mind, though, that small businesses often follow a more streamlined process.

Applications Many companies use written applications simply as an initial screening mechanism. Questions about education and experience will determine whether a candidate gets any further consideration. In other words, the application is primarily a tool for rejecting unqualified candidates rather than for actually choosing qualified candidates.

Interviews Virtually every company uses interviews as a central part of the selection process. In larger companies, the HR department does initial interviews and then sends qualified candidates to the hiring manager for the actual selection. The hiring manager usually recruits coworkers to participate in the process.

Although employers often give interviews heavy weight in hiring decisions, interviews often say surprisingly little about whether a candidate will perform on the job. Too many managers use the interview as a get-to-know-you session instead of focusing on the needs of the position. This is unfortunate, for recent research suggests that employee satisfaction increases as the difficulty of the interview increases. Canadian employees reported a 3 percent increase in satisfaction when interviews were rated 10 percent more difficult.[11]

To help ensure that interviews better predict performance, experts recommend a **structured interview** process: developing a list of questions beforehand and asking the same questions to each candidate. The most effective questions are typically behavioural: they ask the candidate to describe a situation he or she faced at a previous job—or a hypothetical situation at the new job—and to explain the resolution. Interviewers should gear the specific questions towards behaviours and experiences that are key for the new position. Consider the following examples of how this could be worded:

- Describe a time when you had to think "outside the box" to find a solution to a pressing problem.

Herb MacKenzie

> **external recruitment** The process of seeking new employees from outside the firm.
>
> **structured interview** An interviewing approach that involves developing a list of questions beforehand and asking the same questions in the same order to each candidate.

Chapter 14 Human Resource Management: Building a Top-Quality Workforce

- If you realized that a coworker was cheating on his expense report, how would you handle the situation?
- What would you do if your boss asked you to complete a key project within an unreasonable timeframe?

Cultural differences also impact interview performance. As the Canadian labour pool becomes more diverse, even domestic companies must be aware of cultural differences. And it isn't simply a matter of legality or ethics. Firms that hire the best people regardless of cultural background will gain a critical edge in our increasingly competitive world.

Most colleges and universities offer comprehensive career services. Especially in today's competitive labour market, you would be wise to visit your career centre early in your college career and use those services to prepare yourself for a smooth transition into the workforce.

Testing Either before or after the interview process (and sometimes at both points), a growing number of companies have instituted employment testing of various sorts. The main categories include skills testing, personality testing, drug testing, and physical exams. Skills testing and personality testing carry a fair amount of legal risk because these tests must measure skills and aptitudes that relate directly to the job itself. Almost 100 percent of Fortune 500 companies do pre-employment drug testing, as do most other companies. Physical exams are also standard, but firms cannot use them just to screen out certain individuals.

References and Background Checks Even if you feel absolutely *certain* that a candidate is right for the job, don't skip the reference check before you make an offer. Research from the Society for Human Resource Management suggests that more than 50 percent of job candidates lie on their résumé in some way. Although it may be tough to verify contributions and accomplishments at former jobs, it's pretty easy to uncover lies about education, job titles, and compensation. And it's quite worthwhile, given that the costs of bringing an unethical employee on board can be staggering. Furthermore, if you happen to hire a truly dangerous employee, you can open the door to negligent hiring lawsuits for not taking "reasonable care." But surprisingly—despite the high risk—employment expert James Challenger estimates that only about 15 percent of candidates are thoroughly vetted by the companies that consider them.[12]

Job Offers After a company finds the right person, the next hurdle is designing the right job offer and getting a candidate to accept it. To hook an especially hot contender, you may need to get creative. A phone call from top management, the royal treatment, and special perks go a long way, but most superb candidates also want to know in very specific terms how their contributions would affect the business. And no matter how excited you are about your candidate, be certain to establish a **probationary period** upfront. This means a specific time frame (typically three to six months) during which a new hire can prove his or her worth on the job. If everything works out, the employee will move from conditional to permanent status; if not, the company can fire the employee fairly easily.

Contingent Workers Companies that experience a fluctuating need for workers sometimes opt to hire **contingent workers**—or employees who don't expect regular, full-time jobs—rather than permanent, full-time workers. Specifically, contingent employees include temporary full-time workers, independent contractors, on-call workers, and temporary agency or contract agency workers. More than 80 percent of Canadian companies report that they are increasingly using contingent, seasonal, intermittent, or consultant employees.[13]

Employers appreciate contingent workers because they offer flexibility, which can lead to much lower costs. But the hidden downside can be workers who are less committed and less experienced. Too much reliance on contingent workers could unwittingly sabotage company productivity and the customer experience.

14-4c Training and Development: Honing the Competitive Edge

For successful companies in almost every field, training and development has become an ongoing process rather than a one-time activity. In an economic downturn, training and development must gather speed in order for companies and individuals to maintain their competitive edge. Experts offer five key reasons that relate directly to a healthy bottom line:

1. Increased innovation in strategies and products.
2. Increased ability to adopt new technologies.
3. Increased efficiency and productivity.
4. Increased employee motivation and lower employee turnover.
5. Decreased liability (e.g., fewer sexual harassment lawsuits).

Training programs take a number of different forms, from orientation, to skills training, to management development, depending on the specific employee and the needs of the organization.

probationary period A specific timeframe (typically three to six months) during which a new hire can prove his or her worth on the job before the hire becomes permanent.

contingent workers Employees who do not expect regular, full-time jobs, including temporary full-time workers, independent contractors, and temporary agency or contract agency workers.

Oops! What were they thinking?

Communication and Consequences: Misbehaving Workers

Or, in some instances, a more appropriate question might be: "*Were they thinking?*" Companies have always been concerned about how their employees communicate with the media, and many companies have very clear media policies. However, today, communications media may simply be the smartphone in someone's pocket, or the security camera in an elevator or hallway. Companies spend tremendous amounts of money to establish and build their brands. A single employee can tarnish a company's reputation through thoughtless or inappropriate behaviour—in seconds, at zero cost. Here are some examples to consider.

At a 2015 industry awards ceremony in Toronto, a female comedian was harassed by an employee of TC Transcontinental who was attending the event. Because of the audience and the upscale nature of the event, the comedian was told to not talk about sex in her routine. But one male member of the audience didn't want to play by those rules. About three minutes into her routine, the sexist comments began. As a result, his employer suspended him and the chief communications officer for his company apologized, "This is not in our culture and values for sure."

The CEO of Centreplate, a company that caters to sports facilities, lost his job when he kicked a puppy in a Vancouver elevator. Caught on video, his behaviour went viral. He subsequently lost his job and was fined $5,000 for animal cruelty.

Hydro One fired an employee caught on Toronto CityNews after he publicly defended sexually explicit obscenities that were shouted at one of the broadcaster's reporters. The $100,000-plus salaried engineer has since been rehired following arbitration. Subsequent public comments suggest that many people are not pleased that he was rehired, even though his company had no choice.

Two executives of BlackBerry were dismissed from their high-paying jobs after their rowdy in-flight behaviour caused their flight to be rerouted to Vancouver.

Two Canadian school employees were fired for inappropriate behaviour. One, an office worker, supplemented her income as a porn actress. The other, 73 years old and a teacher in a private school, was fired after it was discovered she acted in erotic films—during the 1960s.

Friends of Amanda Todd, a teenager who committed suicide following months of bullying, started a Facebook page that quickly filled with tributes to her memory. When one Ontario man posted a derogatory comment on the site, supporters worked to identify him and then reported him to his employer. Retailer Mr. Big and Tall soon fired him.

A City of Calgary worker was fired for using the city's computer system for personal reasons during work hours. An arbitration panel found that the city had not engaged in any form of progressive discipline and had failed to establish that termination was warranted. However, the panel refused to order that the employee be rehired because, after his termination, he sent two lengthy Facebook messages to coworkers and his Facebook contacts. In the messages, he was extremely derogatory to his manager. The panel concluded that through his own actions, he had undermined the trust necessary for an employer/employee relationship.

Lessons? There are many ways that employees can be held accountable for after-work behaviour, even decades later. Smartphone videos and security cameras provide evidence that was not previously available to substantiate thoughtless behaviour. Social media postings may last forever. Once they're out there, the sender has lost control over where they go and who will see them. For those who are not thinking, it's time to think.[14]

Sources: Leah Eichler, "Misbehaving Workers Are Always On the Clock," *The Globe and Mail*, May 30, 2015; *CityNews* website, "Five Cases of People Who Lost Their Jobs Over Off-Hours Conduct," *Canadian Press*, May 14, 2015; Marsha Lederman, "Transcontinental Employee Suspended After Heckling Female Comic at Awards Show, globeandmail.com, May 20, 2015; " Des Hague, Former CEO of Centreplate, Sentenced for Animal Cruelty," cbc.ca, April 15, 2015; "Shawn Simoes, Man Fired For FHRITP Incident, Rehired By Hydro One," huffingtonpost.ca, November 2, 2015; "Panel Found Termination Unjust, But Refused Reinstatement," advocatedaily.com, n.d.

Orientation Once you hire new employees, **orientation** should be the first step in the training and development process. Effective orientation programs typically focus on introducing employees to the company culture (but without sacrificing need-to-know administrative information). Research consistently shows that strong orientation programs significantly reduce employee turnover, which lowers costs.

The Boeing aerospace company has mastered the art of employee orientation. Boeing Military Aircraft and Missile Systems revamped its orientation process to include mentoring, meetings with senior executives, and an after-work social program. A highlight of the orientation—meant to crystallize the "wow" factor of working at Boeing—is the chance to take the controls of an F/A-18 fighter plane flight simulator. Management rightfully sees the program as a chance to develop "future

> **orientation** The first step in the training and development process, designed to introduce employees to the company culture and provide key administrative information.

leaders . . . the ones who will make sure that Boeing continues to be a great place to work."[15]

On-the-Job Training On-the-job training is popular because it's very low cost: Employees simply begin their jobs—sometimes under the guidance of more experienced employees—and learn as they go. For simple jobs this can make sense, but simple jobs are disappearing from the Canadian market due to the combined impact of offshoring and technology. On-the-job training can also compromise the customer experience. Have you ever waited for much too long in a short line at the grocery store because the clerk couldn't figure out how to use the cash register? Multiplied across hundreds of customers, this kind of experience undermines a company's brand.

Formal apprenticeship programs tend to be a more effective way of handling on-the-job training. **Apprenticeship** programs mandate that each beginner serve as

on-the-job training A training approach that requires employees to simply begin their jobs—sometimes guided by more experienced employees—and to learn as they go.

apprenticeships Structured training programs that mandate that each beginner serve as an assistant to a fully trained worker before gaining full credentials to work in the field.

management development Programs to help current and potential executives develop the skills they need to move into leadership positions.

an assistant to a fully trained worker for a specified period of time before gaining full credentials to work in the field. In Canada, apprenticeships are fairly common in trades such as plumbing and bricklaying. In Europe, apprenticeships are much more common across a wide range of professions, from banking to optometry.

Off-the-Job Training Classroom training happens away from the job setting but typically during work hours. Employers use classroom training—either on- or off-site—to teach a wide variety of topics from new computer programming languages, to negotiation skills, to stress management, and more. Going one step further than classroom training, some employers train workers off-site on "real" equipment (e.g., robots) similar to what they will actually be using on the job. This approach is called *vestibule training*. Police academies, for instance, often use vestibule training for firearms. Job simulation goes even further than vestibule training by attempting to duplicate the *exact* conditions that the trainee will face on the job. This approach makes sense for complex, high-risk positions such as astronaut or airline pilot.

Computer-Based Training Computer-based training—mostly delivered via the Web—now plays a crucial role in off-the-job training. Broadband technology has turbocharged audio and visual capabilities, which support engaging and interactive online training programs. Online training also standardizes the presentation of the material because it doesn't depend on the quality of the individual instructor. And the Web helps employers train employees wherever they may be in the world, at their own pace and convenience. But there is a key drawback: it takes a lot of discipline to complete an online program, and some people simply learn better through direct human interaction.

Management Development As the bulk of top-level Canadian executives move towards retirement, developing new leaders has become a priority in many organizations. **Management development** programs help current and potential executives develop the skills they need to move into leadership positions. These programs typically cover specific issues that face the business but also less tangible yet equally important topics, such as communication, planning, business analysis, change management, coaching, and team-building skills.

14-4d Evaluation: Assessing Employee Performance

Straightforward, frequent feedback is a powerful tool to improve employee performance. The best managers

Herb MacKenzie

Sales managers often use a form of vestibule training to give feedback to salespeople immediately after a sales call.

ODD JOBS

Herb MacKenzie

As you contemplate your post-education career, chances are good that you are mostly considering the more typical fields, where people you know have built successful careers. Although there are many satisfying options, a number of people have built rewarding careers in fields that initially appear somewhat odd. A few examples:

- **Flavourist:** Also known as flavour chemists, flavourists synthesize and re-create natural flavours. Pay for these specialists is up to $100,000 per year. Tim Hortons employs professional coffee tasters to ensure that "every cup, every day, in every store" tastes the same.

- **Pet food taster:** Just like food for humans, dog food needs to be inspected. Since pet food makers can't use dogs to test the food, this delicious cuisine requires professional taste testers.

- **Master sommelier:** Sommeliers help restaurant diners decide which wines complement their meals. They also help restaurants craft their wine lists. Pay is an impressive $80,000 to $160,000 per year.

- **Psychic:** If you want to earn $60 to $110 per hour without any certification required, consider that psychics are in demand, especially whenever the world is experiencing any kind of turbulence or upheaval. (Have you ever wondered why more psychics haven't won the lottery?)

- **Chicken sexer:** Actually, this is a serious job. Young chickens huddle together for warmth, but someone has to look at each one to determine which are boys and which are girls. The boys, well, few survive. The girls, though, have future careers in egg production.

The following jobs have reportedly been advertised on Workopolis: erection superintendent (for a construction company, Mammoth Erection in Aurora, Ontario); full-time wiener peeler (for a meat company); S&M coordinator (that's sales and marketing); master handshaker; change magician; and chief biscuit dunker. It seems there is a job for everybody.[16]

---

provide informal feedback on an ongoing basis so that employees always know where they stand. But most companies also require that managers give formal feedback through periodic **performance appraisals**, usually every six months or once a year. Typically, managers conduct the appraisals by sitting down with each employee on a one-to-one basis and comparing actual results to expected results. Performance appraisals impact decisions regarding compensation, promotions, training, transfers, and terminations.

The HR role in performance appraisals begins with the strategic process of creating evaluation tools that tie directly into the company's big-picture objectives. Then, on a day-to-day basis, HR coordinates the actual appraisal process, which typically involves volumes of paperwork. HR must also ensure that managers are trained in how to provide relevant, honest, objective feedback and that workers at every level know how to respond if they believe their appraisal is unfair.

Giving evaluations tends to be awkward for everyone involved, and unfortunately, uncomfortable people tend to make mistakes. (The same is true of receiving them.) As you read the following list, you'll probably find that you've been at the receiving end of at least a couple of the most common appraisal goofs:

1. **Gotcha!:** Too many managers use the performance appraisal as a chance to catch employees doing something wrong rather than doing something right.

2. **The once-a-year wonder:** Many companies mandate annual reviews, but some managers use that as an excuse to give feedback only once a year.

3. **Straight from the gut:** Although "gut feel" can have real value, it's no substitute for honest, relevant documentation of both expectations and accomplishments.

4. **What have you done for me lately?:** Many managers give far too much weight to recent accomplishments, discounting the early part of the review period.

5. **The "me filter":** While appraisals are a bit subjective by their very nature, some managers filter every comment through their personal biases. Here are some examples:

   - **Positive leniency:** "I'm a nice guy, so I give everyone great scores."

> **performance appraisal** A formal process that requires managers to give their subordinates feedback on a one-to-one basis, typically by comparing actual results to expected results.

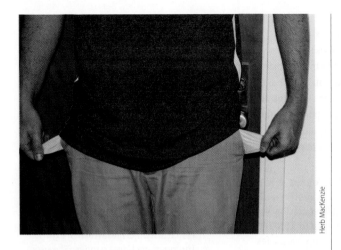
Herb MacKenzie

- **Negative leniency:** "I have high expectations, so I give everyone low scores."
- **Halo effect:** "I like this employee, so I'll give her top scores across the board."

For a performance appraisal to be effective, the manager must focus on fairness, relevance, objectivity, and balance. Equally important, the manager should give feedback on an ongoing basis to eliminate surprises and maximize performance.

14-4e Compensation: Show Me the Money

The term **compensation** covers both pay and benefits. Most people, when they think about compensation, think about cash. Yet your paycheque is only part of the picture. Many companies also offer noncash benefits such as extended health benefits, which can be worth up to 30 percent of each employee's pay. The core HR functions include researching, designing, and managing effective compensation systems.

From a company perspective, compensation—both cash and noncash—represents a big chunk of product costs, especially in labour-intensive businesses such as banks, restaurants, and airlines. Although many firms opt to cut labour costs as far as possible, others boost compensation above the norm to find and keep the best workers. In fact, research suggests that companies that offer higher than average compensation generally outperform their competitors in terms of total return to shareholders—both stock price and dividend payouts.[17]

compensation The combination of pay and benefits that employees receive in exchange for their work.

wages The pay that employees receive in exchange for the number of hours or days that they work.

salaries The pay that employees receive over a fixed period, most often weekly or monthly. Most professional, administrative, and managerial jobs pay salaries.

benefits Noncash compensation, including programs such as extended health care, vacation, and child care.

Regarding specific individuals and positions, companies typically base compensation on a balance of the following factors:

- *Competition:* How much do competing firms offer for similar positions?
- *Contribution:* How much does a specific person contribute to the bottom line?
- *Ability to pay:* How much can the company afford?
- *Cost of living:* What would be reasonable in light of the broader local economy?
- *Legislation:* What does the government mandate?

The most common compensation systems in Canada are wages and salaries. **Wages** refer to pay in exchange for the number of hours or days that an employee works. As of January 2016, minimum wage rates across Canadian provinces varied from $10.30 per hour in New Brunswick to $11.25 per hour in Ontario. The highest minimum wage rate was in Northwest Territories: $12.50 per hour.[18] Lower wages can sometimes be paid for inexperienced workers or for workers in specific sectors. Each province and territory also requires that overtime be paid to employees who work in excess of a specified number of hours per day or per week; this varies by province. The Canada Labour Code—which affects federal government employees and federally regulated companies—requires companies to pay wage earners overtime, 50 percent more than their standard wage, for every hour worked over 40 hours per week.

Salaries, on the other hand, cover a fixed period, most often a week or a month. Most professional, administrative, and managerial jobs pay salaries. While salaries are usually higher than wages, salaried workers do not qualify for overtime, which means that sometimes a low-level manager's overall pay may be less than the pay of wage-based employees who work for that manager.

Pay for Performance In addition to wages and salaries, many organizations link some amount of worker pay directly to performance. The idea, of course, is to motivate employees to excel. Exhibit 14.3 lists some common approaches.

As you look over the various variable pay options, which would you find most motivating? Why? What type of business might use each form of variable pay? Why?

14-4f Benefits: From Birthday Cakes to Death Benefits

Benefits represent a significant cost for employers, but for many years workers took benefits for granted. But keep in mind that employers don't *need* to give you sick

WACKY BENEFITS

While most benefits are optional, you would not be unreasonable to expect your firm to offer standard perks, such as paid vacation days and sick time. However, a handful of creative companies have developed a package of perks to create a unique, compelling corporate culture. A sampling:

- **Bass Pro Shops** reserves a special parking space for its Employee of the Month.

- **Google** encourages its employees to bring their dogs to work—one of many creative perks, which range from free gourmet meals to an on-site massage therapist.

- **GoDaddy**, the Internet domain and Web-hosting firm, holds monthly team-boosting events on company time, including such gems as whitewater rafting, gold panning, competitive cooking courses, and trapeze classes.

- **OpenText Corporation** has a fully equipped employee lounge (with video games and foosball), which leads to an outdoor patio connected to a pathway through the University of Waterloo's environmental reserve.

- **EllisDon Corporation**, a familiar name in commercial construction across Canada, owns and operates "Windjammer Landing Resort" in St. Lucia. It offers discounted accommodation packages for employees and their families.

- **Siemens Canada** has an employee suggestion program where all ideas are evaluated for financial impact—decreased cost or increased revenue—and employees can earn a bonus of up to $100,000.

- **FactSet Research** takes food seriously. Besides free lunches, employees at the financial research and software company have regular summer barbecues, ice cream socials, and visits from local food trucks. The latter have included a cupcake truck, a pie truck, a "weenie" truck, and a cheese truck, whose menu includes grilled cheese, gazpacho, and watermelon.[19]

Nothing can replace a sound financial package and a strong retirement program, but a nice nap, a "weenie," a trip to St. Lucia, and a doggie kiss can certainly make work more fun!

Herb MacKenzie

days, vacations, or overtime pay beyond what is legally mandated. A number of budget-minded employers stick to the legally mandated basics: Canada/Quebec Pension Plan, workers' compensation, and employment insurance. However, socially responsible employers—and companies that seek a competitive advantage through a top-notch workforce—tend to offer far more. Optional benefits usually include some or all of the following:

- Paid vacation days and holidays
- Paid sick days
- Extended health care and dental insurance

Exhibit 14.3 Performance Pay Options

VARIABLE PAY SYSTEM	DESCRIPTION
COMMISSION	Commission involves payment as a percentage of sales. Usually, larger commissions go with smaller base pay.
BONUSES	Bonuses are lump sum payments, typically to reward strong performance from individual employees.
PROFIT SHARING	Profit-sharing plans reward employees with a share of company profits above and beyond predetermined goals.
STOCK OPTIONS	Stock options are the right to buy shares of company stock at some future date for the price of the shares on the day the company awarded the options.
PAY FOR KNOWLEDGE	This approach involves awarding bonuses and pay increases in exchange for increases in knowledge such as earning an MBA.

© Cengage Learning

- Retirement programs
- Product discounts

A smaller number of companies also offer less traditional benefits such as discounted child care facilities, eldercare assistance, fitness programs, tuition reimbursement, and paid time off for volunteering. During periods of economic hardship, companies that do offer "extras" may focus attention on perks that boost morale without committing the company to outrageous costs.

In the past decade, a growing number of companies have begun to offer **cafeteria-style benefits**. This approach involves giving each employee a set dollar amount that must be spent on company benefits. The key to these plans is choice, which allows employees to tailor their benefits to their individual needs.

Over the past couple of decades, employees across the Canadian economy have demanded more flexibility from their employers, and companies have responded. Flexible scheduling options include flextime, telecommuting, and job sharing. A Conference Board of Canada survey found that 78 percent of employers offered flextime, 57 percent offered telecommuting, and 34 percent offered job sharing. Flexible working arrangements were more common in the public sector than in the private sector.[20]

Flextime A **flextime** plan gives workers some degree of freedom in terms of when they start and finish their workday as long as they complete the required number of hours. Typically, companies with flextime scheduling oblige their employees to start work between mandated hours in the morning—say, anytime between 7 a.m. and 10 a.m.—to take lunch between certain hours in the middle of the day, and to complete work at the end of eight hours. This approach ensures that everyone is present during core hours for communication and coordination but provides choice outside those parameters. Flextime tends to increase employee morale and retention. But it makes less sense in jobs that entail extensive teamwork and customer interaction. It also requires careful management to avoid abuse.

The **compressed workweek**, a version of flextime scheduling, allows employees to work a full-time number of hours in less than the standard workweek. The most popular option is to work four 10-hour days rather than five eight-hour days. Major companies such as Intel have developed successful compressed workweek programs at a number of their facilities.

While **telecommuting** sounds great at first glance, it has drawbacks as well as benefits for organizations and employees alike, as you'll see in Exhibit 14.4.

Telecommuting Working remotely—most often from home—is a growing phenomenon on a global scale. In some countries, as many as 50 percent of employees work entirely from home. In Canada, while 51 percent of employees report that flexible work location is important, only 35 percent of executives report that their company offers this possibility. Softchoice, a leading IT solutions and managed services provider, found that nearly 80 percent of employees they surveyed highly valued the ability to access their work from a remote location, and more than half of them worked remotely at least one day per week. Seventy percent reported that they would change employers if they found one that offered greater work flexibility.[21] Telecommuters are increasingly likely to come from a diverse range of industries because many jobs now involve knowledge work.

Job Sharing Job sharing allows two or more employees to share a single full-time job. Typically, job-share participants split salary and responsibility equally. Employees benefit because they get reduced hours and a more manageable schedule, while still retaining their ability to work and gain valuable experience. Companies benefit from higher employee morale, better retention, and having two dedicated employees committed to one role. Sometimes, savvy employers can match older, experienced workers with younger, less experienced workers. The older worker gets more free time and can ease into retirement; the younger worker gets mentored by a knowledgeable worker and becomes a valuable employee more quickly. Despite the benefits, only one in ten Canadians have reported trying a job-share experience.[22]

14-4g Separation: Breaking Up Is Hard to Do

Employees leave jobs for a number of different reasons. Experiencing success, they may be promoted or lured to another firm. Experiencing failure, they may be fired.

cafeteria-style benefits An approach to employee benefits that gives all employees a set dollar amount that they must spend on company benefits. Employees can choose to allocate their spending however they wish within broad limitations.

flextime A scheduling option that allows workers to choose when they start and finish their workdays as long as they complete the required number of hours.

compressed workweek A version of flextime scheduling that allows employees to work a full-time number of hours in less than the standard workweek.

telecommuting Working remotely—most often from home—and connecting to the office via phone lines, fax machines, and broadband networks.

Exhibit 14.4 An Analysis of Telecommuting[23]

	BENEFITS	DRAWBACKS
ORGANIZATION	Lower costs for office space, equipment, and upkeep. Higher employee productivity due to better morale, fewer sick days, and more focused performance. Access to a broader talent pool (not everyone needs to be local).	Greater challenges maintaining a cohesive company culture. Greater challenges fostering teamwork. Greater challenges monitoring and managing far-flung employees.
EMPLOYEE	Much more flexibility. Zero commute time (less gas money). Better work–life balance. Every day is casual Friday (or even pyjama day!). Fewer office politics and other distractions.	Less fast-track career potential. Less influence within the organization. Weaker connection to the company culture. Isolation from the social structure at work.

Source: "Flexible Hours and Telecommuting—Not the Ticket to the Top of Corporate America, Five Questions for Susan DePhillips," *Workforce Management*, September 2005, http://www.workforce.com/section/02/article/24/14/66.html.

Or in response to changing business needs, their employer may transfer them or lay them off. And of course, employees also leave jobs for completely personal reasons such as family needs, retirement, or a change in career aspirations.

When companies terminate employees, they must proceed very carefully to avoid wrongful termination lawsuits. The best protection is honesty and documentation. Employers should always document sound business reasons for termination and share those reasons with the employee.

But employees can still lose their jobs for reasons that have little to do with their individual performance. Reasons include economic slumps, global competition, business bankruptcies or closings, and the efficiencies of outsourcing. By early 2016, with crude oil prices down almost 70 percent, political changes both provincially and federally, and continued pressure for greater environmental stewardship within the oil and gas industry, unemployment in Alberta had risen from a very low 4.4 percent to 7.4 percent, its highest in 20 years and, for the first time in nearly two decades, higher than the national average. Estimates are that more than 100,000 people have lost their jobs, and more will soon do so.[24] As companies have become leaner, the remaining workers have experienced enormous stress. Managers can mitigate the trauma most effectively by showing empathy

> Even a small layoff shocks and demoralizes survivors so much that voluntary quit rates rise an average of 31 percent above previous levels.
>
> *Wall Street Journal*

and concern for employees who remain and by treating the laid-off employees with visible compassion.

14-5 Legal Issues: HR and the Long Arm of the Law

Even when the company is right—even when the company *wins*—employment lawsuits can cost millions of dollars and deeply damage the reputation of your organization, as we briefly discussed earlier in this chapter. To avoid employment lawsuits, most firms rely on HR to digest the complex, evolving web of employment legislation and court decisions and to ensure that management understands the key issues.

The bottom-line goal of most employment legislation is to protect employees from unfair treatment by employers. Some would argue that the legislation goes so far that it hinders the ability of companies to grow. But regardless of your personal perspective, the obligation of an ethical employer is to understand and abide by the law as it stands, even if you're working within the system to change it.

The most influential piece of employment legislation may well be the **Employment Equity Act**.

Employment Equity Act
Legislation designed to improve the status of specific designated groups, most particularly women, aboriginal peoples, persons with disabilities, and members of visible minorities.

MOTIVATED, PASSIONATE, CREATIVE, AND DRIVEN: SO WHAT?

Herb MacKenzie

f you're smart in today's digital world, you're using social media. And if you're like 332 million other people on LinkedIn, you probably describe yourself as a motivated, passionate, creative, and driven professional with extensive experience. Every year, LinkedIn does an analysis of overused buzzwords in personal profiles. Keeping in mind that your profile is your opportunity to establish your brand—to tell the world why you are different from and better than any other potential employee—you may want to check out the latest analysis of overused buzzwords and update your profile. While you're at it, add a few new connections, remembering that the more people who know you're looking, the more likely you'll find a job. Here are the most recent top ten overused buzzwords on LinkedIn profiles:

1. Motivated
2. Passionate
3. Creative
4. Driven
5. Extensive experience
6. Responsible
7. Strategic
8. Track record
9. Organizational
10. Expert

And the top words show up year after year, suggesting that you should spend more time demonstrating how creative you are by crafting a profile that describes how uniquely valuable you truly are.[25]

It applies to all federally regulated employers that have 100 or more employees, including firms in industries such as banking and financial services, communications, transportation, and all parts of the public service. The purpose of the act is

> to achieve equality in the workplace so that no person shall be denied employment opportunities or benefits for reasons unrelated to ability and, in the fulfilment of that goal, to correct the conditions of disadvantage in employment experienced by women, aboriginal peoples, persons with disabilities and members of visible minorities by giving effect to the principle that employment equity means more than treating persons in the same way but also requires special measures and the accommodation of differences.[26]

In addition, the federal government has implemented the Federal Contractors Program, which requires provincially regulated contractors with 100 or more employees that have secured a federal government contract valued at $1 million or more to commit to employment equity in their workplace. Employers found in noncompliance may forfeit their right to bid on further federal government contracts.

employment standards legislation Legislation that defines minimum standards in the workplace.

reverse discrimination Occurs when someone is denied an opportunity because of preferences given to members of designated groups who may be less qualified.

Only Quebec has specific provincial employment equity legislation: *An Act Respecting Equal Access to Employment in Public Bodies*. It covers employers such as school boards, municipalities, transit authorities, colleges and universities, health and social services, and other public bodies. The province also has an Affirmative Action Contract Compliance Program that has similar objectives to the Federal Contractors Program. Ontario implemented employment equity legislation under the former NDP government, but it was repealed in 1995 by the Conservative government. Only one territory, Nunavut, has employment equity legislation. Article 23 of the *Nunavut Land Claims Agreement* speaks to increasing employment of Inuit in government positions. It is important to recognize, however, that all Canadian provinces have human rights legislation designed to prevent systemic discrimination and to overcome historic inequities that such discrimination in the past may have caused.[27]

Employment standards legislation, or *labour standards legislation*, defines minimum standards in the workplace. Such legislation has been passed by the federal government and by all provinces and territories in Canada. This legislation varies across jurisdictions but generally covers the same issues: hours of work, minimum wage, pay equity, statutory (paid) holidays, vacations and vacation pay, bereavement and sick leave, maternity and parental leave, employee health and safety, and termination and severance pay.

HR managers are responsible for not only knowing this legislation in detail but also ensuring that management throughout their firm implements the legislation effectively, wherever it's applicable.

14-5a Employment Equity: The Active Pursuit of Equal Opportunity

Since employment equity and human rights legislation has been passed throughout Canada, there has been considerable debate regarding whether it has resulted in **reverse discrimination**. White males, in particular, have argued that they may be denied opportunities when preference is given to members of designated groups who may be less qualified. Some members of designated groups have also argued against employment equity as they have been concerned that others would view their hires or promotions as unearned, given to them only because of their membership in a group. Supporters of such legislation counter that everyone who benefits from equal opportunity programs must—by law—have relevant and valid qualifications. They argue that proactive measures are the only workable way to right past wrongs and to ensure truly equal opportunity.

Employment equity programs are not insulated from claims of discrimination. The *Canadian Charter of Rights and Freedoms* specifically allows such programs. However, the Supreme Court of Canada points out that such programs may be challenged for being "under-inclusive" or for contravening the right of equality. Employment equity programs and laws pertaining to them will continue to be tested and refined. Their long-term fate remains unclear, but achieving the underlying goal—a diverse workplace with equal opportunity for all—stands to benefit both business and society.

14-5b Harassment: Eliminating Hostility

Both federal and provincial legislation prohibits harassment in Canada. The *Canadian Human Rights Act* defines **harassment** as any unwanted physical or verbal conduct that offends or humiliates a person. The Canadian Human Rights Commission accepts harassment complaints based on 11 grounds: sex, sexual orientation, age, religion, race, colour, national or ethnic origin, marital status, family status, mental or physical disability, and pardoned conviction. Harassment is a serious offence, for it interferes with a person's ability to perform well in the work environment and may even lead to adverse job-related outcomes for the victim. Harassment can take many forms: threats; intimidation; verbal abuse; unwelcome remarks or jokes about race, religion, disability, or age; the display of sexist, racist, or other offensive pictures or posters; sexually suggestive remarks or gestures; unnecessary physical contact, such as touching, patting, pinching, or punching; and physical assault, including sexual assault.

Not just the perpetrator is liable for harassment; employers may share accountability if they did not take "reasonable care" to prevent and correct harassing behaviour. When a former employee of Penguin Canada launched a $523,000 lawsuit alleging sexual harassment by the company CEO, she claimed damages of $423,000 from the company and $100,000 in personal damages from the alleged offender. As a result of the allegations, the CEO was fired from his position, although other terms of the settlement have not been disclosed.[28]

Simply adopting a written harassment policy is not sufficient to mitigate responsibility. Taking "reasonable care" means taking proactive steps—such as comprehensive training—to ensure that everyone in the organization understands that the firm will not tolerate harassment. The firm would also be wise to have a system in place for complaints, with protection against retaliation against those who complain.

> **harassment** Any unwanted physical or verbal conduct that offends or humiliates a person.

Effective human resource management can create an unbeatable competitive edge. A fair, productive, empowering workplace pays off in bottom-line results. In good times, a core goal of human resource management is to find, hire, and develop the best talent. While that function remains crucial in tough economic times, the focus changes to managing HR costs while maintaining morale. Looking forward, a growing number of firms will most likely outsource traditional HR tasks such as payroll and benefits administration to companies that specialize in these areas. HR departments will then be able to focus on their core mission: working with senior management to achieve business goals by cultivating the firm's investment in human resources.

THE BIG PICTURE

careers in human resources: Human Resources Manager

Plan, organize, lead, and coordinate the personnel or labour relations activities of an organization. Identify staff vacancies and recruit, interview, and select applicants, ensuring a strong match between personnel and positions. Establish, maintain, and implement a competitive pay and benefit structure and ensure that policies remain in compliance with federal, provincial, and municipal laws. Establish and conduct employee orientation and training programs. Provide current and prospective employees with information about company policies, pay, benefits, and promotional opportunities. Counsel and coach management, as necessary, on human resources issues. Maintain accurate human resources records. Keep current regarding professional and technical knowledge.

STUDY TOOLS 14

IN THE BOOK, YOU CAN:

☐ Rip out the Chapter Review card at the back of the book to have a summary of the chapter and key terms handy.

ONLINE AT NELSON.COM/STUDENT YOU CAN:

☐ Work through key concepts with a Guided Learning Question.

☐ Prepare for tests with quizzes.

☐ Review the key terms with Flash Cards (online or printer-ready).

☐ Explore practical examples of chapter concepts with Connect a Concept exercises.

Learning like never before.

4LTR PRESS

nelson.com/student

15
Managing Information and Technology:
Finding New Ways to Learn and Link

LEARNING OBJECTIVES
After studying this chapter, you will be able to...

15-1 Explain the basic elements of computer technology—including hardware, software, and networks—and describe key trends in each area

15-2 Discuss the reasons for the increasing popularity of cloud computing

15-3 Describe how data becomes information and how decision support systems can provide high-quality information that helps managers make better decisions

15-4 Explain how Internet-based technologies have changed business-to-consumer and business-to-business commerce

15-5 Describe the problems posed by the rapid changes in Internet-based technologies and explain ways to deal with these problems

After you finish this chapter, go to page 257 for STUDY TOOLS

15-1 Information Technology: Explosive Change

Over the past few decades, computer and communications hardware and software have changed dramatically. The capabilities of hardware have increased by orders of magnitude. In the late 1950s, for example, you would have needed fifty 60 cm disks—costing tens of thousands of dollars—to store five megabytes of data. Today, you can buy a flash memory device about the same size as a postage stamp that stores several gigabytes of data—thousands of times more data than that entire 1950s disk array—for less than $50. And in terms of processing power, Apple's iPad tablet can complete more than three billion mathematical operations per second, making it faster than many multimillion-dollar supercomputers from the early 1990s.[1] While more difficult to quantify with specific statistics, it's also clear that software has become more powerful, more flexible, and easier to use.

But perhaps an even more important development than the increased power of hardware and sophistication of software is the degree to which today's technology is linked by networks. These networks allow businesses to coordinate their internal functions, serve their customers, and collaborate with their suppliers and partners in ways that could not have been envisioned even a quarter of a century ago. Networks have not only improved the efficiency and effectiveness of existing businesses, they've also opened up entirely new business opportunities. Of course, these new linkages pose challenges and threats as well as benefits and opportunities; a quarter of a century ago, people hadn't heard of computer viruses, spyware, phishing, or spam (except for the meat product variety). Over the course of this chapter, we'll take a look at both sides of this rapidly changing story.

15-1a The Role of the IT Department

Many business organizations have an information technology (IT) department to manage their information resources. But the role of this department varies significantly from one company to another. In some firms, the IT department plays a strategic role, making and implementing key decisions about the technologies the firm will use. In other organizations, the role of IT is largely operational; managers in functional departments make the key decisions about the computer and information resources their areas need, and the IT department simply maintains these resources and provides technical support to employees.

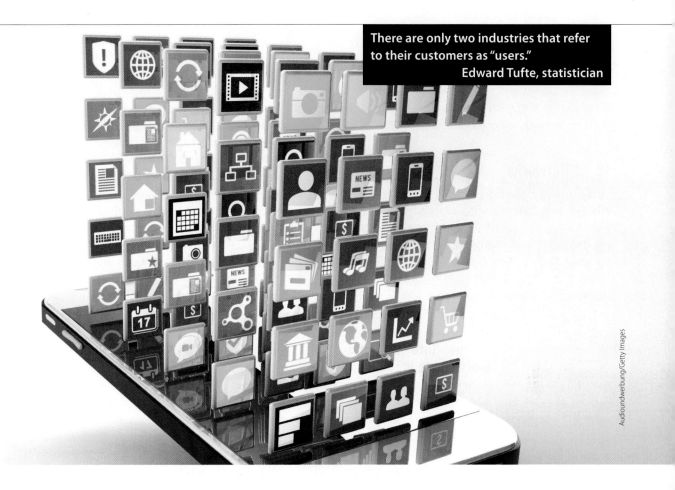

Audioundwerbung/Getty Images

15-1b Hardware and Software

Hardware refers to the physical components used to collect, input, store, organize, and process data and to display and distribute information. This hardware includes the various components of a computer system, as well as communications and network equipment. Examples include barcode scanners, hard drives, printers, routers, and smartphones.

Software refers to the programs that provide instructions to a computer so that it can perform a desired task. There are two broad categories of software: system software and application software. Both types of software have used the tremendous increase in hardware capabilities to become more powerful and easier to use.

System software performs the critical functions necessary to operate the computer at the most basic level. The fundamental form of system software is the operating system, which controls the overall operation of the computer. It implements vital tasks such as managing the file system, reading programs and data into main memory, and allocating system memory among various tasks to avoid conflicts.

Operating system software also provides the interface that enables users to interact with the computer. Early operating systems required users to type complex commands with very precise syntax in order to carry out tasks such as running programs or opening, saving, or deleting files. If you made an error while typing a command, your computer would just sit there until you typed the correct command. Today's operating systems are much simpler and more intuitive. The *graphical user interface* (or GUI—pronounced "gooey") allows users to enter commands by clicking on icons on the computer screen or by tapping or swiping them on devices with a touch screen.

Utility programs supplement operating system software in ways that increase the security or abilities of the computer system. Examples include firewalls, antivirus software, and antispyware programs. Over the years, operating systems have incorporated many features that were originally provided by utility programs.

Applications software is the software that helps users perform desired tasks. *Horizontal applications software*, such as word processing, spreadsheet, and personal information management software, is used by many different businesses and occupations. *Vertical applications software* is designed for a specific

hardware The physical tools and equipment used to collect, input, store, organize, and process data and to distribute information.

software Programs that provide instructions to a computer so that it can perform a desired task.

system software Software that performs the critical functions necessary to operate the computer at the most basic level.

applications software Software that helps a user perform a desired task.

industry or profession. For example, brokerage firms have special software that allows them to transact business on the stock market, and product designers have computer-aided design (CAD) software that enables them to produce technical drawings in three dimensions.

15-1c Networks

Today, most firms (and many households) use networks to enable users to communicate with one another and to share both files and hardware resources. A network links computer resources using either a wired or wireless connection. For privacy and security reasons, firms usually want to prevent outsiders from obtaining access to their networks, but they sometimes allow customers or suppliers partial access to their private networks to strengthen their relationships with these important stakeholders.

Internet The world's largest computer network; essentially a network of computer networks all operating under a common set of rules that allow them to communicate with one another.

broadband Internet connection An Internet connection that is capable of transmitting large amounts of information very quickly.

The Internet and the World Wide Web The development and growth of the Internet is one of the great networking stories of the past two decades. The **Internet** is often referred to as the world's largest computer network. It's actually a network of networks, consisting of hundreds of thousands of smaller networks operating under a common set of protocols (rules) so that they can communicate with one another.

One common way to experience the Internet is through the World Wide Web. Many people think that the Internet and the Web are the same thing, but they aren't. The Internet supports the Web and provides access to it, but only about one-quarter of the traffic on the Internet involves the Web. (Other traffic includes but isn't limited to e-mail, VoIP phone calls, Internet chat, online gambling, and machine-to-machine communications.)[2] Still, the Web is an incredibly rich environment; it consists of billions of pages documents—the number grows significantly every day—written and linked together using hypertext markup language (HTML).[3]

The increased availability of broadband Internet connections has fuelled the popularity of Internet applications. A **broadband connection** has the capability to transmit large amounts of data very quickly, allowing users to quickly download large files such as music, games, and movies. According to the Organization for Economic Co-operation and Development (OECD), the United States has the largest number of broadband subscribers, but the country with the largest percentage of households with broadband subscriptions is Korea. Iceland, Sweden, and Denmark were just behind Korea in terms of broadband penetration of households. Canada was number twelve and the United States ranked number sixteen for percentage of households with broadband access.[4]

TABLET, SMARTPHONE, CHEQUE PLEASE!

Andy Post

People love to eat out but hate waiting for the bill. Jay Johns, vice-president of strategy implementation at Applebee's, says: "When you are ready, that five minutes [of] waiting for the credit-card transaction feels like 20." Sit-down restaurants are addressing that problem by experimenting with tabletop devices, tablets, and smartphone applications that let customers order food and drinks, play games, read news, watch videos, *and* pay their bills.

Although not widely adopted, the devices are popular with customers. At Applebee's restaurants in the United States, 70 percent of customers use them. The management at New York City's La Guardia Airport uses iPads to accomplish the same thing for travellers who are waiting at their gates. Customers don't have to get up. With one of the airports iPads, travellers can have anything from a cheeseburger to a beer delivered to their seat. Sales have increased by double digits as a result.

Another reason why restaurants like the devices is that they can show photos or videos of dessert options 20 minutes after the main meal has been delivered. The result? At Chili's restaurants, dessert orders have increased by 30 percent.

The devices are also preprogrammed for 18 to 20 percent tips (which can be adjusted up or down). Since 90 percent of customers accept the preprogrammed amount, wait staff earn more than the typical 15 percent rate.

Finally, customers can swipe their credit cards without waiting for the bill and can e-mail themselves a receipt.[5]

Sources: S. McCartney, "The Middle Seat: Boarding Gate Makeover: Purgatory No More," *The Wall Street Journal*, August 23, 2012; Nassauer, "Screens Get a Place at the Table," *The Wall Street Journal*, May 31, 2012; "Using the RM Handheld for Payment Processing," *Restaurant Manager* website; Jeff Macke, "Ziosk Could Put Waiters Out of Work, But Not How You think," *Yahoo Finance*, October 10, 2014, finance.yahoo.com.

But even today's broadband connections are too slow and inefficient for many business and scientific applications. Such projects often require high-definition video and audio files to be shared among multiple sites at the same time. Beginning in 1996, several leading research universities, corporations, and other organizations formed a coalition to create a new generation of Internet technology based on fibre-optic cable. The resulting network became known as **Internet2** (or **I2**).

Access to I2 was initially limited to dues-paying members of the Internet2 consortium, which today consists of over 200 major universities as well as leading high-tech corporations, government agencies, and international organizations.[6] However, under an initiative begun in 2001, members of the I2 consortium can sponsor access to the network for other research and educational organizations that otherwise would be unable to qualify for membership. This initiative has given many elementary schools, high schools, community colleges, libraries, and museums access to I2 resources.[7]

Internet2 isn't just a faster way to surf the Web or send e-mail. In fact, such routine uses of the current Internet aren't even allowed. Instead, it is a noncommercial network that uses high-speed connectivity to improve education, research, and collaboration. Member organizations see Internet2 as a way to bring together their researchers, scientists, and engineers at various locations in a way that allows real-time collaboration on complex and important topics. It also allows corporations to collaborate with other companies, universities, and organizations located thousands of miles apart. One mission of the Internet2 consortium is to "facilitate the development, deployment and use of revolutionary internet technologies."[8] So the benefits of Internet2 will eventually become commonplace on the Internet that the rest of us use.

Intranets and Extranets An **intranet** is a private network that has the same look and feel as the Web and uses the same Web browser software to display documents but limits access to the employees of single firm (or members of a single organization). When properly implemented, intranets enhance communication and collaboration among employees and provide an effective way to distribute information and applications throughout the organization. Employees can usually log onto their company's intranet from remote locations using password-protected Internet access, allowing them to use company resources when working on the road or from home.

Firms sometimes also create **extranets** by giving key stakeholders, such as customers and suppliers, limited access to certain areas of their intranet. Extranets enable firms to provide extra services and information to their external stakeholders. For example, the firm might allow customers to check on the status of their order or suppliers to check on the state of the firm's inventory to plan shipments of parts and materials.

15-2 Cloud Computing: The Sky's the Limit!

In most companies, employees use applications and access data stored on their own computers or their companies' servers. But a new trend called **cloud computing** is challenging that approach. Cloud computing means using Internet-based storage capacity, applications, and processing power to supplement or replace internally owned computer resources.

You're already familiar with consumer-focused cloud computing services if you share photos on Shutterfly, store your music on Apple's iCloud storage services, or use a service like Dropbox to access and share documents and files. These services clearly offer significant benefits, such as the ability to store large files without taking up valuable space on your computer's hard drive and the convenience of being able to access your documents, music, or photos from any computer (and many mobile devices) with an Internet connection.

Until recently, most businesses were reluctant to embrace cloud computing, citing concerns about security and reliability. But the rapid increase in the number of firms using cloud-based services suggests that businesses are becoming convinced that the advantages of cloud computing outweigh the risks. The chief technology officer at a leading cloud data host says: "We're definitely having more conversations about security with small- and medium-sized customers, and we're also selling more security services to those customers than ever before. It's on the rise."[9]

And for some organizations, moving to the cloud may actually

Internet2 (I2) A new high-tech Internet with access limited to a consortium of member organizations (and other organizations these members sponsor). I2 utilizes technologies that give it a speed and capacity far exceeding the current Internet.

intranet A private network that has the look and feel of the Web and is navigated using a Web browser but that limits access to a single firm's employees (or a single organization's members).

extranet An intranet that allows limited access to a selected group of stakeholders, such as suppliers or customers.

cloud computing The use of Internet-based storage capacity, processing power, and computer applications to supplement or replace internally owned information technology resources.

increase data security. One industry expert says, "Small and medium businesses are insane not to leverage the advantages of cloud computing. It ends up being almost in all cases a security upgrade because they can't otherwise afford the practices." The executive director of a food bank, who works with 150 employees, 5,000 volunteers, and a small technology budget said that basic data security practices were "well above our [in-house] technological and intellectual capacity." So they put their critical data and supplier network in the cloud. "It was a no-brainer," he says. "I can't be worried about whether there's someone hacking our system."[10] Now his cloud provider does that for him. More specifically, the cloud offers to its users the ability to:

- Access a vast array of computing resources without the need to invest heavily in expensive new hardware, software, and IT personnel.

- Quickly adjust the amount of computer resources to meet their needs—and pay *only* for the resources that are *actually used*. This lowers costs and eliminates the problem of excess capacity. In fact, the cost reductions are often so great that even very small firms can afford to take advantage of sophisticated and powerful cloud computing resources.

- Encourage collaboration among employees and business partners. Cloud resources aren't confined to a specific platform or operating system,

data Raw, unprocessed facts and figures.

information Data that have been processed in a way that makes them meaningful to their user.

so it is easy for people using different computer systems to share files and programs. In addition, many cloud-based applications include tools specifically designed to facilitate collaboration.

- Take advantage of incredible gains in processing speed. Not only does cloud computing give users access to more resources, but it also enables them to use those resources more efficiently by taking advantage of a technique called *massively parallel computing*, which can combine the processing power of hundreds (or even thousands) of computers to work on different elements of a problem *simultaneously*. The result is that data processing projects that used to take weeks to complete on a firm's internal computer resources can be completed in less than a day using cloud resources.[11]

15-3 Information Technology and Decision Making: A Crucial Aid

One vital function of information technology—at least in relationship to business—is to transform data into useful information for decision makers. To make decisions, managers must have information about the current state of their business, their competitive environment, and the trends and market conditions that offer new opportunities. Where does this information come from? How can it be made more useful? How can managers process the information to make better decisions?

15-3a Data and Information

Let's start by distinguishing between data and information. **Data** are the facts and figures a firm collects. Data in their raw form have limited usefulness because they lack the context needed to give them meaning. Data become **information** when they are processed, organized, and presented in a way that makes them useful to a decision maker. Sometimes firms can obtain useful information from external sources, but sometimes they must create information by processing their own data. Given today's competitive environment, the speed with which managers obtain good quality information can be a crucial competitive advantage.

Internally, every department of an organization generates facts and figures that the firm must store and track. Every time a financial transaction is completed, for

Cloud computing may revolutionize the role of IT departments.

iStockphoto/Thinkstock.com

example, the firm's accounting system must record the specific accounts affected. Similarly, a firm's HR department must enter new data every time an employee is hired, fired, or promoted; changes jobs; or retires. Firms must also keep track of the names, addresses, and credit information of each customer. This is hardly a complete list, but you get the picture; firms must store mountains of data and convert it into useful information.

Typically, today's businesses store their data in **databases**, which are files of related data organized according to a logical system and stored on hard drives or some other computer-accessible storage media. It isn't unusual for a company to have many different databases, each maintained by a different department or functional area to meet its specific needs. For example, the HR department might have a database of employee pay rates, and the marketing department might have another database of customer history.

Once all of these data are stored, the firm must convert them into information. One common method is to *query* a database. A query is a request for the database management software to search the database for data that match criteria specified by the user. Suppose, for instance, that a marketing manager plans to introduce a product upgrade. She can enter a query that asks for the e-mail addresses of all customers who have purchased the product in the past year. She can use this information to send a targeted e-mail message, promoting the upgrade to the customers who are most likely to buy it.

> To err is human—
> and to blame it
> on a computer is
> even more so.
>
> Robert Orben, comedy writer
> and speechwriter

15-3b Characteristics of Good Information

We've seen that businesses have many sources of information. But not all information is of good quality. High-quality information is:

- **Accurate:** It should be free of errors and biases.
- **Relevant:** It should focus on issues that are important to making a decision.
- **Timely:** It should be available in time to make a difference.
- **Understandable:** It must help the user grasp its meaning.
- **Secure:** Confidential information must be secure from hackers and competitors.

15-3c Using Information Technology to Improve Decision Making

A company's information technology (IT) department often works closely with managers throughout the organization to support decision making. In fact, many companies develop **decision support systems (DSSs)** that give managers access to large amounts of data and the processing power to convert the data into high-quality information quickly and efficiently.

Over the past two decades, a new class of decision support systems has evolved to take advantage of the dramatic increase in data storage and processing capabilities. Called **business intelligence systems**, these systems help businesses discover subtle and complex relationships hidden in their data. Such systems can be a source of competitive advantage for the businesses that develop them.

One of the most common approaches to implementing a business intelligence system is to create a data warehouse and use data mining to discover unknown relationships. A **data warehouse** is a very large, organization-wide database that provides a centralized location for storing data from both the organization's own databases

database A file consisting of related data organized according to a logical system and stored on a hard drive or some other computer-accessible media.

decision support system (DSS) A system that gives managers access to large amounts of data and the processing power to convert these data into high-quality information, thus improving the decision-making process.

business intelligence system A sophisticated form of decision support system that helps decision makers discover information that was previously hidden.

data warehouse A large, organization-wide database that stores data in a centralized location.

Wireless networks and smartphones allow individuals to connect to the Internet from almost anywhere.

Butterfly Hunter/Shutterstock.com

and external sources. **Data mining** uses powerful statistical and mathematical techniques to analyze the vast amounts of data in a data warehouse to identify useful information that had been hidden. In recent years, data mining has had considerable success in areas as diverse as fraud and crime detection, quality control, scientific research, and even professional sports. For example, when the San Francisco Giants used data mining to decide when to increase seat prices for a single game ticket, ticket revenues jumped by 6 percent.[12]

15-3d Expert Systems

Managers who use decision support systems usually already know quite a bit about the problem and how they want to solve it. They just need access to the right data and a system to "crunch the numbers" in a way that provides relevant, accurate, and timely information to help them make their decisions. But what happens when the problem is beyond the expertise of the manager? One way to deal with this problem is to set up an **expert system (ES)** to guide the manager through the decision-making process.

To develop expert systems, programmers ask experts in the relevant area to explain how they solve problems. They then devise a program to mimic the expert's approach, incorporating various rules or guidelines that the human expert uses. The finished program will ask a user a series of questions, basing each question on the response to the previous question. The program continues to ask questions until it has enough information to reach a decision and make a recommendation.

Expert systems routinely solve problems in areas as diverse as medical diagnoses, fraud detection, and consumer credit evaluation. The troubleshooting systems many companies have on the customer support pages of their websites are another type of expert system. If your product doesn't work, the troubleshooter will ask a series of questions designed to diagnose the problem and suggest solutions. Based on your responses to each question, the system selects the next question as it starts narrowing down the possible reasons for the problem until it identifies the cause and offers a solution. Often you can solve your problem without waiting on hold to talk to a human expert over the phone.[13]

Despite impressive results in many fields, expert systems have their limitations. Programming all of the decision rules into the system can be time consuming, complicated, and expensive. In fact, it's sometimes impossible because the experts themselves can't clearly explain how they make their decisions—they just "know" the answer based on their years of experience. If the experts can't clearly explain how they reach their conclusions, then programmers can't include the appropriate decision rules in the system. Finally, an expert system has little flexibility and no common sense. It probably won't be able to find a solution to a problem that's even a little different from the specific type of problem it was programmed to solve.[14]

> The Internet? Is that thing still around?
>
> Homer Simpson

15-4 Information Technology and the World of E-commerce

Over the past 20 years, advances in information technology have had a dramatic and widespread impact on how companies conduct their business. In this chapter, we'll just concentrate on just one key area: the growth and development of e-commerce.

E-commerce refers to the marketing, buying, selling, and servicing of products over a network (usually the Internet). You're probably most familiar with **business-to-consumer (B2C) e-commerce**. You participate in this form of e-commerce when you purchase songs from iTunes, use Expedia to make travel arrangements, or buy stocks through an online broker. However, **business-to-business (B2B) e-commerce**, which consists of markets where businesses sell supplies, components, machinery, equipment, or services to other businesses, actually accounts for a *much* larger volume of e-commerce.

While both B2C and B2B e-commerce involve exchanging goods over the Internet, they differ in

data mining The use of sophisticated statistical and mathematical techniques to analyze vast amounts of data to discover hidden patterns and relationships among data, thus creating valuable information.

expert system (ES) A decision support system that helps managers make better decisions in an area where they lack expertise.

e-commerce The marketing, buying, selling, and servicing of products over a network (usually the Internet).

business-to-consumer (B2C) e-commerce E-commerce in which businesses and final consumers interact.

business-to-business (B2B) e-commerce E-commerce in markets where businesses buy from and sell to other businesses.

Noah Graham/NBAE/Getty Images

some important ways, as shown in Exhibit 15.1. Given these structural differences, it isn't surprising that the two markets operate so differently.

While B2B and B2C are the most obvious forms of e-commerce, they aren't the *only* forms. For example, in C2C (consumer-to-consumer) e-commerce, consumers buy from and sell to other consumers—think eBay and Craigslist. And in B2G (business-to-government), e-commerce businesses sell information, goods, and services to government agencies.

15-4a Using Information Technology in the B2C Market

Firms in the B2C market use information technology in a variety of ways. In this section, we'll describe how firms use technology in general and the Internet in particular to attract new customers and strengthen the loyalty of existing customers.

Web 2.0 A major goal for most firms today is to develop stronger relationships with their customers. The Internet has proven to be an excellent tool for fostering such relationships—although it took a while for businesses to discover the best way to do so. In the early days of e-commerce, most companies tried to maintain tight control over the content presented on their websites. These websites presented information about products and allowed customers to place orders for goods and services but offered little opportunity for user participation or involvement. However, by the early years of the 21st century, innovative businesses were developing ways to make e-commerce more interactive and collaborative. In doing so, they not only forged stronger relationships with the customers who posted this content, but also created a richer, more interesting, and more useful experience for *others* who visited the site. This new approach became known as **Web 2.0**.

Many Web 2.0 sites rely on users (or members) to provide most of their content. For instance, the online encyclopedia Wikipedia uses wiki software to allow users to comment on and contribute to its articles. And social networking sites such as Facebook and Twitter wouldn't exist without user-created material. The more users who participate on these sites, the more useful (and entertaining) they become—and the easier it is for them to attract even more visitors and contributors.

Interestingly, many companies have found that techniques used to encourage collaboration among their customers can be used to accomplish the same result with their employees. Major corporations such as HP and Procter & Gamble now use Web 2.0 techniques to help

Want to Go Green? There Are Apps for That!

Looking for ways to be more environmentally responsible? If you own a smartphone or tablet, a good strategy is to check out the "green" apps available for your device. Some apps help you find places to recycle, others help you identify "green" businesses, and yet others provide tips to improve your fuel economy while driving. These apps not only allow you to be "green," they also allow you to save some "green" (as in money). Most green apps are priced under $5, and several of them are free. Even the ones that cost a few bucks often quickly pay for themselves by helping you save on gas consumption or utility bills.

The greatest numbers of green apps are available for the iPhone and Android phones, but several are also available for other types of smartphones and for tablets. Here's an "apps sampler" to illustrate some of the possibilities:

- *Go Green*: Provides the user with a new environmental suggestion each time the app is accessed.
- *Good Guide*: Provides ratings for thousands of products to help you pick the ones that are good for both you and the environment.
- *EcoChallenge*: Presents two challenges a week, such as "Cook a meal for your friends using only local produce," that can easily be integrated into daily lives. Users can compare their progress with others on Facebook. The app provides a calculator so that you can measure your progress and impact as well as useful information and research related to each challenge.
- *Ecorio*: A Google app that allows the users to compute their carbon footprint and suggests way to reduce their impact on the environment.
- *Light Bulb Finder*: Helps you choose energy-saving light bulbs for any light fixture, bulb style, feature (dimmable, three-way), and wattage, and then stores that information by room and fixture.

Keep in mind that this is far from a complete list. There are hundreds of additional apps that can help you in your quest to be green, and more are being developed all the time. So be sure to check for new green apps on a regular basis.[15]

Sources: Jaymi Heimbuch, "7 Best Green Apps for Mobile Phones," PlanetGreen.com website; Matylda Czarnecka, "The Top Ten Apps to Make You More Green," TechCrunch website; Deborah Zabarenko, "Green Apps that Can Save You Money," Reuters website; Google website; Jonathan Strickland, "5 Green Mobile Apps," How Stuff Works website, science.howstuffworks.com.

their own employees work more effectively together. The use of Web 2.0 technologies within organizations is called Enterprise 2.0.[16]

Advertising on the Internet Many B2C companies have large target markets, so advertising is an important part of their

> **Web 2.0** Websites that incorporate interactive and collaborative features to create a richer, more interesting, and more useful experience for their users.

Exhibit 15.1 Key Differences between B2C and B2B E-commerce

	B2C	B2B
TYPE OF CUSTOMERS	Individual final consumers	Other businesses
NUMBER OF CUSTOMERS IN TARGET MARKET	Very large	Often limited to a few major business customers
SIZE OF TYPICAL INDIVIDUAL TRANSACTION	Relatively small (usually a few dollars to a few hundred dollars)	Potentially very large (often several thousand dollars, sometimes several million dollars)
CUSTOMER BEHAVIOUR	May do some research, but many purchases may be based on impulse.	Usually does careful research and compares multiple vendors. May take bids.
COMPLEXITY OF NEGOTIATIONS	Purchase typically involves little or no negotiation. Customer usually buys a standard product and pays the listed price.	Often involves extensive negotiation over specifications, delivery, installation, support, and other issues.
NATURE OF RELATIONSHIP WITH CUSTOMERS	Firm wants to develop customer loyalty and repeat business but seldom develops a close working relationship with individual customers.	Buyers and sellers often eventually develop close and long-lasting relationships that allow them to coordinate their activities.

© Cengage Learning

marketing strategy. Internet advertising revenue has grown rapidly in Canada in recent years, increasing from $98 million in 2000 to $3,082 million in 2013. While this amount represents only 24 percent of all the money companies spent on advertising in 2013, it is more than double what was spent the year before. Companies now spend more on Internet advertising than on radio advertising. If the current trend continues, that amount may soon surpass the amount spent on newspaper advertising.[17]

Firms in B2C markets also use opt-in e-mail as an advertising medium. Opt-in e-mails are messages the receiver has explicitly chosen to receive. Customers often opt in when they register their products online and click to indicate that they would like to receive product information from the company. Because the customer has agreed to receive the message, opt-in e-mails tend to reach interested consumers. And because e-mail requires no envelopes, paper, or postage, it's much less expensive than direct mail.

Viral Marketing The Internet has also proven to be an effective medium for **viral marketing**, which attempts to get customers to communicate a firm's message to friends, family, and colleagues. Despite its name, legitimate viral marketing doesn't use computer viruses. Effective viral marketing campaigns can generate a substantial increase in consumer awareness of a product. As a strategy, viral marketing isn't unique to the Internet; even before the World Wide Web, marketers were adept at *buzz marketing*, the use of unconventional (and usually low-cost) tactics to stimulate word-of-mouth product promotions. But the Internet has made it possible to implement such strategies in clever ways and reach large numbers of people very quickly. Many viral marketing campaigns in recent years have used social media such as Facebook, Twitter, and YouTube.

Handling Payments Electronically B2C e-commerce normally requires customers to pay at the time the purchase is made. Clearly, the use of cash and paper cheques isn't practical. In Canada, most payments in the B2C market are made by credit cards. To ensure that such transactions are secure, most sites transmit payment information using a secure socket layer (SSL) protocol. You can tell if a site on which you're doing business is using SSL in two fairly subtle ways. First, the URL will begin with https:// instead of simply http://. (Note the "s" after http in the address.) Also, a small closed-lock icon will appear near the bottom of your Web browser (the exact location depends on the specific browser you are using).

Another common method of payment is to use a **cybermediary**—an Internet-based company that specializes in the secure electronic transfer of funds. By far the best-known cybermediary is PayPal. According to figures on its website, PayPal has over 169 million accounts worldwide.[18]

viral marketing An Internet marketing strategy that tries to involve customers and others not employed by the seller in activities that help promote the product.

cybermediary An Internet-based firm that specializes in the secure electronic transfer of funds.

A final way of making electronic payments is **electronic bill presentment and payment**. This is a relatively new method in which bills are sent to customers via e-mail. The bill includes a simple mechanism (such as clicking on a button-shaped icon) that allows the customer to make a payment once the amount of the bill has been verified. Many banks now offer this service, as do services such as Quicken.

15-4b Using Information Technology in the B2B Market

B2B e-commerce generally requires a very different approach than B2C e-commerce. B2B transactions often involve much larger sums of money and require much more negotiation than B2C transactions; they also often result in long-term supply chain relationships that require close collaboration between buyer and seller. A *supply chain* is the network of organizations and activities needed to obtain materials and other resources, produce final products, and get those products to their final users. Forging tight and efficient supply chain relationships can be a key competitive advantage for firms.

An effective supply chain requires close coordination between a company and its suppliers. Information technology can provide the tools needed to foster this coordination. For example, the extranets we mentioned earlier can allow suppliers to keep tabs on their customers' inventories, thus anticipating when to make shipments of parts or materials.

Many firms involved in B2B business also make use of specialized Internet sites, called **e-marketplaces**, which provide a platform for businesses in specific B2B markets to interact. These platforms generally allow buyers in the market to solicit bids by posting requests for proposals (RFPs) on the site. Suppliers can then respond by bidding on RFPs that interest them.

E-marketplaces provide a number of advantages to their participants:

- Compared to older methods, they reduce time, effort, and the cost of doing business for both buyers and sellers.

- Because they are Internet based, they don't require expensive dedicated connections between firms, so even smaller firms can afford to participate.

- They enable sellers and buyers to contact and negotiate with a large number of market participants on the other side of the market, thus maximizing the chances of finding good matches.

> In 2013, every day users spent an average of 20 billion minutes on Facebook and 2 billion minutes on Skype.
>
> ZDNet, eWeek

- They often provide additional services—beyond simple trade—that allow firms to exchange information and collaborate, thus forging tighter supply chain relationships.

In recent years, many firms have begun using another information technology known as **radio frequency identification (RFID)** to improve the efficiency of their supply chains. This technology stores information on a microchip and transmits it to a reader when it's within range—up to several thousand feet. The chips can be extremely small—some are difficult to see with the naked eye—and can be embedded in most types of tangible products. The chips are usually powered by the energy in the radio signal sent by the reader, so they don't even need batteries.

RFID chips can store and transmit all sorts of information, but most commonly they transmit a serial number that uniquely identifies a product, vehicle, or piece of equipment. This type of information can be used to help track goods and other resources as they move through a supply chain. Deliveries can be recorded automatically and electronically without the need for manual record-keeping. The chips also can make taking inventory much quicker and simpler because the items in stock identify themselves to readers. And the chips can be used to reduce the chances of theft. The result of these advantages is lower cost and a more efficient supply chain.

Australia-based Qantas Airlines uses RFID chips to eliminate paper itineraries, boarding passes, and luggage tags. To check in, frequent fliers "wave" a Quantas ID card with an embedded RFID chip while standing in front of a ticket kiosk. Likewise, frequent fliers receive permanent "Q Bag Tags" with RFID chips to attach to their luggage. So, when dropping bags off, they wave their Qantas ID card again to identify themselves, and put their luggage on the luggage belt. Automatically, the luggage is weighed and the Q Bag Tag is scanned, matching the bag to the ID card. At the gate, customers flash ID cards to receive seat assignments. Qantas customer Jake Coverdale says: "It's bloody good, actually. I go to America and Europe a lot and I think this is the best check-in in the world. It's incredibly efficient."[19]

electronic bill presentment and payment A method of bill payment that makes it easy for the customer to make a payment, often by simply clicking on a payment option contained in an e-mail.

e-marketplace A specialized Internet site where buyers and sellers engaged in business-to-business e-commerce can communicate and conduct business.

radio frequency identification (RFID) A technology that stores information on small microchips that can transmit the information any time they are within range of a special reader.

USE TWO-FACTOR AUTHENTICATION ON YOUR GMAIL ACCOUNT SO YOU'RE NOT "MUGGED IN LONDON"

Giorgio Magini/iStockphoto.com

If you've ever gotten an e-mail from a friend claiming to have been "mugged in Spain" or "mugged in London," then chances are his Gmail account has been hacked. This happens several thousand times daily, and the hacked accounts are then used to send spam and phishing attacks. In the "mugged in Spain or London" scams, hackers take over someone's Gmail account and then, posing as the Gmail account holder, send emails to the account holder's contacts claiming to have been mugged while travelling abroad. Their new bank card won't arrive for several days, and they need you—dear friend or family member—to wire money via Western Union or MoneyGram. Someone often does. Google estimates that, on average, African- and Eastern European-based hackers make $500 a day from these scams.

How does this happen? Simple: people use the same password repeatedly for their online accounts. Google's Chief Technology Advocate says: "If you have ever used the same password in more than one place, you have reduced your overall safety record to whichever site had the lowest amount of protection. If you use your password in two places, it is not a valid password." Then, when hackers crack one password, they've got access to all of your accounts.

To prevent this from happening to you, sign up for Gmail's two-factor authentication. Authentication simply means making sure users are who they say they are. Two-factor means that it takes more than a password, the first factor, to gain access. Google will send a verification code, the second factor, to your smartphone. Enter the code after your password. Since the hacker doesn't have your phone, your Gmail account is safe. Also, Google requires you to reauthorize any device you use to read your Gmail every 30 days. What happens if you lose your phone? Nearly all smartphones can be remotely wiped and shut down. Also, set up your Gmail account with a "recovery e-mail" to receive verification codes. But make sure it has a different password! Two-factor authentication is easy. Use it wherever available for your online accounts.[20]

15-5 Challenges and Concerns Arising from New Technologies

So far we've concentrated on the benefits of advances in information technology—and it's clear that these benefits are enormous. But rapid technological advances also pose challenges and create opportunities for abuse. These problems affect businesses, their customers, and their employees, as well as the general public. In this section, we'll look at annoyances, security concerns, and legal and ethical issues.

15-5a Malware

The Internet—for all its advantages—creates the possibility that unwanted files and programs may land on your computer. In many cases, this happens without your knowledge, much less your permission. Some of these files and programs are relatively benign (even useful), but others can create major problems. Software that is created and distributed with malicious intent is called **malware** (short for "malicious software"). Spyware, computer viruses, and worms are all examples of malware.

Spyware is software that installs itself on your computer without permission and then tracks your computer behaviour in some way. It might track which Internet sites you visit to learn more about your interests and habits in order to send you targeted ads. Or, more alarmingly, it might log every keystroke (thus capturing passwords, account numbers, and user names to accounts as you enter them), allowing someone to steal your identity. Some spyware even goes beyond passive watching and takes control of your computer, perhaps sending you to websites you didn't want to visit.

Computer viruses are programs that install themselves on computers without the users' knowledge or permission and spread from one computer to another—sometimes very rapidly by attaching themselves to other files that are transferred from computer to computer. Viruses

malware A general term for malicious software, such as spyware, computer viruses, and worms.

spyware Software that is installed on a computer without the user's knowledge or permission for the purpose of tracking the user's behaviour.

computer virus Software that can spread from one computer to another without the knowledge or permission of computer users by attaching itself to e-mails or other files.

are often attached to e-mails, instant messages, or files downloaded from the Internet. Some viruses are little more than pranks, but others can cause great harm. They can erase or modify data on your hard drive, prevent your computer from booting up, or find and send personal information you've stored on your computer to people who want to use it for identity theft. **Worms** are similar to viruses, except that they are independent programs that can spread across computer networks without being attached to other files.

How can you protect yourself from spyware and viruses? Take these commonsense steps:

- Perform regular backups. This can come in handy should a virus tamper with (or erase) the data on your hard drive. Store the backed-up data in a separate place.

- Install high-quality antivirus and antispyware software and keep them updated. (Today's Internet security software usually has the ability to download and install updates automatically, but they may need to be configured to do so.)

- Update your operating system regularly so that any security holes it contains are patched as soon as possible.

- Don't open e-mail messages or attachments if you don't know and trust the sender.

- Don't download files from websites unless you are sure they are legitimate. And be sure to read the licensing agreement of any programs you install, especially those of freeware you download from the Internet. The wording of these agreements will often indicate whether other programs (such as spyware) will be installed along with your free program.

15-5b Spam, Phishing, and Pharming

Spam refers to unsolicited commercial e-mails, usually sent to huge numbers of people with little regard to whether they are interested in the product or not. It's hard to get exact measures of the amount of spam that is sent each year, but experts agree that it now comprises the vast majority of all e-mail in Canada. It clogs e-mail inboxes and makes it tough for people to find legitimate messages among all the junk. Spam filters exist that help detect and eliminate spam, but spammers are very good at eventually finding ways to fool these filters.[21]

Many countries are enacting laws in order to try to control spam. Canada's Anti-Spam Legislation came into effect July 1, 2014. This law makes it illegal to send electronic messages to promote or market a product or organization without the consent of the person who is receiving it. This law also requires companies to properly identify themselves and provide an opportunity for customers to unsubscribe to the electronic mailing list. Under this law it is important that companies be able to show they have the consent of the receiver of the messages.[22]

Phishing is another common use of spam. Phishers send e-mail messages that appear to come from a legitimate business, such as a bank or retailer. The e-mail attempts to get recipients to disclose personal information, such as their social insurance or credit card numbers, by claiming that there is a problem with their account—or sometimes simply that the account information needs to be verified or updated. The messages appear authentic; in addition to official-sounding language, they include official-looking graphics, such as corporate logos. The e-mail also usually provides a link to a website where the recipient is supposed to log in and enter the desired information. When the victims of the scam click on this link, they go to a website that can look amazingly like the site for the real company—but it's not. It's a clever spoof of the site where the phishers collect personal information and use it to steal identities.

One of the best ways to avoid such scams is to be skeptical of e-mail requests for personal information; reputable businesses almost *never* ask you to divulge such information via email. Also, never click on a link in an e-mail message to go to a website where you have financial accounts—if the message is from a phisher, that link is used to direct you to the fake site where the phishers hope that you'll mistakenly enter your username and password. Instead, use a link to the site that you've bookmarked, or type in the link to the real site yourself.

Not content with phishing expeditions, some scam artists have now taken to **pharming**. Like phishing, pharming uses fake websites to trick people into divulging personal information. But pharming is more sophisticated and difficult to detect than phishing because it doesn't

iStockphoto/Thinkstock.com

worm Malicious computer software that, unlike viruses, can spread on its own without being attached to other files.

spam Unsolicited e-mail advertisements, usually sent to very large numbers of recipients, many of whom may have no interest in the message.

phishing A scam in which official-looking e-mails are sent to individuals in an attempt to get them to divulge private information such as passwords, user names, and account numbers.

pharming A scam that seeks to steal identities by routing Internet traffic to fake websites.

"IN THE SPACE OF ONE HOUR, MY ENTIRE DIGITAL LIFE WAS DESTROYED."

PN_Photo/iStockphoto.com

Wired magazine writer Mat Honan says: "In the space of one hour, my entire digital life was destroyed. First my Google account was taken over, then deleted. Next my Twitter account was compromised, and used as a platform to broadcast racist and homophobic messages. And worst of all, my AppleID account was broken into, and my hackers used it to remotely erase all of the data on my iPhone, iPad, and MacBook."

How did this happen? Did malicious software transmit this information? No. The hackers, posing as Honan, simply called customer service representatives at Amazon and Apple to gain access to his accounts.

Social engineering uses deception, manipulation, and influence to exploit human psychology to gain access to buildings, systems, or data. And it's surprisingly easy and effective, especially with friendly customer service representatives. Plus, with work histories available on LinkedIn, and friends and hobbies on Facebook and Twitter, it's not hard for hackers to construct a personal profile containing your address, e-mails, phone numbers, and even the last four digits of your credit cards. One fraud investigator says: "The more information there is about you out there, the more information there is for someone to steal."

What's the solution? Don't use the same usernames, passwords, e-mails, and security questions and answers for each account.

Instead, use two-factor authentication and password management software (which remembers and generates different secure passwords), and regularly back up data for all devices.[23]

---

require the intended victim to click on a bogus e-mail link. Instead, it uses techniques to redirect Internet traffic to the fake sites. Thus, even if you type in the *correct* URL for a website you want to visit, you still may find yourself on a very realistic-looking pharming site. One way to check the validity of the site is to look for the indications that the site is secure, such as the https:// in the URL and the small closed-lock icon mentioned earlier.[24]

Computers aren't the only devices plagued by these threats and annoyances. Smartphone users are facing increasing problems with spam delivered via text messaging. Even more alarming, some scammers have found ways to take their phishing expeditions to smartphones—a practice known as "smishing." A typical smishing ploy is to use text messaging to entice smartphone users to visit the scammer's fake website asking you to provide personal or financial information.[25]

15-5c Hackers: Break-Ins in Cyberspace

Hackers are skilled computer users who use their expertise to gain unauthorized access to other people's computers. Not all hackers intend to do harm, but some—called black hat hackers, or crackers—definitely have malicious intent. They may attempt to break into a computer system to steal identities or to disrupt a business.

Protecting against hackers requires individuals and businesses to be security conscious. Some of the precautions used against hackers, such as making frequent backups, are similar to those used to protect against viruses. Another key to protecting against hackers is to make sure that all data transmitted over a network are encrypted, or sent in encoded form that can only be read by those who have access to a key. Security experts also suggest that organizations restrict access to computer resources by requiring users to have *strong passwords*. According to Microsoft, strong passwords are at least fourteen characters in length, include a mix of letters, numbers, and special characters, and don't contain any common words or personal information.[26]

Unfortunately, users struggle to remember strong passwords, so they reuse one or two. "Having the same password for everything is like having the same key for your house, your car, your gym locker, your office," says a representative from PayPal. With password management software, users memorize just one master password. The software works with any browser on any computer, tablet, or smart phone. It generates unique, strong passwords, synchronizes encrypted data across devices, and autofills forms so that you don't have to manually enter personal information or passwords.[27]

Firewalls are another important tool against hackers and other security threats. A firewall uses hardware or

---

hacker A skilled computer user who uses his or her expertise to gain unauthorized access to the computers (or computer systems) of others, sometimes with malicious intent.

firewall Software and/or hardware designed to prevent unwanted access to a computer or computer system.

Just because they can, doesn't mean they should.

Some companies monitor everything in their corporate e-mail accounts without notifying employees. Two recent court cases limited what companies can do with personal information on company computers. Meanwhile, there have been rulings related to work-related e-mails.

Indeed, 60 percent of companies monitor employees' e-mail. But why? The most common reasons are to minimize legal liability by becoming aware of employee misconduct, to increase productivity by reducing nonwork activities, to maintain security so that proprietary information is not shared with outsiders, and to conduct internal investigations when conditions warrant, such as with regard to sexual harassment allegations.

E-mail-monitoring programs typically scan for keywords and competitor's names. For example, financial firms might search for "promise," "guarantee," or "high yield," while health care companies search for "patient information" or "client file." They also scan for profanity. At a leading financial firm, employees are advised that their communications should be "professional, appropriate and courteous at all times." That means the company scans e-mails and texts for profanity on all company-issued devices. When forbidden phrases are used, pop-up boxes instruct employees to change the language or not send the message. If employees persist, the system then blocks such messages from being sent.

But just because companies have the right to scan employee e-mail doesn't mean they should. Before scanning, employers should make clear what constitutes proper e-mail use, what circumstances will prompt monitoring, how long monitored information will be retained, and what the company will do with it. Likewise, monitoring should be done only for legitimate business or legal reasons, in proportion to the harm the company could suffer if it doesn't monitor (i.e., criminal activity), and only after obtaining legal approval from company lawyers. Finally, with employees increasingly using their own devices at work, such as smartphones and tablets, employers need to differentiate between employer-provided e-mail for work only and mixed mailboxes for professional and personal issues.[28]

What do YOU think?

- How concerned are you that your corporate e-mail account can be monitored without your permission?
- When do you think it is reasonable for companies to monitor employee email accounts?
- What should companies do in terms of monitoring e-mail if employees are using personal devices to access those accounts? Is monitoring still acceptable in that case?

---

software (or sometimes both) to create a barrier that prevents unwanted messages or instructions from entering a computer system. As threats from spyware, hackers, and other sources have developed, the use of firewalls has become commonplace.

> Good passwords are bad for people, and bad passwords are good for criminals.
>
> Michael Jones, Chief Technology Advocate, Google

15-5d Ethical and Legal Issues

Information technology raises a number of legal and ethical challenges, such as the need to deal with privacy issues and to protect intellectual property rights. These issues are controversial and don't have simple solutions.

Personal Privacy Firms now have the ability to track customer behaviour in ways that were never before possible. This allows firms to offer better, more personalized service. But all of this extra information comes at the expense of your privacy. Does the fact that firms know so much about your preferences and behaviour make you a bit nervous?

Does it also bother you that your e-mail messages lack confidentiality? When you send an e-mail, it can end up being stored on several computers, the server of your e-mail

provider, the server of your recipient's provider, and your recipient's own computer. Also, if you send the e-mail from your company's system, it's likely to be stored when the company backs up its information. If you thought that deleting an e-mail message from your own computer erased it permanently and completely, you need to think again.

The list of other ways in which information technology can erode your personal privacy is long and getting longer. For example, many countries now embed RFID chips in their passports and driver's licences. Some privacy experts are concerned that such chips will make it easy for government organizations to track individuals. One reason government officials gave for embedding RFID chips in passports and driver's licences was to make it harder for criminals and terrorists to forge IDs. However, one hacker has publicly shown that the information on these chips can be read from a distance of several yards, which has led to fears that identity thieves could use similar techniques to obtain personal information and perhaps even create convincing copies of these important ID documents. Encryption and protective sleeves, however, can prevent unauthorized scanning. Thieves are more likely to steal your actual ID or passport the old-fashioned way.[29]

The bottom line is that there's no simple way to solve privacy concerns. Privacy is an elusive concept, and there is no strong consensus about how much privacy is enough.

Protecting Intellectual Property Rights

Intellectual property refers to products that result from creative and intellectual efforts. There are many types of intellectual property, but we'll focus on the ones that are protected by copyright law, such as books, musical works, computer programs, and movies. Copyright law gives the creators of this property the exclusive right to produce, record, perform, and sell their work for a specified time period.

Piracy of intellectual property occurs when someone reproduces and distributes copyrighted work without obtaining permission from—or providing compensation to—the owner of the copyrighted material. When piracy becomes widespread, creators of intellectual property receive much less income for their efforts. This can substantially reduce their incentive to continue developing creative material.

The Business Software Alliance estimates that, globally, 43 percent of all business software installed on personal computers in 2013 was pirated, resulting in the loss of more than $62 billion in revenue to software companies. In several smaller countries, including Georgia, Bangladesh, and Libya, the rate of piracy was over 80 percent. Among larger nations, the piracy rate in China exceeded 74 percent, while in India it was 60 percent.

> **intellectual property**
> Property that is the result of creative or intellectual effort, such as books, musical works, inventions, and computer software.

Nintendo is just one of many companies concerned about piracy of their intellectual property.

© Jochen Tack/imagebroker/First Light

The good news is that the piracy rate was much lower in Canada at 25 percent, and in the United States it is only 18 percent. But given the huge size of the US software market, even this relatively low rate of piracy still resulted in losses of over $9.7 billion in revenue for software companies. Faced with such a widespread problem, many software publishers have become very aggressive at prosecuting firms and individuals engaged in software piracy.[30]

Given how lucrative piracy can be, it's unlikely that this problem will go away anytime soon. You can expect the companies hurt by these practices to continue aggressively prosecuting pirates and to work on new technologies that make pirating digital media more difficult.

THE BIG PICTURE

Information technology plays a vital role in virtually every aspect of business operations. For instance, marketing managers use information technology to learn more about customers, reach them in novel ways, and forge stronger relationships with them—as we showed in our discussion of Web 2.0. Operations managers use RFID technologies to coordinate the movement of goods within supply chains and to keep more accurate inventory records. And financial managers use IT to track financial conditions and identify investment opportunities. Managers in all areas of a business can use decision support systems to improve their decision making. They also can apply techniques such as data mining to obtain interesting new insights hidden in the vast streams of data that flow into their companies.

Cloud computing represents the newest and one of the most exciting approaches to how companies acquire and utilize IT resources. The use of cloud-based resources has the potential to lower costs and increase flexibility; it also offers the ability to magnify computation power to levels previously impossible to envision. If cloud computing can overcome concerns about security and stability, it is likely to continue growing in popularity, which could result in significant changes to the role IT departments play within their organizations.

The rapid changes in IT in recent years—especially those related to the rise of the Internet as a business venue—have opened up exciting new commercial opportunities. But these changes have also created a host of legal and ethical challenges and security questions. One thing is certain: business organizations that find ways to leverage the advantages of new IT developments while minimizing the accompanying risks are most likely to enjoy competitive success.

careers in information technology:
Information Technology Support Specialist

Responsible for installing and configuring software, responding to employee and customer issues within the ticket management system, interacting with sales, engineering, and product managers to address complex customer issues, escalating relevant problems to appropriate functional and management teams, contributing potential technical workarounds, and acting as a technical expert for IT solutions within a global IT team.

The ideal candidate has a bachelor's degree in computer science or information technology, at least one year of experience with Windows and Unix/Linux administrative services, Web services, and configuration and release management, possesses strong analytical, problem solving, and customer communication skills, is self-motivated, and works effectively with little instruction.

STUDY TOOLS 15

IN THE BOOK, YOU CAN:
☐ Rip out the Chapter Review card at the back of the book to have a summary of the chapter and key terms handy.

ONLINE AT NELSON.COM/STUDENT YOU CAN:
☐ Work through key concepts with a Guided Learning Question.

☐ Prepare for tests with quizzes.

☐ Review the key terms with Flash Cards (online or printer-ready).

☐ Explore practical examples of chapter concepts with Connect a Concept exercises.

16 Operations Management:
Putting It All Together

LEARNING OBJECTIVES
After studying this chapter, you will be able to…

16-1 Define operations management and describe how the role of operations management has changed over the past 50 years

16-2 Discuss the key responsibilities of operations managers

16-3 Describe how operations managers face the special challenges posed by the provision of services

16-4 Explain how changes in technology have revolutionized operations management

16-5 Describe the strategies operations managers have used to improve quality of goods and services

16-6 Explain how lean and green practices can help both the organization and the environment

After you finish this chapter, go to page 274 for STUDY TOOLS

16-1 Operations Management: Producing Value in a Changing Environment

Operations management is concerned with managing all of the activities involved in creating value by producing goods and services and distributing them to customers. When operations managers do their job well, a firm produces the right goods and services in the right quantities and distributes them to the right customers at the right time—all the while keeping quality high and costs low. Obviously, the decisions of operations managers can have a major impact on the firm's revenues and costs and thus on its overall profitability.

operations management Managing the activities involved in creating value by producing goods and services and distributing them to customers.

efficiency Producing output or achieving a goal at the lowest cost.

effectiveness Using resources to create the greatest value by providing customers with goods and services that offer a better relationship between price and perceived benefits.

16-1a Responding to a Changing Environment

Operations management practices have changed dramatically over the past half-century. New technologies, shifts in the structure of the economy, challenges posed by global competition, and concerns about the impact of production on the environment have fuelled this revolution. Let's begin by identifying the key changes that have characterized the practice of operations management over the past 50 years.

From a Focus on Efficiency to a Focus on Effectiveness For operations managers, **efficiency** means producing a product or service at the lowest cost, whereas, **effectiveness** means producing products and services that *create value* by providing customers with goods and services that offer a better relationship between price and perceived benefits. In other words, effectiveness means finding ways to give customers more for their money—while still making a profit.

In the 1960s, the focus of operations management was mainly on efficiency. The goal was to keep costs low so that the firm could make a profit while keeping prices competitive. In today's highly competitive global markets, efficiency remains important. But operations managers now realize that keeping costs (and prices) low is only part of the equation. Customers usually buy goods that offer the best value, and these aren't always the same as the goods that sell for the lowest price. A product that offers better features, more attractive styling, and higher quality may provide more

Success is simple. Do what's right, the right way, at the right time.
Arnold H. Glasgow, psychologist

value—and attract more customers—than a product with a lower price. Thus, today's operations managers have broadened their focus to look at benefits as well as costs.

From Goods to Services **Goods** are tangible products that you can see and touch. *Durable goods* are expected to last three years or longer; examples include furniture, cars, and appliances. *Nondurable goods*, such as toothpaste and paper towels, are used up more quickly and are often perishable. **Services** are activities that yield benefits but don't directly result in a physical product. Examples include legal advice, entertainment, and medical care. Goods are consumed, while services are experienced. As we move through the chapter, we'll see that the differences between goods and services directly affect many operations management decisions.

Over the past 50 years the number of Canadians working in manufacturing has declined. The reduction in the number of people working in manufacturing is due in part to the mechanization of many production processes. During this same period of time the number of Canadians working in service jobs has increased. The increase in the

> Nothing is less productive than to make more efficient what should not be done at all.
>
> Peter F. Drucker

number of people working in services has sharpened the focus on the operational processes in services.[1]

From Mass Production to Mass Customization Fifty years ago, one common production strategy was to keep costs low by producing large quantities of standardized products. The goal of this *mass production* strategy was to achieve reductions in average cost by taking advantage of specialization and the efficient use of capital. But today's technologies allow many firms to pursue *mass customization*—the production of small quantities of customized goods and services that meet more precisely the needs of specific customers—with very little increase in costs.

From Local Competition to Global Competition For the first 25 years after the Second World War, global competition was limited, largely because the production facilities and infrastructure in many European and Asian nations had been severely damaged during the war.

By the early 1970s, the economies of Japan, Germany, and other war-ravaged nations had been rebuilt, and many of their major

goods Tangible products.

services Intangible products.

Chapter 16 Operations Management: Putting It All Together

Exhibit 16.1 | Operations Management: Fifty Years of Change

Characteristics of Operations Management Fifty Years Ago

- Focus on Minimizing Costs
- Production of Goods
- Mass Production
- Simple Supply Chains
- Exploit the Environment

Factors Promoting Change

- Improvements in Production and Information Technologies
- Rise of Global Competition and Global Opportunities
- Recognition of Quality as a Source of Competitive Advantage
- Adoption of Marketing Perspective and Customer Focus
- Recognition of Serious Environmental Problems

Characteristics of Operations Management Today

- Focus on Creating Value
- Provision of Services
- Mass Customization
- Complex Value Chains
- Sustain the Environment

© Cengage Learning

companies boasted efficient new production facilities with state-of-the-art technology. Also, many Japanese firms had adopted new techniques that greatly improved the quality of their products. With lower labour costs, impressive technology, and world-class quality, these foreign producers quickly began to take market share from North American firms. In more recent years, firms in Korea, India, and China have also become formidable competitors.

From Simple Supply Chains to Complex Value Chains Over the past 50 years, the increasingly competitive and global nature of markets has brought about major changes in how firms produce and distribute their goods and services. Many supply chains today span multiple organizations located in many different countries. The shift from a cost perspective to a value perspective has led operations managers to extend their view beyond the traditional supply chain to encompass a broader range of processes and organizations known as a *value chain*.

From Exploiting the Environment to Protecting the Environment In the 1960s, many operations managers viewed the natural environment as something to exploit. The emphasis on keeping costs low made it tempting to dispose of wastes as cheaply as possible— often by dumping them into rivers, lakes, or the atmosphere. But the serious consequences of environmental pollution have become increasingly apparent. Operations managers at socially responsible companies have responded by adopting a variety of green practices to produce goods and services in more environmentally responsible ways.

Exhibit 16.1 summarizes the discussion of the key ways in which operations management has changed over the past 50 years. We'll look at these changes in greater detail as we move through this chapter. But first let's take a look at some of the key tasks operations managers perform.

16-2 | What Do Operations Managers Do?

Understanding the marketing definition of "product" plays a pivotal role in understanding what operations managers do. A product is more than a physical good—it includes a whole set of tangible and intangible features (sometimes called the *customer benefit package*) that create value for consumers by satisfying their needs and wants. For example, when you purchase a car made by General Motors, you not only get the physical automobile, you also get (among other things) a warranty and (for many models) a year of OnStar services.

Marketing research typically determines which features a product should include to appeal to its target customers. Although operations managers don't normally have the primary responsibility for designing these goods and services, they provide essential information and advice during the product design process, especially regarding the challenges and constraints involved in creating actual products on time and within budget.

Once the actual goods and services are designed, operations managers must develop the processes needed to produce them and get them to the customer. A **process** is a set of related activities that transform inputs into outputs, thus adding value. Once these processes are designed, operations managers also play a key role in determining where they will be performed, what organizations will perform them, and how the processes will be organized and coordinated.

The most obvious processes are those directly involved in the production of goods and services. But there are many other processes that play necessary "supporting roles." For example, purchasing and inventory management processes make sure that the firm has an adequate supply of high-quality materials, parts, and components needed to produce the goods without delays or disruptions.

Let's take a closer look at some of the functions operations managers perform to move goods and services from the drawing board to the final user.

16-2a Process Selection and Facility Layout

Once a product is designed, operations managers must determine the best way to produce it. This involves determining the most efficient processes, deciding the best sequence in which to arrange those processes, and designing the appropriate layout of production and distribution facilities. Well-designed processes and facility layouts enable a firm to produce high-quality products effectively and efficiently, giving it a competitive advantage. Poorly designed processes can result in production delays, quality problems, and high costs.

There are several ways to organize processes. The best approach depends on considerations such as the volume of production and the degree of standardization of the product.

- Firms often use a *product layout* when they produce goods that are relatively standardized and produced in large volumes. This type of layout organizes machinery, equipment, and other resources according to the specific sequence of operations that must be performed. The machinery used in this type of layout is often highly specialized, designed to perform one specific task *very* efficiently. One classic example of a product layout is an assembly line, where the product being produced moves from one station to another in a fixed sequence, with the machinery and workers at each station performing specialized tasks. Services that provide a high volume of relatively standardized products also use flow-shop processes. For example, fast food restaurants often use a simple product layout to prepare sandwiches, pizzas, or tacos in a standard sequence of steps.

- A *process layout* is used by many firms that need to produce small batches of goods that require a degree of customization. This approach arranges equipment according to the type of task performed. For example, in a machine shop, all of the drills may be located in one area, all of the lathes in another area, and all of the grinders in yet another. Unlike assembly lines and other product layouts, a process layout doesn't require work to be performed in a specific sequence; instead, the product can be moved from one type of machinery to another in whatever sequence is necessary. Thus, process layouts can be used to produce a variety of products without the need for expensive retooling. But this flexibility sometimes comes at the cost of longer processing times and more complex planning and control systems. Also, because the machinery and equipment used in a process layout are usually more general-purpose in nature and may be used to produce a greater variety of goods, workers must be more versatile than those employed in a product layout.

- A *cellular layout* falls between the product layout and the process layout. It groups different types of machinery and equipment into self-contained cells. A production facility might have several cells, each designed to efficiently produce a family of parts (or entire products) that have similar processing requirements. Like an assembly line, the product moves from one station in the cell to the next in a specific sequence. However, unlike most assembly lines, cells are relatively small and are designed to be operated by a few workers who perform a wider array of tasks than assembly-line workers.

- A *fixed position layout* is used for goods that must be produced at a specific site (such as a building) or that are so large and bulky that it isn't feasible to move them from station to station (such as a ship or a commercial airplane). Even some services, such as concerts or sporting events that are performed at a specific location, use this approach. In a fixed position layout, the good or service stays in one place, and the employees, machinery, and equipment are brought to the fixed site when needed during various stages of the production process.

16-2b Facility Location

There is an old saying in real estate that the three most important factors determining the value of a property are location, location, and location. There is no doubt that the location is also important to operations managers. The location of facilities

process A set of related activities that transform inputs into outputs, thus adding value.

Exhibit 16.2 Factors That Affect Location Decisions

GENERAL LOCATION FACTORS	EXAMPLES OF SPECIFIC CONSIDERATIONS
ADEQUACY OF UTILITIES	Is the supply of electricity reliable? Is clean water available?
LAND	Is adequate land available for a facility? How much does the land cost?
LABOUR MARKET CONDITIONS	Are workers with the right skills available? How expensive is labour?
TRANSPORTATION FACTORS	Is the location near customers and suppliers? Is appropriate transportation nearby?
QUALITY OF LIFE FACTORS	What is the climate like? Are adequate health care facilities available?
LEGAL AND POLITICAL ENVIRONMENT	Does the local government support new businesses? What are the local taxes, fees, and regulations?

© Cengage Learning

can have an important influence on the efficiency and effectiveness of an organization's processes.

For some types of facilities, the location decision is dominated by one key consideration. A coal mine, for instance, must be located where there's coal. But for many other types of facilities, the decision is more complex. Exhibit 16.2 identifies several key factors that operations managers evaluate when they decide where to locate a facility. The importance of each factor in Exhibit 16.2 varies depending on the specific type of industry. For example, many service firms are interested primarily in locating close to their markets, whereas manufacturing firms may be more concerned about the cost and availability of land and labour and access to transportation facilities.

16-2c Inventory Control: Don't Just Sit There

Inventories are stocks of goods or other items held by an organization. Manufacturing firms usually hold inventories of raw materials, components and parts, work-in-process, and finished goods. Retail firms

inventory Stocks of goods or other items held by organizations.

are unlikely to hold work-in-process or raw materials, but they usually do hold inventories of finished goods that they sell as well as basic supplies that the business needs.

Deciding how much inventory to hold can be a real challenge for operations managers because increasing or decreasing the amount of inventory involves both costs and benefits. For example, the benefits of holding larger inventories include the following:

- **Smoother production schedules:** A candy maker might produce more candy than it needs in August and September and hold the excess in inventory so that it can meet the surge in demand in the weeks before Halloween without investing in more production capacity.

- **Protection against stock-outs and lost sales:** Holding larger inventories reduces the chance of stock-outs and lost sales due to supply disruptions or unexpected surges in demand.

- **Reduced ordering costs:** Every time a company orders supplies, it incurs paperwork and handling costs. Holding a larger average inventory reduces the number of orders the firm must make and thus reduces ordering costs.

But holding large inventories involves costs as well as benefits:

- **Tied-up funds:** Items in inventory don't generate revenue until they're sold, so holding large inventories can tie up funds that could be better used elsewhere within the organization.

- **Additional holding costs:** Large inventories require more storage space, which can mean extra costs for heating, cooling, taxes, insurance, and so on.

- **Increased risk:** Holding large inventories exposes the firm to the risk of losses due to spoilage, depreciation, and obsolescence.

Operations managers determine the optimal amount of inventory by comparing the costs and benefits associated with different levels of inventory. In our discussion of lean production later in this chapter, we'll see that a recent trend has been towards finding ways to reduce inventory levels at every stage of the supply chain.

16-2d Project Scheduling

It is a complex and expensive endeavour to build a new production facility, develop a new commercial airplane, or film a movie. It's vital to plan and monitor projects like these carefully to avoid major delays or cost overruns.

Exhibit 16.3 Activities Involved in Presenting a Play

ACTIVITY		IMMEDIATE PREDECESSOR(S)	TIME (WEEKS)
A	Select Play	None	**2**
B	Select Cast	**A** (must know play to know what roles are available)	**4**
C	Design Sets	**A** (must know play before sets can be designed)	**4**
D	Design Costumes	**A** (must know play to determine what costumes are needed)	**5**
E	Buy Materials for Sets	**C** (set must be designed to determine types and quantities of materials needed to build it)	**2**
F	Buy Materials for Costumes	**D** (costumes must be designed before materials for costumes are determined)	**2**
G	Build Sets	**E** (must have materials in order to build the sets)	**4**
H	Make Costumes	**B, F** (must have materials in order to make the costumes, and must know actors' sizes to ensure that costumes fit)	**6**
I	Initial Rehearsals	**B** (actors must be selected for each role before they can rehearse their parts)	**2**
J	Final Dress Rehearsal	**G, H, I** (costumes and sets must be completed, and initial rehearsals performed, before the final rehearsal can occur)	**1**
K	Perform Play (end of project)	**J**	**N/A**

© Cengage Learning

The **critical path method (CPM)** is one of the most important tools that operations managers use for such projects. We can illustrate the basic idea behind this tool by looking at a simple example: a theatre company wants to stage a play. Exhibit 16.3 presents the steps involved in this project.

Notice that Exhibit 16.3 identifies **immediate predecessors** for all of the activities except A. *Immediate predecessors* are activities that must be completed before other activities can begin. For example, it is clear that the cast for the play cannot be determined until the play has been selected, so activity A (selecting the play) is an immediate predecessor to activity B (selecting the cast). Similarly, since sets can't be built without lumber, paint, and other materials, activity E (buying materials for the sets) is an immediate predecessor for activity G (building the sets).

Using the Critical Path Method to Focus Efforts Now look at Exhibit 16.4, which is a CPM network for the theatre project. This network shows how all of the activities in the theatre project are related to one another. The direction of the arrows shows the immediate predecessors for each activity. Notice that arrows go from activities B (selecting the cast) *and* F (purchasing material for the costumes) to activity H (making the costumes). This indicates that *both* of these activities are immediate predecessors for

activity H—the costumes can't be made without material, and they must be made in the correct sizes to fit the actors. But also notice that no arrow links activities B and C. This shows that these are independent activities; in other words, the theatre company doesn't have to select the cast before it designs the sets (or vice versa).

We can use Exhibit 16.4 to illustrate some basic concepts used in CPM analysis. A *path* is a sequence of activities that *must be completed in the order specified by the arrows* for the overall project to be completed. You can trace several paths in our example by following a series of arrows from start to finish. For example, one path is A → B → I → J → K, and another path is A → C → E → G → J → K.

The **critical path** consists of the sequence of activities that takes the longest to complete. A *delay in any activity on a critical path is likely to delay the completion of the entire project*. Thus, operations managers watch activities on the critical path

critical path method (CPM) A project management tool that illustrates the relationships among all the activities involved in completing a project and identifies the sequence of activities likely to take the longest to complete.

immediate predecessors Activities in a project that must be completed before some other specified activity can begin.

critical path The sequence of activities in a project that is expected to take the longest to complete.

Exhibit 16.4 · A CPM Network for Staging a Play

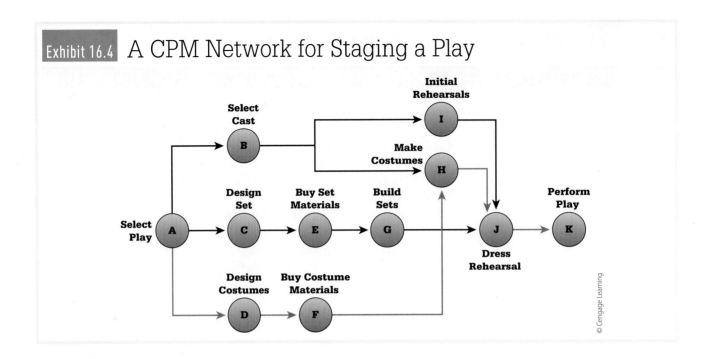

© Cengage Learning

very carefully and take actions to help ensure they remain on schedule. We've shown the critical path for the theatre project (A → D → F → H → J → K) with red arrows on our diagram.

Distinguishing between the critical path and other paths can help operations managers allocate resources more efficiently. Activities that aren't on the critical path can be delayed without causing a delay in the overall completion of the project—as long as the delay isn't too great. In CPM terminology, these activities have *slack*. When operations managers see delays in critical path activities, they may be able to keep the project on track by diverting manpower and other resources from activities with slack to activities on the critical path.

value chain The network of relationships that channels the flow of inputs, information, and financial resources through all of the processes directly or indirectly involved in producing goods and services and distributing them to customers.

vertical integration Performance of processes internally that were previously performed by other organizations in a supply chain.

outsourcing Arranging for other organizations to perform supply chain functions that were previously performed internally.

16-2e Designing and Managing Value Chains

Perhaps the most important function of operations management is the design and management of value chains. A **value chain** is the network of relationships that channels the flow of inputs, information, and financial resources through all of the processes directly or indirectly involved in producing goods and services and distributing them to customers.

An organization's value chain clearly includes its supply chain, which consists of the organizations, activities, and processes involved in the physical flow of goods, from the raw materials stage to the final consumer. In fact, some organizations use the terms *value chain* and *supply chain* interchangeably. But a value chain is a broader concept; in addition to the supply chain, it includes activities and processes involved in *acquiring customers*—such as contract negotiations and customer financing—as well as activities and processes involved in *keeping customers* by providing services after the sale, such as performing warranty repairs, offering call centre assistance, and helping customers recycle used goods. In a value chain, the main focus is on the customer; in contrast, the supply chain is more oriented towards traditional production relationships.[2]

One of the most important issues that operations managers examine when they design value chains is the tradeoff between vertical integration and outsourcing. **Vertical integration** occurs when a firm attempts to gain more control over its value chain by either developing the ability to perform processes previously performed by other organizations in the chain or by acquiring those organizations. **Outsourcing** is essentially the opposite of vertical integration; it involves arranging for other organizations to perform value chain functions that were previously performed internally.

In recent years, the trend in value chain design has been to rely more on outsourcing and less on vertical integration. Outsourcing allows a firm to shed functions it doesn't perform well in order to focus on its areas of strength.

It also frees people, money, and other resources that had been tied up in the outsourced activities, allowing these resources to be employed in more profitable ways.

Even when a firm decides to perform processes itself, it still faces a choice: should it perform these functions domestically, or should it offshore these activities? **Offshoring** means moving processes previously performed domestically to a foreign location. It is important to realize that offshoring is *not* the same thing as outsourcing processes to other organizations. Offshoring doesn't require outsourcing; a firm often offshores processes by directly investing in its *own* foreign facilities. Similarly, outsourcing doesn't require a firm to go offshore; activities can be outsourced to other *domestic* firms. Despite this distinction, many firms have combined these approaches by hiring organizations in other countries to perform some of the processes that they previously performed at their own domestic facilities.

It is also worth noting that offshoring can go in both directions. Just as Canadian firms offshore processes to other countries, some foreign companies offshore some of their processes to Canada. For example, several Japanese automakers now have production facilities in Canada.

One common reason for offshoring by Canadian firms is to take advantage of less expensive labour. But other factors can also play a role. Land and other resources may be less expensive in developing nations than in Canada. And some foreign governments, eager to attract investments, may offer financial incentives or other inducements. In addition, many foreign markets are growing much more rapidly than the relatively mature Canadian market. Firms often find it advantageous to locate production facilities close to these rapidly growing markets.

While foreign outsourcing can often reduce costs, it also can complicate value chains and create coordination problems. And it can expose the firm to certain types of risks. When a firm outsources important functions, it may have to entrust others in its value chain with confidential information and intellectual property, such as copyrighted materials or patented designs. These strategic assets have less legal protection in some countries than in Canada, so providing access to foreign firms may increase the risk that the firm's intellectual property will be pirated or counterfeited. This issue has been of greatest concern when firms have outsourced some of their supply chain functions to organizations in China.[3]

Given the trend towards offshoring and outsourcing, value chains (and the supply chains at their core) have become increasingly complex, often involving many different organizations and processes located in many different countries. Modern operations managers rely on sophisticated *supply chain management software* to streamline the communications among supply chain participants and to help them plan and coordinate their efforts.

The newest versions of **enterprise resource planning (ERP)** software take supply chain management to its highest level. ERP initially focused on integrating the flow of information among *all* aspects of a single organization's operations—accounting, finance, sales and marketing, production, and human resources. But the newest versions go beyond a single organization to help manage activities along an entire supply chain or value chain. The common information system makes it easier for organizations throughout the chain to communicate and coordinate their activities.

ERP systems do have some drawbacks. They are complex, expensive, and difficult to implement, and they require users to learn new ways to enter and access data. Productivity can actually fall until users become accustomed to these new methods. Despite these challenges, ERP systems have become very popular. And they continue to evolve and take advantage of new technologies. One of the newest developments is the arrival of Web-based ERP systems that can be "rented" from online providers—a strategy that reduces the need to invest in new hardware and software. Web-based ERP services are an example of a relatively new trend in IT known as *cloud computing*.[4]

16-3 Implications of a Service-Based Economy: Responding to Different Challenges

Exhibit 16.5 illustrates how services differ from tangible goods. These differences present a number of challenges to service providers. One key challenge arises because customers often participate in the provision of services, which means that service providers have less control over how the process is carried out, how long it takes to complete, and whether the result is satisfactory. For instance, the accuracy of a doctor's diagnosis depends on how honestly and completely the patient answers the doctor's questions. And the amount of time the doctor spends with each patient will depend on the seriousness of the problem and the complexity of the diagnosis and treatment.

offshoring Moving production or support processes to foreign countries.

enterprise resource planning (ERP) Software-based approach to integrate an organization's (and in the sophisticated versions, a value chain's) information flows.

Exhibit 16.5 Differences between Goods and Services

GOODS	SERVICES
Are tangible: They have a physical form and can be seen, touched, handled, etc.	Are intangible: They can be "experienced," but they don't have a physical form.
Can be stored in an inventory.	Must be consumed *when* they are produced.
Can be shipped.	Must be consumed *where* they are provided.
Are produced independently of the consumer.	Often require the customer to be actively involved in their production.
Can have at least *some* aspects of their quality determined objectively by measuring defects or deviations from desired values.	Intangible nature means quality is based mainly on customer perceptions.

© Cengage Learning

16-3a Designing the Servicescape

Because of the interaction between customers and service providers, the design of service facilities often must take the experiences of the participants into account. A **servicescape** is the environment in which the customer and service provider interact. A well-designed servicescape can have a positive influence on the attitudes and perceptions of both the customer and those who provide the service. A poor servicescape can have the opposite effect.[5]

The design of servicescapes centres on three types of factors: ambience; functionality; and signs, symbols, and artifacts.

- *Ambience* refers to factors such as decor, background music, lighting, noise levels, and even scents. For example, massage therapists often use low light, soothing background music, and pleasant scents to create a relaxing atmosphere for a massage.

- *Functionality* involves how easy is it for the customer to move through the facility and find what they are looking for.

- *Signs, symbols,* and *artifacts* convey information to customers and create impressions. Obviously, signs like "Place Your Order Here" and "Pick Up Your Order Here" provide useful information that helps consumers manoeuvre through the service encounter. But other signs and symbols can be used to create favourable impressions. For instance, lawyers and accountants often prominently display their diplomas, professional certifications, and awards in their offices to communicate their qualifications and accomplishments to their clients.

servicescape The environment in which a customer and service provider interact.

16-3b How Big Is Big Enough?

Because services are intangible and often must be experienced at the time they are created, service providers can't produce the service in advance and store it to meet temporary surges in demand. This can create challenges for operations managers because the demand for many types of services varies significantly, depending on the season, the day of the week, or the time of day. During peak lunch and dinner hours, popular restaurants tend to be very busy—often with crowds waiting to get a table. The same restaurants may be nearly empty during the mid-afternoon or late at night. Given such fluctuations in demand, the selection of *capacity*—the number of customers the service facility can accommodate per time period—becomes a crucial consideration.

If the capacity of a service facility is too small, customers facing long waits during periods of peak demand may well take their business elsewhere. But a facility large enough to handle peak capacity is more expensive to build; costs more to heat, cool, and insure; and may have substantial excess capacity during off-peak periods. Operations managers must weigh these drawbacks against the ability to handle a larger number of customers during peak hours.

Many service firms try to minimize this tradeoff by finding ways to spread out demand so that big surges don't occur. One way to do this is to give customers an incentive to use the service at off-peak times. Many bars and restaurants have "happy hours" or "early-bird specials." Similarly, movie theatres have lower prices for matinee showings, and resort hotels offer reduced rates during their off seasons.

16-4 The Technology of Operations

Now let's take a close look at how technology has revolutionized operations management. Some new technologies involve increasingly sophisticated machinery and equipment. Others reflect advances in software and IT. The impact of these advances is greatest when the automated machinery is directly linked to the new software running on powerful new computers.

16-4a Automation: The Rise of the Machine

For the past half-century, one of the biggest trends in operations management has been the increased **automation** of many processes. Automation means replacing human operation and control of machinery and equipment with some form of programmed control. Automated systems have become increasingly common and increasingly sophisticated.

Automation began in the early 1950s with primitive programmed machines. In recent decades, **robots** have taken automation to a whole new level. Robots are reprogrammable machines that can manipulate materials, tools, parts, and specialized devices in order to perform a variety of tasks. Some robots have special sensors that allow them to "see," "hear," or "feel" their environment. Many robots are mobile and can even be guided over rugged terrain.

Firms have found that robots offer many advantages:

- They often perform jobs that most human workers find tedious, dirty, dangerous, or physically demanding.

- They don't get tired, so they can work very long hours while maintaining a consistently high level of performance.

- They are flexible; unlike old dogs, robots *can* be taught new tricks because they are reprogrammable.

Robots are most commonly used for tasks such as welding, spray painting, and assembling products, but they can do many other things ranging from packaging frozen pizza to disposing of hazardous wastes.

16-4b Software Technologies

Several types of software have become common in operations management, and as the processing power of computers has improved, the capabilities of these applications have become increasingly sophisticated. Some of the most common examples include:

- **Computer-aided design (CAD)** software provides powerful drawing and drafting tools that enable users to create and edit blueprints and design drawings quickly and easily. Current CAD programs allow users to create three-dimensional drawings.

- **Computer-aided engineering (CAE)** software enables users to test, analyze, and optimize their designs through computer simulations. CAE software can help engineers find and correct design flaws *before* production.

- **Computer-aided manufacturing (CAM)** software takes the electronic design for a product and creates the programmed instructions that robots and other automated equipment must follow to produce that product as efficiently as possible.

Today, computer-aided design and computer-aided manufacturing software are often combined into a single system, called **CAD/CAM**. This enables CAD designs to flow directly to CAM programs, which then send instructions directly to the automated equipment on the factory floor to guide the production process.

When a CAD/CAM software system is integrated with robots and other high-tech equipment, the result is **computer-integrated manufacturing (CIM)**, in which the whole design and production process is highly automated. The speed of computers, the ability to reprogram computers rapidly, and the integration of all these functions make it possible to switch from the design and production of one good to that of another quickly and efficiently. CIM allows firms to produce custom-designed products for individual consumers quickly and at costs almost as low as those associated with mass production techniques, thus allowing firms to pursue the strategy of mass customization mentioned at the beginning of this chapter.

16-5 Focus on Quality

Almost everyone agrees that quality is important. But the concept of quality is tough to define—even expert opinions differ. For our purposes, we'll adopt the view that quality is defined in terms of how well a good or service satisfies customer preferences.

Why is quality so important? First, better quality clearly improves effectiveness (creates value) since consumers perceive high-quality goods as having greater value than low-quality goods. Also, finding ways to increase quality can lead to greater efficiency because the cost of poor quality can be very high. When a firm detects defective products, it must scrap, rework, or repair

---

automation Replacing human operation and control of machinery and equipment with some form of programmed control.

robot A reprogrammable machine capable of manipulating materials, tools, parts, and specialized devices in order to perform a variety of tasks.

computer-aided design (CAD) Drawing and drafting software that enables users to create and edit blueprints and design drawings quickly and easily.

computer-aided engineering (CAE) Software that enables users to test, analyze, and optimize their designs.

computer-aided manufacturing (CAM) Software that takes the electronic design for a product and creates the programmed instructions that robots must follow to produce that product as efficiently as possible.

(CAD/CAM) A combination of software that can be used to design output and send instructions to automated equipment to perform the steps needed to produce this output.

computer-integrated manufacturing (CIM) A combination of CAD/CAM software with flexible manufacturing systems to automate almost all steps involved in designing, testing, and producing a product.

them. And the costs of poor quality can be even higher when a firm *doesn't* catch defects before shipping products to consumers. These costs include handling customer complaints, warranty repair work, loss of goodwill, and the possibility of bad publicity or lawsuits. In the long run, firms often find that improving quality reduces these costs by more than enough to make up for their investment.

These ideas aren't especially new. W. Edwards Deming, viewed by many as the father of the quality movement, first proposed the relationship between quality and business success in the early 1950s. His ideas, which came to be known as the *Deming Chain Reaction*, are summarized in Exhibit 16.6.

W. Edwards Deming is considered the father of the quality movement.

Klip Brundage/Aurora Photos

Total Quality Management

The first result of this newfound emphasis on quality was the development of an approach called **total quality management (TQM).** There are several variations, but all versions share the following characteristics:

- **Customer focus:** TQM recognizes that quality should be defined by the preferences and perceptions of customers.

- **Emphasis on building quality throughout the organization:** TQM views quality as the concern of every department and every employee.

- **Empowerment of employees:** Most TQM programs give teams of workers the responsibility and authority to make and implement decisions to improve quality.

16-5a Waking Up to the Need for Quality

In the years immediately after the Second World War, most Japanese goods had a reputation for being cheap and shoddy. Then during the 1950s, many Japanese firms sought advice from Deming and other quality gurus. They learned to view quality improvement as a *continuous* process that was the responsibility of all employees in the organization. During the 1950s and 1960s, the quality of Japanese goods slowly but steadily improved.

By the early 1970s, many Japanese firms had achieved a remarkable turnaround, with quality levels that exceeded those of companies in most other countries (including Canada) by a wide margin. This improved quality was a major reason why Japanese firms rapidly gained global market share, often at the expense of North American firms that had faced little competition in years immediately following the Second World War.

16-5b How North American Firms Responded to the Quality Challenge

When operations managers at North American firms realized how far they trailed the Japanese in quality, they made a real effort to change their ways. Like the Japanese a few decades earlier, North American business leaders began to view improving the quality of their goods and services as a key to regaining international competitiveness.

total quality management (TQM) An approach to quality improvement that calls for everyone within an organization to take responsibility for improving quality and that emphasizes the need for a long-term commitment to continuous improvement.

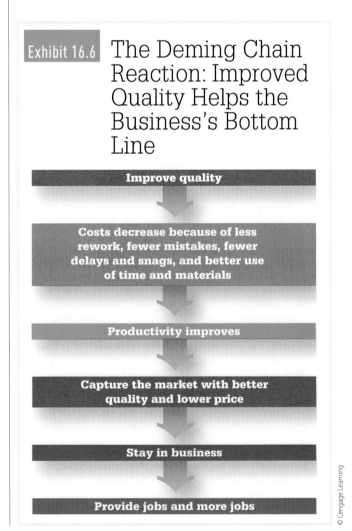

Exhibit 16.6 The Deming Chain Reaction: Improved Quality Helps the Business's Bottom Line

Improve quality

Costs decrease because of less rework, fewer mistakes, fewer delays and snags, and better use of time and materials

Productivity improves

Capture the market with better quality and lower price

Stay in business

Provide jobs and more jobs

© Cengage Learning

ROBOTS MAKE WAREHOUSE WORK EASIER AND MORE EFFICIENT

When you go to the grocery store, you push a shopping cart up and down each aisle looking for the items on your list. When you buy something on Amazon.ca to be delivered to your home, the same thing happens. Workers in Amazon's distribution centres walk miles a day finding items stored on shelves and bins, putting them in grocery-style carts, and then pushing the carts to packers, who put customers' orders into boxes for shipping.

But instead of the 20 items that you hunt for in the grocery store, Amazon's "pickers" need to find tens of thousands of items in immense warehouses to fill the thousands of daily customer orders. When orders surge during the holiday shopping season, Amazon increases the staff in its largest centres to handle the increased volume.

But what if there was a way to make Amazon's already efficient distribution centres five times more productive?

Instead of people walking the aisles, imagine orange robots, several feet wide and high, with 5-foot-high shelves atop them, roaming the aisles to retrieve items needed to complete orders. The robots arrive at packing stations, where lights and lasers point out which items on which shelves go into orders. After items are retrieved from its shelves, the robot moves on to other packing stations and the robot behind it moves into the vacated spot, providing the next item in the order.

Kiva Systems sells this robotics warehouse system. Amazon was so impressed with its incredible productivity increases that it paid $775 million to buy the company.[6]

Sources: G. Fowler, "Holiday Hiring Call: People vs. Robots," *The Wall Street Journal*, December 20, 2010; R. Greenfield, "Meet the Little Orange Robots Making Amazon's Warehouses More Humane," March 20, 2012; J. Letzing, "Amazon Adds That Robotic Touch," *The Wall Street Journal*, March 20, 2012; M. Wohlsen, "Warehouse 'Bots' Do Battle to Make Same-Day Delivery a Reality," *Wired*, September 28, 2012.

Amazon.com screenshot detail

- **Focus on prevention rather than correction:** TQM pursues a strategy of preventing mistakes that create defects.

- **Long-run commitment to continuous improvement:** TQM requires firms to adopt a focus on making improvements in quality a way of life.

In many cases, North American firms using TQM attempt to reduce defects by applying techniques that make the manufacturing process "mistake proof." These techniques are often simple procedures built into the production process that either prevent workers from making mistakes or help workers quickly catch and correct mistakes if they do occur. A simple example would be providing assembly workers with "kits" that contain exactly enough parts to complete one unit of work at a time. If the worker completes an assembly and sees a part leftover, it's clear that a mistake has been made, and he or she can correct it on the spot.[7]

The Move to Six Sigma During the 1990s, another approach to quality improvement, known as **Six Sigma**, became increasingly popular. Six Sigma shares some of the same elements as TQM, such as an organization-wide focus on quality, emphasis on finding and eliminating causes of errors or defects (prevention rather than correction), and a long-term focus on continuous quality improvement. Also like TQM, it relies on teams of workers to carry out specific projects to improve quality. At any given time, a firm may have several Six Sigma projects under way, with the goal of each being to achieve the Six Sigma level of quality.

But Six Sigma differs from TQM in other respects. Unlike TQM, it has a single unifying measure: to reduce defects of any operation or process to a level of no more than 3.4 per million opportunities. Attaining this level of quality is a rigorous and challenging goal. Six Sigma also differs from TQM in its reliance on extensive (and expensive) employee training and reliance on expert guidance. The techniques used in the Six Sigma approach are quite advanced, and their application requires a high level of expertise.

16-5c Quality Standards and Quality Initiatives

Firms also try to implement quality improvement by launching programs designed to achieve certification or recognition from outside authorities. Two common approaches are to participate in national quality programs and to seek certification under the International Organization for Standardization's ISO 9000 standards.

> **Six Sigma** An approach to quality improvement characterized by very ambitious quality goals, extensive training of employees, and a long-term commitment to working on quality-related issues.

APPLE STORES: PREDICTED TO FAIL, HAVE HIGHEST SALES IN RETAIL

When launched a decade ago, Apple's retail stores were widely predicted to fail. This year, more than one quarter billion people will visit Apple's 326 stores, or four times the number of visitors to Walt Disney's four largest theme parks. Why? Quality built on problem solving, highly trained staff, and a customer focus built around empathy.

At Apple stores, high-quality service rests on a sales philosophy of not selling but helping customers solve problems. The Apple training manual reads: "Your job is to understand all of your customers' needs—some of which they may not even realize they have." David Ambrose, a former Apple store employee, says: "You were never trying to close a sale. It was about finding solutions for a customer and finding their pain points."

Apple "geniuses," who staff the "Genius Bars" in each store, are trained at Apple headquarters and "can take care of everything from troubleshooting your problems to actual repairs." Geniuses are regularly tested on their knowledge and problem-solving skills to maintain their certification. Other Apple store employees are highly trained and are not allowed to help customers until they've spent two to four weeks shadowing experienced store employees.

The acronym APPLE instructs employees how to empathetically engage with customers: "Approach customers with a personalized warm welcome," "Probe politely to understand all the customer's needs," "Present a solution for the customer to take home today," "Listen for and resolve any issues or concerns," and "End with a fond farewell and an invitation to return." And when customers are frustrated and become emotional, the advice is to "Listen and limit your responses to simple reassurances that you are doing so. 'Uh-huh,' 'I understand,' etc."

The results from Apple's retail approach speak for themselves: Apple retail sales average $4,406 per square foot, higher than Tiffany jewellery stores ($3,070), Coach luxury retail ($1,776), and Best Buy ($880), a full-service computer and electronics store.[8]

pio3/Shutterstock.com

In Canada, **Excellence Canada** (formerly the National Quality Institute, or NQI) has certification and training programs and annually recognizes organizations with the Canada Awards for Excellence. Founded by Industry Canada, Excellence Canada began in 1992. The organization has developed several training programs relating to quality, customer service, and process management. The mission of Excellence Canada is to help improve organizational performance and recognize excellence.[9]

The United States has the **Baldrige National Quality Program**. The US Congress passed the Malcolm Baldrige National Quality Improvement Act of 1987 in an effort to encourage American firms to become more competi-

> **Quality is more than quantity. One home run is much better than two doubles.**
>
> Steve Jobs, co-founder of Apple

tive in the global economy by pursuing improvements in quality and productivity. As with the Canadian awards, companies participating in this program receive benefits even if they don't win the award.[10]

ISO 9000 Certification Founded in 1947, ISO is a network of national standards institutes in more than 162 nations that have worked together to develop over 19,500 international standards for a wide variety of industries. ISO standards ensure that goods produced in one country will meet the requirements of buyers in another country. This benefits consumers by enabling them to buy from foreign sellers with confidence; the result is greater choice. It also benefits sellers by allowing them to compete more successfully in global markets.[11]

Most of the standards established by the ISO are industry-specific. But in 1987, the ISO developed and published the **ISO 9000** family of standards. The goal of this effort was to articulate an international consensus on good quality-management practices that could be applied to virtually any company. Similar to the other

Excellence Canada (formerly the National Quality Institute, or NQI) A national program established by Industry Canada in 1992 to promote quality improvements and healthy workplaces.

Baldrige National Quality Program A national program to encourage American firms to focus on quality improvement.

ISO 9000 A family of generic standards for quality management systems established by the International Organization for Standardization.

SMALL CHANGES IN RESTAURANT OPERATIONS LEAD TO BIG SAVINGS AND PRODUCTIVITY

1001nights/iStockphoto.com

In all businesses, doing more with less is the core of operations management. Increasing productivity is particularly important in low-profit-margin industries, such as restaurants, where relatively small cost decreases and speed increases can mean the difference between being profitable and going out of business. So what do restaurants do to be more efficient and effective without hurting food quality and service?

- At a restaurant in a major tourist area, which serves 1,400 diners on Saturday nights, the $39 Chilean Sea Bass is partly cooked for 5 minutes at 1 P.M., for 5 more minutes at 6 P.M., and then for 1 more minute just before being served at dinner.

- A steak house reduced costs by ordering meat from one vendor, increasing volume price discounts, and decreasing delivery costs, producing annual savings of $8,000 per restaurant.

- At a fast food chicken restaurant, they quit using chicken diapers (not what you think) to absorb the liquid in packaged chicken shipped to restaurants, saving $800,000 a year.

- A pizza restaurant saved $164,000 a year by eliminating small pizza boxes.

- Speed is another way to increase productivity. The customers at one coffee and doughnut restaurant can now use a smartphone app to pay, saving six seconds per order.

- Finally, at another restaurant, shift managers post the cost of martini glasses, $2.61, and spoons, $1.90, to remind staff to avoid breakage or accidentally throwing them in the trash.[12]

© Courtesy of Stoner, Inc. and NIST

Many leading companies now make quality the responsibility of every employee in every department.

quality initiatives we've discussed, ISO 9000 standards define quality in terms of the ability to satisfy customer preferences and require the firm to implement procedures for continuous quality improvement.

There are several standards in the ISO 9000 family, but it is ISO 9001 that specifies the requirements for a quality-management system. (Other ISO 9000 standards are concerned with documentation, training, and the economic and financial aspects of quality management.) More than 160 countries have national standards organizations that participate in the ISO. These countries have representatives that sit on committees that have developed over 19,000 international standards.[13]

16-6 The Move to Be Lean and Green: Cutting Costs and Cutting Waste

Lean production refers to a set of strategies and practices to eliminate waste, which is defined as any function or activity that uses resources but doesn't create value. Eliminating waste can lead to dramatic improvements in efficiency. For example, Louis Vuitton produces

> **lean production** An approach to production that emphasizes the elimination of waste in all aspects of production processes.

some of the most expensive handmade bags and purses in the world. To increase productivity, it switched to teams of 6 to 12 workers who learned to complete multiple production steps. So instead of having three workers separately gluing, stitching, and finishing the edges of a flap over and over, one worker would do all three steps. Because of that, says CEO Ives Carcelle, "We were able to hire 300 new people without adding a factory."[14]

16-6a Reducing Investment in Inventory: Just-in-Time to the Rescue

One of the hallmarks of lean systems is tight control on inventories. In part, this reflects recognition of the costs of holding large inventories. But the lean approach offers another reason for minimizing inventories. Large inventories serve as a buffer that enables the firm to continue operations when problems arise due to poor quality, faulty equipment, or unreliable suppliers. This makes it easier for firms to live with these problems rather than correct them. Advocates of lean production argue that, in the long run, it is more efficient to improve quality, keep equipment in good working order, and develop reliable supply relationships than to continue compensating for these problems by holding large inventories.

Lean manufacturing avoids overproduction and holding large inventories of finished goods by using **just-in-time (JIT) production** methods. The JIT approach produces only enough goods to satisfy current demand. This approach is called a *pull system* because actual orders "pull" the goods through the production process. The workers at the end of the production process produce just enough of the final product to satisfy actual orders and use just enough parts and materials from preceding stages of production to satisfy their needs. Workers at each earlier stage are expected to produce just enough output at their workstations to replace the amount used by the processes further along the process— and in so doing, they withdraw just the needed amount of parts and other supplies from even earlier processes.

JIT techniques obviously result in very small inventories of finished goods and work-in-process. But lean firms also hold only small inventories of materials and parts, counting on suppliers to provide them with these items as they need them to meet current demand. In a lean system, all organizations in the supply chain use the JIT approach so that inventories are minimized at each stage. Clearly, this type of system requires incredible coordination among all parts of the supply chain; in fact, the movement towards JIT is a key reason why supply chain management has become so crucial.

just-in-time (JIT) production A production system that emphasizes the production of goods to meet actual current demand, thus minimizing the need to hold inventories of finished goods and work-in-process at each stage of the supply chain.

Ultra-Lean Production: Subaru's Zero-Landfill Automobile Plant

Most companies using lean production techniques eliminate waste to decrease costs. Subaru Motors' North American assembly plant in the United States eliminates waste to decrease costs *and* improve the environment. Its goal: to be a zero-landfill manufacturer and eliminate 100 million annual pounds of landfill waste.

When it began, its managers started "dumpster diving" to analyze and eliminate everything that went into its onsite dumpsters. Denise Coogan, manager of safety and environmental compliance, says: "I'd get into a suit and go into the dumpster and look at what was being thrown out each day." Thanks to dumpster diving, Subaru eliminated 100 pounds of scrap steel per car by asking suppliers to make steel rolls in the exact sizes needed for each part.

Subaru previously used a robot-based method of welding steel car frames that produced slag, a waste-metal byproduct. Subaru found a Spanish company that used the copper in slag as an input for its manufacturing process. At first, Subaru increased its costs and reduced landfill waste by paying the Spanish company to take the slag, also paying shipping costs from the United States to Spain. Eventually, however, Subaru came up with a new welding method that reduced slag by 75 percent, thus reducing landfill waste and its costs.

At Subaru, 99.9 percent of waste is recycled or reused as raw materials. Wood pallets are reused and then shredded into mulch for gardens. Misshapen plastic bumpers are ground into plastic pellets, which are then melted and reshaped into new bumpers. Even Styrofoam, used to ship and protect engine parts from Japan to the United States, is reused up to seven times before being recycled. Subaru ships back 930 tons of Styrofoam to Japan each year to be reused to ship parts back to the plant. Even with the shipping costs, that saves about $1.5 million each year.

How well has Subaru's plant performed relative to its zero-landfill goal? For over a decade, it hasn't sent any waste to a landfill. None. To put that in perspective, Subaru's automotive plant produces less waste than your family does on a daily basis.[15]

JIT does have some potential drawbacks. The most serious problem is that it can leave producers vulnerable to supply disruptions. If a key supplier is unable to make deliveries due to a natural disaster or some other problem, the firms farther down the supply chain may quickly run out of supplies and have to shut down production.

16-6b Lean Thinking in the Service Sector

Employing lean principles in the service sector can be quite a challenge because customers often participate in providing the service. This means that a service firm usually has less control over how processes are conducted. But many service firms have benefited from creatively applying lean techniques. WestJet Airlines is well known for its efforts to reduce waste. It uses only one type of aircraft (the Boeing 737) to standardize maintenance and minimize training costs. WestJet uses self-service check-in kiosks and paperless boarding passes in order to streamline the process of moving passengers through the airport. The company has won several awards for its innovative programs as well as for its corporate culture, including being named one of Canada's Top 100 Employers.[16]

16-6c Green Practices: Helping the Firm by Helping the Environment

Many of today's leading firms have also tried to become "greener" by finding environmentally friendly ways to carry out the processes needed to produce and distribute their goods and services. Green practices include designing facilities to be more energy efficient; using renewable energy sources such as wind, solar, or geothermal power when possible; making use of recyclable materials; switching to paints, lubricants, cleaning fluids, and solvents that are less harmful to the environment; and even providing labelling to help consumers find out which products are the most environmentally friendly.

The long-term goal of many green practices is to achieve *sustainability*, which means finding ways to meet the organization's current objectives while protecting and preserving the environment for future generations. One impediment to even greater acceptance of sustainability initiatives is that some sustainability efforts—such as switching to renewable sources of energy—add to costs.[17] But many firms have found that other sustainability efforts can actually benefit the bottom line. A recent study found that firms employing best-in-class sustainability practices not only saw an 8 percent drop in sustainability-related costs but also experienced a 16 percent increase in customer retention.[18]

In the late 1990s, the International Organization for Standardization developed a set of standards called **ISO 14000**. This new set of standards focuses on environmental management. As with ISO 9000, the term ISO 14000 actually refers to a family of standards. The broadest of these is ISO 14001. In order to receive ISO 14001 certification, a firm must:

- demonstrate the ability to identify and control the environmental impact of their activities,
- make a commitment to continually improve their environmental performance, and
- implement a systematic approach to setting environmental targets and to achieving those targets.

It is important to note that ISO 14000 standards do not establish specific goals for environmental performance; doing so would be very difficult, since ISO is intended to be a generic set of standards that apply to all industries, and each specific industry faces different environmental challenges.[19]

> **ISO 14000** A family of generic standards for environmental management established by the International Organization for Standardization.

O perations managers are responsible for "putting it all together" by developing and implementing the processes needed to produce goods and services and distribute them to the target market. Their decisions affect both revenues and costs, going a long way towards determining whether a firm makes a profit or suffers a loss.

The responsibilities of operations managers require them to work closely with other managers throughout their organizations. For example, they must work with marketers and designers to ensure that the desired goods and services move from the drawing board to the final customer on time and within budget. They must work closely with financial managers to ensure that the company invests in the capital goods needed to produce goods and services in the most efficient manner. And they must work effectively with human resources managers to attract and develop workers who possess the knowledge and skills needed to become world-class competitors. Operations managers must even go beyond their own organization and work effectively with the suppliers and distributors who comprise the firm's value chain.

Operations managers must continuously adapt to changes in technology and in competitive conditions. Key challenges in recent years have centred on the need to continuously improve product quality while finding ways to reduce costs and protect the environment. You can expect the goals of becoming ever leaner—and ever greener—to remain a major focus of operations managers in years to come.

careers in operations management:
Plant Supervisor

Responsible for supervising production and warehouse crews, monitoring and maintaining a safe working environment, timely completion of records, keeping lines of communication open between the plant, management, scheduling, and sales, coordinating overtime and reviewing production schedules to make sure each piece of equipment has the appropriate manpower, and cross-training employees for multiple tasks and jobs. The ideal candidate has a bachelor's degree, two to four years of manufacturing experience, strong interpersonal, communication, and team-building skills, good analytical and problem-solving skills, the ability to analyze cost performance data to improve operations and reduce costs, and a willingness to work evenings, night shifts, weekends, and holidays.

STUDY TOOLS 16

IN THE BOOK, YOU CAN:

☐ Rip out the Chapter Review card at the back of the book to have a summary of the chapter and key terms handy.

ONLINE AT NELSON.COM/STUDENT YOU CAN:

☐ Work through key concepts with a Guided Learning Question.

☐ Prepare for tests with quizzes.

☐ Review the key terms with Flash Cards (online or printer-ready).

☐ Explore practical examples of chapter concepts with Connect a Concept exercises.

Appendix 1
Labour Unions and Collective Bargaining

LEARNING OBJECTIVES

After studying this appendix, you will be able to ...

A1-1 Describe the basic structure of unions

A1-2 Discuss the key provisions of the laws that govern labour–management relations

A1-3 Explain how labour contracts are negotiated and administered

A1-4 Evaluate the impact unions have on their members' welfare and the economy

A **labour union** is a group of workers who have organized in order to pursue common work-related goals, such as better wages and benefits, safer working conditions, and greater job security. Few topics in the world of business generate more controversy than labour unions—they have many passionate supporters, but they also have equally fierce detractors. To their supporters, unions protect workers from exploitation by powerful employers, give them a voice in the labour market, and help them achieve a better standard of living. But critics say that unions have undermined the competitiveness of firms in the intensely competitive global marketplace and that they are out of touch with economic reality and the needs of today's workers.

Two terms often used in describing the relationships between unions and management are labour relations and industrial relations. **Labour relations** usually refers to all aspects of union–management relations. **Industrial relations** is a broader term referring to the study of employment in union *and* non-union organizations.[1]

As is the case with many controversial topics, evidence can be found to support the positions of both critics and defenders. The purpose of this appendix is to help you understand the role that unions play in today's economy and the challenges and opportunities unions face as we continue through the second decade of the 21st century.

A1-1 The Basic Structure of Unions

Unions can be organized in two basic ways. **Craft unions** represent workers who have the *same skill* or who work in the *same profession*. Unions representing workers in construction trades and the National Hockey League Players Association (NHLPA) are examples of craft unions. **Industrial unions** represent workers who are employed in the *same industry* regardless of their specific skills or profession. Although industrial unions may have some highly skilled workers among their members, many of the workers they represent are semiskilled or unskilled workers. The Canadian Auto Workers (CAW) union is an example of an industrial union.

labour union A group of workers who have organized to work together to achieve common job-related goals such as higher wages, better working conditions, and greater job security.

labour relations Refers to all aspects of union–management relations.

industrial relations A broad term referring to the study of employment in union and non-union organizations.

craft union A union composed of workers who share the same skill or work in the same profession.

industrial union A union composed of workers employed in the same industry.

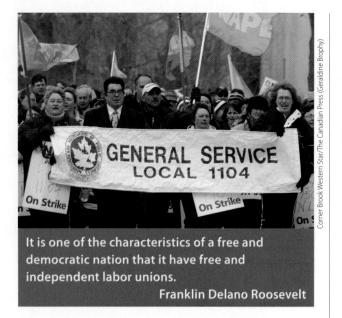

It is one of the characteristics of a free and democratic nation that it have free and independent labor unions.

Franklin Delano Roosevelt

The basic building blocks of a union are its local unions (often just called locals). Most unionized workers interact with their union through their local. The local provides union members with the opportunity to participate directly in union affairs by attending meetings and other union-sponsored functions. The initial stages of a grievance procedure (which we'll describe later in this appendix) are carried out at the local level, and it's usually the locals that organize workers to carry out strike activities when labour disputes arise.

Many Canadians belong to unions that have their head offices in other countries, mainly the United States. These unions are often referred to as *international unions. National unions* are those that operate only in Canada. In many industrial unions, the national union negotiates a master contract, after which each local union negotiates a local contract to address issues and problems unique to its own situation.

Many unions in Canada belong to the Canadian Labour Congress (CLC). This organization provides a high-profile national voice for the labour movement. With more than 3 million members across the country, the CLC can influence government policy with regard to issues such as employment insurance and workplace safety.

National Labor Relations Act (Wagner Act) Landmark pro-labour law enacted in the United States in 1935. This law significantly affected Canadian labour laws.

The CLC represents Canadian workers at international conferences, encourages its members to voice their support for union causes, and provides resources for efforts to increase union membership.[2]

A1-2 Labour Laws

Exhibit A1.1 lists the major federal laws dealing with labour unions and provides a brief description of their key provisions. Notice that the first law was enacted in 1867 as part of the process for Canada to become a country but did not specifically deal with the rights of workers to organize or with the way unions carry out their functions. This lack of legal recognition (and protection) helps explain why the labour movement struggled in our nation's early history.

Like most of Canada's laws, the laws dealing with labour relations were based mainly on British law. However, in later years, Canadian labour relations legislation was greatly influenced by US laws. A significant difference between Canadian laws and those of the United States and the United Kingdom is the division of power between the federal government and the provinces and territories. During some periods in our history, such as the Great Depression years and the Second World War, the federal government enacted labour laws that applied to all workers, but the provinces have regained control of labour legislation. For the most part, labour laws enacted by the provinces and territories are similar in nature.

Early labour relations legislation favoured the employer, with little or no protections for the workers. The **National Labor Relations Act (Wagner Act)**, passed in the United States in 1935, had a significant impact on Canadian law. The *Wagner Act* entrenched the right of employees to join a union and engage in union activities and required companies to bargain in good faith with unions. Canadian law followed this pattern. The federal government strengthened labour relations legislation during the Second World War due mainly to the *War Measures Act*. Under the *War Measures Act*, the federal government took back control of labour relations issues from the provinces. During this period, many provinces took the opportunity to update their own legislation to bring it in line with the federal government's. There was little labour unrest during the war even though wage increases

Exhibit A1.1	History of Federal Labour Legislation in Canada[3]	

DATE	LAW	MAJOR PROVISIONS
1867	*Constitution Act* (originally the *British North America Act*)	■ Outlined what the federal government had jurisdiction over and what the provinces had jurisdiction over ■ Gave provinces authority over labour issues except for certain industries such as shipping and national railways
1872	*Trade Union Act*	■ Allowed workers to organize
1872	*Criminal Amendment Act*	■ Made violence and intimidation illegal during strikes or attempts to unionize
1900	*Conciliation Act*	■ Allowed the Minister of Labour to appoint conciliation officers or board to settle industrial disputes
1903	*Railway Labour Disputes Act*	■ Allowed the federal government to appoint a three-person conciliation board
1906	*Conciliation and Labour Act*	■ Updated previous acts
1907	*Industrial Disputes Investigation Act*	■ Required that any strike or lockout be postponed until the dispute was investigated
1944	*Industrial Disputes Investigations Act* replaced by Order in Council	■ Right to form and join unions ■ Protection against unfair labour practices ■ Compulsory collective bargaining
1948	*Industrial Relations and Disputes Act*	■ Compulsory union recognition and bargaining ■ Compulsory conciliation
1967	*Public Service Staff Relations Act*	■ Gave federal government employees the right to bargain collectively
1970	*Canada Labour Code*	■ Applied only to employees under federal jurisdiction

Sources: Frank Kehoe and Maurice Archer, *Canadian Industrial Relations: Text, Cases & Simulations*, 11th ed., Century Labour Publications; "Average Hourly Wages of Employees by Selected Characteristics and Profession, Unadjusted Data, by Province (Monthly)," Statistics Canada website, www.statcan.gc.ca, accessed July 19, 2009.

were minimal when given at all. Workers and unions were asked to do their part for the war effort, and they generally did so. The postwar period was not so calm. Many unions called strikes to back up their demands for wage increases.

The *Canada Labour Code* covers labour relations issues for firms operating under federal jurisdiction. This law covers four main areas: industrial relations regulations, fair employment practices, employee safety and standardized working conditions (such as number of hours worked), and wages. The industrial relations regulations cover issues such as a worker's right to join a union, how unions will be certified, and procedures for bargaining. The fair employment section prohibits an employer from discriminating on grounds such as a person's race or religion during the hiring process. The safety of employees section sets the requirements for healthy and safe work environments.

The section dealing with hours worked and wages covers issues such as minimum wage requirements, maximum number of hours worked, and the requirement to pay overtime and provide vacation time. This section is included so that employees will be treated consistently regardless of where they work. Most provinces have enacted similar legislation to cover workers where the *Canada Labour Code* does not apply. Exhibit A1.2 shows the number of Canadians who belong to unions.

Number of Canadians Who Belong to a Union or Have Union Coverage (as of September 2015)[4]

	UNION COVERAGE (THOUSANDS)	% CHANGE (SEPTEMBER 2014 TO SEPTEMBER 2015)
CANADA	4,721.6	31.1
NEWFOUNDLAND AND LABRADOR	80.7	−4.4
PRINCE EDWARD ISLAND	22.0	5.3
NOVA SCOTIA	126.1	6.9
NEW BRUNSWICK	92.3	−1.3
QUEBEC	1,427.7	1.7
ONTARIO	1,555.4	−3.4
MANITOBA	204.5	4.9
SASKATCHEWAN	151.2	−2.5
ALBERTA	460.0	9.1
BRITISH COLUMBIA	601.6	5.8

Sources: "Average Hourly Wages of Employees by Selected Characteristics and Occupation, Unadjusted Data, by Province (Monthly)," Statistics Canada website, www.statcan.gc.ca, accessed October 12, 2015.

A1-3 Collective Bargaining: Reaching an Agreement

Collective bargaining is the process by which representatives of union members and employers attempt to negotiate a mutually acceptable labour agreement. By law, both sides must bargain in good faith, meaning that they must take the process seriously and make an effort to reach an agreement that is acceptable to both sides.

A1-3a Subjects of Bargaining

There is no set list of topics that are always discussed during collective bargaining, but certain subjects are *mandatory subjects of bargaining*. Mandatory topics are those that deal with wages and benefits, hours of work, and other terms directly related to working conditions. If one side makes a proposal covering one of these topics, the other side cannot legally refuse to discuss it. For instance, if the union proposes a pay raise or a more flexible work schedule, a refusal by management to engage in good faith discussions concerning these proposals would be an unfair labour practice.

Unions and management sometimes want to discuss topics beyond the mandatory subjects. In general, as long as a topic doesn't involve a violation of the law, these other topics are considered *permissible* subjects of bargaining. That is, the two sides are free to bargain over them, but neither side can be *required* to do so. Proposals to engage in illegal activities—such as a proposal that would involve discrimination against older workers—aren't permissible.

A1-3b Approaches to Collective Bargaining

There are two basic approaches to collective bargaining: distributive bargaining and interest-based bargaining.

Distributive bargaining is the traditional approach to collective bargaining. The two sides negotiate, but they don't explicitly cooperate. Each side usually assumes that a gain for one party is a loss for the other, resulting in an adversarial bargaining environment.

In distributive bargaining, the two parties typically enter negotiations with predetermined positions and specific proposals. In fact, union negotiators often present

collective bargaining The process by which representatives of union members and employers attempt to negotiate a mutually acceptable labour agreement.

distributive bargaining The traditional adversarial approach to collective bargaining.

a long "laundry list" of demands at the beginning of negotiations. Many of the demands may be inflated in order to give the negotiators some room to bargain. For example, the union may initially demand a 10 percent raise, even though it knows that the employer will never agree to a raise that large. Sometimes, management negotiators offer their own demands at the beginning of the negotiation; in other cases, they simply receive the union proposals and promise to respond at a future bargaining session.

After the two sides have presented their initial positions, they work through the specific demands, with each side accepting, rejecting, or making counter-proposals in response to positions taken by the other side. This is often a very time-consuming process. The parties use every persuasive technique at their disposal—including logic, flattery, and blustery threats—to convince the other side to accept (or at least move closer to) their positions. The possibility of a strike or lockout often becomes a major concern if the two sides struggle to reach agreements.

Interest-based bargaining takes a different approach. Rather than beginning with predetermined positions and a long list of inflated demands, each side identifies concerns it wants to discuss. During the negotiations, the two sides explore the issues in depth and work together to find mutually acceptable solutions. They often form teams consisting of members from both sides to work on specific issues. The goal is to find a "win–win" outcome that benefits both sides.

The success of interest-based bargaining hinges on the ability of the two sides to establish and maintain a high level of trust. Both sides must be willing to share information and explore options with open minds. Such a level of trust isn't always present in the collective bargaining arena, but when it is, interest-based bargaining can be very successful. One report states that interest-based bargaining often "makes it possible to generate and consider options to satisfy particular interests that may never have been considered before."[5]

Regardless of the approach the parties take to collective bargaining, the contract doesn't become official until the employees covered under the contract ratify it. The exact ratification procedure varies among unions, but it almost always requires a majority of union members to vote in favour of the agreement.

A1-3c Dealing with Impasse

Collective bargaining negotiations don't always proceed smoothly towards settlement. Sometimes after months of effort, the two sides find that they remain so far apart on one or more issues that they see no way to reach a settlement—a situation known as an *impasse*. In such cases, one of the two sides may try to pressure the other

Rick Madonik/Toronto Star via Getty Images

Past contract negotiations between auto workers union and General Motors.

to change its position by calling for a work stoppage. A **strike** occurs when the workers initiate the stoppage by refusing to report to work. A **lockout** occurs when the employer refuses to allow workers access to their work site. Lockouts, although rare, have become more common in recent years. Some high-profile lockouts have occurred in professional sports. The National Hockey League owners declared a lockout that ultimately resulted in the cancellation of the entire 2004–05 NHL season.[6]

During a work stoppage, unions often use picketing and boycotts to apply additional pressure to the employer. **Picketing** occurs when workers walk outside the employer's place of business carrying signs to inform the public about their position. Workers belonging to other unions often support the striking workers by refusing to cross the picket line. Picketing is legal as long as it's peaceful and as long as picketers don't prevent people who don't support the union's position from entering the business. A **boycott** occurs when striking workers and their supporters refuse to do business with the employer during a

interest-based bargaining A form of collective bargaining that emphasizes cooperation and problem solving in an attempt to find a "win–win" outcome that benefits both sides.

strike A work stoppage initiated by a union.

lockout An employer-initiated work stoppage.

picketing A union tactic during a labour dispute in which union members walk near the entrance of an employer's place of business carrying signs to publicize their position and concerns.

boycott A tactic in which a union and its supporters and sympathizers refuse to do business with an employer with which they have a labour dispute

Striking workers often picket to publicize their position.

labour dispute. This tactic is legal as long as the boycott is limited to the products and services of the firm with which the union has a direct dispute.

Strikes and lockouts are costly to both sides. The workers lose wages, and the employer loses revenue (and perhaps) profits. Unions sometimes pay strike benefits to workers, and workers may be able to find temporary jobs. But these sources of income often fall far short of what the strikers would have earned on their regular jobs.

Businesses often try to continue operating during a strike by using managers and other non-union personnel or by hiring replacement workers—a practice that's become more common in recent years. But it's costly to recruit, select, hire, and train large numbers of new employees. And when the striking workers are highly skilled, it may be impossible to find enough skilled replacement workers to maintain operations.

Because of the costs and uncertainties associated with strikes and lockouts—and the bitterness and resentment that often linger after they end—both unions and employers have an incentive to try to avoid such work stoppages.

Rather than resort to strikes and lockouts when an impasse looms, the two sides sometimes agree to bring in a neutral third party to move the process towards settlement. Two different approaches are possible:

- **Conciliation/mediation** involves bringing in an outsider, who attempts to help the two sides reach an agreement. Conciliation officers and mediators are skilled facilitators who are good at reducing tensions and providing useful suggestions for compromise. The authority of the conciliation officers or mediators and the processes they use vary across the country because these procedures generally fall under provincial jurisdiction.

- **Arbitration** involves bringing in an outsider with the authority to impose a binding settlement on both parties. An arbitrator will listen to both sides, study the issues, and announce a settlement. Arbitration is rare in the case of private-sector collective bargaining, but the public (government) sector uses it frequently to settle disputes.

Administering a Collective Bargaining Agreement

Labour contracts tend to be long, complex documents. Disagreements about how to interpret the various clauses are not unusual. When workers believe that their employer has treated them unfairly under the terms of the contract, they can file a complaint, called a **grievance**. Labour contracts generally spell out a specific procedure for dealing with grievances.

Grievance procedures usually include a number of steps. The first step normally involves informal discussions between the complaining worker and a supervisor. In many cases, an officer of the local union (usually called a *union steward*) becomes involved at this early stage. If the two parties can't settle the grievance informally, the next stage often involves putting the grievance in writing and discussing it with a manager above the supervisor's level. Each successive step involves higher levels of management and union representation. The process continues until the issue is settled or the union drops the complaint. The last step in the grievance procedure normally involves binding arbitration, which means that both parties agree to accept the arbitrator's decision as final.

A1-4 The State of the Unions: Achievements, Problems, and Challenges

Let's conclude our discussion by looking at the impact unions have on the compensation of employees, job security, and worker productivity and at the challenges unions face as they move further into the 21st century.

A1-4a Unions and Compensation

Evidence from a variety of studies suggests that union workers do earn higher wages than non-union workers

conciliation/mediation A method of dealing with an impasse between labour and management that entails bringing in a neutral third party to help the two sides reach agreement by reducing tensions and making suggestions for possible compromises.

arbitration A process in which a neutral third party has the authority to resolve a dispute by rendering a binding decision.

grievance A complaint by a worker that the employer has violated the terms of the collective bargaining agreement.

with similar skills performing similar jobs. Although different studies report somewhat different results, some studies find that, on average, union workers earn as much as 10 to 20 percent more than non-union workers performing similar work—and in some occupations, the differences are even larger. Exhibit A1.3 compares the average hourly wage in September 2015 for union and non-union workers across Canada. In addition to higher wages, union workers also often have better benefits.

A1-4b Unions and Job Security

The terms of labour contracts and the presence of grievance procedures provide due process to workers who are fired or punished for arbitrary reasons. Union workers who believe their employer has unfairly dismissed them can seek reinstatement through the grievance procedure. If their grievance succeeds, their firm may be required to reinstate them and award back pay. Although non-union workers have gained some defences against arbitrary dismissal over the years, their protection isn't as extensive or well defined as it is for union members.

But union workers do face a different type of problem with their job security. It isn't unusual for workers in heavily unionized sectors of the economy to experience layoffs during economic downturns. And many heavily unionized industries in North America have lost jobs due to factors such as automation and steadily increasing foreign competition over the past three decades. Faced with these threats, several unions have agreed to wage cuts and other concessions in an attempt to preserve jobs. Even with these concessions, both temporary layoffs and permanent job losses have remained more common in heavily unionized segments of the economy than in most other sectors of the economy.

A1-4c Unions and Productivity

Critics of labour unions commonly argue that unions negotiate work rules that hurt productivity, which ultimately undermines competitiveness in the global economy. They contend that work rules too often require employers to use more labour than is necessary for various tasks and make it difficult for firms to innovate and introduce more efficient methods. Indeed, critics argue that these union-imposed inefficient work rules are a major reason some firms have lost their ability to compete in the global market.

But defenders of unions argue that unions increase productivity by reducing worker turnover—experienced

Exhibit A1.3 Average Hourly Wage for Union and Non-union Workers across Canada (September 2015)[7]

	UNION ($/HOUR)	NON-UNION ($/HOUR)	DIFFERENCE
CANADA	29.13	23.80	5.33
NEWFOUNDLAND AND LABRADOR	29.12	22.09	7.03
PRINCE EDWARD ISLAND	26.47	17.39	9.08
NOVA SCOTIA	26.47	19.80	6.67
NEW BRUNSWICK	26.92	18.90	8.02
QUEBEC	27.19	21.68	5.51
ONTARIO	30.36	24.30	6.06
MANITOBA	27.38	21.30	6.08
SASKATCHEWAN	28.68	24.45	4.23
ALBERTA	33.56	27.95	5.61
BRITISH COLUMBIA	28.84	23.55	5.29

"Average Hourly Wages of Employees by Selected Characteristics and Occupation, Unadjusted Data, by Province (Monthly)," Statistics Canada website, www.statcan.gc.ca, accessed October 12, 2015.

Job security has become a major concern of many union workers.

Colin McConnell/Toronto Star via Getty Images

workers tend to be more productive than newly hired workers—and by improving worker morale. Some defenders also point out that craft unions often require their workers to undergo extensive training, such as apprenticeship programs, that greatly improves their skills.

Real-world evidence has failed to resolve the issue. Some studies have shown that unions decrease productivity, whereas others have found evidence of increases. These mixed results suggest that productivity doesn't depend so much on whether a plant is unionized but rather on how well management and the union cooperate to find solutions to the challenges they face. That's one of the reasons many labour experts believe that the use of interest-based bargaining holds such promise.[8]

Labour unions have been around for many years, and as the work environment changes, so has the structures of unions. In today's competitive business world, labour unions are facing more challenges and opportunities than ever before. The members of most unions are getting older, and unions are facing the challenge of getting younger workers involved. Economies around the world have been struggling, and this situation puts pressure on unions to compromise on their negotiating positions. Unions are also having to deal with anti-union sentiments.

THE BIG PICTURE

Appendix 2
Business Law

LEARNING OBJECTIVES
After studying this appendix, you will be able to …

A2-1 Explain the purposes of laws and identify the major sources of law in Canada

A2-2 Describe the characteristics of a contract and explain how the terms of contracts are enforced

A2-3 Describe how both title and risk pass from the seller to the buyer when a sale occurs

A2-4 Provide an overview of the legal principles governing agency, intellectual property, and bankruptcy

A-1 The Purpose and Origin of Laws

Laws are those rules governing the conduct and actions of people within a society that are enforceable by the government. Business—in fact, civilization as a whole—simply couldn't function without the rule of law. Can you imagine buying a car, borrowing money, investing in securities, or starting a business if there were no enforceable rules governing these activities? We need laws to accomplish the following:

- Promote stability and order.
- Protect individuals from physical or mental harm.
- Protect property from damage or theft.
- Promote objectives and standards of behaviour that society deems desirable.
- Discourage objectives and standards of behaviour that society deems undesirable.

A2-1a Sources of Law

Just as laws have many purposes, they arise from many sources.

Constitutional Law A **constitution** is a code that establishes the fundamental rules and principles that govern a particular organization or entity. A constitution provides the basis for all other laws within that entity. In Canada, constitutional law establishes and allocates power between the federal and provincial governments and limits government exercise of power. It is the supreme law of Canada. For example, when Canada's tobacco companies challenged British Columbia's *Tobacco Damages and Health Care Costs Recovery Act* as being unconstitutional, the Supreme Court of Canada had to make a ruling. It ultimately declared the act constitutional, by a vote of 9 to 0. Had the court found the act to be in conflict with the Constitution, it would have been declared unconstitutional and thus enforceable.[1]

Statutory Law Legislative bodies enact many more specific laws called **statutory laws**. Federal acts or statutes are laws passed by the Canadian Parliament, comprising the House of Commons and the Senate. To become law, legislation must be passed by the House of Commons and then approved by the Senate. An example is the

laws Rules that govern the conduct and actions of people within a society that are enforced by the government.

constitution A code that establishes the fundamental rules and principles that govern a particular organization or entity.

statutory law Laws that are the result of legislative action.

We are in bondage to the law in order that we may be free.

Marcus Tullius Cicero

Sergign/Shutterstock.com

administrative law Laws that arise from regulations established by government.

common law Laws that result from rulings, called precedents, made by judges who initially hear a particular type of case (also called case law).

Criminal Code of Canada. Provincial acts or statutes are laws passed by provincial legislatures (at the provincial level, there is no Senate). An example is the *Tobacco Control Act of Saskatchewan*. Bylaws are laws passed by city or municipal governments. The legislative bodies are elected town, city, or regional councils. Bylaws address a broad range of issues, from levying business taxes, to requiring business licences, to zoning and parking.

Administrative Law This is one of the primary legal areas where business interacts with government. The best-known sources of **administrative laws**—which are laws established by government agencies—are the federal and provincial commissions and agencies created and given authority to regulate specific types of activities. Often, such activities are commercial. Exhibit A2.1 lists some of these bodies and identifies the areas they regulate. (Keep in mind that this list is far from complete.)

Common (and Civil) Law The body of laws that arise from court decisions is known as common law, or case law. **Common law** governs areas that are not covered by statutory or administrative law. Common law is also used when courts decide on the correct interpretation of statutes or administrative regulations that are in dispute.

When a court that first hears a case dealing with a specific issue renders a decision, it sets a *precedent*. This means that other courts are expected to use this ruling as a guide when hearing cases of a similar nature. Relying on precedents makes the legal process more efficient—courts dealing with the same types of cases don't have to "reinvent the wheel." Precedents also make legal rulings more predictable, so that the parties involved in a dispute know how and why the court is likely to rule. Courts very

Exhibit A2.1 Examples of Federal, Provincial, and Municipal Regulatory Agencies

AGENCY*	MAJOR GOAL OF REGULATION
CANADIAN TRANSPORTATION AGENCY (F)	Manages dispute resolution and economic regulation in the Canadian transportation industry
CANADIAN RADIO-TELEVISION AND TELECOMMUNICATIONS COMMISSION (F)	Regulates and supervises all aspects of the Canadian broadcasting system
CANADIAN WHEAT BOARD (F)	Markets wheat and barley for the best possible price within Canada and internationally on behalf of more than 75 000 western Canadian farmers
NOVA SCOTIA LIQUOR COMMISSION (P)	Regulates alcoholic beverage distribution and sales in Nova Scotia
LAW SOCIETY OF BRITISH COLUMBIA (P)	Sets and enforces standards of professional conduct for lawyers in British Columbia
MANITOBA SECURITIES COMMISSION (P)	Protects investors and promotes fair and efficient investment business practices throughout Manitoba
HALIFAX ZONING BOARD OF APPEALS (M)	Hears appeals concerning denials of permit applications

* F = federal; P = provincial; M = municipal

rarely contradict a precedent. In fact, when they do, it often makes headlines.

Common law, however, does not apply in Quebec. Instead, the province of Quebec is governed by the *Civil Code of Quebec*, which is based on French civil law. In practice, civil law is very similar to common law, but in principle, they are very different. Civil law does not recognize that courts make law through their decisions; that is, they are not bound by precedents. Courts in Quebec decide individual cases based on their interpretation of the general principles defined in the Civil Code. Of course, Quebec is still bound by federal law in those areas defined as federal responsibility under the Constitution.

A2-1b Civil versus Criminal Law

There are two major branches of law in Canada: civil law and criminal law.

Civil law deals with disputes between private citizens. These disputes are settled in the courts when one of the parties initiates a lawsuit against the other. The most common types of cases brought before civil courts involve breach of contract (see the next section) and torts. A **tort** is a private wrong that results in physical or mental harm to an individual or damage to that person's property. *Intentional torts* arise from willful acts. *Unintentional torts* arise because of careless or irresponsible behaviour, known as **negligence**.

Criminal law involves cases in which the Crown investigates and prosecutes individuals who have harmed society. The most serious **crimes**, which are considered inherently evil, are called *felonies*. Less serious crimes are called *misdemeanours*. Exhibit A2.2 summarizes the key differences between civil and criminal law cases.

The same wrongful act may result in both civil and criminal trials. For example, an individual who kills someone can be tried for the crime of murder. At the same time, the family of the murder victim may bring action in civil court for wrongful death or for other torts such as battery (intentional and wrongful physical contact). Because the standard of proof is lower in civil actions, the accused may be found not guilty in the criminal case while still being held liable in the civil court. The O.J. Simpson case in the United States is a famous example. Simpson was found not guilty of the crime of murder in the criminal case. But a civil court found him liable for the wrongful death of Ron Goldman and for battery against both Goldman and Simpson's ex-wife, Nicole Brown.[2]

tort A private wrong that results in physical or mental harm to an individual or damage to that person's property.

negligence An unintentional tort that arises due to carelessness or irresponsible behaviour.

crime A wrongful act against society defined by law and prosecuted by the state.

Exhibit A2.2 Differences between Civil and Criminal Law Cases

	CIVIL LAW	CRIMINAL LAW
Nature of action and parties involved	Lawsuits to settle disputes between private individuals	Prosecution of parties charged with wrongdoings against society
Examples of cases	Intentional torts such as slander, libel, invasion of privacy, wrongful death; unintentional torts arising from negligence; breach of contract	Felonies such as robbery, theft, murder, arson, identity theft, extortion, and embezzlement, as well as less serious crimes called misdemeanours
Possible outcomes	Liable or not liable	Guilty or not guilty
Standard of proof (what is needed for plaintiff to win the case)	Preponderance of evidence (a much less stringent requirement than beyond reasonable doubt)	Proof beyond a reasonable doubt
Goal of remedy	Compensate injured party for harm suffered	Punish wrongdoer and deter similar behaviour
Common remedies	Monetary damages (payments of money to compensate the injured party), injunctions against certain types of behaviour, or requirements for specific performance	Fines and/or imprisonment

A2-2 Contracts: The Ties That Bind

Business law refers to the application of laws and legal principles to business relationships and transactions. A **contract** is one of the most important concepts in business. In basic terms, a contract is an agreement that is enforceable in a court of law. Some people think that contracts must be formal written documents that include complex legal language. But most types of contracts don't have to be in writing. In fact, courts sometimes decide that a contract exists because two parties *behave* in a way that indicates that they have a contractual agreement. A contract that is explicitly spelled out in writing or in words is called an *express contract*. A contract based on the behaviour of the parties is called an *implied contract*. Although harder to prove, an implied contract can be just as valid as an express contract.

A2-2a What Makes a Contract Enforceable?

All valid contracts must satisfy four conditions. In addition, some types of contracts must satisfy a fifth requirement. Let's take a look at each requirement.

business law The application of laws and legal principles to business relationships and transactions.

contract An agreement that is legally enforceable.

consideration Something of value that one party gives another as part of a contractual agreement.

statute of frauds A requirement that certain types of contracts must be in writing in order to be enforceable.

breach of contract The failure of one party to a contract to perform his or her contractual obligations.

statute of limitations The time period within which a legal action must be initiated.

compensatory damages Monetary payments a party that breaches a contract is ordered to pay in order to compensate the injured party for the actual harm suffered by the breach of contract.

1. There must be *mutual assent*. This means that there must be an offer freely given by one party and freely accepted by the other. The offer must be serious and reasonably certain so that both parties (and possibly the court) can determine what the parties intended. The other party's acceptance must be voluntary, unconditional, and clearly communicated to the party making the offer.

2. *Both* parties must offer **consideration**, meaning that they each must offer something of value to the other. Consideration might be money, property, or other assets, or it might be a promise to perform a specific act or provide a specific service. It could even be a promise to *refrain* from performing a certain act that the party could otherwise legally carry out. The promise by one party to provide a gift to another party is not an enforceable contract because the party receiving the gift does not provide consideration.

3. The parties must have the *legal capacity* to enter into a contract. Most individuals are free to enter into contracts and are expected to live up to the terms of these agreements. But common law recognizes that certain individuals are not competent to enter into a binding agreement. For instance, *minors* (in most provinces, anyone under the age of 18) are assumed to lack the maturity and experience to understand the nature of a contractual agreement. Thus, the law provides minors with the right to *disaffirm* (cancel) most types of contracts they enter into with adults. Courts may also rule that people who are mentally impaired lack the legal capacity to enter into contracts.

4. The contract must be for a *legal purpose*. This is almost a no-brainer. Remember, contracts are legally enforceable agreements. It wouldn't make sense for a court to enforce an agreement requiring one or both of the parties to break the law!

5. Most contracts do not have to be in writing to be valid. But there are some notable exceptions to this generalization. According to the **statute of frauds**, certain types of complex or important contracts must be in writing to be enforceable. Examples include contracts for the sale of land, contracts that cannot be completed within a year of their formation, and contracts involving the sale of goods valued at more than a specified amount, which varies by jurisdiction.

A2-2b What Happens When a Party Fails to Satisfy the Terms of a Contract?

A **breach of contract** occurs when one of the parties fails to satisfy the terms of the agreement. In such cases, the injured party can seek a remedy by suing in a civil court. But the injured party must seek a remedy within a reasonable time. The time period in which a lawsuit must be initiated is called the **statute of limitations**. After this time period has expired, the courts will not hear a lawsuit. In criminal law, a statute of limitations extends for a six-month period with respect to lesser (summary) crimes and misdemeanours. There is no statute of limitations in Canada for serious offences: major theft, rape, or murder. In civil law, there is a 10-year statute of limitations for uncollected debt.

The most common remedy enforced by courts for the breach of a contract is **compensatory damages**. These are monetary payments the party that breached

According to the statute of frauds, certain types of contracts must be in writing to be enforceable.

© Stockbyte/Getty Images

contract with a team and then decides he doesn't want to play for that team. A court probably wouldn't force the goalie to play for that team because that would represent involuntary servitude. But it might issue an injunction preventing the player from playing for any other team (even in a rival league) for the term of the contract.

A2-3 Sales: Transferring Ownership

A **sale** occurs when **title** (legal ownership) to a good passes from one party to another in exchange for a price. Each province has a version of the *Sale of Goods Act*. While there are minor differences in the legislation depending on the particular jurisdiction, general principles are in force. The law with respect to the sale of goods is a specialized branch of contract law. "Goods" refers to personal, tangible property in its portable form. This means that land sale is not covered by this legislation, nor is the sale of services. Precedents established by case law govern the sale of services.

Sales contracts must have all of the elements of contracts that we mentioned in the previous section—mutual assent, consideration, legal capacity, and legal purpose. But the law interprets some of these elements more leniently for sales contracts than for most other types of contracts. For example, courts can enforce sales contracts even if important elements, such as the price of the goods being sold or the means of delivery, are not specified in the agreement. A number of terms can be implied into the contract, for the law provides rules for "filling in" missing information in a sales contract. What is important under the law is the clear intent of the two parties to enter into a sales contract. Let's see how the law deals with two other important issues involving sales contracts.

the contract must pay to the injured party in order to compensate for the *actual losses* that result from the breach. Sometimes, if a contract has been breached—but without causing any real harm—the court will award the "injured" party a small monetary payment (such as $1), called *nominal damages*. At the other extreme, the court may order a party who breaches a contract to pay *punitive damages*. These are monetary payments that *exceed* (often far exceed) the amount needed to compensate the injured party for actual losses. Their purpose is to punish the party at fault and to deter similar behaviour in the future. But punitive damages are *not* applied in cases concerned with breach of contract alone; instead, they are awarded in cases dealing with torts where the party being sued engaged in excessively reckless or malicious behaviour.

Even though monetary damages are the most common remedy for a breach of contract, the courts sometimes employ other types of remedies. For instance, when a contract involves the sale of some *unique* item—such as a rare coin or an unusual piece of artwork—that the injured party could not obtain from anyone but the other party to the contract, the courts may require the remedy of **specific performance**. This requires the party who breached the contract to do exactly what the terms of the contract state. In the case of our example, this would require the actual sale of the coin or artwork.

Finally, courts also sometimes issue injunctions against the party that breaches a contract. An *injunction* is a court order that prevents someone from performing a certain act. For example, suppose a star hockey goalie signs a

A2-3a How and When Does Title Pass from Seller to Buyer?

If the sales contract includes conditions that determine when the title to the goods passes from seller to buyer, the law states that these conditions are binding. However, if the sales contract does not specify when the title passes, the law

specific performance A remedy for breach of contract in which the court orders the party committing the breach to do exactly what the contract specifies.

sale A transaction in which title (legal ownership) to a good passes from one party to another in exchange for a price.

title Legal evidence of ownership.

provides specific guidelines that the parties can apply. In general, these rules are based on the principle that title passes when the seller's performance of duties related to the delivery of the good has been completed.

A2-3b Which Party Assumes Risk of Loss If the Goods Are Lost, Damaged, or Destroyed During the Process of Transferring Them from Seller to Buyer?

According to the law, if the contract specifies who bears the risk, then the courts must apply those terms. If the contract is silent on this issue, the law provides guidelines for the courts to use when assigning risk. Interestingly, these rules don't always assign the risk to the party who actually has title to the good. One important principle is that if one party breaches the contract, risk of loss usually falls on that party. Otherwise, the law rules generally place the risk of loss on the party that is most likely to have insurance against a loss or on the party that is in the best position to prevent a loss.

 ### Other Legal Principles: What the Law Says about Agency, Bankruptcy, and Intellectual Property

Business law is a broad field, so it is impossible to adequately cover all of its aspects in a short appendix. We'll close by taking a brief look at three other important topics: principal–agent relationships, protection of intellectual property, and bankruptcy.

principal–agent relationship A relationship in which one party, called the principal, gives another party, called the agent, the authority to act and enter into binding agreements on the principal's behalf.

principal A party that agrees to have someone else (called an agent) act on his or her behalf.

agent A party that agrees to represent another party, called the principal.

scope of authority (for an agent) The extent to which an agent has the authority to act for and represent the principal.

A2-4a Principal–Agent Relationships

A **principal–agent relationship** exists when one party, called the **principal**, gives another party, called the agent, the authority to act and enter into binding contracts on the principal's behalf. Some employees are **agents** for their employers. For example, when a loan officer at a bank grants a loan to a borrower, or when a salesperson enters into a sales contract with a customer,

they are acting as agents for their employers. But not all employees have the authority to act as agents. An agent's **scope of authority** is the extent to which the agent has the authority to represent the principal. This authority can arise in several ways. *Express authority* is authority that is explicitly spelled out, either orally or in writing. *Implied authority* is not explicitly spelled out but is based on the court's recognition that agents must have the authority to act in certain ways in order to perform their duties. *Apparent authority* arises when the principal *behaves* in a way that leads third parties to reasonably believe that the principal–agent relationship exists, even when no such agency actually exists. When a principal is responsible for creating the perception of an agency relationship, the courts will hold the principal liable for any contracts the apparent agent enters into that are within the scope of the apparent agency.

Agents and principals each have certain duties to the other. For example, the duties of an agent to a principal include the following:

- **Loyalty:** Agents must act solely in the interests of the principal. In other words, an agent is supposed to do what is best for the principal rather than what is best for the agent or a third party.

- **Performance:** Agents must use any special skills or knowledge they possess and make a sincere effort to carry out their assigned duties.

- **Notification:** Agents must keep the principal informed on all matters relevant to their relationship.

- **Obedience:** Agents must obey all lawful instructions issued by the principal in the course of carrying out their duties.

- **Accounting:** Agents must keep accurate records of any expenses or resources used in the course of fulfilling their responsibilities and make these records available to the principal.

The obligations of the principal to the agent include the following:

- **Compensation:** The principal must provide reasonable compensation for services performed. The compensation must be made in a timely manner.

- **Reimbursement:** The principal must reimburse the agent for any reasonable and necessary expenses the agent incurs while acting for the principal.

- **Indemnification:** Principals must protect agents from personal losses they might suffer when carrying out their principal's lawful instructions.

- **Safe working conditions:** The principal must provide safe equipment, working premises, and conditions for agents.

- **Cooperation:** Principals must cooperate with and assist their agents in the performance of their duties.

In general, as long as agents act within the scope of their authority, the principal is liable for contracts the agent enters into when acting for the principal. In cases where the principal is undisclosed—so that the third party is not aware of the fact that the agent is acting on behalf of someone else—the agent also may be held liable if the contract is breached.

Agents are personally responsible for any torts they commit. But the principal may also be liable for an agent's torts if the agent is representing the principal and is acting within the scope of authority granted by the principal. This reflects a common law principle called *respondeat superior*, which means "let the master be held accountable." However, principals are not responsible for crimes committed by their agents unless they authorize or participate in the criminal act.

A2-4b Intellectual Property

The term **property** refers to the legal right of an owner to exclude non-owners from having access to a particular resource. While we generally think of property in terms of land, buildings, and physical goods, the law also recognizes **intellectual property**—for example, the right of an inventor, innovator, writer, or artist to own their creations and prevent others from copying or using these creations without their permission. Three common types of intellectual property rights are patents, trademarks, and copyrights.

A **patent** gives an inventor a legal monopoly over that invention for a limited time period. During that period, others may not copy the invention without the inventor's approval. It is important to note that a mere idea is not patentable. To obtain a patent, an inventor must create a new *application* that is as follows:

- **Non-obvious:** The application must represent some insight that was not readily apparent from existing knowledge in the field.

- **Novel:** The application must represent a new and different use of this insight.

- **Useful:** The application must be more than a mere curiosity; it must result in a useful outcome.

In Canada, patents are granted by the Canadian Patent Office, part of the Canadian Intellectual Property Office. To receive a patent, the inventor must file an application and pay a filing fee. The application must clearly explain the purpose of the invention, how it differs from current products in the same field, and how it would be produced and used. The Patent Office will grant a patent only after a thorough investigation of the application to make sure it satisfies the criteria mentioned above—a process that often takes several years.

Most patents offer protection for 20 years, but there are exceptions. For example, patents for designs are for only 10 years. While the patent is in force, its holder can sue anyone who *infringes* on the patent by using or producing the invention without permission. If the holder's suit is successful, the courts typically award the inventor damages for the unauthorized use and often apply additional court remedies. For example, the courts might require the violator to destroy items that infringe on the patent and bar the violator from similar infringements in the future. However, once the patent expires, the invention becomes part of the public domain—meaning that others are free to use and market the invention without obtaining permission from the inventor. Patents, while they are held, apply only in the country where application was made and approved. A Canadian patent does not prevent a firm in the United States from using or selling the same invention, unless the patent holder has also applied for and received a US patent.

A **trademark** is a distinctive mark, symbol, word, phrase, or motto used to uniquely identify the goods of a particular business. When you see the "swoosh," you know it's a Nike product. Similarly, many customers immediately think of Maxwell House coffee when they hear the phrase "good to the last drop."

Trademarks can be acquired in two ways. First, a company can acquire a trademark simply by being the first to use some distinctive mark in commerce. However, this type of trademark typically is confined to the specific geographic area in which the company sells its products. The second way to acquire a trademark is to be the first to register the mark with the Canadian Intellectual Property Office. A registered trademark gives the company nationwide protection—even if it only sells its products in a limited area.

The registration of a trademark initially provides protection from unauthorized use for a 15-year period, but this protection can be renewed every 15 years, as long as the renewal fee is paid and the trademark user continues its use. Firms often use the symbol ® to indicate that their trademark is registered, or the symbol ™ if their trademark is unregistered. Owners of a trademark can sue others who

property The legal right of an owner to exclude non-owners from having access to a particular resource.

intellectual property Property that results from intellectual or creative efforts.

patent A legal monopoly that gives an inventor the exclusive right over the invention for a limited period of time.

trademark A mark, symbol, word, phrase, or motto used to identify a company's goods.

SHAKING YOUR BOOTY EARNS LITTLE RESPECT

How much do you suppose a professional cheerleader earns? When the *Globe and Mail* posed this question, comments from respondents included:

- Is it really even a job?
- There are 16 games a year … this is a hobby.
- Well, it's not like they are doing anything important.
- Stop moaning and quit.

Herb MacKenzie

Many other comments were even less respectful. Do these women deserve such little respect? A look at the bios of many of them reveals that they are often students, and at least 20 or so have gone on to earn a medical degree; a few even practise their "hobby" while working their day job. One real risk is that if they get hurt while cheerleading, they cannot claim workers' compensation and may even lose their other income.

For others who perform 16 games a year, it certainly isn't a hobby. Image meeting Tom Brady, quarterback for the New England Patriots, at a party. You ask him where he works. Would you expect him to say, "Well, I really don't work. But I got this great hobby that pays me $8 million a year"? (And that's less than one-quarter of what Russel Wilson, Ben Roethlisberger, Philip Rivers, and Eli Manning each earn—$31 million and above, all for enjoying the same hobby).

At the other extreme, there are hundreds of people who are, arguably, involved in the same hobby, but who are lucky to earn $1,000 a year (and less in Canada, of course). These are the cheerleaders. Ever since 1954, when the first NFL cheerleader squad appeared with the Baltimore Colts, cheerleaders have worked hard for little respect and less pay. Few moan, and fewer quit. They must follow strict fitness and weight guidelines (and some have had to perform the "jiggle test" to check their weight); they continually report for and practise routines; they appear for photoshoots, autograph signings, and community events; and they perform physically demanding and potentially dangerous activities; yet they earn only a fraction of what their teams pay to the

team mascot: $23,000 to $65,000 a year. Oh, but the perks! One team provided its cheerleaders with a free ticket (for a friend or relative, presumably) and free parking. Others have provided such things as free sunglasses, tanning deals, gym memberships, and hair and makeup deals.

But, as Bob Dylan often sings, "The times, they are a changin'." The Oakland Raiders cheerleaders won a wage-theft lawsuit and now earn $9 per hour, or just over $3,000 per year. The team also must pay $1.25 million to former Raiderettes. The Bengals, Bills, Buccaneers, and Jets cheerleaders have all brought lawsuits against their teams, seeking minimum wage. Things would be better in Canada if our cheerleaders made the minimum wage. (Our minimum wages are higher.) None of our CFL cheerleaders get paid, but the Toronto Argonauts do pay a small honorarium, and the Calgary Stampeders are considering doing so. For the more savvy cheerleaders, maybe cheering for the Toronto Raptors would be a better alternative. Courtside is a lot warmer than outdoors in the fall, and Raptors cheerleaders get paid for all rehearsals, games, and appearances. According to the team choreographer, they "definitely make more than minimum wage."

Perhaps minimum wage is the least amount of respect cheerleaders should get. After all, if teams did not believe that cheerleaders added value to their franchise, they wouldn't be used.[3]

---

make unauthorized use of it in civil court. If the owner of the trademark is successful, the courts may award damages. The courts will also bar the infringer from further use of the trademark.

Trademark protection may be lost if the general public begins using the trademark to refer to a general *type* of good rather than with a good produced by a *specific company*.

(When this happens, the mark is said to be "genericized.") At one time, the names aspirin, zipper, and escalator (among many others) were trademarks. However, over time people began using these terms to refer to a general class of goods. Once this happened, the courts ruled that they had become generic terms and were no longer entitled to trademark protection.[4]

A **copyright** gives authors, artists, or other creative individuals the exclusive right to own, produce, copy, and sell their own creative works and to license others to do so. Copyrights are granted only for original works that display some degree of creative or intellectual content. Still, this covers a lot of territory; copyrights protect a variety of works from unauthorized use, including books, plays, paintings, musical compositions, motion pictures, video games, and computer programs. The period of protection is the creator's remaining life plus an additional 50 years after the creator's death. For some materials—for example, sound recordings—protection is simply for 50 years.

As with holders of patents and trademarks, owners of copyrighted material can sue unauthorized users of their property in civil court. If the court rules favourably, it may award the plaintiff any profits earned by the infringer, as well as damages for any other harm suffered. The court may also order the destruction of any infringing works and bar the infringer from future violations.

It is important to realize that copyrights don't provide complete protection against *all* use of the covered material. Under *fair use doctrine*, parts of a copyrighted work may be used without the creator's explicit permission if certain conditions are met. For example, a teacher can distribute copies of small sections of a copyrighted book to students in order to illustrate a key concept. Similarly, critics, reviewers, and commentators are generally allowed to quote limited passages of copyrighted material without explicit permission.

A2-4c **Bankruptcy**

Bankruptcy refers to procedures governed by law that provide the means for debtors who are unable to meet their obligations to discharge their debts and get a fresh start. Bankruptcy proceedings can be voluntary or involuntary. The difference between the two is who initiates the bankruptcy; debtors initiate voluntary bankruptcies, while creditors initiate *involuntary bankruptcies*. Either way, the goal of bankruptcy law—also referred to as insolvency law—is to provide fair treatment to both debtors and creditors.

Businesses that are considering voluntary bankruptcy may attempt a negotiated settlement. Creditors, individually or as a group, may meet with the debtor and, depending on the circumstances, may agree to let the debtor continue operations or may agree that the debtor should cease operations. Many businesses use a skilled negotiator during these meetings, particularly if a number of creditors are involved, as one or more may attempt to push through an agreement that gives them preferential treatment over other creditors. If a negotiated settlement is to succeed, then everyone must agree to the terms of the settlement.

When a negotiated settlement cannot be reached, the debtor will need to seek a **trustee in bankruptcy**. This person will hold legal responsibility for administering the affairs of the bankrupt party, corporation, or person. The trustee begins by preparing a statement of the debtor's assets and obligations and, if the debtor wishes to continue operating the business, then prepares a **proposal** to the creditors. If the proposal is accepted by the creditors, the debtor then has some time to reorganize operations and may be able to turn the business to profitability. Creditors will normally agree to the proposal if they see the likelihood of getting more money than they would if they force the debtor into bankruptcy. New debts that the debtor might incur—usually at a higher rate of interest—are not covered by the proposal. When a debtor defaults on the terms of the proposal, bankruptcy generally follows.

Any creditor can sue a debtor based on outstanding debts. Secured creditors may also take individual action against specific assets. This is a fairly common action as secured creditors are generally not concerned about the circumstances of other creditors. Depending on the specific asset, this could also force the business to cease operations. Finally, one or more creditors may petition a debtor into bankruptcy, and this is likely to happen when the debtor's situation appears to be hopeless. A **petition** is simply a statement of what the debtor owes and to whom. It is filed in the bankruptcy court, and if the petition is successful, the debtor is declared bankrupt, and the court issues a **receiving order**. The debtor is now officially bankrupt, and the trustee now assumes responsibility for all of the debtor's assets.

Creditors must now file a **proof of claim** with the trustee. This is a formal notice of the amount they are owed. If the trustee accepts the validity of the claim, the creditor is now in a position to share in the distribution of any monies that become available for distribution. Some claimants have superior status. First in line—no surprise—is the Canada Revenue Agency.

copyright The exclusive legal right of authors, artists, or other creative individuals to own, use, copy, and sell their own creations and to license others to do so.

trustee in bankruptcy The person who holds legal responsibility for administering the affairs of bankrupt companies or persons.

proposal A contractual agreement between an insolvent debtor and creditors that would allow the debtor to reorganize and continue operations.

petition A statement of what a creditor owes and to whom. It is filed in bankruptcy court, and if it is successful, the debtor is declared bankrupt.

receiving order A court order that follows a successful petition. It officially declares a debtor as bankrupt and transfers legal control of the debtor's assets to the trustee.

proof of claim A formal notice by a creditor to the trustee concerning what is owed and the nature of the debt.

Any debts to it are not considered to be part of the debtor's estate and must be paid first. Suppliers who have made shipments to the debtor within the previous 30 days may reclaim their goods, assuming that they are still in their original condition. Then there is a pecking order: secured, preferred, and unsecured creditors. Secured creditors, as mentioned, have claim against one or more specific assets. Preferred creditors include funeral expenses, the trustee (for his or her expenses), employees (limited to $2,000 each for unpaid work over the previous six months), municipalities (for taxes), and landlords (for outstanding rents). Finally, unsecured creditors share what is left, assuming that something is left. They receive a share of the remaining monies proportionate to their claim.

Laws are the rules governing the conduct and actions of people or any other type of entity and are enforceable by the government. Laws protect members of society from physical and mental harm, and their property from theft or damage. They also encourage socially desirable behaviour and discourage socially undesirable behaviour. The Canadian Constitution is the supreme law within Canada. Other laws arise from legislative action, administrative regulation, and court decisions.

Business law refers to the application of laws and legal principles to business relationships and transactions. Business law is so broad that we could not hope to cover all of its applications in an appendix. But we have provided an overview of several key concepts:

- A contract is an agreement that is enforceable in a court of law.

- A sale occurs when legal title passes from one party to another in exchange for a price.

- A principal–agent relationship exists when one party, called the principal, gives another party, called the agent, the authority to act and enter into binding contracts on the principal's behalf.

- Bankruptcy refers to procedures governed by law that provide the means for debtors who are unable to meet their obligations to discharge their debts and get a fresh start.

- Intellectual property results from someone's creative or intellectual efforts. The creator's ownership rights in intellectual property are protected by patents, copyrights, and trademarks.

careers in law: Corporate Lawyer

Responsible for reviewing and drafting contracts, policies, and procedures, coordinating transactions, advising management on various legal and compliance issues including litigation, and preparing or supervising the preparation of stock plans, equity agreements, proprietary matters agreements, benefit plans, and benefit plan prospectuses. The ideal candidate has a doctoral degree, at least four years of experience, an active law licence, and substantive knowledge of corporate/commercial transactions, corporate governance and securities laws, and commercial contracts, plus strong written and verbal skills, high personal and professional integrity, and the ability to listen and effectively explain complex legal issues to nonlawyers and concisely translate complicated issues into actionable recommendations and solutions.

Appendix 3
Personal Finance

Personal financial management issues affect all of us, young and old alike. How successfully we manage our financial resources affects where we live, how well we can provide for our families, and when (or perhaps even if) we'll be able to comfortably retire. The financial decisions you make and habits you develop now will affect your personal and financial future.

A3-1 Your Budget

One of the first steps in getting control over your financial situation is to develop a **budget**, which is a detailed forecast of your expected cash inflows (income) and cash outflows (expenditures). You can use your budget to develop your financial plan and to monitor your progress towards achieving your financial goals.

A3-1a How Do I Get Started?

You can get a good handle on what should be included in your budget by carefully tracking and analyzing all of your financial transactions for several weeks. This takes discipline and careful record keeping, but once you know where your money comes from and where it goes, you'll have what you need to prepare your budget.

There are many approaches to setting up your budget. If you don't want to build your budget from scratch, you can check out several free online personal finance sites that can help you get started. If you want more bells and whistles—and more support—than the free sites provide, you can purchase a commercial program such as Quicken®. Basic versions of these programs typically cost less than $100 and provide a wide range of features such as online banking services, financial calculators, and stock quotes. Most also give you the ability to export data into tax preparation software, making tax filing much simpler.

If you are comfortable with Microsoft Excel® (or other spreadsheet software), another option is to build your own budget. Excel has many built-in budget templates to help you get started, and even more are available online. These templates are generic, so you may want to tweak them to suit your own circumstances. You won't get all of the features provided by the commercial packages, but that isn't necessarily a bad thing. Some people actually find all

budget (personal) A detailed forecast of financial inflows (income) and outflows (expenses) in order to determine your net inflow or outflow for a given period of time.

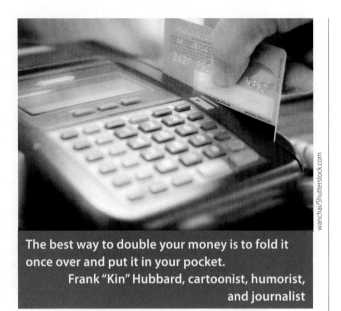

The best way to double your money is to fold it once over and put it in your pocket.
Frank "Kin" Hubbard, cartoonist, humorist, and journalist

of the bells and whistles in the commercial applications overwhelming and prefer the straightforward simplicity of a spreadsheet template. Also, the process of "building" the budget yourself may give you a sense of personal satisfaction and a greater appreciation for the budget relationships than you'd get using online or commercial personal finance software packages.

Assessing Revenues: Where Does My Money Come From? The budget starts with a forecast of your income—the money you bring in. This revenue can come from many different sources. For many people, the pay from their job is their primary source of revenue. But the major source of income for entrepreneurs may be the profits they earn from their businesses. Some people also derive a substantial amount of income from financial investments, such as stocks and bonds; others earn rental income. Retirees may depend on pensions, Canada Pension Plan, Old Age Security, and private investments for much of their income.

Assessing Expenses: Where Does It All Go? Once you have identified the amount of income you expect from various sources, you can turn your focus to the spending side of your budget. To set your budget, you'll need to be very specific about where your money goes. As we've already mentioned, carefully tracking your expenditures over a period of several weeks can help you identify your spending patterns. Many people who do this are surprised by some of the habits they uncover. You may find that you're spending a lot more than you

discretionary costs
Expenditures for which the spender has significant control in terms of the amount and timing.

non-discretionary costs
Costs that the spender must incur but has little or no control over.

savings account An interest-bearing account holding funds not needed to meet regular expenditures.

thought for Tim Hortons coffee, video games, or clothes. Once you discover your spending patterns, you'll be in a better position to determine the categories of spending to include in your budget and to estimate the amount you'll spend in each category.

Understanding Your Spending Habits Your expenditures can be classified into discretionary and non-discretionary categories. The costs you have the most control over are your **discretionary costs**. Perhaps you like dining out, nightclubbing, or shopping. Perhaps you just have expensive taste in coffee. David Bach, author of several books on managing your personal finances, challenges you to look at your "latté factor," meaning the little vices we each find hard to resist. You'll find that something as little as a $4 cup of coffee per workday can cost you $1,040 each year ($4 × 5 days per week × 52 weeks). Once you realize the true cost of these "latté factors," you'll have a greater incentive to bring them under control.[1] Your budget can help you impose the discipline you need to accomplish this goal.

Non-discretionary costs are costs you have little control over, such as your rent or car payments, which are set by contract. Your lifestyle may lock you into other costs that are at least partly non-discretionary. For example, given your need to get to school and work, you may have to spend a significant amount of money on gas and car maintenance every month. But with a little flexibility and creativity, you may find that some of these costs aren't *completely* non-discretionary. For instance, you might be able to significantly reduce your expenses for gas and car maintenance by carpooling or using public transit.

You may also want to consider your attitude towards spending. Are you most likely to spend too much money when you are depressed or stressed out? Look at this aspect carefully and try to be as honest as possible with yourself. The final thing you should consider is who you are with when you spend money. You may find that you tend to spend much more money while hanging out with certain friends.

After you have prepared your budget, you'll need to keep track of your actual expenses and compare them to your budget. Also, you'll periodically need to adjust your budget for significant changes in your lifestyle, employment status, and financial goals.

A3-2 Your Savings: Building a Safety Net

A **savings account** is an interest-earning account that is intended to satisfy obligations that your chequing account cannot handle. Think of your savings account as a "safety net" for unexpected financial challenges, such as a major

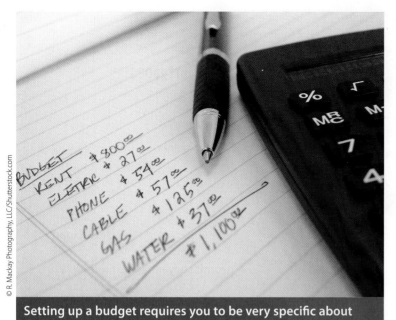

Setting up a budget requires you to be very specific about where your money goes.

can obtain is your history. A **credit history** is a summary of open and closed credit accounts and the manner in which those accounts have been paid. A good credit history can make it easier for you to borrow money when you really need it—such as when you want to buy a car or your first house.

One way that companies evaluate your creditworthiness is by using a scoring system. Your individual **credit score (credit rating)** is based on several factors, including your payment history, the amount you owe, the type of credit used, and the length of time you've held various credit accounts. Other factors considered include your age, whether you rent or own your home, and whether you have declared bankruptcy in the past. Another factor that is considered when evaluating your creditworthiness is your **net worth**. Your net worth is a numerical measure of the value of all your assets minus the total of all your debts.[4]

repair on your car or even the loss of your job. Many financial experts suggest that you have enough money in your savings to cover at least three to six months of your monthly expenses. The good news is that if you're lucky enough to avoid major problems, your savings account will earn you a bit of interest income.

One technique for establishing a sizable savings balance is to "pay yourself first." One way to do this is to have a predetermined amount from each pay automatically deposited into your savings account. Once you've accumulated enough in your savings account to provide an adequate safety net, you can use the "pay yourself first" approach to achieve other financial goals.[2]

Interest rates on savings accounts vary from bank to bank, so you should shop around for the best rate. In recent years, online banks have often provided higher rates than the other banks. Savings accounts, along with some other investments, are covered by the **Canada Deposit Insurance Corporation (CDIC)**. The CDIC is a Crown corporation established to maintain stability and public confidence in the nation's financial system. The CDIC protects the individual deposits of member companies up to $100,000.[3]

A3-3 Your Credit: Handle with Care!

Credit refers to your ability to obtain goods or resources without having to make immediate payment. One of the most important determinants of the amount of credit you

A3-3a Credit Cards: Boon or Bane?

Now let's look at a specific source of credit that is near and dear to many students' hearts: the **credit card**. A credit card allows its holder to make a purchase now and pay the credit issuer later.

There are several benefits to having and using credit cards. The most obvious is that credit cards are more convenient and safer than carrying a lot of cash. Credit cards also make it easy to track your expenditures because you have access to a monthly summary of charges. And many credit cards offer perks, such as discounts on certain products, extended warranties on purchases, or frequent flyer miles. Another benefit of the responsible use of credit cards is that it can improve your credit score (rating) by allowing you to establish a history of prompt payments. This can make it easier for you to borrow money when you really need it.

One downside of having a credit card is that the "buy now,

Canada Deposit Insurance Corporation (CDIC) A Crown corporation created to maintain stability and public confidence in the nation's financial system, primarily by insuring bank deposits.

credit Allows a borrower to buy a good or acquire an asset without making immediate payment and to repay the balance at a later time.

credit history A summary of a borrower's open and closed credit accounts and the manner in which those accounts have been paid.

credit score (credit rating) A numerical measure of a consumer's creditworthiness.

net worth A measure of the value of all your assets minus the total of all your debts.

credit card A card issued by a bank or finance company that allows the cardholder to make a purchase now and pay the credit card issuer later.

© R. Mackay Photography, LLC/Shutterstock.com

pay later" aspect of credit card use makes it hard for people to maintain financial discipline. Another problem is that interest rates on unpaid card balances tend to be very high. Many card issuers also impose a variety of fees that can make a noticeable dent in your wallet. And making late payments or failing to pay what you owe can damage your credit history, hurting your chances of getting additional credit when you need it.

A3-3b The Devil in the Details: Understanding Your Credit Card Agreement

Before you accept a credit card, make sure you read the credit card agreement and understand the main conditions for using that card. Some things to look for include the following:

- **Grace period:** A **grace period** is the period of time that you have to pay your balance before interest fees are assessed. Some credit card companies expect to receive their payment within 21 days of the credit card statement date. So it becomes very important to get these bills paid as soon as possible to avoid the interest and other fees.

- **Interest rate:** The percentage financing cost charged on unpaid balances.

- **Late fees:** Fees that may be assessed if a payment is not received within the grace period.

- **Other fees:** These include annual fees (a charge just for the privilege of having a card, whether you use it or not), over-the-limit fees (if your charges exceed your credit limit), and balance transfer fees (if you transfer a balance from one card to another). This isn't a complete list, but it does reflect many of the common types of fees you might incur. Not all cards are subject to all of these charges; the specific types and amounts of fees can vary

grace period The period of time that the credit card holder has to pay outstanding balances before interest or fees are assessed.

loan The money provided today by the financial institution in exchange for future repayments of principal and interest.

promissory note The written promise to repay the bank for a loan.

collateral The asset the bank takes as security for a loan.

mortgage A loan from the bank that is used to purchase a house.

considerably from one issuer to another, which is why reading the fine print is important.

A3-3c Loans and Mortgages

Credit cards work for smaller every-day purchases, but when you are buying something larger like a car or house, you will need to the spread the payments over a longer period of time. Spreading the payments over a longer period of time makes the monthly amount you have to pay smaller. The money provided today by the financial institution in exchange for future repayments of principal and interest is called a **loan**. When you get a loan from the bank you will need to sign a **promissory note**. The promissory note is a written promise to repay the bank. The promissory note states all the conditions of the loan, including these: the monthly payment, how long you need to make payments, and what the bank has taken for collateral. **Collateral** is what the bank takes as security for the loan. Collateral for a car loan usually would be the car. If payments are not made on the loan, the bank can take back the car and sell it to pay off the outstanding balance of the loan.

A **mortgage** is similar to a loan except the money received from the bank is used to purchase a house. A mortgage is usually for larger amount and therefore the payments are spread over a longer period of time. In the case of a mortgage, the collateral is usually the house.

A3-3d Using Credit Cards Wisely: The Need for Discipline

Although many young adults manage their credit cards without major problems, others are stunned when the credit card bill arrives. Many never read their credit card agreements, so they are taken by surprise by the higher-than-expected interest charges and fees. Others simply lack discipline. They succumb to the temptations of a "buy now, pay later" mentality and run up big bills that they can't afford to pay.

The first rule when you have credit card difficulties is to "PUT THE CARD DOWN!" When you find yourself in trouble, stop using the card so that you don't compound your difficulties. Make sure you don't use the card again until you've gotten your spending habits under control.

Once you have eliminated the temptation to dig a deeper hole, the next step is to make sure you consistently pay a substantial amount each month towards retiring the debt on that card. Given how high interest rates are on unpaid balances for most credit cards, it is usually a good idea to place a very high priority on eliminating these balances as quickly as possible.

If you can't seem to shake the habit of overspending, consider using cash or a **debit card** instead of a credit card. While a debit card looks like a credit card, there is a big difference. When you use a debit card, money is immediately withdrawn from your bank account, so you "feel the pain" just as if you'd paid in cash. Many people spend less when they use cash or debit cards than when they use credit cards.

> The best time to plant a tree was twenty years ago. The next best time is now.
>
> Chinese proverb

A3-4 Your Investments: Building for the Future

Investing involves reducing consumption today in order to acquire assets that build future wealth. In a very real way, investing is like the concept of sowing and reaping. A farmer plants a seed (makes an investment) in anticipation of a harvest (return), which is much larger than the seed that was planted. When it comes to investing, early is better than late—but late is better than never.

A3-4a Building Wealth: The Key Is Consistency—And An Early Start!

Don't talk yourself out of investing just because you don't have much to invest. Even if you start with a small amount, your wealth

iStockphoto/Thinkstock

will eventually grow to become a significant amount as long as you stick with it. And the earlier you start, the better off you'll be. To see this, take a look at Exhibit A3.1, which compares how big your retirement nest egg will be at age 65 for different monthly investment amounts beginning at different ages (and assuming you earn an annual return of 8 percent). A 30-year-old who invests $60 per month will end up with $137,633 at age 65. Compare this to someone who begins investing $60 per month at age 20, and the results are startling. The investor who starts at age 20 directly invests only $7,200 more ($60 per month for 120 more months) than the investor who starts at age 30. But the earlier investor ends up with a nest egg of $316,472—almost $179,000 more than that of the investor who started at age 30.

The reason for this result is that, over time, you earn interest not only on the money you directly invest but also on the interest you've earned in previous years, a process known as compounding. The earlier you begin investing, the more powerful the compounding effect becomes. By the time an investor reaches age 65, any dollars invested at age 20 have been compounded for a very long time, resulting in a big increase in the nest egg. The message of Exhibit A3.1 is clear: An early start to investing can lead to dramatically more money when it comes time to retire.

A3-4b Financial Securities: What Are My Investment Options?

Now that we've demonstrated the importance of investing, let's look at some specific types of financial instruments you might want to include in your investment portfolio. Our brief discussion can't hope to cover all of the possibilities, so we'll focus only on some of the most common financial investments. But keep in mind that, in addition to the financial instruments we describe in this section, many people also hold much of their wealth in other assets. The largest single asset for many households is the equity they have in their home.

Let's begin by looking at *common stock,* which represents ownership in a corporation. Common stock offers the possibility of two types of financial returns. The first, called a *dividend,* is a distribution of profits paid out to the shareholders. Dividends

debit card A card issued by the bank that allows the customer to make purchases as if the transaction involved cash. The customer's bank account is immediately reduced when the purchase is made.

investing Reducing consumption in the current time period in order to build future wealth.

Exhibit A3.1 Growing Your Investment: Starting Early Makes a Difference

MONTHLY SAVINGS	STARTING AGE			
	20	30	40	50
$30	$158,236	$68,816	$28,531	$10,381
$60	$316,472	$137,633	$57,062	$20,762
$90	$474,709	$206,449	$85,592	$31,143
$120	$632,945	$275,266	$114,123	$41,525
$150	$791,181	$344,082	$142,654	$51,906

Note: Figures in the table show the amount accumulated at age 65. Results are based on an assumed rate of return of 8 percent, compounded monthly.

are paid only if the corporation's board of directors declares them—and there is no legal requirement for them to do so. If a corporation is in poor financial shape, its board of directors may decide it is unable to pay a dividend. But even if a company is highly profitable, its board may decide to reinvest (retain) its profits rather than pay dividends to shareholders.

Investors can earn a second type of return, called a *capital gain*, if the market price of their stock rises relative to the price they paid for it. But stock prices can go down as well as up. So it is possible for investors to experience capital losses as well as capital gains. Clearly, investing in common stock entails a significant degree of risk. But historically, the average rate of return on stocks has been better than the return on many types of investments.

In addition to common stock, some corporations offer another type of stock, called *preferred stock*. The two types of stock have some important differences. From the perspective of many investors, the most important distinction is that owners of preferred stock are more likely to receive a dividend than owners of common stock. Preferred stock is normally issued with a stated dividend, and common shareholders can't be paid any dividend until the preferred dividend

> Rather go to bed without dinner than to rise in debt.
>
> Benjamin Franklin

is paid in full. Still, even preferred shareholders have no guaranteed legal right to receive a dividend.

A *corporate bond* is another type of corporate security, but quite different from stock. A bond is a formal IOU issued by a corporation. Shareholders are the owners of a corporation, whereas bondholders are its creditors. Most bonds are long-term debts that mature (come due) 10 to 30 years after they are issued, although bonds with shorter and longer maturities are sometimes issued.

As creditors, bondholders are legally entitled to receive interest payments from the issuing corporation every year until the bond matures and to receive an amount known as the *principal* (or "face value") when the bond matures. But bondholders don't have to hold their bonds until they mature. Like stocks, bonds can be bought and sold on securities markets, and their prices can rise and fall. So, like shareholders, bondholders can experience capital gains or losses.

Because the issuing corporation is legally required to pay interest and principal on a fixed schedule, returns on bonds are more predictable than returns on shares. How-ever, even bonds pose some risk. During an economic downturn, firms may default (fail to make) their legally required bond payments.

Government bonds are IOUs issued by government entities when they need to borrow money. As with corporate bonds, government bonds normally pay their holders a stated rate of interest until they mature. Government bonds can be issued by federal, provincial, or local governments.

Certificates of deposit, *term deposits*, and *guaranteed investment certificates* are offered by banks and other companies, such as credit unions. They are similar to savings accounts but are issued for a fixed term, which could be as short as one month or as long as five years. The rate of interest paid on the investments is often higher than the rate on a regular savings account but usually lower than the interest rate on corporate bonds and most government bonds. These investments with longer maturity dates typically earn a higher interest rate than those with shorter terms. Some of these types of investments can be cashed before maturity, but you often incur a substantial penalty if you do that. One advantage of these investments is that they are usually insured by the Canada Deposit Insurance Corporation. Because of this insurance and the predictable rate of return, these investments are considered to be among the safest investment options. The tradeoff is that they offer lower returns than most other types of investments.

Mutual fund companies sell shares to investors and pool the resulting funds to invest in financial instruments such as corporate stocks, corporate bonds, government bonds, or other assets. Some mutual funds invest mainly in bonds, others invest mainly in stocks, and others in government bonds. Some invest in specific sectors of the economy, such as technology or energy, while others invest in broader portfolios. Most mutual funds are professionally managed, with the fund's manager selecting the specific securities the fund will hold. This professional management appeals to many investors who don't have the time or expertise to evaluate investment alternatives. But it is also expensive—mutual funds charge fees to cover the cost of managing the fund and to meet other expenses. Investors must pay fees even if the funds perform poorly.

Exchange-traded funds (ETFs) are similar to mutual funds in that they represent ownership in a broad portfolio of securities. However, unlike mutual funds, they are bought and sold just like shares of corporate stock. ETFs are a relatively new investment vehicle (first marketed in 1993), but they have become quite popular in recent years.

A *tax-free savings plan* allows investors to deposit up to $5,000 a year. This money can be invested in a savings account, mutual funds, stocks, or other financial securities. The advantage of a tax-free savings plan is that you do not have to pay income tax on the interest or dividends the money in the plan earns.

A3-4c Acquiring Financial Assets: The Role of a Broker

Investors normally acquire many of their financial assets, including shares of common and preferred stock, corporate bonds, and certain other financial assets (such as ETFs), by purchasing them in securities markets. However, individual investors can't directly participate in these markets. Instead, they normally rely on the services of a brokerage firm to buy and sell securities.

When choosing a broker, it's important to consider both the costs and the level of service. In addition to carrying out your trades, a *full-service broker* provides a wide range of services, including research to identify good investment opportunities, financial planning, and tax advice. Most full-service brokerage firms charge commissions based on the dollar value of the orders their clients place. They also charge fees for the services they provide. In contrast, *discount brokers* buy and sell securities for their clients but offer few additional services. The commissions and fees charged by discount brokers are usually significantly lower than those of full-service brokers. Many discount brokerage firms charge flat fees of a few dollars per trade for simple transactions.

In recent years, competition among brokerage firms has blurred the distinction between full-service and discount brokers. Many full-service firms lowered their commissions, and discount brokers have begun offering investment advice and other services. Most major brokerage firms now offer their clients both discount and full-service options.

Before entrusting a brokerage firm with your financial transactions, you should check out its background. Each province and territory has a securities commission that regulates the securities industry for its area.

A3-4d Building a Portfolio: A Few Words about Diversification, Risk, and Return

The financial securities we've described are not mutually exclusive. It is possible—and usually desirable—to invest in a diversified financial portfolio consisting of a variety of stocks, bonds, guaranteed investment certificates, government bonds, and other assets.

The main advantage offered by diversification is that it reduces your risk. If you put a large part of your wealth into one specific investment, you could be wiped out if that investment goes sour. If you invest in several different assets, then losses in some are likely to be offset by gains in others. But diversification also has a downside: It not only reduces risk but also reduces the possibility of earning exceptionally high returns.

One widely accepted financial principle is that a trade-off exists between risk and return; in other words, investments with the potential for generating high returns tend to be riskier than investments that offer lower returns. For example, stock prices sometimes decline sharply, so investing in stocks is considered quite risky. But historically, the long-run average return on stocks has been significantly higher than the average return on bonds, which offer safer, more predictable returns.

In general, younger investors are less concerned about risk than older investors. When you are young, you have more time to recover from adverse results, so you may be willing to take more risks and be more aggressive in pursuit of higher returns. If you invest mostly in stocks when you are young, and the stock market crashes, you still have time to recoup your losses and take advantage of future increases in stock prices. But older investors who hold a lot of stock might find that the same crash wiped out much of their wealth just when they were counting on it to supplement their retirement income. Older investors often become more conservative, adjusting their portfolio to include a greater percentage of relatively safe assets such as government bonds, bonds of corporations with strong credit ratings, and guaranteed investment certificates.

A3-4e But What Is My Best Investment? (Hint: Look in the Mirror!)

So far we have focused on investing in financial assets. But in many ways, the most important investment you can make is in yourself, by devoting your time, effort, and money to your education, training, health, and fitness. Some argue that the earnings difference between those who have a university or college degree and those who have completed high school is getting smaller. Others argue that the difference in earnings between high school and university and college graduates over their lifetime could be more than a million dollars.[5]

Strategies to Become More Marketable One way to increase your marketability and your starting salary is to secure an internship during your college or university years. Such internships usually offer little or no monetary compensation, but they pay off in other ways. They give students a chance to gain firsthand experience that supplements what they learn in the classroom and helps them determine whether a specific career is right for them. And the internship experience looks great on a résumé. The laws regarding unpaid internships in Canada fall under provincial jurisdiction, so there are some wide variations across the country.[6]

Other Work Opportunities Don't despair if you are unable to secure an internship. There are other ways to gain work experience in your field of interest. Consider taking a pay cut from your temporary job to gain experience in your career field. Or perhaps consider doing volunteer work in that field: you'll be doing a good deed, and you'll be learning the ropes in your chosen field. Taking a temporary cut to gain relevant work experience often pays for itself many times over when you leave college or university and pursue a full-time position.

A3-4f Investing for the Long Term

One of the most important reasons people invest is to build up a nest egg for retirement or other long-term objective. While your retirement might seem like it is a long time off, investing for your golden years now can really pay off because it allows you to take advantage of the compounding effects we talked about earlier. Paying for a university or college education is another reason for investing for the long term.

© Monkey Business Images/Shutterstock

One of the most popular ways to build wealth for retirement is to set up an individual retirement account or a **registered retirement savings plan (RRSP)**. You can put your retirement savings money into stocks, government bonds, mutual funds, or any other type of financial security. One major advantage of an RRSP is the tax advantage over investments that are not in a tax-sheltered plan. The amount you deposit into an RRSP can be used as a deduction on your income tax. Another tax advantage to an RRSP is that any interest you earn or any dividends paid on stock held in your plan are tax-exempt until you start taking money out of your plan. In most cases, you will be withdrawing from the plan after you have retired, when you will have less income and so will be paying less tax on the money. Of course, if you take money out of your retirement savings plan at any time, you will have to pay tax on the amount withdrawn. Some people also use the tax-free savings plan described earlier for retirement savings.

A **Registered Education Savings Plan (RESP)** is similar to a retirement savings plan in many ways except instead of using the money for retirement, the money is used to pay for a university or college education. The RESP is designed to make it easy for people to save for their children's post-secondary education. The money deposited into a RESP is tax deferred until it is withdrawn to pay for college or university. As an extra incentive to get people to invest in a RESP, the government will contribute as well.

registered retirement savings plan (RRSP)
An individual retirement account that provides tax benefits to individuals who are investing for their retirement.

Registered Education Savings Plan (RESP) A savings account that provides tax benefits to individuals who are investing for their children's education.

Making sound personal financial decisions requires careful thought and discipline. You should start by establishing a budget; doing so will help you understand your current financial situation, plan for the future, and monitor your progress towards achieving your goals. One of your first goals should be to set aside savings to provide adequate protection against unforeseen financial challenges. One good strategy to build your savings is to "pay yourself first." Another key to financial success is to make careful decisions with respect to your credit cards and other forms of credit. Next, you should turn your attention to investing to build your wealth over time. You'll discover many different opportunities, each with its own pros and cons. No single investment strategy is foolproof, but two principles that have stood the test of time are: (1) start investing early to take full advantage of compounding and (2) diversify your investments against risk.

1

1. Annie Murphy Paul, "Your Head Is in the Cloud," March 12, 2012, *Time*, http://www.time.com/time/magazine/article/0,9171,2108040,00.html.

2. Deborah Blum, "Food That Lasts Forever," March 12, 2012, *Time*, http://www.time.com/time/magazine/article/0,9171,2108051,00.html.

3. Judith Warner, "High Status Stress," March 12, 2012, *Time*, http://www.time.com/time/magazine/article/0,9171,2108019,00.html.

4. PEN Canada, "Public Photography Is Not a Crime," June 21, 2013, http://o.canada.com/news/pen-canada-public-photography.

5. Bryan Walsh, "Nature Is Over," March 12, 2012, *Time*, http://www.time.com/time/magazine/article/0,9171,2108014,00.html.

6. Harriet Barovick, "Niche Aging," March 12, 2012, *Time*, http://www.time.com/time/magazine/article/0,9171,2108022,00.html.

7. Canadian Federation of Independent Business, "Falling dollar, oil prices, send business confidence to post-recession low," news release, January 28, 2016, http://www.cfib-fcei.ca/english/article/8064-falling-dollar-oil-prices-send-business-confidence-to-post-recession-low.html.

8. Imagine Canada website, "Key Facts About Canada's Charities," http://www.imaginecanada.ca/resources-and-tools/research-and-facts/key-facts-about-canada%E2%80%99s-charities.

9. Ari Levy, "Google Parent Alphabet Passes Apple Market Cap at the Open," *cnbc.com*, February 2, 2016, http://www.cnbc.com/2016/02/01/google-passes-apple-as-most-valuable-company.html; Excite declines buying Google, *Business Excellence*, October 10, 2010, http://www.bus-ex.com/article/top-ten-bad-business-decisions?page=0,6; Marguerite Reardon, "Google: Oops, We Spied on Your Wi-Fi," *cnet.com*, May 14, 2010, http://www.cnet.com/news/google-oops-we-spied-on-your-wi-fi; Mitch Wagner, "Google's Pac-Man Cost $120M in Productivity," *pcworld.com*, n.d., http://www.pcworld.com/article/197130/googles_pacman_cost_120_million_in_productivity.html; "101 Dumbest Moments in Business," *fortune.com*, January 16, 2008, http://archive.fortune.com/galleries/2007/fortune/0712/gallery.101_dumbest.fortune/38.html.

10. Simon, "Green Nudge: Nudging Litter into the Bin," *inudgeyou.com*, February 16, 2012, http://inudgeyou.com/archives/819; Richard H. Thaler and Cass R. Sunstein, *Nudge: Improving Decisions About Health, Wealth, and Happiness* (New York: Penguin, 2009).

11. GNI Per Capita 2007 World Bank Data, revised October 17, 2008, http://siteresources.worldbank.org/DATASTATISTICS/Resources/GNIPC.pdf; *CIA World Factbook China*, updated December 18, 2008, https://www.cia.gov/library/publications/the-world-factbook/geos/ch.html; *CIA World Factbook Russia*, updated December 18, 2008, https://www.cia

.gov/library/publications/the-world-factbook/geos/rs.html; *CIA World Factbook Hong Kong*, updated December 18, 2008, https://www.cia.gov/library/publications/the-world-factbook/geos/hk.html.

12. Andy Blatchford, "Trudeau Casts Doubt on Liberals' Balanced-Budget Vow, Cites Fading Economy," *canadianbusiness.com*, February 11, 2016, http://www.canadianbusiness.com/business-news/trudeau-shies-away-from-liberals-balanced-budget-vow-cites-fading-economy; Anu Bararia, "Oil to Drag on Canada Economy but No Recession or Rate Cut: Poll," *reuters.com*, January 14, 2016, http://ca.reuters.com/article/businessNews/idCAKCN0US1TJ20160114; Ashley Csanady, "Government Debt in Canada Set to Top $1.3 Trillion in 2016: Fraser Institute," *nationalpost.com*, January 5, 2016, http://news.nationalpost.com/news/canada/canadian-politics/government-debt-in-canada-set-to-top-1-3-trillion-in-2016-fraser-institute; Andy Blatchford, "Household Debt Still Rising, but Most Canadians in Decent Shape: Experts," *cbc.ca*, December 30, 2015, http://www.cbc.ca/news/business/debt-yearend-1.3383632; David Parkinson, "Canada's Household Debt Burden Hits Record High in Third Quarter," *theglobeandmail.com*, December 14, 2015, http://www.theglobeandmail.com/report-on-business/economy/canadas-household-debt-burden-hits-record-in-third-quarter/article27742769.

13. American Customer Satisfaction Index, ASCI Scores, http://www.theacsi.org/index.php?option=com_content&view=article&id=21&Itemid=116.

14. "Interbrand Releases 2015 Best Global Brands Report," October 4, 2015, *interbrand.com*, http://interbrand.com/?newsroom=interbrand-releases-2015-best-global-brands-report.

15. Andy Riga, "Tech Tornado Wiped Out 21,000 Jobs; Cuts Went Deep. Montreal Sector Poised to Rebound Once Industry Comes Back to Life," *Gazette* (Montreal), November 23, 2002, B1.

16. Michael Addady, "How Apple's Record-breaking iPhone 6 Sales Could Actually Be a Big Problem," *time.com*, August 5, 2015, http://time.com/3985924/apple-sales-iphone; "Apple Loses Its Way," *Advertising Age*, December 28, 2013, http://adage.com/article/news/biggest-advertiser-disasters-2012/238930; Mark Miller, "Apple Core: iPad Rises as iPhone 5 Goes Downmarket," January 10, 2013, *BrandChannel*, http://www.brandchannel.com/home/post/2013/01/10/Apple-iPad-iPhone-Value-011013.aspx.

17. Steven Levy, "Honey, I Shrunk the iPod. A Lot." September 19, 2005, *Newsweek*; John Brodie, "Behind Apple's Strategy: Be Second to Market," August 29, 2005, *Harvard Business School Working Knowledge*, http://hbswk.hbs.edu/item.jhtml?id=4970&t=technology; John Letzing, "What's to Become of Microsoft's Answer to the iPod?" July 29, 2009, *Marketwatch*, http://www.marketwatch.com/story/microsofts-zune-continues-to-struggle-2009-07-29.

18. Daniel Ferry, "Why Investors Should Demand Employee Satisfaction," July 5, 2012, *The Motley Fool*, http://beta.fool.com/catominor/2012/07/05/

why-investors-should-demand-employee-satisfaction/6603; Jeffrey Henning, "Employee Satisfaction & Stock Performance," on Fri, August 6, 2010, Voice of Vovici (blog), http://blog.vovici.com/blog/?Tag=Employee%20Satisfaction%20Surveys, accessed January 17, 2011; "Giving Employees What They Want: The Returns Are Huge," May 4, 2005, *Knowledge@Wharton*, http://knowledge.wharton.upenn.edu/article/1188.cfm; "How Investing in Intangibles—Like Employee Satisfaction—Translates into Financial Returns," January 9, 2008, *Knowledge@Wharton*, http://knowledge.wharton.upenn.edu/article.cfm?articleid=1873.

19. Michael Shulman, "Nearly Half of Canadians Over 50 Have 25% of What They Need to Retire: Survey," September 9, 2015, *ctvnews.ca*, http://www.ctvnews.ca/business/nearly-half-of-canadians-over-50-have-25-of-what-they-need-to-retire-survey-1.2554039.

20. David Kaplan, "eMarketer: E-Commerce Expected to Grow Double Digits through 2012," March 17, 2011, *PaidContent*, http://paidcontent.org/article/419-emarketer-e-commerce-expected-to-grow-double-digits-through-2012; Jeffrey Grau, "Retail E-Commerce Update," December 2008, *eMarketer*, http://www.emarketer.com/Reports/All/Emarketer_2000545.aspx.

21. Statistics Canada, "Population Projections of Visible Minority Groups, Canada, Provinces, and Regions: 2001–2017," Cat. no. 91-541-XIE, based on the reference scenario.

22. Ibid.; Ernest Gundling and Anita Zanchettin with Aperian Global, *Global Diversity: Winning Customers and Engaging Employees Within World Markets* (Boston, MA: Nicholas Brealey International, 2007); Alain Bélanger and Éric Caron Malenfont, "Ethnocultural Diversity in Canada: Prospects for 2017," *Canadian Social Trends*, Winter 2005, 18–21.

23. "Multicultural Programming," *Rogers Communications*, http://www.rogers.com/web/content/multicultural_programs?cm_mmc=Redirects-_-Cable_EN-_-Channel_ThemePacks-_-multicultural; "Diverse Languages for Diverse Needs," *TD Canada Trust*, https://www.td.com/corporate-responsibility/diversity/serving-diverse-needs/diverse-languages-for-diverse-needs.jsp.

24. "Diversity at Work," *hrcouncil.ca*, http://hrcouncil.ca/hr-toolkit/diversity-workforce-matters.cfm.

25. "Attitudes of Young People Toward Diversity," February 2005, *CIRCLE* (fact sheet), http://www.civicyouth.org/PopUps/FactSheets/Attitudes%202.25.pdf.

26. Central Intelligence Agency, "The World Factbook," https://www.cia.gov/library/publications/the-world-factbook/fields/2177.html.

27. "World Population Prospects, 2015 Revision," http://esa.un.org/unpd/wpp/Publications/Files/Key_Findings_WPP_2015.pdf.

28. Julian Sancton, "Book Review: 'Overdressed,' by Elizabeth L. Cline," June 21, 2012, *bloomberg.com*, http://www.businessweek.com/articles/2012-06-21/book-review-overdressed-by-elizabeth-l

-dot-cline; Eliana Dockterman, "How U.S. Clothing Brands Are Getting Greener," *Time*, August 20, 2012, http://www.time.com/time/magazine/article/0,9171,2121658,00.html.

29. "Common Environmental Labels and Claims in Canada," *Innovation, Science and Economic Development Canada*, https://www.ic.gc.ca/eic/site/oca-bc.nsf/eng/ca02523.html; Matthew Knight, "It's Not Easy Being Green," July 23, 2008, *CNN*, http://www.cnn.com/2008/TECH/science/07/16/greenwash; Carl Frankel, "When Green Marketing Becomes Greenwashing," December 11, 2008, *Matter Net-work*, http://featured.matternetwork.com/2008/12/short-history-green-marketing.cfm; Temma Ehrenfield, "Green or Greenwash," *Newsweek*, July 14, 2008, 56.

30. Benefits Canada Staff, "Why Employee Loyalty Is Declining," July 18, 2014, *profitguide.com*, http://www.profitguide.com/manage-grow/human-resources/why-employee-loyalty-is-declining-67639.

31. Sue Shellenbarger, "Pending Job Flexibility Act Received Mixed Reviews," *WSJ Career Journal*, http://www.careerjournal.com/columnists/workfamily/20010426-workfamily.html; Les Christie, "Bad Attitudes in the Workplace," September 6, 2005, *CNNMoney*, http://money.cnn.com/2005/08/24/pf/workplace_morale/?section=money_pf; John Ellis, "Inspiring Worker Loyalty One Tough Job," July 1, 2005, *East Bay Business Times*, http://www.bizjournals.com/eastbay/stories/2005/07/04/focus1.html.

32. "Sustainability: Balancing Opportunity and Risk in the Consumer Products Industry, 2007 Report," *Deloitte*, http://www.deloitte.com/dtt/cda/content/us_cb_sustainability-study_june2007opt.pdf; Sarah Fister Gale, "While Everything Else Stops, Green Still Means Go," January 18, 2009, *GreenBiz*, http://greenbiz.com/feature/2009/01/19/green-still-means-go.

33. Statistics Canada, http://www.statcan.gc.ca/tables-tableaux/sum-som/l01/cst01/labr69a-eng.htm; "Beijing Tops China's Hourly Minimum Wage," September 30, 2015, *chinadaily.com*, http://www.chinadaily.com.cn/china/2015-09/30/content_22017853.htm.

34. Jason Beaubien, "Asian Tsunami Devastates Sri Lankan Fishing Industry," January 10, 2005, *NPR Morning Edition*, http://www.npr.org/templates/story/story.php?storyId=4276161; Sally Pook, "Phuket Tourism Industry Crippled by Mass Cancellations," January 8, 2005, *Cyber Diver News Net-work*, http://www.cdnn.info/news/travel/t050111.html; Veronique de Rugy, "Homeland Security Scuffle," October 15, 2004, *National Review*, http://www.nationalreview.com/comment/rugy200410150840.asp; Reuters, "Bush Brushes Aside Rebuilding Cost Concerns," *MSNBC*, http://www.msnbc.msn.com/id/9374106.

35. Daniel Pink, "Pomp and Circumspect," *New York Times*, June 4, 2005, http://www.nytimes.com/2005/06/04/opinion/pomp-and-circumspect.html?_r=1.

2

1. Adapted from "Making Ethical Decisions: The Six Pillars of Character," *Josephson Institute of Ethics*, http://josephsoninstitute.org/med/med-2sixpillars.

2. "For the First Time in a Decade, Lying, Cheating, and Stealing Among American Students Drops," November 20, 2012, *Josephson Institute*,

http://charactercounts.org/pdf/reportcard/2012/ReportCard-2012-PressRelease-HonestyIntegrityCheating.pdf; Linette Ho, "Classroom Cheating on the Rise; School Isn't About Education Any More; It's About Getting Good Grades and That Increases the Pressure," *Vancouver Sun*, March 28, 2012, A13.

3. Josh Levs, "Big Three Auto CEOs Flew Private Jets to Ask for Taxpayer Money," November 19, 2008, *CNN*, http://www.cnn.com/2008/US/11/19/autos.ceo.jets.

4. "Divorce Duel Reveals Welch's Perks," September 6, 2002, *CNNMoney*, http://money.cnn.com/2002/09/06/news/companies/welch_ge.

5. Barney Gimbel, "Why We'll Miss the Disney Trial," December 27, 2004, *Fortune*, http://money.cnn.com/magazines/fortune/fortune_archive/2004/12/27/8217949/index.htm; Peter Bart, "Disney's Basket Cases," March 7, 2004, *Variety*, http://www.variety.com/article/VR1117901299.html?categoryid=1&cs=1.

6. Vincent Donovan, "The Whistleblower: Sylvie Therrien, a Former EI Fraud Investigator Who Leaked Information About the Government's Efforts to Reduce Payouts, Says Her Decision to Come Forward Has Taken a Huge Personal Toll," *Toronto Star*, January 30, 2016, IN.1; Carly Weeks, "Experts Raise Alarm over Drug Prices," *Globe and Mail*, September 28, 2015, A7; "'Most Hated Man in America' Resigns as Turing Pharmaceuticals CEO Day After Securities Fraud Arrest," *Telegraph-Journal* (Saint John, NB), December 19, 2015, A10; Rosie DiManno, "2013 Was a Stuporific Year for Stupidity," *Toronto Star*, December 31, 2013, A1; Megan O'Toole, "U of T to Review Spence's PhD Thesis for Plagiarism; May Lead to Hearing," *National Post*, January 12, 2013, A13; Norma Greenaway, "Former PM Paid Taxes on Only Half of $225,000;," *Calgary Herald*, May 20, 2009, A1; David Kesmodel and John Wilke, "Whole Foods Is Hot, Wild Oats a Dud—So Said 'Rahodeb,'" July 12, 2007, *Wall Street Journal*, http://online.wsj.com/article/SB118418782959963745.html.

7. "National Business Ethics Survey (NBES) (2013)" Ethics Resource Center, https://www.ethics.org/research/eci-research/nbes/nbes-reports/nbes-2013; "State of Ethics in Large Companies, 2015," Ethics Resource Center, https://www.ethics.org/newsite/research/eci-research/nbes/nbes-reports/large-companies.

8. Felicity Barringer, "Clorox Courts Sierra Club, and a Product Is Endorsed," March 26, 2008, *New York Times*, http://www.nytimes.com/2008/03/26/business/businessspecial2/26cleanser.html; Sarah Ellison, "Kraft Limits on Kids' Ads May Cheese Off Rivals," *Wall Street Journal*, January 13, 2005, http://www.aef.com/industry/news/data/2005/3076; Anonymous, "SNC-Lavalin Hopes Algeria Police Raid Will Help to Shed Light on Wrongdoing," *Daily Commercial News*, June 13, 2013, 1–2; Canada News Wire (Ottawa), "Tim Hortons Announces New Cage-Free Egg Policy," February 1, 2016; Tanya Talaga, "Season Ends for ORNGE Heli-Novela," *Toronto Star*, August 3, 2012, A8; Andy Sharman, "VW Schedules Pit Stop for 11M Cars," http://www.ft.com/cms/s/0/341f56d4-a4b9-11e5-a91e-162b86790c58.html#axzz3zKDinpJg; Mike Spector, "VW's U.S. Chief Apologizes, Says Engineers at Fault," *Wall Street Journal*, October 9, 2015, B1.

9. *Sevenly*, www.sevenly.org; Evan Kirkpatrick, "How Sevenly CEO Dale Partridge Is Changing the World $7 at a Time," March 4, 2013, *Forbes*,

http://www.forbes.com/sites/evankirkpatrick/2013/03/04/how-sevenly-ceo-dale-partridge-is-changing-the-world-7-at-a-time/#760b11115ff8; Gewn Moran, "Doing Good One T-Shirt at a Time," June 7, 2012, *Entrepreneur*, http://www.entrepreneur.com/article/223517.

10. Bob Leduc, "Complaining Customers Are Good for Business," May 11, 2004, *Virtual Marketing Newsletter*, http://www.marketingsource.com/newsletter/05-11-2004.html.

11. Misty Harris, "Maple Leaf Winning Back Its Customers," *Edmonton Journal*, January 23, 2009, A17; "Culture Starts at the Top," *National Post*, November 18, 2010, FP12; Derek DeCloet, "Cold Cuts and Hard Truths," *Globe and Mail*, September 3, 2011, B3.

12. Jeannine Stein, "O.B. Ultra Tampons Are Coming Back, and the Company Apologizes with a Song," December 8, 2011, *Los Angeles Times*, http://articles.latimes.com/2011/dec/08/news/la-heb-ob-tampons-return-20111208; o.b. video apology message, http://articles.latimes.com/2011/dec/08/news/la-heb-ob-tampons-return-20111208, bot.

13. Kyle Stock, "Chipotle's Sales Have Dropped by 10.3 Million Burritos," February 2, 2016, *Bloomberg*, http://www.bloomberg.com/news/articles/2016-02-02/chipotle-s-sales-have-dropped-by-10-3-million-burritos?cmpid=BBD020316_BIZ; Ginger Christ, "Taking a Bite Out of the Leadership Burrito," January 6, 2016, http://ehstoday.com/blog/chipotle-taking-bite-out-leadership-burrito; Susan Berfield, "The Sustainable Locally Sourced Free-Range Humanely Raised Made-To-Order Toxic Burrito," *Bloomberg Business*, December 28, 2015–January 10, 2016, 44–49; Yahoo! Finance Canada, https://ca.finance.yahoo.com/echarts?s=CMG#symbol=CMG;range=6m.

14. "It's Win-Win When Business Partners with Charities and Nonprofits!" Imagine Canada, news release, March 5, 2009, http://www.imaginecanada.ca.

15. Linda Dunlop, "Cause Marketing Makes a Winning Business Strategy," *Toronto Star*, November 10, 2015, A10; "News & Polls," *Ipsos Marketing Canada*, http://ipsos-na.com/images/news-polls/media/7032-infographic.jpg.

16. *Telus*, http://community.telus.com/how-we-give/community-boards.

17. "Canada's Greenest Employers," 2015 Winners: http://www.canadastop100.com/environmental; *Home Depot Canada*, https://www.homedepot.ca/en/home/corporate-information/media-relations/2015/july-8-2015.html; *IKEA Canada*, http://www.ikea.com/ms/en_CA/this-is-ikea/people-and-planet/index.html; "Top 50 Socially Responsible Corporations: 2014," June 5, 2014, *mcleans.ca*, http://www.macleans.ca/work/bestcompanies/top-50-socially-responsible-corporations-2014; *Hemlock Printers*, http://www.hemlock.com/sustainability/carbon_neutrality_&_zero.

18. *McDonald's Canada*, http://www.about mcdonalds.com/mcd/sustainability/planet/minimizing-waste.html.

19. Elizabeth Weise, "In a Drought, Should We Drink Sewage? Singapore Does," *usatoday.com*, http://www.usatoday.com/story/tech/2015/06/02/singapore-water-recycled-sewer-water-newater-california-drought/27958823; Meera Senthilingam, "Drinking Sewage: Solving Singapore's Water Problem," *cnn.com*, http://www.cnn.com/2014/09/23/living/newater-singapore.

20. Kay Johnson, "Selling to the poor," *Time, Bonus Section*, May 2005; C.K. Prahalad and

Allen Hammond, "The payoff for investing in poor countries," *Harvard Business School Working Knowledge*, http://hbswk.hbs.edu/item.jhtml?id=3180&t=nonprofit&noseek=one.

21. *Tree Canada*, https://treecanada.ca/en/programs/grow-clean-air/how-become-carbon-neutral.

22. Jerry Hirsch, "Plug-in Hybrid Sales Soar," July 21, 2012, *Los Angeles Times*, http://articles.latimes.com/2012/jul/21/business/la-fi-0721-autos-electric-vehicles-20120721; "Marketing, Business and Sustainable Development," *Business and Sustainable Development*, http://www.bsdglobal.com/markets/green_marketing.asp.

23. "Corruption Perceptions Index 2015," *Transparency International*, http://www.transparency.org/cpi2015.

24. "Bribe Payers Index 2011," *Transparency International*, http://www.transparency.org.

25. Thomas Donaldson, "Values in Tension," *Harvard Business Review*, September–October 1996.

26. *Sears Canada*, http://www.searscsr.ca/Our-Products/Ethical-Sourcing/Code-of-Vendor-Conduct.aspx.

3

1. Conference Board of Canada, "Canadian Outlook: Economic Forecast," Spring 2015; Nick Cunningham, "How Long Can OPEC Maintain Its Current Strategy?" June 1, 2015, *Time*, http://time.com/3903198/opec-oil-strategy/; Gordon Isfeld, "Canada's Economy Shrinks for First Time in Four Years as Oil Shock Sinks In," May 29, 2015, *financialpost.com*, http://business.financialpost.com/news/economy/canadas-economy-shrinks-for-first-time-in-four-years-as-oils-collapse-takes-toll.

2. Conference Board of Canada, "Canadian Economy to Remain Sluggish Through 2016, but No Recession," news release 16-43, http://www.conferenceboard.ca/press/newsrelease/16-02-04/canadian_economy_to_remain_sluggish_through_2016_but_no_recession.aspx; Kip Beckman, Conference Board of Canada, "Global Economic Trends and Forecasts, Winter 2016," http://www.conferenceboard.ca/temp/2d94da80-390e-432a-b74e-e863daf5b1b3/7693_worldoutlook_winter2016.pdf; Statistics Canada, "Housing Starts by Province," http://www.statcan.gc.ca/tables-tableaux/sum-som/l01/cst01/manuf05-eng.htm; Gordon Isfeld, "Canada's Economy Shrinks for First Time in Four Years as Oil Shock Sinks In," May 29, 2015, *financialpost.com*, http://business.financialpost.com/news/economy/canadas-economy-shrinks-for-first-time-in-four-years-as-oils-collapse-takes-toll; "2016 Salary Increases to Be Lower Than Anticipated: Survey," February 12, 2016, *hrreporter.com*, http://www.hrreporter.com/articleview/26779-2016-salary-increases-to-be-lower-than-anticipated-survey.

3. Department of Finance Canada, "Annual Financial Report of the Government of Canada Fiscal year 2014–2015," http://www.fin.gc.ca/afr-rfa/2015/report-rapport-eng.asp; Ashley Csanady, "Government Debt in Canada Set to Top $1.3 Trillion in 2016: Fraser Institute," *nationalpost.com*, January 5, 2016, http://news.nationalpost.com/news/canada/canadian-politics/government-debt-in-canada-set-to-top-1-3-trillion-in-2016-fraser-institute.

4. Department of Finance Canada, "Annual Financial Report of the Government of Canada Fiscal year 2014–2015."

5. Trading Economics, "Canada Money Supply M1 1975–2015," http://www.tradingeconomics.com/canada/money-supply-m1.

6. *Bank of Canada*, www.bankofcanada.ca.

7. Tavia Grant, "Canada's Aging Population Expected to Head West," September 17, 2014, *globeandmail.com*, http://www.theglobeandmail.com/report-on-business/economy/canadas-aging-population-projected-to-exacerbate-health-care-strain/article20651306; CBC News, "Canada Seniors Population to Jump, Workforce Decline by 2063, September 18, 2014, *cbc.ca*, available http://www.cbc.ca/news/business/canada-s-seniors-population-to-jump-workforce-decline-by-2063-1.2770359; Statistics Canada, "Population Projections: Canada, the Provinces and Territories, 2013 to 2063," http://www.statcan.gc.ca/daily-quotidien/140917/dq140917a-eng.htm; Statistics Canada, "Immigration and Ethnocultural Diversity in Canada," http://www12.statcan.gc.ca/nhs-enm/2011/as-sa/99-010-x/99-010-x2011001-eng.cfm.

8. Gwyn Morgan, "Canada's Monopoly Healthcare System Is Financially Unsustainable," March 3, 2015, *globeandmail.com*, http://www.theglobeandmail.com/report-on-business/monopoly-service-not-working-for-canadian-health-care/article23238707.

9. EPA Region 9 Newsletter, "Creating Green Jobs Through Recycling," February 2011, *EPA*, http://www.epa.gov/region9/newsletter/feb2011/greenjobs.html; "Pay as You Throw Fact Sheet for State Officials," July 26, 2011, *EPA*, http://www.epa.gov/osw/conserve/tools/payt/tools/state.htm; "More Recycling Will Create 1.5 Million New U.S. Jobs," November 14, 2011, *Recycling Works Campaign*, http://www.recyclingworkscampaign.org/2011/11/more-jobs-less-pollution.

10. Adam Minter, "For Chinese Students, Bring-Your-Desk-to-School Day," September 12, 2012, *Bloomberg TV*, http://www.bloomberg.com/news/2012-09-12/for-chinese-students-bring-your-desk-to-school-day.html.

11. Statistics Canada, "Federal Government Employment in Census Metropolitan Areas," *The Daily*, November 28, 2011.

12. Trading Economics, "Canada GDP 1960–2016," http://www.tradingeconomics.com/canada/gdp.

13. Statistics Canada, "Labour Force Survey, January 2016," http://www.statcan.gc.ca/daily-quotidien/160205/dq160205a-eng.htm.

14. Statistics Canada, "Canadian Economic Accounts, Fourth Quarter 2014 and December 2014," http://www.statcan.gc.ca/daily-quotidien/150303/dq150303a-eng.htm; "Provincial Outlook–June 2015–Changing of the Guard," *Royal Bank of Canada*, http://www.rbc.com/economics/economic-reports/provincial-economic-forecasts.html.

15. Statistics Canada, "Consumer Price Index, December 2015," http://www.statcan.gc.ca/daily-quotidien/160122/dq160122a-eng.htm.

4

1. *CIA – The World Factbook*, www.cia.gov; "Global Economic Outlook 2015 – Key Findings," *Conference Board*, www.conference-board.org.

2. *US Census Bureau*, www.census.gov; *Statistics Canada*, www.statcan.gc.ca.

3. "Country Comparisons," *CIA—The World Factbook*, www.cia.gov.

4. Brian S. Hall, "One Big Concern About Facebook and China," December 10, 2014, finance.yahoo.com; Craig Smith, "By the Numbers: 200+ Amazing Facebook User Statistics," February 23, 2015, *DMR Digital Market Marketing Ramblings*, expandedramblings.com; Berit Block, "Facebook: Around the World in 800 Days," May 17, 2012, *Comscore*, www.comscore.com; Aaron Smith, Laurie Segall, and Stacy Cowley, "Facebook Reaches One Billion Users," October 4, 2012, *CNNMoney*, money.cnn.com.

5. Natasha Lomas, "ABI: Africa's Mobile Market to Pass 80% Subscriber Penetration in Q1 Next Year," November 28, 2012, *TechCrunch*, techcrunch.com; Pia Heikkila, "1B Cell Phone Users and No Apple iPhone in India's Breakneck Mobile-Apps Market," September 15, 2012, *International Business Times*, www.ibtimes.com; Sumnina Udas, "Bringing Toilets and Dignity to India's Poor," September 17, 2012, *CNN*, www.cnn.com.

6. "2014 Ranking of the Top 100 Brands", *Interbrand*, interbrand.com; Dave Kiley and Burt Helm, "The Greatest Trust Offensive," *BusinessWeek*, September 17, 2009, businessweek.com.

7. "Insperiences," *Trendwatching* newsletter, www.trendwatching.com; Lisa Smith, "The Good and Bad of Globalization," May 11, 2007, *Forbes*, http://www.forbes.com/2007/05/11/globalization-outsourcing-nafta-pf-education-in_ls_0511investopedia_inl.html; "Advantages and Disadvantages of International Trade," *Economic Concepts*, www.economicconcepts.com.

8. Michael Porter, *The Competitive Advantage of Nations* (New York: Free Press, 1998), 73–74.

9. "World Trade Report 2014: Trade and Developemnt: Recent Trends and the Role of the WTO," *World Trade Organization*, www.wto.org.

10. "Canadian International Merchandise Trade," December 2014, Cat. no. 65-001-X, Statistics Canada, www.statscan.gc.ca; "Economic Indicators, by Province and Territory (monthly and quarterly) (Canada)" Statistics Canada, www.statscan.gc.ca.

11. Paul Ausick, "P&G Only One of Many Hit by Foreign Exchange Rates (PG, PEP, KMB, CL, KO, PM, MCD, F, CCL)," June 20, 2012, *Wall Street Journal*, 247wallst.com.

12. Neha Gupta, "What Is Countertrade?," March 11, 2010, *Barter News Weekly*, www.barternewsweekly.com; Dan West, "Countertrade—An Innovative Approach to Marketing," *BarterNews* 36 (1996), barternews.com; *Global Offset and Countertrade Association*, www.globaloffset.org.

13. Ellen Barry, "Have Car, Need Briefs? In Russia, Barter Is Back," February 8, 2009, *New York Times*, www.nytimes.com.

14. "Mattel Issues New Massive China Toy Recall," Associated Press, August 14, 2007, *MSNBC*, www.msnbc.msn.com; Eric S. Lipton and David Barboza, "As More Toys Are Recalled, Trail Ends in China," June 19, 2007, *New York Times*, http://www.nytimes.com.

15. E. Yellin, *Your Call Is (Not That) Important to Us* (New York: Simon and Schuster, 2009); Carolyn Beeler, "Outsourced Call Centers Return, to U.S. Homes," August 25, 2010, *NPR*, www.npr.org.

16. Curtis, "Thinking Outside the Border," *Minority Business Entrepreneur*, September–October 2005, www.export.gov.

17. Stacy Meichtry and John Stoll, "Fiat Nears Stake in Chrysler That Could Lead to Takeover," January 20, 2009, *Wall Street Journal*, online .wsj.com; "eBay to Acquire Skype", Press Release, September 12, 2005, *Skype*, www.skype.com.

18. Ted Burnham, "What Pizza Hut's Crown Crust Pizza Says About Global Fast Food Marketing," May 2, 2012, *NPR*, www.npr.org; Nina Africano, "McDonald's International: Top Ten Most Unusual Around the World," September 3, 2010, *AOL Travel*, news.travel.aol .com; www.mcdonalds.com; *Dominos*, www .dominos.com; *Serious Eats*, slice.seriouseats.com; *How Stuff Works*, recipes.howstuffworks.com; William Mellor, "McDonald's No Match for KFC in China as Colonel Rules Fast Food," January 26, 2011, *Bloomberg*, www.bloomberg.com; Erik German, "Morocco Loving the McArabia," May 30, 2010, *Global Post*, globalpost.com.

19. David Barboza, "Intel to Build Advanced Chip-Making Plant in China," March 27, 2007, *New York Times*, http://www.nytimes.com.

20. Cynthia Churchwell, "Rethink the Value of Joint Ventures," May 10, 2004, *Harvard Business School Working Knowledge*, hbswk.hbs.edu.

21. Anna Molin, "IKEA Regrets Cutting Women from Saudi Ad," October 1, 2012, *Wall Street Journal Online*, online.wsj.com.

22. Michael Schuman, "Hyundai Grows Up," July 2005, *Time Global Business*, time.com; Cathie Gandel, "At 5 Feet 10 Inches, I Was Too Tall for Tokyo: My Turn," *Newsweek*, December 12, 2005; Moon Ihlwan, "Hyundai Bets Big on India and China," January 30, 2008, *Business Week*, www.businessweek.com; "Maruti, Hyundai, Tata Motors Lose Market Share to Smaller Firms in 2010," April 10, 2011, *India Times*, articles .economictimes.indiatimes.com.

23. "Rural Market India Brand Equity Foundation," *IBEF*, www.ibef.org; "Selling to Rural India," *Springwise Newsletter*, June 2003, www .springwise.com; "Red herring: Selling to the Poor," April 11, 2004, *The Next Practice*, www .thenextpractice.com; Tim Weber, "Are You Ready for Globalization 2.0?" January 28, 2005, *BBC News*, news.bbc.co.uk.

24. 2014 statistics, *Internet World Stats*, www .internetworldstats.com; Nin-Hai Tseng, "Why China Won't Charge It," February 14, 2011, *CNNMoney*, http://money.cnn.com/2011/02/14/ news/international/china_credit_cards.fortune/ index.htm.

25. "Doing Business 2015: Going Beyond Efficiency," www.doingbusiness.org.

26. Will Sarni, "Water Works," *Interbrand*, www .interbrand.com; Brian Dumaine, "2030: China's Coming Water Crisis," December 14, 2012, *Fortune*, tech.fortune.cnn.com; "WaterFacts, 2012," *Water.Org*, water.org.

27. "Shadow Market: 2011 Global Software Piracy Study," May 2012, *Business Software Alliance*, portal.bsa.org.

28. "USTR Releases 2002 Inventory of Trade Barriers," press release, April 2, 2002, www .useu.be; "U.S. Targets Non-tariff Barriers to Global Trade," news release, April 3, 2002, www .usconsulate.org.hk; Foreign Affairs, Trade and Development Canada, www.international.gc.ca.

29. Debt Relief Under the Heavily Indebted Poor Countries Initiative: Fact Sheet, September 30, 2014, *IMF*, www.imf.org; Debt Relief Under the Heavily Indebted Poor Countries (HIPC) Initiative: Fact Sheet, December 16, 2010, *IMF*, www.imf.org.

30. Daniel Workman, "Top 10 Exporting Countries Causing the US Trade Deficit," April 27, 2010, Suite101 website, www.suite101.com, accessed February 11, 2011.

31. "European Union: People 2015," *CIA—The World Factbook*, www.theodora.com; "European Union: Economy 2015," www.theodora.com; *The European Union*, europia.eu.

32. Sarah Dilorenzo, "With Economy Faltering, Debt Crisis Raging, Europe Is Down on Euros on Their 10th Birthday," December 30, 2011, *Canadian Business*, www.canadianbusiness.com; Janet Davison, "European Debt Crisis Puts More Than Just Money at Stake," December 9, 2011, *CBC News*, http://www.cbc.ca/news/business/ story/2011/12/09/f-euro-history-identity.html; "Flaherty Calls Europe's Debt Woes 'Dire'," November 25, 2011, *CBC News*, http://www .cbc.ca/news/politics/story/2011/11/25/flaherty -economy-speech.html.

33. "Creativity and Prosperity: The Global Creativity Index," January 2011, *Martin Prosperity Institute*, martinprosperity.org; "The Bloomberg Innovation Index," *Bloomberg*, www .bloomberg.com.

5

1. Statistics Canada, Business Register Division, Correspondence, January 26, 2016. (Note: Numbers are not comparable to those reported in previous editions of this text because methodological changes have been made in data collection and reporting. For more information, see http://www23.statcan.gc.ca/imdb-bmdi/ document/1105_D16_T9_V1-eng.htm.

2. Ibid.

3. Murray McNeill, "The Lesson Learned: Put Breakup Rules in Writing," *Winnipeg Free Press*, September 2, 2006, B4.

4. *Supra* note 1.

5. Loblaw Companies Limited, *2014 Annual Report.*

6. Mark Kearney and Randy Ray, *I Know That Name!* (Toronto: Dundurn Press, 2002), 48–50.

7. Sherritt International Corp. trading information, https://ca.finance.yahoo.com/q?s=s.to&ql=1, January 18, 2016.

8. Kroeker Farms, http://www.kroekerfarms.com.

9. G. Wilson, "How to Rein in the Imperial CEO," *Wall Street Journal*, July 9, 2009, A15; Reuters, "GM Appoints CEO Mary Barra Chairman," https://ca.finance.yahoo.com/news/gm-appoints -ceo-mary-barra-chairman-201316897–sector.html.

10. C. Huhigg & D. Kocieniewski, "How Apple Sidesteps Billions in Taxes," *New York Times*, April 28, 2012, A1; J. Drucker and H. Zschiegner, "Inside Google's $1 Billion-a-Year Tax Cutting Strategy," October 21, 2010, *Bloomberg BusinessWeek*, http://www.businessweek.com/ technology/google-tax-cut/google-terminal.html; S. Gustin, "Apple's Tax Avoidance: Evil Scheming, Good Business, or Both?," May 1, 2012, *Time*, http://business.time.com/2012/05/01/apples -tax-avoidance-evil-scheming-good -businessor-both; J. Lowder, "The Double Irish and the Dutch Sandwich: The Explainer's Field Guide to Exotic Tax Dodges," *Slate*, http:// www.slate.com/articles/news_and_politics/ explainer/2011/04/the_double_irish_and_the _dutch_sandwich.html; I. Sherr and S. Tibken, "Apple to Pay Dividend, Plans $10 Billion Buyback, March 19, 2012, *Wall Street Journal*,

http://online.wsj.com/article/SB10001424052702 304724404577291071289857802.html.

11. Tim Kiladze and Janet McFarland, "The Trouble with Equity-Based Pay and the Elusive Quest for a Remedy," *Globe and Mail*, December 5, 2015, B8; Janet McFarland, "The Say-on-Pay Shift," *Globe and Mail*, September 29, 2015, B1; Dan Healing, "Observers See Hope for Lower Growth in Executive Pay," *Calgary Herald*, June 12, 2015, C7; Janet McFarland, "Investors Balk at Excessive Pay," *Globe and Mail*, June 6, 2015, B9; Eric Atkins, "CN Caps CEO's Bonus Because of Rise in Train Derailments, Injuries," March 26, 2105, B6; J. Lublin, "Say-on-Pay Votes Show Results," March 1, 2012, *Wall Street Journal*, http://online.wsj.com/article/SB10001424 052970204571404577255641531516510.html.

12. *Co-operatives and Mutuals Canada*, www .canada.coop; "Top 300 Co-operatives Have a Turnover of USD $2.3tn," *International Co-operative Alliance*, http://ica.coop/en/media/news/ top-300-co-operatives-have-turnover-usd-23tn; "New Research on Co-ops in Canada: $5 Billion and 600,000 Jobs," *Canadian CED Network*, https://ccednet-rcdec.ca/en/new-in-ced/2015/09/ 23/new-research-co-ops-canada-50-billion-and -600000-jobs.

13. "Key Facts About Canada's Charities," *Imagine Canada*, http://www.imaginecanada.ca/ resources-and-tools/research-and-facts/key-facts -about-canada%E2%80%99s-charities.

14. "Franchising Fast Facts," *Canadian Franchise Association*, http://www.cfa.ca/tools_resources/ franchise-research-facts.

15. "McDonald's Worldwide," *McDonald's Canada*, http://www.mcdonalds.ca/ca/en/our _story/mcdonalds_worldwide.html.

16. *Restaurant Brands International*, http://www .rbi.com. See also *Investors Section*, http://investor .rbi.com.

17. *Wee Piggies & Paws*, https://weepiggies.com.

18. Julie Bennett, "Franchising Attracts More Women, Minorities," *Startup Journal*, accessed through *Entrepreneur.com*, http://www .entrepreneur.com/franchises/franchisezone/ startupjournal/article61324.html.

19. See *Entrepreneur.com* for individual franchisors, http://www.entrepreneur.com/ franchises/subway/282839-2.html.

20. "Frequently Asked Questions," Tim Hortons, http://www.timhortons.com/ca/en/corporate/ franchise-ca-faq.php.

21. *Molly Maid*, www.mollymaid.ca.

22. R. Gibson, "Franchising—Have It Whose Way?," *Wall Street Journal*, May 17, 2010, R6; R. Gibson, "Burger King Franchisees Can't Have It Their Way," *Wall Street Journal*, January 21, 2012, B1; S. Needleman, "Tough Times for Franchising," *Wall Street Journal*, February 9, 2012, B7; P. Ziobro and K. Benn, "Burger King to Raise Price of Its $1 Double Cheeseburger," *Wall Street Journal*, February 17, 2010, http://online.wsj.com/ article/SB10001424052748703444804575071522 969658634.html.

6

1. Industry Canada, "Key Small Business Statistics—August 2013," http://www.ic.gc.ca/eic/ site/061.nsf/eng/02804.html and http://www.ic.gc .ca/eic/site/061.nsf/eng/02805.html; Matt Lundy, "Canadians Increasingly Becoming Entrepreneurs and Small Business Owners," October 3, 2012,

Canadian Business, www.canadianbusiness.com; Fondation de l'entrepreneurship, "Canadian Entrepreneurship Status 2010," http://www.bdc .ca/EN/about/sme_research/Pages/default.aspx.
2. Matthew Miller and Duncan Greenberg, "The Forbes 400," September 17, 2008, Forbes, http:// www.forbes.com/2008/09/16/forbes-400-billionaires -lists-400list08_cx_mn_0917richamericans_land .html.
3. Fondation de l'entrepreneurship, supra note 1, 13.
4. Wendy Gillis, "iPoo Bathroom App Pays Off for Jokesters," Toronto Star, June 12, 2012; Dylan Love, "Stupid iPhone Apps That We Can't Believe Are Real," March 30, 2015, Business Insider, http://www.businessinsider.com/stupid-iphone -apps-2011-6?op=1; Geoffrey A. Fowler, "Appsurd: In Silicon Valley, It's Hard to Make a Joke," June 5, 2012, Wall Street Journal, http:// online.wsj.com/article/SB1000142405270230350 5504577404284117534706.html.
5. Guy Kawasaki, "The Top 10 Mistakes of Entrepreneurs," presented to the UC Berkeley Hass School of Business, March 11, 2013, YouTube, http://www.youtube.com/watch?v =HHjgK6p4nrw,.
6. Wells Fargo news release: "More than Half of Small Business Owners Work at Least Six-Day Weeks, Still Find Time for Personal Life," August 9, 2005, https://www.wellsfargo .com/press/20050809_GallupPersonalLife; Discover Financial Services: "Discover Polls Reveal True Character of the American Entrepreneur," October 22, 2007, http:// investorrelations.discoverfinancial.com/ phoenix.zhtml?c=204177&p=irol-newsArticle &ID=1065373&highlight; "Small Business Owners Working Longer Hours," May 26, 2009, Rent to Own, http://rtoonline.com/Content/ Article/may09/smal-business-owners-work -hours-survey-052609.asp.
7. Brian Wu and Anne Marie Knott, "Entrepreneurial Risk and Market Entry," SBA Office of Advocacy, January 2005, http://www.sba.gov/ advo/research/wkpbw249.pdf.
8. "Failure: Use It as a Springboard to Success," US SBA Online Library, http://www.sba.gov/ library/successXIII/19-Failure-Use-it.doc.
9. Alice E. Vincent, "Rejection Letters: The Publishers Who Got It Embarrassingly Wrong …," November 7, 2012, Huffington Post, http://www .huffingtonpost.co.uk/2012/05/16/publishers-who -got-it-wrong_n_1520190.html#slide=more226527; also supra note 7.
10. Sian Beilock, "Creativity Happens When You Least Expect It," February 8, 2012, Psychology Today, http://www.psychologytoday.com/blog/ choke/201202/creativity-happens-when-you-least -expect-it.
11. Keith McFarland, "What Makes Them Tick," Inc 500, http://www.inc.com/resources/ inc500/2005/articles/20051001/tick.html; Kwame Kuadey, "Bootstrapping Your Startup? Make Money Before You Spend It," June 12, 2012, Young Entrepreneurs Council, http://theyec.org/bootstrap ping-your-startup-make-money-before-you-spend-it.
12. "How to Finance a New Business," April 2008, Consumer Reports, http://www.consumerreports .org/cro/money/credit-loan/how-to-finance-a-new -business/overview/how-to-finance-a-new-business -ov.htm.
13. John Tozzi, "Credit Cards Replace Small Business Loans," August 20, 2008, Business Week, http://www.businessweek.com/smallbiz/content/

aug2008/ sb20080820_288348.htm?chan=smallbiz _smallbiz+index+page_top+small+business+stories.
14. "Start-up Information," Delaware Small Business Development Center, http://www.delawaresbdc .org/DocumentMaster.aspx?doc=1003#6.
15. Mike Freeman, "San Diego's Investing Angels," January 31, 2013, San Diego Union Tribune, http:// www.utsandiego.com/news/2013/jan/31/Tech -Coast-Angels-fund-local-start-ups/?page=1#article -copy; "Financial Assistance," Small Business Administration, http://www.sba.gov/services/ financialassistance/index.html.
16. LendingClub, www.lendingclub.com; Grouplend, www.grouplend.com.
17. Sarah Barmak, "Rich and Ready to Take Risks," Maclean's, January 26, 2015, 38–39; National Angel Capital Organization, www .nacocanada.com; "2013 Report on Angel Investing Activity in Canada," www.nacocanada.com.
18. Shane Dingman, "Who Needs Silicon Valley? Canadian Startups Scoring Bigger Deals," February 11, 2015, Globe and Mail, http://www .theglobeandmail.com/report-on-business/small -business/sb-money/business-funding/who-needs -silicon-valley-canadian-startups-scoring-bigger -deals/article22904528; Danny Bradbury, "Canadian Tech Firms Are Getting Funded, but Gaps Remain," http://business.financialpost.com/ entrepreneur/canadian-tech-firms-are-getting -funded-but-gaps-remain/?__lsa=a6d9-9dd8.
19. Eric Spitznagel, "Odd Jobs: Prosthetic Dog-Testicle Maker," April 25, 2012, http://www .businessweek.com/articles/2012-04-25/odd-jobs -prosthetic-dog-testicle-maker#disqus_thread; Heather Levin, "6 Weird But Successful Small Business Ideas," September 11, 2011, http://www .moneycrashers.com/weird-successful-small -business-ideas/; Kate Bassett, "Kids Up North: Rent-a-Chicken in Traverse City Makes Urban Farming Child's Play," May 24, 2010, http://www .mynorth.com/My-North/May-2010/Kids-Up -North-Rent-a-Chicken-in-Traverse-City-Makes -Urban-Farming-Child-rsquos-Play.
20. Jenny Lee, "Publisher Finds Successful Niche: Figure 1 Business Uses Three Financing Models to Get Books to Print," Vancouver Sun, March 27, 2015, E1.
21. Paul Grescoe, The Mavericks (Toronto: McGraw-Hill Ryerson, 1999).
22. "E-Commerce Award—June 2002," Anything Left-Handed, http://www.anythingleft-handed .co.uk/pressreleases.html.
23. Rhonda Abrams, "Focus on Success, Not Failure," USA Today, May 7, 2004, http://www .usatoday.com/money/smallbusiness/columnist/ abrams/2004-05-06-success_x.htm.
24. Innovation, Science and Economic Development Canada, "Key Small Business Statistics—July 2012," https://www.ic.gc.ca/eic/site/061.nsf/ eng/02717.html.
25. "Is Entrepreneurship for You?," US Small Business Administration, http://www.sba.gov/ starting_business/startup/areyouready.html.
26. Industry Canada, "Analysis of Regulatory Compliance Costs: Part II," Small Business Quarterly 12, no. 4 (February 2011): 2; Industry Canada, Small Business and Research Policy Branch, "Small Business and Regulatory Burden: 3. Impact on Small Business," http://www.ic.gc.ca/eic/site/sbrp-rppe.nsf/eng/ rd01340.html.
27. Susan Cranston, "Benefits for Small Business," November 14, 2012, http://www.theglobeandmail .com/globe-investor/personal-finance/financial

-road-map/advmanulife/advmanulifearchives/ benefits-for-small-business/article4571713.
28. Steve Strauss, "Five Reasons Why Franchises Flop," February 28, 2005, USA Today, http:// www.usatoday.com/money/smallbusiness/ columnist/strauss/2005-02-28-franchise_x.htm.
29. "Business Plan Basics," US SBA, http://www .sba.gov/starting_business/planning/basic.html.
30. "Inventor of the Week," Lemulson-MIT, http://web.mit.edu/invent/iow/epperson.html; "Top 10 Accidental Inventions," Science Channel, http://science.discovery.com/brink/top-ten/ accidental-inventions/inventions-01.html.
31. Industry Canada, "Key Small Business Statistics–August 2013," http://www.ic.gc.ca/eic/ site/061.nsf/eng/02804.html and http://www.ic.gc .ca/eic/site/061.nsf/eng/02802.html.
32. Industry Canada, "Key Small Business Statistics—August 2013," http://www.ic.gc.ca/eic/ site/061.nsf/eng/02802.html.
33. Industry Canada, "Key Small Business Statistics—August 2013," http://www.ic.gc.ca/eic/ site/061.nsf/eng/02802.html; SBA Office of Advocacy, "Frequently Asked Questions," SBA, http:// www.sba.gov/advo/stats/sbfaq.pdf.
34. Industry Canada, "Key Small Business Statistics—August 2013," http://www.ic.gc.ca/eic/ site/061.nsf/eng/02802.html.
35. Slavica Singer, José Ernesto Amorós, and Daniel Moska Arreola, "Global Entrepreneurship Monitor, 2014 Global Report," Babson College, Universidad del Desarrollo, and Universiti Tun Abdul Razak, Technológico de Monterrey, and London Business School, http://www .gemconsortium.org/docs/3616/gem-2014-global -report.
36. Supra note 35, "Global Entrepreneurship Monitor, 2014 Global Report."

7

1. Deloitte IASPlus, www.iasplus.com.
2. "The 10 Worst Corporate Accounting Scandals of All Time," www.accounting-degree.org: Drew Hasselback, "Livent Auditor Deloitte Ordered to Pay $84.8 Million for Failing Detect Fraud," Financial Post, April 6, 2014, business.financial .com; "Canada: Four Former Nortel Executives Charged with Accounting Fraud," CorpWatch, www.corpwatch.org.
3. Association of Certified Fraud Examiners, "2012 Global Fraud Study: Report to the Nations on Occupational Fraud and Abuse" www.acfe.com; B. Carlino, "The Not-So-Usual Suspects," Accounting Today, December 2011, 9; S. Ostrowski, "Fraud Prevention: How to Implement Internal Controls to Prevent Employee Theft," Smart Business Cleveland, February 2012, 90; J. Wojcik, "Employee Theft, Fraud Pose Growing Challenge," Business Insurance, October 17, 2011, 6.
4. E. Chancellor, "The Bookkeeper of Venice," Wall Street Journal, November 7, 2012, online .wsj.com; J. Gleeson-White, Double Entry: How the Merchants of Venice Created Modern Finance, (New York: W.W. Norton, 2013).
5. "Revenue Recognition on the Sale of Virtual Goods," April 9, 2010, Ernst & Young, www .ey.com; P. Gobry, "How Zynga Makes Money," September 28, 2011, Business Insider, http://www .articles.businessinsider.com; C. Kyle, "Accounting for Gift Cards," November 2007, Journal of Accountancy, www.journalofaccountancy.com; F. McKenna, "Social Media's Phony Accounting,"

Forbes, May 7, 2012, 150–55; M. Lynley, "Zynga Closes 'PetVille' and Several Other Games," December 31, 2012, *Wall Street Journal*, blogs .wsj.com.

6. "How to Efficiently Read an Annual Report," February 5, 2010, *Investopedia*, www.investopedia .com; "How to Read a 10-K," July 1, 2011, *US SEC*, www.sec.gov; McDonald's Corporation, "Form 10-K," US SEC, February 25, 2013, www.aboutmcdonalds.com.

7. "Corporate Intelligence: The Bloodhounds of Capitalism," *The Economist*, January 5, 2013, http://www.economist.com; "FBI Forensic Accountants: Following the Money," March 9, 2012, *Federal Bureau of Investigation*, http:// www.fbi.gov; R. Albergotti, "Job Churn Hits Insider Probe," *Wall Street Journal*, August 11, 2012, B1; C. Davis, R. Farrell, and S. Ogilby, "Characteristics and Skills of the Forensic Accountant," *American Institute of CPAs*, http://www.aicpa.org; S. Freeman, "How Forensic Accounting Works," *Howstuffworks*, http://science.howstuffworks.com; J. Palazzolo, "FCPA Inc: The Business of Bribery," *Wall Street Journal*, October 2, 2012, B1; M. Tan, "Paul McCartney—Heather Mills Divorce Settlement the Bitter End," *People*, March 31, 2008, http:// www.people.com; Matthew McClearn, "Catch and Release," *Canadian Business*, July 14, 2011, www.canadianbusiness.com; Stan Luxenberg, "Forensic Teams Dig into Legal Disputes for Clients," *Crain's New York Business*, September 25, 2006; Jeff Stimpson, "Forensic Accounting: Exponential Growth," *Practical Accountant*, February 2007; Peter Vogt, "CFE: Certified Fraud Examiner?," *MSN Encarta*, August 2006, http://www.investigation.com.

8. Albrecht, Stice, Stice, and Swain, *Accounting Concepts and Applications*, 9th ed. (Cengage Learning), 758.

8

1. R.C. Moyer, J.R. McGuigan, and R.P. Rao, *Fundamentals of Contemporary Financial Management*, 2nd ed. (Boston: Cengage Learning), 3; E.F. Brigham and J.F. Houston, *Fundamentals of Financial Management*, 11th ed. (Boston: Cengage Learning), 2.

2. *The Essentials of Finance and Budgeting* (Cambridge: Harvard Business School Press, 2005), 177–81.

3. Joseph E. Stiglitz, *Freefall* (New York: W.W. Norton, 2010), 31–32; "Financial Crisis Inquiry Commission," *Financial Crisis Inquiry Report* (Official Government Edition, January 2011), 109–14.

4. J. Mackey, M. Friedman, and T. Rodger, "Rethinking the Social Responsibility of Business," *Reason*, October 1, 2005, http://reason.com; *Dove Campaign for Real Beauty*, www.dove.us; *Tim Hortons*, www.timhortons.com; *McDonald's*, www.mcdonalds.com.

5. The approximate "finance charge" of not taking the discount on credit can be computed using the following formula:

$$\begin{array}{l} \text{Cost of} \\ \text{not taking} = \\ \text{discount} \end{array} \begin{pmatrix} \dfrac{\% \text{ discount}}{(100 - \% \text{ discount})} \times \dfrac{365}{(\text{Credit Period} - \text{Discount Period})} \end{pmatrix}$$

where % discount is the discount the buyer receives for paying on or before the last day the discount is available and the credit period is the number of days before payment of full invoice amount is due.

6. Traci Mack and John D. Wolken, "Financial Services Used by Small Businesses," *Federal Reserve Bulletin*, October 2006, A181.

7. M. Pilon, "What Is Commercial Paper and Why Does It Matter?" October 7, 2008, *Wall Street Journal*, http://blogs.wsj.com.

8. *Google Financial Statements*, http://balance -sheets.findthecompany.com.

9. Berkshire Hathaway Inc., "Historical Prices, Google Prices," http://www.google.com.

10. Ibid.

11. "Why Do Companies Issue Debt and Bonds?," *Investopedia*, www.investopedia.com.

12. "#WOW! Twitter Soars 73% in IPO," November 7, 2013, *CNN*, money.cnn.com; Jillian D'Onfro, "The Question That Twitter's CEO Asks at Every Product Meeting," *Yahoo Finance*, finance.yahoo.com, May 29, 2015; U-Jin Lee, "One Reason Twitter (TWTR) Stock Closed Higher," May 28, 2015, thestreet.com.

13. Kerry Gillespie, "Pan Am Games Countdown: 30 for 30," *Toronto Star*, June 9, 2015, www .thestar.com; "Pan Am Party: Accounting on a Grand Scale," *D&A Magazine*, January/February 2015, 37–41; *Pan Am / Parapan Am Games*, www .toronto2015.ordg.

14. Matthew Boyle and Olga Kharif, "Getting Tough with Customers," *BusinessWeek* March 9, 2009, 30.

15. Y. Takahashi and M. Ramsey, "Honda Profit Tumbles: Thai Floods Hit U.S. Output," October 31, 2011, *Dow Jones NewsPlus*, www .djnewsplus.com.

16. Jessica Leeder, "New Fund Has a Taste for Organic Food," *Globe and Mail*, September 4, 2011, www.theglobeandmail.com; *Investeco*, www.investeco.com; "Green and Social Venture Capital," *Green VC*, www.greenvc.org/green -and-social-venture-capital.html; Kelly Fairchild, "30 Entrepreneurs Who Are Saving the World," November 1, 2009, *Inc. Magazine*, http://www .inc.com/magazine/20091101/30-entrepreneurs -who-are-saving-the-world.html; Natasha Tiku, "Do-Gooder Finance," February 1, 2008, *Inc. Magazine*, www.inc.com/magazine/20080201/ do-gooder-finance.html; *Underdog Ventures*, http://www2.underdogventures.com.

9

1."Fast Facts About the Canadian Banking System," *Canadian Bankers Association*, www.cba.ca.

2. "Trust Company," *Canadian Encyclopedia*, www.theCanadianencyclopedia.ca.

3. *Credit Union Central of Canada*, www .cucentral.ca.

4. "2012 Dogs of the Dow," www.dogsofthedow .com; J. Buckingham, "In Dividends We Trust," *Forbes*, November 21, 2011, 80; S. Marnjian, "Dividends for 100 Years," October 2, 2009, www.fool.com,; S. Russolillo and B. Conway, "'Dogs' Strategy Paid Dividends for Second Year in a Row," *Wall Street Journal*, January 3, 2012, online.wsj.com.

5. *Office of the Superintendent of Financial Institutions*, osfi-bsif.gc.ca.

6. *Financial Consumer Agency of Canada*, fcac -acfc.gc.ca.

7. Ibid.

8. *Canadian Securities Administrators*, securities -administrators.ca.

9. *Cooperative Capital Markets Regulatory System*, ccmr-ocrmc.ca.

10. *Canadian Securities Administrators*, securities -administrators.ca.

11. Investors Industry Regulatory Organization, iiroc.ca.

12. "How to Invest in a Bond," *SmartMoney*, June 2, 2011, http://www.smartmoney.com; S. Anand, "Mixing It Up," *Wall Street Journal*, March 4, 2013, R12; Z. Faux, "Kodak Court Loss Leaves Less for Bondholders," May 29, 2012, *Bloomberg Financial*, http://www.bloomberg.com; J. Marte, "Should You Sell Your Bonds?" *Wall Street Journal*, March 11, 2013, http://articles .marketwatch.com; M. Wirz and D. Mattioli, "Kodak's Bonds Fading Fast," *Wall Street Journal*, July 19, 2011, B1.

13. Dan Caplinger, "Are Bond Buyers This Crazy?," *Motley Fool*, http://www.fool.com; A. Gara, "Issuers Plan for 2112 with 'Century' Bonds," *Forbes*, April 12, 2012, http://www.forbes.com.

14. Richard Lehmann, "The Coming Bond Default Wave," *Forbes*, September 18, 2008, http:// www.forbes.com/forbes/2008/1013/130.html.

15. C. Chang, W. Nelson, and D. White, "Do Green Mutual Funds Perform Well?," *Management Research Review* 35 (2012): 693–708; M. Orlitzky, "Payoffs to Social and Environmental Performance," *Journal of Investing* 14 (2005): 403–441; M. Orlitzky, F. Schmidt, and S. Rynes, "Corporate Social and Financial Performance: A Meta-Analysis," *Organization Studies* 24 (2003): 403–441; V. Vyvyan, C. Ng, and M. Brimble, "Socially Responsible Investing: The Green Attitudes and Grey Choices of Australian Investors," *Corporate Governance* 15 (2007): 370–81.

16. *NYSE*, nyse.com; *Nasdaq*, Nasdaq.com.

17. http://online.wsj.com/article/SB100014241 27887324296604578177292540656504.html; N. Huang, "How to Pick the Best Index Funds," February 2013, *Kiplinger's Person Finance*, http:// www.kiplinger.com/article/investing/T041-C000 -S002-how-to-pick-the-best-index-funds.html; P. Merriman, "10 Ways Index Funds Can Save Your Retirement," Market Watch, December 19, 2012, http://www.marketwatch.com/story/10-ways -index-funds-can-save-your-retirement-2012-12-19; *Canadian Imperial Bank of Commerce*, cibc .com; Robb Engen, "Mutual Fund Fees and the High Cost of Canadian Funds," September 12, 2011, Boomerandecho.com.

18. "Insider Trading," *Investopedia*, www .investopedia.com,; R. Heakal, Defining Illegal Insider Trading, *Investopedia*, September 25, 2010, www.investopedia.com; M. Rothfeld, J. Eaglesham, and C. Bray, "SAC Hit with Record Insider Penalty," *Wall Street Journal*, March 16, 2013, A1; J. Stewart and S. Wermiel, "Setting a Precedent," *Wall Street Journal*, November 17, 1987; *Canadian Securities Administrators*, securities-administrators.ca; "Prohibited Insider Trading," www.yourlaws.ca.

10

1. Government of Canada, "2013–2014 Annual Report on Government of Canada Advertising Activities," http://www.tpsgc-pwgsc.gc.ca/pub-adv/ rapports-reports/2013-2014/deppub-advexp-eng .html#tab1.

2. Scott Deveau, "Number of Chinese Tourists Taking Flight," *National Post*, February 15, 2011, 5.

3. Chris Williams, "Mayweather Could Make $250M to $275M," www.boxingnews24.com, May 8, 2015.

4. *American Customer Satisfaction Index*, http://www.theacsi.org/customer-satisfaction-benchmarks/benchmarks-by-company.

5. Rama Ramaswami, "Eight Reasons to Keep Your Customers Loyal," January 12, 2005, *Mulitchannel Merchant*, http://multichannelmerchant.com/opsandfulfillment/advisor/Brandi-custloyal.

6. June Campbell, "The Psychology of Color in Marketing," *UCSI*, http://www.ucsi.cc/webdesign/color-marketing.html; Al Martinovic, "Color Psychology in Marketing," June 21, 2004, *ImHosted*, http://developers.evrsoft.com/article/web-design/graphics-multimedia-design/vRoman, "Colors That Sell," May 30, 2015, *ImHosted*, http://developers.evrsoft.com/article/web-design/graphics-multimedia-design/colors-that-sell.shtml; Pam Belluck, "Reinvent Wheel? Blue Room. Defusing a Bomb? Red Room," May 30, 2015, *New York Times*, http://www.nytimes.com/2009/02/06/science/06color.html.

7. "Nike's Revenue in Greater China from 2009 to 2014, by Segment (in Millions U.S. Dollars)," *Statistics Portal*, http://www.statista.com/statistics/241724/nikes-sales-in-the-asia-pacific-region-by-area-since-2007; Andria Cheng, "Shoe Makers Gunning for Olympian Feat," May 9, 2008, *Market Watch*, http://www.marketwatch.com/news/story/story.aspx?guid={781CC2E2-2B3F-4FF5-A0C5-0FB962D7E204}; Matt Townsend and Robert Fenne, "Nike Climbs to Record as Orders Surge, Profit Rises," September 24, 2010, *Bloomberg BusinessWeek*, http://www.businessweek.com/news/2010-09-24/nike-climbs-to-record-as-orders-surge-profit-rises.html; Laurie Burkitt, "In China, Nike Sets Out to Alter Sports Mindset" *Wall Street Journal*, http://online.wsj.com/article/SB10001424052970204450804576624900309968790.html.

8. Arti Patel, "20 Tim Hortons Secret Menu Items Approved by Readers," July 15, 2015, *Huffington Post Canada*, http://www.huffingtonpost.ca/2014/07/14/tim-hortons-secret-menu_n_5585430.html; Debbie Siegelbaum, "Secret Menus: Fast Food 'Hacks' for In-the-Know Customers," September 3, 2014, *BBC News*, http://www.bbc.com/news/world-us-canada-28990400; Dan Myers, "Wild Fast-Food Secret Menu Items," October 30, 2013, *foxnews.com*, http://www.foxnews.com/leisure/2013/10/30/7-wild-secret-fast-food-menu-items; Alaina McConnell, "14 Secret Menu Items You Can Order at Fast Food Restaurants," December 22, 2012, *Financial Post*, http://business.financialpost.com/business-insider/14-secret-menu-items-you-can-order-at-fast-food-restaurants.

9. "Facebook: Friend, Foe, or Frenemy?," May 27, 2010, *Newsweek*, http://www.newsweek.com/blogs/techtonic-shifts/2010/05/26/facebook-friend-foe-or-frenemy-.html. Diane Buckner, "Biggest Marketing Fails of 2014," December 29, 2014, *CBC News*, http://www.cbc.ca/m/touch/news/story/1.2877875; Matt Kwong, "Coors Light Scare," July 9, 2014, *CBC News*, http://www.cbc.ca/news/canada/toronto/coors-light-scare-7-guerrilla-marketing-blunders-1.2700447; Leslie Ferenc, "Direct Energy Suspends Plan to Charge Fee on Cancelling," *Toronto Star,* March 16, 2012, B1; Hugh Adami, "Angry Customers Forced Change, Direct Energy Says," *Ottawa Citizen*, March 18, 2012, B1; Jason Frost, Direct Energy

Direct Mail Letter, Undated, and Water Heater Rental Terms and Conditions, revised April 2, 2012; Amanda Sibley, "8 of the Biggest Marketing Faux Pas of All Time," http://blog.hubspot.com/blog/tabid/6307/bid/33396/8-of-the-Biggest-Marketing-Faux-Pas-of-All-Time.aspx; Michael Posner, "The Gaffe at the Gap," *Globe and Mail,* October 13, 2010, A3.

10. Jacquelyn Stevens and Marc McAree, "'Greenwashing' Environmental Claims Give Rise to Legal Liability," *Fabricare Canada,* September–October 2014, pp. 25–27; Rebecca Harris, "Greenwashing: Cleaning Up by 'Saving the World,'" *Marketing*, http://www.marketingmag.ca/brands/greenwashing-cleaning-up-by-saving-the-world-77259; Adam Kingsmith, "Pretty Little Industrial liars, Pt. 1," *DeSmog Canada*, http://www.desmog.ca//2013/06/20/pretty-little-industrial-liars-pt-1, accessed May 30, 2015; CBC *Marketplace* http://www.cbc.ca/news/canada/10-worst-household-products-for-greenwashing-1.1200620.

11. Press Release: "Environment a Fair-Weather Priority for Consumers," June 3, 2008, *Penn, Schoen & Bergland*, http://www.psbresearch.com/press_release_Jun3-2008.htm; Gloria Sin, "Green Fashion: Is It More Than Marketing Hype?" May 28, 2008, *Fast Company*, http://www.fastcompany.com/articles/2008/05/green-fashion-hype.html; "Green Fashion: Formerly Hippie, Now Hip!," February 21, 2008, *CBS News*, http://www.cbsnews.com/stories/2008/02/21/earlyshow/living/beauty/main3855868.shtml.

11

1. "Characteristics of a Great Name, the Brand Name Awards," *Brighter Naming*, www.brandnameawards.com.

2. Adam Bass, "Brand Extensions: Marketing in Inner Space," *Brand Channel*, www.brandchannel.com; Reena Jana, "Brand Extensions We Could Do Without," August 7, 2006, *BusinessWeek*, http://www.businessweek.com/stories/2006-08-06/online-extra-brand-extensions-we-could-do-without.

3. Kathie Canning, "2014 State of the Industry Research Study: Full Speed Ahead," www.storebrands.info.

4. "Not on the List? The Truth About Impulse Purchases," January 7, 2009, *Knowledge@Wharton*, http://knowledge.wharton.upenn.edu/article.cfm?articleid=2132.

5. "3M: Commitment to Sustainability," *GreenBiz Leaders*.

6. "Wacky Warning Labels 2009 Winners Announced," August 16, 2009, *Foundation for Fair Civil Justice*, http://www.foundationforfairciviljustice.org/news/in_depth/wacky_warning_labels_2009_winners_announced; Bob Dorigo Jones, "Wacky Warning Labels Show Toll of Frivolous Lawsuits," June 8, 2012, *Bob Dorigo Jones*, http://www.bobdorigojones.com; Bob Dorigo Jones, "Deadline for Entering 15th Annual Wacky Warning Labels™ Contest Is May 15," May 7, 2012, *Bob Dorigo Jones*, www.bobdorigojones.com.

7. Dawn C. Chmielewski, "Binge-viewing Is Transforming the Television Experience," February 1, 2013, *Los Angeles Times*, http://articles.latimes.com/2013/feb/01/entertainment/la-et-ct-binge-viewing-20130201; David Hinkley, "Americans

Spend 34 Hours a Week Watching TV, According to Nielsen Numbers," September 19, 2012, *Daily News*, http://www.nydailynews.com/entertainment/tv-movies/americans-spend-34-hours-week-watching-tv-nielsen-numbers-article-1.1162285; Stine Thorhauge, "How People Spend Their Time Online," May 24, 2012, *MindJunpers*, http://www.mindjumpers.com/blog/2012/05/time-spend-online; "US Consumer Online Behavior Survey Results 2007_Part One: Wireline Usage," February 19, 2008, *International Data Corporation*, http://www.idc.com/getdoc.jsp?containerId=prUS21096308; Dan Frommer, "Why Video On Demand Is Still Cable's Game to Lose," September 5, 2008, *Business Insider*, http://www.businessinsider.com/2008/9/why-video-on-demand-is-still-cable-s-game-to-lose; Glenn Abel, "Streaming Vids Boost Netflix Profits," January 29, 2009, *Download Movies 101*, http://download movies101.com/wordpress-1/2009/01/29/streaming-vids-boost-netflix-profits; "Casting the Big Movie Download Roles," September 7, 2007, *eMarketer*, http://www.emarketer.com/Article.aspx?id=1005346; Clark Fredricksen, "Time Watching TV Still Tops Internet" December 15, 2010, *eMarketer*, http://www.emarketer.com/blog/index.php/time-spent-watching-tv-tops-internet; "Average Time Spent Online per US Visitor in 2010," January 11, 2011, *ComScore Data Mine*, http://www.comscoredatamine.com/2011/01/average-time-spent-online-per-u-s-visitor-in-2010; Erick Schonfeld, "How People Watch TV Online and Off," January 8, 2012, *TechCrunch*, http://techcrunch.com/2012/01/08/how-people-watch-tv-online; Chris Breikss, "Infographic: Canadian Internet Usage Statistics on Mobile, Search and Social," *6S Marketing*, 6smarketing.com.

8. William C. Taylor, "Permission Marketing," December 18, 2007, *Fast Company*, http://www.fastcompany.com/34360/permission-marketing.

9. Bruce Horowitz, "Budweiser's Clydesdale Wins Ad Meter by a Nose," February 4, 2013, *USA Today*, http://www.usatoday.com/story/money/business/2013/02/04/clydesdale- ad-wins-by-a-nose/1889693; Bruce Horovitz, "Two Nobodies from Nowhere Craft Winning Super Bowl Ad," February 4, 2009, *USA Today*, http://www.usatoday.com/money/advertising/admeter/2009admeter.htm.

10. Paul Herbig, Tristate University, International Marketing Lecture Series, Session 6, International Advertising, www.tristate.edu, June 1, 2005; Karl Moore and Mark Smith, "Taking Global Brands to Japan," *Conference Board* website, www.conference-board.org, June 1, 2005.

11. "2013 Actual + 2014 Estimated Canadian Internet Advertising Revenue Survey Detailed Report," *iab Interactive Advertising Bureau*, iabcanada.com.

12. Pamela Parker, "EMarketer: Among Online Ads, Search to Gain Most New Dollars in 2011," *EMarketer*, June 11, 2008, *SearchEngine Land*, http://searchengineland.com/emarketer-among-online-ads-search-to-gain-most-new-dollars-in-2011-80707; "eMarketer: Search Is Vital in a Recession," *Adweek* staff, February 25, 2009, *Brandweek*, http://www.brandweek.com/bw/content_display/news-and-features/digital/e3i195c363 ab252f976a2dabde4d8ef2549.

13. "2013 Actual + 2014 Estimated Canadian Internet Advertising Revenue Survey Detailed Report," *iab Interactive Advertising Bureau*, www.iabcanada.com.

14. Meghan Keane, "Social Media Claims More of Our attention," August 2, 2010, *eConsultancy*, http://econsultancy.com/us/blog/6366-social-media-might-claim-a-lot-of-our-attention-but-email-s-not-dead-yet; Erik Qualman, "Social Media ROI Examples & Video," November 12, 2009, *Socialnomics*, http://socialnomics.net/2009/11/12/social-media-roi-examples-video; Lauren Fisher, "The ROI of Social Media: 10 Case Studies," July 16, 2011, *The Next Web*, http://thenextweb.com/socialmedia/2011/07/16/the-roi-of-social-media-10-case-studies.

15. Eric Caron Malenfant, André Lebel, and Laurent Martel, "Projections of the Diversity of the Canadian Population, 2006 to 2031," Statistics Canada, statcan.gc.ca; Howard Lichtman, "Ethnic Media and Cultural Diversity," Canadian Director's Council Media Digest 2014–15, 98-99; Sarah Cunningham-Scharf, "5 Multicultural Marketing Pitfalls to Avoid," May 8, 2015, marketingmag.ca.

16. Abram Sauer, "Brandchannel's 2004 Product Placement Awards," February 21, 2005, http://www.brandchannel.com/start1.asp? fa_id=251; Dale Buss, "A Product Placement Hall of Fame," June 22, 1998, *BusinessWeek*, http://www.businessweek.com/1998/25/b3583062.htm.

17. "The Canadian Media Directors' Council Media Digest, 2014–2015," pp. 9, 41.

18. Angela Moscaritolo, "Number of U.S. Video Game Players Falls," September 5, 2012, *PC Magazine*, http://www.pcmag.com/article2/0,2817,2409313,00.asp; "Advertisers Support Games Through New Placements," December 12, 2012, *eMarketer*, http://www.emarketer.com/Article/US-Gamers-Race-Mobile/1009543; "Massive Summary Research—Significant Findings," Massive, http://www.massiv-eincorporated.com/casestudiesa.html; "IN-game Advertising Is a Massive Market," May 15, 2011, *The Telegraph*, http://www.telegraph.co.uk/technology/news/5312188/In-game-advertising-is-a-massive-market.html; Mike Shields, "Report: Video Game Ads to Reach $1 Bil. by 2012," March 4, 2008, *AdWeek*, http://www.adweek.com/news/television/report-video-game-ads-reach-1-bil-2012-95119; "Let the Games Begin Advertising!," April 6, 2007, *eMarketer*, http://www.emarketer.com/Article.aspx?1004739&R= 1004739.

19. Google MentalPlex, http://www.google.com/mentalplex/MP_faq.html#4; YouTube DVD Collection, http://www.youtube.com/theyoutubecollection.

20. The Canadian Director's Council Media Digest 2014–15, 7–9.

21. "23 Hilariously Unfortunate Ad Placements," March 18, 2013, *MSN*, http://now.msn.com/bad-ad-placement-funny-photos-show- awkward-ad-choices.

22. Bruce Philip, "Publicity Stunts Are a High-Risk, High-Reward Gamble for Brands," *Marketing*, February 9, 2015, marketingmag.ca.

23. Russ Martin, "Social Scanner: HootSuite Makes Big Moves," *Marketing*, September 4, 2014, marketingmag.ca; Russ Martin, "SXSW: HoortSuite on Why Social Needs a Human Touch," *Marketing*, March 12, 2015, marketingmag.ca; Trevor Melanson, "Is Hoostsuite Canada's Next Billion-Dollar Tech Titan?," *Canadian Business*, January 9, 2013, canadianbusiness.com; *HootSuite*, hootsuite.com.

12

1. "Supermarket Facts," *FMI*, http://www.fmi.org/facts_figs/?fuseaction=superfact.

2. Stephen Budiansky, "Math Lessons for Locavores," August 19, 2010, *The New York Times*, http://www.nytimes.com/2010/08/20/opinion/20budiansky.html.

3. Jamie Sturgeon, "Think Online Shopping Is Exploding in Canada? Hardly," December 18, 2014, *Global News*, http://globalnews.ca/news/1734035/think-online-shopping-is-exploding-in-canada-hardly.

4. Hollie Shaw, "Online Retail Sales to Hit $34-Billion in Canada by 2018," June 23, 2013, *Financial Post*, http://business.financialpost.com/news/retail-marketing/online-retail-sales-to-hit-40-billion-in-canada-by-2018.

5. Fireclick Index, "Top Line Growth," *Fireclick*, http://index.fireclick.com/fireindex.php?segment=0; "For Third Year Running, L.L. Bean Ranks Number One in Customer Service," January 12, 2010, *National Retail Federation*, http://www.nrf.com/modules.php?name=News&op=viewlive& sp_id=653; "Amazon.com Tops in Customer Service, According to NRF Foundation/American Express Survey," January 17, 2012, *National Retail Federation,* http://www.nrf.com/modules.php?name=News&op=viewlive&sp_id=1293.

6. Allison Rice, "Unique Pricing Strategies That Get Publicity and New Customers," April 10, 2012, *Amsterdam Printing*, http://blog.amsterdamprinting.com/2012/08/10/unique-pricing-strategies-that-get-publicity-and-new-customers; "Twitter Index: Tax on IE7, Drake vs Chris Brown," *Yahoo! Celebrity Philippines*, June 14, 2012, https://ph.celebrity.yahoo.com/news/twitter-index-tax-ie7-drake-vs-chris-brown-135709902.html.

7. "Sales soften at Costco," March 4, 2009, *Retail Analysis IGD*, http://www.igd.com/analysis/channel/news_hub.asp?channelid=1&channelitemid=9&nidp=&nid=5616.

8. Chris Morran, "Don't Be Shocked When Lowe's Won't Sell You a $2,999 Fridge Mistakenly Priced at $298," April 17, 2015, *consumerist.com*, http://consumerist.com/2015/04/17/dont-be-shocked-when-lowes-wont-sell-you-a-2999-fridge-mistakenly-priced-at-298/#more-10202083; Pete Evans, "Lenovo Offers $100 for Laptop Pricing Glitch," May 27, 2014, *CBC News*, http://www.cbc.ca/news/business/lenovo-offers-100-for-laptop-pricing-glitch-1.2655392; Bob Tedeschi, "Pricing Errors on the Web Can Be Costly," *New York Times*, http://partners.nytimes.com/library/tech/99/12/cyber/commerce/13commerce.html; "All You Ever Wanted to Know About the Travelocity 'Guarantee,'" *FlyerTalk Forum*, http://www.flyertalk.com/forum/online-travel-booking-bidding-agencies/552951-all-you-ever-wanted-know-about-travelocity-guarantee.html; "8 Biggest Pricing Errors in History," n.d., *Money Super Market*.

9. "Loss Leader Strategy," *Investopedia*, http://www.investopedia.com/terms/l/lossleader.asp; Al Norman, "Walmart Not Crying over Spilt Milk," August 22, 2008, *Huffington Post*, http://www.huffingtonpost.com/al-norman/wal-mart-not-crying-over_b_120684.html.

10. Andrew Jacobs, "Once-Prized Tibetan Mastiffs Are Discarded as Fad Ends in China," April 17, 2015, *newyorktimes.com*, http://www.nytimes.com/2015/04/18/world/asia/once-prized-tibetan-mastiffs-are-discarded-as-fad-ends-in-china.html?_r=0; Jenny Cosgrave, "World's Most Expensive Dog? Pup Sold for $2 Million," March 19, 2014, *www.cnbc.com*, http://www.cnbc.com/id/101506484; David Howell, "Firm Bought for $1-Billion Sold for $2; Deal to Pick Up Debt Good News for Coal Workers," *Calgary Herald,* October 2, 2014, B1.

11. Steven Greenhouse, "How Costco Became the Anti Walmart," July 17, 2005, *New York Times*, http://www.nytimes.com/2005/07/17/business/yourmoney/17costco.html?adxnnl=1&pagewanted=1&adxnnlx=1122004143-8Vfn2DFl1MJfernM1navLA; Matthew Boyle, "Why Costco Is So Addictive," October 25, 2006, *CNNMoney*, http://money.cnn.com/magazines/fortune/fortune_archive/2006/10/30/8391725/index.htm.

12. Andrew Shirley, "Knight Frank Luxury Investment Index Update 2014," *knightfrankblog.com*, http://www.knightfrankblog.com/wealthreport/news-headlines/knight-frank-luxury-investment-index-update-2014; Katya Kazakina and Mary Romano, "These 10 Pieces of Art Just Sold for Almost $800 Million," *bloomberg.com*, http://www.bloomberg.com/news/articles/2015-05-14/these-10-pieces-of-art-just-sold-for-almost-800-million; "The Top 100 Most Expensive Cars of All Time," November 13, 2014, *Gizmag*, http://www.gizmag.com/100-most-expensive-cars-of-all-time/32237.

13

1. "Famous Canadians," *biography.com*, http://www.biography.com/people/groups/famous-canadians; Matt Melvin, "The Roller Coaster Ride of Mark Zuckerberg," 2011, *Teen Ink*, http://www.teenink.com/nonfiction/academic/article/292887; "First Jobs of the Rich and Famous," April 12, 2014, *parade.com*, http://parade.com/81638/parade/stars-first-jobs-of-the-rich-and-famous.

2. Katimavik, https://www.katimavik.org.

3. "The Worst Business Decisions of All Time," October 17, 2012, *Wall Street Journal*, http://247wallst.com/2012/10/17/the-worst-business-decisions-of-all-time/3; "Top Ten Bad Business Decisions," October 10, 2010, *Business Excellence*, http://www.bus-ex.com/article/top-ten-bad-business-decisions.

4. "The Importance of Being Richard Branson," January 12, 2005, *Knowledge@Wharton*, http://knowledge.wharton.upenn.edu/article/1109.cfm.

5. Robert Tanner, "Equity Theory–Why Employee Perceptions About Fairness Do Matter," https://managementisajourney.com/equity-theory-why-employee-perceptions-about-fairness-do-matter.

6. Steve Lohr, "A New Game at the Office," December 5, 2005, *New York Times*, http://select.nytimes.com/gst/abstract.html?res=F00F12FE38550C768CDDAB0994DD404482.

7. "Canada's 50 Best Employers," November 7, 2014, *macleans.ca*, http://www.macleans.ca/work/bestcompanies/canadas-50-best-employers-of-2014.

8. "Canada's Best Employers 2015: The Top 50 Large Corporations," November 10, 2014, *canadianbusiness.com*, http://www.canadianbusiness.com/lists-and-rankings/best-jobs/2015-best-employers-top-50.

9. Derek Gottfrid, "Self-Service, Prorated Super Computing Fun," November 1, 2007, *New York Times,* http://open.blogs.nytimes.com/2007/11/01/self-service-prorated-super-computing-fun; "NY Times AWS Cloud Computing Mistake Costs $240," November 5, 2008, *Green Data Center,* http://www.greenm3.com/gdcblog/2008/11/5/nytimes-aws-cloud-computing-mistake-cost-240.html; Galen Gruman, "Early Experiments in Cloud Computing," April 7, 2008, *InfoWorld,* http://www.infoworld.com/d/cloud-computing/early-experiments-in-cloud-computing-020.

10. Darrell Rigby, "Don't Get Hammered by Management Fads," May 21, 2001, *bain.com,* http://bain.com/publications/articles/dont-get-hammered-by-management-fads.aspx.

11. Bruce Tulgan and Carolyn A. Martin, "Managing Generation Y—Part 1, Book Excerpt," September 28, 2001, *BusinessWeek,* http://www.businessweek.com/smallbiz/content/sep2001/sb20010928_113.htm; Bruce Tulgan and Carolyn A. Martin, "Managing Generation Y—Part 2, Book Excerpt," October 4, 2001, *BusinessWeek,* http://www.businessweek.com/smallbiz/content/oct2001/sb2001105_229.htm; Stephanie Armour, "Generation Y: They've Arrived at Work with a New Attitude," November 6, 2005, *USA Today,* http://www.usatoday.com/money/workplace/2005-11-06-gen-y_x.htm; Gary Hamel, "The Facebook Generation vs. the Fortune 500," March 24, 2009, *Wall Street Journal Blogs,* http://blogs.wsj.com/management/2009/03/24/the-facebook-generation-vs-the-fortune-500; Penelope Trunk, "What Gen Y Really Wants," July 5, 2007, *Time,* http://www.time.com/time/magazine/article/0,9171,1640395,00.html; Molly Smith, "Managing Generation Y as They Change the Workforce," January 8, 2008, *Reuters,* http://www.reuters.com/article/pressRelease/idUS129795+08-Jan-2008+BW20080108; Dan Schawbel, "Millennial Branding Survey Reveals that Gen-Y Is Connected to an Average of 16 Co-Workers on Facebook," January 9, 2012, *Millennial Branding,* http://millennialbranding.com/2012/01/millennial-branding-gen-y-facebook-study.

12. "The Cow in the Ditch: How Anne Mulcahy Rescued Xerox," Special Section: Knowledge at Wharton, November 16–29, 2005, http://knowledge.wharton.upenn.edu/index.cfm?fa=viewArticle&id=1318&specialId=41.

13. Chris Sorensen, "Working Hard, Hardly Working," October 3, 2015, *macleans.ca,* http://www.macleans.ca/work/trendswork/working-hard-hardly-working-our-problem-with-productivity; "Expedia's 2015 Vacation Deprivation Study," November 16, 2015, *prnewswire.com,* http://www.prnewswire.com/news-releases/expedias-2015-vacation-deprivation-study-europe-leads-world-in-paid-vacation-time-while-americans-and-asians-lag-300178727.html; Tony Schwartz, "Relax! You'll Be More Productive," February 9, 2013, *New York Times,* http://www.nytimes.com/2013/02/10/opinion/sunday/relax-youll-be-more-productive.html?pagewanted=all&_r=0.

14. Carol Toller, "If You're Happy, They Know It," *Canadian Business,* January 2016, 36–40; Katie Underwood, "Friends with Benefits," *Chatelaine,* February 2016, 82–83; Alana Semuels, "Every Move, Tracked," April 8, 2013, *Los Angeles Times,* http://www.latimes.com/business/la-fi-harsh-work-tech-20130408,0,7804529.story.

14

1. Joel Schlesinger, "Samsung Promotes Innovation, Culture," *National Post,* December 5, 2015, FP12.

2. Mark Kennedy, "Canadians Under 54 Will Have to Wait Longer to Get Old Age Pension: Budget," *nationalpost.com,* http://news.nationalpost.com/news/canada/canadians-under-54-will-have-to-wait-longer-to-get-old-age-pension-budget.

3. Associated Press, "Facing Young Workers' High Job Expectations," *Los Angeles Times,* June 27, 2005; Bruce Tulgan, *Not Everyone Gets a Trophy* (San Francisco: Jossey-Bass, 2009).

4. "Famous Canadians," *biography.com,* http://www.biography.com/people/groups/famous-canadians; "First Jobs of the Rich and Famous," September 15, 2005, *CNN,* http://www.cnn.com/2005/US/Careers/09/16/first.job; *Sean Connery.com,* April 10, 2013, http://www.seanconnery.com/biography; "Celebrities' First Jobs," November 3, 2009, *Oprah.com,* http://www.oprah.com/entertainment/Oprahs-Live-Newscast-and-Celebrities-First-Jobs.

5. Louise Chenier and Elise Wohlbold, Conference Board of Canada, "Women in Senior Management: Where Are They?," August 2011.

6. Tiziana Barghini, "Educated Women Quit Work as Spouses Earn More," March 8, 2012, *Reuters,* http://www.reuters.com/article/2012/03/08/us-economy-women-idUSBRE8270AC20120308; US Department of Labor, "Highly Achieved Women Leaving the Traditional Workforce," Final Report, March 2008, http://www.choose2lead.org/Publications/Are%20We%20Losing%20the%20Best%20and%20the%20Brightest.pdf.

7. Mai Nguyen, "Make a Small Firm Feel Big," *Canadian Business,* December 2015, 41.

8. Alexandra Posadzki, "Top CEOs Earned Average of $8.96 Million in 2014, New Study Shows," Canadian Press, January 4, 2016.

9. Jenny Green, "The Boomers Are Coming," *University Affairs,* August 2015, 16–23.

10. "SHRM Human Capital Benchmarking Study, 2008 Executive Summary," 14, *SHRM,* http://www.shrm.org/Research/Documents/2008%20Executive%20Summary_FINAL.pdf; "Effective Recruiting Tied to Stronger Financial Performance," August 16, 2005, *Watson Wyatt Worldwide,* http://www.watsonwyatt.com/news/press.asp?ID=14959.

11. Alexandra Bosanac, "The Harder the Interview, the Happier You'll Be in the Job," December 18, 2015, *canadianbusiness.com,* http://www.canadianbusiness.com/lists-and-rankings/best-jobs/the-harder-the-interview-the-happier-youll-be-in-the-job.

12. Jeanne Sahadi, "Top Five Resume Lies," December 9, 2004, *CNN Money,* http://money.cnn.com/2004/11/22/pf/resume_lies.

13. Oxford Economics, "Workforce 2020: Country Fact Sheet: Canada," http://www.successfactors.com/en_us/lp/oxford-economics-workforce-hub-pr.html#.VpJ5gFkgmjN.

14. Leah Eichler, "Misbehaving Workers Are Always on the Clock," *Globe and Mail,* May 30, 2015, B19; Canadian Press, "Five Cases of People Who Lost Their Jobs Over Off-Hours Conduct," May 14, 2015, *CityNews,* http://www.citynews.ca/2015/05/13/five-cases-of-people-who-lost-their-jobs-over-off-hours-conduct; Marsha Lederman, "Transcontinental Employee Suspended After Heckling Female Comic at Awards Show," May 20, 2015, *globeandmail.com,* http://www.theglobeandmail.com/life/tc-transcontinental-employee-suspended-after-heckling-female-comic-at-awards-show/article24506521; "Des Hague, Former CEO of Centreplate, Sentenced for Animal Cruelty," April 15, 2015, *cbc.ca,* http://www.cbc.ca/news/canada/british-columbia/des-hague-former-ceo-of-centerplate-sentenced-for-animal-cruelty-1.3034701; "Shawn Simoes, Man Fired For FHRITP Incident, Rehired By Hydro One," November 2, 2015, *huffingtonpost.ca,* http://www.huffingtonpost.ca/2015/11/02/shawn-simoes-hydro-one_n_8453012.html; "Panel Found Termination Unjust, but Refused Reinstatement," *advocatedaily.com,* http://www.advocatedaily.com/Panel-found-termination-unjust-but-refused-reinstatement.html.

15. Daryl Stephenson, "New Employee Experience Aims for Excitement Beyond the First Day," May 2002, *Boeing Frontiers Online,* http://www.boeing.com/news/frontiers/archive/2002/may/i_mams.html.

16. Hollie Shaw, "What Really Goes into a Cup of Tim's," *Gazette* (Montreal), June 28, 2010, A12; Jane Genova, "Employed as a Psychic: Earn $110 to $60 Hourly," October 11, 2010, *aoljobs,* http://jobs.aol.com/articles/2010/10/11/psychic-earn-110-to-60-hourly; "The 10 Weirdest Jobs You've Never Heard Of," October 13, 2013, *news.com.au,* http://www.news.com.au/finance/work/the-10-weirdest-jobs-youve-never-heard-of/story-e6frfm9r-1226750579336; Elizabeth Bromstein, "The 'Most Unusual' Job Titles in Canada (Plus 20 More Weird Job Titles)," November 4, 2014, *Workopolis.com,* http://careers.workopolis.com/advice/the-most-unusual-job-titles-in-canada-plus-20-more-weird-job-titles.

17. Sean McFadden, "Labor-Intensive," *Boston Business Journal,* November 19, 2004, http://www.bizjournals.com/boston/stories/2004/11/22/smallb1.html; Stanley Holmes and Wendy Zelner, "Commentary: The Costco Way," April 11, 2004, *bloomberg.com,* http://www.bloomberg.com/bw/stories/2004-04-11/commentary-the-costco-way; Todd Raphael, "Study: Moderation in Hiring Practices Boosts Business Performance," Workforce Management, August 19, 2005, http://www.workforce.com/articles/study-moderation-in-hiring-practices-boosts-business-performance.

18. Retail Council of Canada, "Minimum Wage by Province," http://www.retailcouncil.org/quickfacts/minimum-wage.

19. "Whitewater Rafting? 12 Unusual Perks," January 20, 2012, *CNN Money,* http://money.cnn.com/magazines/fortune/best-companies/2012/benefits/unusual.html; "10 Best Companies to Work For (2016)," *Financial Post,* http://www.canadastop100.com/fp10.

20. Crystal Hoganson, "Work and Life: The Balancing Act," Conference Board of Canada, November 2011.

21. Sissi Wang, "70% of Employees Would Quit Their Jobs for a Remote-Working One," October 16, 2015, *canadianbusiness.com,* http://www.canadianbusiness.com/innovation/70-of-employees-would-quit-their-jobs-for-a-remote-working-one.

22. Reva Seth, "Could Job-Sharing Improve Your Work-Life Balance?" *BrighterLife.ca,* http://brighterlife.ca/2013/09/12/could-job-sharing-improve-your-work-life-balance.

23. "Flexible Hours and Telecommuting—Not the Ticket to the Top of Corporate America," September 2005, *Workforce Management,* http://www.workforce.com/section/02/article/24/14/66.html.

24. Stephen Ewart, "Fallout from Plunging Oil Prices Shook the Country," *Calgary Herald*, December 26, 2015, B1; John Shmuel, "As Alberta Leads Canada's Job Slump, Economic Activity Shifts from West to East," February 5, 2016, *financialpost.com*, http://business.financialpost.com/news/economy/canadas-economy-loses-5700-jobs-unemployment-rate-hits-two-year-high.

25. Susan Adams, "Ten Buzzwords to Cut from Your LinkedIn Profile in 2015," January 21, 2015, *www.forbes.com*, http://www.forbes.com/sites/susanadams/2015/01/21/ten-buzzwords-to-cut-from-your-linkedin-profile-in-2015/#363ce85d4227.

26. Employment Equity Act, Department of Justice Canada, http://laws-lois.justice.gc.ca/eng/acts/E-5.401/FullText.html.

27. Government of Canada, "Employment Equity in Federally Regulated Workplace," http://www.esdc.gc.ca/en/jobs/workplace/human_rights/employment_equity/index.page; Government of Quebec, "An Act Respecting Equal Access to Employment in Public Bodies," http://www2.publicationsduquebec.gouv.qc.ca/dynamicSearch/telecharge.php?type=2&file=/A_2_01/A2_01_A.html; Government of Nunavut, "Agreement Between the Inuit of the Nunavut Settlement Area and Her Majesty the Queen in Right of Canada," http://www.gov.nu.ca/sites/default/files/files/013%20-%20Nunavut-Land-Claims-Agreement-English.pdf, all accessed February 6, 2016.

28. John Barber, "Sexual Harassment Suit Rocks Penguin Canada, Former CEO," *Globe and Mail*, http://www.theglobeandmail.com/books/sexual-harassment-suit-rocks-penguin-canada-former-ceo/article1601868.

15

1. John Markoff, "The iPad in Your Hand:," May 9, 2011, *New York Times*, http://bits.blogs.nytimes.com/2011/05/09/the-ipad-in-your-hand-as-fast-as-a-supercomputer-of-yore; M. Grothaus, "iPad2 Would Have Bested 1990s-Era Supercomputers," May 9, 2011, *TUAW*, http://www.tuaw.com/2011/05/09/ipad-2-would-have-bested-1990s-era-supercomputers.

2. C. Anderson, "The Web Is Dead. Long Live the Internet," September 2010, *Wired*, http://www.wired.com/magazine/2010/08/ff_webrip/all/1.

3. "The Size of the World Wide Web (The Internet)," April 2, 2013, *WorldWideWebSize.com*, http://www.worldwidewebsize.com.

4. "OECD Broadband Portal," July 23, 2015, *OECD*, www.oecd.org.

5. S. McCartney, "The Middle Seat: Boarding Gate Makeover," *Wall Street Journal*, August 23, 2012, D3; Nassauer, "Screens Get a Place at the Table," *Wall Street Journal*, May 31, 2012, D1; "Using the RM Handheld for Payment Processing," *Restaurant Manager*, www.rmpos.com; Jeff Macke, "Ziosk Could Put Waiters Out of Work, but Not How You think," October 10, 2014, *Yahoo Finance*, finance.yahoo.com.

6. "Internet2 Member and Partner List," *Internet2*, http://www.internet2.edu/resources/listforweb.pdf.

7. *Muse*, http://k20.internet2.edu/about/goals.

8. "About Us," *Internet2*, http://www.internet2.edu/about.

9. J. Bussey, "Seeking Safety in Clouds," *Wall Street Journal*, September 15, 2011, http://online.wsj.com/article/SB10001424053111904060604576572930344327162.html.

10. Ibid.

11. Derek Gottfrid, "Self-Service, Prorated Super Computing Fun," *New York Times*, November 1, 2007, http://open.blogs.nytimes.com/2007/11/01/self-service-prorated-super-computing-fun; "NY Times AWS Cloud Computing Mistake Costs $240," November 5, 2008, http://www.greenm3.com/2008/11/nytimes-cloud-c.html; Galen Gruman, "Early Experiments in Cloud Computing," April 7, 2008, *Info World*, http://www.infoworld.com/d/virtualization/early-experiments-in-cloud-computing-020.

12. "The Price Is Right," *The Economist*, January 9, 2012, http://www.economist.com/blogs/gametheory/2012/01/sports-ticketing.

13. Effy Oz, *Management Information Systems*, 5th ed. (Mason: Course Technology, Cengage Learning, 2006), 332–38; "Expert Systems," *AlanTuring.Net*, http://www.cs.usfca.edu/www.AlanTuring.net/turing_archive/pages/Reference%20Articles/what_is_AI/What%20is%20AI07.html.

14. David M. Kroenke, *Experiencing MIS* (Toronto: Pearson Prentice Hall, 2008), 340–41; "What Are Expert Systems?," *Thinkquest.org*, http://library.thinkquest.org.

15. Jaymi Heimbuch, "7 Best Green Apps for Mobile Phones," *PlanetGreen.com*, http://planetgreen.discovery.com/feature/green-phone/green-apps-mobile-phones.html; Matylda Czarnecka, "The Top Ten Apps to Make You More Green," *TechCrunch*, http://techcrunch.com/2010/08/10/top-ten-green-apps; Deborah Zabarenko, "Green Apps That Can Save You Money," *Reuters*, http://2011/02/18/green-apps-that-can-save-you-money; *Google*, play.google.com; Jonathan Strickland, "5 Green Mobile Apps," *HowStuffWorks*, www.science.howstuffworks.com.

16. Dion Hinchcliffe, "Web 2.0 Definition Updated and Enterprise 2.0 Emerges," *ZDNet*, http://blogs.zdnet.com; "The Ethics of Web 2.0: YouTube vs. Flickr, Revver, Eyespot, Bliptv, and Even Google," *Lessig.org*, www.lessig.org; Doug Beizer, "Twitter, Blogs and Other Web 2.0 Tools Revolutionize Government Business," March 6, 2009, *Federal Computer Week*, http://fcw.com/articles/2009/03/09/web-2.0-in-action.aspx.

17. Canadian Media Directors' Council, *Media Digest 14/15, Marketing*, p. 7.

18. *PayPal*, www.paypal.com.

19. S. McCartney, "The Middle Seat: The Trump Card at Check-In," *Wall Street Journal*, December 29, 2011, D1.

20. "Advanced Sign-In Security for Your Google Account," http://googleblog.blogspot.com/2011/02/advanced-sign-in-security-for-your.html; "Getting Started with 2-Step Verification," https://support.google.com/accounts/bin/answer.py?hl=en&topic=1056283&answer=185839; "Recovery Email Address," *Google*, http://support.google.com/accounts/bin/answer.py?hl=en&p=oz&ctx=ch_b%2F0%2FUpdateAccountRecoveryOptions&answer=183726.

21. David Utter, "Spammers Target Email Newsletters," January 19, 2007, *WebProWorld Security Forum*, www.securitypronews.com; Anick Jesdanun, "Spammers Turn to Images to Fool Filters," June 28, 2006, *USA Today*, http://www.usatoday.com/tech/news/computersecurity/wormsviruses/2006-06-28-spam-images_x.htm.

22. *Government of Canada Anti-Spam Legislation*, www.fightspam.gc.ca.

23. J. Brodkin, "Amazon Fixes Security Flaw Hackers Used Against Wired's Mat Honan, ArsTechnica," August 7, 2012, *artstechnica.com*, http://arstechnica.com/security/2012/08/amazon-fixes-security-flaw-hackers-used-against-wireds-mat-honan; J. Goodchild, "Social Engineering: The Basics," December 20, 2012, *CSO Online*, http://www.csoonline.com/article/514063/social-engineering-the-basics; S. Kapner, "Hackers Press the "Schmooze" Button," *Wall Street Journal*, October 31, 2011, C1; B. Luscombe, "10 Questions," *Time*, August 29, 2011, 64.

24. "Pharming: Is Your Trusted Website a Clever Fake?," *Microsoft*, January 3, 2007, www.microsoft.com; "Online Fraud: Pharming," *Symantec*, www.symantec.com; "Advisory: Watch Out for Drive-By-Pharming Attacks," *Pharming.org*, www.pharming.org.

25. M. Huffman, "'Smishing' Emerges as New Threat to Cell Phone Users," *Consumer Affairs*, http://www.consumeraffairs.com/news04/2006/11/smishing.html; E. Millis, "'SMiShing' Fishes for Personal Data Over Cell Phone," February 24, 2009, *CNet*, http://news.cnet.com/8301-1009_3-10171241-83.html; L. Musthaler, "How to Avoid Becoming a Victim of SMiShing," March 7, 2013, *NetworkWorld*, http://www.networkworld.com/newsletters/techexec/2013/030813bestpractices.html.

26. Microsoft Safety & Security Center, "Create Strong Passwords," http://www.microsoft.com/security/online-privacy/passwords-create.aspx.

27. MacLeod Law Firm, "Does Monitoring Emails Breach an Employee's Right to Privacy?," March 25, 2013, macleodlawfirm.ca; S. Woo, "What Makes a Password Stronger," *Wall Street Journal*, June 23, 2011, D2.

28. C. Bryan-Low and A. Lucchetti, "George Carlin Never Would've Cut It at the New Goldman Sachs," *Wall Street Journal*, July 29, 2010, A1; R. Mantel, "Watch Your Emails; Your Boss Is," *Wall Street Journal*, May 2, 2010, 3; D. Mirchin, "Monitoring Employee Online Activity: Landmark Case Establishes Guidelines," *Information Today*, February 2012, 32–33; M. Riedy and J. Wen, "Electronic Surveillance of Internet Access in the American Workplace," *Information and Communications Technology Law* 19(1) (2010): 87–99; D. Searcey, "Law Journal: Some Courts Raise Bar on Reading Employee Email," *Wall Street Journal*, November 19, 2009, A17; J. Sipior and B. Ward (2009), "A Framework for Employee E-Mail Privacy Within the United States," *Journal of Internet Commerce* 8 (2010): 161–79; P. Tam, E. White, N. Wingfield, and K. Maher, "Snooping E-Mail by Software Is Now a Workplace Norm," *Wall Street Journal*, March 9, 2005, B1.

29. Government of Canada, "The ePassport," www.cic.gc.ca; Government of Ontario, www.ontario.ca; Dan Goodin, "Passport RFIDs Cloned Wholesale by $250 eBay Shopping Spree," February 2, 2009, *The Register*, http://www.theregister.co.uk/2009/02/02/low_cost_rfid_cloner; Bob Unruh, "Life with Big Brother," February 28, 2009, *World Net Daily*, http://www.worldnetdaily.com/index.php?fa=PAGE.view&pageId=90008; Mark Baard, "RFID Driver's Licenses Debated," October 6, 2004, *Wired*, http://www.wired.com/politics/security/news/2004/10/65243; A. Ramos, W. Scott, D. Lloyd, K. O'Leary, and J. Waldo, "A Threat Analysis of RFID Passports," *Communications of the ACM*, December 2009, 38–42.

30. BSA Global Software Survey June 2014, "The Compliance Gap," *Business Software Alliance*, globalstudy.bsa.org.

16

1. John R. Baldwin and Ryan Macdonald, "The Canadian Manufacturing Sector: Adapting to Challenges," Statistics Canada, Cat. no. 11F0027M-No. 057, 2009; Giuseppe Berlingieri, "Outsourcing and the Shift from Manufacturing to Services," September 25, 2014, www.voxeu.org.

2. David A. Collier and James R. Evans, *OM*, 2nd ed. (Mason: South-Western, Cengage Learning, 2010), 27–28.

3. "Outsourcing: Ripoff Nation," BW Smallbiz Front Line, Winter 2006, *BusinessWeek*, http://www.businessweek.com/magazine/content/06_52/b4015435.htm?chan=rss_topStories_ssi_5; Steve Dickinson, "Outsourcing in China: Five Basic Rules for Reducing Risk," *ezinearticles.com*, http://ezinearticles.com/? Outsourcing-in-China:-Five-Basics-for- Reducing-Risk&id=17214.

4. David Stodder, "ERP and Cloud Computing: Delivering a Virtual Feast," May 20, 2010, *Information Week*, http://www.informationweek.com/news/software/bi/224701329.

5. M.J. Bitner, "Servicescapes: The Impact of Physical Surroundings on Customers and Employees," *Journal of Marketing*, April 1992, 57–71.

6. G. Fowler, "Holiday Hiring Call: People vs. Robots," *Wall Street Journal*, December 20, 2010, B1; R. Greenfield, "Meet the Little Orange Robots Making Amazon's Warehouses More Humane," March 20, 2012, http://www.theatlanticwire.com/technology/2012/03/meet-little-orange-robots-making-amazons-warehouses-more-humane/50094; J. Letzing, "Amazon Adds That Robotic Touch," *Wall Street Journal*, March 20, 2012, B1; M. Wohlsen, "Warehouse 'Bots' Do Battle to Make Same-Day Delivery a Reality," September 28, 2012, *Wired*, http://www.wired.com/business/2012/09/warehouse-robot-battle.

7. Kerri Simon, "Poka Yoke Mistake Proofing," *iSixSigma*, www.isixsigma.com; Mark Hendricks, "Make No Mistake," *Entrepreneur*, October 1996, www.entrepreneur.com.

8. Y. Kane and I. Sherr, "Penney Picks Boss from Apple," *Wall Street Journal*, June 15, 2011, A1.

9. Excellence Canada, www.excellence.ca.

10. "Baldrige FAQs: Applying for the Malcolm Baldrige National Quality Award," National Institutes of Standards and Technology, http://www.nist.gov/baldrige/about/faqs_applying.cfm.

11. "About ISO," *ISO*, http://www.iso.org/iso/about.htm; "ISO Standards," *ISO*, http://www.iso.org/iso/iso_catalogue.htm.

12. R. Flandez, "Restaurant Chains Look for Creative Ways to Cut Costs," *Wall Street Journal*, November 18, 2007, B7; A. Gasparro, "Restaurant Chains Feel the Need for Speed," *Wall Street Journal*, August 29, 2012, http://online.wsj.com/article/SB10000872396390444914904577619743014442300.html; A. Petersen, "When 1,400 Come for Dinner," *Wall Street Journal*, November 11, 2010, D1.

13. *ISO*, www.iso.org.

14. "At Vuitton, Growth in Small Batches," *Wall Street Journal*, June 27, 2011, B1.

15. E. Hromadka, "Green Manufacturing: Innovative Design, Improved Processes and Recycling Efforts in Indiana," *Indiana Business*, May 2008, 10; B. Kenney, "The Zero: How to Green," *Industry Week*, <date?> 36–43. J. McIntosh, "A Solid Program to Reduce Waste," *Toronto Star*, September 27, 2008, W21; A. Robinson and D. Schroeder, "Greener and Cheaper," *Wall Street Journal*, March 23, 2009, R4; C. Woodyard, "It's Waste Not, Want Not at Super Green Subaru Plant," *USA Today*, February 19, 2009, 1B.

16. *WestJet*, www.westjet.com.

17. One reason renewable energy is more expensive than energy from carbon-based sources such as coal or oil is that the market prices of such carbon-based sources do not reflect their environmental costs.

18. "Sustainability Initiatives Cut Costs 6–10%," *Environmental Leader*, http://www.environmentalleader.com/2009/06/09/sustainability-initiatives-cut-costs-by-6-10.

19. "ISO 14000 Essentials," *ISO*, http://www.iso.org/iso/iso_14000_essentials.

Appendix 1

1. Larry Suffield, *Labour Relations*, 2nd ed. (Toronto: Pearson Prentice Hall, 2007), 2.

2. *Canadian Labour Congress*, canadianlabour.ca.

3. Frank Kehoe and Maurice Archer, *Canadian Industrial Relations: Text, Cases & Simulations*, 11th ed., Century Labour Publications; "Average Hourly Wages of Employees by Selected Characteristics and Profession, Unadjusted Data, by Province (Monthly)," *Statistics Canada*, www.statcan.gc.ca.

4. "Average Hourly Wages of Employees by Selected Characteristics and Occupation, Unadjusted Data, by Province (Monthly)," *Statistics Canada*, www.statcan.gc.ca.

5. Federal Mediation and Conciliation Service, "Interest-Based Bargaining," http://www.fmca.gov/internet/itemDetail.asp?categoryID=131&itemID=15804.

6. J. Klein, "NHL and Players Union Reach Tentative Agreement," *New York Times*, January 6, 2013, http://www.nytimes.com/2013/01/07/sports/hockey/nhl-players-union-lockout-agreement.html?_r=0.

7. "Average Hourly Wages of Employees by Selected Characteristics and Occupation, Unadjusted Data, by Province (Monthly)," *Statistics Canada*, www.statcan.gc.ca.

8. "Union Members Summary, Economic News Release," January 21, 2011, *Bureau of Labor Statistics*, http://bls.gov/news.release/union2.nr0.html; "Union Membership-2009," *UAW*, http://www.uaw.org/sites/default/files/inionmembership2009.pdf.

Appendix 2

1. Cristin Schmitz, "Big Tobacco Can Be Sued for Health Bill," *National Post*, September 30, 2005, A4.

2. "Simpson Civil Trial Explainer," *CNN*, http://www.cnn.com/US/9609/16/simpson.case/index.html; Wendy McElroy, "Civil vs. Criminal Remedies for Intentional Wrongs by August 13, 2004," *Future of Freedom Foundation*, http://www.fff.org/comment/com0408f.asp.

3. Shannon Ryan, "Time for NFL to End Use of Cheerleaders," January 7, 2016, *Chicago Tribune*, http://www.chicagotribune.com/sports/columnists/ct-ryan-ending-nfl-cheerleaders-spt-0107-20160107-column.html; Sophia Harris, "Are NFL Cheerleaders Being Exploited?" September 4, 2014, www.cbc.ca, http://www.cbc.ca/news/business/are-nfl-cheerleaders-being-exploited-1.2754361; Andrew Brandt, "Bargain-Bin Brady," September 30, 2015, http://mmqb.si.com/mmqb/2015/09/30/tom-brady-contract-nfl-patriots-salary-cap; "NFL Cheerleader Salaries (Hourly Wage in 2016)," January 24, 2016, http://www.totalsportek.com/news/nfl-cheerleader-salaries-2015/; Joe Dorish, "Hottest Kansas City Chiefs Cheerleaders," examiner.com, December 7, 2012, http://www.examiner.com/article/hottest-kansas-city-chiefs-cheerleaders; Audra Williams, "Gimme an F; Catching a Ball Can Make You a Millionaire–Why Doesn't Cheering Deserve a Living Wage?" *National Post*, October 3, 2015, WP3.

4. "Trademarks vs. Generic Terms," *International Trademark Association*, http://www.inta.org/TrademarkBasics/FactSheets/Pages/TrademarksvsGenericTermsFactSheet.aspx; Mary Bellis, "When a Brand Name Becomes Generic," http://inventors.about.com/b/2006/01/29/when-a-brand-name-becomes-generic-genericized-trademarks.htm; "What Is Generic Trademarks?" *Legal Match*, http://www.legalmatch.com/law-library/article/generic-trademarks.html.

Appendix 3

1. David Bach, *The Automatic Millionaire* (New York: Broadway Books, 2004).

2. Farmoosh Torabi, "4 Financial Habits of Highly Successful People," *Time*, January 14, 2015, http://time.com.

3. *Canada Deposit Insurance*, www.cdic.ca.

4. "How to Check Your Credit Report," November 16, 2012, CBC News, www.cbc.ca.

5. James Bradshaw, "University Education No Guarantee of Earnings Success," September 25, 2011, *Globe and Mail*, theglobeandmail.com.

6. "What Is the Law?" *Internship Association of Canada*, internassociation.ca.

Index

Note: Entries in **bold** are key terms.

Sandburg, Sheryl, 54
Sarbanes-Oxley Act, 27
Saudi Arabia, IKEA catalogue in, 61
savings accounts, 294–295
say-on-pay votes, 77
Scarborough, Michelle, 90
scope of authority of agents, 288
scope of marketing, 153–154
scratch, starting business from, 93
Sears Canada, 31
seasonal unemployment, 48
secondary data, 164
secondary securities market, 142, 143–145
secret menus of fast food chains, 161
securities. *See* financial securities
securities brokers
    career as, 150
    choosing, 145, 299
    role of, 136
securities dealers, 136
security for computers, 253, 254
Seinfeld, Jerry, 226
selection of employees, 229–230
selective distribution, 197
self, investing in, 300
self-employment, 84
self-regulatory organizations, 137
self-reliance of entrepreneurs, 87
Selling Era, 154
selling expenses, 105
separation from employment, 231, 236–237
service-based economies
    capacity of facilities, 266
    designing servicescape, 266
    overview of, 265
services, 170–171, 259, 266
servicescape, 266
service utility, 194
Sevenly, 25
shareholders, 73
shareholders' equity, 103
shareholders' equity statements, 106
shareholder value and social responsibility, 117–118
Shaw, JoAnne, 79
Sherritt International, 73
Shkreli, Martin, 21
shopping products, 173
short-term financing, sources of, 122–124
Siemens, 109, 173–174, 235
signs and symbols of servicescape, 266
Silver, Spencer, 95
Six Sigma, 269
skimming pricing, 202–203
sleep deprivation, 219
small business. *See also* entrepreneurship
    definition of, 95
    funding for, 89–90
    impact on economy, 95–96
    launching, 92–93
    opportunities for, 90–91
    threats to, 92
    tools for success, 93–94
small business confidence index, 4
Smashing Place, The, 91
Smith, Adam, 41
Smith, Fred, 87
Smith, Mike, 212
SNC-Lavalin, 24
social audit, 32
social environment
    marketing and, 162
    overview of, 11–13

Social Era, 155
socialism, 46
social media
    HootSuite, 190
    power of, 46
    promotion and, 184
social responsibility. *See also* ethics and social responsibility
    donations to charity and, 123
    green investing strategy and, 141
    green venture capital firms and, 131
    marketing and, 166–167
    overview of, 22–23
    shareholder value and, 117–118
    stakeholder approach to, 23–30
sociocultural differences and global trade, 60–61
software, 243, 267
sole proprietorships, 68, 69–70
spam, 253
span of control, 219
specialty products, 173
specific performance, 287
speed-to-market, 9
Spence, Chris, 21
Spencer, Percy, 95
spending habits, 294
spin-offs, 77
sponsorships, 185
spontaneous financing, 123
S&P/TSX Composite Index, 148
spyware, 252
staff managers, 220
stakeholders, 23, 100
stamps, as investment, 205
standard of living, 4
Standard & Poor's 500, 148
Starbucks, 161
statements of cash flows, 105–106
statements of retained earnings, 106
static budgets, 120
statute of frauds, 286
statute of limitations, 286
statutory laws, 283–284
Stevens, Didier, 6
stock (securities) exchanges, 143–144
stock index, 148
stock returns, 136
store brands, 177
store retailers, 196–197
strategic alliances, 60
strategic goals, 217
strategic planning, 214, 215–218
strategies, 217
stress and social status, 3
strikes, 279, 280
Stronach, Frank, 86
strong passwords, 254
structural unemployment, 48
structured interviews, 229–230
students and ethics, 19
styles of leadership, 221–222
Subaru zero-landfill automobile plant, 272
subprime mortgages, 120
success, tools for, 93–94
Sumac Ridge Estate Winery, 91
supply, 44, 203, 205
supply chain management, 198–200
supply chains, 198, 199, 260, 264
supply curve, 44
survey research, 165
sustainability, 13, 273

LEARNING OUTCOMES

1-1 (P. 2)

Define business and discuss the role of business in the economy. A business is any activity that provides goods and services in an effort to earn a profit. Profit is the money that a business earns in sales minus expenses such as the cost of goods and the cost of salaries. Profit potential provides a powerful incentive for people to start their own businesses or to become entrepreneurs. Successful businesses create wealth, which increases the standard of living for virtually all members of a society.

Helder Almeida/Thinkstock.com

1-2 (P. 4)

Explain the evolution of modern business. Business historians typically divide our business history into five distinct eras, which overlap during the periods of transition.

- *Industrial Revolution:* From the mid-1700s to the mid-1800s, technology fuelled a period of rapid industrialization. Factories sprang up in cities, leading to mass production and specialization of labour.

- *Entrepreneurship Era:* During the second half of the 1800s, large-scale entrepreneurs emerged, building business empires that created enormous wealth, but often at the expense of workers and consumers.

- *Production Era:* In the early 1900s, major businesses focused on further refining the production process, creating huge efficiencies. The assembly line, introduced in 1913, boosted productivity and lowered costs.

- *Marketing Era:* After the Second World War, consumers began to gain power. As goods and services flooded the market, the marketing concept emerged: a consumer-first orientation as a guide to business decision making.

- *Relationship Era:* With the technology boom in the 1990s, businesses have begun to look beyond the immediate transaction, aiming to build a competitive edge through long-term customer relationships.

1-3 (P. 5)

Discuss the role of not-for-profit organizations in the economy. Not-for-profit organizations often work hand in hand with business to improve the quality of life in our society. Not-for-profits are business-*like* establishments that contribute to economic stability and growth. Similar to businesses, not-for-profits generate revenue and incur expenses. Their goal is to use any revenue above and beyond expenses to advance the goals of the organization rather than to make money for its owners. Some not-for-profits—such as museums, schools, and theatres—can act as economic magnets for communities, attracting additional investment.

KEY TERMS

1-1

value The relationship between the price of a good or a service and the benefits it offers its customers.

business Any activity that provides goods and services in an effort to earn a profit.

profit The money a business earns in sales (or revenue) minus expenses, such as the cost of goods and the cost of salaries (Revenue − Expenses = Profit [or Loss]).

loss When a business incurs expenses that are greater than its revenue.

entrepreneurs People who risk their time, money, and other resources to start and manage businesses.

standard of living The quality and quantity of goods and services available to a population.

quality of life The overall sense of well-being experienced by either an individual or a group.

1-3

not-for-profit organizations Business-*like* establishments that employ people and produce goods and services with the fundamental goal of contributing to the community rather than generating financial gain.

1-4

factors of production Four fundamental elements—natural resources, capital, human resources, and entrepreneurship—that businesses need to achieve their objectives. Some combination of these factors is crucial for an economic system to create wealth.

1-5

business environment The setting in which business operates. The five key components are

CHAPTER IN REVIEW 1

economic environment, competitive environment, technological environment, social environment, and global environment.

speed-to-market The rate at which a new product moves from conception to commercialization.

business technology Any tools—especially computers, telecommunications, and other digital products—that businesses can use to become more efficient and effective.

World Wide Web The service that allows computer users to easily access and share information on the Internet in the form of text, graphics, video, and animation.

e-commerce Business transactions conducted online, typically via the Internet.

demographics The measurable characteristics of a population. Demographic factors include population size and density and specific traits such as age, gender, and race.

free trade An international economic and political movement designed to help goods and services flow more freely across international boundaries.

General Agreement on Tariffs and Trade (GATT) An international trade agreement that has taken bold steps to lower tariffs and promote free trade worldwide.

The Business Environment

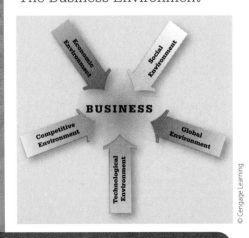

© Cengage Learning

The Relationship between Not-for-Profits and For-Profit Businesses

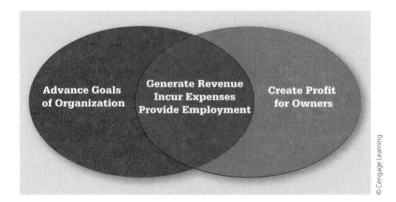

© Cengage Learning

1-4 (P. 7)

Outline the core factors of production and how they influence the economy. The four factors of production are the fundamental resources that both businesses and not-for-profit organizations use to achieve their objectives.

- *Natural resources:* All inputs that offer value in their natural state, such as land, fresh water, wind, and mineral deposits. The value of natural resources tends to rise with high demand, low supply, or both.

- *Capital:* The manmade resources that an organization needs to produce goods or services. The elements of capital include machines, tools, buildings, and technology.

- *Human resources:* The physical, intellectual, and creative contributions of everyone who works within an economy. Education and motivation have become increasingly important as technology replaces manual labour jobs.

- *Entrepreneurship:* Entrepreneurs take the risk of launching and operating their own businesses. Entrepreneurial enterprises can create a tidal wave of opportunity by harnessing the other factors of production.

1-5 (P. 7)

Describe today's business environment and discuss each key dimension. Accelerating change marks every dimension of today's business environment.

- *Economic environment:* The Canadian economy remains relatively strong because the government actively supports free enterprise and fair competition.

- *Competitive environment:* As global competition intensifies, leading-edge companies have focused on long-term customer satisfaction as never before.

- *Technological environment:* The recent technology boom has transformed business, establishing new industries and burying others.

- *Social environment:* The Canadian population continues to diversify. Consumers are gaining power, and society has higher standards for business behaviour.

- *Global environment:* The Canadian economy works within the context of the global environment. A key factor is rapid economic growth in China and India.

1-6 (P. 15)

Explain how current business trends may influence your career choices. With automation picking up speed, many traditional career choices have become dead-ends. But some things—including empathy, creativity, change management, and great communication—can't be digitized. Having these skills can provide you with personal and financial opportunity.

LEARNING OUTCOMES

2-1 (P. 16)

Define ethics and explain the concept of universal ethical standards. Ethics is a set of beliefs about right and wrong, good and bad. Who you are as a human being, your family, and your culture all play a role in shaping your ethical standards. The laws of each country usually set minimum ethical standards, but truly ethical standards typically reach beyond minimum legal requirements. Despite some significant cultural and legal differences, people around the globe tend to agree on core values, which can serve as a starting point for universal ethical standards across a wide range of situations. Those values include trustworthiness, respect, responsibility, fairness, caring, and citizenship.

Universal Ethical Standards

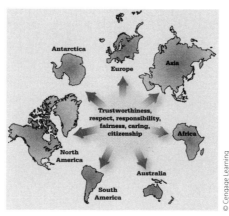

© Cengage Learning

2-2 (P. 18)

Describe business ethics and ethical dilemmas. Business ethics is the application of right and wrong, good and bad, in a business setting. Ethical dilemmas arise when you face business decisions that throw your values into conflict. These are decisions that force you to choose among less than ideal options because whatever choice you make will have some significant negative consequences.

Ethical Dilemma

© Cengage Learning

2-3 (P. 20)

Discuss how ethics relates to both the individual and the organization. Ethical choices begin with ethical individuals. To help people make good choices, experts have developed frameworks for reaching ethical decisions. While the specifics vary, the core principles of most decision guides are similar:

- Do you fully understand each dimension of the problem?
- Who would benefit? Who would suffer?
- Are the alternatives legal? Are they fair?
- Does your decision make you feel comfortable at a "gut feel" level?
- Could you defend your decision on the nightly TV news?
- Have you considered and reconsidered your responses to each question?

While each person is responsible for his or her own actions, the organization can also have a dramatic influence on the conduct of individual employees. An ethical culture—which includes ethical leadership from top executives and accountability at every level of the organization—has an outsized impact on individual conduct. But formal ethics programs also play a crucial role. A written code of ethics—a

KEY TERMS

2-1

ethics A set of beliefs about right and wrong, good and bad.

universal ethical standards Ethical norms that apply to all people across a broad spectrum of situations.

2-2

business ethics The application of right and wrong, good and bad in a business setting.

ethical dilemma A decision that involves a conflict of values; every potential course of action has some significant negative consequences.

2-3

code of ethics A formal, written document that defines the ethical standards of an organization and gives employees the information they need to make ethical decisions across a range of situations.

whistleblowers Employees who report their employer's illegal or unethical behaviour to either the authorities or the media.

2-4

social responsibility The obligation of a business to contribute to society.

stakeholders Any groups that have a stake—or a personal interest—in the performance and actions of an organization.

consumerism A social movement that focuses on four key consumer rights: (1) the right to be safe, (2) the right to be informed, (3) the right to choose, and (4) the right to be heard.

planned obsolescence The strategy of deliberately designing products to fail in order to shorten the time between purchases.

CHAPTER IN REVIEW 2

Sarbanes–Oxley Act US federal legislation that sets higher ethical standards for public corporations and accounting firms. Key provisions limit conflict-of-interest issues and require financial officers and CEOs to certify the validity of their financial statements.

corporate philanthropy All business donations to not-for-profit groups, including money, products, and employee time.

cause-related marketing Marketing partnerships between businesses and not-for-profit organizations, designed to spike sales for the company and raise money for the not-for-profit organization.

corporate responsibility Business contributions to the community through the actions of the business itself rather than donations of money and time.

sustainable development Doing business to meet the needs of the current generation, without harming the ability of future generations to meet their needs.

carbon footprint The amount of greenhouse gases that a firm emits throughout its operations, both directly and indirectly.

green marketing Developing and promoting environmentally sound products and practices to gain a competitive edge.

2-6

social audit A systematic evaluation of how well a firm is meeting its ethics and social responsibility goals.

document that lays out the values and priorities of the organization—is the cornerstone of a formal ethics program. Other key elements include ethics training and a clear enforcement policy for ethical violations.

2-4 (P. 22)

Define social responsibility and examine the impact on stakeholder groups. Social responsibility is the obligation of a business to contribute to society. Enlightened companies carefully consider the priorities of all stakeholders—groups that have an interest in their actions and performance—as they make key decisions. Core stakeholder groups for most businesses are listed below, along with key obligations.

- *Employees:* Treat employees with dignity, respect, and fairness. Ensure that hard work and talent pay off. Help workers balance emerging work–life priorities.

- *Customers:* Provide quality products at fair prices. Ensure that customers are safe and informed. Support consumer choice and consumer dialogue.

- *Investors:* Create an ongoing stream of profits. Manage investor dollars according to the highest legal and ethical standards. Support full disclosure.

- *Community:* Support not-for-profit groups that improve the community and fit with your company. Minimize the environmental impact of your business.

The Spectrum of Social Responsibility

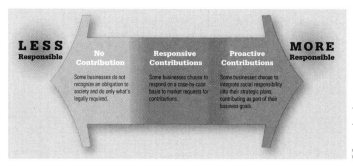

© Cengage Learning

2-5 (P. 31)

Explain the role of social responsibility in the global arena. Social responsibility becomes more complex in the global arena due largely to differences in the legal and cultural environments. Bribery and corruption are key issues, along with concern for human rights and environmental standards.

Social Responsibility Issues in the Global Arena

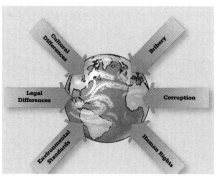

© Cengage Learning

2-6 (P. 32)

Describe how companies evaluate their efforts to be socially responsible. Many companies—even some entire industries—monitor themselves. The process typically involves establishing objectives for ethics and social responsibility and then measuring achievement of those objectives on a systematic, periodic basis. Other groups play watchdog roles as well. Key players include activist customers, investors, unions, environmentalists, and community groups.

LEARNING OUTCOMES

3-1 (P. 34)
Define economics and discuss the global economic crisis.
Economics—the study of how people, companies, and governments allocate resources—offers vital insights regarding the forces that impact every business on a daily basis. Understanding economics helps businesspeople make better decisions, which can lead to greater short-term and long-term profitability. Macroeconomics is the study of broad economic trends. Microeconomics focuses on the choices made by smaller economic units, such as individual consumers, families, and businesses.

Globally, there has been an economic slowdown over the last several years, and it is predicted to continue. The most troubled region is Latin America, but things are only a bit better in Europe. The Asia–Pacific region has slowed well below the growth experienced there in recent years. Because the global economies are now so interdependent, when trouble is experienced in any major region of the world, the pain is felt elsewhere as well. The economies of Canada and the United States will most likely grow, but at slower rates than we are used to, and Canada's growth is very much dependent on what happens in the United States, the one country that is at least seeing some sunny periods.

3-2 (P. 37)
Analyze the impact of fiscal and monetary policy on the economy. Fiscal policy and monetary policy refer to efforts to shape the health of the economy. Fiscal policy involves government taxation and spending decisions designed to encourage growth and boost employment. Monetary policy refers to decisions by the Bank of Canada that influence the size of the money supply and the level of interest rates. Both fiscal and monetary policies played a pivotal role in mitigating the impact of the recent financial crisis and establishing a framework for recovery. Canada was thereby able to weather the crisis better than many other countries. These tools can also help sustain economic expansions.

Equilibrium

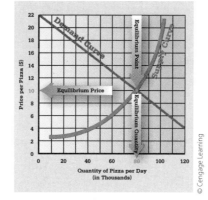

© Cengage Learning

3-3 (P. 40)
Explain and evaluate the free market system and supply and demand. Capitalism, also known as the free market system, is based on private ownership, economic freedom, and fair competition. In a capitalist economy, individuals, businesses, and not-for-profit organizations privately own the vast majority of enterprises. As businesses compete against one another, quality goes up, prices remain reasonable, and choices abound, raising the overall standard of living.

The interplay between the forces of supply and demand determines the selection of products and prices available in a free market economy. Supply refers

KEY TERMS

3-1
economy A financial and social system of how resources flow through society, from production, to distribution, to consumption.

economics The study of the choices that people, companies, and governments make in allocating society's resources.

macroeconomics The study of a country's overall economic issues, such as the employment rate, the gross domestic product, and taxation policies.

microeconomics The study of smaller economic units such as individual consumers, families, and individual businesses.

3-2
fiscal policy Government efforts to influence the economy through taxation and spending.

budget surplus Overage that occurs when revenue is higher than expenses over a given period of time.

budget deficit Shortfall that occurs when expenses are higher than revenue over a given period of time.

federal debt The sum of all the money that the federal government has borrowed over the years and not yet repaid.

monetary policy Bank of Canada decisions that shape the economy by influencing interest rates and the supply of money.

money supply The total amount of money within the overall economy.

M1 money supply Includes all currency plus chequing accounts and traveller's cheques.

M2 money supply Includes all of M1 money supply plus most savings accounts, money market accounts, and certificates of deposit.

CHAPTER IN REVIEW 3

open market operations The Bank of Canada function of buying and selling government securities, which include treasury bonds, notes, and bills.

bank rate The rate of interest the Bank of Canada charges when it loans funds to banks.

reserve requirement A rule that specifies the minimum amount of reserves (or funds) a bank must hold, expressed as a percentage of the bank's deposits.

3-3

economic system A structure for allocating limited resources.

Canada Deposit Insurance Corporation (CDIC) A federal Crown corporation that insures deposits in banks and thrift institutions for up to $100,000 per customer, per bank.

capitalism An economic system—also known as the private enterprise or free market system—based on private ownership, economic freedom, and fair competition.

pure competition A market structure with many competitors selling virtually identical products. Barriers to entry are quite low.

monopolistic competition A market structure with many competitors selling differentiated products. Barriers to entry are low.

oligopoly A market structure with only a handful of competitors selling products that are either similar or different. Barriers to entry are typically high.

monopoly A market structure with one producer completely dominating the industry, leaving no room for any significant competitors. Barriers to entry tend to be virtually insurmountable.

natural monopoly A market structure with one company as the supplier of a product because the nature of that product makes a single supplier more efficient than multiple, competing ones. Most natural monopolies are government sanctioned and regulated.

supply The quantity of products that producers are willing to offer for sale at different market prices.

to the quantity of products that producers are willing to offer for sale at different market prices at a specific time. Demand refers to the quantity of products that consumers are willing to buy at different market prices at a specific time. According to economic theory, markets will naturally move towards the point at which supply and demand are equal: the equilibrium point.

3-4 (P. 45)

Explain and evaluate planned market systems. In planned economies, the government—rather than individual choice—plays a pivotal role in controlling the economy. The two main types of planned economies are socialism and communism. Planned economies aim to create more equity among their citizens but tend to be more prone to corruption and less effective at generating wealth than market-based economies.

3-5 (P. 47)

Describe the trend towards mixed market systems. Most of today's nations have mixed economies, falling somewhere along a spectrum that ranges from pure planned at one extreme to pure market at the other. Over the past 30 years, most major economies around the world have moved towards the market end of the spectrum, although recently—in the wake of the global financial crisis—Canada has added more planned elements to the economy.

3-6 (P. 47)

Discuss key terms and tools to evaluate economic performance. Because economic systems are so complex, no one measure captures all the dimensions of economic performance. But each measure yields insight on overall economic health.

- *Gross domestic product (GDP):* The total value of all final goods and services produced within a nation's physical boundaries over a given period of time.

- *Unemployment rate:* The percentage of workers of employment age who don't have jobs and who are actively seeking employment.

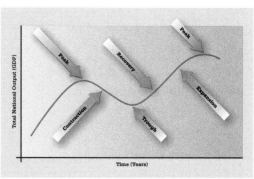
Business Cycle

© Cengage Learning

supply curve The graphed relationship between price and quantity from a supplier standpoint.

demand The quantity of products that consumers are willing to buy at different market prices.

demand curve The graphed relationship between price and quantity from a customer demand standpoint.

equilibrium price The price associated with the point at which the quantity demanded of a product equals the quantity supplied.

3-4

socialism An economic system based on the principle that the government should own and operate key enterprises that directly affect public welfare.

communism An economic and political system that calls for public ownership of virtually all enterprises, under the direction of a strong central government.

3-5

mixed economies Economies that embody elements of both planned and market-based economic systems.

privatization The process of converting government-owned businesses to private ownership.

3-6

gross domestic product (GDP) The total value of all final goods and services produced within a nation's physical boundaries over a given period of time.

unemployment rate The percentage of people in the labour force of employment age who do not have jobs and are actively seeking employment.

business cycle The periodic contraction and expansion that occurs over time in virtually every economy.

contraction A period of economic downturn, marked by rising unemployment and falling business production.

recession An economic downturn marked by a decrease in the GDP for two consecutive quarters.

depression An especially deep and long-lasting recession.

recovery A period of rising economic growth and employment.

expansion A period of robust economic growth and high employment.

inflation A period of rising average prices across the economy.

hyperinflation An average monthly inflation rate of more than 50 percent.

disinflation A period of slowing average price increases across the economy.

deflation A period of falling average prices across the economy.

consumer price index (CPI) A measure of inflation that evaluates the change in the weighted-average price of goods and services that the average consumer buys each month.

producer price index A measure of inflation that evaluates the change over time in the weighted-average wholesale prices.

productivity The basic relationship between the production of goods and services (output) and the resources needed to produce them (input), calculated via the following equation: Output / Input = Productivity.

- *Business cycle:* The periodic expansion and contraction that occurs over time in virtually every economy.

- *Inflation rate:* The rate at which prices are rising across the economy. The government tracks the consumer price index and the producer price index.

- *Productivity:* The relationship between the goods and services that an economy produces and the inputs needed to produce them.

NOTES

LEARNING OUTCOMES

4-1 (P. 52)

Discuss business opportunities in the world economy. Advancing technology and falling trade barriers have created unprecedented international business opportunities. Despite the global crisis that began in 2008, high-population countries—such as China, India, Indonesia, and Brazil—continue to offer the most potential for global trade due to both their size and their relatively strong economic growth rates.

4-2 (P. 54)

Explain the key reasons for and against international trade. The benefits of international trade for individual firms include access to factors of production, reduced risk, and an inflow of new ideas from foreign markets. The disadvantages of international trade include lost jobs and industries to countries with lower paid workers and foreign ownership of domestic companies, particularly resource-based industries. Overall, industries tend to succeed on a global basis in countries that enjoy a competitive advantage. A country has an absolute advantage in a given industry when it can produce more of a good than other nations, using the same amount of resources, and a country has a comparative advantage when it can make products at a lower opportunity cost than other nations. Unless they face major trade barriers, the industries in any country tend to produce products for which they have a comparative advantage. Michael Porter developed a model to help countries evaluate their comparative advantage.

4-3 (P. 56)

Describe the tools for measuring international trade. Measuring the impact of international trade on individual nations requires a clear understanding of balance of trade, balance of payments, and exchange rates.

- *Balance of trade:* A basic measure of the difference between a nation's exports and its imports.

- *Balance of payments:* A measure of the total flow of money into or out of a country, including the balance of trade, plus other financial flows such as foreign loans, foreign aid, and foreign investments.

- *Exchange rates:* A measure of the value of one nation's currency relative to the currency of other nations. The exchange rate has a powerful influence on how global trade impacts both individual nations and their trading partners.

4-4 (P. 58)

Analyze strategies for reaching global markets. Firms can enter global markets by developing foreign suppliers, foreign customers, or both. Two strategies for acquiring foreign suppliers are outsourcing and importing. Key strategies for developing foreign markets include exporting, licensing, franchising, and direct investment. Exporting is relatively low cost and low risk, but it offers little control over how the business unfolds. Direct investment, at the other end of the spectrum, tends to be high cost and high risk, but it offers more control and higher potential profits.

4-5 (P. 60)

Discuss barriers to international trade and strategies to surmount them. Most barriers to trade fall into the following categories: sociocultural differences, economic differences, and legal/political differences. Each country has

KEY TERMS

4-2

opportunity cost The opportunity of giving up the second-best choice when making a decision.

absolute advantage The benefit a country has in a given industry when it can produce more of a product than other nations using the same amount of resources.

comparative advantage The benefit a country has in a given industry if it can make products at a lower opportunity cost than other countries.

4-3

balance of trade A basic measure of the difference in value between a nation's exports and imports, including both goods and services.

trade surplus Overage that occurs when the total value of a nation's exports is higher than the total value of its imports.

trade deficit Shortfall that occurs when the total value of a nation's imports is higher than the total value of its exports.

balance of payments A measure of the total flow of money into or out of a country.

balance of payments surplus Overage that occurs when more money flows into a nation than out of that nation.

balance of payments deficit Shortfall that occurs when more money flows out of a nation than into that nation.

exchange rates A measurement of the value of one nation's currency relative to the currency of other nations.

countertrade International trade that involves the barter of products for products rather than for currency.

4-4

foreign outsourcing Contracting with foreign suppliers to produce products, usually at a fraction of the cost of domestic production (also called contract manufacturing).

importing Buying products domestically that have been produced or grown in foreign nations.

exporting Selling products in foreign nations that have been produced or grown domestically.

foreign licensing Authority granted by a domestic firm to a foreign firm for the rights to produce and market its product or to use its trademark/patent rights in a defined geographic area.

foreign franchising A specialized type of foreign licensing in which a firm expands by offering businesses in other countries the right to produce and market its products according to specific operating requirements.

direct investment When firms either acquire foreign firms or develop new facilities from the ground up in foreign countries (also called foreign direct investment).

joint ventures When two or more companies join forces—sharing resources, risks, and profits but not actually merging companies—to pursue specific opportunities.

partnership A voluntary agreement under which two or more people act as co-owners of a business for profit.

strategic alliance An agreement between two or more firms to jointly pursue a specific opportunity without actually merging their businesses. Strategic alliances typically involve less formal, less encompassing agreements than partnerships.

4-5

sociocultural differences Differences among cultures in language, attitudes, and values.

infrastructure A country's physical facilities that support economic activity.

protectionism National policies designed to restrict international trade,

a different mix of barriers. Often countries with the highest barriers have the least competition, which can present a real opportunity for the first international firms to break through. The best way to surmount trade barriers is to cultivate a deep understanding of a country before beginning business. And because conditions change rapidly in many nations, learning and responding is a continual process.

4-6 (P. 64)

Describe the free trade movement and discuss key benefits and criticisms. Over the past two decades, the emergence of regional trading blocs, common markets, and international trade agreements has moved the world economy much closer to complete free trade. Key players include the following:

- General Agreement on Tariffs and Trade (GATT) and the World Trade Organization (WTO)
- The World Bank
- The International Monetary Fund (IMF)
- The North American Free Trade Agreement (NAFTA)
- The European Union (EU)

The free trade movement has raised the global standard of living, lowered prices, and expanded choices for millions of people, but critics are troubled by worker abuse, large-scale pollution, cultural homogenization, and the growing economic gap between the haves and the have-nots.

usually with the goal of protecting domestic businesses.

tariffs Taxes levied against imports.

quotas Limitations on the amount of specific products that may be imported from certain countries during a given time period.

voluntary export restraints (VERs) Limitations on the amount of specific products that one nation will export to another nation.

embargo A complete ban on international trade of a certain item or a total halt in trade with a particular nation.

4-6

free trade The unrestricted movement of goods and services across international borders.

General Agreement on Tariffs and Trade (GATT) An international trade treaty designed to encourage worldwide trade among its members.

World Trade Organization (WTO) A permanent global institution to promote international trade and to settle international trade disputes.

World Bank An international cooperative of 188 member countries working together to reduce poverty in the developing world.

International Monetary Fund (IMF) An international organization of 188 member nations that promotes international economic cooperation and stable growth.

trading bloc A group of countries that has reduced or even eliminated tariffs, allowing for the free flow of goods among the member nations.

common market A group of countries that has eliminated tariffs and harmonized trading rules to facilitate the free flow of goods among the member nations.

North American Free Trade Agreement (NAFTA) The treaty among Canada, the United States, and Mexico that eliminated trade barriers and investment restrictions over a 15-year period starting in 1994.

European Union (EU) The world's largest common market, composed of 28 European nations.

LEARNING OUTCOMES

5-1 (P. 68)

Describe the characteristics of the three basic forms of business ownership. A sole proprietorship is a business that is owned, and usually managed, by a single person. A partnership is an arrangement where two or more people act as co-owners of a business. A corporation is a legal entity created by filing a document, known as "articles of incorporation," either provincially or federally. A corporation is considered to be distinct from its owners, who have limited liability for the company's debts.

5-2 (P. 69)

Discuss the advantages and disadvantages of a sole proprietorship. A sole proprietorship is the simplest and least expensive form of ownership to establish. The single owner has the flexibility to run the business without seeking the approval of other owners. If the business succeeds, the sole proprietor retains all of the profits. And, the earnings of a sole proprietorship are taxed only as income of the owner, with no separate tax levied on the business. A key disadvantage of a sole proprietorship is that the single owner has unlimited liability for the business's debts. The sole owner may also work long hours and assume heavy responsibilities. Sole proprietorships can have difficulty raising funds for expansion. Finally, because the law views sole proprietorships as simply an extension of the person who owns the company, this form of ownership has a limited life.

5-3 (P. 70)

Evaluate the pros and cons of the partnership as a form of ownership. In a general partnership, each co-owner takes an active role in management. Unlike sole proprietorships, a general partnership offers the advantages of pooled financial resources and the benefits of a shared workload and complementary skills. The earnings are taxed only as income to the partners; there is no separate tax on the business itself. A major disadvantage of a general partnership is that each owner has unlimited liability for the debts of the company. Also, disagreements among partners can complicate decision making. Finally, the death or withdrawal of a partner can create instability in the management and financing of the company.

A limited partnership must have at least one general partner and at least one limited partner. The general partner actively manages the company and accepts unlimited liability for the company's debts. The limited partner invests money (and possibly other resources) in the business and shares in its profits but cannot actively manage the partnership.

The newest form of partnership is the limited liability partnership. Under this arrangement, all partners have the ability to manage their company and some degree of limited liability for the debts of their firm. This type of partnership can be formed only by professional businesses, such as law or accounting firms.

5-4 (P. 72)

Explain why corporations have become the dominant form of business ownership. A corporation is a legal entity created by permission of the federal or a provincial government. All shareholders (owners) have limited liability for company debts. Corporations can raise capital by issuing bonds or shares of stock,

KEY TERMS

5-1

sole proprietorship A form of business ownership with a single owner who usually actively manages the company.

partnership A voluntary agreement under which two or more people act as co-owners of a business for profit.

general partnership A partnership in which all partners can take an active role in managing the business and have unlimited liability for any claims against the firm.

corporation A form of business ownership in which the business is considered a legal entity that is separate and distinct from its owners.

articles of incorporation The document filed with the appropriate government to establish the existence of a new corporation.

limited liability When owners are not personally liable for claims against their firm. Limited liability owners may lose their investment in the company, but their personal assets are protected.

5-3

limited partnership A partnership that includes at least one general partner who actively manages the company and accepts unlimited liability and one limited partner who gives up the right to actively manage the company in exchange for limited liability.

limited liability partnership (LLP) A form of partnership in which all partners have the right to participate in management and have limited liability for company debts.

5-4

public corporation A corporation whose shares of stock are widely held by the public.

private corporation A corporation owned by only a few shareholders and whose shares of stock are not publicly traded.

corporate bylaws The basic rules governing how a corporation is organized and how it conducts its business.

shareholder An owner of a corporation.

institutional investor An organization that pools contributions from investors, clients, or depositors and uses these funds to buy stocks and other securities.

board of directors The individuals who are elected by shareholders of a corporation to represent their interests.

annual report A yearly statement of the firm's financial condition and its future expectations.

acquisition A corporate restructuring in which one firm buys another. After the acquisition, the target firm (the one being purchased) ceases to exist as an independent entity, while the acquiring firm continues to operate.

merger A corporate restructuring that occurs when two formerly independent business entities combine to form a new organization.

divestiture The transfer of total or partial ownership of some of a firm's assets to investors or to another company.

5-5

cooperative A corporation formed to meet the common needs of its members, where it is owned equally by each of them.

not-for-profit corporation A corporation that does not seek to earn a profit and that differs in several fundamental respects from general corporations.

Crown corporation A government-owned organization that provides services to Canadians where it would not be possible for other firms to do so.

which gives them an advantage when it comes to financing growth—a key reason most large businesses are corporations. Other advantages are unlimited life, easy transfer of ownership, and the ability to take advantage of professional management. One disadvantage of a corporation is the complexity and expense involved in its formation. Another is that any profits distributed to shareholders are taxed twice— once as income to the corporation and then again as income to the shareholders. Other disadvantages are more extensive government regulation and the possibility of conflicting interests between owners and professional management.

An acquisition occurs when one corporation buys controlling interest in another; the firm being acquired ceases to exist. A merger occurs when two firms combine and form a new entity. A horizontal merger (or acquisition) is between firms in the same industry. A vertical merger is between firms at different stages in the production process for a good or service. A conglomerate merger is between firms in unrelated industries. Divestiture occurs when a firm transfers total or partial ownership of some of its assets to investors or to another company.

5-5 (P. 78)

Describe three additional corporate forms: cooperatives, not-for-profit corporations, and Crown corporations. Cooperatives are member-owned, and each member has equal ownership. Profits are distributed to members based on how much they use the co-op, not on how many shares they hold. Not-for-profit corporations have social rather than profit goals. They do not have shareholders and cannot pay dividends. Earnings are not taxed. Crown corporations are government-owned enterprises that provide services to Canadians in sectors where private industry cannot.

5-6 (P. 79)

Evaluate the advantages and disadvantages of franchising. A franchise is a licensing arrangement under which the franchisor allows another the franchisee to use its name, trademark, patents, copyrights, business methods, and other property in exchange for payments and other considerations. The franchisor gains revenue without investing its own money. Franchisees gain the right to use a well-known brand name and proven business methods and to receive training and support from franchisors. But, franchisors often find that dealing with a large number of franchisees can be complex. Also, if a few franchisees behave irresponsibly, their actions can have a negative impact on the entire organization. For franchisees, the main drawbacks are the fees they must pay to the franchisor and the loss of control over management of their business. Franchisees also require franchisor approval before they can expand or sell their franchise.

5-6

franchise A licensing arrangement whereby a franchisor allows franchisees to use its name, trademark, products, business methods, and other property in exchange for monetary payments and other considerations.

franchisor The business entity in a franchise relationship that allows others to operate their business using resources it supplies in exchange for money and other considerations.

franchisee The party in a franchise relationship that pays for the right to use resources supplied by the franchisor.

distributorship A type of franchising arrangement in which the franchisor makes a product and licenses the franchisee to sell it.

business format franchise A broad franchise agreement in which the franchisee pays for the right to use the name, trademark, and business and production methods of the franchisor.

franchise agreement The contractual arrangement between a franchisor and franchisee that spells out the duties and responsibilities of both parties in detail.

LEARNING OUTCOMES

6-1 (P. 80)

Explain the key reasons to launch a small business. Launching a business is tough, but the advantages of business ownership can far outweigh the risks and the hard work. Most people who take the plunge are seeking some combination of independence and flexibility, or greater financial success, or they simply want the challenge. But some are seeking survival and simply have no other options.

For Entrepreneurs, the Potential Rewards Outweigh the Issues

© Cengage Learning

6-2 (P. 86)

Describe the typical entrepreneur's mindset and characteristics. Not all small business owners are entrepreneurs. The difference is attitude: from day one, true entrepreneurs aim to dominate their industry. The entrepreneurial personality typically includes some combination of the following characteristics: vision, self-reliance, energy, confidence, tolerance of uncertainty, and tolerance of failure. While these qualities are very helpful, they aren't essential; it's clearly possible to succeed with a number of different personality types.

Entrepreneurial Characteristics

Herb MacKenzie/© Cengage Learning

6-3 (P. 89)

Discuss funding options for small businesses. For many entrepreneurs, finding the money to fund their business is the top challenge of their start-up year. The vast majority of new firms are funded by the personal resources of the founder, including personal accounts (e.g., credit cards), family, and friends. Other key funding sources are bank loans, angel investors, and venture capital firms.

6-4 (P. 90)

Analyze the opportunities and threats that small businesses face. Small businesses enjoy some key advantages but also face daunting obstacles as they fight for a foothold in the turbulent marketplace.

KEY TERMS

6-1

entrepreneurs People who risk their time, money, and other resources to start and manage a business.

6-2

internal locus of control A deep-seated sense that the individual is personally responsible for what happens in his or her life.

external locus of control A deep-seated sense that forces other than the individual are responsible for what happens in his or her life.

6-3

angel investors Individuals who invest in start-up companies with high growth potential in exchange for a share of ownership.

venture capital firms Companies that invest in start-up businesses with high growth potential in exchange for a share of ownership.

6-4

market niche Small segment of a market with fewer competitors than the market as a whole. Market niches tend to be quite attractive to small firms.

6-5

Canada Business Network A federal government service designed to maintain and strengthen the nation's economy by aiding, counselling, assisting, and protecting the interests of small businesses.

business plan A formal document that describes a business concept, outlines core business objectives, and details strategies and timelines for achieving those objectives.

BUSINESS LAUNCH OPTIONS

- Starting from scratch
- Buying an established business
- Buying a franchise

STRATEGIES FOR SUCCESS:

- Gain experience
- Learn from others
- Educate yourself
- Access Canada Business resources
- Develop a plan

© Cengage Learning

Opportunities:

- *Market niches:* Many small firms are uniquely positioned to exploit small but profitable market niches.

- *Personal customer service:* With a smaller customer base, small firms can develop much more personal relationships with individual customers.

- *Lower overhead costs:* Many small firms can hold down overhead costs by hiring fewer managers and fewer specialized employees.

- *Technology:* The Web has played a powerful role in opening new opportunities for small business in both local and global markets.

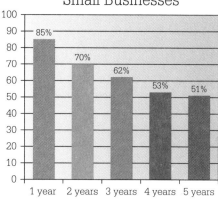

Exhibit 6.2 Survival Rates of Canadian Small Businesses

Source: Industry Canada, "Key Small Business Statistics—August 2013," available http://www.ic.gc.ca/eic/site/061.nsf/eng/02808.html, accessed March 30, 2015.

Threats:

- *High risk of failure:* Starting a new business involves a lot of risk, but the odds improve significantly after the five-year mark.

- *Lack of knowledge and experience:* Entrepreneurs often have expertise in a particular area but lack the background to run a successful business.

- *Too little money:* Lack of start-up money is a major issue for most new firms because ongoing profits don't usually begin for months or even years.

- *Bigger regulatory burden:* Small firms spend more as a percentage of revenue than big firms, simply complying with federal information-reporting requirements.

6-5 (P. 92)

Discuss ways to become a new business owner and tools to facilitate success. Starting a business from scratch comes to mind first for most people. But buying an established business, or even a franchise, can be an excellent choice as well. Each choice involves a range of pros and cons; broadly speaking, though, it's less risky to buy an established business or franchise, but more satisfying (at least for some people) to start a new venture from scratch. Whichever path you choose—whether you're an ambitious entrepreneur or simply a small business owner—several strategies can help you succeed over the long term: gain experience in your field, learn from others, educate yourself, access Canada Business Network resources, and develop a business plan.

6-6 (P. 95)

Explain the size, scope, and economic contributions of small business. Small businesses play a vital role in the Canadian economy, contributing between 25 and 41 percent to Canada's GDP. Canada has more than 1.1 million small businesses; 98 percent of all businesses in Canada employ fewer than 100 employees. However, they employ over 7.7 million Canadians—nearly 70 percent of the private sector labour force. Canadian women are a big force in small business: almost 14 percent are wholly owned by women, and a further 18 percent are owned in equal partnership between women and men. The entrepreneurship rate around the world varies dramatically from country to country, ranging from a high of 37.4 percent in Cameroon to a low of 2.1 percent in Suriname. The differences among countries seem to depend largely on the national per capita income, the opportunity costs for entrepreneurs, and the national culture and political environment.

LEARNING OUTCOMES

7-1 (P. 98)
Define accounting and explain how accounting information is used by a variety of stakeholders. Accounting is a system for recognizing, organizing, analyzing, and reporting information about the financial transactions of an organization. This information is important to many different stakeholders. Owners want to know whether their firm made a profit or suffered a loss. Creditors want to ensure the firm can repay any loans they make. Employees want to know whether their company is performing well enough to provide job security and a good pay raise. The Canada Revenue Agency wants to know how much taxable income is earned during each period.

7-2 (P. 100)
Identify the purposes and goals of accounting standards.
International Financial Reporting Standards (IFRS) are rules that govern the practice of financial accounting. The goal of IFRS is to ensure that the information generated by financial accounting is relevant, reliable, consistent, and comparable.

7-3 (P. 101)
Describe the key elements of the major financial statements. The balance sheet shows the firm's financial position at a specific point in time by reporting the value of its assets, liabilities, and owners' equity. The income statement shows the net income (profit or loss) the firm earns over a stated period of time by deducting expenses from revenues. The statement of cash flows shows the inflows and outflows of cash that result from a firm's operations, its financing activities, and its investing activities in a given time period, and the net change in the amount of available cash the firm has over that time period.

7-4 (P. 106)
Describe several methods stakeholders can use to obtain useful insights from a company's financial statements. In addition to looking at the numbers in financial statements, it's also important to examine the independent auditor's report, the management discussion, and the endnotes. The auditor's report indicates whether the statements were prepared in accordance to accounting standards and fairly present the financial condition of the company. The management discussion puts the numbers in context. Endnotes often disclose key information that isn't directly available in the statements. It's also a good idea to compare the figures reported in current statements to those from earlier statements to see how key account values have changed.

7-5 (P. 110)
Explain the role of managerial accounting and describe the various cost concepts identified by managerial accountants. Managerial accounting provides information to an organization's managers and other internal stakeholders so that they can make better decisions. One key type of information is the classification and measurement of costs. Explicit (or out-of-pocket) costs involve monetary payments. Implicit costs arise when a company gives up an opportunity to use an asset in an alternative way. Fixed costs don't change when a firm changes its rate of output. Variable costs rise when production increases and fall when it decreases. Direct costs are tied to the production of a specific good, while indirect

KEY TERMS

7-1
accounting A system for recognizing, organizing, analyzing, and reporting information about the financial transactions that affect an organization.

7-2
financial accounting The branch of accounting that prepares financial statements for use by owners, creditors, suppliers, and other external stakeholders.

International Financial Reporting Standards (IFRS) An international set of accounting standards that are used in the preparation of financial reports.

generally accepted accounting principles (GAAP) A set of accounting standards that is used in the preparation of financial statements. Replaced in Canada on January 1, 2011, with International Financial Reporting Standards (IFRS).

7-3
balance sheet A financial statement that reports the financial position of a firm at a particular point in time by identifying and reporting the value of the firm's assets, liabilities, and owners' equity.

accounting equation Assets = Liabilities + Owners' equity. This states that the value of a firm's assets is, by definition, exactly equal to the financing provided by creditors and owners for the purchase of those assets.

assets Resources owned by a firm.

liabilities Claims against the firm's assets.

owners' equity The claims a firm's owners have against their company's assets (often called shareholders' equity on balance sheets of corporations).

income statement The financial statement that reports the revenues, expenses, and net income that resulted from a firm's operations over an accounting period.

revenues Increases in a firm's assets that result from the sale of goods, provision of services, or other activities intended to earn income.

accrual-basis accounting The method of accounting that recognizes revenue when it is earned and matches expenses to the revenues they helped produce.

expenses Resources that are used up as the result of business operations.

net income The difference between the revenue a firm earns and the expenses it incurs in a given time period.

statement of cash flow The financial statement that identifies a firm's source and uses of cash in a given accounting period.

7-4

horizontal analysis Analysis of financial statements that compares account values reported on these statements over two or more years to identify changes and trends.

7-5

managerial (or management) accounting The branch of accounting that provides reports and analysis to managers to help them make informed business decisions.

cost The value of what is given up in exchange for something.

out-of-pocket cost A cost that involves the payment of money or other resources.

implicit cost The opportunity cost that arises when a firm uses owner-supplied resources.

fixed costs Costs that remain the same when the level of production changes within some relevant range.

variable costs Costs that vary directly with the level of production.

costs are incurred as the result of a firm's overall operations and are not tied directly to a specific good.

7-6 (P. 112)

Describe how financial managers use key ratios to evaluate their firm.
Financial managers look at four basic types of ratios:

1. *Liquidity ratios*, such as the current ratio, provide insights into whether the firm will have enough cash to pay its short-term liabilities as they come due.

2. *Asset management ratios* tell financial managers how effectively a firm is using various assets to generate revenues for their firm.

3. *Leverage ratios* measure how the firm relies on debt in its capital structure.

4. *Profitability ratios*, such as return on assets and return on equity, measure the firm's overall success at using resources to create a profit for its owners.

direct costs Costs that are incurred directly as the result of some specific cost object.

indirect costs Costs that are the result of a firm's general operations and are not directly tied to any specific cost object.

activity-based costing (ABC) A technique to assign product costs based on links between activities that drive costs and the production of specific products.

7-6

financial ratio analysis Computing ratios that compare values of key accounts listed on a firm's financial statements.

liquid asset An asset that can quickly be converted into cash with little risk of loss.

liquidity ratios Financial ratios that measure the ability of a firm to obtain the cash it needs to pay its short-term debt obligations as they come due.

asset management ratios Financial ratios that measure how effectively a firm is using its assets to generate revenues or cash.

financial leverage The use of debt in a firm's capital structure.

leverage ratios Ratios that measure the extent to which a firm relies on debt financing in its capital structure.

profitability ratios Ratios that measure the rate of return a firm is earning on various measures of investment.

LEARNING OUTCOMES

8-1 (P. 116)

Identify the goal of financial management and explain the issues financial managers confront as they seek to achieve this goal.
Historically, the goal of financial management has been to *maximize the value of the firm to its owners*. But many of today's businesses have adopted a broader perspective, believing that they have responsibilities not just to shareholders but also to customers, employees, and other stakeholders. Treating these other stakeholders well often builds value, which benefits shareholders, but other stakeholder groups sometimes have goals that conflict with those of shareholders. When this happens, financial managers generally adopt the policies they believe are most consistent with the interests of ownership. Another challenge that financial managers face is the need to find the appropriate balance between risk and return. The *risk-return tradeoff* suggests that sources and uses of funds that offer the potential for high rates of return tend to be riskier than those that offer lower returns.

8-2 (P. 118)

Explain how the budget process can help managers plan, motivate, and evaluate their organization's performance. Budgeting facilitates planning by translating goals into measurable quantities and requiring managers to identify the specific resources needed to achieve them. The budgeting process can help with both motivation and evaluation. Employees tend to be more highly motivated when they understand the goals they are expected to accomplish and believe they are ambitious but achievable. Managers can compare actual performance to budgeted figures to determine whether various departments and functional areas are making adequate progress towards achieving their organization's goals.

8-3 (P. 122)

Evaluate the major sources of funds available to meet a firm's short-term and long-term financial needs. Established firms have several sources of short-term funds, including bank loans, trade credit, factoring, and commercial paper. Trade credit arises when suppliers ship materials, parts, or goods to a firm without requiring immediate payment. Banks extend short-term loans to firms with

Major Financial Planning Tools

TOOL	PURPOSE
Budgeted income statement	Forecasts the sales, expenses, and revenue for a firm in some future time period.
Budgeted balance sheet	Projects the types and amounts of assets a firm will need in order to carry out its plans and shows the amount of additional financing the firm will need to acquire these assets.
Cash budget	Projects the timing and amount of cash flows so that management can determine when it will need to arrange for external financing and when it will have extra cash to pay off loans or invest in other assets.

© Cengage Learning

KEY TERMS

8-1

financial capital The funds a firm uses to acquire its assets and finance its operations.

finance The functional area of business that is concerned with finding the best sources and uses of financial capital.

risk The degree of uncertainty regarding the outcome of a decision.

risk–return tradeoff The observation that financial opportunities that offer high rates of return are generally riskier than opportunities that offer lower rates of return.

8-2

budgeting A management tool that explicitly shows how firms will acquire and use the resources needed to achieve its goals over a specific time period.

operating budgets Budgets that communicate an organization's sales and production goals and the resources needed to achieve these goals.

financial budgets Budgets that focus on the firm's financial goals and identify the resources needed to achieve these goals.

master budget Presentation of an organization's operational and financial budgets that represents the firm's overall plan of action for a specified time period.

budgeted income statement A projection showing how a firm's budgeted sales and costs will affect expected net income (also called a pro forma income statement).

budgeted balance sheet A projected financial statement that forecasts the types and amounts of assets a firm will need to implement its future plans and how the firm will finance those assets (also called a pro forma balance sheet).

cash budget A detailed forecast of future cash flows that helps financial managers identify when their firm is likely to experience temporary shortages or surpluses of cash.

8-3

trade credit Spontaneous financing granted by sellers when they deliver goods and services to customers without requiring immediate payment.

spontaneous financing Financing that arises during the natural course of business without the need for special arrangements.

factor A company that provides short-term financing to firms by purchasing their accounts receivables at a discount.

line of credit A financial arrangement between a firm and a bank in which the bank preapproves credit up to a specified limit, provided that the firm maintains an acceptable credit rating.

revolving credit agreement A guaranteed line of credit in which a bank makes a binding commitment to provide a business with funds up to a specified credit limit at any time during the term of the agreement.

commercial paper Short-term (and usually unsecured) promissory notes issued by large corporations.

retained earnings The part of a firm's net income it reinvests.

covenant A restriction that lenders impose on borrowers as a condition of providing long-term debt financing.

8-4

equity financing Funds provided by the owners of a company.

debt financing Funds provided by lenders (creditors).

capital structure The mix of equity and debt financing a firm uses to meet its permanent financing needs.

good credit ratings. Factors provide immediate cash to firms by purchasing their accounts receivable at a discount. Major corporations sometimes raise funds by selling commercial paper, which are short-term IOUs.

Firms that want to build up their permanent financial base have two basic options. First, they can rely on equity financing, which consists of funds provided by owners. The second option is long-term debt financing.

8-4 (P. 125)

Identify the key issues involved in determining a firm's capital structure. Capital structure refers to the mix of equity and debt financing a firm uses to meet its financing needs. Debt financing enables the firm to finance activities without requiring the owners to put up more money. When the firm earns more on borrowed funds than it pays in interest, the excess goes to the owners, thus magnifying the return on their investment. And the interest payments on debt are tax deductible. However, the interest payments and the requirement to repay the amount borrowed can put a strain on companies when business conditions are poor. Equity financing is safer and more flexible than debt financing. But dividend payments are not tax deductible. And issuing new stock can dilute the ownership share of existing stockholders.

8-5 (P. 128)

Describe how financial managers acquire and manage current assets. Firms must have cash, but cash earns little or no interest. Firms with a surplus of cash often hold cash equivalents such as T-bills, commercial paper, and money market mutual funds to earn interest. Accounts receivable are what customers who buy on credit owe to a firm. Firms must establish credit policies that balance the higher sales generated by accounts receivable against the risk that credit customers might not make their payments. Inventories are the stocks of materials, work in process, and finished goods a firm holds. For many firms, the costs of storing, handling, and insuring inventory items are significant. In recent years, many firms have become very aggressive about keeping inventories as low as possible.

Impact of Capital Structure

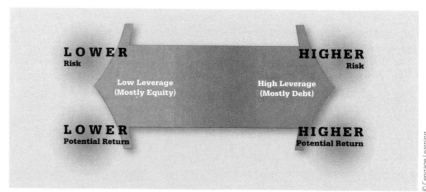

© Cengage Learning

8-6 (P. 130)

Explain how financial managers evaluate capital budgeting proposals to identify the best long-term investment options for their company. Capital budgeting is the process financial managers use to evaluate major long-term investment opportunities. Capital budgeting investments are expected to generate cash flows for many years, so financial managers must take the time value of money into account. The time value of money recognizes

8-5

cash equivalents Safe and highly liquid assets that many firms list with their cash holdings on their balance sheet.

Treasury bills (T-bills) Short-term marketable IOUs issued by the government.

money market mutual funds A mutual fund that pools funds from many investors and uses these funds to purchase very safe, highly liquid securities.

8-6

capital budgeting The process a firm uses to evaluate long-term investment proposals.

time value of money The principle that a dollar received today is worth more than a dollar received in the future.

present value The amount of money that, if invested today at a given rate of interest, would grow to become some future amount in a specified number of time periods.

net present value (NPV) The sum of the present values of expected future cash flows from an investment minus the net cost of that investment.

that the sooner a cash flow is received, the sooner it can be reinvested to earn more money. Financial managers take the time value of money into account by computing the present values of all cash flows the proposal will generate. The present value of a sum of money received in the future is the amount of money today that will become that future amount if it is invested at a specified rate of interest. The net present value (NPV) of the project is the sum of the present values of all the estimated future cash flows, minus the initial cost of the investment. If the NPV of a project is positive, it will increase the value of the firm. If the NPV is negative, it will decrease the value of the firm.

Decision Rule for Capital Budgeting

RESULT OF NPV CALCULATION	DECISION
NPV ≥ 0	Accept proposal ✓
NPV < 0	Reject proposal ✗

© Cengage Learning

NOTES

LEARNING OUTCOMES

9-1 (P. 134)

Explain the role of financial markets in the economy and identify the key players in these markets. Financial markets transfer funds from savers (individuals and organizations willing to defer the use of some of their income in order to earn a financial return and build their wealth) to borrowers (individuals and organizations that need additional funds to achieve their financial goals). Key players in these markets include depository institutions and nondepository institutions. Depository institutions, such as banks, trust companies, credit unions, and *caisses populaires*, accept chequing or savings deposits (or both) from individuals, businesses, and other institutions and then lend these funds to borrowers. Nondepository institutions include institutional investors, such as mutual funds, pension funds, and insurance companies, that don't accept deposits but amass financial capital from other sources and use these funds to acquire portfolios of many different assets.

9-2 (P. 136)

Identify the key regulations that govern the way financial markets operate. Financial markets work well only when savers and borrowers have confidence in the soundness of key financial institutions and in the fairness of the market outcomes. To ensure that investors have confidence in financial markets, federal, provincial, and private efforts regulate financial institutions and the markets. The stability of Canada's financial markets is due in part to the risk management programs put in place by the federal government through the Office of the Superintendent of Financial Institutions and the Financial Consumer Agency of Canada and through legislation such as the *Bank Act*. While many countries have a national body that regulates security markets, Canada has provincial and territorial security commissions. Canada is moving towards one regulatory body across the country. This move has been slow mainly because it requires the agreement of all provincial and territorial bodies. Although the individual security commissions retain ultimate control over the securities markets, they rely on self-regulatory organizations (SROs) to oversee the operations of these markets.

9-3 (P. 137)

Describe and compare the major types of securities that are traded in securities markets. The three basic types of securities are common stock, preferred stock, and bonds. Common stock represents the basic ownership in a corporation. Owners of common stock usually have voting rights and the right to receive a dividend if the corporation's board declares one. Some corporations also issue preferred stock. Owners of preferred stock must receive their stated dividend before any dividend can be paid to common shareholders. Preferred shareholders also have a preferred claim on assets over common shareholders should the company go bankrupt, but they normally do not have voting rights. Bonds are long-term IOUs issued by corporations or government entities. Firms must pay interest on the bonds they issue and must pay the face value to the bondholder when the bond matures.

KEY TERMS

9-1

financial markets Markets that transfer funds from savers to borrowers.

depository institution A financial intermediary that obtains funds by accepting chequing and savings deposits and then lending those funds to borrowers.

trust company A financial intermediary similar to a bank that obtains funds by accepting chequing and savings deposits and then lending those funds to borrowers.

credit union A depository institution that is organized as a cooperative, meaning that it is owned by its depositors.

Caisse Populaire A depository institution that is organized as a cooperative, meaning that it owned by its depositors.

securities broker A financial intermediary that acts as an agent for investors who want to buy and sell financial securities. Brokers earn commissions and fees for the services they provide.

securities dealer A financial intermediary that participates directly in securities markets, buying and selling stocks and other securities for its own account.

investment bank A financial intermediary that specializes in helping firms raise financial capital by issuing securities in primary markets.

9-2

self-regulatory organizations (SROs) Non-governmental organizations operating in the securities industry that develop and enforce rules and standards governing the behaviour of their members.

9-3

common stock The basic form of ownership in a corporation.

capital gain The return on an asset that results when its market price rises above the price the investor paid for it.

preferred stock A type of stock that gives its holder preference over common shareholders in terms of dividends and claims on assets.

bond A formal debt instrument issued by a corporation or government entity.

maturity date The date when a bond will come due.

par value (of a bond) The value of a bond at its maturity; what the issuer promises to pay the bondholder when the bond matures.

coupon rate The interest paid on a bond expressed as a percentage of the bond's par value.

current yield The amount of interest earned on a bond expressed as a percentage of the bond's current market price.

convertible security A bond or share of preferred stock that gives its holder the right to exchange it for a stated number of shares of common stock.

financial diversification A strategy of investing in a wide variety of securities in order to reduce risk.

mutual fund An institutional investor that raises funds by selling shares to investors and uses the accumulated funds to buy a portfolio of many different securities.

net asset value per share The value of a mutual fund's securities and cash holdings minus any liabilities, divided by the number of shares of the fund outstanding.

exchange traded fund (ETF) Shares traded on securities markets that represent the legal right of ownership over part of a basket of individual stock certificates or other securities.

Characteristics of Corporate Securities

SECURITY	TYPE	BASIC RETURN	CLAIM ON ASSETS IF FIRM IS LIQUIDATED	VOTING RIGHTS
Common stock	Equity (ownership)	Dividend (distribution of profits), but only if declared by board of directors	Residual claim (after claims of preferred shareholders and bondholders are satisfied)	Yes
Preferred stock	Equity (ownership)	Dividend—not guaranteed, but with preference in payment over common dividend	Claim on assets before common shareholders but after bondholders	No
Corporate bond	Debt (long-term IOU)	Interest: Legally required payment expressed as a percentage of the bond's par value	Claim on assets must be satisfied before paying common or preferred shareholders. Claim is sometimes secured by pledge of specific assets.	No

© Cengage Learning

9-4 (P. 142)

Explain how securities are issued in the primary market and traded on secondary markets. The primary securities markets are where corporations sell newly issued securities to raise financial capital. There are two ways securities can be issued in primary markets. In public offerings, the securities are sold to the general public. In private placements, the securities are sold to a select group of accredited investors. Secondary markets are where previously issued securities are traded. The two major types of secondary markets are securities exchanges and the over-the-counter market. Securities exchanges list and trade stocks of corporations that satisfy their listing requirements and that pay listing fees. The stocks of corporations not listed on an exchange are sold on the over-the-counter market through a network of securities dealers.

9-5 (P. 145)

Compare several strategies that investors use to invest in securities. Income investors choose securities such as bonds and preferred stocks that tend to generate relatively steady and predictable flows of income. Market timers try to time their purchases of specific stocks to buy low and sell high on a short-term basis. Value investors try to find undervalued stocks. Growth investors often look for stocks in small companies with innovative products and the potential for exceptional growth. Investors using a buy-and-hold approach invest in a broad portfolio of securities with the intention of holding them for a long period of time.

9-6 (P. 148)

Interpret the information provided in the stock quotes available on financial websites. Investors can track broad movements in stock prices by following stock indexes. There are several indexes; the Dow Jones Industrial Average, the Standard & Poor's 500, and the S&P/TSX Composite Index are some of the best known. Many websites provide in-depth information about individual stocks, including each stock's price, volume (number of shares traded), market capitalization (total market value of outstanding shares), earnings per share and other key statistics.

9-4

primary securities market The market where newly issued securities are traded. The primary market is where the firms that issue securities raise additional financial capital.

secondary securities market The market where previously issued securities are traded.

public offering A primary market issue in which new securities are offered to any investors who are willing and able to purchase them.

private placement A primary market issue that is negotiated between the issuing corporation and a small group of accredited investors.

initial public offering (IPO) The first time a company issues stock that may be bought by the general public.

underwriting An arrangement under which an investment dealer agrees to purchase all the shares of a public offering at an agreed-upon price.

stock (or securities) exchange An organized venue for trading stocks and other securities that meet its listing requirements.

Toronto Stock Exchange Canada's stock exchange for larger companies.

TSX Venture Exchange Canada's stock exchange for smaller companies.

market makers Securities dealers that make a commitment to continuously offer to buy and sell the stock of a specific corporation listed on the NASDAQ exchange or traded in the OTC market.

over-the-counter market (OTC) The market where securities that are not listed on exchanges are traded.

electronic communications network (ECN) An automated, computerized securities trading system that automatically matches buyers and sellers, executing trades quickly and allowing trading when securities exchanges are closed.

9-5

market order An order telling a broker to buy or sell a specific security at the best currently available price.

limit order An order to a broker to buy a specific stock only if its price is below a certain level, or to sell a specific stock only if its price is above a certain level.

9-6

stock index A statistic that tracks how the prices of a specific set of stocks have changed.

Dow Jones Industrial Average An index that tracks stock prices of 30 large, well-known corporations.

Standard & Poor's 500 (S&P 500) A stock index based on prices of 500 major US corporations in a variety of industries and market sectors.

S&P/TSX Composite Index A benchmark used to measure the price performance of Canadian stock trading on the Toronto Stock Exchange.

NOTES

LEARNING OUTCOMES

10-1 (P. 152)
Discuss the objectives, the process, and the scope of marketing.
Marketing means delivering value to your customers with the goal of satisfying their needs and achieving long-term profitability for your organization. Goods and services meet customer needs by providing "utility" (or satisfaction) on an ongoing basis. Marketing has moved well beyond the scope of traditional goods and services to include people, places, events, and ideas. Much nontraditional marketing involves both public and private not-for-profit organizations, which measure their success in nonmonetary terms. Over the past century, marketing has evolved through a number of phases. The marketing era gave birth to the marketing concept, which is still in force today: a philosophy that customer satisfaction—now and in the future—should be the central focus of the entire organization.

10-2 (P. 155)
Identify the role of the customer in marketing. Successful marketers always place the customer front and centre, with a focus on customer relationship management: acquiring, maintaining, and growing profitable customer relationships by consistently delivering unmatched value. Effective data management and one-on-one personalization are key customer relationship tools. The result of an effective customer-first strategy is loyal customers, who may even be willing to pay more for your product.

10-3 (P. 156)
Explain each element of marketing strategy. Marketing strategy essentially involves determining who your *target audience* is and how you will reach it. Choosing the right target begins with *market segmentation:* dividing your market into segments or groups of people with similar characteristics. Then you need to determine the best *marketing mix*—the most effective combination of product, pricing, distribution, and promotion strategies to reach your target market. Finally, you must continually monitor each element of the *marketing environment* to ensure that you respond quickly and effectively to change.

10-4 (P. 162)
Describe the consumer and business decision-making process.
Understanding how customers make decisions will help you meet their needs. When people buy for their own personal consumption, a number of forces influence them, including cultural, social, personal, and psychological factors. For high-risk decisions, they generally follow a decision process, but for low-risk decisions, they often just follow rules of thumb. When people buy for business, they typically are more methodical, driven by product specifications.

10-5 (P. 163)
Discuss the key elements of marketing research. Marketing research involves gathering, interpreting, and applying information to uncover opportunities and challenges. Primary and secondary data offer complementary strengths and weaknesses. Observation research tools involve gathering data without interacting

KEY TERMS

10-1
marketing The activity, set of institutions, and processes for creating, communicating, delivering, and exchanging offerings that have value for customers, clients, partners, and society at large.

utility The ability of goods and services to satisfy consumer "wants."

form utility The power of a good or a service to satisfy customer "wants" by converting inputs into a finished form.

time utility The power of a good or a service to satisfy customer "wants" by providing goods and services at a convenient time for customers.

place utility The power of a good or a service to satisfy customer "wants" by providing goods and services at a convenient place for customers.

ownership utility The power of a good or a service to satisfy customer "wants" by smoothly transferring ownership of goods and services from seller to buyer.

marketing concept A business philosophy that makes customer satisfaction—now and in the future—the central focus of the entire organization.

10-2
customer relationship management (CRM) The ongoing process of acquiring, maintaining, and growing profitable customer relationships by delivering unmatched value.

value A customer perception that a product has a better relationship than its competitors between the cost and the benefits.

customer satisfaction When customers perceive that a good or service delivers value above and beyond their expectations.

customer loyalty When customers buy a product from the same supplier again and again—sometimes even paying more for it than they would for a competitive product.

10-3

marketing plan A formal document that defines marketing objectives and the specific strategies for achieving those objectives.

market segmentation Dividing potential customers into groups of similar people, or segments.

target market The group of people who are most likely to buy a particular product.

consumer marketers (aka business-to-consumer or B2C) Marketers who direct their efforts towards people who are buying products for personal consumption.

business marketers (aka business-to-business or B2B) Marketers who direct their efforts towards people who are buying products to use either directly or indirectly to produce other products.

demographic segmentation Dividing the market into smaller groups based on measurable characteristics about people, such as age, income, ethnicity, and gender.

geographic segmentation Dividing the market into smaller groups based on where consumers live. This process can incorporate countries, cities, or population density as key factors.

psychographic segmentation Dividing the market into smaller groups based on consumer attitudes, interests, values, and lifestyles.

behavioural segmentation Dividing the market based on how people behave towards various products. This category includes both the benefits that consumers seek from products and how consumers use the product.

with the research subjects, while survey tools involve asking research subjects direct questions.

10-6 (P. 166)

Explain the roles of social responsibility and technology in marketing.
The surging social responsibility movement and dramatic advances in technology have had a significant influence on marketing. In addition to seeking long-term profitability, socially responsible marketers actively contribute to meeting the needs of the broader community. Key areas of concern include fair labour practices (especially in foreign markets), environmentalism, and involvement in local communities. The digital boom of the past decade has revolutionized marketing, shifting the balance of power from producers to consumers. The Internet has also created marketing opportunities, helping businesses realize new efficiencies, facilitating more customized service, and generating new promotional opportunities.

marketing mix The blend of marketing strategies for product, price, distribution, and promotion.

environmental scanning The process of continually collecting information from the external marketing environment.

market share The percentage of a market controlled by a given marketer.

10-4

consumer behaviour Description of how people act when they are buying, using, and discarding goods and services for their own personal consumption. Consumer behaviour also explores the reasons behind people's actions.

cognitive dissonance Consumer discomfort with a purchase decision, typically for a major purchase.

business buyer behaviour How people act when they are buying products to use either directly or indirectly to produce other products.

10-5

marketing research The process of gathering, interpreting, and applying information to uncover marketing opportunities and challenges and to make better marketing decisions.

secondary data Existing data that marketers gather or purchase for a research project.

primary data New data that marketers compile for a specific research project.

observation research Marketing research that does not require the researcher to interact with the research subject.

survey research Marketing research that requires the researcher to interact with the research subject.

10-6

green marketing The development and promotion of products with ecological benefits.

mass customization The creation of products tailored for individual consumers on a mass basis.

LEARNING OUTCOMES

11-1 (P. 170)

Explain "product" and identify product classifications. A product can be anything that a company offers to satisfy consumer needs and wants. The possibilities include not only physical goods but also services and ideas. A product also includes all the attributes that consumers associate with it, such as name, image, and guarantees. Goods and services fall along a spectrum from pure goods to pure services. Most products fall somewhere between the two ends, incorporating elements of both goods and services. Products typically encompass three layers: the core benefit, the actual physical good or delivered service, and the augmented product. Customers buy consumer products for personal consumption and business products to contribute to the production of other products.

11-2 (P. 173)

Describe product differentiation and the key elements of product planning. Product differentiation means making your product different from—and better than—the competition. Product planning offers the opportunity to achieve differentiation through elements such as better quality, better features and benefits, and a stronger brand. These elements are the foundation of an effective product strategy.

Product Quality Indicators

PRODUCT CATEGORY	SOME QUALITY INDICATORS
INTERNET SEARCH ENGINES	Fast, relevant, far-reaching results
CHILDREN'S TOYS	Safety, expert endorsements, educational and entertainment
COFFEE	Taste, brand, price, country of origin, additives (or lack of)

© Cengage Learning

11-3 (P. 178)

Discuss innovation and the product life cycle. Innovation can range from small modifications of existing products to brand new products that change how people live. Either way, for a business to thrive in the long term, effective new product development is vital. The new product development process is meant to streamline product development. The six steps include idea generation, idea screening, analysis, development, testing, and commercialization. After introduction, successful new products move through a life cycle. The first stage is the *introduction* phase, when a product first hits the market. Marketing generates awareness and trial. During the *growth* phase, sales rise rapidly and profits usually peak. Competitors enter the category. Marketing focuses on gaining new customers. During the *maturity* phase, sales usually peak, while profits fall. Competition intensifies as growth stops. Marketing aims to capture customers from competitors. During the *decline* phase, sales and profits drop. Marketers consider discontinuing products.

11-4 (P. 182)

Analyze and explain promotion and integrated marketing communications. Promotion is marketing communication that influences consumers by informing, persuading, and reminding them about products. The

KEY TERMS

11-1

product Anything that an organization offers to satisfy consumer needs and wants, including both goods and services.

pure goods Products that do not include any services.

pure services Products that do not include any goods.

consumer products Products purchased for personal use or consumption.

business products Products purchased to use either directly or indirectly in the production of other products.

11-2

product differentiation The attributes that make a good or service different from other products that compete to meet the same or similar customer needs.

quality level How well a product performs its core functions.

product consistency How reliably a product delivers its promised level of quality.

product features The specific characteristics of a product.

customer benefit The advantage a customer gains from specific product features.

product line A group of products that are closely related to one another, in terms of either how they work or the customers they serve.

product mix The total number of product lines and individual items sold by a single firm.

cannibalization When a producer offers a new product that takes sales away from its existing products.

CHAPTER IN REVIEW 11

brand A product's identity—including product name, symbol, design, reputation, and image—that sets it apart from other players in the same category.

brand equity The overall value of a brand to an organization.

line extensions Similar products offered under the same brand name.

brand extension A new product, in a new category, introduced under an existing brand name.

licensing Purchasing the right to use another company's brand name or symbol.

cobranding When established brands from different companies join forces to market the same product.

national brands Brands that the producer owns and markets.

store brands Brands the retailer both produces and distributes (also called private labels).

11-3

product life cycle A pattern of sales and profits that typically changes over time.

11-4

promotion Marketing communication designed to influence consumer purchase decisions through information, persuasion, and reminders.

integrated marketing communication The coordination of marketing messages through every promotional vehicle to communicate a unified impression about a product.

11-5

positioning statement A brief statement that articulates how the marketer would like the target market to envision a product relative to the competition.

11-6

promotional channels Specific marketing communication vehicles, including traditional tools, such as advertising, sales promotion, direct marketing, and personal selling, and newer tools, such as product

most effective promotion builds strong, ongoing relationships between customers and companies. The current promotional environment is changing rapidly. Thanks to technology, consumers have more control over how, when, and even if they receive promotional messages. Media have splintered across an array of entertainment options, and consumer viewing patterns have changed. In response, marketers are seeking increasingly creative means to reach their target customers. Their goal is to zero in on the right customers at the right time with the right message. The goal of integrated marketing communications (IMC) is to ensure that consumers receive a unified, focused message regardless of the message source. To make this happen, marketers must break through the clutter, coordinating their messages through various promotional vehicles. Everyone who manages the marketing message must have information about the customer, the product, the competition, the market, and the strategy of the organization. And clearly, solid teamwork is crucial. The result of effective IMC is a relevant, coherent image in the minds of target customers.

11-5 (P. 184)

Discuss development of the promotional message. The promotional message should be a big idea—a meaningful, believable, and distinctive concept that cuts through the clutter. Finding the big idea begins with the positioning statement—a brief statement that articulates how you want your target market to envision your product relative to the competition. A creative development team—often spearheaded by advertising agency professionals—uses the positioning statement as a springboard for finding a big idea. The ideas themselves are typically based on either a rational or an emotional premise, with humour as a recurrent favourite.

11-6 (P. 184)

Discuss the promotional mix and the various promotional tools. The promotional mix is the combination of promotional tools that a marketer chooses to best communicate the big idea to the target audience. In today's rapidly changing promotional environment, new promotional tools have emerged and secondary promotional tools have burst into the mainstream. Examples include Internet advertising (especially paid search advertising), search engine optimization, social media, product placement, advergaming, buzz marketing, and sponsorships. Yet traditional promotional tools retain enormous clout in terms of both spending and impact on the market. Mainstream advertising has split among a growing array of media options. Sales promotion, designed to stimulate immediate sales, is a quickly growing area. Public relations, designed to generate positive, unpaid media stories about a company or its products, also aims to boost brand awareness and credibility. Personal selling, designed to close sales and build relationships, continues to play a dominant role in the promotional mix. Selecting the right mix of promotional tools poses an ongoing challenge for many marketers.

Buzz Marketing Travels along Social Networks

BUZZ MARKETING

© Cengage Learning

placement, advergaming, and online minimovies.

product placement The paid integration of branded products into movies, television, and other media.

advergaming Video games created as a marketing tool, usually with brand awareness as the core goal.

buzz marketing The active stimulation of word of mouth via unconventional and often relatively low-cost tactics. Other terms for buzz marketing are guerrilla marketing and viral marketing.

sponsorship A deep association between a marketer and a partner (usually a cultural or sporting event), which involves promotion of the sponsor in exchange for either payment or the provision of goods.

advertising Paid, non-personal communication, designed to influence a target audience with regard to a product, service, organization, or idea.

sales promotion Marketing activities designed to stimulate immediate sales activity through specific short-term programs aimed at either consumers or distributors.

consumer promotion Marketing activities designed to generate immediate consumer sales, using tools such as premiums, promotional products, samples, coupons, rebates, and displays.

trade promotion Marketing activities designed to stimulate wholesalers and retailers to push specific products more aggressively over the short term.

public relations (PR) The ongoing effort to create positive relationships with all of a firm's different "publics," including customers, employees, suppliers, the community, the general public, and the government.

publicity Unpaid stories in the media that influence perceptions about a company or its products.

personal selling The person-to-person presentation of products to potential buyers.

push strategy A marketing approach that involves motivating distributors to heavily promote—or "push"—a product to the final consumers, usually through heavy trade promotion and personal selling.

pull strategy A marketing approach that involves creating demand from the ultimate consumers so that they "pull" your products through the distribution channels by actively seeking them.

NOTES

LEARNING OUTCOMES

12-1 (P. 192)

Define distribution and differentiate between channels of distribution and physical distribution. Distribution is the element of the marketing mix that involves getting the right product to the right customers in the right place at the right time. A channel of distribution is the path a product takes from the producer to the consumer; physical distribution is the actual movement of products along that path. Distributors add value by reducing the number of transactions—and the associated costs—required for goods to flow from producers to consumers. Distributors can also add a range of different utilities:

- *Form utility:* Provides customer satisfaction by converting inputs into finished products.
- *Time utility:* Adds value by making products available at a convenient time for consumers.
- *Place utility:* Satisfies customer needs by providing the right products in the right place.
- *Ownership utility:* Adds value by making it easier for customers to actually possess the goods and services they purchase.
- *Information utility:* Boosts customer satisfaction by providing helpful information.
- *Service utility:* Adds value by providing fast, friendly, personalized service.

Exhibit 12.1 Reducing Transactions through Marketing Intermediaries

20 Contacts

9 Contacts

Source: From BOONE/KURTZ/MACKENZIE. *Contemporary Marketing*, 3E. © 2013 Nelson Education Ltd. Reproduced by permission. www.cengage.com/permissions

© Cengage Learning

KEY TERMS

12-1

distribution strategy A plan for delivering the right product to the right person at the right place at the right time.

channel of distribution The network of organizations and processes that links producers to consumers.

physical distribution The actual physical movement of products along the distribution pathway.

direct channel A distribution process that links the producer and the customer with no intermediaries.

channel intermediaries Distribution organizations—informally called middlemen—that facilitate the movement of products from the producer to the consumer.

utility The value, or usefulness, that a good or a service offers a customer.

retailers Distributors that sell products directly to the ultimate users, typically in small quantities that are stored and merchandised on the premises.

wholesalers Distributors that buy products from producers and sell them to other businesses such as retailers, not-for-profit organizations, institutional accounts, and the government.

12-2

independent wholesaling businesses
Independent distributors that buy products from a range of different businesses and sell those products to a range of different customers.

merchant wholesalers Independent distributors that take legal possession, or title, of the goods they distribute.

CHAPTER IN REVIEW 12

agents/brokers Independent distributors that do not take title of the goods they distribute (even though they may take physical possession on a temporary basis).

12-3

multichannel retailing Providing multiple distribution channels for consumers to buy a product.

wheel of retailing A classic distribution theory that suggests that retail firms and retail categories become more upscale as they go through their life cycles.

12-4

supply chain All organizations, processes, and activities involved in the flow of goods from their raw materials to the final consumer.

supply chain management (SCM) Planning and coordinating the movement of products along the supply chain, from the raw materials to the final consumers.

logistics A subset of supply chain management that focuses largely on the tactics involved in moving products along the supply chain.

modes of transportation The various transportation options—such as planes, trucks, and railways—for moving products through the supply chain.

12-5

penetration pricing A new-product pricing strategy that aims to capture as much of the market as possible through rock-bottom prices.

everyday low pricing (EDLP) Long-term discount pricing, designed to achieve profitability through high sales volume.

high/low pricing A pricing strategy designed to drive traffic to retail stores by special sales on a limited number of products and higher everyday prices on others.

12-2 (P. 195)

Describe the various types of wholesaler distributors. Wholesalers buy products from the producer and sell them to other businesses and organizations. The two key categories of wholesalers are:

- *Merchant wholesalers*, which take legal title to the goods they distribute. Full-service merchant wholesalers provide a wide array of services, whereas limited-service merchant wholesalers offer more focused services.

- *Agents and brokers*, which connect buyers and sellers in exchange for commissions, but without taking legal ownership of the goods they distribute.

12-3 (P. 195)

Discuss strategies and trends in store and non-store retailing. Retailers are the final stop before the consumer on the distribution path. The two main retail categories are store and non-store, but the line between the two has blurred as more and more retailers pursue multichannel approaches, with online and offline outlets supporting each other. Key non-store retail approaches include online retailing, direct response retailing, direct selling, and vending. As competition intensifies, more and more retailers (both store and non-store) are distinguishing themselves by offering customers an entertainment-like experience.

Retailing

RETAILING

Store   Non-store

© Cengage Learning

Retailers Add Value for Consumers

Product Selection
Look and Feel
Customer Service
Location
Promotion
Pricing
TARGET MARKET

© Cengage Learning

12-4 (P. 198)

Explain the key factors in physical distribution. As marketers manage the movement of products through the supply chain, they must make decisions regarding each of the following factors:

- *Warehousing:* How many warehouses do we need? Where should we locate our warehouses?

- *Materials handling:* How should we move products within our facilities? How can we best balance efficiency with effectiveness?

- *Inventory control:* How much inventory should we keep on hand? How should we store and distribute it? What about taxes and insurance?

Exhibit 12.3 Elements of the Supply Chain

Raw Materials

Logistics (transportation, coordination, etc.)

Warehouse/Storage

Production

Warehouse/Storage

Logistics (transportation, coordination, etc.)

Distributors–Marketing and Sales

© Cengage Learning

loss leader pricing Closely related to high/low pricing, loss leader pricing means pricing a handful of items—or loss leaders—temporarily below cost to drive traffic.

skimming pricing A new-product pricing strategy that aims to maximize profitability by offering new products at a premium price.

12-6

breakeven analysis The process of determining the number of units a firm must sell to cover all costs.

profit margin The gap between the cost and the price of an item on a per product basis.

odd pricing The practice of ending prices in numbers below even dollars and cents in order to create a perception of greater value.

• *Order processing:* How should we manage incoming and outgoing orders? What would be most efficient for our customers and suppliers?

• *Customer service:* How can we serve our customers most effectively? How can we reduce waiting times and facilitate interactions?

• *Transportation:* How can we move products most efficiently through the supply chain? What are the key tradeoffs?

12-5 (P. 200)

Outline core pricing objectives and strategies.

Many marketers continually evaluate and refine their pricing strategies to ensure they meet their goals. The goals themselves may shift in response to the changing market. Key objectives and strategies include the following:

• Building profitability

• Driving volume

• Meeting the competition

• Creating prestige

Pricing Considerations

© Cengage Learning

12-6 (P. 203)

Discuss pricing in practice, including the role of consumer perceptions.
While most marketers are familiar with economics, they often don't have the information they need to apply it to their specific pricing strategies. Because of this, most companies *consider* market-based factors—especially customer expectations and competitive prices—but they *rely* on cost-based pricing: What should we charge to cover our costs and make a profit? Common approaches include breakeven analysis and fixed margin pricing. Many marketers also account for consumer perceptions, especially the link between price and perceived quality. If no other information is available, consumers will often assume that higher priced products are higher quality. Odd pricing means ending prices in dollars and cents rather than round numbers (e.g., $999.99 rather than $1,000) in order to create a perception of greater value.

© Cengage Learning

NOTES

LEARNING OUTCOMES

13-1 (P. 208)

Discuss the role of management and its importance to organizational success.
In formal terms, the purpose of management is to achieve the goals of an organization through planning, organizing, leading, and controlling organizational resources. Managers provide vision for their company and inspire others to follow their lead.

Most medium and large companies have three basic management levels: top management, middle management, and first-line (or supervisory) management. Managers must draw on a wide range of skills, but most of their abilities cluster into three key categories: technical skills, human skills, and conceptual skills. All three skill sets are essential for management success but in different proportions at each managerial level.

Management Hierarchy

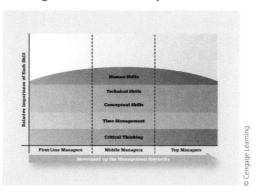

© Cengage Learning

13-2 (P. 210)

Explain key theories and current practices of motivation. Research suggests that people's thoughts and feelings play a vital role in motivation. Key theories that incorporate this perspective include Maslow's hierarchy of needs, Theory X and Theory Y, job enrichment, expectancy theory, and equity theory. In today's business environment, leading-edge firms nourish distinctive, positive cultures that tend to create productive employees who are deeply attached to both their work and their companies. Many also focus on training and education, which are especially motivating for the growing cadre of employees who identify themselves based on their field of expertise rather than their organization.

Maslow's Hierarchy of Needs

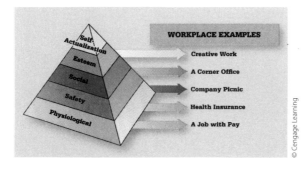

© Cengage Learning

13-3 (P. 214)

Outline the categories of business planning and explain strategic planning. The four main categories of business planning are strategic planning, tactical planning, operational planning, and contingency planning. Strategic planning, handled by top managers, sets the broad direction of the organization, typically over a five-year horizon. Strategic planning guides the entire planning

KEY TERMS

13-1

management Achieving the goals of an organization through planning, organizing, leading, and controlling organizational resources, including people, money, and time.

planning Determining organizational goals and action plans for how to achieve those goals.

organizing Determining a structure for both individual jobs and the overall organization.

leading Directing and motivating people to achieve organizational goals.

controlling Checking performance and making adjustments as needed.

top management Managers who set the overall direction of the firm, articulating a vision, establishing priorities, and allocating time, money, and other resources.

middle management Managers who supervise lower level managers and report to higher level managers.

first-line management Managers who directly supervise non-management employees.

technical skills Expertise in a specific functional area or department.

human skills The ability to work effectively with and through other people in a range of different relationships.

conceptual skills The ability to grasp a big-picture view of the overall organization, the relationship between its various parts, and its fit in the broader competitive environment.

13-2

Maslow's hierarchy of needs theory Motivation theory that suggests human needs fall in a hierarchy and that as each need is met, people become motivated to meet the next highest need in the pyramid.

Theory X and Theory Y Motivation theory that suggests that management attitudes towards workers fall into two opposing categories based on management assumptions about worker capabilities and values.

job enrichment The creation of jobs with more meaningful content, under the assumption that challenging, creative work will motivate employees.

expectancy theory Motivation theory that deals with the relationships among individual effort, individual performance, and individual reward.

equity theory Motivation theory that proposes perceptions of fairness directly affect worker motivation.

13-3

strategic planning High-level, long-term planning that establishes a vision for the company, defines long-term objectives and priorities, determines broad action steps, and allocates resources.

tactical planning More specific, shorter-term planning that applies strategic plans to specific functional areas.

operational planning Very specific, short-term planning that applies tactical plans to daily, weekly, and monthly operations.

contingency planning Planning for unexpected events, usually involving a range of scenarios and assumptions that differ from the assumptions behind the core plans.

mission The definition of an organization's purpose, values, and core goals, which provides the framework for all other plans.

SWOT analysis A strategic planning tool that helps management evaluate an organization in terms of internal strengths and weaknesses and external opportunities and threats.

process because all other plans—and most major management decisions— stem from the strategic plan. Given fierce competition and often unpredictable change, most large firms revise their strategic plans on a yearly basis.

13-4 (P. 218)

Discuss the organizing function of management. The organizing function of management entails creating a logical structure for people, their jobs, and their patterns of interaction. In choosing the right structure for a specific company, management must consider many different factors, including the goals and strategies of the firm, its products, and its size. Management must also make decisions about the degree of centralization, the span of management control, and the type of departmentalization. Company structures tend to follow one of three different patterns: line, line-and-staff, and matrix.

13-5 (P. 221)

Explain the role of managerial leadership and the key leadership styles. Effective business leaders motivate others to achieve the goals of their organization. Most experts agree that true leaders are trustworthy, visionary, and inspiring. Other key leadership traits include empathy, courage, creativity, intelligence, fairness, and energy. While leaders have a range of different styles, three main approaches include autocratic, democratic, and free rein. The best leaders tend to use all three approaches, shifting style in response to the needs of the followers and the situation.

13-6 (P. 222)

Describe the management control process. Controlling means monitoring the performance of the firm—or individuals within the firm—and making improvements when necessary. As the environment changes, plans change. And as plans change, the control process must change to ensure that the company achieves its goals. The control process has three main steps:

1. Establish clear performance standards.
2. Measure actual performance against standards.
3. Take corrective action if necessary.

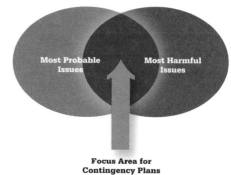

Contingency Planning Paradigm

Most Probable Issues

Most Harmful Issues

Focus Area for Contingency Plans

© Cengage Learning

strategic goals Concrete benchmarks that managers can use to measure performance in each key area of the organization.

strategies Action plans that help the organization achieve its goals by forging the best fit between the firm and the environment.

13-4

organization chart A visual representation of the company's formal structure.

degree of centralization The extent to which decision-making power is held by a small number of people at the top of the organization.

span of control Span of management; refers to the number of people a manager supervises.

departmentalization The division of workers into logical groups.

line organizations Organizations with a clear, simple chain of command from top to bottom.

line-and-staff organizations
Organizations with line managers forming the primary chain of authority in the company and staff departments working alongside line departments.

line managers Managers who supervise the functions that contribute directly to profitability: production and marketing.

staff managers Managers who supervise the functions that provide advice and assistance to the line departments.

matrix organizations Organizations with a flexible structure that brings together specialists from different areas of the company to work on individual projects on a temporary basis.

13-5

autocratic leaders Leaders who hoard decision-making power for themselves and typically issue orders without consulting their followers.

democratic leaders Leaders who share power with their followers. While they still make final decisions, they typically solicit and incorporate input from their followers.

free-rein leaders Leaders who set objectives for their followers but give them freedom to choose how they accomplish those goals.

NOTES

LEARNING OUTCOMES

14-1 (P. 224)

Explain the importance of human resources to business success. A world-class workforce can lead straight to world-class performance. Human resource managers can directly contribute to that goal by recruiting top talent, promoting career development, and boosting organizational effectiveness. Yet HR departments typically face numerous challenges in making this happen.

14-2 (P. 224)

Discuss key HR issues in today's economy. As the economy and society continue to change rapidly, a number of issues have emerged that directly affect human resources. Older workers have begun to retire, while younger workers often bring an unprecedented sense of entitlement. Many women are leaving traditional jobs yet are still under-represented in management positions. Workers are actively seeking more flexibility and a better work–life balance. The growing wage gap between senior managers and the average employee has created tension for a number of stakeholders. Outsourcing remains challenging. And the number of costly employee lawsuits has skyrocketed in the last couple of decades.

© Cengage Learning

14-3 (P. 227)

Outline challenges and opportunities that the human resources function faces. While HR workers tend to have strong people skills, many lack the business acumen to contribute directly to broad company objectives, and other departments often view HR as either irrelevant or adversarial. HR can respond to these issues by demonstrating that it understands the strategic goals of the company, the core customers, and the competition. The best HR departments use this knowledge to raise the value of the firm's human capital, which in turn increases the value of the firm itself.

14-4 (P. 227)

Discuss human resource planning and core human resources responsibilities. HR planning objectives must flow from the company's master plan, and HR strategies must reflect company priorities. The first step should be to determine where the firm currently stands in terms of HR and to forecast future needs. Other key areas of focus follow:

- *Recruitment:* The key to recruitment is finding qualified candidates who fit well with the organization. The right people

© Cengage Learning

KEY TERMS

14-1

human resource (HR) management The management function focused on maximizing the effectiveness of the workforce by recruiting world-class talent, promoting career development, and determining workforce strategies to boost organizational effectiveness.

14-2

job analysis The examination of specific tasks that are assigned to each position, independent of who might be holding the job at any specific time.

job description An explanation of the responsibilities for a specific position.

job specifications The specific qualifications necessary to hold a particular position.

internal recruitment The process of seeking employees who are currently within the firm to fill open positions.

external recruitment The process of seeking new employees from outside the firm.

structured interview An interviewing approach that involves developing a list of questions beforehand and asking the same questions in the same order to each candidate.

probationary period A specific timeframe (typically three to six months) during which a new hire can prove his or her worth on the job before the hire becomes permanent.

contingent workers Employees who do not expect regular, full-time jobs, including temporary full-time workers, independent contractors, and temporary agency or contract agency workers.

orientation The first step in the training and development process, designed to introduce employees to the company culture and provide key administrative information.

on-the-job training A training approach that requires employees to simply begin their jobs—sometimes guided by more experienced employees—and to learn as they go.

apprenticeships Structured training programs that mandate that each beginner serve as an assistant to a fully trained worker before gaining full credentials to work in the field.

management development Programs to help current and potential executives develop the skills they need to move into leadership positions.

performance appraisal A formal process that requires managers to give their subordinates feedback on a one-to-one basis, typically by comparing actual results to expected results.

compensation The combination of pay and benefits that employees receive in exchange for their work.

wages The pay that employees receive in exchange for the number of hours or days that they work.

salaries The pay that employees receive over a fixed period, most often weekly or monthly. Most professional, administrative, and managerial jobs pay salaries.

benefits Noncash compensation, including programs such as extended health care, vacation, and child care.

cafeteria-style benefits An approach to employee benefits that gives all employees a set dollar amount that they must spend on company benefits. Employees can choose to allocate their spending however they wish within broad limitations.

flextime A scheduling option that allows workers to choose when they start and finish their workdays as long as they complete the required number of hours.

can come from either internal or external labour pools.

- *Selection:* Choosing the right person from a pool of candidates typically involves applications, interviews, tests, and references. The terms of the job offer itself play a role as well.

- *Training:* The training process begins with orientation but should continue throughout each employee's tenure. Options include on-the-job training, off-the-job training, and management development.

- *Evaluation:* Performance feedback should happen constantly. But most firms also use formal, periodic performance appraisals to make decisions about compensation, promotions, training, transfers, and terminations.

- *Compensation:* Compensation includes both pay and benefits. Interestingly, companies that offer higher compensation generally outperform their competitors in terms of total return to shareholders.

- *Separation:* Employees leave their jobs for both positive and negative reasons. When the separation is not voluntary—e.g., layoffs or termination—fairness and documentation are critical.

Variable Pay System

- Commission
- Bonuses
- Profit sharing
- Stock options
- Pay for knowledge

14-5 (P. 237)

Explain the key federal legislation that impacts human resources. The most influential piece of employment legislation may well be the *Employment Equity Act*. Its purpose is to ensure equality in the workplace. The federal government has also implemented the Federal Contractors Program, which requires larger provincially regulated contractors that have secured a federal government contract valued at $1 million or more to commit to employment equity in their workplace. Employment standards legislation has been passed by the federal government and by all provinces and territories in Canada. Such legislation defines minimum standards in the workplace. Only Quebec has provincial employment equity legislation, and, among Canada's territories, Nunavut does. It is important to recognize, however, that all Canadian provinces have human rights legislation designed to prevent systemic discrimination and to overcome historic inequities that such discrimination in the past may have caused.

EMPLOYEE EVALUATION

Employee   Manager
Feedback should be continual

© Cengage Learning

Considerations for Compensation

Cost of Living
Legislation
Competition
Contribution
Ability to Pay

D.D Images/Shutterstock.com

FLEXIBLE SCHEDULING
- Flextime
- Telecommuting
- Job Sharing

© Cengage Learning

compressed workweek A version of flextime scheduling that allows employees to work a full-time number of hours in less than the standard workweek.

telecommuting Working remotely—most often from home—and connecting to the office via phone lines, fax machines, and broadband networks.

14-5

Employment Equity Act Legislation designed to improve the status of specific designated groups, most particularly women, aboriginal people, persons with disabilities, and members of visible minorities.

employment standards legislation Legislation that defines minimum standards in the workplace.

reverse discrimination Occurs when someone is denied an opportunity because of preferences given to members of designated groups who may be less qualified.

harassment Any unwanted physical or verbal conduct that offends or humiliates a person.

NOTES

LEARNING OUTCOMES

15-1 (P. 242)

Explain the basic elements of computer technology—including hardware, software, and networks—and describe key trends in each area. Hardware is the physical equipment used to collect, store, organize, and process data and to distribute information. Software consists of computer programs that provide instructions to a computer. System software performs the critical functions necessary to operate the computer at the most basic level. Applications software helps users perform a desired task. Most firms (and many households) now use networks to communicate quickly and efficiently and to share files and hardware resources. The Internet is a vast network of computer networks. The part of the Internet used most by the general public is the World Wide Web, which consists of billions of documents written and linked together using hypertext markup language (HTML). Many organizations have developed intranets that have the same look and feel as the Internet but are limited to servers within an organization. Extranets are intranets that provide limited access to specific stakeholders, such as customers or suppliers.

15-2 (P. 245)

Discuss the reasons for the increasing popularity of cloud computing. Cloud computing means going beyond a company's firewall to store data and run applications using Internet-based resources. Cloud computing allows firms to obtain storage space, processing power, and software without investing heavily in internally owned IT resources. Cloud computing also makes it easier for people in different organizations to collaborate because resources in the cloud are not tied to a specific type of hardware or operating system. Several high-profile security breaches of cloud services in recent years have caused serious concerns. Unless such security lapses are brought under control, they may ultimately limit acceptance of cloud computing.

15-3 (P. 246)

Describe how data becomes information and how decision support systems can provide high-quality information that helps managers make better decisions. Data are raw facts and figures. Data becomes information when it is processed, organized, and presented in a way that is meaningful to a decision maker. Many companies develop decision support systems (DSSs) that give managers access to large amounts of data

HIGH-QUALITY INFORMATION IS	
1. Accurate	Free from errors and omissions.
2. Relevant	Concerns issues that are important to the decision maker.
3. Timely	Available in time to make a difference to the decision maker.
4. Understandable	Presented in a way that allows decision makers to grasp its meaning and significance.
5. Secure	Stored and presented in a way that prevents hackers and other unauthorized parties from obtaining access to it.

KEY TERMS

15-1

hardware The physical tools and equipment used to collect, input, store, organize, and process data and to distribute information.

software Programs that provide instructions to a computer so that it can perform a desired task.

system software Software that performs the critical functions necessary to operate the computer at the most basic level.

applications software Software that helps a user perform a desired task.

Internet The world's largest computer network; essentially a network of computer networks all operating under a common set of rules that allow them to communicate with one another.

broadband Internet connection An Internet connection that is capable of transmitting large amounts of information very quickly.

Internet2 (I2) A new high-tech Internet with access limited to a consortium of member organizations (and other organizations these members sponsor). I2 utilizes technologies that give it a speed and capacity far exceeding the current Internet.

intranet A private network that has the look and feel of the Web and is navigated using a Web browser but that limits access to a single firm's employees (or a single organization's members).

extranet An intranet that allows limited access to a selected group of stakeholders, such as suppliers or customers.

© Cengage Learning

15-2

cloud computing The use of Internet-based storage capacity, processing power, and computer applications to supplement or replace internally owned information technology resources.

15-3

data Raw, unprocessed facts and figures.

information Data that have been processed in a way that makes them meaningful to their user.

database A file consisting of related data organized according to a logical system and stored on a hard drive or some other computer-accessible media.

decision support system (DSS) A system that gives managers access to large amounts of data and the processing power to convert these data into high-quality information, thus improving the decision-making process.

business intelligence system A sophisticated form of decision support system that helps decision makers discover information that was previously hidden.

data warehouse A large, organization-wide database that stores data in a centralized location.

data mining The use of sophisticated statistical and mathematical techniques to analyze vast amounts of data to discover hidden patterns and relationships among data, thus creating valuable information.

expert system (ES) A decision support system that helps managers make better decisions in an area where they lack expertise.

15-4

e-commerce The marketing, buying, selling, and servicing of products over a network (usually the Internet).

business-to-consumer (B2C) e-commerce E-commerce in which businesses and final consumers interact.

and the processing power to convert the data into high-quality information. Firms sometimes develop expert systems to help decision makers when they must deal with problems beyond their expertise. To develop an expert system, programmers ask experts in the relevant area to provide step-by-step instructions describing how they solve a problem. The programmers then write software that mimics the expert's approach and guides the decision maker towards a good solution.

15-4 (P. 248)

Explain how Internet-based technologies have changed business-to-consumer and business-to-business commerce. Information technology, and especially the Internet, has revolutionized the way firms interact with their customers in both the business-to-consumer (B2C) and business-to-business (B2B) markets. In the B2C market, the Internet has enabled firms to reach broader markets, advertise in new ways, and take customer relationship marketing to a new level. One strategy has been to create more interactive websites that encourage customers to collaborate and provide content—an approach referred to as Web 2.0.

In the B2B market, e-marketplaces enable firms to negotiate with suppliers or customers more effectively and share information that leads to better coordination and collaboration.

15-5 (P. 252)

Describe the problems posed by the rapid changes in Internet-based technologies and explain ways to deal with these problems. The rapid development of Internet-based technologies has created several challenges and raised several controversial issues. The Internet has made it easier for malware such as spyware and computer viruses to land on your computer, undermining the security of your information and the stability of your system. Performing regular backups and keeping antivirus and antispyware software and operating systems updated can reduce these threats. Spam is unsolicited commercial e-mail, usually sent to huge numbers of people with little regard for whether they have any interest in the message. Spam filters are available, but spammers are good at finding ways to fool the filters. Phishing and pharming are scams that use fake websites to trick people into divulging private information. One of the most controversial impacts of information technology has been the potential loss of personal privacy. Another issue involves intellectual property. The Internet has made it possible to share videos, music, and computer programs with huge numbers of people, leading to a surge in the illegal sharing of copyrighted material.

business-to-business (B2B) e-commerce E-commerce in markets where businesses buy from and sell to other businesses.

Web 2.0 Websites that incorporate interactive and collaborative features to create a richer, more interesting, and more useful experience for their users.

viral marketing An Internet marketing strategy that tries to involve customers and others not employed by the seller in activities that help promote the product.

cybermediary An Internet-based firm that specializes in the secure electronic transfer of funds.

electronic bill presentment and payment A method of bill payment that makes it easy for the customer to make a payment, often by simply clicking on a payment option contained in an e-mail.

e-marketplace A specialized Internet site where buyers and sellers engaged in business-to-business e-commerce can communicate and conduct business.

radio frequency identification (RFID) A technology that stores information on small microchips that can transmit the information any time they are within range of a special reader.

15-5

malware A general term for malicious software, such as spyware, computer viruses, and worms.

spyware Software that is installed on a computer without the user's knowledge or permission for the purpose of tracking the user's behaviour.

computer virus Software that can spread from one computer to another without the knowledge or permission of computer users by attaching itself to e-mails or other files.

worm Malicious computer software that, unlike viruses, can spread on its own without being attached to other files.

spam Unsolicited e-mail advertisements, usually sent to very large numbers of recipients, many of whom may have no interest in the message.

phishing A scam in which official-looking e-mails are sent to individuals in an attempt to get them to divulge private information such as passwords, user names, and account numbers.

pharming A scam that seeks to steal identities by routing Internet traffic to fake websites.

hacker A skilled computer user who uses his or her expertise to gain unauthorized access to the computers (or computer systems) of others, sometimes with malicious intent.

firewall Software and/or hardware designed to prevent unwanted access to a computer or computer system.

intellectual property Property that is the result of creative or intellectual effort, such as books, musical works, inventions, and computer software.

NOTES

LEARNING OUTCOMES

16-1 (P. 258)
Define operations management and describe how the role of operations management has changed over the past 50 years.
Operations management oversees all of the activities involved in producing and distributing goods and services. When operations managers do their job well, their firms produce the *right* goods and services in the *right* quantities and distribute them to the *right* customers at the *right* time—all the while keeping quality high and costs low. Operations management has undergone profound changes over the past half century. One change has been a switch in focus from efficiency to effectiveness. *Efficiency* means achieving a goal at the *lowest cost. Effectiveness* means *creating value* by satisfying wants. Other key changes include more emphasis on the provision of services, a switch from mass production to customized production, a focus on global markets (and global competition), reliance on complex value chains, and recognition of the need to protect the environment.

16-2 (P. 260)
Discuss the key responsibilities of operations managers. Operations managers often play a role in the design of products by helping designers understand the challenges and constraints involved in producing high-quality products on time and within budget. Once the design is finalized, operations managers must determine the best production processes to convert inputs into outputs; design a facility layout that creates an efficient flow of materials, parts, and work in process through the production process; select the best locations for facilities; make decisions about how much inventory to hold; determine how to allocate resources needed to complete complex projects; and manage value chains to coordinate the functions of all of the organizations and processes directly or indirectly involved in producing goods and services and distributing them to customers.

16-3 (P. 265)
Describe how operations managers face the special challenges posed by the provision of services. Customers often participate in the provision of services, so service providers have only limited control over the ways in which their processes are carried out, how long they take to complete, and whether the result is satisfactory. A *servicescape* is the environment in which the customer and service provider interact. A well-designed servicescape can create a better service experience for both the customer and the provider. Another challenge facing service providers involves determining the proper capacity of service facilities. If the capacity of a service facility is too small, customers facing long waits during peak periods may take their business elsewhere. But a facility large enough to handle peak capacity is more expensive to build and operate and may have substantial excess capacity during off-peak periods. Many service firms try to spread out demand so that big surges don't occur by offering price discounts to customers during off-peak times.

16-4 (P. 266)
Explain how changes in technology have revolutionized operations management. Rapid changes in both machinery and equipment and in software and information technologies have revolutionized operations

KEY TERMS

16-1
operations management
Managing the activities involved in creating value by producing goods and services and distributing them to customers.

efficiency Producing output or achieving a goal at the lowest cost.

effectiveness Using resources to create the greatest value by providing customers with goods and services that offer a better relationship between price and perceived benefits.

goods Tangible products.

services Intangible products.

16-2
process A set of related activities that transform inputs into outputs, thus adding value.

inventory Stocks of goods or other items held by organizations.

critical path method (CPM) A project management tool that illustrates the relationships among all the activities involved in completing a project and identifies the sequence of activities likely to take the longest to complete.

immediate predecessors Activities in a project that must be completed before some other specified activity can begin.

critical path The sequence of activities in a project that is expected to take the longest to complete.

value chain The network of relationships that channels the flow of inputs, information, and financial resources through all of the processes directly or indirectly involved in producing goods and services and distributing them to customers.

vertical integration Performance of processes internally that were previously performed by other organizations in a supply chain.

outsourcing Arranging for other organizations to perform supply chain functions that were previously performed internally.

offshoring Moving production or support processes to foreign countries.

enterprise resource planning (ERP) Software-based approach to integrate an organization's (and in the sophisticated versions, a value chain's) information flows.

16-3

servicescape The environment in which a customer and service provider interact.

16-4

automation Replacing human operation and control of machinery and equipment with some form of programmed control.

robot A reprogrammable machine capable of manipulating materials, tools, parts, and specialized devices in order to perform a variety of tasks.

computer-aided design (CAD) Drawing and drafting software that enables users to create and edit blueprints and design drawings quickly and easily.

computer-aided engineering (CAE) Software that enables users to test, analyze, and optimize their designs.

computer-aided manufacturing (CAM) Software that takes the electronic design for a product and creates the programmed instructions that robots must follow to produce that product as efficiently as possible.

CAD/CAM A combination of software that can be used to design output and send instructions to automated equipment to perform the steps needed to produce this output.

management. The biggest change in machinery and equipment has been the increasing use of automation, which means replacing human operation and control of machinery and equipment with programmed control. The development of software applications to allow computer-aided design (CAD), computer-aided engineering (CAE), and computer-aided manufacturing (CAM) has given firms the flexibility to design, test, and produce goods more quickly and efficiently than ever before. When these powerful software applications are integrated with robots and other automated equipment, the result is called computer-integrated manufacturing. This tight integration allows firms to produce customized goods quickly and at low cost, a process called mass customization.

16-5 (P. 267)

Describe the strategies operations managers have used to improve quality of goods and services. In recent years, firms have adopted programs such as total quality management (TQM) and Six Sigma to improve quality. TQM and Six Sigma both view quality improvement as a continuous process that is the responsibility of everyone within the organization. Both approaches also empower workers and make use of teams to solve quality-related problems. But Six Sigma incorporates more specific quality goals and relies on more sophisticated techniques that require a higher degree of expertise. Another way firms have tried to improve efficiency has been to launch programs designed to achieve certification or recognition from outside authorities. Two common approaches are to participate in Excellence Canada's programs and to seek certification under the International Organization for Standardization's ISO 9000 standards.

16-6 (P. 271)

Explain how lean and green practices can help both the organization and the environment. Lean production refers to a set of strategies and practices to eliminate waste and thus make organizations more efficient, responsive, and flexible. Inventory control is one of the key areas where waste often occurs. Many lean firms have adopted just-in-time production methods to minimize the amount of parts, work-in-process, and finished products they hold in inventory. Many firms have also become "greener" by finding environmentally friendly ways to produce and distribute their goods and services. Green practices include designing facilities to be more energy efficient; using renewable energy; making use of recyclable materials; switching to paints, lubricants, cleaning fluids, and solvents that are less harmful to the environment; and providing labeling to help consumers find out which products are the most environmentally friendly.

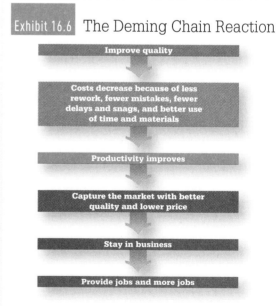

Exhibit 16.6 The Deming Chain Reaction

Improve quality

Costs decrease because of less rework, fewer mistakes, fewer delays and snags, and better use of time and materials

Productivity improves

Capture the market with better quality and lower price

Stay in business

Provide jobs and more jobs

Source: From COLLIER/EVANS, Operations Management: Goods, Service, and Value Chains, 2E. © 2007 Cengage Learning.

© Cengage Learning

computer-integrated manufacturing (CIM) A combination of CAD/CAM software with flexible manufacturing systems to automate almost all steps involved in designing, testing, and producing a product.

16-5

total quality management (TQM) An approach to quality improvement that calls for everyone within an organization to take responsibility for improving quality and that emphasizes the need for a long-term commitment to continuous improvement.

Six Sigma An approach to quality improvement characterized by very ambitious quality goals, extensive training of employees, and a long-term commitment to working on quality-related issues.

Excellence Canada (formerly the National Quality Institute, or NQI) A national program established by Industry Canada in 1992 to promote quality improvements and healthy workplaces.

Baldrige National Quality Program A national program to encourage American firms to focus on quality improvement.

ISO 9000 A family of generic standards for quality management systems established by the International Organization for Standardization.

16-6

lean production An approach to production that emphasizes the elimination of waste in all aspects of production processes.

just-in-time (JIT) production A production system that emphasizes the production of goods to meet actual current demand, thus minimizing the need to hold inventories of finished goods and work-in-process at each stage of the supply chain.

ISO 14000 A family of generic standards for environmental management established by the International Organization for Standardization.

NOTES

LEARNING OUTCOMES

A1-1 (P. 275)

Describe the basic structure of unions. A labour union is a group of workers who have organized in order to pursue common job-related objectives, such as securing better wages and benefits, safer working conditions, and greater job security. Unions can be organized either as craft unions, which consist of members who share the same skill or profession, or as industrial unions, which consist of workers in the same industry. The most basic unit of a union is the "local." This is the level at which most members have an opportunity to get directly involved in union activities. Most locals belong to a national (or international) union. The national union provides training, legal support, and bargaining advice to locals; organizes new locals; and sometimes takes an active role in the collective bargaining process. Many national unions belong to the Canadian Labour Congress, which serves as the national voice for the labour movement.

A1-2 (P. 276)

Discuss the key provisions of the laws that govern labour–management relations. The first law involving labour relations was enacted in 1867 as part of the process for Canada to become a country, but it did not specifically deal with the rights of workers to organize. Like most of Canada's laws, the laws dealing with labour relations were mainly based on British law. In later years, Canadian labour relations legislation was greatly influenced by American laws. In Canada, there is a division of power between the federal government and the provinces and territories. The Great Depression and the Second World War significantly influenced labour legislation. The *Wagner Act* in the United States, which entrenched the right of employees to join a union and engage in union activities and required companies to bargain in good faith with unions, greatly influenced Canadian law. The *Canada Labour Code* covers labour-relations issues for firms operating under the federal government's jurisdiction. This law covers four main areas: industrial relations regulations, fair employment practices, employee safety, and standardized working conditions (such as number of hours worked and wages). Most provinces have enacted similar legislation to cover workers where the *Canada Labour Code* does not apply.

A1-3 (P. 278)

Explain how labour contracts are negotiated and administered. The process by which representatives of labour and employers attempt to negotiate a mutually acceptable labour agreement is called collective bargaining. There are two broad basic approaches to collective bargaining. In distributive bargaining, the process tends to be adversarial. The sides begin with predetermined positions and an initial set of demands. They then use persuasion, logic, and even threats to gain as much as they can. The other approach is called interest-based bargaining. In this approach, the two sides do not present initial demands. Instead, they raise issues and concerns and try to work together to develop mutually beneficial solutions.

Negotiations sometimes break down. An impasse occurs when it becomes obvious that a settlement is not possible under current conditions. When an impasse is reached, a strike may be called by the union, or a lockout may be called by the employer. However, both sides may agree to either conciliation/mediation

KEY TERMS

A1-1

labour union A group of workers who have organized to work together to achieve common job-related goals such as higher wages, better working conditions, and greater job security.

labour relations Refers to all aspects of union–management relations.

industrial relations A broad term referring to the study of employment in union and non-union organizations.

craft union A union composed of workers who share the same skill or work in the same profession.

industrial union A union composed of workers employed in the same industry.

A1-2

National Labor Relations Act (Wagner Act) Landmark pro-labour law enacted in the United States in 1935. This law significantly affected Canadian labour laws.

A1-3

collective bargaining The process by which representatives of union members and employers attempt to negotiate a mutually acceptable labour agreement.

distributive bargaining The traditional adversarial approach to collective bargaining.

interest-based bargaining A form of collective bargaining that emphasizes cooperation and problem solving in an attempt to find a "win–win" outcome that benefits both sides.

strike A work stoppage initiated by a union.

lockout An employer-initiated work stoppage.

APPENDIX IN REVIEW 1

picketing A union tactic during a labour dispute in which union members walk near the entrance of an employer's place of business carrying signs to publicize their position and concerns.

boycott A tactic in which a union and its supporters and sympathizers refuse to do business with an employer with which they have a labour dispute.

conciliation/mediation A method of dealing with an impasse between labour and management that entails bringing in a neutral third party to help the two sides reach agreement by reducing tensions and making suggestions for possible compromises.

arbitration A process in which a neutral third party has the authority to resolve a dispute by rendering a binding decision.

grievance A complaint by a worker that the employer has violated the terms of the collective bargaining agreement.

or arbitration to try to settle their differences and reach an agreement without resorting to such work stoppages. Conciliation officers or mediators can only make suggestions and encourage the two sides to settle. If one or both sides reject their efforts, then the process is likely to fail. In contrast, an arbitrator has the authority to render a binding decision. Arbitration is common in the public sector but rare in the private sector.

When workers believe they have been unfairly treated under the terms of the contract, they may file a grievance. Most labour agreements contain a formal grievance procedure that identifies a specific series of steps involved in settling a complaint. The final step usually involves binding arbitration.

A1-4 (P. 280)

Evaluate the impact unions have on their members' welfare and the economy. Most studies find that union workers earn higher wages and receive more benefits than non-union workers with similar skills performing the same type of job. Union contracts and the grievance procedure also provide union members with more protection from arbitrary discipline (including firings) than non-union workers enjoy. However, unionized industries in the private sector haven't provided much job security. Total employment in many highly unionized industries has fallen dramatically in recent years.

Many critics argue that unions undermine worker productivity by imposing rules and restrictions that reduce the ability of firms to innovate and by requiring employers to use more labour than necessary to produce goods and services. But union supporters suggest that unions reduce worker turnover and encourage worker training, thus increasing productivity. Research on this topic has not yielded clear-cut evidence in support of either position.

LEARNING OUTCOMES

A2-1 (P. 283)

Explain the purposes of laws and identify the major sources of law in Canada. Laws are those rules—enforced by the government—that set parameters for the conduct and actions of people within a society. These rules promote order and stability, protect individuals from physical or mental harm, protect property from damage or theft, promote behaviour that society deems desirable, and deter behaviour that society deems undesirable. Laws come from several sources. Constitutional law is based on a constitution and is the supreme law of Canada. Statutory law is enacted by a legislative body, such as the Canadian Parliament or a provincial legislature. Administrative laws are established and enforced by government agencies. Common law (also called case law) is law based on court decisions.

A2-2 (P. 286)

Describe the characteristics of a contract and explain how the terms of contracts are enforced. A contract is an agreement that is enforceable in a court of law. A valid contract must be characterized by (1) mutual assent, (2) consideration, (3) legal capacity, and (4) legal purpose. In addition, according to the statute of frauds, certain types of contracts, such as those that will take more than a year to complete or those involving the sale of goods worth more than a specified value, must be in writing.

A breach of contract occurs if one of the parties does not live up to the terms of the agreement. When one party breaches a contract, the other party can sue in a civil court. If the court agrees that a party breached the contract, it orders some type of remedy. The most common remedy is compensatory damages, or money the party that breached the contract must pay to the injured party to compensate for the actual harm suffered. In cases where the contract calls for the sale of a unique good, the courts may apply a remedy known as specific performance, which requires the party that breached the contract to do exactly what the contract says. Finally, the courts may issue injunctions (court orders) that prevent the party that breached the contract from taking some action.

A2-3 (P. 287)

Describe how both title and risk pass from the seller to the buyer when a sale occurs. A sale occurs when the title to a good passes from one party to another in exchange for a price. Sales of goods are covered by the *Sale of Goods Act*. Sales of services are based on precedents established by common law. A sales contract must contain the same basic elements as other contracts. However, the law has relaxed the requirements for some of these elements. For example, under the law, courts may recognize a sales contract even if certain key facts of the agreement (such as the price of the good) aren't explicitly spelled out. In such cases, the law provides guidelines for supplying the missing details. One key sales contract issue involves when the title actually passes from one party to another. If the contract is silent about this, the law generally holds that the title passes when the seller has completed all duties related to the delivery of the good. Another key issue involves which party bears the risk if the goods are lost, damaged, or destroyed during the transfer from seller to buyer. If the contract doesn't specify which party assumes the

KEY TERMS

A2-1

laws Rules that govern the conduct and actions of people within a society that are enforced by the government.

constitution A code that establishes the fundamental rules and principles that govern a particular organization or entity.

statutory law Laws that are the result of legislative action.

administrative law Laws that arise from regulations established by government.

common law Laws that result from rulings, called precedents, made by judges who initially hear a particular type of case (also called case law).

tort A private wrong that results in physical or mental harm to an individual or damage to that person's property.

negligence An unintentional tort that arises due to carelessness or irresponsible behaviour.

crime A wrongful act against society defined by law and prosecuted by the state.

A2-2

business law The application of laws and legal principles to business relationships and transactions.

contract An agreement that is legally enforceable.

consideration Something of value that one party gives another as part of a contractual agreement.

statute of frauds A requirement that certain types of contracts must be in writing in order to be enforceable.

breach of contract The failure of one party to a contract to perform his or her contractual obligations.

APPENDIX IN REVIEW 2

statute of limitations The time period within which a legal action must be initiated.

compensatory damages Monetary payments a party that breaches a contract is ordered to pay in order to compensate the injured party for the actual harm suffered by the breach of contract.

specific performance A remedy for breach of contract in which the court orders the party committing the breach to do exactly what the contract specifies.

A2-3

sale A transaction in which title (legal ownership) to a good passes from one party to another in exchange for a price.

title Legal evidence of ownership.

A2-4

principal–agent relationship A relationship in which one party, called the principal, gives another party, called the agent, the authority to act and enter into binding agreements on the principal's behalf.

principal A party that agrees to have someone else (called an agent) act on his or her behalf.

agent A party that agrees to represent another party, called the principal.

scope of authority (for an agent) The extent to which an agent has the authority to act for and represent the principal.

property The legal right of an owner to exclude non-owners from having access to a particular resource.

intellectual property Property that results from intellectual or creative efforts.

patent A legal monopoly that gives an inventor the exclusive right over the invention for a limited period of time.

trademark A mark, symbol, word, phrase, or motto used to identify a company's goods.

risk, the law normally places the risk on the party that is most likely to have insurance against a loss or on the party that is in the best position to prevent a loss.

A2-4 (P. 288)

Provide an overview of the legal principles governing agency, intellectual property, and bankruptcy. A principal–agent relationship exists when one party (the principal) gives another party (the agent) the authority to act and enter into binding agreements on the principal's behalf. As long as agents act within their scope of authority, principals are legally liable for any contracts their agents enter into while representing them. Not all employees have the authority to act as agents, but many do. A loan officer at a bank and a salesperson at a store are both employees of and agents for their companies.

Intellectual property refers to the right of inventors, innovators, authors, and artists to own their creations and prevent others from copying, distributing, or selling these creations without their permission. Patents protect the intellectual property rights of inventors. Most patents give the inventor exclusive rights to their invention for 20 years. Copyrights protect the intellectual property rights of authors, artists, and other creative individuals. Copyrights normally extend for 50 years beyond the author's or artist's life. Trademarks, which are marks, symbols, words, phrases, or mottos that identify a company's goods, are another form of intellectual property. Registered trademarks are protected for 10 years, and the protection can be extended for an unlimited number of additional 15-year periods.

Bankruptcy provides a way for debtors who are unable to meet their obligations to discharge their debts and get a fresh start. Bankruptcy proceedings can be either voluntary or involuntary (i.e., debtor or creditor initiated). Creditors may seek a negotiated settlement. If this fails, they will need a trustee in bankruptcy. This person will prepare a proposal, which may or may not be acceptable to the creditors. Any creditor can sue a debtor based on outstanding debts. Secured creditors may also take individual action against specific assets. Finally, one or more creditors may petition a debtor into bankruptcy. Creditors may then share in any monies that are available. In order of claim, they are special creditors, secured creditors, preferred creditors, and, finally, unsecured creditors.

copyright The exclusive legal right of authors, artists, or other creative individuals to own, use, copy, and sell their own creations and to license others to do so.

trustee in bankruptcy The person who holds legal responsibility for administering the affairs of bankrupt companies or persons.

proposal A contractual agreement between an insolvent debtor and creditors that would allow the debtor to reorganize and continue operations.

petition A statement of what a creditor owes and to whom. It is filed in bankruptcy court, and if it is successful, the debtor is declared bankrupt.

receiving order A court order that follows a successful petition. It officially declares a debtor as bankrupt and transfers legal control of the debtor's assets to the trustee.

proof of claim A formal notice by a creditor to the trustee concerning what is owed and the nature of the debt.

APPENDIX IN REVIEW 3
Personal Finance

LEARNING OUTCOMES

A3-1 (P. 293)
Apply the principles of budgeting to your personal finances. A budget is a detailed schedule that documents your expected financial inflows (revenues earned and received) and outflows (expenses incurred and paid) in order to determine your net inflow or outflow for a given period of time. You can use your budget to develop your financial plan and to monitor your progress towards achieving your financial goals. One key part of the budgeting process is accurate estimation of revenues. The other key to setting up a budget is to assess your expenses. You should also consider the factors that affect your spending habits. Certain types of expenditures, called discretionary costs, can be adjusted fairly easily. Other expenditures, referred to as non-discretionary, are more difficult to cut—at least in the short run.

A3-2 (P. 294)
Identify strategies to help build a sufficient savings. A savings account is an interest-bearing account that is intended to satisfy obligations that cannot be handled by a chequing account. Many financial experts suggest that your savings account should be able to cover six months of your expenses. One technique for establishing a sizable savings balance is to "pay yourself first." This technique is accomplished by automatically depositing a predetermined amount into your savings account with each paycheque.

A3-3 (P. 295)
Explain the importance of using credit wisely. Credit refers to your ability to obtain goods or resources without having to make immediate payment. One of the most important determinants of the amount of credit you can obtain is your credit history. Financial companies determine your creditworthiness by obtaining your credit score (rating). Your credit score (rating) is a numerical indicator of your creditworthiness.

A credit card allows its holder to make a purchase now and pay the credit card issuer later. Credit cards are more convenient and safer than carrying a lot of cash. They also make it easy to track your expenditures because you have access to a monthly summary of charges. And many cards offer perks, such as discounts on certain products, extended warranties on purchases, or frequent-flyer miles. Another benefit of the responsible use of credit cards is that it can improve your credit score (rating) by allowing you to establish a history of prompt payments.

One downside of having a credit card is that the "buy now, pay later" aspect of credit card use makes it hard for some people to maintain financial discipline. Another problem is that interest rates on unpaid balances tend to be very high. Many card issuers also impose a variety of fees that can make a noticeable dent in your wallet. And making late payments or failing to pay what you owe can damage your credit history, hurting your chances of getting additional credit when you need it.

Before you accept a credit card, you should read and understand all of the main conditions for using that card. Among the major areas to consider are (1) the grace period, the period of time that you have to pay your balance before interest or fees are assessed; (2) the interest rate as well as any (3) late fees that may be assessed if a payment is not received within a grace period; and (4) other fees, such as annual fees, over-the-credit-limit fees, and balance-transfer fees.

The first rule when you have credit card difficulties is to just stop using the card. Then commit to setting up (and sticking to) a budget and putting a consistent

KEY TERMS

A3-1
budget (personal) A detailed forecast of financial inflows (income) and outflows (expenses) in order to determine your net inflow or outflow for a given period of time.

discretionary costs Expenditures for which the spender has significant control in terms of the amount and timing.

non-discretionary costs Costs that the spender must incur but has little or no control over.

A3-2
savings account An interest-bearing account holding funds not needed to meet regular expenditures.

Canada Deposit Insurance Corporation (CDIC) A Crown corporation created to maintain stability and public confidence in the nation's financial system, primarily by insuring bank deposits.

A3-3
credit Allows a borrower to buy a good or acquire an asset without making immediate payment and to repay the balance at a later time.

credit history A summary of a borrower's open and closed credit accounts and the manner in which those accounts have been paid.

credit score (credit rating) A numerical measure of a consumer's creditworthiness.

net worth A measure of the value of all your assets minus the total of all your debts.

credit card A card issued by a bank or finance company that allows the cardholder to make a purchase now and pay the credit card issuer later.

grace period The period of time that the credit card holder has to pay outstanding balances before interest or fees are assessed.

loan The money provided today by the financial institution in exchange for future repayments of principal and interest.

promissory note The written promise to repay the bank for a loan.

collateral The asset the bank takes as security for a loan.

mortgage A loan from the bank that is used to purchase a house.

debit card A card issued by the bank that allows the customer to make purchases as if the transaction involved cash. The customer's bank account is immediately reduced when the purchase is made.

A3-4

investing Reducing consumption in the current time period in order to build future wealth.

registered retirement savings plan (RRSP) An individual retirement account that provides tax benefits to individuals who are investing for their retirement.

Registered Education Saving Plan (RRSP) A savings account that provides tax benefits to individuals who are investing for their children's education.

amount of money towards retiring the debt on that card. Another useful tip is to use cash or a debit card instead. Many people tend to spend more when they pay with a credit card than when they pay with cash.

For larger purchases, like a car or a house, the bank or other financial institution can provide a loan or mortgage.

A3-4 (P. 297)

Discuss key wealth-building principles and the financial instruments that may be part of a wealth-building strategy.

Investing involves reducing consumption today in order to build future wealth. One key to investing is consistency—make it a habit to invest something every month. Another key is to begin as soon as possible, even if you can invest only a little. The time value of money says that a dollar invested today is worth more than a dollar invested later because the earlier a dollar is invested, the longer it can earn a return.

There are several different types of financial assets you might want to consider. Each has its own advantages and disadvantages. One tradeoff involves risk and return. Investments that offer the potential for higher returns tend to be riskier than investments that offer lower returns.

Corporate stock represents shares of ownership in a corporation. Investing in stock offers the possibility of receiving dividends, which are a distribution of a company's profits to its shareholders. It also offers the potential for capital gains, which are increases in the market value of stocks. However, neither dividends nor capital gains are guaranteed. Corporate bonds are formal IOUs issued by corporations. Bonds typically pay a stated rate of interest until they mature (come due). Once a bond matures, the issuer is obligated to pay the bondholder an amount known as the principal (or face value) of the bond.

Government bonds are IOUs issued by a government entity. All levels of governments issue bonds.

Certificates of deposit, term deposits, and guaranteed investment certificates are offered by banks and other depository institutions. They are similar to savings accounts but are issued for a fixed term—ranging from a month to as long as five years. One advantage of these types of investments is that they are insured by the Canada Deposit Insurance Corporation. Because of this insurance and their predictable rate of return, these investments are considered to be among the safest investment options. But they generally pay less interest than bonds and most other investments.

Mutual funds offer investors shares that represent ownership in a variety of financial securities, such as stocks, corporate bonds, and government bonds. These funds are professionally managed. The managers select the specific securities that the fund holds. Exchange-traded funds are "market baskets" of securities that are traded much like individual shares of stock.

Tax-free savings plans allow investors to purchase stocks, bonds, or mutual funds or invest in other savings. The interest or dividends from investments in tax-free savings accounts are tax-exempt.

One of the most important reasons people invest is to build up a nest egg for retirement. While your retirement might seem like it is a long time off, investing for your golden years now can really pay off because it allows you to take advantage of compounding. One of the most popular ways to build wealth for retirement is to set up a registered retirement savings plan. You can put your retirement savings money into stocks, government bonds, mutual funds, or any other type of financial securities. One major advantage of retirement savings is the tax advantage over investments that are not in a tax-sheltered plan.

Similar to a retirement savings plan is the registered education savings plan. This plan allows people to save for their children's post-secondary education. The registered education saving plan defers the income tax until the money is withdrawn to pay for college or university. An added incentive with the RESP is that the government will also add money into the plan.